W9-CZD-429

THE SCARECROW AUTHOR BIBLIOGRAPHIES

1. John Steinbeck (Tetsumaro Hayashi).   1973.
   See also no. 64.
2. Joseph Conrad (Theodore G. Ehrsam).   1969.
3. Arthur Miller (Tetsumaro Hayashi). 2nd ed., 1976.
4. Katherine Anne Porter (Waldrip & Bauer).   1969.
5. Philip Freneau (Philip M. Marsh).   1970.
6. Robert Greene (Tetsumaro Hayashi).   1971.
7. Benjamin Disraeli (R.W. Stewart).   1972.
8. John Berryman (Richard W. Kelly).   1972.
9. William Dean Howells (Vito J. Brenni).   1973.
10. Jean Anouilh (Kathleen W. Kelly).   1973.
11. E.M. Forster (Alfred Borrello).   1973.
12. The Marquis de Sade (E. Pierre Chanover).   1973.
13. Alain Robbe-Grillet (Dale W. Frazier).   1973.
14. Northrop Frye (Robert D. Denham).   1974.
15. Federico Garcia Lorca (Laurenti & Siracusa).   1974.
16. Ben Jonson (Brock & Welsh).   1974.
17. Four French Dramatists: Eugène Brieux, François de Curel,
    Emile Fabre, Paul Hervieu (Edmund F. Santa Vicca).   1974.
18. Ralph Waldo Ellison (Jacqueline Covo).   1974.
19. Philip Roth (Bernard F. Rodgers, Jr.). 2nd ed., 1984.
20. Norman Mailer (Laura Adams).   1974.
21. Sir John Betjeman (Margaret Stapleton).   1974.
22. Elie Wiesel (Molly Abramowitz).   1974.
23. Paul Laurence Dunbar (Eugene W. Metcalf, Jr.).   1975.
24. Henry James (Beatrice Ricks).   1975.
25. Robert Frost (Lentricchia & Lentricchia).   1976.
26. Sherwood Anderson (Douglas G. Rogers).   1976.
27. Iris Murdoch and Muriel Spark (Tominaga &
    Schneidermeyer).   1976.
28. John Ruskin (Kirk H. Beetz).   1976.
29. Georges Simenon (Trudee Young).   1976.
30. George Gordon, Lord Byron (Oscar José Santucho).   1976.
31. John Barth (Richard Vine).   1977.
32. John Hawkes (Carol A. Hryciw).   1977.
33. William Everson (Bartlett & Campo).   1977.
34. May Sarton (Lenora Blouin).   1978.

35. Wilkie Collins (Kirk H. Beetz).   1978.
36. Sylvia Plath (Lane & Stevens).   1978.
37. E.B. White (A.J. Anderson).   1978.
38. Henry Miller (Lawrence J. Shifreen).   1979.
39. Ralph Waldo Emerson (Jeanetta Boswell).   1979.
40. James Dickey (Jim Elledge).   1979.
41. Henry Fielding (H. George Hahn).   1979.
42. Paul Goodman (Tom Nicely).   1979.
43. Christopher Marlowe (Kenneth Friedenreich).   1979.
44. Leo Tolstoy (Egan & Egan).   1979.
45. T.S. Eliot (Beatrice Ricks).   1980.
46. Allen Ginsberg (Michelle P. Kraus).   1980.
47. Anthony Burgess (Jeutonne P. Brewer).   1980.
48. Tennessee Williams (Drewey Wayne Gunn).   1980.
49. William Faulkner (Beatrice Ricks).   1981.
50. Lillian Hellman (Mary Marguerite Riordan).   1980.
51. Walt Whitman (Jeanetta Boswell).   1980.
52. Jack Kerouac (Robert J. Milewski).   1981.
53. Herman Melville (Jeanetta Boswell).   1981.
54. Horatio Alger, Jr. (Scharnhorst & Bales).   1981.
55. Graham Greene (A.F. Cassis).   1981.
56. Henry David Thoreau (Boswell & Crouch).   1981.
57. Nathaniel Hawthorne (Jeanetta Boswell).   1982.
58. Jean Genet (R.C. Webb).   1982.
59. August Derleth (Alison Morley Wilson).   1983.
60. John Milton (Michael A. Mikolajczak).   1983.
61. Algernon Charles Swinburne (Kirk H. Beetz).   1982.
62. George Washington Cable (William H. Roberson).   1982.
63. Christine de Pisan (Edith Yenal).   1982.
64. John Steinbeck (Tetsumaro Hayashi).   1983.
        See also no. 1
65. John G. Neihardt (John Thomas Richards).   1983.
66. Yvor Winters (Grosvenor Powell).   1983.
67. Sean O'Casey (E.H. Mikhail).   1984.
68. Tennyson (Kirk H. Beetz).   1984.
69. Floyd Dell (Judith Nierman).   1984.

TENNYSON
A Bibliography, 1827-1982

by Kirk H. Beetz

Scarecrow Author Bibliographies No. 68

The Scarecrow Press, Inc.
Metuchen, N.J., and London
1984

Library of Congress Cataloging in Publication Data

Beetz, Kirk H., 1952–
   Tennyson : a bibliography, 1827–1982.

   (Scarecrow author bibliographies ; no. 68)
   Includes indexes.
   1. Tennyson, Alfred Tennyson, Baron, 1809–1892--
Bibliography. I. Title.
Z8866.B43 1984   016.821'8   84–1274
[PR5581]
ISBN 0-8108-1687-3

CONTENTS

Acknowledgments   v

A Note on Sources   vi

Introduction   1

Bibliography   11

Author-Editor Index   479

Subject Index   505

iii

ACKNOWLEDGMENTS

My thanks for their assistance to: Barbara A. King; Betty Kimura, Librarian, Department of English, University of California, Davis; Theodore F. Gould, Reference Librarian, Peter J. Shields Library, University of California, Davis; Peter L. Hays, Professor, Department of English, University of California, Davis; and Peter A. Dale, Associate Professor, University of California, Davis.

My thanks for answering questions concerning copyrights to: Jonathan Dodd of Dodd, Mead & Company, Inc., New York; Betty Kish, Copyrights and Permissions, Bobbs-Merrill Trade Division, Indianapolis; J. Nulls of Macmillan Publishers, Ltd., London; Marian Redman, Permissions, Routledge & Kegan Paul, PLC, London; and E. Soschin, Manager, Permissions, Charles Scribner's Sons, New York.

Copyright Acknowledgment

A NOTE ON SOURCES

The following were particularly helpful during the research for the present book: Theodore G. Ehrsam, Robert H. Deily, and Robert M. Smith's "Alfred Lord Tennyson," in <u>Bibliographies of Twelve Victorian Authors</u> (entry 2756); John Olin Eidson's <u>Tennyson in America</u> (entry 3328); and Edgar F. Shannon, Jr.'s <u>Tennyson and the Reviewers</u> (entry 3496) and "The Critical Reception of Tennyson's <u>Maud</u>" (entry 3539).

INTRODUCTION

In more than five thousand publications, scholars and critics have picked apart Tennyson and his works; they have analyzed his canon as a whole down to the phonemes of individual words. Poems obscure and famous have been subjected to psychoanalytic, structural, symbolic, philosophical, historical, and linguistic analysis. Tennyson's stature as a poet has been debated in redundant detail; the merits of the poems have been debated in even greater detail. In spite of the efforts of thousands of scholars and critics, writing about Tennyson for over one hundred years, a genuine critical consensus about Tennyson and his works remains elusive.

Few, at present, would quarrel with the notion that Tennyson is an important poet; most would agree that he is a great poet; yet the greatness or deficiencies of his individual works remains a matter of controversy. Idylls of the King now seems to be the poet's most admired work, although In Memoriam is again rising in favor; in the past, In Memoriam, The Princess, "Ulysses," and "Locksley Hall" have been critical favorites, and each has been condemned as foolish and mindless, structurally confused and disorganized, trite, poorly characterized, and unimportant. This wide variation of opinions, from admiration to disdain, makes generalizations about Tennyson and his work difficult; even today, fine scholars and critics disagree. Those who study Tennyson should beware of even the most commonly accepted generalizations about his work.

That scholars would generalize about Tennyson is reasonable; few have the will or interest to slog through the poet's canon and over five thousand secondary works. That the old generalizations of the past--the old truisms--often break down when closely examined should not be cause for despair among those who wish to understand Tennyson; the truisms served the purpose of organizing large amounts of information so that critics could think about the major issues of the poet's work. The lack of unanimity of opinion is a sign of the vitality of Tennyson's work and of Tennysonian studies.

Biographies

Biographers generally portray Tennyson as a paradigm for his time. For instance, Harold Nicolson, in 1923 (entry 2971), sees Victorian society as split into two distinct personalities--a point of view that remains commonplace--and he thus portrays Tennyson as a divided poet. According to Nicolson, Tennyson the lyricist was brilliant, a poet whose lyrics blended sound and image wonderfully; however, Tennyson the narrative poet was dull, hypocritically moralistic, and prone to filling his works with Victorian clichés. Nicolson's contention that there were two Tennysons has undergone several permutations over the past sixty years, yet it still retains currency. Although most critics would now deny Nicolson's denigration of Tennyson's nonlyrical poetry, many still seek to find in the poet the representation of the divided Victorian spirit, often finding in Tennyson's character and poetry a conflict between Romantic passion and a desire to conform.

One biographer who expressed no such division was Hallam Tennyson, the poet's son. In <u>Alfred Lord Tennyson: A Memoir</u>, 1897 (entry 1955), Hallam Tennyson presents a man who was consistent in probity and friendship. Like Nicolson, he perceives in his father the representative Victorian man: in this case, an upright, stalwart Victorian who was true to his Queen and her society's ethos. Unlike Nicolson's biography, Hallam Tennyson's does not try to prove an arguable thesis; through carefully edited letters and other manuscript notes, Tennyson's biography shows an ideal Victorian gentleman who devoted his life to poetry.

On this last, biographers universally seem to agree. Charles Tennyson, the poet's grandson, in his 1949 biography (entry 3417), presents a man whose life was poetry. Nicolson perceives in the poems the essence of the man, and so does Charles Tennyson, but the latter goes further: he sees in his grandfather's life the essence of poetry. Charles Tennyson writes his biography in part as a response to Nicolson and Hallam Tennyson; he seeks to rehabilitate the poet from what he believes to be Nicolson's harsh, anti-Victorian portrayal, and to broaden the poet's character beyond that revealed in Hallam Tennyson's book. Where Nicolson finds the poet to be stupid and ignorant, Charles Tennyson finds an intelligent and well-informed man who understood science and social issues well enough to discuss them ably with the leading scientists and social leaders of Victorian England. Where Hallam Tennyson shows a serenely contented family man whose strength of character was forged in early years of trouble when critics responded cruelly to his poetry, Charles Tennyson presents a deeply troubled man whose didactic poetical works such as <u>The Princess</u> and <u>Maud</u> were not wholly responses to earlier criticism of his lyrical poetry, but, rather, expressions of his concern for and understanding of the great social and political issues of his day. According to Charles Tennyson, his grandfather represented in his life and work the strengths and weaknesses of the Victorian character and was a man acutely aware of the intellectual and social issues of his day, as well as someone who devoted himself to fulfilling the demands of his art.

For three decades, Charles Tennyson's biography was widely

regarded as the standard one.   However, a biography by Robert
Bernard Martin was published in 1980 (entry 4970) and might supplant that by Tennyson.   Critics have responded well to Martin's
book; many think it the new standard biography.   It follows the
same tack as that of Charles Tennyson, although it tries less
overtly to correct possible misinterpretations of the poet's character by Nicolson and others.   Martin expresses a more subtle
understanding of Tennyson's relationship to poetry than previous
biographers have shown.   The greatest asset of Martin's book may
be its erudition; Martin had access to records previously unavailable to biographers.

Of the major biographies on Tennyson, Martin's may be the
most complete.   In contrast, Nicolson's, while influential, may be
the most shallow.   Nicolson's effort to prove a thesis seems to
have led him to miss significant aspects of Tennyson's character.
His book remains of interest primarily because of its influence and
presentation of a point of view that was predominant in the post-
World War I era.   Hallam Tennyson's biography remains a standard reference because of its wealth of research materials: its presentation of letters, notes, and commentary make it important reading for those interested in the serious study of Tennyson.   With the
publication of Martin's biography, Charles Tennyson's book may fade
into simply historical significance; however, many readers have been
inspired by Charles Tennyson's observations and insights, and the
book remains, at present, a standard resource.   Martin's book may
be the best written of all biographies on Alfred, Lord Tennyson; it
is likely to appeal to readers new to Tennyson as well as to serious
students of the poet.

Editions

Hallam Tennyson's 1907 (entry 2465) edition of Alfred, Lord
Tennyson's works has long been the standard one, although some
poems not included have been uncovered by scholars since its publication.   In 1969, Christopher Ricks published an annotated edition
(entry 4145).   Most scholars seem agreed that Ricks's edition is
the single outstanding version of Tennyson's works, although both
the 1907 version and Ricks's are generally considered acceptable for
scholarly references.   Given the great value of Ricks's edition, its
publishers would do Tennysonian students a favor by reprinting it;
it is presently hard to find outside of libraries.

An interesting publication from 1973 is A Variorum Edition
of Tennyson's "Idylls of the King," edited by John Pfordresher (entry 4419).   Pfordresher provides much information on the composition of Idylls of the King and on its various texts.   Those who are
interested in the Arthurian poems will find Pfordresher's edition
valuable.

As of this writing, the letters of Tennyson are being published by Harvard University Press.   Although it is too early to

assess the merits of the edition, one can note that its editors,
Cecil Y. Lang and Edgar F. Shannon, Jr., are skilled scholars
who have already made significant contributions to literary research. Certainly, anyone with a serious interest in Tennyson
should be aware of the Lang and Shannon edition of his letters.

General State of Criticism

The broad issues of Tennysonian criticism have remained
fundamentally the same from the time the poet became established
to the present. Early in Tennyson's career, critics doubted his
staying power; they often saw his poetry as a minor offshoot of
Keats's Romantic lyricism. Tennyson's friends, most notably
Arthur Hallam, in "On Some of the Characteristics of Modern
Poetry, and on the Lyrical Poems of Alfred Tennyson," in Englishman's Magazine, 1831 (entry 9), argued that Tennyson was an
important poet, but their bias blinded them to his early poetic
weaknesses. Both the early praise and the early attacks, such as
John Wilson Croker's in the 1833 Quarterly Review (entry 22), quite
naturally missed the major critical issue of the past one hundred
years: Tennyson's stature as a poet.

After the publication of In Memoriam, that question became
an important issue for critics. As Tennyson added work upon work
to his canon, Victorian critics became assured of Tennyson's rank
among poets. For them, he grew from a minor Romantic to one
of the best of his age, to a genius to be compared with Milton and
Virgil. Much of the criticism of the 1880s and 1890s is almost
obsequious in its extravagant praise of Tennyson. When Tennyson
died in 1892, few critics doubted that he was a great poet.

The reaction against the Victorian era rarely brought deni-
grations of his importance. Instead, the reassessment of him
brought doubt about his stature among great poets. Critics generally agreed that Tennyson was an important representative of his
time, but they often ranked him as the best of a bad lot; he was a
stupid poet in an era of stupid poetry, and his poetry was not to be
ranked anywhere near that of Milton. His plays were held in even
lower esteem. Thus Nicolson's biography of 1923 was much as he
claimed it to be: a rehabilitation of Tennyson's reputation, at least
as a lyrical poet.

The next broad shift in critical views of Tennyson's poetic
stature began with Charles Tennyson's biography of 1949 and became generally accepted with the publication of Jerome Buckley's
Tennyson: The Growth of a Poet in 1960 (entry 3696), an introductory study that influenced a generation of Tennysonian scholars.
Buckley presents Tennyson as a poet whose stature is not to be
doubted, although the relative merits of his individual poems might
be debated. The 1960s saw a boom in publications on Tennyson,
many of them marked by their authors' confidence in Tennyson's
genius and status as one of the world's great poets. The present

critical climate retains much of the assuredness of the 1960s: Tennyson is an undoubtedly major poet. He is a popular subject for dissertations, which often echo the worshipful tone of the criticism of the 1880s.

The issue of Tennyson's stature should not be regarded as settled. Much of his current high esteem may be a matter of fashion, with critics writing about him because he is regarded as a major poet and because publications on major authors bring scholars more favor than ones on minor writers. The reaction of the early twentieth century grew in part out of a sensible dismay at the sometimes mindless approbation of Tennyson; such a reaction may come again.

Another significant critical view also began in the Victorian era: Tennyson's works as representative of their time. Even when critics doubt the merits of the poems and plays as works of art, they seldom deny their importance as expressions of Victorian sensibilities. The Victorian critics often viewed the poet's works as expressing the essence of their society; they saw the poetry as a defense of their time, and Tennyson as their voice speaking to posterity. Later critics have used the poetry to hold Victorian mores up to ridicule, for insight into social trends and historical events, or for illustrating the development of English poetry. Whatever their views of the merits of Tennyson's poetry and Victorian society, critics have generally agreed that the poetry has historical importance. Nonetheless, students of Tennyson should beware the seeming unanimity of opinion; when individual works are considered, the notion of Tennyson as spokesman for his age can become confusing.

The Princess, with its commentary on the status of women, and Maud, with its contemporary social topics, certainly seem to be expressions of their age. Poems such as "Locksley Hall" and In Memoriam have been analyzed as expressions of a Victorian ethos. But such views of Idylls of the King become more debatable. Some critics see Idylls of the King as an expression of Victorian ideals, others as Tennyson's apocalyptic vision of the inevitable decay of Victorian society, and still others as no more than a botched attempt to modernize medieval legends. Plays such as Queen Mary and Harold also produce contradictory views of their possible expressions of Victorian manners and ideas.

Another issue that long held currency, but which seems to have faded for the present, concerns Tennyson's nature as a poet. The standard debate has been over whether Tennyson was essentially a lyrical or a narrative poet. Critics have explained failings in Idylls of the King by asserting that the narrative mode was inhospitable to Tennyson's talents. The general weight of critical opinion until the 1970s was that Tennyson's strengths were in imagery and poetic music, not in ideas and storytelling. Idylls of the King has risen greatly in critical esteem during the last twenty years and the issue of the poet's lyrical versus narrative talents seems to be unimportant to most Tennysonians. Debate over

Tennyson's lyrical and narrative achievement, as opposed to his talents, also seems to be abating. Questions about the merits of the poet's plays still command a small amount of attention, but the critical consensus seems to be that the plays are of secondary importance.

In Memoriam

From its publication in 1850, In Memoriam's critics have been alternately puzzled and amused by the poem's ambiguities and themes. The reviewers of the 1850s found the poem "monotonous" (entry 182), "capricious" (entry 188), and a "masterpiece" (entry 247), and compared it favorably to the poems of Spenser and Shakespeare (entry 211). George Henry Lewes (entry 225) went so far as to dub Tennyson "our greatest living poet" on the basis of In Memoriam. The poem's religious themes troubled some critics, who found them heretical; other critics found comfort in what they believed was the poem's ultimate affirmation of faith.

Readers of In Memoriam have remained divided about its meaning and merits since 1850. By the time of Tennyson's death, critics in general were sure that In Memoriam was the poet's most representative work. With the decline in critical estimation of lyrical poetry that marked twentieth-century scholarship, In Memoriam also sank in estimation, although critics of the late 1970s and early 1980s seem to have revived the poem's reputation.

The first major assessment of In Memoriam was published in 1884, John Franklin Genung's Tennyson's "In Memoriam": Its Purpose and Structure (entry 1066). Genung's purpose was to show how the poem fit into Tennyson's poetic development. The book's emphasis on structure highlights an approach to understanding the poem that succeeding critics have found fruitful. For instance, Andrew Cecil Bradley used structural analysis to reveal In Memoriam's merits in his 1901 A Commentary on Tennyson's "In Memoriam" (entry 2218). He saw the poem as being divided into four major sections, each of which was organized into subsections united by themes. Bradley's Commentary remains the most influential study of In Memoriam.

Although T. S. Eliot (entry 3242) and others regarded the poem as an important work, Baum summed up general critical opinion from 1901 to 1950 by noting that In Memoriam had parts that might be admired, but that the work as a whole was unsuccessful. The next major study of the poem focused on its sources and on bibliographical issues, rather than evaluating it: Eleanor B. Mattes's "In Memoriam": The Way of a Soul, 1951 (entry 3481) was the publication of a 1945 dissertation. Her speculations on sources for the poem in the works of Wordsworth and others, and her datings of the times of composition for portions of the poem, have been to varying degrees superseded by subsequent research, but her approach to studying In Memoriam opened up new avenues for critical understanding of it as a unified work.

In the late 1950s, studies of In Memoriam diversified. In
1958, E. D. H. Johnson evaluated the poem as an expression of Tennyson's artistic development, which he called "The Way of the Poet" (entry 3654). On the other hand, in his 1959 essay "The Two
Kingdoms of In Memoriam" (entry 3681), John D. Rosenberg ex-
plains that the poem is Tennyson's effort to unite "evolutionary
science and Christian faith." In 1962, Martin J. Svaglic submitted
an alternative view of the structure of the poem, arguing that it
has nine divisions (entry 3792).

The 1960s saw a general revaluation of Tennyson's works,
and during this decade interest in In Memoriam increased. In 1964,
K. W. Grandsen published a keynote work, Tennyson: "In Memoriam" (entry 3849), an introductory study that sets forth the problems
the poem poses for critics. Subsequent studies tend to fragment the
poem in order to understand individual parts. Notable exceptions
include Robert Langbaum's 1970 "The Dynamic Unity of In Memoriam" in The Modern Spirit (entry 4216) and Alan Sinfield's 1971 The
Language of Tennyson's "In Memoriam" (entry 4283). This last is
a linguistic analysis that has become a standard reference for those
who study the poem.

A useful summary of criticism, particularly of the 1960s and
1970s, is Joseph Sendry's "In Memoriam: Twentieth-Century Criticism," in Victorian Poetry, Summer 1980 (entry 5026).

Idylls of the King

Idylls of the King was published in fragments over a forty-
seven-year period, beginning with "Morte d'Arthur" in 1842 and cul-
minating in the complete series in 1889. The diversity of the stories in the complete work, as well as the many years of Tennyson's
life that it represents, has encouraged some critics to regard Idylls
of the King as diffuse and unorganized. Most of the major studies
of the work, however, have tried to show that it is unified and
meaningful.

Victorian critics were naturally at a disadvantage when discussing Idylls of the King. Only at the end of the nineteenth century was it whole; thus most of the early critics had to content themselves with discussing its parts. The first major study appeared in
1878 and focused on the 1859 Idylls of the King, which contained only "Enid," "Vivien," "Elaine," and "Guinevere" (the titles of the
first three became "Geraint and Enid," "Merlin and Vivien," and
"Lancelot and Elaine"). Henry Elsdale's 1878 Studies in the Idylls
(entry 876) presents an analysis of allegory in the poems. His allegorical reading is typical of other Victorian analyses and is an
early example of a popular approach to interpreting the entire work.

Probably the next major study is Harold Littledale's Essays
on Lord Tennyson's "Idylls of the King" of 1893 (entry 1675). Littledale's commentary is intended for the general reader and provides

an excellent introduction to the poetry and its background. In contrast to Littledale's book, Mungo William MacCallum's 1894 Tennyson's "Idylls of the King" and Arthurian Story from the XVIth Century (entry 1804) provides a more detailed examination of Tennyson's antecedents. Like Elsdale, MacCallum also presents an allegorical interpretation of the poetry. MacCallum's book was the major reference for the Arthurian background of Idylls of the King until the 1960s. Another valuable study from the 1890s is Richard D. Jones's 1895 The Growth of the "Idylls of the King" (entry 1869), which notes Tennyson's revisions of the poetry. Many scholars are still interested in Tennyson's method of composition and Jones's work is still helpful in this regard.

The twentieth century brought with it a reevaluation of Tennyson. Early on, the Idylls of the King retained its interest for scholars, as represented by Condé Bénoist Pallen in his interesting 1907 study The Meaning of the Idylls of the King (entry 2361), but a critical consensus developed that held the poetry vague, disjointed, and anachronistic. The notion that Tennyson was a lyrical poet out of his element prevailed during most of the middle of the twentieth century, and Idylls of the King became, for many scholars, a literary curiosity, although the general public seemed to retain an interest in the poem.

Interest in the Idylls of the King grew in the 1960s as the whole of Tennyson's canon was subjected to fresh scrutiny. The shift to viewing the poetry seriously again may have its origins in F. E. L. Priestly's essay, "Tennyson's Idylls," in the University of Toronto Quarterly in 1949 (entry 3440). Priestly argues that the poem is a serious effort to express important ideas; he sees it as an allegorical representation of Tennyson's faith and distrust of materialism.

In 1967, Clyde de L. Ryals's From the Great Deep: Essays on Idylls of the King (entry 4015) was published. In it, Ryals examines the work "as a philosophical poem." Later, in his 1969 book, Perception and Design in Tennyson's Idylls of the King (entry 4143), John R. Reed argues that the poetry has a clear "moral design" that "was one of long standing in Christian tradition." Also concerned with the poetry's structure and meaning, J. Philip Eggers presents in his 1971 King Arthur's Laureate (entry 4276) an informative examination of the development of Idylls of the King and its relationship to the time of its composition. Following these three significant studies came a notably original one by John D. Rosenberg, his 1973 The Fall of Camelot (entry 4421). In it, Rosenberg argues that Idylls of the King is "self-fulfilling prophecy" that "validates itself, like Scripture, by foretelling in one passage what is fulfilled in the next" and is also "a kind of literary second coming of Arthur."

Bibliography

No good analytical bibliography of primary works has, as

yet, been published.   The standard concordance is A. E. Baker's 1914 A Concordance to the Poetical and Dramatic Works of Alfred, Lord Tennyson (entry 2756).   Baker's A Tennyson Dictionary of 1916 (entry 2809) is also the standard reference for characters and place-names in Tennyson's works.

    The first attempt at a complete enumerative bibliography of secondary works is Theodore G. Ehrsam, Robert H. Deily, and Robert M. Smith's "Alfred Lord Tennyson" in their 1936 Bibliographies of Twelve Victorian Authors (entry 3241).   This work is supplemented by Joseph G. Fucilla in Modern Philology for 1939 (entry 3280).

    In 1930 appeared Marjorie Moreland Bowden's Tennyson in France (entry 3101), which describes the reception in France of Tennyson's works.   A similar work by John Olin Eidson, Tennyson in America: His Reputation and Influence from 1827 to 1858 (entry 3328), provides a detailed and still useful study of the reputation of Tennyson in America.   In addition, Edgar Finley Shannon, Jr.'s Tennyson and the Reviewers: A Study of His Literary Reputation and the Influence of the Critics upon His Poetry, 1827-1851, published in 1952 (entry 3496), presents a detailed examination of the responses of British critics to Tennyson's early works.   Shannon's 1953 "The Critical Reception of Tennyson's 'Maud,'" in PMLA (entry 3539), is a well researched extension of his book.

    The organization of the present bibliography is chronological, with works gathered together by year of publication from 1827 to 1983.   Within each year, books, if any were published, are listed first, followed by dissertations and then periodical listings.   Within each section--books, dissertations, and periodicals--works are listed alphabetically by author.   The bibliographic list is followed by two indexes, author-editor and subject.   The entries in each are organized alphabetically and are followed by the relevant entry numbers for listed publications.

THE BIBLIOGRAPHY

1827

In 1826, Simpkin and Marshall of London published Poems by Two Brothers (dated 1827). The "Two Brothers" were Alfred and Charles Tennyson, although Frederick Tennyson also contributed to the book.

Periodicals

1 Gentleman's Magazine, 97, part I (June 1827), 609.
Review of Poems by Two Brothers. Finds the poems "amiable" and elegant.

2 Literary Chronicle and Weekly Review, May 19, 1827, p. 308.
Review of Poems by Two Brothers. Likes the volume as a whole and remarks that it "contains several little pieces of considerable merit."

1829

Alfred Tennyson entered a poetry contest at Cambridge and won. The competition topic was Timbuctoo, and not surprisingly his winning poem, when published, was titled Timbuctoo: A Poem which Obtained the Chancellor's Medal at the Cambridge Commencement, 1829.

Periodical

3 Athenaeum, July 22, 1829, p. 456.
Review of Timbuctoo. Enthusiastically praises the poem.

1830

With the publication of Poems, Chiefly Lyrical in 1830, Tennyson's literary career truly begins.

Periodicals

4 [Bell, Robert?] Atlas, 5 (June 27, 1830), 411.

Review of Poems, Chiefly Lyrical. Bell is suggested as the author by E.F. Shannon in his Tennyson and the Reviewers (entry 3496). The review's remarks are friendly.

5 Felix Farley's Bristol Journal, Sept. 25, 1830, p. [4].
Review of Poems, Chiefly Lyrical. Very favorable review.

6 Literary Gazette, Oct. 16, 1830.
Review of The Gem: A Literary Annual for 1831 (published in October 1830). Negatively mentions Tennyson's poems "Anacreontics," "No More," and "A Fragment," in The Gem. Mentioned on page 5 of Tennyson and the Reviewers by E.F. Shannon (entry 3496).

7 Spectator, 3 (Aug. 21, 1830), 637-639.
Review of Poems, Chiefly Lyrical. Faults Tennyson's use of archaic words but likes his inventiveness.

1831

Periodicals

8 [Fox, William Johnson.] Westminster Review, 14 (Jan. 1831), 210-224.
Review of Poems, Chiefly Lyrical. Reprinted: J.D. Jump, ed., Tennyson: The Critical Heritage, pages 21-33 (entry 4013); and I. Armstrong, Victorian Scrutinies, pages 71-83 (entry 4333).
Hallam Tennyson in his Alfred Lord Tennyson (entry 1955, page 49), and Charles Tennyson and Christine Fall in their Alfred Tennyson (entry 4016, page 67), identify the author as John Bowing instead of W.J. Fox. They are virtually alone in their identification.
Fox writes: "That these poems will have a very rapid and extensive popularity we do not anticipate. Their very originality will prevent their being generally appreciated for a time." The review is generally positive, with strictures against Tennyson for becoming too indulgent of his fancy and glibness.

9 [Hallam, Arthur Henry.] "On Some of the Characteristics of Modern Poetry, and on the Lyrical Poems of Alfred Tennyson." Englishman's Magazine, 1 (Aug. 1831), 616-628.
Review of Poems, Chiefly Lyrical. Reprinted: The Poems of Arthur Henry Hallam (entry 1672); The Writings of Arthur Hallam (entry 3329); J.D. Jump, ed., Tennyson: The Critical Heritage, pages 34-49 (entry 4013); J.D. Hunt, ed., Tennyson: In Memoriam, pages 51-59 (entry 4214); and I. Armstrong, Victorian Scrutinies, pages 84-101 (entry 4333).
This article is almost universally regarded as an important assessment of Tennyson and an important influence on Tennyson's early aesthetics.
Hallam writes: "We have remarked five distinctive excellencies of his [Tennyson's] own manner. First, his luxuriance of imagination, and at the same time his control over it. Secondly,

his power of embodying himself in ideal characters, or rather moods
of character, with such accuracy of adjustment that the circumstances of the narrative seem to have a natural correspondence with
the predominant feeling and, as it were, to be evolved from it by
assimilative force. Thirdly, his vivid, picturesque delineation of
objects, and the peculiar skill with which he holds all of them fused,
to borrow a metaphor from science, in a medium of strong emotion.
Fourthly, the variety of his lyrical measures and the exquisite mod-
ulation of harmonious words and cadences to the swell and fall of
the feelings expressed. Fifthly, the elevated habits of thought, implied in these compositions, and importing a mellow soberness of
tone, more impressive to our minds than if the author had drawn
up a set of opinions in verse, and sought to instruct the understanding rather than to communicate the love of beauty to the heart."

10 [Hunt, Leigh.] Tatler, Feb. 24 and 26, 1831, pp. 593-594 and
601-602.
    Review of Poems, Chiefly Lyrical. Comments on Alfred
and Charles Tennyson. Very favorable assessment.

11 New Monthly Magazine, 33 (March 1831), 111-112.
    Review of Poems, Chiefly Lyrical. Compares Tennyson
with Keats and asserts that they are similar poets.

                              1832

        Tennyson's Poems was published by Edward Moxon in London
in 1832 (although the volume was dated 1833). This volume of poetry will be hereinafter referred to as Poems, 1833.

12 Athenaeum, Dec. 1, 1832, pp. 770-772.
    Review of Poems, 1833. Tennyson has many faults, accord-
ing to the reviewer, including being "fanciful to the verge (nay, till
he is often utterly lost to us, within the precincts) of unintelligibil-
ity." Nonetheless, the reviewer confesses "reverence and respect
for his genius."

13 [Bell, Robert?] Atlas, 7 (Dec. 16, 1832), 842.
    Review of Poems, 1833. Although noting some faults in
Poems, 1833, the reviewer asserts that "there is more true relish
in it of that which constitutes the soul of genuine poetry than in a
thousand such books as are daily published under its name."

14 [Jerdan, William?] Literary Gazette, Dec. 8, 1832, pp. 772-
774.
    Review of Poems, 1833. Disparaging of Poems, 1833, al-
though complimentary of Tennyson's talents.

15 North, Christopher (pseudonym for John Wilson). "Noctes
Ambrosianae." Blackwood's Edinburgh Magazine, 31, part I
(Feb. 1832), 277.
    On Poems, Chiefly Lyrical. Tennyson "has--genius," in
spite of some quirks.

16 _____ . Blackwood's Edinburgh Magazine, 31 (May 1832), 721-
741.
    Review of Poems, Chiefly Lyrical. Reprinted: Museum of
Foreign Literature and Science, 21 (Aug. 1832), 128-138; Essays,
Critical and Imaginative (entry 416); and, in part, J. D. Jump, ed.,
Tennyson: The Critical Heritage, pages 50-65 (entry 4013); and I.
Armstrong, Victorian Scrutinies, pages 102-124 (entry 4333).
    "To Christopher" in Poems, 1833, is a response to the pres-
ent review. The poem provided some of the motivation for J. W.
Croker's notorious remarks in The Quarterly Review (entry 22).
    With wit and sarcasm, North attacks the overly enthusiastic
reviews of Poems, Chiefly Lyrical. His commentary is balanced in
spite of its witticisms, and he acknowledges Tennyson's merits even
while noting the poet's weaknesses. North asserts: "Alfred is an
owl: all that he wants is to be shot, stuffed and stuck into a glass
case, to be made immortal in a museum." (These comments are
about Tennyson's "The Owl.") North also comments: "But though
it might be a mistake of ours, were we to say that he [Tennyson]
has much to learn, it can be no mistake to say that he has not a
little to unlearn, and more to bring to practice, before his genius
can achieve its destined triumphs."

17 Spectator, 5 (Dec. 15, 1832), 1190-1191.
    Review of Poems, 1833. Reviewer asserts that Poems, 1833,
is inferior to Poems, Chiefly Lyrical with the exception of "Eleanor."

1833

Periodicals

18 Albion, n. s. 1 (June 1, 1833), 176.
    Agrees with J. W. Croker's (Quarterly Review, April 1833,
entry 22) assessment of Tennyson's poetry.

19 "Alfred Tennyson." Athenaeum, Nov. 16, 1833, p. 772.
    Reprinted: Museum of Foreign Literature and Science, 24
(March 1834), 257-258.

20 Athenaeum, April 13, 1833, p. 234.
    Defends Tennyson against the criticism of J. W. Croker in the
Quarterly Review (entry 22). Asserts that Tennyson "has much fine
poetry about him."

21 [Bulwer, Edward?] New Monthly Magazine, 37 (Jan. 1833),
    69-74.
    Review of Poems, 1833. Condemns Tennyson's poetry for too
much affectation and the advocates of Tennyson for misleading Tennyson with excessive praise.

22 [Croker, John Wilson.] Quarterly Review, 49 (April 1833), 81-96.
    Review of Poems, 1833. Reprinted: Select Journal of Foreign
Literature, 2 (July 1833), 106-121; and J. D. Jump, ed., Tennyson:

The Critical Heritage (entry 4013). Replied to by the Athenaeum
(entry 20) and the Sun (entry 31). See also J.S. Mill's response in
the London Review, 1835 (entry 36).
    This heavy-handed sarcastic review was unhappily remembered
by Tennyson for the rest of his life. Some scholars hold the review
in large part responsible for the almost decade-long gap between Tennyson's publications. Croker ties Tennyson to the so-called Cockney
School of poetry, which he had attacked while savaging the poetry of
Keats in the Quarterly Review in 1818.

23 Cunningham, Allan. "Biographical and Critical History of the
        Last Fifty Years." Athenaeum, Nov. 16, 1833, p. 772. Re-
        printed: Revue des Deux Mondes, Nov. 1833, p. 396.
        Cunningham likes Tennyson's imagination but not Tennyson's
odd diction. Various critics, Cunningham asserts, regard Tennyson
as "the chief living hope of the Muse."

24 [d'Haussey, Baron?] "Alfred Tennyson." L'Europe littéraire,
        March 6 and 15, 1833.
        This particularly thoughtful analysis provides two readings of
Tennyson's poetry. The first discusses him as a possible successor
to Byron. The second seeks to place Tennyson's work in the poetic
tradition.

25 [Forster, John?] True Sun, Jan. 19, 1833, p. [3].
        Review of Poems, 1833. A thoughtful discussion that praises
Tennyson's imagination but finds his wealth of imagery sometimes
tiresome.

26 [Fox, William Johnson?] Monthly Repository, n.s. 7 (Jan. 1833),
        30-41.
        Review of Poems, Chiefly Lyrical and Poems, 1833. Praises
the artistry of Tennyson's poetry.

27 Metropolitan, 6 (Jan. 1833), 9.
        Review of Poems, 1833. Favorable review.

28 Perriwig, John. Revue de Paris, April 1833, pp. 7-8.
        Attacks Tennyson's poetry as derivative and clumsy.

29 Revue des Deux Mondes, Nov. 1833, p. 396.
        Comments on Allan Cunningham's article from the Athenaeum
(entry 23). The commentator regards Tennyson as strikingly original.

30 Select Journal, 2 (July 1833), 106-121.
        Review of Poems, 1833.

31 Sun, April 9, 1833, p. [3].
        Defends Tennyson against the criticism in the Quarterly Re-
view (entry 22) by J.W. Croker. Asserts that Tennyson merely suf-
fers from faults common in young writers and is basically a good
poet.

32 Tait's Edinburgh Magazine, 2 (Jan. 1833), 540.
      Review of Poems, 1833. Finds the work good but beneath
expectations raised by Poems, Chiefly Lyrical.

1834

Book

33 [Thurston, Charles T.] The Sister's Tragedy. London: 1834.
      The author is identified by E. D. Shannon in Tennyson and
the Reviewers (page 30; entry 3496) from the catalogue of the Bodle-
ian Library. This play derived from Tennyson's "The Sisters" in
Poems, 1833.

Periodicals

34 "Alfred Tennyson." Le Voleur, Dec. 20, 1834.
      Mentioned by Margorie Bowden in Tennyson in France (entry
3101), page 11. Places Tennyson in the tradition of Thomas Moore.

1835

Book

35 Coleridge, Samuel Taylor. Specimens of the Table Talk of the
      Late Samuel Taylor Coleridge. [Ed. Henry N. Coleridge.]
London: 1835.
      Tennyson on pages 164-165 of Volume II.

Periodical

36 [Mill, John Stuart.] (Signed "A.") London Review, 1 (July 1835),
      402-424.
      Review of Poems, Chiefly Lyrical and Poems, 1833. Reprinted:
J. D. Jump, ed., Tennyson: The Critical Heritage (entry 4013), pages
84-97.
      Mill praises Tennyson's poetry and asserts that Poems, 1833,
is superior to Poems, Chiefly Lyrical. He remarks: "The poems
which we have quoted from Mr. Tennyson prove incontestably that he
possesses, in an eminent degree, the natural endowment of a poet--
the poetic temperament. And it appears clearly, not only from a comparison of the two volumes, but of different poems in the same volume, that with him, the other element of poetic excellence--intellec-
tual culture--is advancing both steadily and rapidly.... [He] is rip-
ening into a true artist."

1836

Periodicals

37 Athenaeum, Nov. 5, 1836.

Discusses Tennyson's "Saint Agnes," which was published in The Keepsake, 1837 (circa 1836). Review of The Keepsake as a whole.

38 [Clarke, James Freeman.] Western Messenger, 2 (Dec. 1836), 323-325.
Review of Poems, Chiefly Lyrical. Clarke says that Tennyson's poetry is beautifully musical but insubstantial.

1837

Periodicals

39 Every Body's Album, 2 (March 1837), 232.
Notice of Poems, Chiefly Lyrical and Poems, 1833. Notes Tennyson as a leading young English poet.

40 [Napier, Macvey?] Edinburgh Review, 66 (Oct. 1837), 108-110.
Review of The Tribute (1837), a volume of verse intended to raise money for Edward Smedley. It discusses Tennyson's contribution, "Stanzas," and cites fifty-eight lines of the poem.

1838

Periodical

41 D., J.S. (John Sullivan Dwight). Christian Examiner, 23 (Jan. 1838), 305-327.
Review of Poems, Chiefly Lyrical and Poems, 1833. Discusses some English criticism of Tennyson. Admires Tennyson's economy of phrasing and particularly likes Tennyson's portraits of women. Dwight asserts: "He [Tennyson] has the true insight, or onsight (Anschauen) as the Germans call it."

1839

Periodical

42 Chasles, Philarète. "De la littérature anglaise actuelle." Revue des Deux Mondes, March 1, 1839, pp. 583-608.
Chasles discusses Tennyson as if Tennyson were no longer going to write poetry. He is unhappy with Tennyson's romanticism.

1840

Periodical

43 Poe, Edgar A. Burton's Gentleman's Magazine, 6 (Feb. 1840), 100-103.

Poe reviews Longfellow's Voices of the Night and points out resemblances between poems by Longfellow and earlier ones by Tennyson.

1841

Periodicals

44 Duyckinck, Evert A. "English Literary Intelligence."
    News-Gong: A Literary Intelligencer, 1 (Dec. 1841). Listed in J.O. Eidson's Tennyson in America (entry 3328), page 168.

45 [Fuller, Margaret.] "Tennyson's Poems." Dial, 2 (July 1841), 135.
    Praises Tennyson's poetry. Fuller remarks: "Tennyson is known by heart, is copied as Greek works were at the revival of literature...."

1842

Tennyson's Poems of 1842 was published by Edward Moxon of London. The new volume of poetry generated much interest among the book-buying public, and the critics produced a deluge of reviews. The 1842 volume will hereinafter be referred to as Poems, 1842.

Periodicals

46 Atlas, 17 (June 25, 1842), 410-411.
    Review of Poems, 1842. Notes Tennyson's maturation as a poet. Commends the "thoughtfulness" of Tennyson's poetry.

47 Boston Miscellany of Literature and Fashion, 2 (Sept. 1842), 140.
    Review of Poems, 1842.

48 Brother Jonathan, 2 (July 16, 1842), 325.
    Review of Poems, 1842. Praises Tennyson's poetry.

49 C. Lady's World of Fashion, 2 (Oct. 1842), 114-117.
    Review of Poems, 1842.

50 C., W.A. (William Arthur Case?) London University Magazine, 1 (Dec. 1842), 286-314.
    Review of Poems, 1842. Points out the beauties of Tennyson's poetry.

51 Cambridge University Magazine, 2 (Oct. 1842), 629-639.
    Review of Poems, 1842. High praise for Tennyson's mastery of poetry.

52 [Chorley, Henry Fothergill.] Athenaeum, Aug. 6, 1842, p. 700-702.

Review of <u>Poems</u>, 1842. Admires the power, sensitivity, and musicality of Tennyson's poems. Unhappy with some of Tennyson's revisions of previously published poems but primarily favorable in point of view.

53 <u>Courier</u> (Boston), July 12, 1842.
   Review of <u>Poems</u>, 1842. Ranks Tennyson among the best of contemporary poets.

54 <u>Democratic Review</u>, 11 (Aug. 1842), 215.
   Review of <u>Poems</u>, 1842.

55 Duyckinck, Evert A. "The Poems of Tennyson." <u>Arcturus</u>,
   3 (Feb. 1842), 235-238.
   Finds Tennyson to be a gentle poet.

56 <u>Echo de la Littérature</u>, 1842, p. 270.
   Review of <u>Poems</u>, 1842. Expresses dismay at Tennyson's revisions of previously published poems.

57 "Editor's Table." <u>Knickerbocker</u>, 20 (Aug. 1842), 208.
   Review of <u>Poems</u>, 1842. Finds the poetry moving. Compare with <u>Knickerbocker</u> reviews of December 1842 (entry 58) and June 1845 (entry 104).

58 "Editor's Table." <u>Knickerbocker</u>, 20 (Dec. 1842), 582.
   Quotes from and lauds C.C. Felton's negative review in the <u>Christian Examiner</u>. Odd contrast to <u>Knickerbocker</u>'s review of August 1842 (entry 57).

59 <u>Evening Post for the Country</u> (New York), July 8, 1842.
   Review of <u>Poems</u>, 1842.

60 <u>Evening Transcript</u> (Boston), Aug. 15, 1842.
   Review of <u>Poems</u>, 1842. Suggests that the poems need editing.

61 [Felton, Cornelius C.] "Tennyson's Poems." <u>Christian Examiner</u>,
   33 (Nov. 1842), 237-244.
   Review of <u>Poems</u>, 1842. Sharp attack on Tennyson's poetry. Portrays Tennyson as effeminate.

62 [Forster, John.] <u>Examiner</u>, May 28, 1842, pp. 340-341.
   Review of <u>Poems</u>, 1842. Praises it as the fulfillment of the promise shown in Tennyson's earlier works. Notes the maturation of Tennyson's art. Singles out "Locksley Hall" for special notice as a "piece of strong, full-blooded, man's writing."

63 [Fuller, Margaret.] "A Review of the Poems of Alfred Tennyson."
   <u>Dial</u>, 3 (Oct. 1842), 273-276.
   Praises the poetry of Tennyson and notes his increasing poetic maturity.

64 [Garden, Francis?] <u>Christian Remembrancer</u>, 4 (July 1842),

42-58.
Review of Poems, 1842. Reprinted in part: J.D. Jump, ed.,
Tennyson: The Critical Heritage (entry 4013), pages 98-102.
      Calls Tennyson the "foremost" of young poets. A cautiously
favorable assessment of Tennyson's latest poetry.

65 [Griswold, Rufus W.] Graham's Magazine, 21 (Sept. 1842),
      152-153.
      Review of Poems, 1842. Mildly favorable view of Tennyson's
poetry.

66 [Hunt, Leigh.] "The Modern School of Poetry." Church of
      England Quarterly Review, 12 (Oct. 1842), 361-376.
      Review of Poems, 1842. Reprinted: J.D. Jump, ed.,
Tennyson: The Critical Heritage (entry 4013), pages 126-136.
      Moderate praise for Poems, 1842. Singles out "The Two
Voices" for particular praise. Hunt comments: "Mr. Tennyson
is at present a kind of philosophical Keats, without the later judgment of that extraordinary genius, and of a turn of mind less naturally and thoroughly given to poetry, in its essence. But there
can be no doubt that he is a genuine poet too in his degree...."

67 J., J. Christian Teacher, n.s. 4 (1842), 414-423.
      Review of Poems, 1842. A favorable review.

68 [Jerdan, William?] Literary Gazette, Nov. 19, 1842, pp. 788-
      789.
      Review of Poems, 1842. Focuses negatively on the changes
made in previously published poems.

69 M., R.M. (Richard Monckton Milnes). Westminster Review,
      38 (Oct. 1842), 371-390.
      Review of Poems, 1842. Reprinted in part: J.D. Jump, ed.,
Tennyson: The Critical Heritage (entry 4013), pages 137-138.
      Quotes extensively from Poems, 1842, and urges Tennyson
to be more of a teacher. Milnes remarks: "His [Tennyson's] command of diction is complete, his sense and execution of the harmo-
nies of verse accurate and admirable; he has only to show that he
has substance (what Goethe used to call stoff) worthy of these media;
that he will not content himself with any ingenuity of conceit or fan-
cifulness of illustration; that, in fine, he comprehends the function
of the poet in this day of ours, to teach still more than he delights,
and to suggest still more than he teaches."

70 Monthly Review, n.s. 2 (July 1842), 369-375.
      Review of Poems, 1842. A balanced review of the strengths
and weaknesses of Poems, 1842, that praises "Locksley Hall" as a
particularly noteworthy poem.

71 Morning Post (Boston), July 12, 1842.
      Review of Poems, 1842. A strongly hostile review that calls
some of Tennyson's poetry "trash." Replied to by New World (entry
73).

72 Morning Post (London), Aug. 9, 1842, p. 6.
    Review of Poems, 1842. The poems "exhibit a strength, a
brilliancy, a truthful earnestness of sentiment--a perfect mastery of
language--an unerring power and discretion in adapting it to the most
effective forms of versification--which, beyond the possibility of a
doubt of question, must entitle Mr. Tennyson to take his stand at
once amongst the most famous of our living poets."

73 New World, 5 (July 16, 1842), 48.
    Review of Poems, 1842. Attacks the Boston Morning Post's
review of Poems, 1842 (entry 71). The reviewer asserts that Tennyson "is a true prophet ... giving utterance to the unapprehended
aspirations of millions."

74 [Poe, Edgar Allan.] Graham's Magazine, 21 (Sept. 1842), 152-
    153.
    Review of Poems, 1842. Poe remarks: "Tennyson has been
praised as a strikingly original poet. He has indeed a bold and af-
fluent fancy, whereby he tricks out common thoughts in dresses so
unique that it is not always easy to identify them; but we have not
seen in his works proofs of an original mind."

75 Revue britannique, Aug. 1842, p. 389.
    Review of Poems, 1842. Favorable view.

76 [Richards, William C.?] Orion, 1 (Sept. 1842), 395.
    Review of Poems, 1842. Favorable.

77 Southern Literary Messenger, 8 (Sept. 1842), 612.
    Review of Poems, 1842.

78 Spectator, 15 (June 4, 1842), 544.
    Review of Poems, 1842. Acknowledges Tennyson's talents in
a generally negative commentary.

79 [Sterling, John.] Quarterly Review, 70 (Sept. 1842), 385-416.
    Review of Poems, 1842. Reprinted: J. D. Jump, ed., Ten-
nyson: The Critical Heritage (entry 4013), pages 103-125: and I.
Armstrong, Victorian Scrutinies (entry 4333), pages 125-147.
    Generally favorable review, although it includes negative re-
marks. Sterling argues that great poets reflect their eras and discusses Tennyson's work from such a point of view. He praises
"Locksley Hall" and dismisses "Morte d'Arthur" as frivolous.

80 Sun, May 28, 1842, p. [4].
    Review of Poems, 1842. Complains about "hazy imagery."
Singles out "Locksley Hall": "Our author's best poem is decidedly
the one entitled 'Locksley Hall,' wherein strength and earnestness of
purpose are visible throughout, relieved and softened off by occasional touches of infinite tenderness."

81 Sun, Sept. 21, 1842.
    Mentioned on page 82 of W. D. Templeman's "A Consideration

of the Fame of 'Locksley Hall'" in Victorian Poetry (entry 3843).
    While discussing the Quarterly Review, the article mentions
Sterling's review (entry 79) and praises Tennyson and "Locksley
Hall."

82 Tait's Edinburgh Magazine, n.s. 9 (Aug. 1842), 502-508.
    Review of Poems, 1842. Detailed argument that Tennyson's
poetry is of the highest quality.

83 Times (Boston), July 14, 1842.
    Review of Poems, 1842. Ambiguous review.

84 Weekly Dispatch, Aug. 21, 1842, p. 406.
    Review of Poems, 1842. An ambiguous commentary.

1843

Periodicals

85 Aytoun, William Edmondstoune. "The Laureate, by Alfred Ten-
        nyson." Tait's Edinburgh Magazine, 10 (May 1843),
        275.
    Reprinted: B. Gaultier, ed., The Book of Ballads, 1890
(entry 1288). A parody.

86 _____. "La Mort d'Arthur: A Fragment--Not by Tennyson."
        Tait's Edinburgh Magazine, 10 (Oct. 1843), 651-652.
    Reprinted: B. Gaultier, ed., The Book of Ballads, 1890
(entry 1289).

87 [Emerson, Ralph Waldo.] "Europe and European Books." Dial,
        3 (April 1843), 517-518.
    "Perhaps Tennyson is too quaint and elegant," remarks Emer-
son. He compares Tennyson with Ben Jonson.

88 Poe, Edgar Allan. "William Ellery Channing." Graham's
        Magazine, 23 (Aug. 1843), 113.
    Defends some of the traits of Tennyson's poetry and asserts
that "Locksley Hall" ranks among the best "compositions of any one
living or dead."

89 [Spedding, James.] Edinburgh Review, 77 (April 1843), 373-391.
    Review of Poems, 1842. Reprinted: Albion, 2 (May 20,
1843), 242; Reviews and Discussions, 1879 (entry 911); J.D. Jump,
ed., Tennyson: The Critical Heritage (entry 4013), pages 139-152.
    Spedding was a close friend and advisor of Tennyson. He of-
fers a careful explication of Tennyson's poetry and answers some
negative criticisms put forth by other reviewers. Spedding asserts:
"The decade during which Mr. Tennyson has remained silent has
wrought a great improvement. The handling in his later pieces is
much lighter and freer; the interest deeper and purer; there is
more humanity with less image and drapery; a closer adherence to

truth; a greater reliance for effect upon the simplicity of Nature.
Moral and spiritual traits of character are more dwelt upon, in
place of external scenery and circumstance. He addresses himself more to the heart and less to the ear and eye." Spedding also
approves of the changes made in previously published poems.

1844

Book

90 Horne, Richard H., and Elizabeth Barrett. "Alfred Tennyson."
    A New Spirit of the Age. London: Smith, Elder, 1844.
    New York: Harper, 1844. Volume II, pp. 3-32.
    Reprinted in part: J. D. Jump, ed., Tennyson: The Critical
Heritage (entry 4013), pages 153-165.
    Interesting discussion of Tennyson's reputation and poetry.
Ranks Tennyson as a first-rate poetic genius.

Periodicals

91 Athenaeum, March 23; April 6, 20, 27; and June 8, 1844, pp.
    270-271, 318-319, 357-358, 381-383, and 525-526, respec-
    tively.
    Three correspondents debate the merits of contemporary poets,
with Tennyson's strengths and faults used, in part, to illustrate
whether or not the poets were expressing the concerns of modern
society.

92 [Butler, Fanny Kemble.] "Tennyson's Poems." United States
    Magazine and Democratic Review, 14 (Jan. 1844), 62-77.
    Review of Poems, 1842. Analyzes Tennyson's revisions of
previously published poems that appear in Poems, 1842. Argues in
extensive detail that the revisions worsened the poems.

93 "Editor's Table." Knickerbocker, 23 (March 1844), 291-293.
    "The May Queen" is mentioned.

94 [Lea, Henry Charles.] Southern Literary Messenger, 10 (April
    1844), 240-246.
    Review of Poems, 1842. Believes Tennyson is unoriginal and
his poetry without value. Suggests Tennyson give up poetry and become a gardener.

95 "Modern Poets--Tennyson, Marston, and Browning." Foreign
    and Colonial Quarterly Review (soon to change to New Quar-
    terly Review), 3 (Jan. 1844), 202-215.
    Praises Tennyson as a genius and singles out his poem
"Ulysses" as especially admirable.

96 Poe, Edgar Allan. "Marginalia." United States Magazine and
    Democratic Review, 15 (Dec. 1844), 580.

Poe says: "I am not sure that Tennyson is not the greatest of poets." He admires in particular "Morte d'Arthur."

97 "Tennyson's Poems." Christian Parlor Magazine, 1 (Dec. 1844), 231-233.
The discussion emphasizes "The May Queen."

1845

Books

98 Fox, William Johnson. "Living Poets and Their Services to the Cause of Political Freedom and Human Progress: Alfred Tennyson." Lectures Addressed Chiefly to the Working Classes. London: Charles Fox, 1845. Volume I, pp. 248-265.

99 Gaultier, Bon (pseudonym for Theodore Martin and William Edmondstoune Aytoun). "The Lay of the Lovelorn." The Book of Ballads. Ed. Bon Gaultier. London: 1845, pp. 13-18.
A parody of "Locksley Hall."

Periodicals

100 B., C. A. (Charles Astor Bristed). "English Poetry and Poets of the Present Day." Knickerbocker Magazine, 25 (June 1845), 534-540.
Contends that Tennyson is a great poet and the best of his time.

101 British Quarterly Review, 2 (Aug. 1845), 46-71.
Review of Poems, 1842. Reprinted: Eclectic Magazine of Foreign Literature, Science and Art, 6 (Oct. 1845), 205-217.
A balanced and friendly discussion.

102 "Editor's Table." Knickerbocker Magazine, 26 (Sept. 1845), 288.
"My Early Love" is mentioned.

103 [Gilfillan, George.] "Alfred Tennyson." Dumfries-shire and Galloway Herald and Register, Oct. 16, 1845, pp. [1] and [4]; and Oct. 23, 1845, pp. [1] and [4].
Reprinted in revised form: Tait's Edinburgh Magazine, 1847 (entry 126).

104 Knickerbocker Magazine, 25 (June 1845), 487-488.
"My Early Love" is mentioned.

105 "Literary Gossip." Broadway Journal, 1 (May 31, 1845), 348.

106 [Poe, Edgar Allan?] "Alfred Tennyson." Broadway Journal, 2 (July 19, 1845), 26.

A few brief comments followed by an extensive extract from
a review by E. P. Whipple (entry 113). Poe declares: "The injus-
tice done in America to the magnificent genius of Tennyson is one
of the worst sins for which the country has to answer."

107 _____. Broadway Journal, 2 (Nov. 29, 1845), 322.
Notice of Poems, 1842. Poe asserts: "This is a very neat,
and altogether tasteful new edition of a poet, who (in our own hum-
ble, but sincere opinion) is the greatest that ever lived."

108 [_____]. "Critical Notices." Broadway Journal, 1 (March
29, 1845), 195-196.
Suggests that Longfellow has plagiarized Tennyson.

109 _____. "Marginal Notes--No. II." Godey's Lady's Book,
31 (Sept. 1845), 120-123.

110 "The Poetry of Alfred Tennyson." Chamber's Edinburgh
Journal, n.s. 4 (July 12, 1845), 25-29.
In a general appreciation of Tennyson's poetry, the author
argues that Tennyson is a passive poet who reflects the past and
the human heart.

111 [Ray, Luzerne.] New Englander, 3 (Jan. 1845), 57-66.
Review of Poems, 1842. Analyzes Tennyson's strengths and
weaknesses in an overall favorable view of Tennyson's poetry.

112 Tuckerman, Henry T. "Thoughts on the Poets--Tennyson."
Columbian Lady's and Gentleman's Magazine, 4 (Aug. 1845),
91-93.
Reprinted: Thoughts on the Poets, 1846 (entry 115). Praises
Tennyson's poetry.

113 [Whipple, Edwin P.] American Whig Review, 2 (July 1845),
45-48.
Review of R. W. Griswold's edition, Poets and Poetry of
England, 1845 (an anthology). Reprinted in part: Broadway Journal,
2 (July 19, 1845), 26-27 (see entry 106).
Whipple disputes Griswold's assessment of Tennyson as a
minor poet. He defends Tennyson's thoughtfulness.

1846

Books

114 Bulwer-Lytton, Edward. The New Timon: A Poetical Romance.
London: Colburn, 1846.
In 1845, Robert Peel persuaded Queen Victoria to grant Tennyson a pension of £200 per year. The pension angered Bulwer-
Lytton, who in The New Timon calls Tennyson "School-Miss Alfred,"
who is "outbabying Wordsworth and outglittering Keates." Tennyson
responded in "New Timon and the Poets," which was published in

<u>Punch</u> without his consent.

Reviewed: <u>Athenaeum</u> (entry 116); <u>Eclectic Review</u> (entry 118); <u>Lowe's Edinburgh Magazine</u> (entry 119); and <u>Times</u> (London) (entry 122).

115 Tuckerman, Henry T. "Tennyson." <u>Thoughts on the Poets.</u>
New York: Francis, 1846. pp. 273-280.
Reprinted from: <u>Columbian Lady's and Gentleman's Magazine</u> (entry 112).

Periodicals

116 <u>Athenaeum</u>, March 14, 1846, pp. 263-264.
Review of E. Bulwer-Lytton's <u>The New Timon</u> (entry 114).
Derogates Bulwer-Lytton's poem and defends Tennyson.

117 Clements, H. H. "Tennyson." <u>New York Illustrated Magazine of Literature and Art,</u> 2 (Sept. 1846), 241-244.
Ranks Tennyson near Milton.

118 <u>Eclectic Review,</u> 19 (April 1846), 419.
Review of E. Bulwer-Lytton's <u>The New Timon</u> (entry 114).
In bitingly colorful language, this review attacks <u>The New Timon.</u>

119 <u>Lowe's Edinburgh Magazine,</u> 1 (June 1846), 566-568.
Review of Bulwer-Lytton's <u>The New Timon</u> (entry 114). Extols Tennyson's virtues at the expense of the author of <u>The New Timon.</u>

120 " 'The New Timon' and Alfred Tennyson's Pension." <u>Punch,</u>
10 (February 7, 1846), 64.
A defense of Tennyson against Bulwer-Lytton.

121 "Tennyson's Poetry." <u>Christian Parlor Magazine,</u> 3 (May 1846), 29.

122 <u>Times</u> (London), June 5, 1846, p. 7.
Review of E. Bulwer-Lytton's <u>The New Timon</u> (entry 114).
Defends Tennyson.

1847

Edward Moxon published Tennyson's <u>The Princess</u> in 1847.

Book

123 Howitt, William, "Alfred Tennyson." <u>Homes and Haunts of The Most Eminent British Poets.</u> London: Bentley, 1847. Volume II, pp. 452-470.
Although dated "1847," this book may have appeared in December 1846. Howitt remarks about Tennyson: "There speaks the man of this moving age. There speaks the spirit baptized into the great spirit of progress."

Periodicals

124 "Alfred Tennyson." Hogg's Weekly Instructor, 6 (Dec. 25, 1847), 231-284.
     Reprinted: Eclectic Magazine of Foreign Literature, 13 (March 1848), 289-295.
     Calls Tennyson "one of the greatest of living poets" but is dissatisfied with the beauty in his poetry; asks that Tennyson become a "prophet-preacher."

125 Forgues, E.D. "Alfred Tennyson." Revue des Deux Mondes, 18 (May 1, 1847), 417-437.
     Reprinted: Originaux et Beau Esprits de L'Angleterre Contemporaine, 1860 (entry 495).
     Complains that Tennyson's poetry is vague and capricious.

126 Gilfillan, George. "Alfred Tennyson." Tait's Edinburgh Magazine, 14 (April 1847), 229-234.
     A revised version of Gilfillan's article in the Dumfries-shire and Galloway Herald and Register, 1845 (entry 103). Reprinted: Eclectic Magazine of Foreign Literature, 11 (June 1847), 161-168; A Second Gallery of Literary Portraits, 1850 (entry 181); Modern Literature and Literary Men, 1857 (entry 443).
     Even though he admires Tennyson's artistry, Gilfillan is unhappy with the poet's "timidity and weakness."

127 "On the Poetry and Poets of the Age." Albion, 6 (Nov. 27, 1847), 568.

128 [Talfourd, Thomas Noon?] Eclectic Magazine of Foreign Literature, Science and Art, 11 (May 1847), 144.
     Reprinted: National Magazine, 1 (Nov. 1852), 434.

1848

Books

129 Sterling, John. Essays and Tales. Ed. Julius C. Hare. London: John W. Parker, 1848. Volume I, pp. 422-462.

130 Whipple, Edwin P. Essays and Reviews. New York: Appleton, 1848. Volume I, pp. 322-330.

Periodicals

131 Albion, 7 (Feb. 19, 1848), 95-96.
     Review of The Princess.

132 American Literary Magazine, 2 (May 1848), 275-281.
     Review of The Princess. The reviewer admires the beauties of the poem's verse but is disturbed by Tennyson's grammatical lapses. The poem also inspires the reviewer to attack women who want equal rights with men.

133   Atlas, 23 (Jan. 15, 1848), 42-43.
      Review of The Princess.   Finds the poem to be uneven in
quality.

134   Bristed, Charles A.   "A Talk about the Princess."   American
      Whig Review, 8 (July 1848), 28-39.
      Bristed creates the characters Fred Peters and the General
and has them repeat the standard criticisms of Tennyson's poetry,
as if in a conversation.   He refutes the criticism as if replying to
his characters.   A significant article.

135   Britannia, Jan. 22, 1848, p. 61.
      Review of The Princess.   Condemns it as the worst of Ten-
nyson's writings.

136   C.   Christian Reformer, or Unitarian Magazine and Review,
      n. s. 4 (Feb. 1848), 11-113.
      Review of The Princess.   Likes the poem.

137   Chronotype (Boston), Feb. 11, 1848.
      Review of The Princess.   Mentioned in J.O. Eidson's Ten-
nyson in America (entry 3328), pages 58 and 171.   The reviewer
admires The Princess, according to Eidson.

138   [Coleridge, Sara.]   Quarterly Review, 82 (March 1848),
      427-453.
      Review of The Princess.   Coleridge tries to maintain a bal-
anced tone while analyzing The Princess as an important work of
literature.

139   Dublin Evening Herald, May 22, 1848, p. [2].
      Review of The Princess.   Views the poem as pleasant but
not meaningful.

140   Dwight, J[ohn] S[ullivan].   Harbinger, 6 (March 18, 1848),
      158.
      Review of The Princess.   Dwight believes that Tennyson has
given The Princess purpose and therefore has made it more real-
istic and meaningful than his previous poetry.

141   Eclectic Review, 23 (April 1848), 415-423.
      Review of The Princess.   Praises Tennyson's choice of sub-
ject but finds the poem uneven in quality.

142   English Review, 9 (June 1848), 286-297.
      Review of The Princess.   Admires the poem's charm, imagery,
and didacticism.

143   Evening Transcript (Boston), Feb. 11, 1848.
      Review of The Princess.

144   F., C.B.   Literary World, 3 (Feb. 12, 1848), 28.
      Review of The Princess.

145 [Forster, John?] Examiner (London), Jan. 8, 1848, pp. 20-21.
        Review of The Princess. Reprinted: Daguerreotype, 2 (Feb.
26, 1848), 80-84; and Littell's Living Age, 16 (March 4, 1848), 441-
445. See for response: Literary World, 1848 (entry 154).
        Contends that The Princess is filled with "first-rate poetry."

146 Gentleman's Magazine, 29 (Feb. 1848), 115-131.
        Review of The Princess. The reviewer notes some imper-
fections in the poem but likes it as a whole.

147 Graham's Magazine, 32 (May 1848), 300.
        Review of The Princess. Admires the poem's beauty.

148 Guardian, Jan. 5, 1848, pp. 13-14.
        Review of The Princess. Praises it.

149 [Hirst, Henry B.?] Illustrated Monthly Courier, 1 (Nov. 1,
        1848), 78-79.
        Review of The Princess. Immoderate praise for Tennyson
and the poem.

150 Holden's Dollar Magazine, 1 (March 1848), 185.
        Review of The Princess.

151 [Hopkins, Manley?] Times (London), Oct. 12, 1848, p. 3.
        Review of Poems, 1842, and The Princess. A sensitive
appreciation marred by some silly language. Argues that Tennyson
writes in the tradition of the late Romantics but is original enough
to have become the leader of a new school of poetry. Regrets that
Tennyson is not as careful a craftsman as he should be. Singles out
"The Two Voices" as Tennyson's "best poem."

152 [Howitt, William?] Howitt's Journal, 3 (Jan. 8, 1848), 28-29.
        Review of The Princess. Likes Tennyson's topic and artistry.

153 [Jerdan, William?] Literary Gazette, Aug. 12, 1848, pp. 530-
        532.
        Review of The Princess. Although The Princess is "true
poetry," its imperfections are so great that they obscure its merits.

154 Literary World, 3 (Feb. 26, 1848), 61-62.
        Review of The Princess. Disputes the Examiner's (entry 145)
assertion that The Princess contains "first-rate poetry." The Princess makes for pleasant reading but is a treatise rather than a poem.

155 [Lowell, James Russell.] Massachusetts Quarterly Review,
        1 (March 1848), 256-259.
        Review of The Princess. Proclaims the poem Tennyson's
best and that Tennyson has gained confidence in himself.

156 Lowe's Edinburgh Magazine, 3 (Feb. 1848), 245-258.
        Review of Poems, 1842, and The Princess. Reprinted in part:
Dumfries and Galloway Standard and Advertiser, Feb. 16, 1848, p. [2].

Discusses Tennyson's political views and provides a favorable analysis of Tennyson's poetry.

157 M. Metropolitan Magazine, 51 (Feb. 1848), 220-229.
Review of The Princess. Presents extracts from the poem. Praises it.

158 Manchester Examiner, Jan. 8, 1848, p. 3.
Review of The Princess. Praises Tennyson's poetry.

159 [Marston, John Westland.] Athenaeum, Jan. 1, 1848, pp. 6-8.
Review of The Princess. Reprinted in part: Dumfries-shire and Galloway Herald and Register, Jan. 6, 1848, p. [4]; Albion, 7 (March 4, 1848), 113. Reprinted: J.D. Jump, ed., Tennyson: The Critical Heritage (entry 4013), pp. 166-171.
Marston writes: "There is so much to admire in this volume that we cannot wish it unwritten,--but so much also to censure that, while we could recognize the whole if tendered as a pledge of genius, we cannot accept it as a due consummation of that faculty." He adds: "Lecture rooms and chivalric lists, modern pedantry and ancient romance, are antagonisms which no art can reconcile." Also: "With the power which Mr. Tennyson has here evinced for the familiar and the ideal regarded separately, it is much to be deplored that by their unskilful combination he has produced simply--the grotesque."

160 Morning Post (London), Jan 22, 1848, p. 3.
Review of The Princess. Ranks Tennyson's achievement in The Princess among the best in poetry. Calls the poem's theme "great."

161 [Patmore, Coventry.] North British Review, 9 (May 1848), 43-72.
Review of Poems, 1842, and The Princess. Perceives The Princess as an allegory for contemporary science.

162 Peterson's Magazine, 13 (April 1848), 155.
Review of The Princess. Discusses Tennyson's social commentary.

163 S. Atlas (Boston), Feb. 11, 1848.
Review of The Princess. Discussed by J.O. Eidson in Tennyson in America (entry 3328), pages 58-59. Predicts popularity for the poem, according to Eidson.

164 Sharpe's London Magazine, 6 (April 1848), 139-141.
Review of The Princess. Tries to appraise the poem fairly as neither entirely good nor bad.

165 Spectator, 21 (Jan. 8, 1848), 41-42.
Review of The Princess. Condemns the Subject and execution of The Princess. Declares that the "subject ... is narrow, uninteresting, unnatural, and absurd, not to say offensive."

166 Sun, Jan. 8, 1848, p. [3].
     Review of The Princess. Praises it as a poem of lasting
value and universal appeal.

167 Sutton, Henry. "The Poet's Mission." Howitt's Journal, 3
     (Jan. 15, 1848), 39-42.
     Sutton interprets "The Lady of Shalott" as an allegory of
a poet's loss of artistic power when he pursues fame.

168 Tait's Edinburgh Magazine, 15 (Aug. 1848), 554-555.
     Review of The Princess. Believes that Tennyson opposes
the feminist movement and derogates the poem as beneath Tennyson's
talent.

169 "A Talk about The Princess." American Whig Review, 8 (July
     1848), 28-39.

170 Times (Sheffield), Jan. 29, 1848, p. 2.
     Review of The Princess. Places it among the best of contem-
porary poems.

171 Tribune (New York), Feb. 14, 1848.
     Review of The Princess. Enthusiastic praise.

                         1849

Book

172 Powell, Thomas. "Alfred Tennyson." The Living Authors of
     England. New York: Appleton, 1849, pp. 36-60.

Periodicals

173 [Chretien, Charles Peter.] Christian Remembrancer, 17 (April
     1849), 381-401.
     Reprinted: I. Armstrong, Victorian Scrutinies (entry 4333),
pages 200-222.
     Review of Poems, 1842, and The Princess. Admires Ten-
nyson's language but little else. Contends that Tennyson is eminent
because his contemporaries are mediocre. Asserts: "Mr. Tennyson
is not a great poet. We can scarcely any longer hope that he will
achieve greatness."

174 [de Vere, Aubrey.] Edinburgh Review, 90 (Oct. 1849), 388-433.
     Review of Poems, 1842, and The Princess. Reprinted:
Eclectic Magazine of Foreign Literature, Science and Art, 19 (Jan.
1850), 66-90.
     De Vere was a friend of Tennyson and heard the poet recite
portions of The Princess long before its publication. His review
emphasizes Tennyson's many poetic assets as illustrated by The
Princess.

175 [Finch, F.M.] "A Frolic with Tennyson." Yale Literary
     Magazine, 14 (Jan. 1849), 112-121.
     Review of The Princess. Finds it to be satirical.

176 Hadley, James. New Englander, 7 (May 1849), 193-215.
     Review of The Princess. Reprinted: Essays, Philological
and Critical, 1873 (entry 738).
     Reviews previous criticisms and methodically analyzes and
defends the poem. An important discussion that retains value
because of its logic.

177 Poe, Edgar Allan. "Fifty Suggestions." Graham's Magazine,
     34 (June 1849), 363-364.

178 _____. "Marginalia." Southern Literary Messenger, 15
     (May 1849), 292-296.

179 [Smith, William Henry.] Blackwood's Edinburgh Magazine, 65
     (April 1849), 453-467.
     Review of Poems, 1842, and The Princess. Reprinted:
Eclectic Magazine of Foreign Literature, 17 (June 1849), 169-182.
     Acknowledges Tennyson as an important poet, then notes his
faults and bad poems, and then notes his good poems. Accuses
Tennyson of bad taste. Likes The Princess, although the poem might
be better.

180 Westminster Review, 51 (July 1849), 265-290.
     Review of Poems, 1842. Devotes much space to "Locksley
Hall," which the reviewer likes.

1850

     Tennyson was appointed Poet Laureate on November 19, 1850.
The year included the publication of In Memoriam, a revised version
(third edition) of The Princess, and a slightly expanded version (sixth
edition) of Poems, 1842. In Memoriam was at first published anon-
ymously, but word of its author's identity quickly reached most critics.

Book

181 Gilfillan, George. "Alfred Tennyson." A Second Gallery of
Literary Portraits. Edinburgh and London: 1850, pp. 214-231.
     Reprinted from Tait's Edinburgh Magazine, 1847 (entry 126).
See entry 126 for other reprintings and annotation.

Periodicals

182 Albion, 9 (Aug. 10, 1850), 381.
     Review of In Memoriam. Calls the poem "monotonous."

183 "Alfred Tennyson." Christian Parlor Magazine, 6 (March 1850),
     145-148.

184 Athenaeum, April 27, 1850, p. 451.
     Discusses Tennyson as a possibility for the poet laureateship.

185 Atlas, 25 (June 15, 1850), 379.
     Review of In Memoriam. Regards the poem as an expression
of genuine sorrow.

186 Ayr Observer, July 16, 1850, p. [2].
     Review of In Memoriam. Mentioned in E. F. Shannon's Ten-
nyson and the Reviewers (entry 3496).

187 B. Nassau Literary Magazine, 10 (Oct. 1850), 62-65.
     Review of In Memoriam. The reviewer objects to Tennyson
asking the public to share his grief.

188 B., S.E. United States Magazine and Democratic Review, 27
     (Sept. 1850), 204-207.
     Review of In Memoriam. The reviewer finds In Memoriam
insincere and too remote from most readers. He asserts: "These
poems are, in a word, capricious and fanciful."

189 Boston Weekly Museum, 3 (Aug. 10, 1850), 69.
     Review of In Memoriam.

190 Britannia, June 29, 1850, p. 410.
     Review of In Memoriam. Likes In Memoriam in spite of some
of the poem's faults.

191 British Quarterly Review, 12 (Aug. 1850), 291-292.
     Review of In Memoriam.

192 [Brownson, Orestes A. ?] Brownson's Quarterly Review, 4 (Oct.
     1850), 539-540.
     Review of In Memoriam. Tennyson is "feeble, diffuse, and
tiresome." A very negative review.

193 C. Christian Reformer, n.s. 6 (July 1850), 439-441.
     Review of In Memoriam.

194 C., E. [John Esten Cooke?] Southern Literary Messenger,
     16 (Nov. 1850), 686-691.
     Review of In Memoriam. Finds the poetry rewarding even
though difficult to penetrate.

195 C., G. Edinburgh News and Literary Chronicle, Aug. 24,
     1850, p. 8, and Sept. 14, 1850, p. 8.
     Discusses the body of Tennyson's published poetry.

196 Caledonian Mercury, June 17, 1850, p. [3].
     Review of In Memoriam. Listed in E. F. Shannon's Tennyson
and the Reviewers (entry 3496).

197 Chivers, Thomas Holley. "Valley of Diamonds." Georgia
     Citizen (Macon), Aug. 2, 1850.

Mentioned by J.O. Eidson in Tennyson in America (entry 3328), page 173. According to Eidson, Chivers hopes that Tennyson will be appointed to the poet laureateship.

198 [Chorley, Henry Fothergill.] Athenaeum, June 22, 1850, p. 662.
Discusses various possibilities for the poet laureateship and mentions Tennyson.

199 [_____.] "Our Weekly Gossip." Athenaeum, Nov. 23, 1850, p. 1218.
Notes less than happily Tennyson's appointment to the poet laureateship.

200 Christian Register, 29 (Aug. 3, 1850), 122.
Review of In Memoriam. The reviewer is troubled by religious aspects of the poem.

201 Court Journal, Aug. 10, 1850, p. 505.
Review of In Memoriam. Admires the poem.

202 Critic (London), n.s. 9 (July 15, 1850), 355-356.
Review of In Memoriam.

203 Dublin University Magazine, 36 (Aug. 1850), 209-224.
Review of In Memoriam, among other works. Tennyson on pages 213-214.

204 Dumfries and Galloway Standard and Advertiser, June 19, 1950, p. [3].
A notice mentioned by E.F. Shannon in Tennyson and the Reviewers (entry 3496).

205 Dumfries and Galloway Standard and Advertiser, July 3, 1850, p. [1].
A notice "made up largely of quotations from the reviews in the Examiner and Spectator," according to E.F. Shannon in Tennyson and the Reviewers (entry 3496), page 173.

206 Eclectic Review, 92 (Sept. 1850), 330-341.
Review of In Memoriam. Admires the poem's universality.

207 "A Few Words about Tennyson." American Whig Review, 12 (Aug. 1850), 176-181.

208 [Forster, John?] Examiner (London), June 8, 1850, pp. 356-357.
Review of In Memoriam. Reprinted: Littell's Living Age, 26 (July 27, 1850), 167-171.
Ranks In Memoriam among the best poems in any language.

209 Gentleman's Magazine, n.s. 34 (July 1850), 59-60.
Notice of In Memoriam.

210 Graham's Magazine, 37 (Sept. 1850), 198-199.
     Review of In Memoriam. Takes issue with its detractors
and finds the poem to be sincere. Admires "Ring Out, Wild Bells."

211 Guardian, June 26, 1850, p. 477.
     Review of In Memoriam. Compares it favorably with the
sonnets of Spenser and Shakespeare.

212 H. Westminster and Foreign Quarterly Review, 53 (July 1850),
     572.
     Notice of In Memoriam.

213 Harper's Monthly Magazine, 1 (Sept. 1850), 570.
     Review of In Memoriam. Admires the tone and sincerity of
the poem.

214 [Hart, John S.] Sartain's Union Magazine of Literature and
     Art, 7 (Oct. 1850), 256.
     Review of In Memoriam. Finds the poetry readable and
pleasurable.

215 Hogg's Instructor, 5 (Aug. 1850), 365-368.
     Review of In Memoriam. Admires its high purpose and
vigor.

216 Holden's Dollar Magazine, 6 (Oct. 1850), 631.
     Review of In Memoriam.

217 Home Journal, Aug. 10, 1850.
     Review of In Memoriam. Mentioned by J.O. Eidson in Ten-
nyson in America (entry 3328), page 174.

218 [Hunt, Leigh.] Leigh Hunt's Journal, Dec. 7, 1850, p. 16.
     Leigh Hunt had been a leading candidate for the poet laure-
ateship, but he here praises Tennyson while announcing Tennyson's
appointment to the position.

219 Inquirer, 9 (June 22, 1850), 389-390.
     Review of In Memoriam. Dislikes the poem.

220 International Weekly Miscellany, 1 (July 8, 1850), 34-35.
     Review of In Memoriam. Borrows comments from the
Spectator of June 8, 1850 (entry 246).

221 [Jerdan, William?] Literary Gazette, June 15, 1850, p. 407.
     Notice of In Memoriam. The writer attributes the authorship
of In Memoriam to "a female hand." (The poem was at first published without Tennyson's name on its title page.) Admires the poem.

222 [Kingsley, Charles.] "Tennyson." Fraser's Magazine, 42
     (Sept. 1850), 245-255.
     Reprinted: Miscellanies, 1859 (entry 460); Literary and
General Lectures and Essays, 1888 (entry 1219); J.D. Jump, ed.,

Tennyson: The Critical Heritage (entry 4013), pages 173-185.
        Kingsley discusses Tennyson's poetry through In Memoriam.
He lauds "Locksley Hall" as "the poem which, as we think deserv-
edly, has had most influence on the minds of the young men of
today." The Princess, he argues, shows Tennyson to be interested in contemporary language and problems. He ranks In Memoriam among the best poems in English and sees it as the fulfillment of themes previously developed in "Locksley Hall." Kingsley
also remarks: "It has been often asked why Mr. Tennyson's great
and varied powers had never been concentrated on one immortal
work. The epic, the lyric, the idyllic faculties, perhaps the dramatic also, seemed to be all there, and yet all sundered, scattered
about in small fragmentary poems. In Memoriam, we think, ex-
plains the paradox. Mr. Tennyson could not write an epos or drama
while he was living one."

223   The Leader, 1 (June 8, 1850), 254.
        Discusses Tennyson as a possibility for the poet laureateship.

224   The Leader, 1 (Nov. 23, 1850), 832-833.
        Happy to announce Tennyson's appointment to the poet laure-
ateship.

225   [Lewes, George Henry.] The Leader, 1 (June 22, 1850), 303-
        304.
        Review of In Memoriam. Reprinted in part: J.D. Hunt, ed.,
Tennyson: In Memoriam (entry 4214), pages 64-69.
        Lewes regards In Memoriam as a work of genius. He as-
serts that "it is erected by our greatest living poet--Alfred Tennyson." In addition, Lewes says: "All who have sorrowed will listen with delight to the chastened strains here poured forth In Memoriam."

226   Literary World, 7 (July 13, 1850), 30-31.
        Review of In Memoriam.

227   [Lushington, Franklin.] Tait's Edinburgh Magazine, 17 (Aug.
        1850), 499-505.
        Review of In Memoriam. Reprinted: J.D. Hunt, ed., Ten-
nyson: In Memoriam (entry 4214), pages 71-84; and I. Armstrong,
Victorian Scrutinies (entry 4333), pages 223-236.
        States that In Memoriam "is the finest poem the world has
seen for very many years."

228   Manchester Examiner and Times, Supplement, June 29, 1850,
        p. 3.
        Review of In Memoriam.

229   [Marston, John Westland.] Athenaeum, June 15, 1850, pp. 629-
        630.
        Review of In Memoriam. Reprinted in part: J.D. Hunt, ed.,
Tennyson: In Memoriam (entry 4214), pages 63-64.
        Marston believes that In Memoriam will provide "solace for

the living" and states that "we feel no sense of hyperbole when the
Poet demands that the very elements shall be solemnized in sym-
pathy while the freight of death passes over the waters...."

230 Mayor, J.E.B. "Locksley Hall." Notes and Queries, 1st ser.
       2 (Aug. 24, 1850), 195.

231 Morning Herald, Sept. 5, 1850, p. 6.
       Review of In Memoriam.

232 Morning Post, Aug. 31, 1850, p. 2.
       Review of In Memoriam. Admires the poem's intellectual
and emotional depth.

233 "New Poetry--Tennyson, Browning, and Taylor." English
       Review, 14 (Sept. 1850), 65-92.
       Reprinted in part: J.D. Hunt, ed., Tennyson: In Memoriam
(entry 4214), pages 85-100.
       The reviewer details the lack of faith in In Memoriam. He
asserts that "despite the really exquisite beauty of much of his
writing, Mr. Tennyson will always be a class poet; he will never
be very generally popular. Then, too, he teaches us nothing; he
needs teaching himself...."

234 [Patmore, Coventry.] North British Review, 13 (Aug. 1850),
       532-555.
       Review of In Memoriam. Reprinted in part: J.D. Hunt, ed.,
Tennyson: In Memoriam (entry 4214), pages 69-71.
       Patmore asserts that In Memoriam is of the highest literary
importance.

235 [_____?] Palladium, 1 (Aug. 1850), 94-100.
       Review of In Memoriam. Ranks Tennyson with George Herbert
as a poet of religion and ranks In Memoriam above the best of contemporary English poetry.

236 Peterson's Magazine, 18 (Sept. 1850), 134.
       Review of In Memoriam. The poem is monotonous.

237 Poe, Edgar Allan. "The Poetic Principle." Home Journal,
       Aug. 31, 1850.
       Reprinted: Sartain's Union Magazine of Literature and Art,
7 (Oct. 1850), 231-239.
       Poe calls Tennyson "the noblest of poets."

238 Prospective Review, 6 (Aug. 1850), 306-331.
       Review of In Memoriam. Reprinted: Eclectic Magazine of
Foreign Literature, 21 (Oct. 1850), 209-219.

239 Revue britannique, June 1850, p. 437.
       Review of In Memoriam. The reviewer seems puzzled by the
poem, but finds sections to admire.

240   Revue britannique, Nov. 1850, p. 225.
      Hails with pleasure Tennyson's appointment to the poet
laureateship.

241   Scotsman, June 12, 1850, p. [3].
      Review of In Memoriam.

242   Sharpe's London Journal, 12 (Aug. 1850), 119-121.
      Review of In Memoriam. Believes Tennyson reaches matu-
rity as a poet with this poem.

243   [Simms, William Gilmore?] Southern Quarterly Review, 18
         (Nov. 1850), 535-536.
      Review of In Memoriam. Complains of the poem's monotony,
although, "It contains undoubtedly a considerable proportion of excellent verse."

244   Singer, S.W. "The 'bar' of Michael Angelo." Notes and
         Queries, 1st ser. 2 (Aug. 10, 1850), 166.

245   [Smith, C.C.] Christian Examiner, 49 (Sept. 1850), 289-290.
      Review of In Memoriam. Finds the poem to be an expression
of intimate emotions.

246   Spectator, 23 (June 8, 1850), 546.
      Review of In Memoriam. Reprinted: Littell's Living Age, 26
(July 27, 1850), 170-171.
      Admires the poem.

247   Sun, Aug. 29, 1850, p. [3].
      Review of In Memoriam. Calls it a "masterpiece."

248   [Tarbox, Increase N.] New Englander, 8 (Nov. 1850), 598-615.
      Review of In Memoriam. Detailed analysis of the poem and
a defense against its detractors.

249   Tribune (New York), Aug. 21, 1850.
      Review of In Memoriam. Discussed by J.O. Eidson in Ten-
nyson in America (entry 3328), pages 81 and 84. According to Eidson, the reviewer believes In Memoriam lacks the liveliness of Tennyson's earlier works but still admires the poem.

250   Westminster Review, 54 (Oct. 1850), 85-103.
      Review of In Memoriam. Admires Tennyson.

1851

Periodicals

251   B. "Shelley and Tennyson." Democratic Review, 28 (Jan.
         1851), 49-54.

252 [Brown, John.] North British Review, 14 (Feb. 1851), 486-
514.
Discusses In Memoriam while reviewing The Remains in
Verse and Prose of Arthur Henry Hallam.

253 Christian Parlor Magazine, 7 (Jan. 1851), 7.
Review of In Memoriam.

254 Eclectic Review, 5th ser. 1 (April 1851), 408-410.

255 Eliza Cook's Journal, 4 (April 5, 1851), 353-355.

256 [Fisher, George P.] Christian Review, 16 (Jan. 1851), 36-50.
Review of Poems, 1842, and In Memoriam.

257 Hogg's Instructor, 6 (1851), 273-275.
Discusses "Locksley Hall."

258 [Hopkins, Manley?] "The Poetry of Sorrow." Times (London),
Nov. 28, 1851, p. 8.
Review of In Memoriam. Reprinted: Literary World, 10
(Jan. 3 and 17, 1852), 11-12 and 48-49; Albion, 11 (Jan 31, 1852),
51-52; Essays from the London Times, 1852 (entry 275); and in
part in J.D. Hunt, ed., Tennyson: In Memoriam (entry 4214),
pages 100-112. Replied to by F.W. Robertson in Two Lectures on
the Influence of Poetry on the Working Classes, 1852 (entry 278).
Satirized in Tait's Edinburgh Magazine, 1852 (entry 290).
Hopkins accuses Tennyson's poetry of being mannered and
Tennyson himself of bad taste and language. He faults In Memoriam
for its tone of grief and of "amatory tenderness" that he maintains
is best suited for address to a woman. He cites LXXIV, lines 5-12
of the poem to support the latter contention.

259 "Illustrations of Tennyson." Notes and Queries, 1st ser. 3
(April 26, 1851), 319-320.

260 " 'In Memoriam.' " People's and Howitt's Journal, 4 (May
1851), 185-186.
Provides a subject list for the sections of In Memoriam.

261 Literary Gazette, Jan. 18, 1851, p. 52.
Notice of In Memoriam.

262 Massey, Gerald. "Tennyson and His Poetry." Christian
Socialist, 2 (Aug. 30, Sept. 6, and Sept. 20, 1851),
140-142, 155-157, and 187-190.
An appreciation of Tennyson's poetry.

263 _____. "Tennyson's 'Princess.' " Christian Socialist,
2 (Sept. 27, Oct. 4, 11, 18, and Nov. 1, 1851), 204-207,
220-222, 236-238, 246-247, and 284-286.
Greatly admires The Princess.

264 Milsand, Joseph. "Alfred Tennyson." Revue des Deux Mondes,
    July 15, 1851, pp. 345-366.
    Reprinted: Littérature anglais et philosophie, 1893 (entry
1680).
    Milsand cites "Locksley Hall" and In Memoriam among other
poems to show that Tennyson has carried poetry to a new realm of
moral thought beyond that of the previous generation of poets.

265 P., H.W. Literary World, 8 (March 8, 1851), 195-196.
    Discusses aspects of In Memoriam worthy of study.

266 "Passage in Tennyson." Notes and Queries, 1st ser. 3 (Jan.
    4, 1851), 10-11.

267 "Queries on Tennyson." Notes and Queries, 1st ser. 3 (June
    21, 1851), 493.

268 S., J. "Death-Verses: A Stroll through the Valley of the
    Shadow of Death with Tennyson." American Whig Review,
    13 (June 1851), 534-544.
    Review of In Memoriam. Finds the poem comforting.

269 [Smith, Albert.] "Lincoln's Inn." The Month, 1 (Aug. 1851),
    106.
    A parody of "Locksley Hall."

270 "Tennyson's 'In Memoriam.' " Notes and Queries, 1st ser.
    3 (June 7, 1851), 458.

271 [Thompson, John R.] "Editor's Table." Southern Literary
    Messenger, 17 (April 1851), 252.
    Mentions the sonnets of Tennyson.

272 W. Sheffield and Rotherham Independent, Jan. 18, 25; Feb.
    1; and March 1, 1851, pp. 6, 6, 6, and 6.
    Review of In Memoriam. Listed in E.F. Shannon's Tennyson
and the Reviewers (entry 3496).

273 W., C.B. "Infidelity in England." New York Recorder, 6
    (Feb. 12, 1851), 181.
    Much of this article focuses on Tennyson. The author be-
lieves that In Memoriam reveals an absence of faith in Tennyson.

274 Wesleyan-Methodist Magazine, 7, part I (June 1851), 587-588.
    Review of In Memoriam. Praises the poem for its Christian
virtues.

1852

    Tennyson's Ode on the Death of the Duke of Wellington was
published by Edwar Moxon in 1852. The poem will hereinafter be
referred to as Duke of Wellington.

Books

275 [Hopkins, Manley?] "Alfred Tennyson: The Poetry of Sorrow."
     Essays from the London Times. New York: Appleton, 1852.
     pp. 38-59. (Appleton's Popular Library).
        Reprinted from the Times (London), 1851 (entry 258); see
for other reprintings and annotation.

276 Moir, David M. "Tennyson." Sketches of the Poetical Lit-
     erature of the Past Half-Century. Second edition. Edinburgh:
     Blackwood, 1852, pp. 312-321.

277 Richardson, D. L. "Criticism of the Day and Tennyson."
     Literary Recreations. London: Thacker, 1852, pp. 291-305.

278 Robertson, Frederick W. Two Lectures on the Influence of
     Poetry on the Working Classes. Brighton: 1852.
        Tennyson on pages 26-34. Reprinted: J. D. Hunt, ed., Ten-
nyson: In Memoriam (entry 4214), pages 113-122.
        Robertson replies to the review of In Memoriam in the London
Times, 1851 (entry 258). He remarks: "So much for the critic of
The Times: wrong when he praises and wrong when he blames:
who finds Shakspere false to the facts of human nature, and quotes
Dr. Johnson as a model poet: who cannot believe in the Poetry of
any expression unless it bear the mint-stamp of a precedent, and
cannot understand either the exaggerations or infinitude of genuine
grief."

Periodicals

279 [Hervey, T. K.] Athenaeum, Nov. 20, 1852, p. 1263.
     Review of Duke of Wellington.

280 Ingleby, C. Mansfield. "Passage in Tennyson." Notes and
     Queries, 1st ser. 6 (Sept. 18, 1852), 272.

281 "Mind and Money-Making." Home Journal, Feb. 14, 1852.
        Comments favorably on the London Times (entry 258) review
of In Memoriam.

282 New Hampshire (signature). Home Journal, Feb. 28, 1852.
        A letter replying to the London Times (entry 258) review of
In Memoriam. Defends the poem. See entry 281, above.

283 "Recollections of Poets Laureate--Tennyson." American Whig
     Review, 15 (June 1852), 520-523.

284 Revue britannique, Nov. 1852, pp. 229-231.

285 Southern Literary Gazette, 2 (Dec. 18, 1852), 284-285.
        Review of Duke of Wellington. Assesses the poem as below
Tennyson's usual poetical achievement.

286 Southern Literary Gazette, 2 (Dec. 25, 1852), 296-297.
    Discusses the London Times (entry 258) review of In
Memoriam.

287 T. "The Mission of Modern Poetry." Yale Literary Magazine,
    18 (Feb. 1852), 133.

288 "Tennyson on Wellington." Evening Transcript (Boston), Dec.
    4, 1852.
    Review of Duke of Wellington. Considers the poem a weak
performance unworthy of Tennyson.

289 "Tennyson's Credence in the Future." Methodist Quarterly
    Review, 34 (July 1852), 358-360.
    A religious interpretation of Tennyson.

290 "The 'Times' and the Poets." Tait's Edinburgh Magazine,
    19 (Jan. 1852), 18-21.
    Reprinted: Albion, 11 (Feb. 7, 1852), 61-62; and Literary
World, 10 (March 20, 1852), 204-206.
    Satirizes the review of In Memoriam in the London Times,
1851 (entry 258).

291 Times (London), Nov. 15, 1852.
    Review of Duke of Wellington. Reprinted: Albion, 11 (Dec.
4, 1852), 585; and Literary World, 11 (Dec. 11, 1852), 374.

292 To-Day, 2 (Nov. 27, 1852), 365-366.
    Review of Duke of Wellington. Empathizes with the poem's
sentiment.

1853

    A slightly altered version of Poems, 1842 (eighth edition)
appeared in 1853, along with the fifth edition and final text of
The Princess.

Book

293 Gannon, Nicholas J. An Essay on the Characteristic Errors
    of Our Most Distinguished Living Poets. Dublin: 1853.

Periodicals

294 Athenaeum, March 5, 1853, pp. 280-281.
    Review of Duke of Wellington.
    Reprinted: Littell's Living Age, 37 (May 14, 1853), 441-443.

295 A Borderer (signature). "Tennyson's 'Oriana.' " Littell's
    Living Age, 38 (July 2, 1853), 2.

296 Etienne, L. "Alfred Tennyson." Revue contemporaine, 6

(March 1853), 205-230.
A generally negative view of Tennyson's poetry that contends that Tennyson is admired because his work is a little better than the poor poetry written by his contemporaries.

297 Evening Transcript (Boston), April 20, 1853.
Mentioned by J. O. Eidson in Tennyson in America (entry 3328), page 177. Eidson says this article is a "Report of a lecture by Oliver Wendell Holmes on Tennyson and Browning."

298 F. Monthly Religious Magazine, 10 (April 1853), 150-158.
Review of In Memoriam. With enthusiastic praise, the reviewer discusses In Memoriam and finds in the poem a positive view of religion.

299 Graham's Magazine, 43 (Sept. 1853), 336.
Review of The Princess (fifth edition). Praises the poem.

300 "Literary and Critical." Times (New York), June 7, 1853.
According to J. O. Eidson in Tennyson in America (entry 3328), page 177, this article compares Tennyson and Alexander Smith.

301 Literary World, 12 (Feb. 5 and 26, 1853), 102-103 and 169.
Discusses Edgar Allan Poe's possible borrowings from Tennyson.

302 Literary World, 12 (April 9, 1853), 290-291.
Review of Duke of Wellington.

303 Putnam's Monthly Magazine, 1 (Jan. 1853), 108.
Review of Duke of Wellington. Defends the poem.

304 Schmitt, Karl. "Alfred Tennyson in Deutschland." Deutsches Museum, 3 (Dec. 15, 1853), 905-908.
A bibliographic article.

305 Southern Literary Messenger, 19 (Nov. 1853), 649-658.
Review of Poems, 1842, and In Memoriam. Tennyson is a poet of the present and the future.

306 "Tennyson." Notes and Queries, 1st ser. 7 (June 4, 1853), 559.

307 "Tennyson on Woman's Rights." Home Journal, Aug. 20, 1853.
Points to The Princess for a favorable view of women's rights.

308 [Thompson, John R. ?] "Editor's Table." Southern Literary Messenger, 19 (March 1853), 184-189.
About "Sweet and Low."

309 Times (New York), March 25, 1853.
Review of Duke of Wellington.

1854

Periodicals

310 Archiv für das Studium der neueren Sprachen und Literature,
16 (1854), 324-328.
Review of In Memoriam.

311 "Art and Literature in London: From Our Own Correspondent."
Tribune (New York), June 8, 1854.
Listed by J. O. Eidson in Tennyson in America (entry 3328),
page 177.

312 "Authors and Artists at Florence." Eliza Cook's Journal, 11
(July 22, 1854), 205.

313 "Esquisse d'un tableau de la littérature anglaise, 1830-1854."
Revue de Paris, Sept. 1854.
Discussed by M. Bowden in Tennyson in France (entry 3101),
page 21.
Tennyson is a tired poet of the past.

314 Fischer, Heinrich. "Englische Poeten der Gegenwart: I.
Alfred Tennyson." Archiv für das Studium der neueren
Sprachen und Literaturen, 15 (1854), 24-40.

315 Revue britannique, Dec. 1854, p. 491.

316 "Tennyson." Eclectic Magazine of Foreign Literature, Science
and Art, 33 (Sept 1854), 73.

317 Tribune (New York), July 22, 1854.
Review of Poems, 1842.

318 W.W. "Wordsworth and Tennyson." Yale Literary Magazine,
19 (July 1854), 298-299.
Believes Tennyson has a special appeal for young Americans.

319 "Winter and the New Year." National Magazine, 4 (Jan. 1854),
15-17.

1855

Tennyson's "Charge of the Light Brigade" had been published
in the Examiner on December 9, 1854. Maud, and Other Poems
was published by Edward Moxon in 1855.

Books

320 "After Reading Maud." Ionica. London: 1855.
A poem.

321 [Bennett, William Cox.] <u>Anti-Maud: By a Poet of the People</u>.
    London: E. Churton, 1855. Reprinted by Booth in 1856.
    A reply to <u>Maud</u>.

322 [Brimley, George.] (Signed "G.B.") "Alfred Tennyson's
    Poems." <u>Cambridge Essays: Contributed by Members of the
    University</u>. London: John W. Parker, 1855, pp. 226-281.
    Reprinted: <u>Essays of the Late George Brimley</u>, 1858 (entry
450); in part by J.D. Jump, ed., <u>Tennyson: The Critical Her-
itage</u> (entry 4013), pages 191-196.
    A detailed analysis of Tennyson's poetry. Particular atten-
tion is paid to "Morte d'Arthur," "Locksley Hall," and "Maud."
Brimley remarks: "<u>Locksley Hall</u> is a grand hymn of human progress, in which the discoveries of science, the inventions of art, the
order and movement of society, the sublime hopes and beliefs of
religion, blend in a magnificent vision of the age, and are sung with
the rapture of a prophet to the noblest music." In a letter dated
November 28, 1855 (published in Hallam Tennyson's <u>Alfred Lord
Tennyson</u>, entry 1955, page 408), Tennyson writes to Brimley: "I
wish to assure you that I quite close with your commentary on
'Maud.' I may have agreed with portions of other critiques on the
the same poem, which have been sent to me; but when I saw your
notice I laid my finger upon it and said, 'There, that is my meaning.' Poor little 'Maud,' after having run the gauntlet of so much
brainless abuse and anonymous spite, has found a critic. Therefore
believe her father (not the gray old wolf) to be / Yours not unthank-
fully, A. Tennyson."

Periodicals

323 "Alfred Tennyson." <u>Putnam's Monthly Magazine</u>, 6 (Oct. 1855),
    382-392.
    A general discussion of Tennyson's poetry. Condemns Ten-
nyson's revisions of his early poems. Praises <u>Maud</u>.

324 <u>Atlas</u>, Aug. 4, 1855, p. 499.
    Review of <u>Maud</u>. It is "a splendid and exquisite poem."

325 [Aytoun, William Edmondstoune.] <u>Blackwood's Edinburgh
    Magazine</u>, 78 (Sept. 1855), 311-321.
    Review of <u>Maud</u>. Reprinted: <u>Littell's Living Age</u>, 47 (Oct.
6, 1855), 51-59.

326 B. <u>Yale Literary Magazine</u>, 20 (Jan. 1855), 136-143.
    Review of <u>In Memoriam</u>.

327 B., J.C. (John Charles Bucknill) <u>Asylum Journal of Mental
    Science</u>, 2 (Oct. 1855), 95-104.
    Review of <u>Maud</u>. Bucknill explains that the madness of the
poem's hero is accurately portrayed.

328 "Bailey and Tennyson." Scottish Review, 3 (Oct. 1855),
      347-357.

329 Banner of Ulster (Belfast), Sept. 6, 1855, p. [4].
       Mentioned in E. F. Shannon's "The Critical Reception of
Tennyson's Maud" (entry 3539).

330 Bentley's Magazine, 38 (Sept. 1855), 262-265.
       Review of Maud.

331 Biblioteca Sacra, 12 (Oct. 1855), 851.
       Review of Maud. A less than happy notice.

332 Birmingham Journal, Aug. 11, 1855, Supplement, p. 3.
       Review of Maud.

333 Brechin Advertiser, Sept. 4, 1855, p. [4].
       Review of Maud. Mentioned in E. F. Shannon's "The Criti-
cal Reception of Tennyson's Maud" (entry 3539).

334 British Quarterly Review, 22 (Oct. 1855), 467-498.
       Review of Maud. Discusses the poem in detail. Accepts the
notion that Tennyson approved of the Crimean War and that Maud is
an expression of a warlike philosophy. Likes Maud but does not
think it a great poem.

335 Christian Reformer, 11 (Oct. 1855), 602-613.
       Review of Maud.

336 [Collins, Wilkie?] The Leader, June 23, 1855.
       Notice of Maud. Reprinted: Albion, 14 (July 21, 1855), 346.

337 [_____?] The Leader, 6 (Aug. 4, 1855), 747-748.
       Review of Maud. E. F. Shannon in "The Critical Reception
of Tennyson's Maud" (entry 3539), page 399, suggests George Henry
Lewes as the possible author of the present article. Favorable
commentary.

338 Critic (London), 14 (Aug. 15, 1855), 386-387.
       Review of Maud. Dislikes the opening thirteen stanzas of the
poem. Finds Maud generally beneath Tennyson's talents.

339 "The Cure for Mammonism." Morning Post (London), Aug. 2,
      1855, p. 6.
      About the possible warlike philosophy of Maud.

340 "Current Literature, English and Foreign." Aberdeen Journal,
      Aug. 29, 1855, p. 6.
      Includes some discussion of the warlike philosophy of Maud.

341 [Curtis, George William.] "Editor's Easy Chair." Harper's
      Monthly Magazine, 11 (Oct. 1855), 701-706.

Review of Maud. Praises the poem, which is "a passionate love poem, full of burning social protest and indignation."

342 [Dallas, Eneas Sweetland.] Times (London), Aug. 25, 1855, pp. 8-9.
Review of Maud. Even though Dallas likes what he perceives as Tennyson's support for the Crimean War over the objections of "peacemongers," he derogates Maud's literary merits, calling the poem "crude."

343 [Dixon, Hepworth.] Atheneaum, Aug. 4, 1855, pp. 893-895.
Review of Maud. Dixon calls it unmusical and asserts: "This volume is not worthy of its author."

344 Döllen, Dr. "Alfred Tennyson." Archiv für das Studium der neueren Sprachen und Literaturen, 17 (1855), 73-82.

345 Dublin University Magazine, 46 (Sept. 1855), 332-340.
Review of Maud. The reviewer likes portions of the poem but finds the work "unsatisfying" overall.

346 Dundee and Perth Saturday Post, Oct. 6, 1855, p. [4].
Review of Maud. Mentioned in E. F. Shannon's "The Critical Reception of Tennyson's Maud" (entry 3539).

347 Ecclesiastic and Theologian, 17 (Sept. 1855), 431-436.
Review of Maud.

348 Eclectic Review, 102 (Nov. 1855), 568-575.
Review of Maud.

349 Edinburgh Advertiser, Sept. 21, 1855, p. [3], and Oct. 5, 1855, p. [3].
Review of Maud. Mentioned in E. F. Shannon's "The Critical Reception of Tennyson's Maud" (entry 3539).

350 Edinburgh Evening Courant, Aug. 2, 1855, p. [3].
Review of Maud. Discussed in E. F. Shannon's "The Critical Reception of Tennyson's Maud" (entry 3539), page 398. According to Shannon, the reviewer regards Maud as utterly unworthy of Ten - nyson. Maud, the reviewer asserts, is "a thing to be blotted, if possible, from the memory."

351 "Editor's Table." Graham's Magazine, 46 (March 1855), 276-277.
Discusses "The Charge of the Light Brigade" and objects to the commemoration in poetry of "a bloody blunder."

352 "Editor's Table." Graham's Magazine, 47 (Oct. 1855), 360-361.
The author believes Maud is superior to Longfellow's Hiawatha (1855) because it is forthright in point of view and deals

with issues of broad and great importance, while Hiawatha deals with an arcane subject. He takes Maud as an example of the general superiority of English over American poets.

353 "Editor's Table." Peterson's Magazine, 27 (March 1855), 252.
Admires the "bold, Homeric strain" of "The Charge of the Light Brigade."

354 "Editor's Tableau." Genius of the West, 4 (Nov. 1855), 347-348.
Review of Maud.

355 [Eliot, George.] "Belles-Lettres in Contemporary Literature." Westminster Review, 64 (Oct. 1855), 596-601.
Review of Maud. Assaults Tennyson' point of view in Maud and accuses him of advocating war.

356 Evening Transcript (Boston), July 31, 1855.
Review of Maud. Discussed in J.O. Eidson's Tennyson in America (entry 3328), page 131.
According to Eidson, the reviewer cites several passages from Maud to illustrate Tennyson's skills and presents a favorable view of the poem.

357 [Ewer, Ferdinand C.] "Editor's Table." Pioneer, 3 (June 1855), 279-280.
Praises "The Charge of the Light Brigade."

358 Express (Edinburgh), Aug. 11, 1855, p. 4.
Review of Maud. A balanced discussion of the poem's strengths and weaknesses. Tennyson thought well of this review.

359 Family Friend, Sept. 1855, pp. 251-254.
Discusses Maud.

360 [Forster, John.] Examiner (London), Aug. 4, 1855, pp. 483-484.
Review of Maud. Reprinted: Littell's Living Age, 46 (Sept. 15, 1855), 54-57.
In a thoughtful analysis of the poem, Forster ranks it high among Tennyson's works.

361 [Fox, William Johnson.] (Signed "Publicola") "The War Poetry of the Laureate." Weekly Dispatch, Aug. 26, 1855, p. 7.
Mentioned in E.F. Shannon's "The Critical Reception of Tennyson's Maud" (entry 3539), p. 402.

362 "Fusion of Authors and Publishers." Home Journal, Oct. 13, 1855.
Review of Maud.

363 [Gladstone, William Ewart?] New Quarterly Review, 4 (Oct.

1855), 393-397.
Review of Maud. Negative review in which Maud is viewed as unhappily atypical of Tennyson's poetry.

364 Globe, Oct. 18, 1855, p. 1.
Discusses Maud while discussing recent issues of English journals.

365 Graham's Magazine, 47 (Oct. 1855), 371-372.
Review of Maud. Views the poem as atypical of Tennyson's poetry.

366 Guardian, Aug. 29, 1855, p. 664.
Review of Maud. Places the poem in the "Spasmodic" school of poetry. Regards it as poor poetry.

367 H., J. "A Criticism Comprehensive and Suggestive." Oxford Chronicle, Sept. 1, 1855, p. 6.
"Dismally dull and dolefully dawdlin'
Tennyson's Maud should be Tennyson's Maudlin."

368 Hale, Edward Everett. North American Review, 81 (Oct. 1855), 544-546.
Review of Maud. Hale defends Maud even though he has ambivalent feelings about the poem. He is unhappy with its conclusion.

369 Havens, Charles E. "The Poems of Alfred Tennyson." Pioneer, 3 (Jan. 1855), 28-34.
Emphasizes Poems, 1842.

370 Home Journal, Sept. 15, 1855.
Review of Maud. Very negative commentary.

371 "Idlewild Evening Lamp." Home Journal, Dec. 15, 1855.

372 Illustrated Times, Aug. 4, 1855, pp. 142-143.
Review of Maud. The reviewer regards it as a successful work of a mature poet and comments favorably on the perceived warlike philosophy of the poem.

373 "Indecent Poetry." Home Journal, Oct. 20, 1855.
Discusses "Fatima."

374 Inquirer, 14 (Sept. 1, 1855), 546-547.
Review of Maud. Finds those qualities that were best in Tennyson's previous poetry are missing from Maud.

375 Inverness Courier, Aug. 2, 1855, p. 2.
Review of Maud.

376 Irish Quarterly Review, 5 (Sept. 1855), 453-472.
Review of Maud.

377 J. Scotsman, Aug. 29, 1855, p. 3.
     Review of Maud. The reviewer finds its premise to be silly,
even though the campaign in Crimea is a justifiable war against an
evil enemy.

378 John Bull, 35 (Aug. 18, 1855), 523-524.
     Review of Maud. Regards Maud as a successful poem.

379 [Kingsley, Charles.] Fraser's Magazine, 52 (Sept. 1855),
     264-273.
     Review of Maud. Kingsley complains that the characters are
not believable and the poem is awkward.

380 Knickerbocker, 46 (Nov. 1855), 525-526.
     Review of Maud. Unhappy with the poem.

381 "The Laureate's View of War." Punch, 29 (Aug. 18, 1855),
     69.
     A poem.

382 Leeds Mercury, Aug. 11, 1855, p. 7.
     Review of Maud. According to E. F. Shannon in "The Critical
Reception of Tennyson's Maud" (entry 3539), page 399, the reviewer
"hailed the poet's achievement" in Maud.

383 Literary Gazette, Aug. 4, 1855, pp. 483-484.
     Review of Maud.

384 "Literature in London." Tribune (New York), Feb. 20, 1855.
     Mentioned in J. O. Eidson's Tennyson in America (entry 3328),
page 178.

385 London Quarterly Review, 5 (Oct. 1855), 213-229.
     Review of Maud.

386 MacPhail's Edinburgh Ecclesiastical Journal, 20 (Sept. 1855),
     120-125.
     Review of Maud. Positive assessment.

387 Manchester Examiner and Times, Aug. 7, 1855, p. 2.
     Attacks Maud for its portrait of villainous commercial enter-
prise and maintains that commerce is "humanising."

388 [Massey, Gerald.] Edinburgh News and Literary Chronicle,
     July 28, 1855, p. 7.
     Review of Maud. Massey regards it as a powerful portrayal
of contemporary life and problems. He likes the differences from
Tennyson's previous works.

389 _____. Hogg's Instructor, 5 (July 1855), 1-14.
     Reprinted: Eclectic Magazine of Foreign Literature, 35 (Sept.
1855), 616-628.
     A general discussion of Tennyson's poetry.

390 [Miller, Hugh?] Witness (Edinburgh), Sept. 1, 1855, p. 2.
Likes Tennyson's point of view in Maud.

391 "More about 'Maud.' " Home Journal, Oct. 20, 1855.

392 Morning Post (London), Sept. 1, 1855, pp. 5-6.
Review of Maud. The reviewer is confused by the poem and
does not like it.

393 News (London), Aug. 17, 1855, p. 2.
Review of Maud.

394 [Patmore, Coventry.] Edinburgh Review, 102 (Oct. 1855),
498-519.
Review of Maud. Patmore is unhappy with Tennyson's effort
to be topical in Maud. He argues: "All great poets, and even
small ones, do and must 'reflect the character of the time,' as the
cant phrase runs; but how? Not by taking the bread out of the
mouth of the demagogue, or by doing the work of the parliamentary
committeeman; but by the possession and consequent reflection of
those peculiarities which constitute the permanent contribution of the
age, whether for ill or for good, to the ever-growing tradition of
civilisation. Such possession and reflection evidently cannot be con-
scious. Accordingly no man reflects our age more truly than Mr.
Tennyson does, when he is not thinking of doing so."

395 Press, 3 (Aug. 11, 1855), 764-765.
Review of Maud. Dislikes the poem.

396 Putnam's Monthly Magazine, 6 (Sept. 1855), 318.
Review of Maud. Praises the poem.

397 Rambler: A Catholic Journal and Review, 4 (Sept. 1855),
240-242.
Review of Maud.

398 Revue britannique, Sept. 1855, pp. 234-236.
Review of Maud. The reviewer believes Tennyson is out of
his element in Maud. The melodies of the verse, he believes, are
suited to more gentle topics.

399 [Roscoe, William Caldwell.] National Review, 1 (Oct. 1855),
377-410.
Reprinted: Poems and Essays of the Late William Caldwell
Roscoe, 1860 (entry 498).
Discusses Poems, 1842, The Princess, In Memoriam, and
Maud.

400 Saturday Evening Post, Sept. 8, 1855.
Review of Maud.

401 Short, Jeremy. "Tennyson's Maud." Peterson's Magazine,
28 (Nov. 1855), 307-309.
Review of Maud.

402   "Smith and the Poet Laureate." Evening Transcript (Boston),
       March 15, 1855.
       Alexander Smith and Tennyson.

403   [Smith, Goldwin.] "The War Passages in 'Maud.' " Saturday
       Review (London), 1 (Nov. 3, 1855), 14-15.
       Reprinted: J. D. Jump, ed., Tennyson: The Critical Her-
itage (entry 4013), pages 186-190.
       Often using sarcasm, Smith condemns Tennyson's complaints
about commercial evils and the poet's seeming advocacy of war for
it own sake. Even so, he avers: "In rejecting the author of Maud
as a practical advisor, let us render full, though superfluous, homage to his poetical powers. Only on the theory that a moral purpose is indispensable to poetry, can it be denied that he is one of
the greatest of poets."

404   Spectator, 28 (Aug. 4, 1855), 813-814.
       Review of Maud. Reprinted: Littell's Living Age, 46 (Sept.
15, 1855), 57-61.
       The reviewer regards Maud as clear and powerful.

405   Sun, Aug. 27, 1855, p. 3.
       Review of Maud.

406   Tablet (Dublin), 16 (Aug. 25, 1855), 539.
       Review of Maud.

407   Tait's Edinburgh Magazine, 22 (Sept. 1855), 531-539.
       Review of Maud. The reviewer calls Tennyson's remarks
about the advocates of peace "a sad artistic blunder" and assaults
the notions of the benefits of war put forth in Maud. In what may
be the most effective of the 1855 attacks on Maud, the reviewer
examines the errors of language and metaphor engendered by the
political topic of the poem.

408   "Tennyson's Battle Ode." Evening Transcript (Boston), Jan.
       16, 1855.
       Admires "The Charge of the Light Brigade."

409   [Thompson, John R.?] Southern Literary Messenger, 21 (Oct.
       1855), 638-639.
       Review of Maud. The reviewer suggests that it could have
been written by "some unhappy lunatic" or a prankster trying to
dupe critics. The poem, he writes, is "a morbid, splenetic, fragmentary effusion" and is unworthy of Tennyson.

410   Times (New York), Nov. 13, 1855.
       Review of Maud. Admires "Come into the Garden, Maud"
but disapproves of Tennyson's revisions of "The Charge of the Light
Brigade."

411   Tribune (New York), Aug. 7, 1855.
       Review of Maud. The poem features beautiful language.

412 W. "New Poetry, English and American." Evening Tran-
     script (Boston), Dec. 19, 1855.
     Review of Maud. Defends the poem.

413 [Whitman, Walt.] "An English and an American Poet."
     American Phrenological Journal, 12 (Oct. 1855), 90-91.
     Review of Maud and Whitman's own Leaves of Grass (1855).
Whitman portrays Tennyson as a poet of aristocratic England and
himself as a poet of the "American freeman." He provides a generally negative view of Maud as a sickly poem. One might find
comparison between the present essay and Whitman's 1887 "A
Word About Tennyson" (entry 1211) of interest.

414 Y. "Value of Half an Hour." Home Journal, Oct. 27, 1855.
     A letter about Maud.

                              1856

Books

415 Mann, R[obert] J[ames]. Tennyson's "Maud" Vindicated: An
     Explanatory Essay. London: Jarrold, [1856].
     Reprinted in part: J. D. Jump, ed., Tennyson: The Critical
Heritage (entry 4013), pages 197-211.
     Tennyson had this to say (in a letter to Mann) about Mann's
Essay: "Thanks for your Vindication. No one with this essay before him can in future pretend to misunderstand my dramatic poem,
'Maud': your commentary is as true as it is full, and I am really
obliged to you for defending me against the egregiously nonsensical
imputation of having attacked the Quakers or Mr. Bright: you are
not aware, perhaps, that another wiseacre accused me of calling
Mr. Layard an 'Assyrian Bull'!" (H. Tennyson, Alfred Lord Tennyson, entry 1955, page 405.)
     This little book provides a detailed explication of Maud; the
commentary is still well thought of by modern scholars and the
book is likely to remain a standard reference for many more years.
Mann summarizes the central theme of Maud as: "the proper function of love is the ennobling and energizing of the human soul" (the
italics are those of Mann). Mann is a physician, and he brings an
interesting understanding of human character to his study.
     For relevant commentary on Mann's book and Maud, see
R. B. Basler's "Tennyson the Psychologist" in South Atlantic Quarterly, 1944 (entry 3349).
     One should note before reading Mann's book that Tennyson
saw the book before its publication and commented on it to Mann.

416 North, Christopher (pseudonym for John Wilson). Essays,
     Critical and Imaginative. Edinburgh: Blackwood, 1856.
     Volume II, pp. 109-152.
     Reprinted from Blackwood's Edinburgh Magazine, May 1832
(entry 16).

Periodicals

417 Alger, W. R. "The Literature of Friendship." North American Review, 83 (July 1856), 104-132.
Discusses In Memoriam among other works. Alger declares
that In Memoriam will be "a shrine for the pilgrims of the heart
as long as a single feature remains in the mighty landscape of
English literature."

418 Arthur's Home Magazine, 8 (Sept. 1856), 180-181.
Review of a gathering of Tennyson's works. Asserts that
Tennyson's early poems are his most effective.

419 [Aytoun, William Edmondstoune.] Blackwood's Edinburgh
Magazine, 80 (Sept. 1856), 365.
Mentions Maud while discussing Thomas Babington Macaulay.

420 Cecilia. "Tennyson's Portraiture of Woman." Southern
Literary Messenger, 22 (Feb. 1856), 97-100.

421 Christian Remembrancer, 31 (April 1856), 268-270.
Review of Maud.

422 "Contemporary Poets." Independent, 7 (Feb. 7, 1856), 48.
Review of Maud.

423 "Country Correspondence." Crayon, 3 (Oct. 1856), 314-316.
Mentions Maud.

424 [Curtis, George William?] "Editor's Easy Chair." Harper's
Monthly Magazine, 12 (Jan. 1856), 262.
Review of Maud. Defends the poem against unreasonable
attacks.

425 Dudley, Arthur. "La Poésie anglais dupuis Shelley." Revue
des Deux Mondes, Feb. 15, 1856, pp. 821-846.
Reviews Maud. Dudley believes that Tennyson is overmas-
tered by his subject and that Maud is insincere.

426 "Editor's Table." Graham's Magazine, 48 (Jan. 1856), 71.
Discusses and defends the versification of Maud.

427 "The English Poet-Laureate." Home Journal, Aug. 16, 1856.

428 [Fulford, William.] "Alfred Tennyson: An Essay in Three
Parts." Oxford and Cambridge Magazine, 1 (Jan., Feb.,
and March 1856), 7-18, 73-81, and 136-145.
Part I emphasizes Tennyson's early poetry; part II focuses
on In Memoriam; and part III emphasizes Maud. A generally friendly assessment of Tennyson's achievements.

429 Gatty, Margaret. "Passage in Tennyson's 'In Memoriam.' "
Notes and Queries, 2nd ser. 1 (Feb. 23, 1856), 161.

430 London University Magazine, 1 (May 1856), 1-11.
    Review of Maud. Proclaims that in Maud Tennyson express-
es the spirit of his era. Admires the poem.

431 "The Lotus-Eater." Evening Bulletin (San Francisco), Aug.
    25, 1856.
    Mentioned in J. O. Eidson's Tennyson in America (entry
3328), page 181.

432 "Modern Light Literature--Poetry." Blackwood's Edinburgh
    Magazine, 79 (Feb. 1856), 125-138.
    Excerpted: National Magazine (England), 8 (June 1856),
562-563.

433 Monthly Review of Literature, Science, and Art, 1 (Jan. 1856),
    19-24.
    Review of Maud.

434 [Morin, E.] National Magazine (USA), 1 (Oct. 1856), 3-5.
    Biographical and critical.

435 S., J. O. "Ruskin on the Ancient and the Modern Poets:
    Homer and Tennyson." Fraser's Magazine, 53 (June 1856),
    648-659.

436 [Stoddard, Richard Henry.] "Alfred Tennyson." National
    Magazine (England), 9 (Nov. 1856), 408-415.

437 "Studies among the Leaves." Crayon, 3 (Jan. 1856), 30-32.
    Review of Maud. Compares Maud to Leaves of Grass. Finds
the works similar in point of view and technique, although Maud is
more "refined in its art."

438 "Tennyson and Jeremy Taylor." Littell's Living Age, 49 (May
    10, 1856), 349.

439 [Thompson, John R. ?] "Editor's Table." Southern Literary
    Messenger, 23 (Dec. 1856), 470-471.
    Discusses "A Farewell."

440 "What Is Poetry?" Putnam's Monthly Magazine, 8 (Oct. 1856),
    371-380.
    Mentions Tennyson's diction.

1857

    Poems, illustrated by Dante Gabriel Rossetti, John Everett
Millais and others, was published by Edward Moxon in 1857. This
edition is sometimes referred to by scholars as the "Pre-Raphaelite
edition" of Tennyson's poems. The book will be hereinafter referred
to as Poems, illustrated, 1857.

Books

441 Bayne, Peter. "Tennyson and His Teachers." Essays in
  Biography and Criticism: First Series. Boston: Gould and
  Lincoln, 1857. Volume I, pp. 50-145.
  Reprinted, revised: Essays, 1859 (entry 459).
  Generally admires Tennyson's poetry, with the notable excep-
tion of Maud. Discusses the major aspects of Tennyson's verse
and asserts that the poet's writings express the essence of modern
life.

442 Freeland, H.W. "Tennyson's 'In Memoriam.'" Lectures
  and Miscellanies. London: Longmans, 1857, pp. 194-200.

443 Gilfillan, George. "Alfred Tennyson." Modern Literature and
  Literary Men. New York: Appleton, 1857, pp. 192-207.
  Reprinted from Tait's Edinburgh Magazine, 1847 (entry 126).
See entry 126 for another reprinting.

Periodicals

444 B., D.G. (D.G. Brinton). "The Beauties of Maud." Yale
  Literary Magazine, 22 (Aug. 1857), 358-361.

445 "Editor's Table." Russell's Magazine, 1 (May 1857), 179 and
  181-182.
  Ranks Tennyson among the best of English poets.

446 Saturday Review (London), 3 (June 27, 1857), 601-602.
  Review of Poems, illustrated, 1857.

447 "Tennyson Queries." Notes and Queries, 2nd ser. 4 (Nov. 14,
  1857), 386.

448 Westminster Review, 12 (Oct. 1857), 590-592.
  Review of Poems, illustrated, 1857.

449 "Woolner's Bust of Tennyson." Albion, 35 (April 11, 1857),
  177.

1858

Books

450 Brimley, George. "Alfred Tennyson's Poems." Essays of the
  Late George Brimley. Ed. William G. Clark. Cambridge
  and London: 1858, pp. 1-103. Reprinted: New York: Rudd
  and Carlton, 1861, pp. 13-128.
  Reprinted from Cambridge Essays, 1855 (entry 322). See for
another reprinting and for annotation.

451 Robertson, Frederick William. Lectures and Addresses.

London: Smith, Elder, 1858.
Tennyson on pages 124-141.

Periodicals

452 Bibliothèque universelle, Jan. 1858, p. 120.
Review of Poems, illustrated, 1857. Praises the book.

453 C., C.C. "Locksley Hall." Yale Literary Magazine, 24 (Nov.
1858), 79-84.

454 H. "Alfred Tennyson and Opium." Times (New York), Jan.
28, 1858.

455 "Isabel: A Portrait." Russell's Magazine, 2 (March 1858),
500-501.

456 L., T.R. (Thomas R. Lounsbury). "Tennyson's Maud as a
Work of Art." Yale Literary Magazine, 24 (Dec. 1858),
89-98.
Tries to make sense of the seeming contradictions in Maud.

457 "Tennyson." Presbyterian Quarterly Review, 6 (March 1858),
656-663 and 681-685.
Excerpted: Evening Transcript (Boston), March 18, 1858.
Emphasizes Tennyson's early poetry.

458 Victor, O.J. Lady's Repository, 18 (July 1858), 420-423.
Review of Maud.
Victor admires Tennyson's previous poetry but not Maud,
which "gloats over tales of war and incidents of the horrible kind."

1859

In 1859, Idylls of the King was published by Edward Moxon.
Only four sections of the eventual twelve-part work were included in
the 1859 edition. The book is hereinafter referred to as Idylls,
1859.

Books

459 Bayne, Peter. "Tennyson and His Teachers." Essays: Biographical, Critical, and Miscellaneous. Edinburgh and London: 1859, pp. 202-280.
Revised version of essay in Essays in Biography and Criticism (entry 441). See for annotation.

460 Kingsley, Charles. "Tennyson." Miscellanies. London: John
W. Parker, 1859. Volume I, pp. 214-233.
Reprinted from Fraser's Magazine, 1850 (entry 222). See
entry 222 for another reprinting and annotation.

461 _____ . "Tennyson." Sir Walter Raleigh and His Time,
     with Other Papers. Boston: Ticknor and Fields, 1859,
     pp. 177-195.

Periodicals

462 "Alfred Tennyson." Littell's Living Age, 62 (July 23, 1859),
     195-201.

463 [Bagehot, Walter.] National Review, 9 (Oct. 1859), 368-394.
     Review of Idylls, 1859. Reprinted: Littell's Living Age, 63
     (Dec. 3, 1859), 579-593; The Collected Works of Walter Bagehot,
     1965 (entry 3901); and J.D. Jump, ed., Tennyson: The Critical
     Heritage (entry 4013), pages 215-240.
     Bagehot analyzes Idylls, 1859, and compares Tennyson with
     Shelley, Keats, and Wordsworth. He remarks: "If we were asked,
     as we shall be asked, why we think Mr. Tennyson to have greater
     powers than Wordsworth, we would venture to allege two reasons.
     In the first place, Mr. Tennyson has a power of making fun. No
     one can claim that, of all powers, for Wordsworth, it is certain
     . . . . Secondly, it may be said that, far more completely than any
     other recent poet, Mr. Tennyson has conceived in his mind, and
     has delineated in his works, a general picture of human life."

464 British Quarterly Review, 30 (1859), 481-508.
     Review of Idylls, 1859. Lauds Tennyson for presenting his
     subject in modern terms.

465 Chamber's Journal, 32 (Aug. 20, 1859), 121-124.
     Review of Idylls, 1859. A favorable but uninsightful commen-
     tary.

466 Constitutional Press, Sept. 1859.
     Review of Idylls, 1859.

467 [Doran, John, and (?) Blackburne (?)] Athenaeum, July 16,
     1859, pp. 73-76.
     Review of Idylls, 1859. Admires the poetry.

468 Eclectic Magazine of Foreign Literature, 48 (Oct. 1859), 247-
     255.
     Review of Idylls, 1859.

469 Eclectic Review, 110 (Sept. 1859), 287-294.
     Review of Idylls, 1859. Discusses characterization and
     imagery.

470 Fraser's Magazine, 60 (Sept. 1859), 301-314.
     Review of Idylls, 1859.

471 [Gladstone, William Ewart.] Quarterly Review, 106 (Oct. 1859),
     454-485.

Reprinted, revised: Gleanings of Past Years, 1879 (entry 908); in part, Gladstone on Tennyson, 1908 (entry 2488); in part, J.D. Jump, ed., Tennyson: The Critical Heritage (entry 4013); and B. Johnson, ed., Famous Reviews, 1914 (entry 2759).

Gladstone discusses Tennyson's works in general and provides commentary on In Memoriam, Idylls of the King (1859), and Maud, in particular. He discusses Arthur Henry Hallam in relation to In Memoriam and the strengths of both In Memoriam and Idylls, 1859. He is unhappy with the militaristic aspects of Maud.

472 [Hasell, Elizabeth J.] Blackwood's Edinburgh Magazine, 86
    (Nov. 1859), 608-627.
    Review of Idylls, 1859. An insightful discussion of Tennyson's art, with words of concern about some of the characterizations.

473 Irish Quarterly Review, 9 (Oct. 1859), 834-859.
    Review of Idylls, 1859.

474 Lee, W. New Rugbeian, Sept. 1859, pp. 267-271.
    Review of Idylls, 1859.

475 London Quarterly Review, 13 (Oct. 1859), 62-80.
    Review of Idylls, 1859. A generally positive commentary on structure and characters.

476 Ludlow, J.M. "Moral Aspects of Mr. Tennyson's 'Idylls of
    the King.' " Macmillan's Magazine, 1 (Nov. 1859), 63-72.
    Admires Tennyson's use of scene to evoke mood and character.

477 [Macmillan, Alexander.] (Signed "A.Y." for "Amos Yates,"
    the pseudonym of Macmillan.) "The Quarterly Review on
    Mr. Tennyson's Maud." Macmillan's Magazine, 1 (Dec.
    1859), 114-115.

478 Maddyn, D. Owen. "The Politics of the Poet Laureate."
    Constitutional Press, June 1859.
    Listed in Ehrsam, et al. "Alfred Lord Tennyson," Bibliographies of Twelve Victorian Authors, 1936 (entry 3241).

479 Masson, Gustave. Correspondence littéraire, Sept. 5, 1859.
    Review of Idylls, 1859. Unhappy with Tennyson's language.

480 Montégut, Emile. "Des premiers poèmes aux Idylles du roi."
    Revue des Deux Mondes, Nov. 15, 1859, pp. 472-496.
    Review of Idylls, 1859. Perceives Tennyson as aloof and spiritual. Wide-ranging essay seeks to assess Tennyson's merits and faults as a poet.

481 [Mozley, Anne.] Bentley's Quarterly, 2 (Oct. 1859), 159-194.
    Review of Idylls, 1859.

482 New Quarterly Review, 8 (July 1859), 336-351.
    Review of Idylls, 1859.

483 [Nichol, John.] Westminster Review, 72 (Oct. 1859), 503-526.
Review of Idylls, 1859. Unhappy with some of Tennyson's
characters.

484 Palgrave, Francis Turner. Under the Crown, nos. 1-2 (1859).
According to Ehrsam, et al. In "Alfred Lord Tennyson"
(entry 3241), page 338, Palgrave discusses a "visit to Portugal with
Tennyson."

485 [Patmore, Coventry.] Edinburgh Review, 110 (July 1859),
247-263.
Review of Idylls, 1859. Patmore states: "Since the definite
formation of the English language no poetry has been written with so
small an admixture of Latin as the 'Idylls of the King,' and what
will sound still stranger in the ears of those who have been in the
habit of regarding the Latin element as essential to the dignity of
poetry, no language has surpassed in epic dignity the English of
these poems."

486 [_____.] North British Review, 31 (Aug. 1859), 148-174.
Review of Idylls, 1859. Patmore particularly admires
"Guinevere."

487 "Poets and Poetry." Tait's Edinburgh Magazine, 26 (Aug.
1859), 464-470.
Review of Idylls, 1859.

488 Revue britannique, July 1859, pp. 237-240.
Review of Idylls, 1859. The reviewer seems a little confused
by the title of Tennyson's book. He discusses Tennyson's style.

489 Saturday Review (London), 8 (July 16, 1859), 75-76.
Review of Idylls, 1859. Unimpressed.

490 Smith, C.C. North American Review, 89 (Oct. 1859), 554-555.
Review of Idylls, 1859.

491 Spectator, 32 (July 23, 1859), 764-766.
Review of Idylls, 1859.

492 [Stirling, James Hutchinson.] "Tennyson and His Poetry."
Meliora, 2 (Oct. 1859), 225-248.
Reprinted: Jerrold, Tennyson, and Macaulay, 1868 (entry
604).
A generally laudatory commentary. Stirling seems to have
difficulty finding anything to dislike in Tennyson's poetry. Discusses
Tennyson's works from Poems, 1842, through Idylls, 1859.

493 "Tennyson's 'Enid.' " Notes and Queries, 2nd ser. 8 (Aug. 20,
1859), 155-156.

494 [Walter, John.] Times (London), Sept. 10, 1859, p. 5.
Review of Idylls, 1859. Admires the poems.

1860

Books

495 Forgues, E. D. "Alfred Tennyson." Originaux et Beau
Esprits de L'Angleterre Contemporaine. Paris: Charpentier,
1860. Volume II, pp. 309-344.
Reprinted from Revue des Deux Mondes, 1847 (entry 125).
See entry 125 for annotation.

496 Gatty, Alfred. The Poetical Character: Illustrated from the
Works of Alfred Tennyson. London: Bell and Daldy, 1860.

497 Reed, Henry. "Elegiac Poetry." Lectures on English Literature, from Chaucer to Tennyson. Philadelphia: Lippincott,
1860, pp. 323-336.

498 Roscoe, William Caldwell. "Tennyson." Poems and Essays
of the Late Roscoe. Ed. Richard Holt Hutton. London:
Chapman and Hall, 1860. Volume II, pp. 1-37.
Reprinted from National Review, 1855 (entry 399).

499 Taylor, Bayard. At Home and Abroad. New York: Putnam,
1860.
Tennyson on pages 445-446.

Periodicals

500 Bacon, George B. "Mr. Tennyson and the Idyls of King
Arthur." New Englander, 18 (Feb. 1860), 1-42.
Review of Idylls, 1859.

501 De Bow's Review, 28 (June 1860), 679-689.
Review of Idylls, 1859.

502 Eclectic Magazine of Foreign Literature, 49 (Jan. 1860), 28-37.
Review of Idylls, 1859.

503 Etienne, L. "Les poètes anglais contemporains: leurs
sentiments sur l'Empereur et sur l'Angleterre." Revue
européenne, Aug. 1860.
Compares Tennyson's poetry negatively to E. B. Browning's
Poems before Congress (1860).

504 Everett, Charles Carroll. North American Review, 90 (Jan.
1860), 1-21.
Review of Idylls, 1859.

505 "Leading Men--Tennyson." Littell's Living Age, 65 (April 7,
1860), 24.

506 M., J. L. "Un poèm de Tennyson." Bibliothèque universelle,

Sept. 1860.
Emphasizing "Lancelot and Elaine," the writer praises Tennyson as one of England's great poets.

507 "Maclise's Illustrations to Tennyson's 'Princess.' "
Dublin University Magazine, 55 (March 1860), 314-320.

508 Meliora, 2 (1860), 225-248.
A general discussion of Tennyson's poetry.

509 Milsand, Joseph. Le Magasin de Librairie, 12 (1860), 321-350.
Review of Idylls, 1859.

510 "A Rainy Day with Tennyson and Our Poets." Dublin University Magazine, 55 (Jan. 1860), 62-65.
Calls Idylls, 1859, "noble."

511 "Religious Aspects of Mr. Tennyson's Poetry." Dublin University Magazine, 55 (March 1860), 353-356.
Reprinted: Eclectic Magazine of Foreign Literature, 50 (May 1860), 52-56.

512 Revue européenne, Sept. 1860, p. 176.
Contrasts Tennyson negatively with Victor Hugo.

1861

Book

513 McNicoll, Thomas. "Alfred Tennyson." Essays on English Literature. London: Pickering, 1861, pp. 248-276.

Periodicals

514 Breachan. "The Bar of Michael Angelo." Notes and Queries, 2nd ser. 12 (July 20, 1861), 56.

515 "Lyell and Tennyson." Saturday Review (London), 11 (June 22, 1861), 631-632.
Reprinted: Littell's Living Age, 70 (Aug. 17, 1861), 417-420.

516 Meissner, L. Archiv für das Studium der neueren Sprachen und Literaturen, 29 (1861), 347-350.
Discusses Timbuctoo.

517 "One of Tennyson's Poems." Boston Review, 1 (Sept. 1861), 436-445.

518 Simpson, William. "Tennyson's 'Princess.' " Notes and Queries, 2nd ser. 12 (Aug. 17, 1861), 129.

519 Taine, Hippolyte Adolphe. "Tennyson: I. Son talent."
     Journal des Débats, April 3, 1861.
     Reprinted: L'Histoire de la littérature anglaise, 1864
(entry 534).

520 _____. "Tennyson: II. Son oeuvre." Journal des Débats,
     April 4, 1861.
     Reprinted: L'Histoire de la littérature anglaise, 1864
(entry 534).
     Admires "Locksley Hall" and Maud but not In Memoriam.

521 _____. "Tennyson: III. Son public." Journal des Débats,
     April 6, 1861.
     Reprinted: L'Histoire de la littérature anglaise, 1864
(entry 534).

522 "Tennyson's Philosophy--In Memoriam." Dublin University
     Magazine, 57 (Feb. 1861), 183-192.
     Reprinted: Eclectic Magazine of Foreign Literature, 52
(April 1861), 183-192.

1862

Books

523 Carroll, Lewis (pseudonym for Charles Lutwidge Dodgson).
     An Index to "In Memoriam." London: Moxon, 1862.

524 Hamerton, Philip Gilbert. "Word Painting and Colour Painting."
     A Painter's Camp in the Highlands and Thoughts about Art.
     London: 1862. Volume II, pp. 252-269.

525 Robertson, Frederick W. Analysis of Mr. Tennyson's "In
     Memoriam." London: Smith, Elder, 1862.
     A popular book that went through many editions during the
nineteenth century.

Periodical

526 Hendrickson, L. National Quarterly Review, 5 (June 1862),
     76-82.
     Discusses Maud.

1863

Book

527 Priolo, Paolo. Illustrations of Alfred Tennyson's Idylls the
     King. London: 1863.
     Not examined.

Periodicals

528 "Alfred Tennyson." Leisure Hour, 12 (Feb. 21 and 28, 1863), 119-124 and 136-140.

529 "Concerning Cutting and Carving." Fraser's Magazine, 67 (Feb. 1863), 213.

530 Corson, Mrs. C. R. New Englander, 23 (Oct. 1863), 638-653. Discusses "The Two Voices."

531 Pearce, Maresco. "The 'In Memoriam' Stanza." Reader, 1 (May 30, 1863), 531.

532 Renaud, Armand. "Alfred Tennyson." Revue contemporaine, 35 (1863), 476-504. Discusses Maud.

533 "Song-Writers." Dublin University Magazine, 61 (May 1863), 601-603.

1864

Tennyson's Enoch Arden, Etc. was published by Edward Moxon in 1864.

Books

534 Taine, Hippolyte A. "Les Contemporaines." Histoire de la Littérature anglaise. Paris: 1864. Volume IV.
Reprinted from Journal des Débats, 1864 (entries 519, 520, and 521). Translated: by H. van Laun. "Poetry--Tennyson." History of English Literature. 1871. Volume II, pp. 518-541. This translation reprinted in part: J. D. Jump, ed., Tennyson: The Critical Heritage (entry 4013), pages 270-277.
Tennyson is representative of his age. A careful study of Tennyson's achievements.

535 Watts, Henry Edward. Alfred Tennyson: A Lecture, Delivered at the Town Hall, Prahan, October 10th, 1864. Melbourne: Mullen, 1864.

Periodicals

536 Atlantic Monthly, 14 (Oct. 1864), 518-520.
Review of Enoch Arden.

537 [Bagehot, Walter.] "Wordsworth, Tennyson, and Browning: or, Pure, Ornate, and Grotesque Art in English Poetry." National Review, 19 (Nov. 1864), 27-67.
Reprinted: Literary Studies, 1879 (entry 904); and in part, J. D. Jump, ed., Tennyson: The Critical Heritage (entry 4013),

pages 282-293.
    Long-winded essay on the nature of literary art, much of
which is illustrated by Tennyson and "Enoch Arden."

538 Baxter, Wynne E. "Tennyson's 'Enoch Arden': Bigamy and
     Desertion." Notes and Queries, 3rd ser. 6 (Sept. 24, 1864),
     258.
     See: Job J.B. Workard (entry 559), below.

539 British Quarterly Review, 40 (Oct. 1864), 463-490.
     Reprinted in translation: Bibliothèque Universelle et Revue
Suisse, n.s. 22 (1865), 540-562; and 23 (1865), 107-128.
     Review of Enoch Arden.

540 Chambers's Journal, 41 (Sept. 24, 1864), 620-622.
     Review of Enoch Arden.

541 Curtis, G.W. Harper's Monthly Magazine, 29 (Oct. 1864),
     675-676.
     Review of Enoch Arden.

542 [Dixon, Hepworth.] Athenaeum, Aug. 13, 1864, pp. 201-202.
     Review of Enoch Arden. Dixon believes "Enoch Arden" is
immoral. He remarks: "Do we wish the young women of this generation to believe that it is a poetical incident rather than a dark
and shameful misfortune to have two husbands alive at the same
time? An agreeable impression!" Dixon fears that the poem may
make bigamy seem less than awful to impressionable people.

543 Dublin University Magazine, 64 (Oct. 1864), 386-396.
     Review of Enoch Arden.

544 [Hasell, Elizabeth J.] Blackwood's Magazine, 96 (Nov. 1864),
     555-572.
     Review of Enoch Arden.

545 [Lancaster, H.H.] North British Review, 41 (Aug. 1864),
     231-252.
     Review of Enoch Arden. Reprinted: Littell's Living Age, 83
(Oct. 22, 1864), 163-174; and Eclectic Magazine of Foreign Literature, 63 (Nov. 1864), 319-321.

546 "The Laureate and His School." Dublin Review, n.s. 2 (1864),
     363-385.

547 Littell's Living Age, 82 (Sept. 24, 1864), 579-587.
     Review of Enoch Arden.

548 London Quarterly Review, 23 (Oct. 1864), 153-169.
     Review of Enoch Arden.

549 Lowell, James Russell. North American Review, 99 (Oct.
     1864), 626.
     Review of Enoch Arden.

550 Ludlow, J.M. Macmillan's Magazine, 10 (Oct. 1864), 486-
     489.
     Discusses "The Northern Farmer, Old Style."

551 "Mr. Tennyson's New Volume." Notes and Queries, 3rd ser.
     6 (Sept. 3, 1864), 186-187.

552 National Review, n.s. 1 (Nov. 1864), 27-67.
     Review of Enoch Arden. Reprinted: Littell's Living Age,
     84 (Jan. 7, 1865), 3-24; and Eclectic Magazine of Foreign Lit-
     erature, 64 (March and April 1865), 273-284 and 415-427.

553 Reader, 4 (Aug. 13, 1864), 187-188.
     Review of Enoch Arden.

554 Revue britannique, Sept. 1864.
     Review of Enoch Arden. Mentioned in M. Bowden's Tenny-
     son in France (entry 3101), page 67. According to Bowden, the
     reviewer believes "Enoch Arden" is successful because of its high
     style.

555 Spectator, 37 (Aug. 27, 1864), 991-992.
     Review of Enoch Arden.

556 St. James Magazine, 11 (1864), 224-238.
     Review of Enoch Arden.

557 Vermorel, A. "Enoch Arden." Nouvelle Revue de Paris,
     Sept. 1864, p. 586.
     Review of Enoch Arden. Vermorel believes that Tennyson
     may find a wider audience outside of England because of Enoch
     Arden, although the volume might hurt the poet's reputation in
     England.

558 Westminster Review, 82 (Oct. 1864), 186-194.
     Review of Enoch Arden.

559 Workard, Job J.B. "Tennyson's 'Enoch Arden': Bigamy and
     Desertion." Notes and Queries, 3rd ser. 6 (Oct. 8, 1864),
     298.
     See: Wynne E. Baxter (entry 538), above.

                              1865

Books

560 Gomont, Henri Augustin. Poètes anglais au XIXe Siècle:
     Tennyson. Metz: Rousseau-Pallez, [1865].
     Reprinted from Revue de l'Est, 1865 (entry 564). See entry
     564 for annotation.

561 Page, H.A. (pseudonym for Alexander Hay Japp). Three

Great Teachers of Our Own Time: Carlyle, Tennyson, and Ruskin. London: Smith, Elder, 1865. Reprinted: Folcroft, Pennsylvania: Folcroft, 1977.
Tennyson on pages 87-186.

Periodicals

562 "Alfred Tennyson, ses derniers poèmes." Bibliothèque universelle, May 1865.

563 Asher, David. Archiv für das Studium der neueren Sprachen und Literaturen, 37 (1865), 238.
Note on "The Northern Farmer, Old Style."

564 Gomont, Henri Augustin. "Poètes anglais au XIXe Siècle: Tennyson." Revue de l'Est, Feb. 1865.
Reprinted: entry 560.
Gomont admires in particular "The Lotos-Eaters," "Oenone," and "The Two Voices." He regards Tennyson as a thoughtful and important poet.

565 "Recent Criticism on Tennyson." Temple Bar, 13 (March 1865), 354-362.

566 [Stephens, F.G.] Athenaeum, Dec. 23, 1865, II, p. 894.
Review of Enoch Arden. Stephens calls "Enoch Arden" an "English literary treasure."

567 "Tennyson, Wordsworth and Browning." Eclectic Magazine of Foreign Literature, 64 (March and April 1865), 273-284 and 415-427.

568 "Tennyson's Baronetcy." Spectator, 38 (Jan. 21, 1865), 65-66.

569 Warren, J. Leicester. "The Bibliography of Tennyson." Fortnightly Review, 2 (Oct. 1865), 385-403.
Reprinted: Littell's Living Age, 87 (Nov. 18, 1865), 289-299; and Eclectic Magazine of Foreign Literature, 66 (Feb. 1866), 159-170.

1866

Books

570 Grant, Charles. "Tennyson." The Last Hundred Years of English Literature. Jena: 1866, pp. 147-162.

571 P., C.H. (?Curtis Hidden Page?) Enoch Arden, by C.H.P.: Not by the "Laureate," but a Timid Hand that Grasped the Poet's Golden Lyre, "and back recoiled--e'en at the sound herself had made." 1866.
Verse.

572 [Shepherd, Richard Herne.] Tennysoniana: Notes Bibliographical Critical on Early Poems of Alfred & C. Tennyson.
London: Pickering, 1866.
A sloppy book that is still referred to by some scholars
even though it is unreliable. Revised and enlarged in 1879 (entry
910).

Periodicals

573 Bede, Cuthbert (pseudonym for Edward Bradley). "Early
Poetry of Alfred Tennyson." Notes and Queries, 3rd ser.
9 (March 10, 1866), 206.

574 Challsteth, A. "American Edition of Tennyson's Poems."
Notes and Queries, 3rd ser. 9 (Jan. 13, 1866), 48.

575 Emerson, G.R. Athenaeum, Aug. 18, 1866, pp. 211-212.

576 Grove, George. "On a Song in 'The Princess.' " Shilling
Magazine, Feb. 1866, pp. 181-184.

577 _____. " 'Tears, Idle Tears': A Commentary." Macmillan's Magazine, 15 (Nov. 1866), 67-72.
On a song from The Princess.

578 "Line from Tennyson." Notes and Queries, 3rd ser. 10 (Nov.
24, 1866), 413-414.

579 Ludlow, J.M. "Mr. Tennyson and the Eyre Defence Fund."
Spectator, 39 (Nov. 3, 1866), 1225-1226.

580 Montégut, Emile. "Enock Arden et les poèmes populaires."
Revue des Deux Mondes, March 15, 1866, pp. 423-442.
Review of Enoch Arden. Admires Tennyson's serenity.

581 "On the Early Poetry of Alfred Tennyson." Notes and Queries,
3rd ser. 9 (Feb. 10, 1866), 111-113.
See also: entry 573.

582 Renaud, Armand. Revue Contemporaine, 49 (Jan. 1866), 265-
284.
The discussion focuses on "Enoch Arden," "Aylmer's Field,"
and "Sea Dreams." Renaud perceives "Enoch Arden" as a humane
poem that focuses on characters. He finds the complaints of immorality brought against the poem by some British reviewers to be un-
warranted.

583 [Scott, Robert?] Quarterly Review, 119 (Jan. 1866), 58-80.
Review of Enoch Arden.

584 Skeat, Walter William. "Grig." Notes and Queries, 3rd ser.
10 (Dec. 29, 1866), 516.

585   Taylor, John. "Tennyson and W.R. Spenser." Notes and
      Queries, 3rd ser. 9 (June 30, 1866), 531.

                            1867

Books

586   Doré, Gustave. Illustrations to Elaine. London: Edward
      Moxon, 1867.

587   _____. Illustrations to Guinevere. London: Edward Moxon,
      1867.

588   _____. Illustrations to the Idylls of the King. London:
      Edward Moxon, 1867-1868 (in four parts).

589   _____. Illustrations to Vivien. London: Edward Moxon,
      1867.
      Reviewed by: Athenaeum (entry 592).

590   Ingram, John K. "Tennyson's Works." Afternoon Lectures
      on English Literature. London: Bell and Daldy, 1867.
      Volume IV, pp. 47-94.
      Ingram believes Tennyson's achievements in Poems, 1842,
remain in some ways unique. He admires Tennyson's early poetry.

591   Trench, Richard Chenevix. "The Sonnets of Charles and Al-
      fred Tennyson." Afternoon Lectures on Literature and Art.
      London: Bell and Daldy, 1867.   Volume IV, p. 163.

Periodicals

592   Athenaeum, Dec. 21, 1867, p. 845.
      Review of G. Doré's Illustrations to Vivien, 1867 (entry 589).

593   Blair, D. "Tennyson's Early Poems." Notes and Queries,
      3rd ser. 12 (Aug. 3, 1867), 98.

594   Bouchier, Jonathan. "Tennyson's 'Elaine.' " Notes and
      Queries, 3rd ser. 11 (April 27, 1867), 336.

595   Gatty, Margaret. "Tennyson: Elaine: Camelot." Notes and
      Queries, 3rd ser. 11 (June 8, 1867), 464-465.

596   "Home of Alfred Tennyson." Hours at Home, 5 (June 1867),
      116-118.

597   "The Laureate Under the Microscope." Chambers's Journal,
      44 (June 29, 1867), 404-407.

598   Spectator, 40 (Jan. 5, 1867), 18.
      Discusses "Lancelot and Elaine."

599 "Studies in Alfred Tennyson." Belgravia, 4 (Dec. 1867), 217-223.

600 "Tennysoniana." Leisure Hour, 16 (Oct. 1, 1867), 653-655.

601 "Tennysoniana." Notes and Queries, 3rd ser. 12 (Oct. 12, 1867), 283.

602 "Tennyson's Early Poems." Notes and Queries, 3rd ser. 12 (Nov. 23, 1867), 415.

1868

　　Tennyson's "Lucretius" appeared in the May 1868 issue of Macmillan's Magazine.

Books

603 Doré, Gustave. Illustrations to Enid. London: Edward Moxon, 1868.

604 Stirling, James Hutchinson. "Alfred Tennyson." Jerrold, Tennyson and Macaulay, with Other Critical Essays. Edinburgh: Edmonston and Douglas, 1868, pp. 51-111. Reprinted from Meliora, Oct. 1859 (entry 492). See entry 492 for annotation.

605 Tainsh, Edward Campbell. A Study of the Works of Alfred Tennyson, D.C.L., Poet Laureate. London: Chapman and Hall, 1868. Reprinted: London: Macmillan, 1893. A solid study of Tennyson's poetry. Reviewed by: Critic (New York) (entry 1707); E. Dowden in Fortnightly Review (entry 608); London Quarterly Review (entry 613); Saturday Review (London) (entry 618); Spectator (entry 621), A. Waugh in Academy (entry 1789); and Westminster Review (entry 1795).

Periodicals

606 Bouchier, Jonathan. "Tennyson's 'Palace of Art.'" Notes and Queries, 4th ser. 1 (April 18, 1868), 364.

607 [Cheetham, Samuel.] "The Arthurian Legends in Tennyson." Contemporary Review, 7 (April 1868), 497-514. Cheetham discusses the similarities and differences between Thomas Malory's Le Morte d'Arthur and Tennyson's versions of the Arthurian stories. He in general finds Tennyson's accounts superior to those of Malory.

608 Dowden, Edward. Fortnightly Review, 9 (May 1868), 582-584. Review of E.C. Tainsh's A Study of the Works of Alfred Tennyson, 1868 (entry 605).

609 "Fashion in Poetry." St. Pauls Magazine, 1 (March 1868), 702-703.

610 Fitzhopkins. "Tennysoniana." Notes and Queries, 4th ser. 1 (June 20, 1868), 577.

611 Jebb, R.C. "On Mr. Tennyson's 'Lucretius.' " Macmillan's Magazine, 18 (June 1868), 97-103.
Reprinted: Every Saturday, 6 (July 25, 1868), 101-104.
A short study of Tennyson's poem.

612 "The Laureate's New Poem." Punch, 54 (May 9, 1868), 205.
Reprinted: Littell's Living Age, 97 (June 27, 1868), 824.
On "Lucretius."

613 London Quarterly Review, 31 (Oct. 1868), 134-136.
Review of E.C. Tainsh's A Study of the Works of Alfred Tennyson, 1868 (entry 605).

614 London Quarterly Review, 31 (Oct. 1868), 249-254.
Discusses "Lucretius."

615 "Mr. Tennyson's 'Death of Lucretius.' " Spectator, 41 (May 2, 1868), 523-524.

616 Nation (New York), 6 (April 30, 1868), 352-353.
Discusses "Lucretius."

617 "Passage in Tennyson." Notes and Queries, 4th ser. 2 (Nov. 28, 1868), 510.

618 Saturday Review (London), 25 (April 18, 1868), 521-522.
Review of E.C. Tainsh's A Study of the Works of Alfred Tennyson, 1868 (entry 605). Reprinted: Littell's Living Age, 97 (June 27, 1868), 814-816.

619 Smedley, Menella B. " 'The Victim.' " Notes and Queries, 4th ser. 2 (Sept. 26, 1868), 307.
Tennyson's poem "The Victim" was set to music by Arthur Sullivan and printed by Ivor Guest, 1867.

620 Smith, George. "On Three Contemporary Poets." Bentley's Miscellany, 64 (July 1868), 61-69.

621 Spectator, 41 (May 16, 1868), 588-589.
Review of E.C. Tainsh's A Study of the Works of Alfred Tennyson, 1868 (entry 605). Reprinted: Littell's Living Age, 97 (June 27, 1868), 804-807.

622 "Tennyson and Longfellow." Littell's Living Age, 98 (Aug. 22, 1868), 450.

623 "Tennyson and M. Doré." Athenaeum, Jan. 4, 11, and 25, 1868, pp. 26, 64, and 138.

624 "Tennyson and the Queen." New Eclectic, 2 (Aug. 1868), 465-468.

625 "Tennyson in His Catholic Aspects." Catholic World, 7 (May 1868), 145-154.

626 "Tennyson's 'Lucretius.' " Tinsley's Magazine, 2 (July 1868), 611-616.

627 Waldmueller, R. (C.E. Duboc). "Alfred Tennyson." Unsere Zeit, 1 (1868), 522-543.

628 _____. "Alfred Tennyson." Illustrierte Deutsche Monatshefte, 25 (Nov. 1868), 214-224.

629 "What Is the Laureate About?" Tinsley's Magazine, 2 (March 1868), 262-267.

1869

Tennyson's The Holy Grail and Other Poems was published in London in 1869 by Strahan and Co.

Books

630 Brightwell, D. Barron. A Concordance to the Entire Works of Alfred Tennyson. London: Edward Moxon, 1869. Updated in 1870 (entry 645).
Brightwell's concordances are good, straightforward examples of literary research. They are still useful.

631 Clough, Arthur Hugh. The Poems and Remains of Arthur Hugh Clough. Ed. Blanche Clough and J.A. Symonds. London: Macmillan, 1869.
Tennyson in volume I, pages 264-269.

631a Dowden, Edward. "Mr. Tennyson and Mr. Browning." Afternoon Lectures on Literature. Dublin: McGee, 1869, pp. 139-179. Reprinted: London: Kegan Paul, 1878. Reprinted, revised: Studies in Literature, 1798-1877, 1906 (entry 2414).
Dowden perceives Tennyson as having faith in science and human progress. He focuses on the ideas of Tennyson and Browning.

632 The Laughter of the Muses: A Satire on the Reigning Poetry of 1869. Glasgow: Thomas Murray, 1869.
A verse satire on the works of Tennyson and Robert Browning.

Periodicals

633 Athenaeum, Dec. 18, 1869, pp. 809-810.
     Review of The Holy Grail.

634 [Austin, Alfred.] "The Poetry of the Period: Mr. Tennyson."
     Temple Bar, 26 (May 1869), 179-194.
     Reprinted, revised: Poetry of the Period, 1870 (entry 643).
     Deprecates Tennyson's stature as a poet. See entry 643 for
more extensive notation.

635 "Mr. Tennyson's New Poems." Literary World, n.s. 1, nos.
     7 and 8 (Dec. 17 and 24, 1869), 97-98 and 120-121.
     Review of The Holy Grail. Finds Tennyson's good charac-
ters dull and the poet's bad characters more interesting.

636 "Mr. Tennyson's New Poems." Spectator, 42 (Dec. 25, 1869),
     1530-1533.
     Review of The Holy Grail.

637 "Modern English Poets." Quarterly Review, 126 (April 1869),
     332-340.

638 National Magazine (London), 6 (1869), 169-174.
     Discusses Tennyson's Arthurian poetry.

639 "Roman Catholic Poets." Temple Bar, 27 (Sept. 1869), 170-
     186; and 28 (Dec. 1869), 33-48.

640 Schrumpf, G.A. "An Unacknowledged Poem of Tennyson."
     Notes and Queries, 4th ser. 4 (Oct. 23, 1869), 345.

641 Tennyson, Alfred. Notes and Queries, 4th ser. 4 (Oct. 30,
     1869), 378.
     A letter dated Sept. 9, 1869, to the Tennyson Society of
Philadelphia.

642 "Weighing Tennyson." Every Saturday, 7 (May 29, 1869),
     699-701.

1870

     In 1870, Tennyson's The Window: or, The Song of the Wrens,
with music by Arthur Sullivan, was published by Strahan and Co. in
London. The song was first printed by Ivor Guest in 1867.

Books

643 Austin, Alfred. "Tennyson." Poetry of the Period. London:
     Bentley, 1870, pp. 1-37.
     Reprinted, revised, from Temple Bar, 1869 (entry 634). Re-
printed: J.D. Jump, ed., Tennyson: The Critical Heritage (entry
4013), pages 294-311.
     Austin asserts: "... Mr. Tennyson has no sound pretensions

to be called a great poet, and will of a certainty not be esteemed such by an unbiased posterity...." Austin also remarks: "There is yet time to revise and recall our hasty and extravagant praises; and Mr. Tennyson's merits are so obvious and so considerable that, when we have plucked off all the false feathers in which we have bedecked him, some very beautiful plumage will remain. But our attempts to glorify ourselves by over-exalting him can do no possible good to anybody; and if we persist in this ridiculous course, it will only ensure our being scoffed at by less partial times as a parcel of indiscriminating dunces."

644 [Aytoun, William Edmondstoune, and Theodore Martin] (jointly under the pseudonym of Bon Gaultier). "The Lay of the Lovelorn" and "Caroline." The Book of Ballads. Edinburgh: Blackwood, 1870. 11th edition, pp. 102-111 and 239-241, respectively.
"Caroline" is probably the work of Martin, while "The Lay of the Lovelorn" is by Aytoun.

645 Brightwell, D. Barron. Concordance to the Works of Alfred Tennyson, Poet Laureate. London: Strahan, 1870.
An updated version of Brightwell's 1869 concordance (entry 630). A solid example of literary research that remains useful.

646 de Laprade, Victor. "Les Contemporaines: Tennyson." Le Sentiment de la Nature chez les Modernes. 2nd edition. Paris: Didier, 1870, pp. 285-289.

647 Friswell, James Hain. "Mr. Alfred Tennyson." Modern Men of Letters Honestly Criticized. London: Hodder and Stoughton, 1870, pp. 145-156.

648 [Shepherd, Richard Herne.] The Lover's Tale: A Supplementary Chapter to Tennysoniana. London: privately printed, 1870.
Only fifty copies printed.

Periodicals

649 Alford, Henry. Contemporary Review, 13 (Jan. 1870), 104-125.
Review of The Holy Grail. A study of the imagery and symbolism of Tennyson's poems. Alford is particularly interested in the allegorical aspects of The Holy Grail.

650 "Alfred Tennyson." Every Saturday, 9 (Jan. 1, 1870), 2.

651 Archiv für das Studium der neueren Sprachen und Literaturen, 47 (1870), 321-322.
Review of Enoch Arden. Pays special attention to "Aylmer's Field."

652 Athenaeum, Dec. 17, 1870, pp. 793-794.
Review of The Window.

653 Blair, D. "Tennyson's 'Idylls of the King.' " Notes and
Queries, 4th ser. 5 (June 4, 1870), 537.

654 Camerini, E. "Alfred Tennyson." Nuova Antologia di Lettere,
Scienze ed Arti, Feb. 1870.

655 Chambers's Journal, 47 (Feb. 26, 1870), 137-140.
Review of The Holy Grail.

656 Eclectic Magazine of Foreign Literature, 74 (March 1870),
339-444.
Review of The Holy Grail.

657 Every Saturday, 9 (Jan. 29, 1870), 76.
Discusses In Memoriam.

658 [Forman, Harry Buxton?] London Quarterly Review, 34 (April
1870), 154-186.
Review of The Holy Grail. Discusses The Idylls of the King,
1859, as well.

659 Fullerton, John. "Alfred Tennyson: His Life and Writings."
Broadway (London), 2nd ser. 3 (Jan. 1870), 507-514.

660 Harper's Monthly Magazine, 40 (March 1870), 610-611.

661 "House of Alfred Tennyson near Haslemere." Every Saturday,
9 (Feb. 26, 1870), 132.

662 [Howells, William Dean.] Atlantic Monthly, 25 (Feb. 1870),
249-250.
Review of The Holy Grail.

663 [Kemble, John?] "Tennyson's Arthurian Poem." Spectator,
43 (Jan. 1, 1870), 1-12.
Review of The Holy Grail.

664 Knowles, James T. "Tennyson's Arthurian Poem." Spectator,
43 (Jan. 1, 1870), 15-17.
Reprinted: H. Tennyson, ed., Tennyson and His Friends,
1911 (entry 2658); and J.D. Jump, ed., Tennyson: The Critical
Heritage (entry 4013), pages 312-317.
Hallam Tennyson notes in his Alfred Lord Tennyson (entry
1955), Volume II, page 126, footnote 2, that Knowles wrote the
following to him: "He [Tennyson] encouraged me to write a short
paper, in the form of a letter to the Spectator, on the inner meaning of the whole poem [The Holy Grail], which I did, simply upon
the lines he himself indicated. He often said, however, that an
allegory should never be pressed too far." Knowles emphasizes
the allegory and moral themes of the poem.

665 "The Laureate's Motto." Notes and Queries, 4th ser. 5 (Jan.
22, 1870), 103.

666 Lawrenny, H. Academy, 1 (Jan. 8, 1870), 91-94.
Review of The Holy Grail. A less than understanding commentary.

667 Littell's Living Age, 106 (1870), 131-150.
Review of The Holy Grail. Includes discussion of the earlier Arthurian poems of Tennyson.

668 "The Modern Poetry of Doubt." Spectator, 43 (Feb. 5, 1870),
166-167.
Reprinted: New Eclectic, 6 (April 1870), 490-494.

669 [Mozley, J.R.] "Mr. Tennyson's 'Holy Grail.' " Quarterly
Review, 128 (Jan. 1870), 1-17.
Review of The Holy Grail. Finds the poetry too ornate.

670 "Mr. Tennyson and the Round Table." British Quarterly Review, 51 (April 1870), 200-206.
Review of The Holy Grail. A generally positive review.

671 "Mr. Tennyson's Arthurian Poems" Dublin Review, 66 (April
1870), 418-429.
Review of The Holy Grail.

672 Nation (New York), 10 (Feb. 17, 1870), 109-110.
Review of The Holy Grail.

673 New Englander, 29 (April 1879), 351-357.
Review of The Holy Grail.

674 "New Poem by Tennyson: Northern Farmer: New Style."
Every Saturday, 9 (Jan. 1, 1870), 2.
"The Northern Farmer, New Style" appeared in The Holy
Grail and Other Poems, 1869.

675 "Old Romance and Modern Poetry." All the Year Round, n.s.
4 (Sept. 17, 1870), 373-379.
Review of The Holy Grail.

676 [Oliphant, Margaret.] Edinburgh Review, 131 (April 1870),
502-539.
Review of The Holy Grail. Discusses the earlier Arthurian
poems of Tennyson as well as The Holy Grail. Offers some insight into Tennyson's imagery.

677 "The Quest of the Sancgreal." St. James's Magazine, n.s. 4
(April 1870), 785-814.
Review of The Holy Grail. Less than happy with the manner
in which Tennyson handles his characters, notably King Arthur.

678 Scherer, Edmond. "Alfred Tennyson." Le Temps, Jan. 11,
1870.
Discusses Tennyson's originality and versatility. Admires
the consistently high quality of Tennyson's poetry.

679 Spectator, 43 (Dec. 31, 1970), 1586-1587.
     Review of The Window.

680 "A Study of Tennyson." Every Saturday, 9 (Feb. 5, 1870),
     90.

681 "A Study of Tennyson." Graphic, May 7, 1870, pp. 538-539.
     Discusses Tennyson's use of architecture in poems.

682 "Tennyson and the Holy Vision." Intellectual Repository and
     New Jerusalem Magazine, 17 (Dec. 1870), 472-476 and
     522-254.
     Review of The Holy Grail.

683 "Tennyson's Two Northern Farmers." Every Saturday, 9 (Jan.
     15, 1870), 34.
     About "The Northern Farmer, Old Style" and "The Northern
Farmer, New Style."

684 Victoria Magazine, 14 (Feb. 1870), 376-383.
     Review of The Holy Grail.

1871

     Tennyson's "The Last Tournament" appeared in the Contem-
porary Review's December issue. Strahan and Co. of London published the Miniature Edition of Tennyson's works in 1871.

Book

685 Forman, Harry Buxton. "Alfred Tennyson." Our Living Poets:
     An Essay in Criticism. London: Tinsley, 1871, pp. 27-69.
     Reviewed by: W.J. Courthope in Quarterly Review (entry
745).

Periodicals

686 "Congreve and Wycherley." Notes and Queries, 4th ser. 7
     (June 3, 1871), 486.

687 Friswell, James Hain. "Tennyson and the 'Plain Dealer.' "
     Notes and Queries, 4th ser. 7 (April 8, 1871), 301.

688 Haweis, Hugh Reginald. St. Paul's Magazine, 7 (Feb. 1871),
     473-487.
     Review of The Window.

689 [Hayward, Abraham.] "Byron and Tennyson." Quarterly
     Review, 131 (Oct. 1871), 354-392.
     Reprinted: Eclectic Magazine of Foreign Literature, 78 (Jan.
1872), 1-20; and Sketches, 1880 (entry 948).

690 Nation (New York), 13 (Dec. 28, 1871), 418-419.
    Review of "The Last Tournament."

691 Saturday Review (London), 32 (Dec. 9, 1871), 754-755.
    Review of "The Last Tournament."

692 Schmidt, Rudolf. "Et digt af Tennyson." For Ide og
    Virkelighed, 1 (1871), 544-564.
    Discusses "Enoch Arden."

693 [Simpson, Richard.] "Mr. Tennyson's Poetry." North British
    Review, 53 (Jan. 1871), 378-425.
    Review of Poems, 1842. Reprinted: Littell's Living Age,
    109 (April 22, 1871), 195-220.

694 Stedman, Edmund Clarence. "Tennyson and Theocritus."
    Atlantic Monthly, 28 (Nov. 1871), 513-526.
    Reprinted: Victorian Poets, 1896 (entry 1909).

695 "Tennysoniana." Notes and Queries, 4th ser. 7 (May 20,
    1871), 431.

1872

Gareth and Lynette was published by Strahan and company
in 1872. In addition, Strahan published The Library Edition of
Tennyson's works, in seven volumes.

Books

696 Matthison, Arthur. Enoch Arden: A Drama in Five Acts,
    Founded on Alfred Tennyson's Great Poem. London: French,
    [c. 1872]. (French's Standard Drama.)

697 Swinburne, Algernon Charles. Under the Microscope. London:
    D. White, 1872.
    Tennyson on pages 36-45. Swinburne remarks: "It seems to
me that the moral tone of the Arthurian story has been on the whole
lowered and degraded by Mr. Tennyson's mode of treatment." Swinburne cites differences between Tennyson's version of the Arthurian
legends and the medieval stories. The assessment of Tennyson's
Arthurian poems is negative.

Periodicals

698 Appleton's Journal, 7 (Jan. 20, 1872), 78-79.
    Discusses Lord Byron and Tennyson.

699 Atlantic Monthly, 30 (Dec. 1872), 747-748.
    Review of Gareth and Lynette.

700 Bede, Cuthbert (pseudonym for Edward Bradley). "Locksley

Hall." Notes and Queries, 4th ser. 9 (June 22, 1872), 518.
Mentions parodies of "Locksley Hall."

701 _____. "Tennyson's 'Death of the Old Year.' " Notes and
Queries, 4th ser. 9 (Feb. 3, 1872), 92.

702 Blair, D. "Tennysoniana." Notes and Queries, 4th ser. 9
(June 8, 1872), 467.
About the state of the texts of Tennyson's poems.

703 Blémont, Emile. "Tennyson." La Renaissance artistique et
littéraire, May 11, 1872.
Makes fun of Tennyson's pretensions and denegrates Tennyson's achievements.

704 Bouchier, Jonathan. "The Metre of 'In Memoriam.' " Notes
and Queries, 4th ser. 10 (Oct. 12, 1872), 293.
See also: A. Dobson (entry 712) and W. Thomas (entry 733).

705 British Quarterly Review, 55 (Jan. 1872), 139-140.
Review of The Library Edition, 1872.

706 Browne, W. H. Southern Magazine, 10 (March 1872), 371-377.
Review of "The Last Tournament."

707 Buchanan, Robert. "Tennyson's Charm." St. Pauls Magazine,
10 (March 1872), 282-303.
A laudatory commentary.

708 Catholic World, 15 (May 1872), 241-254.
Review of "The Last Tournament."

709 "Cleopatra." Notes and Queries, 4th ser. 10 (Dec. 21, 1872),
499.

710 [Colvin, Sidney.] Fortnightly Review, 18 (Dec. 1872), 757-758.
Review of Gareth and Lynette.

711 Congregationalist, 1 (Dec. 1872), 718-726.
Review of "The Last Tournament."

712 Dobson, Austin. "The Metre of Tennyson's 'In Memoriam.' "
Notes and Queries, 4th ser. 10 (Oct. 26, 1872), 338.
See also: J. Bouchier (entry 704) and W. Thomas (entry
733).

713 "Dora." Notes and Queries, 4th ser. 10 (July 6, 1872), 8.

714 Furnivall, F. J. "Tennyson's Arthurian Poem." Notes and
Queries, 4th ser. 10 (Nov. 2, 1872), 348-349.

715 Gatty, Alfred. "What Keeps a Spirit Wholly True?" Notes
and Queries, 4th ser. 10 (Nov. 9, 1872), 381.

716 [Howells, William Dean.] Atlantic Monthly, 29 (Feb. 1872), 236-237.
Review of "The Last Tournament."

717 Hutton, R[ichard] H[olt]. "Tennyson." Macmillan's Magazine, 27 (Dec. 1872), 143-167.
Not entirely happy with Tennyson's characterizations in the Arthurian poems. Mentions Algernon Charles Swinburne's Under the Microscope.

718 [Knight, Joseph.] Athenaeum, Oct. 26, 1872, pp. 521-524.
Review of Gareth and Lynette. Knight dislikes the characterization of Arthur, although he admires the work as a whole.

719 "The Last of the Arthurian Legends." Chambers's Journal, 49 (Dec. 14, 1872), 813-816.
Review of Gareth and Lynette.

720 Leary, T. H. L. "Tennyson's 'Last Tournament.' " Gentleman's Magazine, 232 (April 1872), 423-430.
Review of "The Last Tournament." Discusses imagery and characterization.

721 "The Metre of Tennyson's 'Charge of the Six Hundred.' " Notes and Queries, 4th ser. 10 (Nov. 16, 1872), 390.

722 Nation (New York), 15 (Nov. 7, 1872), 301-302.
Review of Gareth and Lynette.

723 "Novelties in Poetry and Criticism." Fraser's Magazine, n.s. 5 (May 1872), 588-596.

724 Oakley, J. H. I. "Tennyson's 'Charge of the Six Hundred.'" Notes and Queries, 4th ser. 10 (Dec. 14, 1872), 479.

725 [Oliphant, Margaret.] Blackwood's Magazine, 112 (Dec. 1872), 760-765.
Review of Gareth and Lynette.

726 "The Poet Laureate." Once a Week, 26 (April 13, 1872), 343-348.

727 Saturday Review (London), 34 (Nov. 2, 1872), 568-569.
Review of Gareth and Lynette.

728 Scribner's Monthly, 3 (Feb. 1872), 508-509.
Review of "The Last Tournament."

729 Simcox, George Augustus. Academy, 3 (Nov. 15, 1872), 423-424.
Review of Gareth and Lynette.

730 Spectator, 45 (Oct. 26, 1872), 1363-1365.
Review of Gareth and Lynette.

731 Stoddard, Richard Henry. "Alfred Tennyson." Appleton's
     Journal, 7 (March 30, 1872), 353-356.

732 "Tennyson's Poem, 'Gareth and Lynette.' " Notes and Queries,
     4th ser. 10 (Dec. 28, 1872), 524.

733 Thomas, William. "The Metre of 'In Memoriam.' " Notes
     and Queries, 4th ser. 10 (Nov. 16, 1872), 403.
     See also: J. Bouchier (entry 704) and A. Dobson (entry
712).

734 Williams, Sparks Henderson. "Tennyson." Notes and Queries,
     4th ser. 9 (April 13, 1872), 301.

                              1873

Books

735 Buchanan, Robert. "Tennyson, Heine, and DeMusset."
     Master-Spirits. London: King, 1873, pp. 54-88.

736 Calverley, Charles Stuart. "First Love." Fly Leaves.
     London: 1873, pp. 32-35.
     "First Love" parodies "Locksley Hall."

737 Devey, J[oseph]. "The Art School." A Comparative Estimate
     of Modern English Poets. London: Edward Moxon, 1873,
     pp. 275-336.
     Devey examines Tennyson's art, skill, and technique.

738 Hadley, James. Essays, Philological and Critical. New York:
     Holt and Williams, 1873, pp. 296-324.
     Reprinted from New Englander, 1849 (entry 176).

739 Irving, Walter (pseudonym for George M. Brody). Tennyson.
     Edinburgh: Maclachlan and Stewart, 1873.
     A twenty-eight-page commentary.

740 Smith, Jephson Huband. Notes and Marginalia, Illustrative of
     the Public Life and Works of Alfred Tennyson, Poet-Laureate.
     London: Blackwood, 1873.
     Reviewed by: Athenaeum (entry 742).

Periodicals

741 Addis, John. "In Memoriam." Notes and Queries, 4th ser.
     11 (May 10, 1873), 388.

742 Athenaeum, Sept. 27, 1873, pp. 393-394.
     Review of J. H. Smith's Notes and Marginalia, 1873 (entry
740).

743 Barry, E. Milner. "Tennyson's Arthurian Poem." Notes and Queries, 4th ser. 11 (March 1, 1873), 183-184.

744 Browne, W. H. Southern Magazine, 12 (Jan. 1873), 106-113. Review of Gareth and Lynette.

745 [Courthope, W. J.] "The State of English Poetry." Quarterly Review, 135 (July 1873), 1-40.
Review of H. B. Forman's Our Living Poets, 1871 (entry 685).

746 Davies, James. "Tennyson's 'Ode on the Death of the Duke of Wellington.' " Notes and Queries, 4th ser. 11 (May 17, 1873), 407.

747 Dees, R. R. "Tennyson's 'Gareth and Lynette.' " Notes and Queries, 4th ser. 11 (March 8, 1873), 207.
See also: J. E. Sandys (entry 766).

748 Furnivall, F. J. "Mr. Hutton and Tennyson's 'King Arthur.' " Notes and Queries, 4th ser. 11 (Jan. 4, 1873), 3-4.

749 G., C. A. L. Victoria Magazine, 20 (Feb. 1873), 308-313.
Review of Gareth and Lynette. Includes criticism of Tennyson's imagery.

750 Gatty, Alfred. "The Idylls of the King: An Allegory." Notes and Queries, 4th ser. 11 (Jan. 11, 1873), 30-31.

751 Hilton, A. C. "Tennyson." Notes and Queries, 4th ser. 11 (March 22, 1873), 238.

752 Himes, John A. "The Religious Faith of Wordsworth and Tennyson as Shown in Their Poems." Lutheran Church Quarterly, 3 (April 1873), 253-267.

753 Hutchinson, J. "Mr. Tennyson as a Botanist." St. Pauls Magazine, 13 (Oct. 1873), 443-452.
Reprinted: Littell's Living Age, 119 (Nov. 8, 1873), 372-377.

754 "I held it truth with him who sings." Notes and Queries, 4th ser. 11 (Feb. 1, 1873), 105.

755 Knowles, James T. "The Meaning of Mr. Tennyson's 'King Arthur.' " Contemporary Review, 21 (May 1873), 938-948.
Knowles repeats some of his comments in the Spectator, 1870 (entry 664), and replies to Swinburne's comments on Tennyson in Under the Microscope (entry 697).

756 London Quarterly Review, 39 (Jan. 1873), 394-405.
Review of Gareth and Lynette.

757 "The Metre of 'In Memoriam.' " Notes and Queries, 4th ser.
    11 (Jan. 11, 1873), 37-38.
    See also: entries 704, 712, and 733.

758 "The Metres of Tennyson." Notes and Queries, 4th ser. 11
    (Feb. 1, 1873), 104-105.

759 "Mr. Tennyson's 'Holy Grail.' " Spectator, 46 (May 10, 1873),
    600-601.

760 "Phases of Sorrow in Tennyson." Victoria Magazine, 20
    (March 1873), 422-438.

761 Picton, J. A. "Tennyson: 'All the swine were sows.' "
    Notes and Queries, 4th ser. 11 (April 26, 1873), 345-346.
    See also: W. W. Skeat (entry 769).

762 Quesnel, Léo. "La Poésie contemporaine en Angleterre."
    Revue bleue, 1873, p. 517.
    An astonishing display of ignorance. Quesnel has either not
    read Tennyson's poetry or does not understand English. Hostile
    toward Tennyson.

763 Ramage, C. T. "The Duke of Wellington." Notes and Queries,
    4th ser. 11 (April 26, 1873), 342.
    See also: entry 764, below, and entry 772.

764 _____. "Ode on the Death of the Duke of Wellington."
    Notes and Queries, 4th ser. 12 (Aug. 2, 1873), 95.
    See also: entry 763, above, and entry 772.

765 Rawnsley, Hardwick Drummond. "Lincolnshire Scenery and
    Character as Illustrated by Mr. Tennyson." Macmillan's
    Magazine, 29 (Dec. 1873), 140-144.
    Reprinted: Every Saturday, 16 (Jan. 3, 1874), 13-15.

766 Sandys, J. Edwin. "Tennyson's 'Gareth and Lynette.' "
    Notes and Queries, 4th ser. 11 (Jan 11, 1873), 44-45.
    See also: R. R. Dees (entry 747).

767 Scribner's Monthly, 5 (Jan. 1873), 397-398.
    Review of Gareth and Lynette.

768 "Sir Tray: An Arthurian Idyl." Blackwood's Edinburgh Mag-
    azine, 113 (Jan. 1873), 120-124.
    A parody of Tennyson's Arthurian poetry.

769 Skeat, Walter William. "All the swine were sows." Notes
    and Queries, 4th ser. 11 (April 26, 1873), 346
    See also: J. A. Picton (entry 761).

770 Spectator, 46 (Feb. 8, 1873), 177-178.
    Discusses Idylls of the King.

771   "Tennyson's Natural History." Notes and Queries, 4th ser.
      12 (July 19, 1873), 55-56.

772   "Tennyson's Ode on the Death of the Duke of Wellington."
      Notes and Queries, 4th ser. 11 (June 7, 1873), 473.
      See also: C. T. Ramage (entries 763 and 764).

773   Westminster Review, 99 (Jan. 1873), 153-154.
      Review of Gareth and Lynette.

1874

      H. S. King and Co. published the Cabinet Edition of Tenny-
son's poetry in 1874.

Book

774   Barot, Odysse. Littérature contemporaine en Angleterre.
      Paris: Charpentier, 1874.
      Includes a discussion of "Locksley Hall."

Periodicals

775   " 'In Memoriam' and the Bible." Leisure Hour, 23 (1874),
      71-73.

776   Picton, J. A. "Dante and Tennyson: Parallel Passages."
      Notes and Queries, 5th ser. 1 (Feb. 21, 1874), 142-143.
      An interesting note on a subject that still seems worth
pursuing.

777   Purton, J. B. "Tennyson." Notes and Queries, 5th ser. 2
      (Oct. 24, 1874), 335.

778   Stedman, Edmund Clarence. "Alfred Tennyson." Scribner's
      Monthly, 8 (May and June 1874), 100-107 and 160-170.

779   Tollemache, Lionel A. "Mr. Tennyson's Social Philosophy."
      Fortnightly Review, 21 (Feb. 1, 1874), 225-247.
      Tollemache believes Tennyson to be a moral poet preoccupied
with the Middle Ages and considers the poet's ideas about morality,
religion, and society commonplace. Nonetheless, Tollemache
observes, Tennyson's gentleness and open-mindedness have had
beneficial effects on British society.

1875

      Tennyson's verse-play Queen Mary: A Drama was published
in London by Henry S. King and Co.

Books

780 Camerini, E. "Alfredo Tennyson." Nuovi profili letterari. Milano: Battezzati e Saldini, 1875. Volume I, pp. 1-35.

781 Cameron, Julia Margaret. Illustrations to Tennyson's Idylls of the King and Other Poems. London: King, 1875.

782 Cranch, Christopher Pearse. "On Re-Reading Tennyson's Princess." The Bird and the Bell: With Other Poems. Boston: Osgood, 1875, pp. 283-284.

783 Gostwick, Joseph. "Tennyson." English Poets: Twelve Essays. New York: Stroefer and Kirchner, 1875.

784 Irving, Walter (pseudonym for George M. Brody). Tennyson's "Queen Mary": A Criticism. Edinburgh: Maclachlan and Stewart, 1875.
An essay attacking Queen Mary.

785 McCrie, George. "Alfred Tennyson." The Religion of Our Literature. London: Hodder and Stoughton, 1875, pp. 110-180.

Periodicals

786 Adams, H. North American Review, 121 (Oct. 1875), 422-429. Review of Queen Mary.

787 Athenaeum, June 26, 1875, pp. 845-848.
Review of Queen Mary. The reviewer does not believe that Queen Mary has the necessary qualities of successful drama. See also: entry 788, below.

788 Athenaeum, July 3, 1875, pp. 13-14.
Review of Queen Mary. The reviewer believes the play inferior to Tennyson's nondramatic works. See also: entry 787, above.

789 British Quarterly Review, 62 (Oct. 1875), 181-193.
Review of the Cabinet Edition and Queen Mary.

790 Browne, W. H. Southern Magazine, 17 (Sept. 1875), 372-380. Review of Queen Mary.

791 Bullen, A. H. "Tennyson and Shelley." Notes and Queries, 5th ser. 4 (Dec. 11, 1875), 464.
See entry 843.

792 Catholic World, 22 (Oct. 1875), 1-12.
Review of Queen Mary.

793 Christian Observer, 74 (Oct. 1875), 761-764.
Review of Queen Mary.

794 Church Times, July 2, 1875, p. 330.
     Review of Queen Mary. Listed in C. Tennyson and C. Fall,
Alfred Tennyson (entry 4016), page 100.

795 [Courthope, W.J.] Quarterly Review, 139 (July 1875), 231-248.
     Review of Queen Mary. Courthope regards the drama as an
idea piece worthy of reading but unworthy of performance.

796 Eclectic Magazine of Foreign Literature, 85 (Aug. 1875), 251.
     Review of Queen Mary.

797 Guardian, June 30, 1875, p. 837.
     Review of Queen Mary.

798 Harper's Monthly Magazine, 51 (Sept. 1875), 598-599.
     Review of Queen Mary.

799 [Hasell, Elizabeth J.] Blackwood's Edinburgh Magazine, 118
     (Sept. 1875), 322-335.
     Review of Queen Mary.

800 [Howells, William Dean.] Atlantic Monthly, 36 (Aug. 1875),
     240-241.
     Review of Queen Mary. Howells describes the drama as a
sloppy work thematically, poetically, and structurally.

801 International Review, 2 (Oct. 1875), 701-702.
     Review of Queen Mary.

802 James, Henry, Jr. Galaxy, 20 (Sept. 1875), 393-402.
     Review of Queen Mary.

803 [Jebb, R.C.?] "Notes on Mr. Tennyson's Queen Mary."
     Macmillan's Magazine, 32 (Sept. 1875), 434-441.
     Generally likes the play although its action sometimes lags.

804 Lang, Andrew. Academy, 7 (June 26, 1875), 649-650.
     Review of Queen Mary. Lang admires Tennyson's character-
izations and thoughtfulness.

805 Literary World (Boston), 6 (June 1875), 14-15.
     Review of Queen Mary.

806 "Locksley Hall." Notes and Queries, 5th ser. 4 (July 31,
     1875), 91-92.

807 Mackay, Charles. "Locksley Hall." Notes and Queries, 5th
     ser. 4 (Oct. 9, 1875), 297-298.

808 Midland Counties Herald, June 24, 1875, Supplement, p. 1.
     Review of Queen Mary. Listed in C. Tennyson and C. Fall,
Alfred Tennyson (entry 4016), page 101.

809 Nation (New York), 21 (July 22, 1875), 60-61.
     Review of Queen Mary.

810 New Englander, 34 (Oct. 1875), 789-790.
     Review of Queen Mary.

811 Noncomformist, June 23, 1875, p. 639.
     Review of Queen Mary. Admires almost everything about
the play.

812 Picton, J.A. "Locksley Hall." Notes and Queries, 5th ser.
     4 (Oct. 30, 1875), 349-350.

813 "Queen Mary." Notes and Queries, 5th ser. 4 (Sept. 18,
     1875), 232-233.

814 "Queen Mary." Unsere Zeit, 2 (1875), 632-636.

815 Raleigh, Walter S. "The Poet Laureate and the Queen's
     English." Notes and Queries, 5th ser. 4 (Aug. 21, 1875),
     148.

816 Rawnsley, Hardwicke Drummond. "Virgil and Tennyson."
     Macmillan's Magazine, 33 (Nov. 1875), 43-49.
     Reprinted: Littell's Living Age, 127 (Dec. 18, 1875),
756-762.

817 Saturday Review (London), 40 (July 3, 1875), 19-21.
     Review of Queen Mary. The reviewer finds the play dreary.

818 Scribner's Magazine, 10 (Sept. 1875), 644-645.
     Review of Queen Mary.

819 Southern Review, n.s. 18 (Oct. 1875), 484-492.
     Review of Queen Mary.

820 Spectator, 48 (June 26, 1875), 820-822.
     Review of Queen Mary. Admires the play's characterizations
and its dramatic qualities. Possibly by Richard Holt Hutton.

821 Times (London), June 19, 1875, p. 12.
     Review of Queen Mary. The reviewer admires the play and
emphasizes its dramatic assets.

1876

     Queen Mary was performed at the Lyceum Theatre in April
1876. The play was edited to a more manageable size from the
published version. Also in 1876, Tennyson's play Harold: A
Drama was published in London by Henry S. King and Co., although
the volume was dated "1877."

Book

822 Taylor, Bayard. "Eustace Green." The Echo Club, and Other
     Literary Diversions. Boston: Osgood, 1876, pp. 87-92.

Periodicals

823 Athenaeum, Dec. 30, 1876, 882-884.
     Review of Harold.

824 Boucher, L. "Les Drames de Tennyson." Revue des Deux
     Mondes, April 15, 1876, pp. 887-909.
     Review of Queen Mary.

825 Clarke, Hyde. "Tennyson's 'Enoch Arden.' " Notes and
     Queries, 5th ser. 5 (March 25, 1876), 255-256.

826 Clarke, Marcus. "Gray's 'Elegy.' " Notes and Queries,
     5th ser. 5 (Jan. 8, 1876), 29-30.

827 Clifford, John R. S. "Parallelism in Tennyson's 'In Memori-
     am.'" Notes and Queries, 5th ser. 6 (July 22, 1876), 66.

828 "Enoch Arden." Notes and Queries, 5th ser. 5 (Feb. 26,
     1876), 166.

829 Hagan, J. O. Irish Monthly, 4 (1876), 572-587.
     Review of Queen Mary.

830 Herald (New York), April 23, 1876, pp. 7 and 10.
     An account of Queen Mary at the Lyceum.

831 [Jebb, R. C. ?] Times (London), Dec. 18, 1876, p. 6.
     Review of Harold. This review was read by Tennyson, who
     thought it well expressed the essence of what is important in the
     character of Harold--according to H. Tennyson in Alfred Lord Ten-
     nyson (entry 1955), volume II, page 186, footnote 1. The reviewer
     remarks: "Nothing in the play seems to us finer than the contrast
     between Harold's own view of his predicament and the casuistry of
     the theologians who seek to re-assure him. He has a foreboding
     that he must suffer the immediate doom of the defiled; but beyond
     that doom he looks up to that Justice which shall give him the re-
     ward of the pure in spirit."

832 "Lyceum." Daily News (London), April 19, 1876, p. 2.
     Discusses the performance of Queen Mary.

833 Malcolm, E. H. "Tennyson's 'Enoch Arden.'" Notes and
     Queries, 5th ser. 5 (June 24, 1876), 526-527.

834 Manuel, J. "Queen Elizabeth and 'Queen Mary.'" Notes and
     Queries, 5th ser. 5 (June 17, 1876), 486.

835   "Mr. Tennyson's Drama on the Stage." Spectator, 49 (April
      22, 1876), 526-527.
      Discusses the performance of Queen Mary. Dislikes the way
the play has been edited but thinks it may be popular with audiences.

836   Pall Mall Gazette, April 20, 1876, p. 11.
      Review of the stage version of Queen Mary. Regards the
play as a failure.

837   "Queen Mary at the Lyceum." Academy, 9 (April 22, 1876),
      392.
      Discusses the portions of the published version of Queen
Mary that were edited out of the stage version.

838   "Queen Mary at the Lyceum." Era, April 23, 1876, p. 12.
      Attacks the stage version of Queen Mary for leaving too
much of importance out of its production. Finds the performance
to be poor. See also: entry 844.

839   "Queen Mary at the Lyceum." Times (London), April 20,
      1876, p. 7.
      Prefers the published version of Queen Mary to the stage
one.

840   Spectator, 49 (Dec. 23, 1876), 1610-1612.
      Review of Harold.

841   Standard, April 19, 1876, p. 3.
      Review of stage version of Queen Mary. Listed in C. Ten-
nyson and C. Fall, Alfred Tennyson (entry 4016), page 103. Friendly review.

842   Stone, Samuel John. "Home Aspect of Mr. Tennyson's Poems."
      Leisure Hour, 25 (1876), 54-56.

843   "Tennyson and Shelley." Notes and Queries, 5th ser. 5 (Jan.
      15, 1876), 41-43.
      See entry 791.

844   "Tennyson's Queen Mary." Era, April 16, 1876, p. 10.
      Unhappy with the focus of the play. See also: entry 838.

                              1877

Books

845   Elsdale, Henry. Studies in Tennyson's "Idylls of the King."
      London: Kegan, Paul, Trench, Trübner, 1877.
      See: H. Elsdale, Studies in the Idylls, 1878 (entry 876).

846   Heywood, J.C. "An Over-rated Poet." How They Strike Me,
      These Authors. Philadelphia: Lippincott, 1877, pp. 126-147.

847   Hutton, Richard Holt. "Tennyson." Literary Essays. Lon-
       don: Macmillan, 1877, pp. 361-436.
         Reprinted (from 1888 edition): J. D. Jump, ed., Tennyson:
       The Critical Heritage (entry 4013), pages 352-394.
         In a general analysis of Tennyson's works, Hutton also re-
       plies to Swinburne's remarks on Tennyson's Arthurian poems (Under
       the Microscope, 1877, entry 697). Assesses Tennyson's strengths
       as a lyric poet and weaknesses as a dramatic poet.

848   Yates, Edmund Hodgson. "Mr. Tennyson at Haslemere."
       Celebrities at Home. London: The World, 1877, pp. 21-29.

Periodicals

849   Atlantic Monthly, 39 (Jan. 1877), 102-103.
         Discusses medieval themes in the works of Tennyson and
       William Morris.

850   British Quarterly Review, 65 (April 1877), 267-268.
       Review of Harold.

851   Clifford, John R. S. "In Memoriam." Notes and Queries,
       5th ser. 8 (Dec. 29, 1877), 514.
       See also: R. M. Spence (entry 864).

852   Craggs, John. "Tennyson's 'To the Queen.'" Notes and
       Queries, 5th ser. 7 (March 17, 1877), 205.

853   Earle, John Charles. "Tennyson's Influence on the Formation
       of Christian Character." Christian Apologist, Jan. 1877,
       pp. 163-174.
         Listed in C. Tennyson and C. Fall, Alfred Tennyson (entry
       4016), page 16.

854   Gatty, Alfred. "Tennyson's 'In Memoriam.'" Notes and
       Queries, 5th ser. 8 (Nov. 17, 1877), 387.

855   Harper's Monthly Magazine, 54 (April 1877), 769-770.
       Review of Harold.

856   [Howells, William Dean.] Atlantic Monthly, 39 (Feb. 1877),
       242-243.
       Review of Harold.

857   International Review, 4 (April 1877), 282-283.
       Review of Harold.

858   Literary World (Boston), 7 (Feb. 1877), 133-134.
       Review of Harold.

859   Longfellow, Henry Wadsworth. "Wapentake to Alfred Tennyson."
       Atlantic Monthly, 40 (Dec. 1877), 731.
         Reprinted: H. Tennyson, Alfred Lord Tennyson (entry 1955),

volume II, page 220.
The poem is as follows:

Wapentake to Alfred Tennyson

Poet! I come to touch thy lance with mine,
Not as a knight who on the listed field
Of tourney touched his adversary's shield
In token of defiance, but in sign
Of homage to the mastery, which is thine
In English song; nor will I keep concealed
And voiceless as a rivulet frost-congealed,
My admiration for thy verse divine.
Not of the howling dervishes of song,
Who craze the brain with their delirious dance,
Art thou, O sweet historian of the heart!
Therefore to thee the laurel-leaves belong,
To thee our love and our allegiance,
For thy allegiance to the poet's art.

Tennyson wrote to Longfellow: "You have sent me a Christmas greeting: more than that, a Christmas gift in the shape of a very perfect flower from your own spacious garden: wherefore I exult and stick it in my cap and defy my foes." (Letter in H. Tennyson's Alfred Lord Tennyson, volume II, page 220, entry 1955).

860 Nation (New York), 24 (Jan. 18, 1877), 43-44.
      Review of Harold.

861 Penn Monthly, 8 (April 1877), 321-325.
      Review of Harold.

862 Saturday Review (London), 43 (Jan. 6, 1877), 21-23.
      Review of Harold.

863 Scribner's Monthly, 13 (March 1877), 718-719.
      Review of Harold.

864 Spence, R. M. "In Memoriam." Notes and Queries, 5th ser.
      8 (Dec. 29, 1877), 514.
      See also: J. R. S. Clifford (entry 851).

865 [Statham, H. H.] "The Dramas of Alfred Tennyson." Edinburgh
      Review, 145 (April 1877), 383-415.
      Statham discusses Queen Mary and Harold. He likes Harold
better than Queen Mary but dislikes the structure of both plays.
Neither one, in his estimation, is a good play.

866 [Symonds, John Addington.] Academy, 11 (Jan. 6, 1877), 1-2.
      Review of Harold. Symonds finds dramatic merit in Harold
and is interested in the play's characters.

867 Taylor, Bayard. "Tennyson." International Review, 4 (May

1877), 397-418.
Reprinted: Critical Essays, 1880 (entry 949).

868 "Tennyson and Bunyan." Notes and Queries, 5th ser. 8 (Sept.
22, 1877), 226.

869 "Tennysoniana." Notes and Queries, 5th ser. 7 (April 7,
1877), 265.

870 "Tennyson's Country." Notes and Queries, 5th ser. (Sept. 1,
1877), 166.

871 "Tennyson's 'Will': Misprints." Notes and Queries, 5th ser.
8 (Aug. 18, 1877), 126.

872 Ward, Julius H. North American Review, 124 (Jan. 1877),
157-159.
Review of Harold.

873 Weiss, J. Radical Magazine, 1 (May 1877), 158-165.
Review of Harold.

874 Westminster Review, n. s. 51 (April 1877), 587-588.
Review of Harold.

1878

Books

875 Dowden, Edward. "Mr. Tennyson and Mr. Browning." Studies
in Literature, 1798-1877. London: Kegan, Paul, Trench,
Trübner, 1878, pp. 191-239.
Reprinted, revised, from: Afternoon Lectures on Literature,
1869. Section II, pp. 195-211, reprinted: J. D. Jump, ed., Tennyson: The Critical Heritage (entry 4013), pages 322-333.

876 Elsdale, Henry. Studies in the Idylls: An Essay on Mr. Tennyson's "Idylls of the King." London: Henry S. King, 1878.
See also: Studies, 1877 (entry 845).
Elsdale analyzes the allegory of the Arthurian poems and
finds it disorganized. The poems have much power, he believes,
but they are inconsistent and poorly related to one another.

877 Hamilton, Walter. "Alfred Tennyson." The Poets Laureate
of England. London: Stock, 1878, pp. 263-300.

878 Heraud, Edith. Lecture on Tennyson as Delivered by Her at
Unity Church, Barnsbury Hall, and Before the Society for the
Fine Arts. London: Simpkin, Marshall, 1878.
Religion in the poetry of Tennyson.

879 Selkirk, J. B. (pseudonym for James Brown). Ethics and

Aesthetics of Modern Poetry. London: Smith, Elder, 1878.
See also: J. B. Selkirk, "Exhumations IV" in Essays in
Criticism, 1966 (entry 4002).
Discusses Tennyson's mysticism.

Periodicals

880 Axon, William Edward Armitage. "Tennyson's 'Northern Farmer.'" Notes and Queries, 5th ser. 10 (Dec. 14, 1878),
466.

881 Bayne, Peter. "Alfred Tennyson: His First Volume." Lit-
erary World (London), n.s. 18 (Sept. 27, 1878), 200-202.
Entries 881 through 891 reprinted in Lessons from My
Masters, 1879 (entry 905).

882 _____. "The Compass and Scheme of In Memoriam."
Literary World (London), n.s. 18 (Nov. 29, 1878), 344-347.

883 _____. "The Dream of Fair Women and Palace of Art."
Literary World (London), n.s. 18 (Oct. 25, 1878), 264-267.

884 _____. "M. Taine on Tennyson and Alfred De Musset."
Literary World (London), n.s. 18 (Oct. 4, 1878), 216-218.
See entry 534.

885 _____. "The Religious Philosophy of In Memoriam." Literary World (London), n.s. 18 (Nov. 22, 1878), 328-330.

886 _____. "Tennyson as a People's Poet." Literary World
(London), n.s. 18 (Nov. 1, 1878), 280-282.

887 _____. "Tennyson's Diction: The Idylls of the King."
Literary World (London), n.s. 18 (Dec. 6, 1878), 360-362.

888 _____. "Tennyson's Oenone, Lotos Eaters, Ulysses, Simeon
Stylites, and In Memoriam." Literary World (London), n.s.
18 (Nov. 15, 1878), 312-315.

889 _____. "Tennyson's Poems on Marriage." Literary World
(London), n.s. 18 (Oct. 11, 1878), 232-234.

890 _____. "The Two Versions of Maud." Literary World
(London), n.s. 18 (Oct. 18, 1878), 248-251.
Discusses Tennyson's revisions of the poem.

891 _____. "The Two Voices." Literary World (London), n.s.
18 (Nov. 8, 1878), 296-298.

892 Bouchier, Jonathan. "Tennyson and Oliver Cromwell." Notes
and Queries, 5th ser. 10 (Aug. 10, 1878), 105.

893 _____. "Tennysoniana." Notes and Queries, 5th ser. 9
(June 29, 1878), 508.

894 Brewer, E. Cobham. "Gareth and Lynette." Notes and Queries, 5th ser. 9 (Jan. 19, Feb. 16, and March 16, 1878), 41-42, 122-123, and 201-202.

895 _____. "Morte D'Arthur." Notes and Queries, 5th ser. 10 (July 13, 1878), 21-22.

896 Healy, John. "Catholic Aspects of Mr. Tennyson's Poetry." Irish Monthly, 6 (1878), 429-439.

897 Lyall, William. "Tennyson: A Criticism." Rose-Belford's Canadian Monthly and National Review, 1 (Oct. 1878), 477-489.

898 Moggridge, M.W. "Idyllic Poetry." Macmillan's Magazine, 38 (June 1878), 108.

899 Quesnel, Léo. "La poésie au XIXe Siècle en Angleterre." Le Correspondant, 110 (March 10, 1878), 802-810.

900 Selkirk, J.B. (pseudonym for James Brown). "Ethics and Aesthetics of Modern Poetry." Cornhill Magazine, 37 (May 1878), 569-583.
    Tennyson on pages 580-583.

901 "Tennyson and Oliver Cromwell." Notes and Queries, 5th ser. 10 (Nov. 16, 1878), 396.

902 "Tennyson: 'Arrive at Last the Blessed Goal.'" Notes and Queries, 5th ser. 10 (July 20, 1878), 54.

903 "Walter Scott: Tennyson." Notes and Queries, 5th ser. 9 (March 23, 1878), 225.

1879

Tennyson's The Lover's Tale was published in London by Kegan Paul in 1879. The poet's play The Falcon was produced at St. James' Theatre, December 1879 to February 1880.

Books

904 Bagehot, Walter. "Wordsworth, Tennyson, and Browning: or, Pure, Ornate, and Grotesque Art in English Poetry." Literary Studies. London: Longmans, Green, 1879. Volume II, pp. 338-390.
    Reprinted from National Review, 1864 (entry 537). See entry 537 for annotation.

905 Bayne, Peter. "Alfred Tennyson." Lessons from My Masters: Carlyle, Tennyson and Ruskin. London: James Clark, 1879, pp. 195-332. New York: Harper and Brothers, 1879, pp.

193-350.
Reprinted from Literary World (London), 1878 (entries 881-891).
Admires Tennyson's poetry. Reviewed by: National Quarterly Review (entry 962) and Spectator (entry 942).

906 Cusins, W.G., ed. Tennyson's Songs Set to Music by Various
    Composers. London: Kegan Paul, 1879.
    Review by: Nation (New York) (entry 961) and Spectator (entry 943).

907 Gatty, Alfred. A Key to Tennyson's "In Memoriam": Being
    a Lecture Delivered at Sheffield and Liverpool. Sheffield:
    Clark and Greenup, 1879. Reprinted: London: Bogue, 1882.
    Reprinted, revised: London: George Bell, 1885.
    Gatty uses his personal knowledge of Hallam from their days
together in school to inform this interesting essay. Reviewed by:
Literary World (Boston) (entry 1027).

908 Gladstone, William Ewart. "Tennyson." Gleanings of Past
    Years. London: John Murray, 1879. New York: Scribner,
    1879. Volume II, pp. 131-179.
    Reprinted from Quarterly Review, 1859 (entry 471). See
entry 471 for other reprintings and for annotation.

909 Payne, Frederic Taylor. Essays on Sir Philip Sidney and
    Alfred Tennyson. London: Hazell, 1879.

910 Shepherd, Richard Herne. Tennysoniana. London: Pickering,
    1879.
    Revised and expanded version of Tennysoniana, 1866 (entry 572).
    A catchall listing of Tennyson's publications, influences on the
poet, his versifications, and of some criticisms. Not complete nor
reliable, but of interest to the specialist in Tennyson. A note on
this book appears in Notes and Queries, by A.L. Mayhew, 1883
(entry 1048).

911 Spedding, James. "Tennyson's Poems." Reviews and Discus-
    sions. London: Kegan Paul, 1879, pp. 277-299.
    Reprinted from Edinburgh Review, 1843 (entry 89). See entry
89 for other reprintings and for annotation.

Periodicals

912 Athenaeum, June 7, 1879, pp. 723-725.
    Review of The Lover's Tale.

913 Axon, William Edward Armitage. "Tennyson's 'Confessions
    of a Sensitive Mind.'" Notes and Queries, 5th ser. 11 (Jan.
    18, 1879), 49; and 11 (May 3, 1879), 355.

914 Bede, Cuthbert (pseudonym for Edward Bradley). "A Passage

in Tennyson's 'Lotos-Eaters.'" Notes and Queries, 5th ser. 12 (Oct. 18, 1879), 307.

915 Brewer, E. Cobham. "Tennyson and Elaine." Notes and Queries, 5th ser. 11 (Feb. 8, 1879), 101-102.

916 _____. "Tennyson's Idylls." Notes and Queries, 5th ser. 12 (July 5, 1879), 1-2; and 12 (Aug. 23, 1879), 142-144.

917 Brightwell, D. Barron. "Tennyson and Washington Irving." Notes and Queries, 5th ser. 12 (July 26, 1879), 65.

918 British Quarterly Review, 70 (July 1879), 133-134. Review of The Lover's Tale.

919 Collins, John Churton. "A New Study of Tennyson." Cornhill Magazine, 41 (Jan. 1879), 36-50; 42 (July 1880), 17-35; and 44 (July 1881), 87-106.
Reprinted: Littell's Living Age, 146 (Aug. 21 and 28, 1880), 483-492 and 544-554; Illustrations of Tennyson, 1891 (entry 1354). See entry 1354 for annotation.

920 Congregationalist, 8 (Aug. 1879), 672-681. Review of The Lover's Tale.

921 Daily Telegraph (London), Dec. 19, 1879, p. 3
Review of the production of The Falcon. Admires the verse but not the dramatic qualities of the play.

922 Gosse, Edmund. Academy, 15 (June 7, 1879), 489. Review of The Lover's Tale.

923 Harper's Monthly Magazine, 59 (Sept. 1879), 629-630. Review of The Lover's Tale.

924 [Howells, William Dean.] Atlantic Monthly, 44 (Aug. 1879), 268-269.
Review of The Lover's Tale.

925 "Locksley Hall." Notes and Queries, 5th ser. 12 (Dec. 13, 1879), 471.

926 "Mr. Tennyson as a Youthful Poet." Literary World (Boston), 10 (June 2, 1879), 200.

927 "Mr. Tennyson's New Play." Pall Mall Gazette, Dec. 31, 1879, p. 12.
Review of the production of The Falcon. The reviewer acknowledges the beauties of the verse and the sound dramatic construction of the play but finds the play empty of interest.

928 "Mr. Tennyson's New Play." Standard (London), Dec. 19, 1879, p. 3.

Review of the production of The Falcon. Essentially positive review with a few caveats.

929 Morning Post (London), Dec. 19, 1879, p. 5.
Review of the production of The Falcon. Listed in C. Tennyson and C. Fall, Alfred Tennyson (entry 4016), page 118. Reviewer thinks the play is an "admirable little piece."

930 Nation (New York), 29 (July 10, 1879), 30-31.
Review of The Lover's Tale.

931 Phillips, W. "Tennyson and Oliver Cromwell." Notes and Queries, 5th ser. 11 (April 26, 1879), 338.

932 "The Poet Laureate and the Knights of the Round Table."
Notes and Queries, 5th ser. 12 (Sept. 27, 1879), 244;
and 12 (Nov. 8, 1879), 371-372.

933 "The Poet Laureat's New Play." Era, Dec. 21, 1879, p. 6.
Review of the production of The Falcon. Likes the production.

934 Robinson, A. Mary F. "Alfred Tennyson." Unsere Zeit,
n.s. 15 (Jan. 15, 1879), 81-94.

935 Rose-Belford's Canadian Monthly and National Review, 3 (Aug.
1879), 221-223.
Review of The Lover's Tale.

936 Russell, John. "Tennyson and the Ettrick Shepherd." Notes
and Queries, 5th ser. 12 (Nov. 15, 1879), 384.

937 Scribner's Monthly, 18 (Aug. 1879), 628.
Review of The Lover's Tale.

938 Shoemaker, W. L. "To the Poet Laureate of England." Literary World (Boston), 10 (Nov. 8, 1879), 363.
A poem.

939 Skeat, Walter William. "Locksley Hall." Notes and Queries,
5th ser. 12 (Dec. 13, 1879), 471.

940 Sparvel-Bayly, J. A. "Tennyson and Oliver Cromwell." Notes
and Queries, 5th ser. 11 (Jan. 18, 1879), 58-59.

941 Spectator, 52 (June 21, 1879), 790-791.
Review of The Lover's Tale.

942 Spectator, 52 (Aug. 16, 1879), 1044-1046.
Review of P. Bayne's Lessons from My Masters, 1879 (entry
905).

943 Spectator, 52 (Dec. 27, 1879), 1652.
Review of W.G. Cusins's Tennyson's Songs Set to Music by
Various Composers (entry 906).

944 "Three Small Books: By Great Writers." Fraser's Magazine, 100 (July 1879), 103-124.
Review of The Lover's Tale on pages 110-116.

945 Times (London), Dec. 20, 1879, p. 11.
Review of the production of The Falcon. Likes the production.

946 Ward, Julius H. "A Tennysonian Retrospect." Atlantic Monthly, 44 (Sept. 1879), 356-361.

947 Westminster Review, n.s. 56 (July 1879), 266-267.
Review of The Lover's Tale.

1880

In 1880, Tennyson's Ballads and Other Poems was published in London by C. Kegan Paul and Co.

Books

948 Hayward, Abraham. "Byron and Tennyson." Sketches of Eminent Statesmen and Writers. London: Murray, 1880. Volume II, pp. 305-359.
Reprinted from Quarterly Review, 1871 (entry 689). See entry 689 for another reprinting.

949 Taylor, Bayard. "Tennyson." Critical Essays and Literary Notes. New York: Putnam, 1880, pp. 1-36.
Reprinted from International Review, 1877 (entry 867).

Periodicals

950 Academy, Jan. 3, 1880, p. 18.
Comments on the production of The Falcon. Dislikes the play and its performance.

951 Blackwood's Edinburgh Magazine, 128 (July 1880), 34-36.

952 British Quarterly Review, 72 (Oct. 1880), 141-150.
Reprinted: Littell's Living Age, 147 (Dec. 25, 1880), 786-795.
Discusses Poems, 1842.

953 Buckley, W.E. "Dream of Fair Women." Notes and Queries, 6th ser. 2 (Dec. 11, 1880), 470.

954 _____. "Palace of Art." Notes and Queries, 6th ser. 2 (Dec. 18, 1880), 492.

955 _____. "Tennyson's 'In Memoriam.'" Notes and Queries, 6th ser. 1 (June 19, 1880), 499-500.

956 Collins, John Churton. "A New Study of Tennyson." Cornhill
    Magazine, 42 (July 1880), 17-35.
    Second of three parts. See entry 919.

957 Gatty, Alfred. "Tennyson's 'Sleeping Beauty.'" Notes and
    Queries, 6th ser. 1 (April 17, 1880), 320-321.

958 Gerhart, Robert Leighton. "Tennyson." Reformed Quarterly
    Review, 27 (Oct. 1880), 538-576.

959 Literary World (Boston), 11 (Dec. 18, 1880), 463.
    Review of Ballads.

960 "Mariana." Notes and Queries, 6th ser. 1 (May 8, 1880),
    382-383.

961 Nation (New York), 30 (Feb. 26, 1880), 160-161.
    Review of W.G. Cusins's Tennyson's Songs Set to Music by
    Various Composers, 1879 (entry 906).

962 National Quarterly Review, 40 (Jan. 1880), 234-240.
    Review of P. Bayne's Lessons from My Masters, 1879
    (entry 905).

963 Peacock, Edward. "'Aylmer's Field' and John's Brand."
    Notes and Queries, 6th ser. 2 (Oct. 16, 1880), 314.
    See entry 968.

964 Reynolds, Llywarch. "Locksley Hall." Notes and Queries,
    6th ser. 1 (April 17, 1880), 326.

965 Saintsbury, George. Academy, 18 (Dec. 4, 1880), 397-398.
    Review of Ballads.

966 Saturday Review (London), 50 (Dec. 4, 1880), 708-709.
    Review of Ballads.

967 Spectator, 53 (Dec. 18, 1880), 1624-1626.
    Review of Ballads.

968 "Tennyson's 'Aylmer's Field' and John's Brand." Notes and
    Queries, 6th ser. 2 (Sept. 25, 1880), 253-254.
    See: E. Peacock (entry 963).

1881

Tennyson's play The Cup was produced at the Lyceum Theatre, January to May 1881.

Books

969 Chignell, T.W. Tennyson: A Lecture, Delivered Before the

Exeter Literary Society. Exeter: Weekly Times (Devon), 1881.

970 Foote, G.W. Atheism and Suicide: A Reply to Lord Tennyson. [London: Freethought Publishing Co., 1881.] Attacks "Despair."

971 Hodgson, S.H. "The Supernatural in English Poetry." Outcast Essays and Verse. London: Longmans, Green, 1881, pp. 99-205.

972 No entry

973 Scharf, Lewis. "Alfred Tennyson." Literary Impressions. Ascherslehen: Schlegel, 1881, pp. 25-36. Publication of a dissertation: See entry 975.

974 Wace, Walter E. (pseud. for William Robertson Nicoll). Alfred Tennyson: His Life and Works. Edinburgh: Macniven and Wallace, 1881. Still occasionally used as a source by scholars. A helpful expression of the Victorian view of Tennyson and his works.

Dissertation

975 Scharf, Lewis. "Alfred Tennyson." Literary Impressions. Leipzig, 1881 (?). Published: See entry 973.

Periodicals

976 "Alfred Tennyson." National Magazine (London), 120 (July, Aug., and Sept. 1881), 47-68, 131-147, and 241-251.

977 Appleton's Journal, 25 (March 1881), 253-256. Review of the production of The Cup.

978 Austin, Alfred. "On a Recent Criticism of Mr. Swinburne's." Macmillan's Magazine, 43 (March 1881), 399-408. Reprinted: The Bridling of Pegasus, 1910 (entry 2621). Austin presents a friendlier view of Tennyson than he does in his Poetry of the Period (entry 643).

979 "Ballads and Other Poems." Notes and Queries, 6th ser. 3 (Feb. 19, 1881), 158.

980 Boodle, R.W. "The Idylls of the King: Their Growth and Meaning." Rose-Belford's Canadian Monthly and National Review, 6 (April 1881), 379-398.

981 British Quarterly Review, 73 (Jan. 1881), 218-219. Review of Ballads.

982   "Catholic Musings on Tennyson's 'In Memoriam.'" Catholic
      World, 34 (Nov. 1881), 205-211.

983   Collins, John Churton.   "A New Study of Tennyson." Cornhill
      Magazine, 44 (July 1881), 87-106.
      Third of three parts.   See entry 919.

984   Colvin, Sidney.   Macmillan's Magazine, 43 (Jan. 1881), 738-
      748.
      Review of Ballads.

985   Congregationalist, 10 (Jan. 1881), 53-60.
      Review of Ballads.

986   "'The Cup' at the Lyceum." Saturday Review (London), 51
      (Jan. 8, 1881), 48-49.
      Review of the production of The Cup.   Generally positive
commentary.

987   Daily News (London), Jan. 4, 1881, p. 6.
      Review of the production of The Cup.   The reviewer dislikes
the play.

988   Dial, 1 (Jan. 1881), 191-192.
      Review of Ballads.

989   Harper's Monthly Magazine, 62 (March 1881), 633.
      Review of Ballads.

990   Lathrop, G. P.   Atlantic Monthly, 47 (March 1881), 425-427.
      Review of Ballads.

991   Literary World (Boston), 12 (Dec. 17, 1881), 477-478.
      Discusses "The Lady of Shalott."

992   "The Lyceum Theatre." Times (London), Jan. 5, 1881, p. 4.
      Review of the production of The Cup.   Likes The Cup better
than The Falcon but finds it mystifying.

993   [Mallock, W. H.]   Edinburgh Review, 154 (Oct. 1881), 486-
      515.
      Review of Ballads.

994   "Mr. Tennyson's New Play." Daily Telegraph, Jan. 4, 1881,
      p. 3.
      Review of the production of The Cup.   Listed in C. Tennyson
and C. Fall, Alfred Tennyson (entry 4016), page 117.   According to
Tennyson and Fall, the review provides the background to the story
of the play and a careful analysis.

995   "A Morning Performance at the Lyceum: Mr. Tennyson's
      'Cup.'" St. James's Magazine, 48 (March 1881), 195-203.

996 Morning Post (London), Jan. 4, 1881, p. 5.
Review of the production of The Cup. Praises the production
and the play.

997 Nation (New York), 33 (July 7, 1881), 15-16.
Discusses The Princess.

998 Nencioni, Enrico. Fanfulla Della Domenica, April 10, 1881.
Review of Ballads.

999 Pall Mall Gazette, Jan. 5, 1881, p. 10.
Review of the production of The Cup. Admires the play.

1000 Placci, C. La Rassegna Nazionale, March 1881, pp. 524-
534.
Review of Ballads.

1001 Potter's American Monthly, 16 (Feb. 1881), 111.
Discussion of Poems, 1842.

1002 Scribner's Monthly, 21 (Feb. 1881), 639-641.
Review of Ballads.

1003 Smith, G.B. International Review, 10 (Feb. 1881), 178-183.
Review of Ballads.

1004 Spectator, Jan. 15, 1881, p. 81.
Review of the production of The Cup. Favorable.

1005 Standard (London), Jan. 4, 1881, p. 3.
Review of the production of The Cup. Admires the dramatic
craftsmanship of the play.

1006 Stoddard, Richard Henry. "A Study of Tennyson." North
American Review, 133 (July 1881), 82-107.

1007 Swinburne, Algernon Charles. "Disgust: A Dramatic Monologue." Fortnightly Review, 36 (Dec. 1881), 715-717.
Swinburne parodies Tennyson's "Despair."

1008 _____. "Tennyson and Musset." Fortnightly Review, 35
(Feb. 1, 1881), 129-153.
Reprinted: Eclectic Magazine of Foreign Literature, 96 (May
1881), 600-616; and Miscellanies, 1886 (entry 1153).
Swinburne believes Alfred de Musset and Tennyson are similar
poets. He rejects Tennyson's moral stance but admires the felici-
tous images of Tennyson's poetry.

1009 "Tennyson's 'Ballads and Other Poems.'" Notes and Queries,
6th ser. 3 (Jan. 29, 1881), 85.

1010 "Tennyson's New Play." Era, Jan. 8, 1881, p. 5.
Review of the production of The Cup. Admires the play.

1011   Wedmore, Frederick. "Mr. Tennyson's New Play."
       Academy, 19 (Jan. 8, 1881), 34-36.
       Review of the production of The Cup.

1012   Wright, W. H. K. "Tennyson's 'Ballads and Other Poems.'"
       Notes and Queries, 6th ser. 3 (March 12, 1881), 217-218.

1882

       Tennyson's play The Promise of May was produced at the
Globe Theatre in October 1882.

Books

1013   Archer, William. "Mr. Alfred Tennyson." English Drama-
       tists of Today. London: Sampson Low, 1882, pp. 334-351.
       A practical discussion of Queen Mary, Harold, The Falcon,
and The Cup. Archer is an experienced man of the stage who
takes a pragmatic view of the plays.

1014   Conway, Moncure Daniel. Laureate Despair: A Discourse
       Given at South Place Chapel, December 11th, 1881. London:
       privately printed, [c. 1882?].

1015   Dawson, Samuel Edward. A Study, with Critical and Explan-
       atory Notes, of Lord Tennyson's Poem The Princess. Mon-
       treal: Dawson Brothers, 1882. Reprinted: Philadelphia:
       West, 1976.
       Dawson greatly admires The Princess. He includes comments
by Tennyson himself on the poem and notes the pioneering presentation of the social oppression of women in the poem. Reviewed by:
Harper's Monthly Magazine (entry 1043); Literary World (Boston)
(entry 1088); and E. Myers in Macmillan's Magazine (entry 1050).

1016   The "De Produndis" of Alfred Tennyson: Remodelled by
       Metamorphosis. London: Allen, 1882.

1017   Scherer, Edmond. "Wordsworth et la poésie moderne de
       l'Angleterre." Etudes critiques sur la littérature contem-
       poraine. Paris: Levy, 1882.

1018   Shepard, William (pseudonym for William Shepard Walsh).
       "Alfred Tennyson." Pen Pictures of Modern Authors. New
       York: Putnam, 1882, pp. 74-85.

1019   Walker, Thomas. Mr. Tennyson's "Despair": A Lecture on
       Its Religious Significance. London: Stock, 1882.
       An essay featuring a favorable view of Tennyson's ideas.

Periodicals

1020   Chamberlain, N. H.   "Tennyson's New Battle Piece."   Literary World (Boston), 13 (March 25, 1882), 97.

1021   Daily News (London), Nov. 13, 1882, p. 2.
        Listed in C. Tennyson and C. Fall, Alfred Tennyson (entry 4016), page 119. Describes the reception of The Promise of May at its first performance.

1022   Era, Nov. 18, 1882, p. 6.
        Review of the production of The Promise of May. A severely negative commentary.

1023   Fambri, Paulo. "Maria Tudor sotto la penna dell' Hugo e del Tennyson." Nuova Antologia di Lettere, Scienze ed Arti, 32 (April 15, 1882), 585-636.
        Discusses Queen Mary.

1024   Fenn, Alice Maude. "The Borderland of Surrey." Century Illustrated Monthly Magazine, 24 (Aug. 1882), 491.

1025   Gatty, Alfred. "Tennyson and Goethe." Spectator, 55 (Aug. 26, 1882), 1111.

1026   Hollowell, J. Hirst. "Mr. Tennyson's 'Despair.'" Congregationalist, 11 (Oct. 1882), 824-831.

1027   Literary World (Boston), 13 (March 11, 1882), 71-72.
        Review of 1882 Bogue edition of A. Gatty's A Key to Tennyson's "In Memoriam" (entry 907).

1028   "Mr. Tennyson's Play." Saturday Review (London), 54 (Nov. 18, 1882), 670-671.
        Review of the production of The Promise of May. Considers the play a failure in plot and characterization.

1029   Nencioni, Enrico. "Maud." Domenica Litteraria, March 19, 1882.

1030   Pall Mall Gazette, Nov. 13, 1882, p. 4.
        Review of the production of The Promise of May. Negative.

1031   Picton, J. A. "In Memoriam." Notes and Queries, 6th ser. 5 (May 27, 1882), 404-405.

1032   Shakespeare, Charles. "Tennyson's 'Despair.'" Modern Review, 3 (July 1882), 462-473.

1033   "Tennyson as Dramatist." Spectator, 55 (Nov. 18, 1882), 1474-1475.
        Focuses on the production of The Promise of May. Finds Tennyson's approach to drama to be poor.

1034 "Tennyson's Literary Career." Literary World (Boston), 13
(Aug. 26, 1882), 280-281.
A brief account that includes a listing of "Mr. Tennyson's
Chief Works" on page 281.

1035 Times (London), Nov. 13, 1882, p. 6.
Review of the production of The Promise of May. Finds the
play formless and ineffective.

1036 Wedmore, Frederick. "The Stage: Tennyson's Play."
Academy, 22 (Nov. 18, 1882), 370-371.
Review of the production of The Promise of May. Wedmore
believes the play might be saved if properly edited.

1037 Wilson, William. "Tennyson's 'New' Song." Athenaeum,
June 17, 1882, p. 763.

1883

In late 1883, Tennyson accepted a barony and became a peer.

Books

1038 Blanloeil, A. Les grands poètes anglais. Paris: Delhomme
et Briguet, 1883.

1039 Gower, Ronald Sutherland. My Reminiscences. London:
Kegan, Paul, Trench, 1883.
Tennyson on pages 176-177.

1040 Mathews, C.E. The Earlier and Less-Known Poems of Alfred Tennyson, Poet-Laureate. Birmingham: Herald Press,
1883.

Periodicals

1041 Buckley, W.E. "Parallel Passages." Notes and Queries,
6th ser. 7 (April 28, 1883), 325-326.

1042 Didier, Eugene L. "Is Tennyson a Plagiarist?" Literary
World (Boston), 14 (Aug. 25, 1883), 272-273.
See also: J. Hooper (entry 1045); and entry 1046.

1043 Harper's Monthly Magazine, 66 (May 1883), 963-964.
Review of S.E. Dawson's A Study..., 1882 (entry 1015).

1044 Harper's Monthly Magazine, 68 (Dec. 1883), 156.
Discusses The Princess.

1045 Hooper, Joseph. "Tennyson as a Plagiarist." Literary
World (Boston), 14 (Oct. 6, 1883), 327-328.
See also: E. L. Didier (entry 1042); and entry 1046.

1046 "Is Tennyson a Plagiarist?" Literary World (Boston),
14 (Sept. 8, 1883), 291.
See also: E. L. Didier (entry 1042) and J. Hooper (entry
1045).

1047 Malan, Edward. "Hallam's Grave." Notes and Queries, 6th
ser. 8 (Sept. 22, 1883), 221-223.

1048 Mayhew, A. L. Notes and Queries, 6th ser. 8 (Oct. 27,
1883), 337.
Note on R. H. Shepherd's Tennysoniana (1879 edition; entry
910).

1049 "Mr. Tennyson's Peerage." Saturday Review (London), 56
(Dec. 15, 1883), 751-752.

1050 Myers, E. Macmillan's Magazine, 47 (April 1883), 492-498.
Review of S. E. Dawson's A Study ..., 1882 (entry 1015).

1051 Nencioni, Enrico. "In Memoriam." Fanfulla della Domenica,
May 1883.

1052 _____ . "The Idylls of the King." Fanfulla della Domenica,
Sept. 1883.

1053 Reardon, Timothy Henry. "Alfred Tennyson, Poet Laureate."
Overland Monthly, 2nd ser. 1 (Jan. 1883), 17-33.
Reprinted: Petrarch and Other Essays, 1897 (entry 1950).

1054 Ritchie, Anne. "Alfred Tennyson." Harper's Monthly Magazine, 68 (Dec. 1883), 21-41.
Reprinted: Records of Tennyson, Ruskin, Browning, 1892
(entry 1408). See entry 1408 for annotation.

1055 Shoemaker, W. L. "To the Detractors of Tennyson." Literary World (Boston), 14 (June 16, 1883), 194.

1056 Spectator, 56 (March 17, 1883), 355-357.
Discusses Poems, 1842.

1057 "Tennyson and Lockhart." Notes and Queries, 6th ser. 8
(June 7, 1883), 18.

1058 "Tennyson and Lockhart." Notes and Queries, 6th ser. 8
(July 21, 1883), 51.

1059 "The Tennyson Peerage." Spectator, 56 (Dec. 8, 1883),
1577-1578.

1060　"Tennysonian Philosophy." Time, 8 (Jan. 1883), 53-59.

1061　"Tennysoniana." Notes and Queries, 6th ser. 8 (Oct. 27, 1883), 337.

1062　"Tennyson's Peerage." Nation (New York), 37 (Dec. 20, 1883), 506.

1063　"Three Representative Poets: Mr. Tennyson, Mr. Swinburne, and Mr. Browning." Scottish Review, 2 (Sept. 1883), 334-358.
Tennyson on pages 334-343.

1064　Van Dyke, Henry J., Jr. "Milton and Tennyson." Presbyterian Review, 4 (Oct. 1883), 681-709.
　　　In a perceptive study, Van Dyke discusses the similarities of the poetry of John Milton and Tennyson. He notes their sensitivity to religious feelings and ideas and their importance as expressors of moral principles. Milton, he notes, is among the greatest of the world's poets; Tennyson ranks lower, but is among the greatest English poets.

1884

　　　Macmillan and Company published Tennyson's The Cup and the Falcon, Becket, and A New Single-Volume of Works, all in 1884.

Books

1065　Andrews, Samuel. Our Great Writers: or, Popular Chapters on Some Leading Authors. London: Stock, 1884.

1066　Genung, John Franklin. Tennyson's In Memoriam: Its Purpose and Its Structure. Boston: Houghton, Mifflin, 1884.
　　　An interesting study that places In Memoriam in the perspective of Tennyson's overall achievement. Reviewed by: Critic (New York) (entry 1078); G. P. Lathrop in Atlantic Monthly (entry 1086); Literary World (Boston) (entry 1088); and E. D. A. Morshead in Academy (entry 1093).

1067　Gilbert, William S. A Respectful Operatic Perversion of Tennyson's "Princess," in Three Acts, Entitled Princess Ida: or, Castle Adamant. London: Chappel, 1884.

1068　Hamilton, Walter. Parodies of the Works of English and American Authors. London: Reeves and Turner, 1884.
Tennyson in Volume I, pp. 3-62 and 142-186; and volume II, pp. 136-141 and 260-280.

1069　Jennings, Henry J. Lord Tennyson: A Biographical Sketch. London: Chatto and Windus, 1884.

Reprinted, revised and expanded: 1892.
W. D. Templeman in his "A Consideration of the Fame of 'Locksley Hall'" in Victorian Poetry, 1963 (entry 3843), page 90, calls this book "valuable." C. Tennyson and C. Fall in their Alfred Tennyson, 1967 (entry 4016), page 4, assert: "The book has little value today." The specialist will find this book interesting reading. Reviewed by: E. D. A. Morshead in Academy (entry 1094); and Saturday Review (London) (entry 1099).

1070   Mallock, W. H. "Tennyson in the Shadow." Atheism and the
        Value of Life. London: Bentley, 1884, pp. 83-146.
        Mallock sees Tennyson as a reflector of the times in which
he writes. Discusses the poet's works through Ballads.

Periodicals

1071   Asher, David. "Tennysons Erhebung in den Pairstand."
        Die Gegenwart, 25 (Jan. 19, 1884), 41.

1072   Athenaeum, March 8, 1884, pp. 319-321.
        Review of The Cup and the Falcon. The reviewer seems
caught up in his own erudition, and Tennyson's dramas serve as
excuses for a discussion of verse drama.

1073   Bede, Cuthbert (pseudonym for Edward Bradley). "Tennyson's
        'Ancle' and 'Ankle.'" Notes and Queries, 6th ser. 9 (April
        26, 1884), 326.

1074   Black, William George. "Tennysoniana." Notes and Queries,
        6th ser. 9 (Jan. 12, 1884), 26.

1075   "Christman Waits." Punch, 87 (Dec. 27, 1884), 303.
        A cartoon of Tennyson.

1076   Cole, Samuel Valentine. "A Salutation." Critic (New York),
        5 (Dec. 6, 1884), 268.

1077   "Contemporary Verse." Times (London), May 5, 1884, p. 3.
        Discusses The Cup and the Falcon. Dislikes the latter play.

1078   Critic (New York), 4 (Feb. 16, 1884), 75.
        Review of J. F. Genung's Tennyson's In Memoriam, 1884
(entry 1066).

1079   "An Early Sonnet by the Poet Laureate." Notes and Queries,
        6th ser. 9 (March 15, 1884), 205.

1080   "An Early Sonnet by the Poet Laureate." Notes and Queries,
        6th ser. 9 (April 26, 1884), 333.

1081   "English History on the Stage." Pall Mall Gazette, Dec. 9,
        1884, p. 1.
        Review of Becket.

1082 Evans, Howard. "Tennyson's 'Holy Grail.'" Congregationalist, 13 (June 1884), 463-471.

1083 [Heron, Robert Matthew.] "The Three Poems 'In Memoriam.'" Quarterly Review, 158 (July 1884), 162-183.
Reprinted: Littell's Living Age, 162 (Aug. 30, 1884), 549-
561.
Discusses poems by Milton, Shelley, and Tennyson.

1084 Hogben, John. "Tennyson's Allusions to Christ." Sunday
Magazine, n.s. 13 (1884), 761-764.

1085 Hoskyns-Abrahall, J. "Tennyson's Inspiration from the
Pyrenees." Academy, 25 (June 14, 1884), 422.
Reprinted: Critic (New York), 4 (June 28, 1884), 310-311.

1086 Lathrop, G.P. Atlantic Monthly, 53 (June 1884), 853-854.
Review of J.F. Genung's Tennyson's In Memoriam, 1884
(entry 1066).

1087 _____. Atlantic Monthly, 54 (July 1884), 117-118.
Review of The Cup and the Falcon.

1088 Literary World (Boston), 15 (Feb. 9, 1884), 42-43.
Review of J.F. Genung's Tennyson's In Memoriam, 1884
(entry 1066).

1089 Literary World (Boston), 15 (Oct. 4, 1884), 332.
Review of S.E. Dawson's A Study ..., 1882 (entry 1015).

1090 Literary World (Boston), 15 (Nov. 1, 1884), 371.
Discusses a selective edition of Tennyson's poetry.

1091 Literary World (Boston), 15 (Dec. 13, 1884), 441.
Discusses "Lady Clare."

1092 Morshead, E.D.A. Academy, 25 (March 8, 1884), 160-161.
Review of The Cup and the Falcon. Unhappy with both plays
but particularly dislikes The Falcon.

1093 _____. Academy, 25 (June 28, 1884), 452.
Review of J.F. Genung's Tennyson's In Memoriam, 1884
(entry 1066).

1094 _____. Academy, 26 (Nov. 22, 1884), 336.
Review of H.J. Jennings's Lord Tennyson, 1884 (entry 1069).

1095 Mackail, John William. Academy, 26 (Dec. 27, 1884), 421-
422.
Review of Becket. A tepid estimate of the play's quality.

1096 Rolfe, William James. "Misquotation, Shakespearian and
Other." Literary World (Boston), 15 (July 12, 1884), 233-
234.

1097 Salt, Henry Stephens. "The Poet Laureate as Philosopher and Peer." To-Day, 1 (Feb. 1884), 135-147.
Reprinted: Literary Sketches, 1888 (entry 1222).

1098 Saturday Review (London), 58 (Dec. 13, 1884), 757-758.
Review of Becket. A tepid review.

1099 Saturday Review (London), 58 (Dec. 27, 1884), 822-823.
Review of H.J. Jennings's Lord Tennyson (entry 1069).

1100 Shepherd, Richard Herne. "The Genesis of Tennyson's 'Maud.'" North American Review, 139 (Oct. 1884), 356-361.

1101 Spectator, 57 (March 8, 1884), 316-317.
Review of The Cup and the Falcon. Admires The Cup but dislikes The Falcon.

1102 Spectator, 57 (Dec. 20, 1884), 1699-1700.
Review of Becket. The reviewer considers Becket a good but not great play.

1103 St. James's Gazette, Dec. 9, 1884, p. 11.
Review of Becket. Interested in characterizations.

1104 "Tennyson on 'The Princess.'" Critic (New York), 4 (May 10, 1884), 223-224.
Reprinted: Academy, 25 (May 24, 1884), 367.

1105 Times (London), Dec. 10, 1884, pp. 5-6.
Review of Becket. Favorable.

1106 Standard, Dec. 9, 1884, p. 5.
Review of Becket.

1107 "Unconsidered Tennysonia Trifles." Critic (New York), 5 (Dec. 6, 1884), 268-269.
See also: W.J. Rolfe, 1885 (entry 1134).

1108 Wallis, Alfred. "A 'Tennyson' Forgery." Notes and Queries, 6th ser. 9 (Feb. 23, 1884), 143-144.

1109 Yorkshire Illustrated Monthly, May 1884, pp. 343-349.
Review of The Cup and the Falcon. Dislikes the plays. Believes Tennyson unsuited to writing drama.

1885

Tennyson's Tiresias and Other Poems was published in London by Macmillan in 1885. Lyrical Poems edited by Francis Turner Palgrave was also published by Macmillan.

Books

1110 Formont, M. "Maud." Du Roman en Vers et de L'Epopée domestique, étude littéraire. Bar-sur-Aube: Lebois, 1885.

1111 Galton, Arthur. "Lord Tennyson." Urbana Scripta. London: Stock, 1885, pp. 36-58.

1112 The Princess: A Sketch Explanatory of Lord Tennyson's Poems. [London: W. Rider, c. 1885.]

1113 Shepard, William (pseudonym for William Shepard Walsh). "Alfred Tennyson." Enchiridion of Criticism. Philadelphia: Lippincott, 1885, pp. 222-234.

Periodicals

1114 Athenaeum, Jan. 3, 1885, 7-9.
      Review of Becket. Admires Becket as poetry and discusses the character Becket.

1115 Bates, Charlotte Fiske. "To the Laureate." Literary World (Boston), 16 (Aug. 8, 1885), 272.
      A poem.

1116 Book Buyer, n.s. 2 (Feb. 1885), 5.
      Mentions Becket.

1117 Caine, Hall. Academy, 28 (Dec. 19, 1885), 403-405.
      Review of Tiresias.

1118 Carlyle, Thomas. "Alfred Tennyson: 1840." Literary World (Boston), 16 (May 30, 1885), 187.

1119 Critic (New York), 6 (Jan. 10, 1885), 14.
      Review of Becket.

1120 Critic (New York), 7 (Aug. 1, 1885), 51-52.
      Review of Lyrical Poems, ed. F. T. Palgrave.

1121 Eclectic Magazine of Foreign Literature, 105 (Sept. 1885), 418-425.
      Review of Becket.

1122 Egan, Maurice Francis. "Saint Thomas of Canterbury and Becket." Catholic World, 42 (Dec. 1885), 382-395.
      Review of Becket. The first work is by Aubrey de Vere. Egan believes de Vere's effort is superior to Becket.

1123 Filon, Augustin. "Lord Tennyson." Revue des Deux Mondes, 71 (Sept. 1885), 70-101.

1124 [Hasell, Elizabeth J.] Blackwood's Edinburgh Magazine, 138 (July 1885), 57-66.
      Review of Becket.

1125 Hawkins, Frederick. Theatre (London), n.s. 5 (Feb. 2, 1885), 53-61.
Review of Becket. Hawkins admires the poetry and characterizations but believes the play would not be successful if performed.

1126 Literary World (Boston), 16 (Jan. 24, 1885), 27.
Review of New Single-Volume Edition.

1127 Literary World (Boston), 16 (Feb. 7, 1885), 39.
Review of Becket.

1128 Literary World (Boston), 16 (July 11, 1885), 239.
Review of Lyrical Poems, ed. F.T. Palgrave.

1129 Literary World (Boston), 16 (Nov. 28, 1885), 431-434.
Discusses Tennyson's poetry with particular attention to "The Day Dream."

1130 "Lord Tennyson's Definition of a King." Present Day, 2 (Jan. 1885), 61.
Review of Becket. Focuses on the nature of the king in the play.

1131 Malan, Edward. "Hallam's Grave." Notes and Queries, 6th ser. 11 (Jan. 24, 1885), 66.

1132 Noel, Roden. "The Poetry of Tennyson." Contemporary Review, 47 (Feb. 1885), 202-224.
Reprinted: Littell's Living Age, 164 (March 28, 1885), 771-784; Eclectic Magazine of Foreign Literature, 104 (April 1885), 459-473; and Essays on Poetry and Poets, 1886 (entry 1151).
Interested in Tennyson's development of characters. Tennyson wrote to Noel: "You are wrong about the 'Idylls of the King,' but wrong in a gracious and noble way, for which I am obliged to you" (H. Tennyson, Alfred Lord Tennyson, page 311, entry 1955).

1133 Pallen, Condé Bénoist. "A Meaning of the 'Idylls of the King.'" Catholic World, 41 (April 1885), 43-54.
See also: C.B. Pallen's The Meaning of the Idylls of the King, 1904 (entry 2361).
A good examination of the allegory of the Idylls of the King.

1134 Rolfe, William James. "More Tennyson Trifles." Critic (New York), 6 (June 27, 1885), 301-302.
See also: entry 1107.

1135 Saturday Review (London), 60 (Dec. 19, 1885), 810-811.
Review of Tiresias.

1136 Spectator, 58 (Oct. 3, 1885), 1319-1320.
Review of Lyrical Poems, ed. F.T. Palgrave.

1137   Spectator, 58 (Nov. 7, 1885), 1466-1467.
       Discusses Tennyson's "Vastness."

1138   Spectator, 58 (Dec. 12, 1885), 1649-1651.
       Review of Tiresias.

1139   Stoddard, Richard Henry. Book Buyer, n.s. 2 (Feb. 1885),
       10.
       Review of Becket.

1140   Times (London), Dec. 9, 1885, p. 8.
       Review of Tiresias.

1141   [Ward, Mary Augusta.] Macmillan's Magazine, 51 (Feb.
       1885), 287-294.
       Review of Becket. Ward likes the play and discusses it as
part of Tennyson's overall literary achievement. She thinks the
play might be successfully staged.

1142   [Watts, Theodore.] Athenaeum, Dec. 26, 1885, 831-834.
       Review of Tiresias. Watts believes the poems are among
Tennyson's best.

1143   Westminster Review, n.s. 67 (April 1885), 581-582.
       Review of Becket.

1144   Woodberry, George Edward. Atlantic Monthly, 55 (April
       1885), 565-566.
       Review of Becket.

                              1886

       In 1886, Tennyson's Locksley Hall Sixty Years After (al-
though dated 1887) and A New Library Edition of Complete Works
(in ten volumes) were published by Macmillan, which also published
a single-volume collection of the poet's works.

Books

1145   Archer, William. About the Theatre. London: T. Fisher
       Unwin, 1886.
       Describes the production of The Promise of May in 1882 on
pages 81-88.

1146   Baret, Adrien. "Tennyson." Morceaux Choises des Clas-
       siques Anglais. Paris: Garnier, 1886.

1147   Beers, Henry Augustin. An Outline Sketch of English Litera-
       ture. New York: Chautauqua Press, 1886.
       Tennyson on pages 284-289.

1148   Chapman, Elizabeth Rachel. "In Memoriam." A Comtist

Lover and Other Studies. London: Unwin, 1886. Part II.
Tennyson wrote to Chapman: "I am grateful to you for your
book which contains an analysis of 'In Memoriam.' I like this much
better than Mr. Gatty's [entry 907], which perhaps you have seen,
and which is too personal to please me. Yours is excellent in taste
and judgment. I like too what you say about Comtism. I really
almost fancy that p. 95 was written by myself. I have been saying
the same thing for years in all but the same words." (H. Tennyson's Alfred Lord Tennyson, entry 1955, Volume II, page 332.)
This work is occasionally referred to incorrectly by scholars,
probably because Hallam Tennyson refers to it incorrectly in his
biography of his father. Chapman's comments are worth study if
for no other reason than Tennyson's evident enthusiasm for her
analysis.
Do not confuse this book with Chapman's summary, A Companion to In Memoriam, 1888 (entry 1214).

1149 Cooke, George Willis. "Tennyson." Poets and Problems.
Boston: Ticknor, 1886, pp. 55-169.

1150 Mayor, Joseph B. "Modern Blank Verse: Tennyson and
Browning." Chapters on English Metre. London: Clay,
1886, pp. 184-196.

1151 Noel, Roden. "The Poetry of Tennyson." Essays on Poetry
and Poets. London: Kegan Paul, Trench, 1886, pp. 223-
255.
Reprinted from Contemporary Review, 1885 (entry 1132).
See entry 1132 for other reprintings and an annotation.

1152 Rolfe, William James. "Tennyson and His Works." The
Young People's Tennyson. Boston: Houghton, Mifflin,
[c1886], pp. 87-118.

1153 Swinburne, Algernon Charles. "Tennyson and Musset."
Miscellanies. London: Chatto and Windus, 1886, pp. 219-
259.
Reprinted from Fortnightly Review, 1881 (entry 1008).
See entry 1008 for another reprinting and an annotation. This
book version of the essay is reprinted in part in J.D. Jump, ed.,
Tennyson: The Critical Heritage (entry 4013), pages 336-347.

Periodicals

1154 Book Buyer, n.s. 3 (Feb. 1886), 27.
Review of Tiresias.

1155 Bouchier, Jonathan. "Sir Walter Scott and Tennyson."
Notes and Queries, 7th ser. 2 (Aug. 14, 1886), 128.

1156 Critic (New York), 8 (Jan. 2, 1886), 4-5.
Review of Tiresias.

1157 Deutsche Rundshau, 47 (1886), 317.
      Review of Tiresias.

1158 Dial, 6 (Jan. 1886), 246-248.
      Review of Tiresias.

1159 Dyneley, Mortimer. "Locksley Hall and Liberalism."
      National Review, 8 (Dec. 1886), 641-647.

1160 Escott, T. H. S. Fortnightly Review, 45 (Feb. 1886), 270-272.
      Review of Tiresias.

1161 Green, S. G. Leisure Hour, 35 (1886), 99-101.
      Review of Tiresias.

1162 Hamann, Albert. Archiv für das Studium der neuren Sprach-
      en und Literaturen, 76 (1886), 338.
      Discusses Enoch Arden.

1163 [Hutton, Richard Holt.] "'Locksley Hall' in Youth and Age."
      Spectator, 59 (Dec. 18, 1886), 1706-1707.
      Reprinted: Criticisms, 1894 (entry 1802).
      Hutton discusses "Locksley Hall" and "Locksley Hall Sixty
Years After." He admires both poems and disagrees with those
critics who believe the later poem is inferior to its predecessor.
Although "Locksley Hall" has many fine passages that evoke the
spirit and thought of its age, Hutton contends that it also has weak
passages that are not incisive. "Locksley Hall Sixty Years After,"
he contends, is more consistent in its excellence even though it may
lack the high moments of the earlier poem. This essay is well
worth the reading for anyone interested in the "Locksley Hall" poems.

1164 "An Imperial Ode by Tennyson." Critic, 8 (May 8, 1886), 235.

1165 London Quarterly Review, 65 (Jan. 1886), 243-247.
      Review of Becket.

1166 [Prothero, Rowland.] "Modern Poetry." Edinburgh Review,
      163 (April 1886), 466-498.
      Review of Tiresias.

1167 Saturday Review (London), 62 (Dec. 25, 1886), 842-843.
      Review of Locksley Hall Sixty Years After.

1168 Spectator, 59 (Dec. 25, 1886), 1750-1751.
      Review of Locksley Hall Sixty Years After.

1169 Westminster Review, 69 (April 1886), 581-582.
      Review of Tiresias.

1170 Woodberry, George Edward. Atlantic Monthly, 57 (March
      1886), 423-426.
      Review of Tiresias.

<u>1887</u>

Books

1171 Belrose, Louise, Jr. <u>To the Poet Laureate</u>. Washington:
      Brentano, 1887.
      A poem.

1172 Bennett, W. C. "Locksley Hall": An Appeal from "Locksley
      Hall Sixty Years After" to "Locksley Hall." London: Hart,
      1887.
      Reprinted from <u>Liberal Home Ruler</u>, 1887 (entry 1184).

1173 Buchanan, Robert Williams. "From Pope to Tennyson."
      <u>A Look Round Literature</u>. London: Ward, 1887, pp. 347-
      358.

1174 Gilchrist, Herbert Harlakenden. <u>Anne Gilchrist: Her Life</u>
      <u>and Writings</u>. London: Unwin, 1887.
      Tennyson mentioned.

1175 Gladstone, William Ewart. <u>Gladstone on the New "Locksley</u>
      <u>Hall."</u> New York: Brentano, 1887.
      Reviewed by: <u>Critic</u> (New York) (entry 1188).

1176 Griswold, Hattie Tyng. "Alfred Tennyson." <u>Home Life of</u>
      <u>Great Authors</u>. Chicago: McClurg, 1887, pp. 197-206.

1177 Hamann, Albert. <u>An Essay on Tennyson's Idylls of the King</u>.
      Berlin: Gaertner, 1887. (Wissenschaftliche beilage zum
      Programm der Luisenschule.)
      Discusses the allegory in <u>Idylls of the King</u>.

1178 Mackay, Eric (pseudonym for George Eric). <u>Vox Clamantis:</u>
      <u>A Comparison, Analytical and Critical, Between the</u>
      <u>"Columbus at Seville" of Joseph Ellis, 1869, and the</u>
      <u>"Columbus" of the Poet Laureate, 1880</u>. London: Stewart,
      [c1887].
      Contends that Tennyson plagiarized from the poem by Ellis.

1179 <u>Mr. Eric Mackay and "Vox Clamantis": A Summary of Inci-</u>
      <u>dents Controverting Assertions Contained in Two Letters</u>
      <u>Addressed to the Editor of "The Birmingham Daily Gazette."</u>
      London: Stewart, 1887.

Periodicals

1180 "Adapting Tennyson to the Stage." <u>Critic</u> (New York), 10
      (April 16, 1887), 192-193.
      About "Lancelot and Elaine."

1181 Bacon, Thomas R. <u>New Englander</u>, 46 (Feb. 1887), 155-167.
      Review of <u>Locksley Hall Sixty Years After</u>.

1182 _____ . New Princeton Review, 3 (March 1887), 265-271.
On Locksley Hall Sixty Years After.

1183 Beeching, H.C. Academy, 31 (Jan. 1, 1887), 1-2.
Review of Locksley Hall Sixty Years After.

1184 Bennett, W.C. "'Locksley Hall': An Appeal from 'Locksley
Hall Sixty Years After' to 'Locksley Hall.'" Liberal Home
Ruler, Jan. 15, 1887.
Reprinted: 1887 (entry 1172).

1185 Canebrake, Thomas. "The Philosophy of Locksley Hall."
Southern Bivouac, 2 (April 1887), 704-708.

1186 Church Review, 49 (March 1887), 283-289.
Review of Locksley Hall Sixty Years After.

1187 Congregationalist Review, 1 (Feb. 1887), 97-105.
Discusses "Locksley Hall."

1188 Critic (New York), 10 (Feb. 12, 1887), 74.
Review of W.E. Gladstone's Gladstone on the New "Locksley
Hall" and Locksley Hall Sixty Years After.

1189 Dowden, Edward. "Victorian Literature." Fortnightly Review,
47 (June 1887), 852-855.

1190 Gardiner, Robert F. "'Locksley Hall': A Prophecy."
Notes and Queries, 7th ser. 3 (June 25, 1887), 512.

1191 Gatty, Alfred. "Locksley Hall Sixty Years After." Notes and
Queries, 7th ser. 3 (April 30, 1887), 347.

1192 Gladstone, William Ewart. "'Locksley Hall' and the Jubilee."
Nineteenth Century, 21 (Jan. 1887), 1-18.
Reprinted: Littell's Living Age, 172 (Jan. 29, 1887), 311-
320; and Eclectic Magazine of Foreign Literature, 108 (March 1887),
317-328.
Gladstone discusses the optimistic faith in progress in
"Locksley Hall" and the pessimism in "Locksley Hall Sixty Years
After." He is unhappy with the point of view of the later poem and
believes it inaccurately represents the progress made since the 1842
publication of the earlier poem.

1193 Hoskyns-Abrahall, J. "Tennyson's Inspiration from the
Pyrenees." Academy, 32 (Dec. 17, 1887), 408-409.

1194 James, A. "Tennyson et Gladstone." La Société nouvelle,
1 (1887).

1195 Literary World (Boston), 18 (Jan. 22, 1887), 25.
Review of Locksley Hall Sixty Years After.

1196 "The Literature of the Last Fifty Years." Blackwood's
Edinburgh Magazine, 141 (June 1887), 740-743.

1197 "'Locksley Hall' Earlier and Later." Leisure Hour, 36
(1887), 137-140.

1198 "London Letter." Critic (New York), 10 (Jan. 15, 1887), 31.
A letter dated December 25, 1886, that mentions Locksley
Hall Sixty Years After.

1199 Nation (New York), 44 (April 7, 1887), 298.
Review of Locksley Hall Sixty Years After.

1200 [Oliphant, Margaret.] Blackwood's Edinburgh Magazine, 141
(Jan. 1887), 129-131.
Review of Locksley Hall Sixty Years After.

1201 Payne, William Morton. Dial, 7 (Feb. 1887), 246-248.
Review of Locksley Hall Sixty Years After.

1202 Rolfe, William James. "The New and the Old 'Locksley
Hall.'" Critic (New York), 10 (Jan. 8, 1887), 19.

1203 _____. "An Old Poem of Tennyson's." Critic (New York),
10 (Jan. 1, 1887), 2.

1204 Royce, Josiah. Harvard Monthly, 3 (Jan. 1887), 127-137.
Review of Locksley Hall Sixty Years After.

1205 Shepherd, Richard Herne. "The Genesis of 'In Memoriam.'"
Walford's Antiquarian Magazine, 11 (June 1887), 407-412.

1206 "Tennysonian and Thackerayan Rarities." Walford's Antiquarian Magazine, 12 (Aug. 1887), 79-83.
Of bibliographic interest.

1207 Thomas, E.M. Book Buyer, 4 (Dec. 1887), 401-403.
Discusses "Enoch Arden."

1208 To-Day, 7 (March 1887), 93-95.
Review of Locksley Hall Sixty Years After.

1209 Van Dyke, Henry. "Vicissitudes of a Palace." New Princeton
Review, 62 (July 1887), 65-74.

1210 [Watts, Theodore.] Athenaeum, Jan. 1, 1887, pp. 31-33.
Review of Locksley Hall Sixty Years After. Watts perceives
the titular poem as a reflection of the last hope of England in the
1880's.

1211 Westminster Review, 128 (April 1887), 131-132.
Review of Locksley Hall Sixty Years After.

1212 Whitman, Walt. "A Word About Tennyson." Critic (New
      York), 10 (Jan. 1, 1887), 1-2.
      Reprinted: November Boughs, 1888 (entry 1226); Democrat-
ic Vistas, 1888 (entry 1227); Complete Prose Works, 1898 (entry
2040); Rivulets of Prose, 1928 (entry 3059); and J.D. Jump, ed.,
Tennyson: The Critical Heritage (entry 4013), pages 348-351.
      Whitman pays homage to Tennyson. He declares: "Yes,
Alfred Tennyson's is a superb character, and will help give illus-
triousness, through the long roll of time, to our Nineteenth Century."
One might find comparison between the present essay and Whitman's
1855 "An English and an American Poet" (entry 413) of interest.

1213 Woodberry, George Edward. Atlantic Monthly, 59 (May 1887),
      705-707.
      Review of Locksley Hall Sixty Years After.

                            1888

Books

1214 Chapman, Elizabeth Rachel. A Companion to "In Memoriam."
      London: Macmillan, 1888.

1215 Cochrane, Robert. "Lord Tennyson." Great Thinkers and
      Workers. London: Chambers, 1888, pp. 50-72.

1216 Dawson, George. "The 'Idylls of the King'" and "Enoch
      Arden." Shakespeare and Other Lectures. Ed. G. St.
      Clair. London: Kegan Paul, Trench, 1888, pp. 471-480
      and 481-485.

1217 Grindon, Leopold Hartley. "The Tennyson Flora." Report
      of the Manchester Field-Naturalist's Society. Manchester:
      1888, pp. 44-73.

1218 Jerome, Jerome Klapka. Sunset: Play in One Act. London:
      French, [c. 1888]. (French's Acting Editions of Plays.)
      Based on Tennyson's "The Sisters."

1219 Kingsley, Charles. "Tennyson." Literary and General Lec-
      tures and Essays. London: Macmillan, 1888, pp. 103-124.
      Reprinted from Fraser's Magazine, 1850 (entry 222). See
entry 222 for other reprintings and for annotation.

1220 Miller, Bessie Porter. "Some Aspects of Womanhood in
      Chaucer, Shakespeare and Tennyson." Shakespeare and
      Chaucer Examinations. Boston: 1888, pp. 307-346.

1221 Nutt, Alfred. Studies of the Legend of the Holy Grail. Lon-
      don: Nutt, 1888.

1222 Salt, Henry Stephens. "The Tennyson Philosophy." Literary

Sketches. London: Swan, Sonnenschein, Lowrey, 1888, pp. 39-58.
Reprinted from To-Day, 1884 (entry 1097).

1223 Shaw, William J. Forward Forever: A Response to Lord Tennyson's "Locksley Hall Sixty Years After." New York: Fowler and Wells, 1888.

1224 Shorter, Clement King. Tennyson. Glasgow: Mackenzie, 1888.
A three-page article.

1225 Taylor, Henry. Correspondence of Henry Taylor. ed. Edward Dowden. London: Longmans, Green, 1888.
Tennyson mentioned throughout.

1226 Whitman, Walt. "A Word About Tennyson." November Boughs. Philadelphia: McKay, 1888, pp. 65-67.
Reprinted from Critic (New York), 1887 (entry 1212). See entry 1212 for other reprintings and for annotation.

1227 _____. "A Word About Tennyson." Democratic Vistas. London: Scott, 1888, pp. 125-129.
Reprinted from Critic (New York), 1887 (entry 1212). See entry 1212 for other reprintings and for annotation.

Periodicals

1228 Bede, Cuthbert (pseudonym for Edward Bradley). "Stanzas by Alfred Tennyson." Notes and Queries, 7th ser. 5 (April 14, 1888), 283.

1229 Boodle, R.W. "Tennyson's Idylls." Rose-Belford's Canadian Monthly and National Review, 13 (April 1888).

1230 Bouchier, Jonathan. "Literary Coincidence: Scott and Tennyson." Notes and Queries, 7th ser. 5 (March 3, 1888), 170.

1231 _____. "Tennyson Queries." Notes and Queries, 7th ser. 6 (Dec. 29, 1888), 513.

1232 Bowker, R.R. "London as a Literary Center." Harper's Monthly Magazine, 76 (May 1888), 816-817.

1233 Dorsey, Anna Vernon. "Tennyson's Idyls: Their Sources and Significance." American Magazine, 7 (April 1888), 737-743.

1234 Fuchs, R. Leipziger Zeitung, 1888, pp. 154 and 163.
Listed in Ehrsam, et al., "Alfred Lord Tennyson," Bibliographies of Twelve Victorian Authors (entry 3241), page 320.

1235 "Is Tennyson a Spiritualist?" Pall Mall Gazette, Dec. 20, 1888.

1236   Jacottet, Henri. "Poètes modernes de L'Angleterre: Alfred
       Tennyson." Bibliothèque Universelle et Revue Suisse, 37
       (March 1888), 449-472; and 38 (April 1888), 89-114.

1237   Literary World (Boston), 19 (Nov. 24, 1888), 413.
       Discusses Tennyson's "Lilian."

1238   Little, Charles J. "Some Words about Tennyson." Methodist
       Review, 70 (March 1888), 203-221.

1239   Mabie, Hamilton Wright. "Tennyson's Earlier Poems."
       Book Buyer, 5 (Dec. 1888), 457-460.

1240   Sarrazin, Gabriel. "Lord Tennyson." Nouvelle Revue, 55
       (Dec. 15, 1888), 812-838.
       Reprinted: La Renaissance de la poésie anglaise, 1889 (entry
       1253).
       Sarrazin discusses the moral and social themes of Tennyson's
poetry.   He is enthusiastic about Idylls of the King.

1241   Saturday Review (London), 65 (May 26, 1888), 637.

1242   Stone, J. M. "A Missing Page from the 'Idylls of the King.'"
       Dublin Review, 103 (Oct. 1888), 259-274.
       Reprinted: Studies from Court and Cloister, 1905 (entry
2395).

1243   Swinburne, Algernon Charles. "Dethroning Tennyson."
       Nineteenth Century, 23 (Jan. 1888), 127-129.
       A satirical essay that mocks those who would assert that
Francis Bacon wrote the plays of Shakespeare.   Swinburne asserts
that Darwin wrote the poetry of Tennyson.

1244   "Tennyson Superseded." Saturday Review (London), 66 (Aug.
       25, 1888), 225.

1245   "Tennysonian Trees." Gardener's Magazine, Dec. 29, 1888.

1246   "Tennyson's Earlier Poems." Bookworm, 2 (1888), 92-93.
       Not examined.

1247   Toynbee, Paget. "To Tennyson." Academy, 34 (Nov. 17,
       1888), 321.
       A poem.

                              1889

       In 1889, Tennyson's Demeter and Other Poems (hereinafter
referred to as Demeter) and a new Single-Volume Edition edition of
his poetry were published by Macmillan and Co.

Books

1248   Austin, Alfred. "To Lord Tennyson." Love's Widowhood
       and Other Poems. London and New York: Macmillan, 1889,
       p. 121.
       The poem is as follows:

                           To Lord Tennyson

            Poet! in other lands, when Spring no more
            Gleams o'er the grass, nor in the thicket-side
            Plays at being lost and laughs to be descried,
            And blooms lie wilted on the orchard floor,
            Then the sweet birds that from AEgean shore
            Across Ausonian breakers hither hied,
            Own April's music in their breast hath died,
            And croft and copse resound not as before.
            But, in this privileged Isle, this brave, this blest,
            This deathless England, it seems always Spring.
            Though graver wax the days, Song takes not wing.
            In Autumn boughs it builds another nest:
            Even from the snow we lift our hearts and sing,
            And still your voice is heard above the rest.

1249   Davidson, Thomas. Prolegomena to "In Memoriam."   Boston:
       Houghton, Mifflin, 1889.
       Focuses on the spiritual aspects of the poem.

1250   Montégut, Emile. "Essais sur Alfred Tennyson: I. Des
       premiers Poèmes aux Idylls du Roi.   II.   Enoch Arden et
       les Poèmes populaires." Ecrivains modernes de l'Angleterre.
       Paris: Hachette, 1889, pp. 261-349.

1251   O'Connor, W. A. "Tennyson's Palace of Art." Essays on
       Literature and Ethics. Manchester: 1889, pp. 25-56.

1252   Robertson, John Mackinnon. "The Art of Tennyson." Essays
       Toward a Critical Method. London: Unwin, 1889, pp. 233-282.
           Reprinted: J. D. Jump, ed., Tennyson: The Critical Heri-
       tage (entry 4013), pages 414-443.
           Robertson likes Tennyson's early poetry better than the poet's
       later work. He particularly dislikes Idylls of the King. He notes
       Tennyson's craftsmanship and often cites the opinions of A. C.
       Swinburne. He calls Tennyson "the Virgil of our time."

1253   Sarrazin, Gabriel. "Alfred Tennyson." La renaissance de
       la poèsie anglaise 1798-1889. Paris: Perrin, 1889, pp.
       149-198.
       Reprinted from Nouvelle Revue, 1888 (entry 1240).

1254   Scherer, Edmond. "Tennyson and Gladstone." Etudes cri-
       tiques sur la littérature contemporaine. Paris: Levy, 1889.
       Volume X.

1255   Schmerler, Heinrich Emil. "Tennyson as a Dramatic Poet."
       Chips from English Literature. Borna: Noske, 1889.

1256 Van Dyke, Henry. The Poetry of Tennyson. New York: Scribner's, 1889.
This book went through many reprintings and revisions during the next two decades. Van Dyke admires Tennyson's poetry and emphasizes the personal and spiritual aspects of it. A highly intelligent critic who understands the fundamentals of poetry, Van Dyke presents a vigorous and interesting study of Tennyson's work. The book's erudition and sound scholarship made it a standard reference for students and scholars for as least a generation. Van Dyke's discussion is still worth reading; I recommend the 1907 edition.
Reviewed by: Igdrasil (entry 1315); Literary World (Boston) in 1890 and 1893 (entries 1320 and 1735); Literary World (London) (entry 1323); Nation (New York) (entry 1328); and W. Watson in Academy (entry 1348).

1257 Walsh, Henry C. "Introduction." Idylls of the King. Philadelphia: Altemus, 1889, pp. iii-ix.

Dissertation

1258 Wüllenweber, Walther. Über Tennysons Königsidylle "The Coming of Arthur" und ihre Quellen: Ein Beitrag zur Geschichte der Artussage. Marburg, 1889.
Published in Archiv für das Studium der neueren Sprachen und Literaturen, 1889 (entry 1287).

Periodicals

1259 Austin, Alfred. "Lord Tennyson's New Volume." National Review, 14 (Dec. 1889), 694-702.
Review of Demeter.

1260 _____. "Tennyson as Eighty." Spectator, 63 (Aug. 10, 1889), 175.
A poem.

1261 Bayne, Thomas. "Tennyson's 'J.S.'" Notes and Queries, 7th ser. 7 (Jan. 19, 1889), 55-56.

1262 Buchan, T. Winter. "Tennyson's 'To-Morrow'--a Coincidence." Academy, 36 (Oct. 26, 1889), 270-271.

1263 Cattle, Frederic. "Some Less-Known Tennysoniana." Bookworm, 2 (1889), 263-264.

1264 Gage, Minot G. "Tennyson: the Man." Unitarian Review, 32 (Dec. 1889), 535-541.

1265 Garrod, H.B. Academy, 36 (Dec. 28, 1889), 413-414.
Review of Demeter.

1266 Gosse, Edmund William. "Tennyson at Eighty." Critic (New York), 15 (Aug. 30, 1889), 105-107.

1267   Hutton, Laurence. "The Miller's Daughter." Book Buyer, 6 (Dec. 1889), 435-436.

1268   [Hutton, Richard Holt.] "Browning and Tennyson." Spectator, 63 (Dec. 21, 1889), 879-880.
        Reprinted: Brief Literary Criticisms, 1906 (entry 2420).

1269   Lamont, Alexander. "Tennyson's Touch with Nature." Sunday Magazine, 18 (June 1889), 378-387.

1270   Lester, George. "The Poets Laureate of England: Alfred, Lord Tennyson." Methodist Recorder, March 21, 1889.

1271   Lounsbury, Thomas Raynesford. "The Two Locksley Halls." Scribner's Magazine, 6 (Aug. 1889), 250-256.
        Lounsbury asserts: "To a large portion of the English-speaking race, perhaps to the larger portion of it, Tennyson is pre-eminently the poet of 'Locksley Hall.' There are others of his productions that will commend themselves with far more effectiveness to minds of a certain order. There are others of them which will be conceded to display more varied if not greater power. But there is no other that has appealed to so wide a circle of sympathies, and, as a result, there is no other that has been so generally read and admired and quoted." Lounsbury believes that "Locksley Hall" is a great poem that gives expression to the hopes and ideas of ordinary people.

1272   Myers, F.W.H. "Tennyson as Prophet." Nineteenth Century, 25 (March 1889), 381-396.
        Reprinted: Littell's Living Age, 180 (March 30, 1889), 811-819; Eclectic Magazine of Foreign Literature, 112 (April 1889), 531-541; Science and a Future Life, 1893 (entry 1682); and J.D. Jump, ed., Tennyson: The Critical Heritage (entry 4013), pages 395-413.
        Myers portrays Tennyson as an optimist "in the darkest hour of the world's thought." He sees the poet as predicting a brighter spiritual future.

1273   Parsons, Eugene. "Tennyson's Art and Genius." Baptist Quarterly Review, 11 (Jan. 1889), 29-47.

1274   Rawnsley, Hardwicke Drummond. "To Lord Tennyson: On His Eightieth Birthday, August 6th, 1889." Macmillan's Magazine, 60 (Aug. 1889), 293.
        A poem.

1275   "The Right Hon. Lord Tennyson, D.C.L., F.R.S." Tinsley's Magazine, 43 (Oct. 1889), 580-584.

1276   Sarrazin, Gabriel. "A Gallic Study of Tennyson." Universal Review, 4 (1889), 529-554.

1277   Scots Observer, 3 (Dec. 21, 1889), 127-128.
        Review of Demeter.

1278 Spectator, 63 (Dec. 21, 1889), 883-884.
Review of Demeter.

1279 "Tennyson at Eighty." Critic (New York), 15 (Aug. 10,
1889), 69.

1280 "Tennyson's Spiritual Service to His Generation." Andover
Review, 12 (Sept. 1889), 291-296.

1281 "Tennyson's Undertones." Spectator, 62 (Feb. 2, 1889),
165-166.

1282 Van Dyke, Henry. "The Bible in Tennyson." Century Illustrated Monthly Magazine, 38 (Aug. 1889), 515-522.

1283 _____. "Tennyson's First Flight." Scribner's Magazine,
6 (Aug. 1889), 242-249.

1284 [Watts, Theodore?] Athenaeum, Dec. 28, 1889, pp. 883-885.
Review of Demeter.

1285 _____. "The Eightieth Birthday." Athenaeum, Aug. 10,
1889, p. 191.
A poem.

1286 Weigand, W. "Lord Tennysons neueste Lyrik." Vossische
Zeitung (Sonntagsbeilage), no. 3 (1889).

1287 Wüllenweber, Walther. "Tennysons Königsidylle The Coming
of Arthur und ihre Quellen." Archiv für das Studium der
neueren Sprachen und Literaturen, 83 (1889), 1-66.
Publication of a dissertation: 1889 (entry 1258).

1890

Books

1288 [Aytoun, William Edmondstoune.] "The Laureate, by Alfred
Tennyson." The Book of Ballads. Ed. Bon Gaultier
(pseudonym for W.E. Aytoun and Theodore Martin). New
York: Worthington, 1890, pp. 129-131.
Reprinted from Tait's Edinburgh Magazine, 1843 (entry 85).
A parody.

1289 [Aytoun, William Edmondstoune.] "La Mort d'Arthur: A
Fragment--Not by Tennyson." The Book of Ballads. Ed.
Bon Gaultier (pseudonym for W.E. Aytoun and Theodore
Martin). New York: Worthington, 1890, p. 191.
Reprinted from Tait's Edinburgh Magazine, 1843 (entry 86).

1290 Bolton, Sarah. "Alfred Tennyson." Famous English Authors
of the Nineteenth Century. New York: Crowell, [c1890],
pp. 256-310.

1291   Cooledge, Charles E.   The Sunny Side of Bereavement as
      Illustrated in Tennyson's "In Memoriam."   1890.
      Mentioned in P. F. Baum's "Alfred Lord Tennyson" in The
Victorian Poets, ed. F. E. Faverty, 1956 (entry 3600), page 30,
footnote 1.

1292   Dawson, W. J.   "Tennyson."   Makers of Modern English.
      New York: Whittaker, 1890, pp. 169-269.

1293   Gaultier, Bon (pseudonym for William Edmondstoune Aytoun
      and Theodore Martin).   "The Biter Bit."   The Book of
      Ballads.   New York: Worthington, 1890, pp. 68-70.

1294   Hatton, Joseph.   "Tennyson and Longfellow."   Old Lamps
      and New.   London: Hutchinson, [c1890], pp. 176-198.

1295   Haweis, Hugh Reginald.   "Tennyson."   Poets in the Pulpit.
      London: Low, 1890, pp. 33-115.

1296   Paget, Walter, and Herbert Dicksee.   Tennyson Pictures.
      London: Nister, 1890.
      Illustrates and comments on some poems by Tennyson.

1297   Reid, Thomas Wemyss.   The Life, Letters, and Friendships
      of Richard Monckton Milnes.   London: Cassell, 1890.
      Milnes had died on August 11, 1885.   He was the friend of
many Victorian authors, including Tennyson.

1298   Walters, John Cuming.   In Tennyson Land: A Brief Account
      of the Home and Early Surroundings of the Poet and an At-
      tempt to Identify the Scenes and Trace the Influence of
      Lincolnshire in His Works.   London: Redway, 1890.
      Compares passages in Tennyson's poetry to the area of
Lincolnshire.   Walters ventures some strong opinions about various
poems by Tennyson.
      Reviewed by: Book Buyer (entry 1302); Igdrasil (entry 1316);
Literary World (Boston) (entry 1321); Literary World (London) (entry
1322); Nation (New York) (entry 1329); Notes and Queries, (entry
1331); and Spectator (entry 1341).

Periodicals

1299   Aldrich, Thomas Bailey.   "Tennyson."   Atlantic Monthly, 65
      (March 1890), 412.
      A poem.

1300   "An Arthurian Journey."   Atlantic Monthly, 65 (June 1890),
      811-829.

1301   Bixby, James T.   "Alfred Tennyson and the Questionings of
      Our Age."   Arena, 2 (June 1890), 57-71.

1302   Book Buyer, 7 (March 1890), 66-67.
      Review of J. C. Walter's In Tennyson Land, 1890 (entry 1298).

1303 Buckley, W.E. "Gwydion: Flur." <u>Notes and Queries</u>, 7th
      ser. 10 (Nov. 22, 1890), 409-410.

1304 Caswell, C.J. "Tennyson's Schooldays." <u>Pall Mall Gazette</u>,
      June 19, 1890.

1305 Cheney, John Vance. "Tennyson." <u>Chautauquan</u>, 11 (May and
      June 1890), 173-178 and 308-312.

1306 "The Coming Laureate." <u>Public Opinion</u> (New York), 8
      (March 22, 1890), 568.

1307 <u>Critic</u> (New York), 16 (Jan. 11, 1890), 13.
      Review of <u>Demeter</u>.

1308 <u>Deutsche Rundschau</u>, 62 (1890), 477.
      Review of <u>Demeter</u>.

1309 Ewing, Thomas J. "Tennyson's 'Voyage of Maeldune.'"
      <u>Notes and Queries</u>, 7th ser. 9 (June 14, 1890), 475-476.

1310 Fruit, John Phelps. "Browning and Tennyson." <u>Modern
      Language Notes</u>, 5 (May 1890), 276-283.

1311 Gladstone, William Ewart. "British Poetry of the Nineteenth
      Century." <u>Speaker</u>, 1 (Jan. 11, 1890), 34.

1312 "Hallam's Remains." <u>Notes and Queries</u>, 7th ser. 10 (Sept.
      27, 1890), 244-245.

1313 <u>Harper's Monthly Magazine</u>, 80 (April 1890), 807.

1314 Higgs, William. "An Open Letter in re the Article Entitled
      'A Poetical Heartbreak.'" <u>New Englander</u>, 53 (Sept. 1890),
      276-283.
      Responds to an article in the August issue of the <u>New Eng-
lander</u> (entry 1335).

1315 <u>Igdrasil</u>, 1 (Feb. 1890), 78.
      Review of H. Van Dyke's <u>The Poetry of Tennyson</u>, 1889
(entry 1256).

1316 <u>Igdrasil</u>, 1 (April 1890), 163.
      Review of J.C. Walters's <u>In Tennyson Land</u>, 1890 (entry
1298).

1317 <u>Independent</u>, 42 (Feb. 6, 1890), 188.
      Review of <u>Demeter</u>.

1318 Lester, George. "Christmas with Lord Tennyson." <u>Fireside
      Magazine</u>, Dec. 1890.

1319 <u>Literary World</u> (Boston), 21 (Jan. 18, 1890), 19-20.
      Review of <u>Demeter</u>.

1320 Literary World (Boston), 21 (Jan. 18, 1890), 20.
      Review of H. Van Dyke's The Poetry of Tennyson, 1889
(entry 1256).

1321 Literary World (Boston), 21 (March 29, 1890), 99.
      Review of J. C. Walters's In Tennyson Land, 1890 (entry
1298).

1322 Literary World (London), 41 (March 7, 1890), 216-217.
      Review of J. C. Walters's In Tennyson Land, 1890 (entry
1298).

1323 Literary World (London), 41 (April 4, 1890), 316-317.
      Review of H. Van Dyke's The Poetry of Tennyson, 1889
(entry 1256).

1324 London Quarterly Review, 74 (April 1890), 86-95.
      Review of Demeter.

1325 "Lord Tennyson." Speaker, 2 (July 19, 1890), 69-70.

1326 Marshall, Ed. "Hallam's Remains." Notes and Queries, 7th
      ser. 10 (Nov. 1, 1890), 354.

1327 "Modern Men: The Laureate." National Observer, 5 (Nov.
      22, 1890), 10-11.

1328 Nation (New York), 50 (Jan. 2, 1890), 20.
      Review of H. Van Dyke's The Poetry of Tennyson, 1889
(entry 1256).

1329 Nation (New York), 50 (March 27, 1890), 265.
      Review of J. C. Walters's In Tennyson Land, 1890 (entry
1298).

1330 New Englander, 53 (Nov. 1890), 492-494.
      Discusses In Memoriam.

1331 Notes and Queries, 7th ser. 9 (April 12, 1890), 299-300.
      Review of J. C. Walters's In Tennyson Land, 1890 (entry
1298).

1332 [Oliphant, Margaret.] Blackwood's Edinburgh Magazine, 147
      (Jan. 1890), 137-140.
      Review of Demeter.

1333 Parsons, Eugene. "Tennyson." Examiner (New York), Feb.
      1890.

1334 Payne, William Morton. Dial, 10 (Feb. 1890), 280-281.
      Review of Demeter.

1335 "A Poetical Heartbreak." New Englander, 53 (Aug. 1890)

126-142.
Responded to by William Higgs in the September issue of the New Englander (entry 1314).

1336 Porter, C. Poet Lore, 2 (1890), 201-207.
Review of Demeter.

1337 [Reeve, Henry.] "Tennyson and Browning." Edinburgh Review, 172 (Oct. 1890), 301-316.
Discusses Poems, 1842.

1338 Rodriguez, Francesco. "Lord Tennyson: Alcuni suoi scritti minori." Nuova Antologia di Lettere, Scienze ed Arti, 112 (July 16, 1890), 318-340.

1339 Salt, Henry Stephens. "Tennyson as a Thinker." Time, 23 (Oct. 1890), 1055-1066.
Reprinted: 1893 (entry 1688).
Salt contends that Tennyson is a poor thinker who is out of touch with the important social movements of his age.

1340 Shepherd, Henry Elliott. "A Study of Tennyson's English." Modern Language Notes, 5 (April 1890), 193-206.

1341 Spectator, 64 (April 19, 1890), 571.
Review of J.C. Walters's In Tennyson Land, 1890 (entry 1298).

1342 "Tennyson: and After?" Fortnightly Review, 53 (May 1, 1890), 621-637.
Discusses possible successors to the poet laureateship.

1343 Thayer, W.R. American (Philadelphia), 19 (Jan. 18, 1890), 273-275.
Review of Demeter.

1344 Urban, Sylvanus. "The Laureate and Mr. Swinburne." Gentleman's Magazine, 268 (April 1890), 431.

1345 Van Dyke, Henry. "The Fame of Tennyson." Independent, 42 (Jan. 16, 1890), 66-67.

1346 Walters, John Cuming. "In King Arthur's Capital." Igdrasil, 2 (Nov. 1890), 49-55.

1347 _____. "Tennyson and Lincolnshire." Scots Observer, 3 (March 1, 1890), 410.
See entry 1298.

1348 Watson, William. Academy, 37 (March 29, 1890), 217-218.
Review of H. Van Dyke's The Poetry of Tennyson, 1889 (entry 1256).

1349   White, James W.   "Tennyson on the Philosophy of the Future
       Life."   Baptist Quarterly Review, 12 (April 1890), 158-182.

1350   Wilcock, A. B.   "Tennyson's Earlier Poems."   Bookworm,
       3 (1890), 317.

1351   Woodberry, George Edward.   Atlantic Monthly, 65 (March
       1890), 421-423.
       Review of Demeter.

1891

Books

1352   Ainger, Alfred.   Tennyson for the Young.   London: Mac-
       millan, 1891.

1353   Church, Alfred John.   The Laureate's Country.   London:
       Seeley, 1891.

1354   Collins, John Churton.   Illustrations of Tennyson.   London:
       Chatto and Windus, 1891.
           Reprinted from Cornhill Magazine, 1879, 1880, and 1881
       (entries 919, 956, and 983).
           With admirable erudition, Collins examines the sources and
       influences for much of Tennyson's poetry.   He compares Tennyson
       to a variety of poets, notably Virgil.   This book is still commonly
       used as a reference by scholars and critics.
           Reviewed by: R. Le Gallienne in Academy (entry 1522);
       and Spectator (entry 1385).

1355   Graham, Peter Anderson.   "Art and Scenery (Lord Tennyson)."
       Nature in Books: Some Studies in Biography.   London:
       Methuen, 1891, pp. 44-65.

1356   Jones, Richard D.   The Ethical Element in Literature.
       Bloomington, Illinois: Public School, [c1891].
       Discusses In Memoriam.

1357   Lester, George.   Lord Tennyson and the Bible.   London:
       Howe, [1891].
       Lester notes Tennyson's use of the Bible.

1358   Rhys, John.   Studies in the Arthurian Legend.   Oxford:
       University Press (Clarendon Press), 1891.

1359   Rodriguez, Francesco.   Studi e saggi: Lord Tennyson:
       Henry W. Longfellow: William Cowper.   Rome: Forzani,
       1891.

1360   Shairp, John Campbell.   "Tennyson."   Aspects of Poetry.
       Boston: Houghton, Mifflin, 1891.

1361 Sharp, Amy. "Alfred Tennyson." Victorian Poets. London: Methuen, 1891, pp. 1-39.
Reprinted: Port Washington, N.Y., and London: Kennikat, 1970. Reviewed by: Speaker (entry 1384).

1362 Wilde, Jane Francesca Elgee. Notes on Men, Women, and Books. London: Ward and Downey, 1891.
Tennyson on pages 286-326. Jane Wilde was a poet and the mother of Oscar Wilde.

1363 Winn, Edith Lynwood. A Vision of Fair Women: A Dramatic Paraphrase Based upon Tennyson's "Dream of Fair Women." Boston: Baker, 1891. (Baker's Novelty List.)

Periodicals

1364 Arnold, Edwin. "A Day with Lord Tennyson." Forum, 12 (Dec. 1891), 536-548.
Reprinted: Forum Papers, ed. C.R. Gaston, 1925 (entry 2999).

1365 Axon, William. "Tennysoniana." Notes and Queries, 7th ser. 11 (April 25, 1891), 326.

1366 Bayne, Thomas. "Carlyle and Lord Tennyson." Notes and Queries, 7th ser. 11 (March 14, 1891), 204.

1367 Buckley, W.E. "Aylmer's Field." Notes and Queries, 7th ser. 12 (Dec. 26, 1891), 509-510.

1368 Caswell, C.J. "A Comitia of Errors." Birmingham Weekly Mercury, April 11, 1891.
Listed in Ehrsam, et al., "Alfred Lord Tennyson" in Bibliographies of Twelve Victorian Authors (entry 3241), page 312.

1369 _____. "Lord Tennyson's Birthday." Notes and Queries, 7th ser. 11 (March 14, 1891), 201-202.

1370 Cook, Albert S. "Literary Factors in Tennyson's 'St. Agnes Eve.'" Poet Lore, 3 (Jan. 1891), 10-17.

1371 _____. "The Literary Genealogy of Tennyson's Ulysses." Poet Lore, 3 (1891), 499-504.

1372 Davies, Joseph J. "Tennyson's Lincolnshire Farmers." Westminster Review, 136 (1891), 132-137.
Reprinted: Littell's Living Age, 191 (Oct. 17, 1891), 183-186.
"Northern Farmer, Old Style" and "Northern Farmer, New Style."

1373 Gatty, Alfred. "Tennyson's 'In Memoriam.'" Notes and Queries, 7th ser. 12 (Aug. 1, 1891), 97.

1374   Graham, Peter Anderson. "Lord Tennyson's Childhood."
        Art Journal, 53 (1891), 13-18 and 46-50.
        Biographical.

1375   Groth, Ernst. "Lord Tennysons neueste Lyrik." Die
        Grenzboten, 50 (Jan. 1891), 417-424.

1376   "Illustrations of Animal Life in Tennyson's Poems." Cornhill
        Magazine, 63 (Feb. 1891), 145-151.
        Reprinted: Littell's Living Age, 188 (March 14, 1891),
694-698.

1377   Literary World (London), 44 (Sept. 18, 1891), 216.
        Discusses Enoch Arden.

1378   Mason, C. "Lord Tennyson's Birthday." Notes and Queries,
        7th ser. 11 (April 18, 1891), 317.

1379   Mount, C.B. "Tennyson's 'Aylmer's Field.'" Notes and
        Queries, 7th ser. 12 (Dec. 26, 1891), 510.
        See also: C.B. Mount in Notes and Queries, 1892 (entry
1555).

1380   Parsons, Eugene. "Tennyson's Quotableness." Chautauquan,
        13 (June 1891), 334-337.

1381   Rand, Theodore H. "Limae Labor." McMaster University
        Journal, 1 (June 1891), 1-11.
        Rand uses Tennyson's revisions as examples of the process
of revising poems.

1382   Saturday Review (London), 72 (Sept. 12, 1891), 312-313.
        Discusses Tennyson's "Daphne."

1383   Shepherd, Henry Elliott. "Some Phases of Tennyson's In
        Memoriam." PMLA, 6 (1891), 41-51.

1384   Speaker, 4 (Aug. 15, 1891), 206-207.
        Review of Amy Sharp's Victorian Poets (entry 1361).

1385   Spectator, 67 (Dec. 12, 1891), 849-850.
        Review of J.C. Collins's Illustrations of Tennyson, 1891
(entry 1354).

1386   Stephenson, Nathaniel Wright. "One Aspect of the 'Idylls
        of the King.'" Harvard Monthly, 11 (Feb. 1891), 187-191.

1387   Tabb, John B. "To Lord Tennyson." Academy, 40 (Aug. 8,
        1891), 115.
        A poem.

1388   "Tennyson's 'In Memoriam.'" Notes and Queries, 7th ser.
        11 (Jan. 31, 1891), 94.

1389 "Tennyson's Poems: Translations." Notes and Queries, 7th
      ser. 12 (Oct. 24, 1891), 332.

1390 Van Dyke, Henry. "On the Study of Tennyson." Century
      Illustrated Monthly Magazine, 42 (Aug. 1891), 502-510.

1391 Warren, Thomas Herbert. "To Lord Tennyson." Spectator,
      66 (April 25, 1891), 593.
      A poem.

1392 [Watts, Theodore.] "Lord Tennyson's New Play." Athe-
      naeum, Oct. 3 and 10, 1891, pp. 461 and 493-494.
      Reprinted: Critic (New York), 19 (Oct. 31, 1891), 238-239.
Discusses The Foresters.

1393 _____. "To Tennyson on His Eighty-second Birthday."
      Athenaeum, Aug. 22, 1891, p. 255.
      Reprinted: Literary World, 22 (Sept. 26, 1891), 332.

                              1892

        Alfred, Lord Tennyson died on October 6, 1892. Many of
the listings for 1892 and 1893 are eulogies and memorials. His
poems The Death of OEnone, Akbar's Dream and Other Poems
(hereinafter referred to as The Death of OEnone) were published in
1892 by Macmillan and Co. His play The Foresters, Robin Hood
and Maid Marian was published by Macmillan and Co. and was
produced at Daly's Theatre in New York in March 1892.

Books

1394 Butler, H. Montagu. A Sermon Preached in the Chapel of
      Trinity College ... in Reference to the Death of Lord Tenny-
      son. Cambridge: Macmillan and Bowes, 1892.

1395 Cheney, John Vance. "Tennyson and His Critics." The
      Golden Guess: Essays on Poetry and the Poets. Boston:
      Lee and Shepard, 1892, pp. 161-201.

1396 Greswell, William. Tennyson and Our Imperial Heritage.
      London: Gower, Dodson, 1892.

1397 Jacobs, Joseph. Tennyson and "In Memoriam": An Appre-
      ciation and a Study. London: Nutt, 1892.
      Reviewed by: Critic (New York) (entry 1705); Literary World
(London) (entry 1737); Nation (New York) (entry 1745); and Spectator
(entry 1766).

1398 Jenkinson, Arthur. Alfred, Lord Tennyson, Poet Laureate:
      A Brief Study of His Life and Poetry. London: Nisbet, 1892.

1399 Lyon, William Henry. "Renan and Tennyson." Five Prophets
      of Today. Boston: Smith, 1892, pp. 21-38.

1400   Macaulay, G. C.   Introduction to Tennyson: "The Marriage
        of Geraint" and "Geraint and Enid."   London and New York:
        Macmillan, 1892.
        Macaulay discusses sources and merits.

1401   Macphail, W. M.   Tennyson's Idylls of the King.   London:
        Hitchcock, 1892.

1402   Mather, Marshall (pseudonym for James Marshall).   "Tenny-
        son the Moodist."   Popular Studies of Nineteenth Century
        Poets.   London: Warne, 1892, pp. 125-152.

1403   Mullany, Patrick Francis.   "Spiritual Sense of In Memoriam."
        Phases of Thought and Criticism.   Boston: Houghton,
        Mifflin, 1892, pp. 183-264.

1404   Napier, George G.   The Homes and Haunts of Alfred, Lord
        Tennyson.   Glasgow: MacLehose, 1892.
        The illustrations are still of interest.   Reviewed by: Review
        of Reviews (London) (entry 1584).

1405   Oliphant, Margaret.   "Alfred Tennyson, 1809-1892."   The
        Victorian Age of English Literature.   New York: Tait,
        [1892].   Volume I, pp. 203-218.

1406   Pain, Barry.   "The Poets at Tea: II. Tennyson, Who Took
        It Hot."   Playthings and Parodies.   New York: Cassell,
        [1892], p. 225.

1407   Parsons, Eugene.   Tennyson's Life and Poetry: And Mistakes
        Concerning Tennyson.   [Chicago: Craig, 1892.]
        Of interest to the specialist in Tennyson because it discusses
        mistakes about Tennyson made by other critics.   Reviewed by:
        Critic (New York) (entry 1454).

1408   Ritchie, Anne.   "Alfred Tennyson."   Records of Tennyson,
        Ruskin, Browning.   New York: Harper, 1892, pp. 3-60.
        Reprinted from: Harper's Monthly Magazine, 1883 (entry
        1054).
              Anne Ritchie was the daughter of William Makepeace Thacker-
        ay and was well acquainted with Tennyson.   Her discussion remains
        valuable to scholars, particularly biographers.
              Ritchie remarks: "Alfred's first verses, so I once heard
        him say, were written upon a slate which his brother Charles put
        into his hand one Sunday at Louth, when all the elders of the party
        were going into church, and the child was left alone.   Charles gave
        him a subject--the flowers in the garden--and when he came back
        from church little Alfred brought the slate to his brother all covered
        with written lines of blank verse.   They were made on the model of
        Thomson's Seasons, the only poetry he had ever read."   She contin-
        ues: "Alfred Tennyson, as he grew up towards manhood, found other
        and stronger inspirations than Thomson's gentle Seasons.   Byron's
        spell had fallen on his generation, and for a boy of genius it must

have been absolute and overmastering. Tennyson was soon to find his own voice, but meanwhile he began to write like Byron." Further: "One thing which cannot fail to strike us when we are looking over the records of these earlier days is the remarkable influence which Alfred Tennyson seems to have had from the very first upon his contemporaries, even before his genius had been recognized by the rest of the world."

On In Memoriam: "In Memoriam, with music in its cantos, belonging to the school of all men's sad hearts, rings the awful De Profundis of death, faced and realized as far as may be by a human soul. It came striking suddenly into all the sweet ideal beauty and lovely wealth which had gone before, with a revelation of that secret of life which is told to each of us in turn by the sorrow of its own soul." On Idylls of the King: "If In Memoriam is the record of a human soul, the Idylls mean the history, not of one man or of one generation, but of a whole cycle, of the faith of a nation failing and falling away into darkness. The first 'Idyll' and the last, I have heard Lord Tennyson say, are intentionally more archaic than the others. 'The whole is the dream of man coming into practical life, and ruined by one sin.'"

Reviewed by: Critic (New York) (entry 1457); Dial (entry 1472); Literary World (London) (entry 1530); National Observer (entry 1562); Saturday Review (London) (entry 1594); and Speaker (entry 1596).

1409 Rowe, F.J. Introduction to The Coming of Arthur and The Passing of Arthur. London: Macmillan, 1892.

1410 Stedman, Edmund Clarence. The Nature and Elements of Poetry. Boston: Houghton, Mifflin, 1892.
Tennyson on pages 68-70.

1411 Sterne, Ernest Staveley. In Memory of Alfred, Lord Tennyson, the English Theocritus. London: Sterne, [c1892].

1412 Swanwick, Anna. "Lord Tennyson." Poets: The Interpreters of Their Age. London: Bell, 1892, pp. 380-387.

1413 Taylor, Achilles. Sermonettes from Tennyson. Birmingham: Leicester and Leamington, 1892.

1414 Wallace, Percy M. Introduction to Tennyson: The Princess. London: Macmillan, 1892.

1415 Waugh, Arthur. Alfred Lord Tennyson: A Study of His Life and Work. London: Heinemann, 1892.
An interesting biography that has been superseded by subsequent ones.
Reviewed by: Critic (New York) (entry 1458); Dial (entry 1713); R. Le Gallienne in Academy (entry 1523); Literary World (Boston), 1893 and 1896 (entries 1735 and 1922); Saturday Review (London), 1892 and 1896 (entries 1592 and 1934); and Spectator (entry 1765).

1416 Winter, William. "Tennyson's 'Foresters.'" Shadows of the
      Stage. Edinburgh: 1892, pp. 269-285.
      Winter's observations on the production of the play at Daly's
Theatre.

Periodicals

1417 Ainger, Alfred. "The Death of Tennyson." Macmillan's
      Magazine, 67 (Nov. 1892), 76-80.
      Reprinted: Lectures and Essays, 1905 (entry 2384).

1418 Aldrich, Thomas Bailey. "Tennyson." Critic (New York),
      21 (Nov. 26, 1892), 289.
      A poem.

1419 "Alfred Baron Tennyson." Gentleman's Magazine, 273 (Nov.
      1892), 535-540.

1420 "Alfred Tennyson." Book News Monthly, 11 (Nov. 1892),
      68-69.

1421 "Alfred Tennyson." Literary World (Boston), 23 (Oct. 22,
      1892), 372-373.

1422 "Alfred Tennyson." Dial, 13 (Oct. 16, 1892), 231-236.
      Includes a bibiliography on pages 235-236.

1423 "Alfred Tennyson." National Observer, 8 (Oct. 8, 1892),
      521-522.

1424 "Alfred Tennyson's Play at Daly's." World (New York),
      March 18, 1892, p. 10.
      Friendly commentary.

1425 Allen, Grant. "Tennyson's Homes at Aldworth and Farring-
      ford." English Illustrated Magazine, 10 (1892), 145-156.

1426 Arnold, Edwin. Critic (New York), 21 (Oct. 15, 1892), 210.
      A poem.

1427 "Art and Architecture in Tennyson's Poetry." American
      Architect and Building News, 38 (Nov. 5, 1892), 87-90.

1428 Athenaeum, April 16, 1892, pp. 491-493.
      Review of The Foresters. Likes the play.

1429 Austin, Alfred. "The Passing of Merlin." Critic (New York),
      21 (Oct. 15, 1892), 210-211.
      Reprinted: Autobiography, 1911 (entry 2651). A poem, as
follows:

The Passing of Merlin

> I am Merlin,
> And I am dying,
> I am Merlin
> Who follow The Gleam.
>   Tennyson's <u>Merlin and the Gleam</u>.

I

Merlin has gone--has gone!--and through the land
The melancholy message wings its way;
To careless-ordered garden by the bay,
Back o'er the narrow strait to island strand,
Where Camelot looks down on wild Broceliand.

II

Merlin has gone, Merlin the Wizard who found,
In the Past's glimmering tide, and hailed him King,
Arthur, great Uther's son, and so did sing
The mystic glories of the Table Round,
That ever its name will live so long as Song shall sound.

III

Merlin has gone, Merlin who followed the Gleam,
And made us follow it; flying tale
Of the Last Tournament, the Holy Grail,
And Arthur's Passing; till the Enchanter's dream
Dwells with us still awake, no visionary theme.

IV

To-day is dole in Astolat, and dole
In Celidon the forest, dole and tears.
In joyous Gard blackhooded lean the spears:
The nuns of Almesbury sound a mournful toll,
And Guinevere kneeling weeps, and prays for Merlin's soul.

V

A wailing cometh from the shores that veil
Avilion's island valley; on the mere,
Looms through the mist and wet winds weeping blear
A dusky barge, which, without oar or sail,
Fades to the far-off fields where falls nor snow nor hail.

VI

Of all his wounds He will be healed now,
Wounds of harsh time and vulnerable life,
Fatigue of rest and weariness of strife,
Doubt and the long deep questionings that plough
The forehead of age, but bring no harvest to the brow.

VII

And there He will be comforted; but we
Must watch, like Bedivere, the dwindling light
That slowly shrouds Him darkling from our sight.
From the great deep to the great deep hath He
Passed, and, if now He knows, is mute eternally.

VIII

From Somersby's ivied tower there sinks and swells
A low slow peal, that mournfully is rolled
Over the long gray fields and glimmering wold,
To where, 'twixt sandy tracts and moorland fells,
Remembers Locksley Hall his musical farewells.

IX

And many a sinewy youth on Cam to-day
Suspends the dripping oar and lets his boat
Like dreaming water-lily drift and float,
While murmuring to himself the undying lay
That haunts the babbling Wye and Severn's dirgeful bay.

X

The bole of the broad oak whose knotted knees
Lie hidden in the fern of Sumner Place,
Feels stirred afresh, as when Olivia's face
Lay warm against its rind, though now it sees
Not Love but Death approach, and shivers in the breeze.

XI

In many a Vicarage garden, dense with age,
The haunt of pairing throstles, many a grange
Moated against the assault and siege of change,
Fair eyes consult anew the cherished Sage,
And now and then a tear falls blistering the page.

XII

April will blossom again, again will ring
With cuckoo's call and yaffel's flying scream,
And in veiled sleep the nightingale will dream,
Warbling as if awake.   But what will bring
His sweet note back?   He mute, it scarcely will be Spring.

XIII

The Seasons sorrow for Him, and the Hours
Droop, like to bees belated in the rain.
The unmoving shadow of a pensive pain

Lies on the lawn and lingers on the flowers,
And sweet and sad seem one in woodbine-woven bowers.

XIV

In English gardens fringed with English foam,
Or girt with English woods, He loved to dwell,
Singing of English lives in thorp or dell,
Orchard or croft; so that, when now we roam
Through them, and find Him not, it scarcely feels like home.

XV

And England's glories stirred Him as the swell
Of bluff winds blowing from Atlantic brine
Stirs mightier music in the murmuring pine.
Then sweet notes waxed to strong within his shell,
And bristling rose the lines, and billowy rose and fell.

XVI

So England mourns for Merlin, though its tears
Flow not from bitter source that wells in vain,
But kindred rather to the rippling rain
That brings the daffodil sheath and jonquil spears,
When Winter weeps away and April reappears.

XVII

For never hath England lacked a voice to sing
Her fairness and her fame, not will she now.
Silence awhile may brood upon the bough,
But shortly once again the Isle will ring
With wakening winds of March and rhapsodies of Spring.

XVIII

From Arthur unto Alfred, Alfred crowned
Monarch and Minstrel both, to Edward's day,
From Edward to Elizabeth, the lay
Of valour and love hath never ceased to sound,
But Song and Sword are twin, indissolubly bound.

XIX

Nor shall in Britain Taliessin tire
Transmitting through his stock the sacred strain.
When fresh renown prolongs Victoria's Reign,
Some patriot hand will sweep the living lyre,
And prove, with native notes, that Merlin was his sire.

1430 _____. "Tennyson's Literary Sensitiveness." National Review, 20 (Dec. 1892), 454-460.

Reprinted: <u>Eclectic Magazine of Foreign Literature</u>, 120 (Feb. 1893), 230-234.
Austin discusses conversations he had with Tennyson and asserts that Tennyson's innocence made him sensitive.

1431   Bayne, Thomas. "Charles Lamb and Lord Tennyson." <u>Notes and Queries</u>, 8th ser. 2 (Sept. 10, 1892), 206.

1432   Beale, Dorothea. "Tennyson." <u>Spectator</u>, 69 (Oct. 29, 1892), 595.
A poem.

1433   <u>Birmingham Gazette</u>, March 29, 1892, p. 4.
Review of <u>The Foresters</u>.

1434   Blakeney, E. H. "The Teaching of Tennyson." <u>Churchman</u>, Dec. 1892.
Reprinted: 1893 (entry 1661).

1435   _____. "Tennysoniana." <u>Academy</u>, 42 (Nov. 19, 1892), 461.

1436   Bleibtreu, Karl. "Tennyson." <u>Zukunft</u>, 1 (Oct. 22, 1892), 169-173.

1437   <u>Book Buyer</u>, 9 (May 1892), 174-175.
Review of <u>The Foresters</u>.

1438   Boswell, R. Bruce. "Lord Tennyson and Mr. Churton Collins: 'The Miller's Daughter.'" <u>Notes and Queries</u>, 8th ser. 1 (April 30, 1892), 359.

1439   Bourdillon, Francis William. "Tennyson." <u>Critic</u> (New York), 21 (Nov. 5, 1892), 256.
A Poem.

1440   Bradley, E. T. "The Burial of Tennyson." <u>Critic</u> (New York), 21 (Nov. 26, 1892), 286-288.

1441   Brandl, Alois. "Tennysons Bruder." <u>Allgemeine Zeitung</u>, 4 (1892-1893), 289-290.

1442   Brooke, Stopford Augustus. "Tennyson." <u>Contemporary Review</u>, 62 (July 1892), 761-785.
A discussion of Tennyson's views on literature, religion, and society.

1443   Brown, Anna Robertson. "Celtic Element in Tennyson's 'Lady of Shalott.'" <u>Poet Lore</u>, 4 (1892), 408-415.

1444   Browne, Irving. "Elucidating Tennyson." <u>Critic</u> (New York), 20 (Jan. 9, 1892), 25.
See also: "'Elucidating' Tennyson" in <u>Critic</u> (New York) (entry 1481).

1445 Buchanan, Robert Williams. "The Galahad of Song." Critic
     (New York), 21 (Oct. 15, 1892), 210.
     A poem.

1446 "The Burial of Tennyson." Pall Mall Budget, 40 (Oct. 13,
     1892), 1502-1505.

1447 Chestnutt, J. "In Memoriam." Notes and Queries, 8th ser.
     2 (Nov. 26, 1892), 430.

1448 "Christianity in Tennyson's Poetry." Pall Mall Budget, 40
     (Nov. 10, 1892), 1659.

1449 Clarke, Henry V. "Alfred Tennyson." Munsey's Magazine,
     7 (May 1892), 189-194.

1450 Cobbe, Frances Power. "Lord Tennyson." Spectator, 69
     (Oct. 15, 1892), 527.

1451 Cole, Samuel Valentine. "The Return." Critic (New York),
     21 (Oct. 22, 1892), 223.
     A poem.

1452 Conway, Moncure Daniel. "Tennyson's Pilgrimage." Open
     Court, 6 (Nov. 17, 1892), 3455-3459.

1453 Critic (New York), 20 (March 26, 1892), 186-187.
     Review of the New York production of The Foresters. The
reviewer is unimpressed.

1454 Critic (New York), 20 (June 25, 1892), 351.
     Mentions E. Parsons's Tennyson's Life and Poetry (entry
1407).

1455 Critic (New York), 21 (Nov. 5, 1892), 245.
     Review of The Death of OEnone.

1456 Critic (New York), 21 (Nov. 26, 1892), 288.
     Notes the failure of the Prince of Wales to attend the funeral
of Tennyson.

1457 Critic (New York), 21 (Dec. 17, 1892), 337.
     Review of A. Ritchie's Records, 1892 (entry 1408).

1458 Critic (New York), 21 (Dec. 31, 1892), 369-370.
     Review of A. Waugh's Alfred Lord Tennyson, 1892 (entry
1415).

1459 Daily Graphic, April 2, 1892, p. 439.
     Discusses the New York production of The Foresters. Likes
the play.

1460 Daily News, March 29, 1892, p. 2.
     Review of The Foresters.

1461 D'Albeville, J.W. "The Origin of Tennyson's 'Rizpah.'"
Bookman (London), 3 (Dec. 1892), 78.

1462 D'Annunzio, G. "Tennyson." Mattino, 1 (1892).

1463 Darmesteter, Mary James. "Tennyson." Revue bleue, 50
(Nov. 12, 1892), 619-623.
Denigrates Tennyson as a thinker but likes his lyricism.

1464 Davies, W.W. "Lord Tennyson's 'The Foresters.'" Notes
and Queries, 8th ser. 1 (May 28, 1892), 432.

1465 "The Death of Tennyson." Spectator, 69 (Oct. 8, 1892),
484-485.

1466 De Blowitz. "Le Poète-Lauréat." Le Gaulois, Oct. 7, 1892.
Asserts that Tennyson's poetry has universal appeal.

1467 de P., F. "Tennyson." Le Temps, Oct. 7, 1892.
The author defends Tennyson against misinformed opinions.

1468 de Vere, Aubrey. "The Land's Vigil." Nineteenth Century,
32 (Nov. 1892), 840.
A poem, as follows:

The Land's Vigil

How many a face throughout the Imperial Isle
From southern shores to Scottish hill or hall,
From Cambrian vales to Windsor's royal pile
Turned sadly towards one house more sad than all,
Turned day by day, fear-blanched! When evening's
More late round such descended many a mile,
How oft sad eyes, fixed on one thought the while.
Not seeing, seemed to see a taper small,
Night after night, flashed from one casement high!
Let these men sing his praise! Others there are
Who fitlier might have sung them in old time,
Since they loved best who loved him in his prime--
Their youth, and his, expired long since and far:--
Now he is gone it seems once more to die.

1469 _____. "In Westminster Abbey." Nineteenth Century,
32 (Nov. 1892), 840-841.
A poem, as follows:

In Westminster Abbey

'Tis well! not always nations are ingrate!
He gave his country of his best; and she
Gave to her bard, in glorious rivalry,
Her whole great heart. A People and a State
Had met, through love a Tomb to consecrate:--

In the Abbey old each order and degree
They knelt, and upward gazing seemed to see
Not that dark vault, but Heaven's expanding gate.
O'er him the death-song he had made they sung:--
Thus, when in Rome the Prince of Painters died,
His Art's last marvel o'er his bier was hung[1]
At once in heavenly hope and honest pride:
Thus England honoured him she loved that day:
Thus many prayed--as England's Saints will pray.

1470 _____. "The Poet." Nineteenth Century, 32 (Nov. 1892),
841.
A poem, as follows:

The Poet

None sang of Love more nobly; few as well;
Of friendship none with pathos so profound;
Of Duty sternliest-proved when myrtle-crowned;
Of English grove and rivulet, mead and dell:
Great Arthur's Legend he alone dared tell;
Milton and Dryden feared to tread that ground;
For him alone o'er Camelot's faery bound
The 'horns of Elfland' blew their magic spell.
Since Shakespeare and since Wordsworth none hath sung
So well his England's greatness; none hath given
Reproof more fearless or advice more sage;
None inlier taught how near to earth is Heaven;
With what vast concords Nature's harp is strung;
How base false pride;--faction's fanatic rage.

1471 de Wyzewa, Téodor. "Lord Tennyson." Le Figaro, Oct. 9,
1892, p. 1.
The author ranks Tennyson as one of England's three best
contemporary writers, along with William Morris and James Froude.

1472 Dial, 13 (Dec. 1, 1892), 339-342.
Review of A. Ritchie's Records, 1892 (entry 1408).

1473 Dieter, Ferdinand. "Alfred Tennyson." Die Gegenwart, 42
(Nov. 12, 1892), 309-312.

1474 Dobson, Austin. "Alfred, Lord Tennyson." Athenaeum, Oct.
8, 1892, p. 483.
Reprinted: Critic (New York), 21 (Oct. 22, 1892), 224-225;
and Collected Poems, 1913 (entry 2717).
A poem, as follows:

---

1. Raffael's Transfiguration.

Alfred, Lord Tennyson
Emigravit, October VI., MDCCCXCII

Grief there will be, and may,
When King Apollo's bay
Is cut midwise;
Grief that a song is stilled,
Grief for the unfulfilled
Singer that dies.

Not so we mourn thee now,
Not so we grieve that thou,
MASTER, art passed,
Since thou thy song didst raise,
Through the full round of days,
E'en to the last.

Grief there may be, and will,
When that the singer still
Sinks in the song;
When that the wingéd rhyme
Fails of the promised prime,
Ruined and wrong.

1475 Dowden, Edward. "Tennyson as a Teacher." Illustrated London News, 101 (Oct. 15, 1892), 490.

1476 "A Dream of Fair Women." Notes and Queries, 8th ser. 2 (Dec. 10, 1892), 478.

1477 "An Early French Estimate of Tennyson." Athenaeum, Oct. 22, 1892, pp. 554-555.

1478 "Early Recollections." Bookman (London), 3 (Nov. 1892), 50-51.

1479 Eclectic Magazine of Foreign Literature, 119 (Dec. 1892), 853-854.
     Review of The Death of OEnone.

1480 Egan, Maurice Francis. "Of Tennyson." Catholic World, 56 (Nov. 1892), 149-157.

1481 "'Elucidating' Tennyson." Critic (New York), 20 (June 25, 1892), 357.
     See also: I. Browne (entry 1444).

1482 Farrar, Frederick William. "Lord Tennyson as a Religious Teacher." Review of Reviews and World's Work (New York), 6 (Dec. 1892), 570-572.

1483 Filon, Augustin. "Lord Tennyson." Journal des Débats, March 11, 1892.

Filon asserts that Tennyson's poetry is essentially musical, although profoundly moral.

1484 "The Foresters." Critic (New York), 20 (April 16, 1892), 232.
A parody.

1485 Formentin, C. "Tennyson chez Stéphane Mallarmé." Echo de Paris, Oct. 8, 1892.
An interview of Mallarmé, who praises Tennyson.

1486 Forshaw, Charles F. "Lord Tennyson on Tobacco." Notes and Queries, 8th ser. 2 (Oct. 22 and Dec. 3, 1892), 326 and 450.

1487 Fowler, William J. "Whittier and Tennyson." Arena, 7 (Dec. 1892), 1-11.

1488 "The Funeral." Spectator, 69 (Oct. 15, 1892), 516-517.

1489 G., S.G. (S.G. Green?) "Browning and Tennyson." Leisure Hour, 39 (April 1890), 231-234.

1490 Garnett, Richard. "Alfred, Lord Tennyson." Illustrated London News, 101 (Oct. 15, 1892), 474.

1491 Gates, Lewis Edwards. "Romantic Elements in Lord Tennyson's Poetry." Harvard Monthly, 15 (Nov. 1892), 45-60.

1492 Gatty, Alfred. "A Line in 'Locksley Hall.'" Notes and Queries, 8th ser. 2 (Nov. 12, 1892), 387.

1493 "The Genius of Tennyson." Spectator, 69 (Oct. 15, 1892), 522-524.
Reprinted: Littell's Living Age, 195 (Nov. 19, 1892), 505-510; and Eclectic Magazine of Foreign Literature, 119 (Dec. 1892), 808-817.

1494 Gentleman's Magazine, 273 (Dec. 1892), 641-642.
Review of The Death of OEnone.

1495 Gilder, Richard Watson. "The Silence of Tennyson." Critic (New York), 21 (Oct. 15, 1892), 204.
Reprinted: Current Opinion, 11 (Dec. 1892), 475; and The Poems of Richard Watson Gilder, 1908 (entry 2487). A poem.

1496 Globe, March 29, 1892, p. 3.
Review of The Foresters. Admires the play.

1497 Gosse, Edmund William. "Tennyson." New Review, 7 (Nov. 1892), 513-532.
Reprinted: Littell's Living Age, 195 (Dec. 17, 1892), 707-713.

1498 Griswold, Hattie Tyng. "The Silent Singer." <u>Dial</u>, 13 (Oct. 16, 1892), 231.
A poem, as follows:

The Silent Singer

Far aback in the years grown misty,
　Far away from the days that be,
Sang a poet of Love and Duty,
　Songs that were set to a brave new key.
Trembled the heartstrings as he swept them,
　Stirred and trembled at great new words;
Great, but sweet to the ears that listened,
　Tender and sweet as the song of birds.

Ever the voice rose high and higher,
　Clearer the note and purer the tone;
Wider the thought and deeper the insight,
　Year by year as the songs were sown.
Soon the music the earth had girdled,
　Every nation had caught the strain;
Echoes sprang from the highest mountain,
　Kindred thought from the farthest plain.

Now at last is the singer silent;
　All of the Idylls are said and sung:
His voice is lost from the autumn spaces,
　The anthem dies on the harp unstrung.
Death's bugle has sounded the final tourney,
　The nations listen, both near and far,--
The last great bard world-crowned with laurel,
　Worn and weary, has "crossed the bar."

1499 "Die Grossen Todten." <u>Deutsche Rundschau</u>, 73 (1892), 308-309.

1500 Hales, John W. "South Grammar School." <u>Gentleman's Magazine</u>, 273 (Dec. 1892), 562-573.

1501 [Halsey, F.W.] "The Laureate's Career." <u>Critic</u> (New York), 21 (Oct. 15, 1892), 204-212.

1502 Hayne, William H. "Tennyson's Early and Late Lyrics." <u>Critic</u> (New York), 21 (Dec. 10, 1892), 332.
A poem.

1503 <u>Herald</u> (Glasgow), March 29, 1892, p. 4.
Review of <u>The Foresters</u>. Generally positive comments.

1504 Huxley, T[homas] H[enry]. "Westminster Abbey: Oct. 12, 1892." <u>Nineteenth Century</u>, 32 (Nov. 1892), 831-832.
Reprinted: <u>Critic</u> (New York), 21 (Nov. 26, 1892), 288. A poem, as follows:

Westminster Abbey
October 12, 1892

Gib diesen Todten mir heraus![1]
(The Minister speaks)

Bring me my dead!
To me that have grown,
Stone laid upon stone,
As the stormy brood
Of English blood
Has waxed and spread
And filled the world,
With sails unfurled;
With men that may not lie;
With thoughts that cannot die.

Bring me my dead!
Into the storied hall,
Where I have garnered all
My harvest without weed;
My chosen fruits of goodly seed;
And lay him gently down among
The men of state, the men of song:
The men that would not suffer wrong:
The thought-worn chieftains of the mind:
Head servants of the human kind.

Bring me my dead!
The autumn sun shall shed
Its beans athwart the bier's
Heaped blooms: a many tears
Shall flow; his words, in cadence sweet and
Shall voice the full hearts of the silent throng.
Bring me my dead!

And oh! sad wedded mourner, seeking still
For vanished hand-clasp: drinking in thy fill
Of holy grief; forgive, that pious theft
Robs thee of all, save memories, left:
Not thine to kneel beside the grassy mound
While dies the western glow; and all around
Is silence: and the shadows closer creep
And whisper softly: All must fall asleep.

1505 Independent, 44 (April 28, 1892), 592.
Review of The Foresters.

1506 Independent, 44 (Nov. 10, 1892), 1598.
Review of The Death of OEnone.

1. Don Carlos.

1507   Jacobs, Joseph. "Alfred Tennyson." Academy, 42 (Oct. 15,
       1892), 335-337.
       An obituary.

1508   Johnson, L. Academy, 42 (Nov. 5, 1892), 403-405.
       Review of The Death of OEnone.

1509   Johnson, Rossiter. "Tennyson, Poe and Admiral Farragut."
       Critic (New York), 21 (Oct. 22, 1892), 224.

1510   Jones, D.M. "The Religious Teaching of Tennyson."
       Wesleyan Methodist Magazine, 115 (1892), 876-880.

1511   Keeling, A.E. "Tennyson." Wesleyan Methodist Magazine,
       115 (1892), 925-932.

1512   Knowles, James. "Apotheosis: Westminster, October 1892
       (An allegory)." Nineteenth Century, 32 (Nov. 1892), 843-844.
       A poem, as follows:

Apotheosis
Westminster, October 1892
(An allegory)

The peasants of Parnassus come to fling
   Their wreaths upon the grave of Orpheus.
Their Master and the Flower of Men lies low,
His coffin resting on a bed of flowers--
And these would scatter flowers above his head.

But there was loftier tribute when the gods,
The deathless gods, descended to this fane
From high Olympos at the festival
Of his translation to the starry realm.
They stood around the portals of the tomb
Invisible, yet dimly felt by all,
In the hush't awe that fell upon the hearts
Of those who came to mourn and honour him.
--Dianna, who had stayed her 'silver wheels'
And called his soul to her from midnight skies;
--Demeter, who had purified with fire[1]
The dark earth-chasm where his bones should rest;
--Persephone, with lap of lasting blooms
To deck his pathway to Elysium;
--Apollo, towering from floor to roof
In sunbeams turn'd to music, while the songs
Of him who lay so still, like incense rose;
--And clear-eyed Pallas who had led his feet

---

1.   As the grave was being hewn out of the hard rock-like founda-
tions of the Abbey, it was filled continually with sparks of fire struck
from the stone and flint.

Secure to topmost heights of Wisdom's hill
--All these were there, and from the crowds of men
Their sovran presence rapt their blessed one
To peace and rest for ever--in their arms--
Amid his kindred gods and demigods.

Great Bard! dear Friend! thy welcome by the gods
Is our sole comfort for the loss of thee;
They will be happier in their golden clime,
And Heaven, when we reach it, more like Home.

1513 König, Robert. "Zu Alfred Tennysons Gedächtnis." Daheim, 29 (Nov. 19, 1892), 102-104.

1514 "The Last Message." Speaker, 6 (Nov. 5, 1892), 553-554.

1515 "The Late Alfred, Baron Tennyson, Poet Laureate." Illustrated London News, 101 (Oct. 15, 1892), 483-490. Reprinted: Neuphilologisches Centralblatt, 7 (1893), 8-11.

1516 "The Late Lord Tennyson." Pall Mall Budget, 40 (Nov. 3, 1892), 1639.

1517 "The Laureate's Career." Critic (New York), 21 (Oct. 15, 1892), 204-209.

1518 "The Laureate's Funeral." Critic (New York), 21 (Oct. 22, 1892), 223-224.

1519 "The Laureateship." Spectator, 69 (Oct. 15, 1892), 517-518.

1520 "The Laureateship." Critic (New York), 21 (Nov. 5, 1892), 255-256.

1521 "The Laureateship." Illustrated London News, 101 (Oct. 15, 1892), 491.

1522 Le Gallienne, Richard. Academy, 41 (Jan. 16, 1892), 55-57. Review of J.C. Collins's Illustrations of Tennyson, 1891 (entry 1354).

1523 _____. Academy, 42 (Nov. 12, 1892), 427-429. Review of A. Waugh's Alfred Lord Tennyson, 1892 (entry 1415).

1524 Lillie, Lucy C. "Tennyson's Home Life." Independent, 44 (Oct. 27, 1892), 1510-1511.

1525 "Literary Notes." Pall Mall Budget, 40 (Aug. 11, 1892), 1190.

1526 Literary World (Boston), 23 (April 23, 1892), 141. Review of The Foresters.

1527 Literary World (Boston), 23 (Oct. 22, 1892), 376-377.
Note on Tennyson.

1528 Literary World (Boston), 23 (Nov. 19, 1892), 401-402.
Review of The Death of OEnone.

1529 Literary World (London), 45 (April 8, 1892), 331-332.
Review of The Foresters.

1530 Literary World (London), 46 (Oct. 21, 1892), 299-300.
Review of A. Ritchie's Records, 1892 (entry 1408).

1531 Literary World (London), 46 (Nov. 4, 1892), 347-348.
Review of The Death of OEnone.

1532 Loliée, Frédéric. "Les Disparus: Alfred Tennyson."
Nouvelle Revue, 79 (Nov. 1892), 175-181.
Discusses Tennyson as a poet for women.

1533 "Lord Tennyson." Pall Mall Budget, 40 (Oct. 6, 1892),
1465-1472 and 1500.

1534 "Lord Tennyson." Saturday Review (London), 74 (Oct. 8,
1892), 405-406.

1535 "Lord Tennyson." Speaker, 6 (Oct. 8, 1892), 429-431.

1536 "Lord Tennyson." Literary World (London), 46 (Oct. 14,
1892), 284-285.

1537 "Lord Tennyson." Westminster Review, 138 (Dec. 1892),
589-596.

1538 "Lord Tennyson and Sir Henry Parkes." Pall Mall Budget,
40 (Nov. 24, 1892), 1750.

1539 "Lord Tennyson's Fancy." Spectator, 68 (April 2, 1892),
458-459.

1540 "Lord Tennyson's Foresters at Daly's Pleases the Public."
Commercial Advertiser, March 18, 1892.
Listed in C. Tennyson and C. Fall, Alfred Tennyson (entry
4016), page 123.

1541 "Lord Tennyson's Funeral." Dial, 13 (Oct. 16, 1892), 236.

1542 "Lord Tennyson's Funeral." Littell's Living Age, 195 (Nov.
19, 1892), 510-512.

1543 "Lord Tennyson's Play." Times, March 19, 1892, p. 7.
Review of the New York production of The Foresters.

1544   Mabie, Hamilton Wright. "The Influence of Tennyson in
       America: Its Sources and Extent." Review of Reviews
       (New York), 6 (Dec. 1892), 553-556.

1545   _____. "Tennyson the Artist." Christian Union, 46 (Oct.
       29, 1892), 786-787.

1546   Mallarmé, Stéphane. "Tennyson vu d'ici." National Observer,
       8 (Oct. 29, 1892), 611-612.
          Reprinted: Revue Blanche, Dec. 1892; and Divagations,
       1897 (entry 1946).
          Mallarmé admires Tennyson's poetry, particularly Maud,
       "Locksley Hall," "The Lotos-Eaters," "OEnone," and In Memoriam.
       He asserts that Tennyson's reputation will improve in France.

1547   Manchester Examiner, March 30, 1892, p. 5.
          Review of The Foresters. Finds the play pleasantly light.

1548   Martin, Theodore. "Tennyson and 'Cymbeline.'" Blackwood's
       Edinburgh Magazine, 152 (Nov. 1892), 767.
          A poem, as follows:

                    Tennyson and "Cymbeline"

          ["My father was reading 'Lear,' 'Troilus and Cressida,'
       and 'Cymbeline,' through the last days of his life. On Wed-
       nesday he asked for his Shakespeare; I gave him the book,
       but said, 'You must not try to read.' He answered, 'I have
       opened the book.' I looked at the book at midnight, when
       I was sitting by him lying dead on the Thursday, and I
       found that he had opened it on one of those passages which
       he called the tenderest of Shakespeare--
                    Hang there, like fruit, my soul,
                    Till the tree die.
       It was probably an answer to a message that I had given
       him from my mother."--Letter from Hallam Tennyson to
       the Chairman of Executive Committee, Shakespeare's Birth-
       place, 14th October 1892.]

       "Bring me my Shakespeare! There! So let it rest!"
          Then, as fair visions from that treasury vast
       Of noble women through his memory passed,
       He turned to find the page, where to his breast
       Her Posthumus in rapturous frenzy pressed
          Divinest Imogen with the wild cry,
          "Hang there, like fruit, my soul, till the tree die,"
       There paused, like one by some sweet thought caressed.

       Was it his "other dearer life in life"[1]
          With Shakespeare's Imogen was mated then?

       _____
       1.   From "The Miller's Daughter."

> Were all the tender heart-warm memories rife,
> Had hallowed her for him, most blest of men,
> "The queen of marriage, a most perfect wife,"[2]
> Soul of his soul, his own dear Imogen?

1549　Matthews, J. "Tennyson's Witness to the Higher Hope."
　　　　 Spectator, 69 (Oct. 29, 1892), 594-595.

1550　Miller, Joaquin. "The Passing of Tennyson." Critic (New
　　　　 York), 21 (Nov. 5, 1892), 256.

1551　"More Tennysoniana." Pall Mall Budget, 40 (Oct. 20, 1892),
　　　　 1558-1559.
　　　　 See also: "Tennyson Supplement" in Pall Mall Budget (entry
1613).

1552　Morris, Lewis. Critic (New York), 21 (Oct. 15, 1892),
　　　　 209-210.
　　　　 A poem.

1553　Moulton, Louise Chandler. "From Over the Sea." Critic
　　　　 (New York), 21 (Nov. 26, 1892), 289.
　　　　 A poem.

1554　　　　　. "Tennyson." Literary World (Boston), 23 (Dec.
　　　　 17, 1892), 476.
　　　　 A poem.

1555　Mount, C.B. "Aylmer's Field." Notes and Queries, 8th ser.
　　　　 1 (June 25, 1892), 524.
　　　　 See also: C.B. Mount in Notes and Queries, 1891 (entry
1379).

1556　Myers, Frederic W.H. "The Height and the Deep." Nine-
　　　　 teenth Century, 32 (Nov. 1892), 833-834.
　　　　 A poem, as follows:

The Height and the Deep

Καὶ αὐτὸς οὐρανὸς ἀκύμων. --Plotinus

1

> When from that world ere death and birth
> 　He sought the stern descending way,
> Perfecting on our darkened earth
> 　His spirit, citizen of day;--
> Guessed he the pain, the lonely years,--
> 　The thought made true, the will made strong?
> Divined he from the singing spheres

2.　From "Isabel."

Eternal fragments of his song?

2

Hoped he from dimness to discern
  The Source, the Goal, that glances through?--
That One should know, and many turn--
  Turn heavenward, knowing that he knew?--
Once more he rises; lulled and still,
  Hushed to his tune the tideways roll;
These waveless heights of evening thrill
  With voyage of the summoned Soul.

3

O closing shades that veil and drown
  The clear-obscure of shore and tree!
O star and planet, shimmering down
  Your sombre glory on the sea!
O Soul that yearned to soar and sing,
  Enamoured of immortal air!
Heart that thro' sundering change must cling
  To dream and memory, sad and fair!

4

Sun, star, and space and dark and day
  Shall vanish in a vaster glow;
Souls shall climb fast their age-long way,
  With all to conquer, all to know:
But thou, true Heart! for aye shalt keep
  Thy loyal faith, thine ancient flame;--
Be stilled an hour, and stir from sleep
  Reborn, rerisen, and yet the same.

1557 "My Tennyson." Speaker, 6 (Oct. 15, 1892), 461-462.
        Reprinted: Littell's Living Age, 195 (Nov. 12, 1892),
446-448.

1558 MacArthur, James. "Discarded Poems of Tennyson's."
      Christian Union, 46 (Oct. 29, 1892), 787-789.

1559 McCarthy, Justin. "The Foresters." Gentleman's Magazine,
      272 (May 1892), 528-534.

1560 Macquoid, Thomas R. "Tennyson's Funeral." Literary
      World (Boston), 23 (Nov. 5, 1892), 388.

1561 National Observer, 7 (April 9, 1892), 540.
      Review of The Foresters.

1562 National Observer, 8 (Oct. 8, 1892), 539-540.
      Review of A. Ritchie's Records, 1892 (entry 1408).

1563   National Observer, 8 (Nov. 12, 1892), 660-661.
        Review of The Death of OEnone.

1564   Nencioni, Enrico. "Lord Tennyson." Nuova Antologia di
        Lettere, Scienze ed Arti, 125 (Oct. 6, 1892), 613-631.
        Praises Tennyson for his poetic skills and his expression
of human aspirations.

1565   Noel, Roden. "The Death of Tennyson." Nineteenth Century,
        32 (Nov. 1892), 835-836.
        A poem, as follows:

                        The Death of Tennyson

            The last of all our mighty bards is low,
            And who is left to wear the conqueror's crown?
            Bays all to ample for a lesser brow.
            I mourn the Master-singer and the friend.
              In at the oriel, as he passed, the moon
            Shone at her full; the stars looked; but no light
            Kindled by human hands confused the beam
            Wherewith God ushered him to worlds unknown,
            After the day's long task, accomplished well.
            He with the failing sense of one who faints
            From life to life beheld them, and the lands
            In elf-light lying, field, moor, autumn wood.
            Meet emblems of a fortune-favoured life,
            And ordered art, a fair, serene domain.

              So that loud-pealing thunderstorm which rapt
            The eagle soul of Byron from our ken
            In yon far land, in Greece, with birth-throes torn
            Of revolution, 'mid the clash and clang
            Of turbulent war, was emblem meet for him,
            Who from hot heart and idol-shattering soul
            Rolled the wild torrent of impetuous song,
            'Whelming old landmarks; exile young and broken,
            Whose dying lips might frame not their last wish
            To that one hired dependent; ah! not so
            Our later master, Tennyson, went forth
            From us but now; for he, from that pure home
            Deserved success had made for him, went forth
            Whispering words of love from his true heart
            To her true heart who loved him through the years.
            One hand on the dear volume he had opened,
            His Shakespeare, slept; well worn with noble use
            Gently as when a child he fell asleep,
            His mother keeping her love-vigil o'er him.
            Then the moon hallowed that sublime repose
            As of pale marble in cathedral gloom.

1566   _____. "Lord Tennyson, with a Few Personal Reminis-
        cences." Atlanta Magazine, 1892, p. 264.

1567 North, Ernest Dressel. "A Tennyson Bibliography." Critic (New York), 21 (Oct. 15, 1892), 211-212.

1568 "A Note on Tennyson." Bookman (London), 3 (Nov. 1892), 44-45.

1569 Oliphant, Margaret. "Alfred Tennyson." Spectator, 69 (Oct. 15, 1892), 528.
Reprinted: Littell's Living Age, 195 (Nov. 19, 1892), 450.
A poem.

1570 Palgrave, F[rancis] T[urner]. "In Pace." Nineteenth Century, 32 (Nov. 1892), 837-839.
A poem, as follows:

In Pace

Sad morrow dawn! when the presaging heart
    Fore-reads the pang, that o'er the whole world's face
    Perchance e'en now, leaping from space to space,
The silent lightnings dart:--

We knew the blow must fall, yet knew it not:
    For who the blank can gauge, though seen afar,
    Th' o'ershadowing eclipse, should Heaven's great Star
The sudden death-clouds blot?

--So, while Hope would not wholly veil her face,
    Nor the great soul had touch'd the further shore,
    I mourn'd the friend of forty years and more
As with love's last embrace.

Now, where the imperial speech from land to land
    Broadens, the death-shock thrills; the lord of song
    Supreme, thought set to music, sweet, yet strong,
Is with the immortal band

Who hail'd as brother the rapt Florentine,
    And those of kindred blood, whom later days
    Have crown'd for us with Phoebus' greenest bays,
Last of the lordly line,

Alfred to Alfred!--Who, with weaker hand,
    Unworthy, should recount thy varied page,
    Thy sweep o'er all the chords from youth to age,
Each Mode at thy command,

Sweet Lydian strain, chasten'd by Doric strength,
    Art lucid, sane, that check'd the o'er-fervent soul,
    Holding in leash all passion, till the goal
Was triumph-touch'd at length,

Our happier Vergil! whose long grasp of years

Gave thee thine Epic to full close to sing--
Then bade us look to Christ, and for thee bring
A farewell without tears:--

Ah yet, 'tis vain! The natural drops must fall
    For something more than the now-silenced strain,
    The sovran singer from his England ta'en,
The magic past recall:--

For as, when great the work, the workman still
    Is greater, all men knew that heart, that head,
    Noble among our noblest; wisdom-led,
Love leading wisdom: till

As from some weightiest judge the sentence slips,
    Wing'd by gay humour, kindly, such the word
    With insight fraught or happy counsel, heard
From those rich resonant lips,

Moved by the generous soul to frailty kind,
    Knowing himself; true to the inmost core;
    Poet, as poets were in years of yore,
High teacher of mankind,

Wisdom in beauty veil'd!--Or England's name
    Broke from the loyal breast, this dear, dear land,
    And, "O may she in strong-arm'd foresight stand
To guard her ancient fame

And Freedom law-obedient, and the throne
    Of Her, the gracious Empress:"--Ah! great Voice
    Now hush'd, for thee, for thee we may rejoice,
Changed to the realm unknown

In peace, safe piloted, safe from earthly fears,
    By that Eternal Love, thy Lord, received:--
    While to thy honour'd grave we bring, bereaved,
Our unavailing tears.

    --Not so! For him who gains the great release,
        Ready for death and life, no tears be shed:
        His own, God knoweth: o'er the loved one fled
    Let the last word be, Peace.

1571   Pall Mall Budget, 40 (Nov. 3, 1892), 1642.
       Review of The Death of OEnone.

1572   Parsons, Eugene. "Mistakes about Tennyson." Dial, 13
       (Nov. 1, 1892), 270.

1573   Paul, Herbert Woodfield. "Tennyson." New Review, 7 (Nov.
       1892), 513-532.
       Reprinted: Littell's Living Age, 195 (Dec. 17, 1892), 713-
718.

1574 Payne, William Morton. Dial, 13 (June 1892), 51.
      Review of The Foresters.

1575 _____. Dial, 13 (Dec. 1, 1892), 344-346.
      Review of The Death of OEnone.

1576 Peacock, Florence. "The Tennysons." Bookman (London),
      3 (Nov. 1892), 49-50.

1577 "Personalia." Critic (New York), 21 (Nov. 26, 1892), 289.

1578 Poet Lore, 4 (1892), 640-643.
      Review of The Death of OEnone.

1579 Price, Thomas R. "What after Lord Tennyson?" Independ-
      ent, 44 (Nov. 3, 1892), 1542-1543.

1580 Prideaux, W. F. "Lord Tennyson and Mr. Churton Collins."
      Notes and Queries, 8th ser. 2 (Aug. 27, 1892), 170-171.

1581 "The Question of the Laureateship." Bookman (London), 3
      (Nov. 1892), 52-55.

1582 Rawnsley, Hardwicke Drummond. "The Laureate Dead."
      Academy, 42 (Oct. 15, 1892), 335.
      Reprinted: Literary World (Boston), 23 (Dec. 17, 1892),
476; and Littell's Living Age, 195 (Dec. 17, 1892), 706. A poem.

1583 _____. "Leaving Aldworth: Oct. 11, 1892." Blackwood's
      Edinburgh Magazine, 152 (Nov. 1892), 768.
      A poem, as follows:

Leaving Aldworth
Oct. 11, 1892

["I chanced to be one of the few who walked from
Aldworth to Haslemere with the great poet's body. I
send you a sonnet which describes the scene as I saw it."]

A steamy thresher murmured from afar
  In the near copse a solitary hound
  Howled broken-heartedly, no other sound
Availed the absolute peacefulness to mar.
Then to the moss-lined laurel-woven car
  We bore the poet, laid the wreaths around,
  And so in silence left his garden ground,
While o'er us gleamed the first pale evening star.

The moon rose black against the dying day,
  And purple grew the dewy woodland dell,
    But from those lamps that lit the funeral wain
    Shone such a glory through the hollow lane,
  We felt, "with him who leads us all is well,"
And bravely followed down the darkened way.

1584   Review of Reviews (London), 6 (Sept. 1892), 298.
       Review of G. G. Napier's The Homes and Haunts of Alfred,
Lord Tennyson, 1892 (entry 1404).

1585   Riley, James Whitcomb. "Tennyson: England, October 5,
       1892." Critic (New York), 21 (Oct. 15, 1892), 211.
       Reprinted: Complete Works, 1913 (entry 2729). A poem,
as follows:

Tennyson
England, October 5, 1892

> We of the New World clasp hands with the Old
> In newer fervor and with firmer hold
>   And nobler fellowship!
> O Master Singer, with the finger-tip
> Of Death laid thus on thy melodious lip!
>
> All ages thou hast honored with thine art,
> And ages yet unborn thou wilt be part
>   Of all songs pure and true!
> Thine now the universal homage due
> From Old and New World--ay, and still
>   The New!

1586   Roberts, Robert. "Recollections of Tennyson." Bookman
       (London), 3 (Nov. 1892), 46-49.

1587   Rolfe, William James. "A Recent Visit to Tennyson." Critic
       (New York), 21 (Nov. 26, 1892), 285-286.

1588   Saint-Cère, Jacques. "Tennyson." Le Figaro, Oct. 7, 1892,
       p. 2.
       Ridicules Tennyson.

1589   "The Sale of Lord Tennyson's Birthplace." Pall Mall Budget,
       40 (Aug. 25, 1892), 1268.

1590   Sangster, Margaret E. "Tennyson." Critic (New York), 21
       (Nov. 5, 1892), 256.
       A poem.

1591   Saturday Review (London), 73 (April 2, 1892), 391-392.
       Review of The Foresters. Admires the play.

1592   Saturday Review (London), 74 (Oct. 22, 1892), 473-474.
       Review of A. Waugh's Alfred Lord Tennyson, 1892 (entry
1415).

1593   Saturday Review (London), 74 (Nov. 5, 1892), 536-537.
       Review of The Death of OEnone.

1594   Saturday Review (London), 74 (Nov. 5, 1892), 545-546.
       Review of A. Ritchie's Records, 1892 (entry 1408).

1595 Simcox, George Augustus. "In Memoriam--Lord Tennyson." Bookman (London), 3 (Nov. 1892), 43-44. A poem.

1596 Speaker, 6 (Oct. 8, 1892), 447-448. Review of A. Ritchie's Records, 1892 (entry 1408).

1597 Spectator, 68 (Feb. 6, 1892), 201-202. Discusses Tennyson's works.

1598 Spectator, 69 (Sept. 3, 1892), 325-327. Discusses Maud.

1599 Stead, William T. "Tennyson the Man: A Character Sketch." Review of Reviews (New York), 6 (Dec. 1892), 557-570.

1600 Steigler, G. "Qui remplacera Tennyson?" Echo de Paris, Oct. 18, 1892.

1601 Stewart, George. "Alfred Tennyson." Cosmopolitan, 14 (Dec. 1892), 169-178.

1602 Stitt, E. F. R. "Love and Duty in Tennyson and Browning." Poet Lore, 4 (1892), 271-274.

1603 Stoddard, Richard Henry. "The Poetry of Lord Tennyson." Independent, 44 (Oct. 20, 1892), 1469-1470.

1604 Tabb, John Banister. "Alfred Tennyson." Independent, 44 (Oct. 27, 1892), 1509.
Reprinted: Critic (New York), 21 (Nov. 5, 1892), 256. A poem.

1605 "Table Talk." Literary World (London), 46 (Oct. 14, 1892), 285-286.

1606 Tennyson, Alfred. "Me mine own fate to lasting sorrow doometh." Notes and Queries, 8th ser. 2 (Nov. 5, 1892), 361.
A sonnet.

1607 "Tennyson." Blackwood's Edinburgh Magazine, 152 (Nov. 1892), 748-766.
A tribute.

1608 "Tennyson." Nation (New York), 55 (Oct. 13, 1892), 276-278.

1609 "Tennyson." Review of Reviews (London), 6 (Nov. 1892), 436-447.

1610 "Tennyson and His Publishers." Bookman (London), 3 (Nov. 1892), 51-52.
Reprinted: Critic (New York), 21 (Dec. 3, 1892), 316.

1611 "Tennyson in Music." Review of Reviews (London), 6 (Nov. 1892), 447.

1612 "Tennyson in Song." Musical Times, 33 (Nov. 1, 1892), 655-656.

1613 "Tennyson Supplement." Pall Mall Budget, 40 (Oct. 13, 1892), 1517-1524.
See also: "More Tennysoniana" in Pall Mall Budget (entry 1551).

1614 "Tennysoniana." Athenaeum, Oct. 15, 1892, p. 517.

1615 "Tennysoniana." Athenaeum, Nov. 26, 1892, pp. 741-742.

1616 "Tennysoniana." Critic (New York), 21 (Oct. 29, 1892), 237-240.

1617 "Tennysoniana." Critic (New York), 21 (Nov. 5, 1892), 254.

1618 "Tennysoniana." Critic (New York), 21 (Nov. 19, 1892), 280-281.

1619 "Tennysoniana." Critic (New York), 21 (Dec. 3, 1892), 315-316.

1620 "Tennysoniana." Dial, 13 (Nov. 1, 1892), 265-267.

1621 "Tennysonaian." Pall Mall Budget, 40 (Oct. 27, 1892), 1608.

1622 "Tennysons Bruder." Allgemeine Zeitung, 2 (1892), 96.

1623 "Tennyson's Forest Idyll." Christian Herald, March 31, 1892, p. 6.
Review of The Foresters.

1624 "Tennyson's 'Maid Marian.'" Notes and Queries, 8th ser. 2 (July 2, 1892), 6.
See also: entry 1625, below.

1625 "Tennyson's 'Maid Marian.'" Notes and Queries, 2 (July 16, 1892), 55.

1626 "Tennyson's Quiet Old Age." Critic (New York), 20 (Feb. 20, 1892), 121.

1627 "Tennyson's Relation to Social Politics." Pall Mall Budget, 40 (Nov. 17, 1892), 1718.

1628 "Tennyson's Theology." Spectator, 69 (Nov. 5, 1892), 642-643.
Reprinted: Eclectic Magazine of Foreign Literature, 56 (Dec. 1892), 853-855.

1629 Terry, F.C. Birbick. "A Dream of Fair Women." Notes and Queries, 8th ser. 2 (Nov. 19, 1892), 407.

1630 Thayer, Stephen Henry. "Alfred Tennyson." Andover Review, 18 (Nov. 1892), 460-478.

1631 Theuriet, André. "Alfred Tennyson." Le Journal, Oct. 17, 1892.
Dislikes Tennyson's work, which the author believes is aimed at women.

1632 Times (London), Oct. 7, 1892.
Reprinted: Eminent Persons, 1896 (entry 1905).

1633 Todhunter, John. "In Westminster Abbey, October 12, 1892." Academy, 42 (Oct. 22, 1892), 361.
Reprinted: Eclectic Magazine of Foreign Literature, 56 (Dec. 1892), 820-821. A poem.

1634 Traill, H.D. "Aspects of Tennyson." Nineteenth Century, 32 (Dec. 1892), 952-966.
Reprinted: Littell's Living Age, 196 (Feb. 11, 1893), 415-425.
A notably interesting discussion of Tennyson's work as a whole.

1635 "Unwelcome Visitors." Critic (New York), 21 (Oct. 22, 1892), 225.

1636 Urban, Sylvanus. "Alfred Baron Tennyson, Born August 5, 1809: Died October 6, 1892." Gentleman's Magazine, 273 (Nov. 1892), 535-540.

1637 Van Dyke, Henry. "In Lucem Transitus." Critic (New York), 21 (Oct. 15, 1892), 211.
Reprinted: Poems, 1923 (entry 2974). A poem, as follows:

Tennyson
In Lucem Transitus, October, 1892

From the misty shores of midnight, touched with splen-
dours of the moon,
To the singing tides of heaven, and the light more clear
than noon,
Passed a soul that grew to music till it was with God
in tune.

Brother of the greatest poets, true to nature, true to art;
Lover of Immortal Love, uplifter of the human heart;
Who shall cheer us with high music, who shall sing, if
thou depart?

Silence here--for love is silent, gazing on the lessening
sail;

> Silence here--for grief is voiceless when the mighty
> minstrels fail;
> Silence here--but far beyond us, many voices crying,
> Hail!

1638 _____. "Tennyson." Critic (New York), 21 (Oct. 15, 1892), 203-204.

1639 Venables, Edmund. "Tennyson's Cambridge Contemporaries." Notes and Queries, 8th ser. 2 (Dec. 3, 1892), 441-442.

1640 Waldau, Otto. "Alfred Tennyson." Illustrirte Zeitung, 99 (Oct. 15, 1892), 439-440.

1641 Walford, E. "Early Notice of Tennyson." Notes and Queries, 8th ser. 1 (March 5, 1892), 185.

1642 Walford, L. B. "London Letter." Critic (New York), 21 (Nov. 5, 1892), 251.

1643 Walkley, A. B. "Maid Marian on the Stage." Theatre (London), 19 (May 1892), 227-231.

1644 Warfield, Ethelbert D. "Tennyson as a Spiritual Teacher." Independent, 44 (Oct. 20, 1892), 1473-1474.

1645 Warren, Thomas Herbert. "In Memoriam: Alfred, Lord Tennyson." Spectator, 69 (Oct. 15, 1892), 528. Reprinted: Littell's Living Age, 195 (Nov. 19, 1892), 450; Critic (New York), 21 (Nov. 26, 1892), 288-289. A poem.

1646 Watson, William. Academy, 41 (April 9, 1892), 341-342. Review of The Foresters.

1647 _____. "Lachrymae Musarum." Illustrated London News, 101 (Oct. 15, 1892), 474. A poem.

1648 _____. "To Lord Tennyson." Critic (New York), 21 (Nov. 26, 1892), 289. Reprinted: Collected Poems, 1899 (entry 2101).

1649 [Watts, Theodore.] Athenaeum, Nov. 19, 1892, pp. 695-697. Review of The Death of OEnone. Watts praises it as an example of Tennyson's poetic powers. He compares Tennyson favorably with the best of nineteenth-century British poets.

1650 _____. "In Westminster Abbey." Nineteenth Century, 32 (Nov. 1892), 842. A poem, as follows:

In Westminster Abbey

"The crowd in the Abbey was very great."--Morning
Newspaper.

I saw no crowd: yet did these eyes behold
What others saw not--his lov'd face sublime
Beneath that pall of death in deathless prime
Of Tennyson's long day that grows not old;
And, as I gazed, my grief seemed over-bold;
And, "Who art thou," the music seemed to chime,
"To mourn that king of song whose throne is time?"
Who loves a god should be of godlike mould.

Then spake my heart rebuking Sorrow's shame:
"So great he was, striving in simple strife
With Art alone to lend all beauty life--
So true to Truth he was, whatever came--
So fierce against the false when lies were rife--
That Love o'erleapt the golden fence of Fame."

1651   _____. "Lord Tennyson." Athenaeum, Oct. 8 and 22,
1892, pp. 482-483 and 555-556.
Watts asserts that Tennyson was modest even though a popular poet.

1652   _____. "Lord Tennyson's Last Volume." Athenaeum,
Nov. 12, 1892, 665.

1653   _____. "The Portraits of Lord Tennyson." Magazine of
Art, 16 (Dec. 1892 and Jan. 1893), 37-43 and 96-101.
Portraits and notes.

1654   Waugh, Arthur. "Tennysoniana." Academy, 42 (Nov. 19,
1892), 461.

1655   Weiss, August. "Tennysons letzte Worte." Allgemeine
Zeitung, Dec. 8, 1892, pp. 1-2.

1656   "Who Will Be Poet Laureate?" Atlantic Monthly, 70 (Dec.
1892), 855-856.

1657   Wilson, Epiphanius. "The Dead Singer." Critic (New York),
21 (Nov. 5, 1892), 256.
A poem.

1658   Winterwood, Geoffrey. "In the Laureate's Footsteps." Good
Words, 33 (1892), 670-678.

1659   Yardley, E. "Charles Lamb and Lord Tennyson." Notes and
Queries, 8th ser. 2 (Oct. 29, 1892), 356.

1893

On February 6, 1893, Henry Irving's version of Becket began its run at the Lyceum and was very successful. Macmillan and Co. published the stage version of Becket, as Arranged for the Stage by Henry Irving in 1893.

Books

1660 "Alfred Tennyson." Pratt Institute: Library School Lectures on General Literature, No. 82. [Brooklyn: Pratt Institute School of Library Service, c. 1893], pp. 643-649. Bibliographical.

1661 Blakeney, E. H. The Teaching of Tennyson. London: c. 1893. Reprinted from Churchman, 1892 (entry 1434).

1662 Bourdillon, Francis William. Sursum Corda. London: Unwin, 1893. Fifty copies printed. Rare.

1663 Brooks, Elbridge Streeter, ed. Tennyson Remembrance Book: A Memorial for the Poet's Reader Friends. Boston: Lothrop, 1893.

1664 Cameron, H. H. Hay. Introduction to Alfred, Lord Tennyson and His Friends by J. M. Cameron (see entry 1665, below). London: Unwin, 1893.

1665 Cameron, Julia Margaret. Alfred, Lord Tennyson and His Friends: A Series of 25 Portraits and Frontispiece in Photogravure from the Negatives of Mrs. Julia Margaret Cameron and H. H. H. Cameron. London: Unwin, 1893. The Camerons were occasional guests at Tennyson's home. Reviewed by: Nation (New York) (entry 1747); and Saturday Review (London) (entry 1759).

1666 Canton, William. "Tennyson." Masson, David, and Others: In the Footsteps of the Poets. London: Isbister, 1893, pp. 333-381.

1667 Carpenter, William Boyd. The Message of Tennyson. London: Macmillan, 1893. Carpenter was the Bishop of Ripon and a friend of Tennyson. He talked with Tennyson about religion and the present book discusses faith in Tennyson's work.

1668 Finlayson, Thomas Campbell. "Tennyson's 'In Memoriam.'" Essays, Addresses, and Lyrical Translations. London: Macmillan, 1893, pp. 1-35.

1669 Francis, Beata. The Scenery of Tennyson's Poems. London:

Bumpus, 1893.
Etchings and Commentary.

1670 Gosse, Edmund. "Tennyson--and After." Questions at Issue.
London: Heinemann, 1893, pp. 175-198.
     Gosse contends that Tennyson's poetry is read by but a small
number of people and will be read by only a small number in the
future. The essay is more an effort to express Gosse's belief in
the elite nature of poetry than an analysis of Tennyson. Perhaps
this essay is responsible for the notion that appears in the works
of some twentieth-century scholars that Tennyson's poetry was not
popular.

1671 Hales, John W. "Alfred Tennyson." Folia Litteraria:
Essays and Notes on English Literature. New York: Macmillan, 1893, pp. 332-336.

1672 Hallam, Arthur Henry. The Poems of Arthur Henry Hallam,
Together with His Essay on the Lyrical Poems of Alfred
Tennyson. Ed. Richard Le Gallienne. London: Mathews
and Lane, 1893.
See entry 9.

1673 Innes, Arthur Donald. "Tennyson in Particular." Seers and
Singers. London: Innes, 1893, pp. 26-49.

1674 Kalisch, Carl. Studier over Tennyson med et kort Omrids
af Digterens Liv. Gad: 1893.
Publication of a dissertation, 1893 (entry 1693).

1675 Littledale, Harold. Essays on Lord Tennyson's Idylls of the
King. London: Macmillan, 1893.
     This book is possibly the best of the nineteenth-century in-
troductions to the Idylls of the King. Aimed at the general reader,
the book discusses each of the Idylls and presents the backgrounds
for the poetry.
     Reviewed by: Critic (New York) (entry 1706); Literary
World (London) (entry 1736); Nation (New York) (entry 1746); Saturday Review (London) (entry 1757); Speaker (entry 1763); and A.
Waugh in Academy (entry 1788).

1676 Luce, Morton. New Studies in Tennyson. London: Baker,
[1893].

1677 Macaulay, G.C. Introduction to The Holy Grail. London:
Macmillan, 1893.

1678 _____. Introduction to Tennyson: Gareth and Lynette.
London: Macmillan, 1893.
Discusses Tennyson's poetic techniques.

1679 Masson, D. In the Footsteps of the Poets. London: Ibister,
1893.
Tennyson on pages 333-381.

1680 Milsand, Joseph. "Alfred Tennyson" and "Idylls of the King." Littérature anglaise et Philosophie. Dijon: Lamarche, 1893, pp. 39-71.
"Alfred Tennyson" reprinted from Revue des Deux Mondes, 1851 (entry 264). See entry 264 for annotation.

1681 Monti, G. "Il Dolore nelle opere dei grandi poeti della fede: Klopstock, Schiller, LaMartine, Tennyson, Elizabeth Browning, Cora Fabbri." La Poesia del dolore. Modena: E. Sarasino, 1893.

1682 Myers, F. W. H. "Tennyson as Prophet." Science and a Future Life. London: Macmillan, 1893, pp. 27-65.
Reprinted from Nineteenth Century, 1889 (entry 1272). See entry 1272 for other reprintings and for annotation.

1683 Negri, Gaetano. "Tennyson e Gladstone." Segni dei Tempi: Profili e bozzetti letterari. Milano: Hoepli, 1893, pp. 55-72. Second edition in 1897, pp. 86-104. See: G. Negri in Die Gesellschaft, 1898 (entry 2074).

1684 Parnell, John. Death of Tennyson. London: 1893.
A one-leaf poem.

1685 Rawnsley, Hardwicke Drummond. "Tennyson." Valete: Tennyson and Other Memorial Poems. Glasgow: MacLehose, 1893, pp. 1-35.
Reviewed by: Speaker (entry 1764).

1686 Ritchie, Anne. "Reminiscences." Alfred, Lord Tennyson and His Friends by J. M. Cameron. London: Unwin, 1893, pp. 9-16.
See entry 1665.

1687 Rupprecht, Johann Georg. Tennysons Naturschilderungen. Leipzig-Reudnitz: Schmidt, 1893.
Publication of a dissertation, 1893 (entry 1694).

1688 Salt, Henry S. Tennyson as a Thinker. London: Reeves, 1893.
Reprinted from Time, 1890 (entry 1339). See entry 1339 for annotation.

1689 Souvenir of Becket by Alfred, Lord Tennyson: First Presented at the Lyceum Theatre 6th Feb. 1893 by Henry Irving. London: Black and White, 1893.
Includes twelve plates.

1690 Stewart, George. Essays from Reviews. Quebec: 1893.
Tennyson in Volume II, pages 9-41.

1691 Walters, J. Cuming. Tennyson: Poet, Philosopher, Idealist: Studies of the Life, Work, and Teaching of the Poet Laureate.

London: Kegan Paul, Trench, Trübner, 1893.
Reprinted: New York: Haskell House, 1971.
Walters' discussion of Tennyson's philosophies and religious views is of particular interest. Walters' attempts to identify the major aspects of Tennyson's poetry.
Reviewed by: Critic (New York) (entry 1822); Nation (New York) (entry 1834); and A. Waugh in Academy (entry 1857).

1692 Winter, William. "Tennyson." Shadows of the Stage. Edinburgh: 1893. Second series, pp. 359-367.

Dissertations

1693 Kalisch, Carl. Studier over Tennyson med et kort Omrids af Digterens Liv. Copenhagen, 1893.
Published: 1893 (entry 1674).

1694 Rupprecht, Johann Georg. Tennysons Naturchilderungen. Leipzig, 1893.
Published: 1893 (entry 1687).

Periodicals

1695 Argyll, Duke of. "At the Laureate's Funeral." National Review, 20 (Jan. 1893), 581-586.

1696 Athenaeum, Feb. 11, 1893, pp. 193-194.
Review of the Lyceum production of Becket. Favorable.

1697 B., Ad. (Adrien Baret?). "Lord Tennyson." Revue chrétienne, 13 (1893), 269-284.

1698 "'Becket' at the Lyceum." Spectator, 70 (Feb. 25, 1893), 253-254.
Review of the Lyceum production of Becket. Likes the play in spite of its faults.

1699 "'Becket' at the Lyceum." Saturday Review (London), 75 (Feb. 11, 1893), 146-147.
Review of the Lyceum production of Becket. Unhappy with the play although admiring the production.

1700 Bouchor, Maurice. "Becket, un drame historique de Tennyson." Revue Hebdomadaire, 10 (March 11, 1893), 275-287.

1701 Burroughs, John. "Whitman's and Tennyson's Relations to Science." Dial, 14 (March 16, 1893), 168-169.
Burroughs discusses the use of modern science in the works of Whitman and Tennyson.

1702 Burton, Richard. "Tennyson." Critic (New York), 22 (Jan. 14, 1893), 24.
A poem.

1703 Church Quarterly Review, 35 (Jan. 1893), 485-506.
Review of Demeter, The Death of OEnone, and The Foresters.

1704 Clarke, Helen A. "How to Study Tennyson's 'In Memoriam.'"
Poet Lore, 5 (Nov. 1893), 574-582.

1705 Critic (New York), 22 (Feb. 4, 1893), 58.
Review of J. Jacobs's Tennyson and "In Memoriam," 1892
(entry 1397).

1706 Critic (New York), 22 (May 6, 1893), 285.
Review of H. Littledale's Essays, 1893 (entry 1675).

1707 Critic (New York), 23 (Oct. 28, 1893), 270.
Review of E.C. Tainsh's Study, 1893 edition (entry 605).

1708 Daily News (London), Feb. 7, 1893, p. 3.
Review of the Lyceum production of Becket. Likes the performance.

1709 Daily Telegraph (London), Feb. 7, 1893, p. 6.
Review of the Lyceum production of Becket. A balanced
appraisal.

1710 Davies, Samuel D. "Shakespeare's 'Miranda' and Tennyson's
'Elaine.'" Poet Lore, 5 (Jan. 1893), 15-25.
Compares the poems to reveal aspects of the poets.

1711 de Vere, Aubrey. "To Alfred Tennyson." Century Illustrated Monthly Magazine, 46 (May 1893), 37.

1712 De Witt, A. "Alfred Tennyson." Presbyterian Reformed
Review, 4 (1893), 112.

1713 Dial, 14 (Jan. 16, 1893), 53-54.
Review of A. Waugh's Alfred Lord Tennyson, 1892 (entry
1415).

1714 "The Drama: 'Becket.'" Critic (New York), 23 (Nov. 18,
1893), 326.
Review of the Lyceum (London) production of Becket. Likes
Henry Irving's performance.

1715 Elliott, J.J. "Poems by Two Brothers." Literary World
(London), 47 (June 30, 1893), 612-613.

1716 Era, Feb. 11, 1893, p. 10.
Review of the Lyceum production of Becket. Favorable.

1717 Everett, Charles Carroll. "Tennyson and Browning as Spiritual
Forces." New World, 2 (June 1893), 240-256.
Reprinted: Essays Theological and Literary, 1901 (entry
2224).

1718 Fields, Annie. "Tennyson." Harper's Monthly Magazine, 86
      (Jan. 1893), 309-312.

1719 "First Editions of Tennyson." Bookworm, 6 (1893), 26.
      Bibliographical.

1720 "The Foresters." National Observer, 10 (Oct. 7, 1893),
      531.
      Discusses the staging of The Foresters.

1721 Guardian (Manchester), Feb. 7, 1893, p. 7.
      Review of the Lyceum production of Becket.   Likes Henry
Irving's performance.

1722 Hale, Edward E., Jr. "Tennyson's Place in Poetry." Dial,
      14 (Feb. 16, 1893), 101-102.

1723 Halsey, John J. "Tennyson as a Creator." Dial, 14 (March
      1, 1893), 135-136.

1724 Harrison, Frederic. "Literary and Municipal Problems in
      England." Forum, 14 (Jan. 1893), 644-648.

1725 Hatton, Joseph. "Becket at the Lyceum." Art Journal, 55
      (April 1893), 105-109.
      Discusses the Lyceum production of Becket.

1726 Hoyt, Arthur S. "Tennyson's Poetry." Homiletic Review,
      25 (1893), 402-407.

1727 Kellogg, D.B. "Why Tennyson Is Not More Read." Critic
      (New York), 22 (Jan. 7, 1893), 11.

1728 Knowles, James T. "Aspects of Tennyson: A Personal
      Reminiscence." Nineteenth Century, 33 (Jan. 1893), 164-188.
      Reprinted: Littell's Living Age, 196 (Feb. 25, 1893), 515-
529.
      Knowles was a close friend of Tennyson and the editor of
Nineteenth Century.   He solicited a series of well written essays
on Tennyson for publication in his magazine.   These essays, listed
in subsequent entries, are among the best written about the poet.
The present essay is of interest to biographers.

1729 _____. "Characteristics of Tennyson." Critic (New York),
      22 (Feb. 4, 1893), 67-68.

1730 Kynaston, Herbert. "Crossing the Bar." National Observer,
      9 (Jan. 7, 21, and 28, 1893), 187, 239, and 265.

1731 Lambert, Agnes. "The Real Thomas Becket." Nineteenth
      Century, 33 (Feb. 1893), 273-292.
      Reprinted: Littell's Living Age, 197 (April 1, 1893), 18-32.
      Includes a laudatory discussion of Tennyson's Becket while
discussing research into Becket's life.

1732 "The Late Lord Tennyson on the Future Life." Spectator, 70 (March 4, 1893), 283-284.

1733 Lathrop, G. P. "Was Tennyson Consistent?" American Catholic Quarterly Review, 18 (Jan. 1893), 101-121. Focuses on The Death of OEnone.

1734 Le Gallienne, Richard. "Poets and Publishers." Speaker, 8 (Nov. 18, 1893), 550.

1735 Literary World (Boston), 24 (Jan. 28, 1893), 22. Review of H. Van Dyke's The Poetry of Tennyson, 1889 (entry 1256) and A. Waugh's Alfred Lord Tennyson, 1892 (entry 1415).

1736 Literary World (London), 47 (March 3, 1893), 192-193. Review of H. Littledale's Essays, 1893 (entry 1675).

1737 Literary World (London), 47 (April 7, 1893), 316. Review of J. Jacobs's Tennyson and "In Memoriam," 1892 (entry 1397).

1738 Looten, C. "Alfred Tennyson." Revue de Lille, Jan. 1893.

1739 "Lord Tennyson." Calcutta Review, 96 (Jan. 1893), 193-202.

1740 "Lord Tennyson's Masters." Bookworm, 7 (1893), 18.

1741 Martin, Edwin. "Tennyson's Friendships." McClure's Magazine, 2 (Dec. 1893), 54-60.

1742 "The Master Artist." Critic (New York), 22 (June 24, 1893), 422. Focuses on Tennyson.

1743 Morning Post (London), Feb. 7, 1893, p. 5. Review of the Lyceum production of Becket.

1744 Myers, F. W. H. "Modern Poets and the Meaning of Life." Nineteenth Century, 33 (Jan. 1893), 93-111. Mentions Tennyson.

1745 Nation (New York), 56 (Jan. 26, 1893), 66. Review of J. Jacobs's Tennyson and "In Memoriam," 1893 (entry 1397).

1746 Nation (New York), 57 (Sept. 14, 1893), 194. Review of H. Littledale's Essays, 1893 (entry 1675).

1747 Nation (New York), 57 (Nov. 9, 1893), 356. Review of J. M. Cameron's Alfred, Lord Tennyson and His Friends, 1893 (entry 1665).

1748 National Observer, 9 (May 13, 1893), 654-655.
      Discusses Poems by Two Brothers.

1749 National Observer, 10 (Aug. 26, 1893), 381-382.
      Discusses In Memoriam.

1750 Painter, F.V.N. "The Homiletic Value of Tennyson."
      Homiletic Review, 25 (1893), 202-208.

1751 Pall Mall Gazette, Feb. 7, 1893, pp. 1-2.
      Review of the Lyceum production of Becket. Dislikes the
play.

1752 Paul, Herbert. "The Classical Poems." Nineteenth Century,
      33 (March 1893), 436-453.
      Reprinted: Littell's Living Age, 197 (May 13, 1893), 407-
418; and Men and Letters, 1901 (entry 2232).
      Part of the "Aspects of Tennyson" series of essays written
at the request of James Knowles (see entry 1728). Paul focuses
on Tennyson's classicism. A useful reference for anyone interested
in its subject.

1753 "Poems, Chiefly Lyrical." Bookworm, 7 (1893), 48.
      Bibliographical.

1754 "The Poetry of Tennyson." Quarterly Review, 176 (Jan.
      1893), 1-39.

1755 Quiller-Couch, Arthur. "On a Proposed Birthday-Book."
      Speaker, 7 (June 24, 1893), 720-721.

1756 Reynolds, Helen M. "Tennyson in Class." Education, 13
      (Feb. 1893), 359-364.

1757 Saturday Review (London), 75 (March 4, 1893), 248-249.
      Review of H. Littledale's Essays, 1893 (entry 1675).

1758 Saturday Review (London), 75 (May 13, 1893), 516-517.
      Discusses Poems by Two Brothers.

1759 Saturday Review (London), 76 (Oct. 21, 1893), 473.
      Review of J.M. Cameron's Alfred Lord Tennyson and His
Friends, 1893 (entry 1665).

1760 Shepherd, Henry Elliott. "Tennyson's 'In Memoriam.'"
      Sewanee Review, 1 (Aug. 1893), 402-409.

1761 Shorey, Paul. "A Word with Tennyson Dissenters." Dial,
      14 (Feb. 16, 1893), 102-103.

1762 Speaker, 7 (Jan. 7, 1893), 14.

1763 Speaker, 7 (April 15, 1893), 434.
      Review of H. Littledale's Essays, 1893 (entry 1675).

1764 Speaker, 8 (Oct. 21, 1893), 444.
Review of H. D. Rawnsley's Valete, 1893 (entry 1685).

1765 Spectator, 70 (Jan. 21, 1893), 82-83.
Review of A. Waugh's Alfred Lord Tennyson, 1892 (entry 1415).

1766 Spectator, 70 (April 29, 1893), 551.
Review of J. Jacobs's Tennyson and "In Memoriam," 1892 (entry 1397).

1767 Stanley, Hiram M. "A Closing Word on Tennyson." Dial, 14 (March 1, 1893), 136.

1768 _____. "Tennyson's Place in Poetry." Dial, 14 (Feb. 1, 1893), 72.

1769 Stead, William T. "Genius and Theology of Tennyson." Our Day, 11 (Jan. 1893), 19-36.

1770 Strachey, Edward. "Talk at a Country House." Atlantic Monthly, 72 (Nov. 1893), 607-617.

1771 "A Study of Tennyson's 'Locksley Hall' and 'Sixty Years After.'" Poet Lore, 5 (1893), 34-39.

1772 Swinburne, Algernon Charles. "Threnody: Alfred, Lord Tennyson, October 6, 1892." Nineteenth Century, 33 (Jan. 1893), 1-3.
Reprinted: Eclectic Magazine of Foreign Literature, 120 (Feb. 1893), 249-250. A poem, as follows:

Threnody
Alfred, Lord Tennyson, October 6, 1892

I

Life, sublime and serene when time had power upon it
and ruled its breath,
Changed it, bade it be glad or sad, and hear what change
in the world's ear saith,
Shines more fair in the starrier air whose glory lightens
the dusk of death.

Suns that sink on the wan sea's brink, and moons
that kindle and flame and fade,
Leave more clear for the darkness here the stars that
set not and see not shade
Rise and rise on the lowlier skies by rule of sunlight
and moonlight swayed.

So, when night for his eyes grew bright, his proud
head pillowed on Shakespeare's breast

Hand in hand with him, soon to stand where shine
    the glories that death loves best,
Passed the light of his face from sight, and sank
    sublimely to radiant rest.

II

Far above us and all our love, beyond all reach of its
    voiceless praise,
Shines for ever the name that never shall feel the
    shade of the changeful days
Fall and chill the delight that still sees winter's light
    on it shine like May's.

Strong as death is the dark day's breath whose blast
    has withered the life we see
Here where light is the child of night, and less than
    visions or dreams are we:
Strong as death; but a word, a breath, a dream is
    stronger than death can be.

Strong as truth and superb in youth eternal, fair as
    the sundawn's flame
Seen when May on her first-born day bids earth exult
    in her radiant name,
Lives, clothed round with its praise and crowned
    with love that dies not, his love-lit
        fame.

III

Fairer far than the morning star, and sweeter far
    than the songs that rang
Loud through heaven from the choral Seven when
    all the stars of the morning sang,
Shines the song that we loved so long--since first
    such love in us flamed and sprang.

England glows as a sunlit rose from mead to
    mountain, from sea to sea.
Bright with love and with pride above all taint of
    sorrow that needs must be,
Needs must live for an hour, and give its rainbow's
    glory to lawn and lea.

Not through tears shall the new-born years behold
    him, crowned with applause of men,
Pass at last from a lustrous past to life that lightens
    beyond their ken,
Glad and dead, and from earthward led to sunward,
    guided of Imogen.

1773 Symonds, John Addington. "Recollections of Lord Tennyson."
    Century Illustrated Monthly Magazine, 46 (May 1893), 32-37.

1774 Tainsh, Edward Campbell. Academy, Sept. 2, 1893.
See: A. Waugh in Academy (entry 1789).

1775 "Tennyson." Eclectic Magazine of Foreign Literature, 120
(Jan. 1893), 31-44.

1776 "Tennysoniana." Sunday Magazine, 22 (Jan., Feb., and
March 1893), 50-53, 122-125, and 201-205. Signed "Nemo."

1777 "Tennyson's Earliest Poems." Critic (New York), 22 (May
20, 1893), 333-335.
Discusses Poems by Two Brothers.

1778 Times (London), Feb. 7, 1893, p. 7.
Review of the Lyceum production of Becket.

1779 Unwin, S. Philip. "Shakespeare, Tennyson, and the Lord
Chief Justice." Speaker, 7 (July 1, 1893), 746.

1780 Van Dyke, Henry. "The Voice of Tennyson." Century Illustrated Monthly Magazine, 45 (Feb. 1893), 539-544.

1781 W., A.B. (Arthur Bingham Walkley). Speaker, 7 (Feb. 11,
1893), 157-158.
Reviews the 1893 edition of Becket. Positive response.

1782 Walford, L.B. "London Letter." Critic (New York), 22
(Feb. 25, 1893), 116.
Discusses the Lyceum production of Becket.

1783 Walsh, Walter. "Tennyson's Great Allegory." Gentleman's
Magazine, 50 (1893), 500-507.

1784 "Was Tennyson Either Gnostic or Agnostic?" Spectator, 70
(Jan. 7, 1893), 10-11.
Reprinted: Littell's Living Age, 196 (Feb. 25, 1893), 561-
564.

1785 Watts, Theodore. "The Portraits of Tennyson." Magazine
of Art, 16 (Jan. 1893), 96-101.
Second of two parts. See entry 1653.

1786 _____. "Tennyson as a Nature Poet." Nineteenth Century,
33 (May 1893), 836-856.
Reprinted: Littell's Living Age, 198 (July 1, 1893), 28-42.
Part of the "Aspects of Tennyson" series of essays. See entry
1728.

1787 _____. "Tennyson as a Poet of Evolution." Nineteenth
Century, 34 (Oct. 1893), 657-672.
Reprinted: Littell's Living Age, 199 (Dec. 9, 1893), 611-622.
Interesting.

1788 Waugh, Arthur. Academy, 43 (May 13, 1893), 413-414.
Review of H. Littledale's Essays, 1893 (entry 1675).

1789 _____. Academy, 44 (Aug. 5, 1893), 106.
Review of 1893 edition of E.C. Tainsh's Study, 1868 (entry
605). See E.C. Tainsh in Academy (entry 1774).

1790 _____. "London Letter." Critic (New York), 23 (Oct. 21,
1893), 260-261.

1791 Webb, W. Trego. "Tennyson's 'Crossing the Bar.'" Spectator, 70 (Feb. 4, 1893), 160.

1792 Wedgwood, Julia. "Tennyson as the Religious Exponent of
His Age." Sunday Magazine, 22 (Jan. 1893), 34-38.

1793 Wedmore, Frederick. "The Stage: Tennyson's Becket."
Academy, 43 (Feb. 18, 1893), 158-159.
Review of the Lyceum production of Becket. Likes the per-
formance.

1794 Weld, Agnes Grace. "Talks with Tennyson." Contemporary
Review, 63 (March 1893), 394-397.
Reprinted: Littell's Living Age, 197 (April 29, 1893), 306-
308.

1795 Westminster Review, 140 (Sept. 1893), 345.
Review of 1893 edition of E.C. Tainsh's Study, 1868 (entry
605).

1796 Woods, M.A. "In Memoriam." Expository Times, 5 (1893).

1797 Zimmern, Helen. "Alfred Tennyson." Velhagen und Klasings
Monatshefte, 7 (Jan. 1893), 499-511.

1894

In 1894, Macmillan published the Complete Single-Volume
Edition of Tennyson's works.

Books

1798 Axson, Stockton. Syllabus of a Course of Six Lectures on
Browning and Tennyson. [Philadelphia: American Society
for the Extension of University Teaching, 1894.] An eleven-
page outline.

1799 Bellezza, Paolo. La vita e le opere di Alfredo Tennyson.
Florence: Rassegna Nazionale, 1894.
Reprinted from La Rasegna Nazionale, 1894 (entry 1816).
Reviewed by: Archiv für das Studium der neueren Sprachen und
Literaturen (entry 1812); and Athenaeum (entry 1813).

1800 Brooke, Stopford Augustus. Tennyson: His Art and Relation
to Modern Life. London: Isbister, 1894. New York: G. P.
Putnam's Sons, 1894.
Brooke presents a careful study of Tennyson's poetry. Although the criticism may seem a little naive by modern standards,
literary historians may find the book interesting because of its
discussion of Tennyson's place in the Victorian era.
Reviewed by: Academy (entry 1810); P. Bayne in Literary
World (London) (entry 1814); Book Buyer (entry 1817); Bookman
(London) (entry 1818); Critic (New York) (entry 1824); A. Elliot in
Edinburgh Review (entry 1884); London Quarterly Review (entry
1833); Nation (New York) (entry 1835); Saturday Review (London)
(entry 1842); Speaker (entry 1846); and Spectator (entry 1848).

1801 Dixon, William Macneile. "Tennyson, Arnold, Browning."
English Poetry from Blake to Browning. London: Methuen,
1894, pp. 188-200.

1802 Hutton, Richard Holt. "Tennyson's Poem on 'Despair'" and
"'Locksley Hall' in Youth and Age." Criticisms on Contemporary Thought and Thinkers: Selected from the Spectator.
London: Macmillan, 1894. Volume II, pp. 197-203 and 204-
212, respectively.
Reprinted from the Spectator, 1886 (entry 1163). See entry
1163 for annotation.

1803 Layard, George Somes. Tennyson and His Pre-Raphaelite
Illustrators: A Book about a Book. London: Stock, 1894.
About the Poems of 1857.
Reviewed by: Critic (New York) (entry 1825); Literary World
(London) (entry 1832); Nation (New York) (entry 1836); Saturday Re-
view (London) (entry 1841); and Studio (entry 1849).

1804 MacCallum, Mungo William. Tennyson's Idylls of the King
and Arthurian Story from the XVIth Century. Glasgow:
MacLehose, 1894.
This book was a major reference for study of the Idylls of
the King, and it remains useful. It has been largely superseded by
studies published in the 1960s and 1970s. MacCallum supplies an
interesting history of Arthurian literature. His discussion of the
allegorical qualities of the Idylls of the King also retains its interest.
Reviewed by: Critic (New York) (entry 1823); A. Elliot in
Edinburgh Review (entry 1884); S. L. Gwynn in Bookman (London)
(entry 1828); Literary World (London) (entry 1831); Nation (New
York) (entry 1835); National Observer (entry 1837); Speaker (entry
1845); Spectator (entry 1847); and A. Waugh in Academy (entry 1858).

1805 Oates, John. The Teaching of Tennyson. London: Stock,
[1894].
Reviewed by: Literary World (London), 1895 and 1899 (entries
1889 and 2117).

1806   Radford, G.H.   "King Arthur."   Shylock and Others: Eight
       Studies.   London: Unwin, 1894, pp. 153-176.

1807   Slater, J.H.   Early Editions: A Bibliographical Survey of the
       Works of Some Modern Authors.   London: Kegan Paul,
       Trench, Trübner, 1894.
       Reviewed by: T.J. Wise in Bookman (London) (entry 1859).

1808   Swinburne, Algernon Charles.   "Tennyson or Darwin?"   Stu-
       dies in Prose and Poetry.   London: Chatto and Windus,
       1894, pp. 141-145.

1809   Wilson, Henry Schütz.   "'Tis Sixty Years Since":   or, The
       Two Locksley Halls.   London: Kegan Paul, Trench, Trübner,
       1894.
       A short study.

Periodicals

1810   Academy, 46 (July 14, 1894), 24-25.
       Review of S.A. Brooke's Tennyson, 1894 (entry 1800).

1811   Adams, Francis.   "Tennyson."   New Review, 10 (March
       1894), 311-323.

1812   Archiv für das Studium der neueren Sprachen und Literaturen,
       93 (1894), 454-457.
       Review of P. Bellezza's La vita e le opere di Alfredo Tenny-
son, 1894 (entry 1799).

1813   Athenaeum, Oct. 13, 1894, pp. 486-489.
       Review of P. Bellezza's La vita e le opere di Alfredo Tenny-
son, 1894 (entry 1799).

1814   Bayne, Peter.   Literary World (London), 49 (May 11, 1894),
       436-437.
       Review of S.A. Brooke's Tennyson, 1894 (entry 1800).

1815   Beatty, Arthur.   "Tennyson's 'In Memoriam.'"   Modern Lan-
       guage Notes, 9 (May 1894), 257-260.

1816   Bellezza, Paolo.   "La vita e le opere di Alfredo Tennyson."
       La Rassegna Nazionale, 75 (June 1, 1893?-Feb. 16, 1894),
       60-89, 246-270, 398-423, and 636-649.
       Reprinted: entry 1799.

1817   Book Buyer, 11 (July 1894), 300.
       Review of S.A. Brooke's Tennyson, 1894 (entry 1800).

1818   Bookman (London), 6 (June 1894), 86-87.
       Review of S.A. Brooke's Tennyson, 1894 (entry 1800).

1819   Brookfield, Mrs. W.H.   "Early Recollections of Tennyson."

Temple Bar, 101 (Feb. 1894), 203-207.
Reprinted: Littell's Living Age, 200 (March 10, 1894), 618-
621. The Brookfields were close friends of Tennyson.

1820 Cambridge Review, 16 (Nov. 22, 1894), 97.
Reviews Tennyson's works.

1821 "Chaucer and Tennyson." National Observer, 11 (March 10,
1894), 428.

1822 Critic (New York), 24 (Jan. 13, 1894), 15-16.
Review of J. C. Walters's Tennyson, 1893 (entry 1691).

1823 Critic (New York), 24 (May 5, 1894), 297-298.
Review of M. W. MacCallum's Tennyson's Idylls of the King,
1894 (entry 1804).

1824 Critic (New York), 24 (June 2, 1894), 369-370.
Review of S. A. Brooke's Tennyson, 1894 (entry 1800).

1825 Critic (New York), 25 (Nov. 24, 1894), 347-348.
Review of G. S. Layard's Tennyson, 1894 (entry 1803).

1826 Davies, Joseph J. "Tennyson's Turncoat." Westminster
Review, 142 (1894), 558-566.

1827 Fields, Annie. "To the Memory of Tennyson." Dial, 17
(Aug. 1, 1894), 57.
A letter, dated July 22, 1894, announcing a plan to build a
memorial to Tennyson "in the form of an Iona cross" on "the western end of the Isle of Wight" and soliciting funds for the project.

1828 Gwynn, Stephen Lucius. Bookman (London), 6 (May 1894),
53-54.
Review of M. W. MacCallum's Tennyson's Idylls of the King,
1894 (entry 1804).

1829 Haddow, R. "Sense in War with Souls: Studies in 'Idylls of
the King.'" Knox College Monthly, 18 (1894-1895), 40-45,
86-91, 131-135, and 215-220.

1830 König, Robert. "Tennyson." Neue Christoterpe, 1894, pp.
125-162.

1831 Literary World (London), 49 (Feb. 23, 1894), 165.
Review of M. W. MacCallum's Tennyson's Idylls of the King,
1894 (entry 1804).

1832 Literary World (London), 49 (March 23, 1894), 275.
Review of G. S. Layard's Tennyson, 1894 (entry 1803).

1833 London Quarterly Review, 82 (July 1894), 381-383.
Review of S. A. Brooke's Tennyson, 1894 (entry 1800).

1834 Nation (New York), 58 (Feb. 22, 1894), 139.
      Review of J.C. Walters's Tennyson, 1893 (entry 1691).

1835 Nation (New York), 58 (June 21, 1894), 471.
      Reviews of S.A. Brooke's Tennyson, 1894 (entry 1800) and
M.W. MacCallum's Tennyson's Idylls of the King, 1894 (entry 1804).

1836 Nation (New York), 59 (Oct. 11, 1894), 270.
      Review of G.S. Layard's Tennyson, 1894 (entry 1803).

1837 National Observer, 11 (Feb. 10, 1894), 323-324.
      Review of M.W. MacCallum's Tennyson's Idylls of the King,
1894 (entry 1804).

1838 Parsons, Eugene. "Tennyson's Theology." Methodist Review,
      76 (1894), 917-927.

1839 "A Proposed Tennyson Memorial." Dial, 16 (June 1, 1894),
      342.

1840 "The 'Round Table' Tennyson." Critic (New York), 24 (Jan.
      20, 1894), 38.

1841 Saturday Review (London), 77 (April 7, 1894), 370.
      Review of G.S. Layard's Tennyson, 1894 (entry 1803).

1842 Saturday Review (London), 77 (April 28, 1894), 450.
      Review of S.A. Brooke's Tennyson, 1894 (entry 1800).

1843 Savage, W.H. "Tennyson's Religion." Arena, 9 (April 1894),
      582-592.

1844 Schooling, J. Holt. "The Handwriting of Alfred, Lord Tenny-
      son." Strand Magazine, 8 (1894), 599-608.
      Still of interest to book collectors.

1845 Speaker, 9 (April 21, 1894), 449-450.
      Review of M.W. MacCallum's Tennyson's Idylls of the King,
1894 (entry 1804).

1846 Speaker, 9 (June 2, 1894), 615-616.
      Review of S.A. Brooke's Tennyson, 1894 (entry 1800).

1847 Spectator, 72 (May 12, 1894), 653-655.
      Review of M.W. MacCallum's Tennyson's Idylls of the King,
1894 (entry 1804).

1848 Spectator, 73 (July 7, 1894), 18-19.
      Review of S.A. Brooke's Tennyson, 1894 (entry 1800).

1849 Studio, 2 (March 1894), 221-222.
      Review of G.S. Layard's Tennyson, 1894 (entry 1803).

1850 Taylor, W.V. "New Lights on Tennyson." Sunday Magazine,
      23 (1894), 344-348.

1851 Teeling, Bartle. "A Visit to the Tennysons in 1839."
      Blackwood's Magazine, 155 (May 1894), 605-621.
      Reprinted: Littell's Living Age, 201 (June 1894), 536-549;
and Eclectic Magazine of Foreign Literature, 123 (July 1894), 79-
92. Of biographical interest.

1852 "Tennysoniana." Academy, 45 (Jan. 20 and 27, 1894), 57-58
      and 81.

1853 Thackeray, Francis St. John. "Dante and Tennyson." Tem-
      ple Bar, 102 (July 1894), 387-397.
      Reprinted: Littell's Living Age, 202 (Aug. 4, 1894), 259-
265; and Eclectic Magazine of Foreign Literature, 123 (Sept. 1894),
352-358.

1854 Traill, Henry Duff. "Aspects of Tennyson: As a Humorist."
      Nineteenth Century, 33 (May 1894), 761-774.

1855 "The Trees and Flowers of Tennyson." Temple Bar, 103
      (Nov. 1894), 358-366.
      Reprinted: Eclectic Magazine of Foreign Literature, 123
(Dec. 1894), 783-788.

1856 Walters, John Cuming. "Tennyson--Poet, Philosopher, and
      Idealist." Academy, 45 (Feb. 10, 1894), 128.

1857 Waugh, Arthur. Academy, 45 (Feb. 3, 1894), 96-98.
      Review of J.C. Walters's Tennyson, 1893 (entry 1691).

1858 _____. Academy, 45 (May 12, 1894), 390-391.
      Review of M.W. MacCallum's Tennyson's Idylls of the King,
1894 (entry 1804).

1859 Wise, T.J. Bookman (London), 6 (May 1894), 49-50.
      Review of J.H. Slater's Early Editions, 1894 (entry 1807).

                              1895

Books

1860 Bellezza, Paolo. "Iuando nacque e quandro mori Alessandro
      Manzoni, con un appendice relativa ad A. Tennyson."
      Anniversari Manzoniani. Florence: 1895.

1861 [Browning, Elizabeth Barrett.] Literary Anecdotes of the
      Nineteenth Century. ed. W. Robertson Nicoll and Thomas J.
      Wise. London: Hodder and Stoughton, 1895. Volume I, pp.
      33-41.

1862 [Forman, H. Buxton.] "Midnight: Lines on the Death of Alfred, Lord Tennyson" and "The Building of the Idylls." Literary Anecdotes of the Nineteenth Century. Ed. W. Robertson Nicoll and Thomas J. Wise. London: Hodder and Stoughton, 1895. Volume I, pp. 29-32 and Volume II, pp. 217-272. "Building" discusses Tennyson's revisions of the Idylls of the King.

1863 Godwin, Edward William. Pastoral Play of Fair Rosamund. [Albany: Brate, 1895.]
An adaptation from Becket.

1864 Gurteen, Stephen Humphreys Villiers. The Arthurian Epic: A Comparative Study of the Cambrian, Breton, and Anglo-Norman Versions of the Story and Tennyson's Idylls of the King. New York: Putnam, 1895.
Interesting reading, although largely superseded by later studies.

1865 Hallam, Arthur Henry. Literary Anecdotes of the Nineteenth Century. Ed. W. Robertson Nicoll and Thomas J. Wise. London: Hodder and Stoughton, 1895. Volume I, pp. 21-27.

1866 Hodgkins, Louise Manning. "Alfred Tennyson." A Guide to the Study of the Nineteenth Century Authors. Boston: Heath, 1895, pp. 58-65.

1867 Howells, William Dean. "Tennyson." My Literary Passions. New York: Harper, [c1895], pp. 113-123.

1868 Jacobs, Joseph. "Alfred Tennyson." Literary Studies. London: Nutt, 1895, pp. 155-171.

1869 Jones, Richard D. The Growth of the "Idylls of the King." Philadelphia: J.B. Lippincott, 1895.
Publication of a dissertation: 1895 (entry 1878).
This fine study of Idylls of the King remains valuable. It includes a discussion of sources for the poetry and a useful list of Tennyson's revisions and other variations.

1870 Jusserand, Jules Jean. "Tennyson." Histoire Abrégée de la Littérature Anglais. Paris: Delagrave, 1895.

1871 Le Gallienne, Richard. "'Tennyson' at the Farm." English Poems. London: Lane, 1895, p. 102.

1872 Luce, Morton. A Handbook to the Works of Alfred, Lord Tennyson. London: Bell, 1895. Reprinted, revised: 1914.
This book is a companion to the Macmillan Single-volume Edition of 1894. It discusses Tennyson's poems in the order in which they appear in the 1894 gathering. Luce emphasizes appreciation over analysis.
Reviewed by: Literary World (Boston) (entry 1923); Literary

182 / TENNYSON

World (London) (entry 1924); London Quarterly Review (entry 1928); and Saturday Review (London) (entry 1933).

1873   Saintsbury, George. "Tennyson." Corrected Impressions: Essays on Victorian Writers. New York: Dodd, 1895. London: Heinemann, 1895, pp. 21-40. Reprinted: The Collected Essays and Papers of George Saintsbury, 1875-1920, 1923. Saintsbury believes Tennyson's work will stand the test of time.

1874   Smalley, George W. "Tennyson." Studies of Men. New York: Harper, 1895, pp. 66-85.

1875   Tennyson, Hallam. Materials for a Life of A. T. 4 volumes. London: privately printed, 1895. This publication is extremely rare and valuable. It contains the basic material used by Hallam Tennyson in his 1897 biography of his father.

1876   Walker, Hugh. "Tennyson: The First Period of Authorship," "The Second Period of Tennyson's Work," "Tennyson and Browning: The Closing Period," "The Dramas," "The Poetry of Nature," "The Influence of Science," "The Social and Political Aspects of the Poets," and "Faith and Doubt." The Greater Victorian Poets: Tennyson, Browning, and Arnold. London: Swan Sonnenschein, 1895. New York: Macmillan, 1895, pp. 16-34, 70-90, 150-155, 174-185, 201-212, 248-251, 260-270, and 320-327, respectively. Reviewed by: Athenaeum (entry 1914); and Literary World (London) (entry 1888).

1877   Wülker, Richard Paul. Die Arthursage in der englischen Literatur. Leipzig: Edelmann, [1895]. Tennyson on pages 37-39. Publication of a dissertation: 1895 (entry 1880).

Dissertations

1878   Jones, Richard. The Growth of The Idylls of the King. Heidelberg, 1895. Published: 1895 (entry 1869). See entry 1869 for annotation.

1879   Niessl von Mayendorf, Erwin. Vier Dramen von Alfred Tennyson: Literargeschichtlich und kritisch Bearbeitet. Vienna, 1895.

1880   Wülker, Richard Paul. Die Arthursage in der englischen Literatur. Leipzig, [1895?]. Published: 1895 (entry 1877).

Periodicals

1881 Althaus, Friedrich. "Alfred Tennyson: Ein Dichterleben."
Nord und Süd, 73 (May 1895), 206-230.

1882 Block, Louis James. "Tennyson's Songs." Poet Lore, 7
(1895), 127-133.

1883 Dorchester, Daniel. "Alfred Tennyson." Methodist Review,
77 (1895), 409-422.

1884 [Elliot, Arthur.] "Mr. Stopford Brooke on Tennyson." Edin-
burgh Review, 181 (April 1895), 485-513.
Review of S. A. Brooke's Tennyson, 1894 (entry 1800) and
M.W. MacCallum's Tennyson's Idylls of the King, 1894 (entry 1804).

1885 Filon, Augustin. "Henry Irving: Les Drames de Tennyson."
Revue des Deux Mondes, Aug. 15, 1895, pp. 869-897.

1886 Jennings, Henry James. "'King Arthur' at the Lyceum."
Gentleman's Magazine, 278 (Feb. 1895), 202-211.

1887 Kitton, F.G. "Tennyson at Aldsworth." Gentleman's Magazine, 278 (Jan. 1895), 53-59.
Reprinted: Littell's Living Age, 204 (Feb. 16, 1895), 434-
438.

1888 Literary World (London), n.s. 52 (Sept. 27, 1895), 220.
Review of H. Walker's The Greater Victorian Poets, 1895
(entry 1876).

1889 Literary World (London), n.s. 52 (Nov. 1, 1895), 344.
Review of J. Oates's The Teaching of Tennyson, 1894 (entry
1805).

1890 London Quarterly Review, 85 (Oct. 1895), 76-95.
Discusses Idylls of the King.

1891 Pollock, Walter Herries. "The Laureateship." National Observer, 13 (Jan. 12, 1895), 233-234.

1892 Rolfe, W.J. "Notes on Tennyson's In Memoriam." Poet
Lore, 7 (1895), 428-435.
General comments. Might be of use to someone making a
detailed study of In Memoriam.

1893 Schuman, A.T. "A Ballade of Poets." Dial, 19 (July 1,
1895), 25.
A poem, as follows:

A Ballade of Poets

Where are the poets of the past
Whose voices rang divinely true?--
Whose thoughts munificent and vast

From stars and suns their music drew?--
To whom the gods a welcome blew,
And lamps from far Parnassus shone? . . .
None dare the heights to which they flew,
Since Alfred Tennyson is gone.

The freshening gale strained spar and mast,
The billows great and greater grew;
The vessel forward sped and fast,
Nor port nor anchorage she knew;
Naught recked they of the circling view,--
Their only end was to sweep on. . . .
Vanished are captain, ship, and crew,
Since Alfred Tennyson is gone.

Now lesser men their fortunes cast
In lesser seas, and zephyrs woo;
Their lutes are thin, they cannot last,--
We listen but to say adieu.
The artificial gems they strew
Of specious glitter fade anon. . . .
Is there no granite left to hew,
Since Alfred Tennyson is gone?

ENVOY

Fled are the mighty bards and few;
The ways of song are barren, wan. . . .
Fled is the perfect manner, too,
Since Alfred Tennyson is gone.

1894   Sweeney, Helen M.   "Tennyson and Holmes: A Parallel."
Catholic World, 60 (Jan. 1895), 521-534.

1895   "The Victorian Garden of Song." Dial, 19 (Nov. 1, 1895),
238-239.

1896   Walters, John Cuming.   "Links with Tennyson's Youth."
Academy, 47 (March 16, 1895), 238.

1896

Books

1897   Adam, Graeme Mercer.   "Alfred (Lord) Tennyson: The Spirit
of Modern Poetry." Beacon Lights of History, by John Lord.
New York: Clarke, [c.1896].   Volume XIII, pp. 437-477.

1898   Barera, Eugenio.   A Critical Essay on the Works of Alfred,
Lord Tennyson. Venice: Visentini, 1896.

1899   de Wyzewa, Teodor.   "Lord Tennyson." Ecrivains étrangers.
Paris: Perrin, 1896, pp. 75-81.

1900 Dixon, William Macneile. A Primer of Tennyson: With a
      Critical Essay. London: Methuen, 1896.
      Reprinted, third edition, as A Primer of Tennyson, 1908. A
dated but still informative basic introduction to Tennyson and his
poetry. A useful bibliography is on pages 145-189.
      Reviewed by: Literary World (London) (entry 1926); and
London Quarterly Review (entry 1927).

1901 Dowden, Edward. "Victorian Literature." Transcripts and
      Studies. London: Kegan Paul, Trench, Trübner, 1896, pp.
      201-205.

1902 Fields, Annie. "Tennyson." Authors and Friends. Boston:
      Houghton Mifflin, 1896, pp. 335-347.

1903 Knight, William. Memoir of John Nichol. Glasgow: Mac-
      Lehose, 1896.

1904 Lindsay, James. "Tennyson." Essays, Literary and Philo-
      sophical. Edinburgh: Blackwood, 1896.

1905 "Lord Tennyson, 1809-1892: Obituary Notice, Friday, October
      7, 1892." Eminent Persons: Biographies Reprinted from the
      Times. London: Macmillan, 1896. Volume V, pp. 272-290.
      Reprinted from the Times (London), 1892 (entry 1632).

1906 Saintsbury, George. "Tennyson." A History of Nineteenth
      Century Literature. London: Macmillan, 1896, pp. 253-268.
      A careful discussion of Tennyson's achievement.

1907 Seaman, Owen. "Ars Postera." The Battle of the Bays.
      New York: Lane, 1896, pp. 58-60.
      Parodies Tennyson's "Lady Clara Vere de Vere."

1908 [Shepherd, Richard Herne.] The Bibliography of Tennyson: A
      Bibliographical List of the Published and Privately-Printed
      Writings of Alfred (Lord) Tennyson, Poet Laureate, from 1827
      to 1894 Inclusive, with His Contributions to Annuals, Maga-
      zines, Newspapers, and Other Periodical Publications, and a
      Scheme for a Final and Definitive Edition of the Poet's Works.
      London: privately printed, 1896.
      Reprinted: New York: Haskell House, 1970.
      Although an unsatisfactory bibliography overall, this book con-
tains much information about Tennyson's publications that might be
useful to bibliographers, book collectors, and other literary researchers.
      Reviewed by: Literary World (London) (entry 1925).

1909 Stedman, Edmund Clarence. "Alfred Tennyson" and "Tennyson
      and Theocritus." Victorian Poets. Boston: Houghton Mifflin,
      1896, pp. 150-200 and 201-233.
      "Tennyson and Theocritus" is reprinted from Atlantic Monthly,
1871 (entry 694).

1910 Thistlethwaite, George Parker. Über die Sprache in Tenny-
      sons Idylls of the King, in ihrem Verhältniss zur Bibel und
      zu Shakespere. Halle: Kaemerer, 1896.
      Publication of a dissertation: 1896 (entry 1912).

1911 Wülker, Richard Paul. "Dramatische Litteratur im 19.
      Jahrhundert: Alfred Tennyson." Geschichte der englischen
      Litteratur von dem ältesten Zeiten bis zur Gegenwart.
      Leipzig: Bibliographisches Institut, 1896, pp. 596-603.

Dissertation

1912 Thistlethwaite, George Parker. Über die Sprache in Tenny-
      sons Idylls of the King, in ihrem Verhältniss zur Bibel und
      zu Shakespere. Halle, 1896.
      Published: 1896 (entry 1910).

Periodicals

1913 Alger, George W. "Tennyson as Poet of the English People."
      Poet Lore, 8 (1896), 325-329.

1914 Athenaeum, Jan. 18, 1896, pp. 80-81.
      Review of H. Walker's The Greater Victorian Poets, 1895
(entry 1876).

1915 Block, Louis J. "The Dramatic Sentiment and Tennyson's
      Plays." Poet Lore, 8 (1896), 512-527.
      Block defends Tennyson's plays and argues that they offer
insight into their historical subjects.

1916 Brachvogel, Udo. "Poe, Longfellow und Tennyson." Nord
      und Süd, 77 (April 1896), 87-96.

1917 Cameron, P. "Idyll of Guinevere." Catholic World, 63 (June
      1896), 328-342.

1918 Critic (New York), 29 (July 18, 1896), 46-47.
      Discusses W. Ward's "Talks with Tennyson" in New Review,
1896 (entry 1937).

1919 Dronsart, M. "Alfred Tennyson d'aprés les memoires pub-
      liées par son fils." Correspondant, Nov. 10 and Dec. 10,
      1896.

1920 Hardin, M.C. "Theology in Tennyson's Poetry." Methodist
      Review, 44 (1896), 315-319.

1921 [Hutton, Richard Holt?] "Newman and Tennyson." Spectator,
      77 (July 18, 1896), 74-75.

1922 Literary World (Boston), 27 (March 7, 1896), 70-71.
      Discusses A. Waugh's Alfred, Lord Tennyson, 1892 (entry
1415).

1923 Literary World (Boston), 27 (March 7, 1896), 71.
      Review of M. Luce's Handbook, 1895 (entry 1872).

1924 Literary World (London), n.s. 53 (Jan. 31, 1896), 92.
      Review of M. Luce's Handbook, 1895 (entry 1872).

1925 Literary World (London), n.s. 53 (Feb. 21, 1896), 170.
      Review of R.H. Shepherd's The Bibliography of Tennyson,
1896 (entry 1908).

1926 Literary World (London), n.s. 53 (April 10, 1896), 343.
      Review of W.M. Dixon's A Primer of Tennyson, 1896 (entry
1900).

1927 London Quarterly Review, 86 (April 1896), 178-179.
      Review of W.M. Dixon's A Primer of Tennyson, 1896 (entry
1900).

1928 London Quarterly Review, 86 (April 1896), 179-180.
      Review of M. Luce's Handbook, 1895 (entry 1872).

1929 Parsons, Eugene. "'In Memoriam' as a Representative
      Poem." Homiletic Review, 32 (1896), 213-219.

1930 _____. "Tennyson's Attitude Towards Skepticism."
      Homiletic Review, 32 (1896), 205-213.

1931 _____. "Tennyson's Women." Chautauquan, 23 (Aug.
      1896), 621-626.

1932 Rawnsley, Hardwicke Drummond. "In Memoriam: Lady
      Tennyson." Academy, 50 (Aug. 22, 1896), 130.
      A poem.

1933 Saturday Review (London), 81 (Feb. 1, 1896), 128-130.
      Review of M. Luce's Handbook, 1895 (entry 1872).

1934 Saturday Review (London), 81 (March 7, 1896), 257.
      Discusses A. Waugh's Alfred, Lord Tennyson, 1892 (entry
1415).

1935 "A Tale by Tennyson." Critic (New York), 28 (Feb. 1,
      1896), 81.

1936 "Tennyson's Birthplace for Sale." Critic (New York), 29 (Sept.
      5, 1896), 149.

1937 Ward, Wilfrid. "Talks with Tennyson." New Republic, 15
      (July 1896), 76-95.
      Reprinted: Littell's Living Age, 210 (Aug. 8, 1896), 323-
335; and Eclectic Magazine of Foreign Literature, 127 (Sept. 1896),
317-328. Discussed in Critic (New York), 1896 (entry 1918).

1938 Webb, W. Trego. "The Rhythm of Tennyson." Calcutta Review, 203 (Jan. 1896), 1-13.
An interesting discussion of the metrics of Tennyson's poetry.

1897

Books

1939 Bailey, Albert Edward. Notes on the Literary Aspects of Tennyson's Princess. Worcester: C. F. Laurence, 1897.

1940 Brown, Calvin S. Enoch Arden and the Two Locksley Halls. Boston: 1897.

1941 Browning, Elizabeth Barrett. The Letters of Elizabeth Barrett Browning. Ed. Frederic G. Kenyon. 2 volumes. London: Smith, Elder, 1897.

1942 Chimenti, Francesco. "Alfredo Tennyson e la sua Poesia." Larghi Orizzonti. Bari: Petruzzelli, 1897, pp. 75-93.

1943 A Chronological List of the Works of Alfred, Lord Tennyson with Some Few Items of Tennysoniana and a Series of Portraits of the Poet Laureate. New York: Grolier Club, 1897. A twenty-four-page listing.

1944 Farrar, Frederick William. "Lord Tennyson." Men I Have Known. New York: Crowell, [c.1897], pp. 1-41.

1945 McDonnell, A.C. XIX.-Century Poetry. London: Black, 1897. (Literary Epoch Series) Tennyson on pages 107-120.

1946 Mallarmé, Stéphane. "Tennyson vu d'Ici." Divagations. Paris: Charpentier, 1897. Reprinted from National Observer, 1892 (entry 1546).

1947 Nencioni, Enrico. "Lord Tennyson." Saggi critici di letteratura inglese. Florence: Le Monnier, 1897, pp. 269-300.

1948 Palgrave, Francis Turner. "The Landscape of Alfred Lord Tennyson." Landscape in Poetry from Homer to Tennyson. London: Macmillan, 1897, pp. 279-297.

1949 Quayle, William Alfred. "The Greater English Elegies." The Poet's Poet and Other Essays. Cincinnati: Curtis and Jennings, 1897, pp. 124-138.

1950 Reardon, Timothy Henry. "Alfred Tennyson, Poet Laureate." Petrarch and Other Essays. San Francisco: Doxey, 1897, pp. 43-96. Reprinted from Overland Monthly, 1885 (entry 1053).

1951 Shorter, Clement King. Victorian Literature. New York:
      Dodd, Mead, 1897.
      Tennyson on pages 10-13.

1952 Smith, Byron Caldwell. A Young Scholar's Letters: Being
      a Memoir of Byron Caldwell Smith. Ed. D.O. Kellogg.
      London: Putnam, 1897.
      Tennyson on pages 48-52.

1953 Stanley, Hiram M. "Tennyson's Rank as a Poet." Essays
      on Literary Art. London: Swan Sonnenschein, 1897, pp.
      13-24.

1954 Strong, Augustus Hopkins. "Tennyson." The Great Poets and
      Their Theology. Philadelphia: Griffith and Rowland,
      [c.1897], pp. 449-524.

1955 [Tennyson, Hallam.] Alfred Lord Tennyson: A Memoir.
      2 volumes. London: Macmillan, 1897.
      Reprinted: New York: Greenwood, 1969.
        This work is one of the most important on Tennyson. Hallam
Tennyson was the son of Alfred Lord Tennyson, and he provides a
valuable firsthand account of much of the poet's life. The Memoir
provides letters to and from Tennyson, memoirs of the poet,
and the poet's own comments on his work and responses to it. This
work is fundamental to the study of Tennyson, although its sympathetic account of the poet's life sometimes seems to gloss over Tennyson's weaknesses. Scholars often refer to this work as simply the
Memoir. Even beginning students of Tennyson and Victorian literature would be well advised to acquaint themselves with the contents
of the Memoir.
        Hallam Tennyson sets the facts of his father's life and career
in order. His efforts influence much of subsequent scholarship on
his father.
        Reviewed by: Academy (entry 1959); R. Ackermann in
Beiblatt zur Anglia (entry 2161); P. Arnstein in Das Litterarische
Echo (entry 2104); Athenaeum (entry 1962); Lady Blennerhassett in
in Deutsche Rundschau (entry 2107); Bookman (London) (entry 1964);
Bookman (New York) (entry 1966); Book Reviews (entry 1967); Church
Quarterly Review (entry 2047); Critic (New York) (entry 1972); G.
Dabbs in Quarterly Review (entry 1973); H.D. Davray in L'Ermitage
(entry 2177); Deutsche Rundschau (entry 2110); Dial (entry 1974); M.
Dronsart in Correspondant (entry 1975); E. Faguet in Quarterly Review (entry 2574); W. Canton in Good Words (entry 1970); J.E. Graham in Scottish Review (entry 2054); S. Gwynn in Macmillan's Magazine (entry 1978); W. Jerrold in Literary World (London) (entry
1981); A. Lang in Longman's Magazine (entry 1984); Literary World
(Boston) (entry 1988); Literature (entry 1990); Littell's Living Age
(entry 1991); London Quarterly Review (entry 2067); A. Lyall in
Edinburgh Review (entry 1992); H.W. Mabie in Atlantic Monthly
(entry 1993) and Outlook (entry 1994); W.H. McKellar in Sewanee
Review (entry 2070); J.H. Millar in Blackwood's Edinburgh Magazine
(entry 1996); Nation (New York) (entry 1999); Overland Monthly (entry

2075); F. Roz in Bibliothèque Universelle et Revue Suisse (entry
2643); St. James Gazette (entry 2004); Saturday Review (London)
(entry 2005); Spectator (entry 2008); F. Thompson in New Review
(entry 2016); G. Valbert in Revue des Deux Mondes (entry 2020);
and H. Van Dyke in Book Buyer (entry 2022).

1956   Van Dyke, Henry. "Preface." In Memoriam, by Alfred,
       Lord Tennyson. New York: Fords, Howard, and Hubert,
       1897, pp. v-xxiii.

1957   Walker, Hugh. Age of Tennyson. London: Bell, 1897.
       Reviewed by: Bookman (London) (entry 1965); Literary World
(London) (entry 1989); and Saturday Review (London) (entry 2078).

Dissertation

1958   Pyre, James F. A. A Study of Tennyson's Blank Verse.
       Wisconsin, 1897.

Periodicals

1959   Academy, 52 (Oct. 9, 1897), 275-277.
       Review of H. Tennyson's Alfred Lord Tennyson, 1897 (entry
1955).

1960   Albee, John. "'Learn' for 'Teach' in Tennyson." Dial, 22
       (March 16, 1897), 177.
       See also: C. S. Brown in Dial (entry 1969).

1961   "Another and a Better Tennyson." Saturday Review (London)
       84 (Nov. 27, 1897), 582-584.

1962   Athenaeum, Oct. 9 and 16, 1897, pp. 481-484 and 521-524.
       Review of H. Tennyson's Alfred Lord Tennyson, 1897 (entry
1955).

1963   Baskerville, W. M. "Lord Tennyson." Methodist Review, 46
       (1897), 323-337.

1964   Bookman (London), 13 (Nov. 1897), 36-38.
       Review of H. Tennyson's Alfred Lord Tennyson, 1897 (entry
1955).

1965   Bookman (London), 13 (Nov. 1897), 51.
       Review of H. Walker's Age of Tennyson, 1897 (entry 1957).

1966   Bookman (New York), 6 (Dec. 1897), 357-360.
       Review of H. Tennyson's Alfred Lord Tennyson, 1897 (entry
1955).

1967   Book Reviews, 5 (Nov. 1897), 115-118.
       Review of H. Tennyson's Alfred Lord Tennyson, 1897 (entry
1955).

1968 Bowen, Robert Adger. "Tennyson." Bookman (New York), 5
(March 1897), 46.
A poem, as follows:

Tennyson

> Life spoke her mystic secrets in thine ear,
>   And Art gave to thee thine own Merlin's spell:
>   While in thy soul, as in an ocean's shell,
> God's everlasting music echoed clear.

1969 Brown, Calvin S. "Tennyson's Fondness for Archaic Words."
Dial, 22 (April 1, 1897), 209.
See also: J. Albee in Dial (entry 1960).

1970 Canton, William. "The Life of Lord Tennyson." Good
Words, 38 (1897), 785-792.
Review of H. Tennyson's Alfred Lord Tennyson, 1897 (entry
1955).

1971 Clark, William. "Tennyson's 'Crossing the Bar.'" Canadian
Magazine, 8 (March 1897), 420-422.

1972 Critic (New York), 31 (Oct. 16, 1897), 213-214.
Review of H. Tennyson's Alfred Lord Tennyson, 1897 (entry
1955).

1973 [Dabbs, George.] Quarterly Review, 186 (Oct. 1897), 492-
528.
Review of H. Tennyson's Alfred Lord Tennyson, 1897 (entry
1955).

1974 Dial, 23 (Oct. 16, 1897), 212-214.
Review of H. Tennyson's Alfred Lord Tennyson, 1897 (entry
1955).

1975 Dronsart, M. "Lord Tennyson." Correspondant, 189 (Nov.
10 and Dec. 10, 1897), 533-550 and 959-980.
Review of H. Tennyson's Alfred Lord Tennyson, 1897 (entry
1955).

1976 Gosse, Edmund William. "Life of Tennyson." North American Review, 165 (Nov. 1897), 513-526.

1977 Graves, Alfred Perceval. "Tennyson in Ireland: A Reminiscence." Cornhill Magazine, 76 (Nov. 1897), 594-602.
Reprinted: Tennyson in Ireland, 1913 (entry 2719).

1978 Gwynn, Stephen. Macmillan's Magazine, 77 (Nov. 1897),
57-66.
Review of H. Tennyson's Alfred Lord Tennyson, 1897 (entry
1955).

1979 Hunt, Theodore Whitfield. "Tennyson's 'In Memoriam.'"
Bibliotheca Sacra, 54 (April 1897), 249-263.
Reprinted: English Literary Miscellany, 1914 (entry 2762).

1980 Independent, 49 (Dec. 9, 1897), 1623.
Discusses In Memoriam.

1981 Jerrold, W. Literary World (London), n.s. 56 (Oct. 15,
1897), 275-277.
Review of H. Tennyson's Alfred Lord Tennyson, 1897 (entry
1955).

1982 Knight, William. "A Reminiscence of Tennyson." Blackwood's Edinburgh Magazine, 162 (Aug. 1897), 264-270.

1983 Koeppel, Emil. "Tennyson." Allgemeine Zeitung, 1897.

1984 Lang, Andrew. Longman's Magazine, 31 (Nov. 1897), 27-39.
Review of H. Tennyson's Alfred Lord Tennyson, 1897 (entry
1955).

1985 Lester, George. "Concerning Lord Tennyson's Knowledge and
Use of the Bible." Methodist Review, 45 (1897), 163-170.

1986 _____. "Tennyson and Christmas." Methodist Review, 46
(1897), 338-350.

1987 Lilly, William Samuel. "The Mission of Tennyson." Fortnightly Review, 61 (Feb. 1, 1897), 239-250.
Reprinted: Studies in Religion and Literature, 1904 (entry
2354).

1988 Literary World (Boston), 28 (Nov. 13, 1897), 389-390.
Review of H. Tennyson's Alfred Lord Tennyson, 1897 (entry
1955).

1989 Literary World (London), n.s. 56 (Dec. 3, 1897), 444.
Review of H. Walker's Age of Tennyson, 1897 (entry 1957).

1990 Literature, 1 (Oct. 23 and 30, 1897), 3-5 and 34-36.
Review of H. Tennyson's Alfred Lord Tennyson, 1897 (entry
1955).

1991 Littell's Living Age, 215 (Oct. 30, 1897), 295-306.
Review of H. Tennyson's Alfred Lord Tennyson, 1897 (entry
1955).

1992 [Lyall, Alfred.] "Alfred Lord Tennyson." Edinburgh Review,
186 (Oct. 1897), 275-306.
Review of H. Tennyson's Alfred Lord Tennyson, 1897 (entry
1955).

1993 Mabie, Hamilton Wright. "The Life of Tennyson." Atlantic

Monthly, 80 (Nov. 1897), 577-589.
Review of H. Tennyson's Alfred Lord Tennyson, 1897 (entry
1955).

1994 _____. Outlook, 57 (Nov. 6, 1897), 577-583.
Review of H. Tennyson's Alfred Lord Tennyson, 1897 (entry
1955).

1995 McGiffert, Margaret C. "Tennyson's Use of Archaic Forms."
Dial, 22 (April 16, 1897), 240-241.

1996 [Millar, J. H.] "Lord Tennyson." Blackwood's Edinburgh
Magazine, 162 (Nov. 1897), 615-629.
Review of H. Tennyson's Alfred Lord Tennyson, 1897 (entry
1955).

1997 Moore, John Murray. "Tennyson's Nature Studies." Literary
and Philosophical Society of Liverpool: Proceedings, 51 (Nov.
1897), 189-215.

1998 Moseley, W. M. "Tennyson and Immortality." Wesleyan
Methodist Magazine, 120 (1897), 859-866.

1999 Nation (New York), 65 (Nov. 11, 1897), 379-381.
Review of H. Tennyson's Alfred Lord Tennyson, 1897 (entry
1955).

2000 O'Connor, V. C. Scott. "Tennyson and His Friends at Freshwater." Century Illustrated Monthly Magazine, 33 (Dec.
1897), 240-268.
Of biographical interest.

2001 Parkin, George R. "Tennyson." Canadian Monthly, 10 (Dec.
1897), 167-172.

2002 Rideing, William H. "Tennyson in the Isle of Wight."
North American Review, 165 (Dec. 1897), 701-710.

2003 Rolfe, William James. "The Metre of 'In Memoriam.'"
Dial, 23 (July 1, 1897), 7.

2004 St. James Gazette, Oct. 6, 1897.
Review of H. Tennyson's Alfred Lord Tennyson, 1897 (entry
1955).

2005 Saturday Review (London), 84 (Oct. 16, 1897), 423-424.
Review of H. Tennyson's Alfred Lord Tennyson, 1897 (entry
1955).

2006 Sinclair, W. "The Religious Poetry of Tennyson." Churchman, n. s. 12 (1897), 435-443 and 475-483.

2007 Smith, C. Alphonso. "The Metre of 'In Memoriam.'" Dial,
22 (June 16, 1897), 351-352.

2008 Spectator, 79 (Oct 16 and 23, 1897), 522-524 and 556-558.
Review of H. Tennyson's Alfred Lord Tennyson, 1897 (entry
1955).

2009 Spender, Harold. "Tennyson: A Study in Poetic Workman-
ship." Fortnightly Review, 62 (Nov. 1897), 778-783.

2010 "Tennyson and Wordsworth." Academy, 52 (Oct. 23, 1897),
331.

2011 "Tennyson as a Dramatist." Academy, 52 (Aug. 14, 1897),
134-135.
Downgrades Tennyson's dramas.

2012 "Tennyson as a Guest." Spectator, 78 (April 3, 1897), 475.

2013 "Tennyson Reference List." Providence Public Library
Monthly Bulletin, 3 (Oct. 1897), 280-283.
Of bibliographic interest.

2014 "Tennyson's Ruling Passion." Spectator, 79 (Aug. 14, 1897),
207-208.

2015 Thompson, Francis. "Academy Portraits. XXIII--Tennyson."
Academy, 51 (April 17, 1897), 428-429.

2016 _____. "The Life of Tennyson." New Review, 17 (Nov.
1897), 536-548.
Review of H. Tennyson's Alfred Lord Tennyson, 1897 (entry
1955).

2017 _____. "The Withheld Poems of Tennyson." Academy, 52
(Oct. 23, 1897), 326-327.

2018 Traill, Henry Duff. "The Literature of the Victorian Era."
Fortnightly Review, 67 (June 1897), 830-831.

2019 Truman, Joseph. "Victoria's Poets." Spectator, 78 (April 3,
1897), 476.
A poem.

2020 Valbert, G. (Victor Cherbuliez). "La vie d'Alfred, Lord
Tennyson." Revue des Deux Mondes, Dec. 1, 1897, pp.
671-682.
Review of H. Tennyson's Alfred Lord Tennyson, 1897 (entry
1955). Finds the biography verbose.

2021 Valdes, Edgar. "The Birds of Tennyson." Temple Bar, 110
(1897), 495-512.
Reprinted: Littell's Living Age, 213 (June 19, 1897), 807-
817.

2022 Van Dyke, Henry. "A Filial Portrait of a Great Poet."

Book Buyer, n.s. 15 (Dec. 1897), 433-441.
Review of H. Tennyson's Alfred Lord Tennyson, 1897 (entry 1955).

2023 Ward, Wilfrid. "Tennyson's Religious Philosophy." Spectator, 79 (Nov. 13, 1897), 681-683.

2024 Weld, Agnes Grace. "Tennyson." Contemporary Review, 72 (Nov. 1897), 689-696.

2025 Wise, Thomas James. "Tennyson Bibliography." Athenaeum, March 27, April 10 and 24, May 22, Sept. 18 and 25, 1897, pp. 417-418, 479-480, 543-544, 681-682, 388-389, and 419-420, respectively.

1898

Books

2026 Armstrong, Richard A. "Alfred Tennyson." Faith and Doubt in the Century's Poets. New York: Whittaker, 1898, pp. 67-90.

2027 Beers, Henry Augustin. From Chaucer to Tennyson. New York: Flood and Vincent, 1898. (Chautauqua Reading Circle Literature)
Tennyson on pages 244-249.

2028 Cary, Elisabeth Luther. Tennyson: His Homes, His Friends, and His Work. New York: Putnam, 1898.
Reviewed by: Critic (New York) (entry 2109); and Literary World (Boston) (entry 2065).

2029 Compton-Rickett, Arthur. Prophets of the Century. London: Ward, Lock, 1898.

2030 Cuthbertson, Evan J. Tennyson: The Story of His Life. London: Chambers, 1898.
A short biography that follows Hallam Tennyson's Alfred Lord Tennyson (entry 1955).
Reviewed by: Literary World (London) (entry 2066).

2031 Forster, Joseph. Great Teachers. London: Redway, 1898.

2032 Griswold, Hattie Tyng. "Alfred Tennyson." Personal Sketches of Recent Authors. Chicago: McClurg, 1898, pp. 11-31.

2033 Merivale, Charles. Atuobiography and Letters of Charles Merivale, Dean of Ely. Ed. Judith Anne Merivale. Oxford: H. Hart, 1898.

2034 Rolfe, William James. "Biographical Sketch" and Bibliogra-

phy of Tennyson's Works." The Poetic and Dramatic Works.
of Alfred Lord Tennyson. Boston: Houghton Mifflin,
[c.1898], pp. xi-xvii and 875-876, respectively.

2035 _____. "Notes and Illustrations." Tennyson's Poetical
Works. Boston: Houghton Mifflin, 1898.

2036 Royce, Josiah. "Tennyson and Pessimism." Studies of Good
and Evil. New York: Appleton, 1898, pp. 76-88.
Royce discusses "Locksley Hall" and "Locksley Hall Sixty
Years After." He is unhappy with the poems because of their
philosophical implications; he calls "Locksley Hall" "unhealthy."
This essay is still useful and interesting.

2037 Stephen, Leslie. "Life of Tennyson." Studies of a Biographer. New York: Putnam, 1898. Volume II, pp. 196-240.
Stephen admires Tennyson's early works more than the later
ones. He emphasizes the profound effect Tennyson's early poems
such as "Locksley Hall" and "The Lotos-Eaters" had on young people when first published.

2038 Ward, William G. Tennyson's Debt to His Environment: A
Study of Tennyson's England as an Introduction to His Poems.
Boston: Roberts, 1898.
A one-hundred-page study that is long on praise.

2039 White, Walter. Journals. London: Chapman and Hall, 1898.
Tennyson on pages 141-168. Of biographical interest for the
middle years of Tennyson's life.

2040 Whitman, Walt. "A Word About Tennyson." Complete Prose
Works. Boston: Small, Maynard, 1898. London: G. P.
Putnam's Sons, 1898, pp. 403-405.
Reprinted from Critic (New York), 1887 (entry 1212). See
entry 1212 for other reprintings and for annotation.

Dissertation

2041 Baker, Myron Eugene. Tennyson and Browning: A Study in
the Conflict of Personality and Art. Wisconsin, 1898.

Periodicals

2042 Axon, William. "An Italian Translator of Tennyson."
Notes and Queries, 9th ser. 1 (June 25, 1898), 503-504.

2043 Barthélemy, A. "Tennyson." Revue Hebdomadaire, March
1898.

2044 Boedeker, Augusta. "Tennyson's 'Idylls of the King.'"
Education, 18 (Feb., March, and April 1898), 355-361.
403-413, and 476-481.

2045 Bouchier, Jonathan. "Mistral and Tennyson." Notes and Queries, 9th ser. 2 (Dec. 17, 1898), 487.

2046 Bricard, Georges. "Alfred Tennyson." La Quinzaine, 22 (May 16, 1898), 259-277.

2047 Church Quarterly Review, 45 (Jan. 1898), 331-356. Review of H. Tennyson's Alfred Lord Tennyson, 1897 (entry 1955).

2048 Ellis, A.S. "Tennyson Family." Notes and Queries, 9th ser. 1 (April 16, 1898), 312-313.

2049 Escott, Thomas Hay Sweet. "Cornish Colour in Tennyson's Poetry." New Century Review, 3 (Jan. 1898), 52-58.

2050 Fischer, Charles. "Tennyson, the Man." Gentleman's Magazine, 285 (Sept. 1898), 265-274.

2051 Ford, C. Lawrence. "'In Memoriam,' LIV." Notes and Queries, 9th ser. 1 (Feb. 5, 1898), 110. See also: R.M. Spence in Notes and Queries (entry 2080).

2052 _____. "Tennysoniana." Notes and Queries, 9th ser. 2 (Dec. 10, 1898), 461-462.

2053 Gosse, Edmund William. "Tennyson's Last Poem." Literature, 2 (Jan. 8, 1898), 23.

2054 Graham, J.E. Scottish Review, 31 (Jan. 1898), 23-51. Review of H. Tennyson's Alfred Lord Tennyson, 1897 (entry 1955).

2055 Henry, H.T. "Lord Alfred Tennyson." American Catholic Quarterly, 23 (1898), 1-27.

2056 Hinckley, Henry B. "Tennyson and Crabbe." Nation (New York), 66 (Jan. 20, 1898), 47-48.

2057 Hope, Henry Gerald. "Tennyson on Havelock, 1857." Notes and Queries, 9th ser. 2 (Sept. 3, 1898), 184.

2058 Hunt, Theodore Whitfield. "Tennyson's 'Idylls of the King.'" Bibliotheca Sacra, 55 (July 1898), 444-458. Reprinted: English Literary Miscellany, 1914 (entry 2762).

2059 Jack, Albert E. "Dr. Rolfe's Notes on Tennyson." Dial, 25 (Dec. 16, 1898), 449-450.

2060 Kellner, Leon. "Tennyson." Die Nation, 15 (Feb. 12, 1898), 288-290.

2061 Kennedy, William Sloane. "Tennyson and Other Debtors to Spenser's 'Faerie Queen.'" Poet Lore, 10 (1898), 492-506.

2062 Kenyon, James Benjamin. "Tennyson in New Aspects."
Methodist Review, 80 (May 1898), 434-453.
Reprinted: Loiterings in Old Fields, 1901 (entry 2225).

2063 "The Laureate of Lincolnshire." Blackwood's Edinburgh
Magazine, 164 (Nov. 1898), 670-675.

2064 Lee, John. "The Passing of Arthur." Literary and Philosophical Society of Liverpool, 52 (1898), 39-56.

2065 Literary World (Boston), 29 (Dec. 10, 1898), 434.
Review of E. L. Cary's Tennyson, 1898 (entry 2028).

2066 Literary World (London), n. s. 58 (Dec. 2, 1898), 436.
Review of E. J. Cuthbertson's Tennyson, 1898 (entry 2030).

2067 London Quarterly Review, 89 (Jan. 1898), 205-231.
Review of H. Tennyson's Alfred Lord Tennyson, 1898 (entry
1955).

2068 "Lord Tennyson." Academy, 53 (Jan. 8, 1898), 34-36.

2069 Luce, Morton. "The Evolution of the Idylls of the King."
Academy, 53 (June 11, 1898), 640-641.

2070 McKellar, W. H. Sewanee Review, 6 (Jan. 1898), 94-100.
Review of H. Tennyson's Alfred Lord Tennyson, 1897 (entry
1955).

2071 Moore, John Murray. "Tennyson as a National Poet." Literary and Philosophical Society of Liverpool, 52 (Sept. 1898),
85-118.

2072 Mustard, Wilfrid Pirt. "Tennyson and Catullus." Nation
(New York), 66 (May 12, 1898), 362-363.

2073 _____. "Tennyson and Horace." Nation (New York), 66
(June 9, 1898), 438-439.

2074 Negri, Gaetano. "Gladstone and Tennyson." Die Gesellschaft,
2 (1898), 762-771.
See: G. Negri's Segni dei Tempi, 1893 (entry 1683).

2075 Overland Monthly, n. s. 31 (March 1898), 255-260.
Review of H. Tennyson's Alfred Lord Tennyson, 1897 (entry
1955).

2076 Parsons, Eugene. "A Literary Biography." Chautauquan, 26
(March 1898), 641-644.

2077 "Reputations Reconsidered: III. Lord Tennyson." Academy,
53 (Jan. 8, 1898), 34-36.

2078 Saturday Review (London), 85 (Jan. 15, 1898), 85-86.
Review of H. Walker's Age of Tennyson, 1897 (entry 1957).

2079 Shields, Charles W. "The Arctic Monument Named for Tennyson by Dr. Kane." Century Illustrated Monthly Magazine, 34 (Aug. 1898), 483-492.

2080 Spence, R. M. "'In Memoriam,' LIV." Notes and Queries, 9th ser. 1 (Jan. 1 and April 9, 1898), 18 and 292.
See also: C. L. Ford in Notes and Queries (entry 2051).

2081 Temple, Joseph. "Tennyson and Bright." Literature, 3 (Aug. 13, 1898), 141.
See also: C. A. Vince in Literature (entry 2084).

2082 "Tennyson and Horace." Nation (New York), 67 (Dec. 22, 1898), 465.

2083 Trent, William Peterfield. "Tennyson and Musset Once More." Bookman (New York), 7 (April 1898), 108-114.
Reprinted: Authority and Criticism, 1899 (entry 2100).

2084 Vince, C. A. "Tennyson and Bright." Literature, 3 (Aug. 27, 1898), 186.
See also: J. Temple in Literature (entry 2081).

2085 Whymper, A. "One of Tennyson's Rustic Friends." Sunday Magazine, 27 (April 1898), 221-223.

2086 "Young and Tennyson." Notes and Queries, 9th ser. 1 (June 25, 1898), 501-502.

1899

Books

2087 Adams, Francis. "Tennyson." Essays in Modernity. London: Lane, 1899, pp. 3-39.

2088 Browning, Robert, and Elizabeth Barrett Browning. The Letters of Robert Browning and Elizabeth Barrett Barrett, 1845-1846. [Ed. Robert B. Browning.] 2 volumes. London: 1899.

2089 Bryden, Robert. "Tennyson." Some Woodcuts of Men of Letters of the Nineteenth Century. London: Dent, 1899.

2090 Dawson, W. J. Makers of Modern Poetry. London: Hodder and Stoughton, 1899.
Tennyson on pages 169-269.

2091 Fischer, Thomas A. Leben und Werke Alfred Lord Tennysons.

Gotha: Perthes, 1899.
Reviewed by: R. Ackermann in Beiblatt zur Anglia (entry
2162); Deutsche Rundschau (entry 2110); and Literature (entry 2119).

2092 Gwynn, Stephen. Tennyson: A Critical Study. London:
Blackie, 1899. (Victorian Era Series)
A sympathetic study of Tennyson's poetry. Gwynn's comments are insightful.
Reviewed by: Athenaeum (entry 2105); Bookman (London)
(entry 2108); Literary World (London) (entry 2118); Literature
(entry 2120); D. O'Brien in Truth (London) (entry 2127); and Spectator (entry 2129).

2093 Hillis, Newell Dwight. "Tennyson's Idylls of the King."
Great Books as Life Teachers. Chicago: Revell, 1899,
pp. 151-177.

2094 Koeppel, Emil. Tennyson. Berlin: Hofmann, 1899.
Reviewed by: R. Ackermann in Beiblatt zur Anglia (entry
2163).

2095 Mustard, Wilfrid Pirt. Tennyson and Virgil. Baltimore:
Lord Baltimore Press, [1899].
Reprinted from: American Journal of Philology, 1899 (entry
2126).

2096 Peck, Harry Thurston. "Human Side of Tennyson." What
Is Good English and Other Essays. New York: Dodd, Mead,
1899, pp. 169-194.
Also in: Bookman (New York) (entry 2594).

2097 Ragey, Le Père. Tennyson. Paris: Delhomme et Briguet,
1899.
An admiring biography that features confusing religious interpretations of Tennyson's poetry.

2098 Scudder, Vida Dutton. "Tennyson and 'In Memoriam.'"
The Life of the Spirit in the Modern English Poets. Boston:
Houghton Mifflin, 1899, pp. 281-290.

2099 Sharp, Elizabeth A. "Introduction." English Idyls: The
Princess: and Other Poems, by Alfred, Lord Tennyson.
London: Scott, [1899], pp. vii-xxviii. (Canterbury Poets)

2100 Trent, William Peterfield. "Tennyson and Musset Once
More." Authority of Criticism. New York: Scribner,
1899, pp. 269-291.
Reprinted from: Bookman (New York), 1898 (entry 2083).

2101 Watson, William. "To Lord Tennyson." The Collected Poems
of William Watson. New York: Lane, 1899, p. 83.
Reprinted from: Critic (New York), 1892 (entry 1648).
A poem.

Dissertation

2102 Margulies, David. "Maud" und "Locksley Hall": Zwei
      literarischkulturgeschichtliche Abhandlungen, mit einer kurzen
      Biographie Tennysons und erklärenden Bemerkungen. Vienna,
      1899.

Periodicals

2103 Allen, Katherine. "Lucretius the Poet and Tennyson's Poem
      'Lucretius.'" Poet Lore, 1899.

2104 Arnstein, P. Das Litterarische Echo, 1 (Jan. 15, 1899),
      522-523.
      Review of H. Tennyson's Alfred Lord Tennyson, 1897 (entry
1955).

2105 Athenaeum, May 6, 1899, pp. 561-562.
      Review of S. L. Gwynn's Tennyson, 1899 (entry 2092).

2106 Bayne, Thomas. "Tennyson's 'The Ancient Sage.'" Notes
      and Queries, 9th ser. 3 (May 13, 1899), 376.

2107 Blennerhassett, Lady. "Alfred Lord Tennyson." Deutsche
      Rundschau, 98 (Feb. 1899), 257-290.
      Review of H. Tennyson's Alfred Lord Tennyson, 1897 (entry
1955).

2108 Bookman (London), 16 (May 1899), 57.
      Review of S. L. Gwynn's Tennyson, 1899 (entry 2092).

2109 Critic (New York), 34 (Jan. 1899), 71-74.
      Review of E. L. Cary's Tennyson, 1898 (entry 2028).

2110 Deutsche Rundschau, 101 (1899), 195.
      Review of H. Tennyson's Alfred Lord Tennyson, 1897 (entry
1955) and T. A. Fisher's Leben und Worke Alfred Lord Tennysons,
1899 (entry 2091).

2111 Draycott, Charles. "A Medley of Voices." Temple Bar, 117
      (July 1899), 418.

2112 Ford, C. Lawrence. "Tennyson's 'The Ancient Sage.'"
      Notes and Queries, 9th ser. 3 (May 13, 1899), 376.
      See also: F. Jarratt and R. M. Spence in Notes and Queries,
(entries 2116 and 2130).

2113 Gregory, D. S. "A Literary Study of 'In Memoriam.'"
      Homiletic Review, 38 (1899), 467-472.

2114 Hodell, Charles W. "The Three Christmases in 'In Memori-
      am.'" Poet Lore, 11 (1899), 451-455.

2115   Jack, Albert E.   "Tennyson Bibliographies."   Dial, 26 (May 16, 1899), 329.

2116   Jarratt, F.   "Tennyson's 'The Ancient Sage.'"   Notes and Queries, 9th ser. 3 (May 13, 1899), 376.
See also: C. L. Ford and R. M. Spence in Notes and Queries, (entries 2112 and 2130).

2117   Literary World (London), n. s. 59 (March 17, 1899), 250.
Discusses J. Oates's The Teaching of Tennyson, 1894 (entry 1805).

2118   Literary World (London), n. s. 59 (May 26, 1899), 489.
Review of S. L. Gwynn's Tennyson, 1899 (entry 2092).

2119   Literature, 4 (Feb. 18, 1899), 171-172.
Review of T. A. Fischer's Leben und Werke Alfred Lord Tennysons, 1899 (entry 2091).

2120   Literature, 4 (April 8, 1899), 354-356.
Review of S. L. Gwynn's Tennyson, 1899 (entry 2092).

2121   Literature, 5 (Dec. 23, 1899), 605-606.
Review of F. Harrison's Tennyson, Ruskin, Mill, 1900 (entry 2144).

2122   Livingston, Luther Samuel.   "The First Books of Some English Authors: The Tennysons."   Bookman (New York), 10 (Oct. 1899), 123-127.
Of bibliographical interest.

2123   Meakin, Budgett.   "Tennyson's 'Timbuctoo.'"   Athenaeum, Nov. 25, 1899, pp. 722-723.

2124   Moore, John Murray.   "Tennyson as a Poet of Humanity."   Literary and Philosophical Society of Liverpool: Proceedings, 53 (1899), 81-105.

2125   Mudge, J.   "Tennyson and His Teachings."   Methodist Review, 81 (1899), 874-887.

2126   Mustard, Wilfrid Pirt.   "Tennyson and Virgil."   American Journal of Philology, 20 (1899), 186-194.
Reprinted: Tennyson and Virgil, 1899 (entry 2095).

2127   O'Brien, D.   Truth (London), 46 (Oct. 5, 1899), 834.
Review of S. L. Gwynn's Tennyson, 1899 (entry 2092).

2128   Read, William A.   "Some Traces of Keats' Influence upon the Language of Tennyson."   Englische Studien, 26 (1899), 326-327.

2129   Spectator, 83 (Oct. 7, 1899), 467-468.
Review of S. L. Gwynn's Tennyson, 1899 (entry 2092).

2130 Spence, R.M. "Tennyson's 'The Ancient Sage.'" Notes and Queries, 9th ser. 3 (April 1, 1899), 248.
See also: C.L. Ford and F. Jarratt in Notes and Queries (entries 2112 and 2116).

2131 "The Spiteful Letter." Notes and Queries, 9th ser. 3 (April 22, 1899), 317.

2132 "Tennyson and the Birds." Saturday Review (London), 87 (April 1, 1899), 393-394.

2133 "Tennyson and Virgil." Academy, 57 (July 22, 1899), 88-89.

2134 "Traductions de Tennyson." L'Intermédiare des Chercheurs et Curieux, 39 (April 10, May 7, and June 30, 1899), 507, 662, and 978; and 40 (July 30, 1899), 163.

2135 "The True Poet of Imperialism." Macmillan's Magazine, 80 (July 1899), 192-195.

2136 Westercamp, F.W. "Tennyson als Dramatiker." Gegenwart, 55 (Feb. 4, 1899), 71-75.

1900

Books

2137 Allen, G.C. Tales from Tennyson. London: Constable, 1900.
Reviewed by: Literary World (London) (entry 2192).

2138 Brooks, Elbridge Streeter. Out Doors with Tennyson. Boston: Lothrop, Lee and Shepard, 1900.

2139 Chesson, Nora Hopper. Tales from Tennyson. London: Tuck, [190-?].

2140 Clark, J. Scott. "Bibliography of Criticism on Tennyson." A Study of English and American Poets. New York: Scribner, 1900, pp. 764-766.

2141 Collier, William Francis. "Alfred, Lord Tennyson." A History of English Literature in a Series of Biographical Sketches. London: Nelson, 1900, pp. 472-479.

2142 Collins, John Churton (ed.). "Introduction." The Early Poems of Alfred Lord Tennyson. London: Methuen, 1900, pp. vii-xlii. Bibliography on pages 315-317.
Collins was an above-average critic and scholar whose "Introduction" remains of interest for its general commentary.
Reviewed by: Athenaeum (entry 2168); Bookman (London) (entry 2170); A.E. Jack in Dial (entry 2244); Literary World (Boston) (entry 2189); Literary World (London) (entry 2191); Saturday Review (London) (entry 2204); Speaker (entry 2206); and Spectator, 1900

and 1901 (entries 2208 and 2269).   See also: J.C. Collins in Critic
(New York) (entry 2176).

2143   Gates, Lewis Edwards.   "Tennyson's Relation to Modern
         Life" and "Nature in Tennyson's Poetry."   Studies and Appre-
         ciations.   New York: Macmillan, 1900, pp. 60-76 and 77-91,
         respectively.
         "Tennyson's Relation to Modern Life" reprinted from Critic
(New York), 1900 (entry 2181).

2144   Harrison, Frederic.   "Tennyson."   Tennyson, Ruskin, Mill
         and Other Literary Estimates.   New York: Macmillan, 1900,
         pp. 1-47.
         Harrison provides a balanced assessment of Tennyson's work.
His views are sometimes unsympathetic, particularly when he discusses Tennyson's thinking, but he never loses sight of Tennyson's
achievements.
         Reviewed by: Athenaeum (entry 2166); Bookman (New York)
(entry 2171); Literary World (Boston) (entry 2188); Literature (entry
2121); Nation (New York) (entry 2199); Saturday Review (London)
(entry 2203); and W.P. Trent in Current Literature (entry 2212).

2145   Herford, Oliver.   "Godiva."   Overheard in a Garden.   New
         York: Scribner, [c.1900], pp. 96-97.

2146   Horton, Robert Forman.   Alfred Tennyson: A Saintly Life.
         London: Dent, 1900.
         Contributes little original to the study of Tennyson's life.
         Reviewed by: Literary World (Boston) (entry 2248); Saturday
Review (London) (entry 2205); and A.M. Stoddart in Bookman (London)
(entry 2209).

2147   Looten, C.   Une Biographie de Tennyson.   Arras: Sueur-
         Charruey, 1900.
         Looten's criticism is interesting, but his account of Tennyson's
life is not.

2148   Masterman, C.F.G.   Tennyson as a Religious Teacher.   Lon-
         don: Methuen, 1900.   Reprinted: New York: Octagon, 1977.
         This book is the fundamental study of Tennyson's religious
views.   Masterman establishes what Tennyson's views were and relates those views to the context of the Victorian era.   Anyone interested in Tennyson's thoughts on religion and the importance of religion to the poetry should consult this book.
         Reviewed by: Literary World (London) (entry 2190); Literature
(entry 2195); and Spectator (entry 2207).

2149   O'Hagen, Thomas.   "Tennyson's 'In Memoriam.'"   Studies in
         Poetry: Critical, Analytical, Interpretive.   Boston: Marlier,
         Callanan, 1900, pp. 1-23.

2150   Parsons, Eugene.   "Introduction" and "Bibliography of First
         Editions."   The Poetical Works of Alfred, Lord Tennyson,

Poet Laureate. New York: Crowell, [c. 1900], pp. iii-xv
and xvii-xviii, respectively.

2151 Rawnsley, Hardwicke Drummond. Memories of the Tennysons. Glasgow: MacLehose, 1900.
The Rawnsleys were friends of the Tennysons in Lincolnshire.
Reviewed by: Academy (entry 2160); Literary World (London)
(entry 2194); Literature (entry 2196); Nation (New York) (entry 2260);
and Saturday Review (London) (entry 2266).

2152 Sharp, Robert Farquharson. "Tennyson." Architects of
English Literature. New York: Dutton, 1900, pp. 314-326.

2153 Sneath, Elias Hershey. The Mind of Tennyson: His Thoughts
on God, Freedom, and Immortality. Westminster: Constable,
1900.
This book provides a study of Tennyson's philosophy and the
relation of the Victorian Age to Tennyson's thought. Sneath's discussion is worth studying.
Reviewed by: Literary World (London) (entry 2193).

2154 Traill, Henry Duff. The New Lucian: Series of Dialogues of
the Dead. London: Chapman, 1900.

2155 Trevvett, Florence. A Child Story from Tennyson's "Enoch
Arden." Chicago: Scroll, 1900.

2156 Van Dyke, Henry. Outline of Lectures on Wordsworth,
Browning, and Tennyson. Princeton: Princeton Press,
[1900].

2157 [Ward, Louisa Edith.] Memorials for My Children and Personal Recollections of Lord Tennyson. Ed. R. W. (Richard
Ward). London?: privately printed, [c. 1900].

2158 Zocco, Irene. Spigolando. Catania: Niccolo Giannotta, 1900.

Periodicals

2159 Academy, 59 (July 21, 1900), 46.
On Tennyson's The Princess. Of bibliographical interest.

2160 Academy, 59 (Nov. 10, 1900), 439-440.
Review of H. D. Rawnsley's Memories, 1900 (entry 2151).

2161 Ackermann, R. Beiblatt zur Anglia, 10 (March 1900), 323-
328.
Review of H. Tennyson's Alfred Lord Tennyson, 1897 (entry
1955).

2162 _____. Beiblatt zur Anglia, 10 (April 1900), 353-354.
Review of T. A. Fischer's Leben und Werke Alfred Lord
Tennysons, 1899 (entry 2091).

2163 _____. Beiblatt zur Anglia, 10 (April 1900), 355-357.
Review of E. Koeppel's Tennyson, 1899 (entry 2094).

2164 "Apparatus for the Study of Tennyson." Literary World
(Boston), 31 (July 1, 1900), 136.
A listing with notes.

2165 Aronstein, P. "Tennyson's Welt-und Lebensanchauung."
Englische Studien, 28 (1900), 54-91.

2166 Athenaeum, Jan. 27, 1900, p. 103.
Review of F. Harrison's Tennyson, Ruskin, Mill, 1900 (entry
2144).

2167 Athenaeum, Feb. 3, 1900, p. 144.
Discusses Tennyson's poetry.

2168 Athenaeum, June 16, 1900, 747-748.
Review of J.C. Collins, ed., Early Poems, 1900 (entry
2142).

2169 Barnes, S.D. "The Faith of Tennyson." Methodist Review,
82 (1900), 582-591.

2170 Bookman (London), 18 (July 1900), 122.
Review of J.C. Collins, ed., Early Poems, 1900 (entry
2142).

2171 Bookman (New York), 11 (March 1900), 88-89.
Review of F. Harrison's Tennyson, Ruskin, Mill, 1900
(entry 2144).

2172 Bouchier, Jonathan. "Literary Parallel: Addison--Tennyson."
Notes and Queries, 9th ser. 6 (July 21, 1900), 45.

2173 Canton, William. "Tennyson's Early Poems." Living Age,
227 (Oct. 20, 1900), 187-192.
Reprinted: Eclectic Magazine of Foreign Literature, 135
(Dec. 1900), 778-783.

2174 Chesterton, Gilbert Keith. "The Literary Portraits of G.F.
Watts, R.A." Bookman (London), 19 (Dec. 1900), 81.

2175 Chesterton, Gilbert Keith, and J.E. Hodder Williams.
"Literary Pictures of the Year: I. Shakespeare, Tennyson,
Dickens." Bookman (New York), 11 (July 1900), 427-434.

2176 Collins, John Churton. Critic (New York), 37 (Dec. 1900),
508-510.
Discusses Early Poems, 1900 (entry 2142).

2177 Davray, Henry D. "La biographie d'Alfred, Lord Tennyson."
L'Ermitage, Dec. 1900.

Review of H. Tennyson's Alfred Lord Tennyson, 1897 (entry
1955). Dislikes the biography's format and tone.

2178 Déjob, Ch. "Les Pauvres Gens de Victor Hugo et Enoch
Arden." Revue des Cours et des Conférences, 1900, p.
751.
Compares Hugo's Les Pauvres Gens to Tennyson's Enoch
Arden. Considers Tennyson's poem to be more subtle and meaning-
ful.

2179 Dutoit, M. "La Vie de Tennyson." Revue des jeunes filles,
Feb. 1900.

2180 Fisher, Charles. "Tennyson's Relations to Science." New
Century Review, 7 (June 1900), 456-465.

2181 Gates, Lewis Edwards. "Tennyson's Relation to Modern
Life." Critic (New York), 36 (June 1900), 530-537.
Reprinted: Studies and Appreciations, 1900 (entry 2143).

2182 Gill, W. K. "The Ornithology of Tennyson." Spectator, 85
(Aug. 25, 1900), 238.
See also: Spectator (entry 2200) and D. Harford-Battersby
(entry 2184).

2183 Haight, Elizabeth Hazelton. "Tennyson's Use of Homeric
Material." Poet Lore, 12 (1900), 541-551.

2184 Harford-Battersby, D. "The Ornithology of Tennyson."
Spectator, 85 (Aug. 25, 1900), 238.
See also: Spectator (entry 2200) and W. K. Gill (entry 2182).

2185 Koeppel, Emil. "Tennysoniana." Englische Studien, 28 (1900),
397-406.

2186 Lee, George. "Tennyson's Religion." American Catholic
Quarterly Review, 25 (Jan. 1900), 119-132.

2187 Lees, Frederic. "Tennyson and the Old Annuals." Literature,
6 (Jan. 27 and Feb. 17, 1900), 87-88 and 155.
See also: A. Waugh in Literature (entry 2214).

2188 Literary World (Boston), 31 (Feb. 3, 1900), 44.
Review of F. Harrison's Tennyson, Ruskin, Mill, 1900 (entry
2144).

2189 Literary World (Boston), 6 (June 2, 1900), 420-421.
Review of J.C. Collins, ed., Early Poems, 1900 (entry 2142).

2190 Literary World (London), n.s. 61 (March 16, 1900), 243.
Review of C.F.G. Masterman's Tennyson as a Religious
Teacher, 1900 (entry 2148).

2191 Literary World (London), n.s. 61 (June 22, 1900), 580-581.
Review of J.C. Collins, ed., Early Poems, 1900 (entry 2142).

2192 Literary World (London), n.s. 62 (Oct. 5, 1900), 235.
Review of G.C. Allen's Tales from Tennyson, 1900 (entry 2137).

2193 Literary World (London), n.s. 62 (Oct. 12, 1900), 253-254.
Review of E.H. Sneath's The Mind of Tennyson, 1900 (entry 2153).

2194 Literary World (London), n.s. 62 (Nov. 30, 1900), 433.
Review of H.D. Rawnsley's Memories, 1900 (entry 2151).

2195 Literature, 6 (Feb. 24, 1900), 168.
Review of C.F.G. Masterman's Tennyson as a Religious Teacher, 1900 (entry 2148).

2196 Literature, 7 (Dec. 8, 1900), 461.
Review of H.D. Rawnsley's Memories, 1900 (entry 2151).

2197 McGill, Anna Blanche. "Some Famous Literary Clans: II.-- The Tennysons." Book Buyer, n.s. 21 (Aug. 1900), 30-37.

2198 Mustard, Wilfrid Pirt. "Tennyson and Homer." American Journal of Philology, 21 (1900), 143-153.

2199 Nation (New York), 70 (June 21, 1900), 483-484.
Review of F. Harrison's Tennyson, Ruskin, Mill, 1900 (entry 2144).

2200 "The Ornithology of Tennyson." Spectator, 85 (Aug. 18, 1900), 203-204.
Reprinted: Living Age, 226 (Sept. 29, 1900), 836-839.
See also: W.K. Gill (entry 2182) and D. Harford-Battersby (entry 2184) in the Spectator.

2201 Ortensi, Ulisse. "Letterati contemporanei: Alfred Tennyson." Emporium, 11 (May 1900), 360-373.

2202 Rees, R. Wilkins. "Crossing the Bar." Academy, 59 (Nov. 24, 1900), 497.
See also: A. Waugh in Academy (entry 2213).

2203 Saturday Review (London), 89 (Jan. 27, 1900), 108-109.
Review of F. Harrison's Tennyson, Ruskin, Mill, 1900 (entry 2144).

2204 Saturday Review (London), 90 (Aug. 11, 1900), 174-175.
Review of J.C. Collins, ed., Early Poems, 1900 (entry 2142).

2205 Saturday Review (London), 90 (Dec. 29, 1900), 830.
Review of R.F. Horton's Alfred Tennyson, 1900 (entry 2146).

2206 Speaker, n.s. 2 (June 30, 1900), 359-360.
Review of J.C. Collins, ed., Early Poems, 1900 (entry 2142).

2207 Spectator, 84 (Feb. 10, 1900), 214.
Review of C.F.G. Masterman's Tennyson as a Religious
Teacher, 1900 (entry 2148).

2208 Spectator, 84 (June 30, 1900), 895-896.
Review of J.C. Collins, ed., Early Poems, 1900 (entry 2142).

2209 Stoddart, A.M. Bookman (London), 19 (Dec. 1900), 88-89.
Review of R.F. Horton's Alfred Tennyson, 1900 (entry 2146).

2210 "Tennyson as a Thinker." Spectator, 85 (Sept. 29, 1900),
402-403.
Reprinted: Living Age, 227 (Nov. 17, 1900), 455-457.

2211 "A Tennyson Letter." Century Illustrated Monthly Magazine,
59 (April 1900), 956-957.

2212 Trent, William Peterfield. Current Literature, 29 (Nov.
1900), 529.
Review of F. Harrison's Tennyson, Ruskin, Mill, 1900 (entry
2144).

2213 Waugh, Arthur. "Crossing the Bar." Academy, 59 (Nov. 17,
1900), 473.
See also: R.W. Rees in Academy (entry 2202).

2214 _____. "Tennyson and the Old Annuals." Literature, 6
(Feb. 3, 1900), 113.
See also: F. Lees in Literature (entry 2187).

1901

Books

2215 Beers, Henry Augustin. "Diffused Romanticism in the Literature of the Nineteenth Century." A History of English
Romanticism in the Nineteenth Century. New York: Holt,
1901, pp. 264-275.

2216 Beljame, Al. (ed.) Introduction. Enoch Arden, by Alfred,
Lord Tennyson. Paris: Librairie Hachette, 1901.
Notes and introduction are in French.

2217 Boase, Frederic. "Tennyson, Alfred." Modern English
Biography. Truro: Netherton and Worth, 1901. Volume III,
p. 913.

2218 Bradley, Andrew Cecil. A Commentary on Tennyson's In
Memoriam. New York: Macmillan, 1901.

With this book, Bradley establishes the foundation for twentieth-century criticism of In Memoriam. His notable contributions to study of the poem include his discussion of the unifying aspects of the poem, such as the three Christmases, his identification of thematic structures that relate various sections to one another, and his interpretations of obscure passages. This book is a standard reference.
Reviewed by: Longman's Magazine (entry 2254); and Speaker (entry 2267).

2219 Carpenter, William Boyd. "Tennyson" and "Tennyson--In Memoriam." The Religious Spirit in the Poets. New York: Crowell, 1901, pp. 162-181 and 182-201, respectively.

2220 Chapman, Edward Mortimer. "The Great Twin Brethren: Tennyson and Browning." A History of English Literature, London: Murray, 1901, pp. 349-393.

2221 Clark, Thomas Arkle. "Alfred Tennyson." Biographies of Great English Authors. Taylorville, Illinois: Parker, 1901.

2222 Courthope, William John. "Byron and Tennyson." Life in Poetry: Law in Taste. London: Macmillan, 1901, pp. 388-418.

2223 Davidson, H. A. The Study of the Idylls of the King. Albany: Williams, 1901.

2224 Everett, Charles Carroll. "Tennyson and Browning as Spiritual Forces." Essays Theological and Literary. Boston: Houghton Mifflin, 1901, pp. 304-327.
Reprinted from: New World, 1893 (entry 1717).

2225 Kenyon, James Benjamin. "Tennyson in New Aspects." Loiterings in Old Fields: Literary Sketches. New York: Eaton and Mains, [1901], pp. 1-48.
Reprinted from: Methodist Review, 1898 (entry 2062).

2226 Kernahan, Coulson. "Tennyson and Some Others." Wise Men and a Fool. New York: Brentano, 1901, pp. 129-147.

2227 Lang, Andrew. Alfred Tennyson. New York: Dodd, Mead, 1901. Edinburgh: Blackwood, 1901. (Modern English Writers Series)
A critical study. Reviewed by: Athenaeum (entry 2237); Literary World (London) (entry 2251); Nation (New York) (entry 2261); and Speaker (entry 2268).

2228 L., L. S. (Luther Samuel Livingston). Bibliography of the First Editions in Book Form of the Works of Alfred, Lord Tennyson. New York: Dodd, Mead, 1901.
A descriptive bibliography. Noted: Nation (New York) (entry 2297).

2229   Luce, Morton. Tennyson. London: Dent, 1901.
       An interesting analysis of Tennyson's poetry.

2230   Moore, John Murray. Three Aspects of the Late Alfred Lord
       Tennyson. Manchester: Marsden, 1901.
       Reviewed by: Literary World (London) (entry 2252).

2231   Mühlefeld, K. Französische und englische Gedichte in
       metrischer Übertragung. Osterode am Harz: 1901.

2232   Paul, Herbert Woodfield. "The Classical Poems of Tennyson."
       Men and Letters. London: Lane, 1901, pp. 1-26.
       Reprinted from: Nineteenth Century, 1893 (entry 1752). See
entry 1752 for another reprinting and for annotation.

2233   Scott, J. Loughran. "Memoir of Alfred Lord Tennyson."
       The Works of Alfred Lord Tennyson. Philadelphia: McKay,
       [c.1901]. Volume I, pp. xiii-lxiv.

2234   Shaylor, Joseph. "Lord Tennyson." Some Favorite Books
       and Their Authors. London: Richards, 1901, pp. 257-259.

2235   Snow, Jane Elliott. Women of Tennyson. Buffalo: Wenborne-
       Summer, 1901.
       Snow identifies types of women characters in Tennyson's
poetry.

2236   Thompson, Alexander Hamilton. "Tennyson and the Victorian
       Poets." A History of English Literature. London: Murray,
       1901, pp. 757-766.

Periodicals

2237   Athenaeum, Oct. 26, 1901, pp. 551-552.
       Review of A. Lang's Alfred Tennyson, 1901 (entry 2227).

2238   Capen, S. H. R. "The Source of 'Enoch Arden.'" Book-Lover
       (San Francisco), 2 (Nov.-Dec. 1901), 458.

2239   Carroll, Lewis (Charles Lutwidge Dodgson). "A Visit to Ten-
       nyson." Strand Magazine, 21 (May 1901), 543-544.
       Reprinted: Book-Lover (San Francisco), 2 (Nov.-Dec. 1901),
476-477. Publication of a letter.

2240   Currier, Mary M. "Affectation in Tennyson's Poetry."
       Writer (Boston), 14 (April 1901), 52-53.

2241   Dessommes, Georges. "Un poète heureux: Tennyson." Re-
       vue de Paris, 1 (Feb. 15, 1901), 777-805.

2242   Didier, Eugene L. "An Illustrious Plagiarist." Literary Era,
       n. s. 8 (April 1901), 228-230.
       Reprinted: Book-Lover (San Francisco), 2 (1901), 374-376.

2243 "In Tennyson's Country." Literary World (London), n.s. 64
(Sept. 13, 1901), 176.

2244 Jack, Albert E. Dial, 30 (March 16, 1901), 192-193.
Review of J.C. Collins, ed., Early Poems, 1900 (entry
2142).

2245 Jessup, A. "Frederick Harrison as a Critic of Tennyson."
Dial, 31 (Nov. 1, 1901), 311.
See also: R.H. Paget in Dial (entry 2262).

2246 Karkaria, R.P. "Tennyson on the Signature in Criticism."
Literature, 8 (June 29, 1901), 571.

2247 Lang, Andrew. "Tennyson and His Commentators." Living
Age, 231 (Dec. 21, 1901), 781-784.

2248 Literary World (Boston), 32 (April 1, 1901), 52.
Review of R.F. Horton's Alfred Tennyson, 1900 (entry 2146).

2249 Literary World (London), n.s. 63 (Feb. 15, 1901), 157.
Discusses The Princess.

2250 Literary World (London), n.s. 63 (May 31, 1901), 522.
Discusses In Memoriam.

2251 Literary World (London), n.s. 64 (Dec. 27, 1901), 542.
Review of A. Lang's Alfred Tennyson, 1901 (entry 2227).

2252 Literary World (London), n.s. 64 (Dec. 27, 1901), 542-543.
Review of J.M. Moore's Three Aspects, 1901 (entry 2230).

2253 Literature, 8 (April 27, 1901), 328.
A possible Tennyson plagiarism.

2254 Longman's Magazine, 38 (Sept. 1901), 474-475.
Review of A.C. Bradley's A Commentary, 1901 (entry 2218).
Although he thinks all commentary on Tennyson's In Memoriam to be
superfluous, the reviewer admires Bradley's effort.

2255 Marble, Annie Russell. "Messages of the Nineteenth Century
Poets." Dial, 30 (Feb. 16, 1901), 97-98.

2256 _____. "Victoria's Poets-Laureate." Critic (New York),
38 (March 1901), 233-236.

2257 "Max Heinrich and Richard Strauss' 'Enoch Arden.'" Music,
20 (Nov. 1901), 396-402.

2258 Mims, Edwin. "Mysticism in Tennyson." Methodist Review,
83 (Jan. 1901), 62-71.

2259 Minckwitz, M.J. "Princess." Allgemeine Zeitung, 32 (Feb.
8, 1901), 4-6.

2260 <u>Nation</u> (New York), 72 (Jan. 24, 1901), 75-76.
Review of H. D. Rawnsley's <u>Memories</u>, 1900 (entry 2151).

2261 <u>Nation</u> (New York), 73 (Dec. 5, 1901), 443-444.
Review of A. Lang's <u>Alfred Tennyson</u>, 1901 (entry 2227).

2262 Paget, R. H. "Frederic Harrison as a Critic of Tennyson."
<u>Dial</u>, 31 (Nov. 15, 1901), 355.
See also: A. Jessup in <u>Dial</u> (entry 2245).

2263 Platner, John Winthrop. "Tennysoniana." <u>Nation</u> (New York),
73 (Sept. 26, 1901), 245.

2264 Rolfe, William James. "The Christmases of 'In Memoriam.'"
<u>Poet Lore</u>, 13 (1901), 151-153.

2265 _____. "Variations in Tennyson." <u>Dial</u>, 30 (May 16,
1901), 327-329.

2266 <u>Saturday Review</u> (London), 91 (Jan. 26, 1901), 112-113.
Review of H. D. Rawnsley's <u>Memories</u>, 1900 (entry 2151).

2267 <u>Speaker</u>, n. s. 4 (Aug. 17, 1901), 559-560.
Review of A. C. Bradley's <u>A Commentary</u>, 1901 (entry 2218).

2268 <u>Speaker</u>, n. s. 5 (Nov. 30, 1901), 256-257.
Review of A. Lang's <u>Alfred Tennyson</u>, 1901 (entry 2227).

2269 <u>Spectator</u>, 86 (Jan. 5, 1901), 26-27.
Review of J. C. Collins, ed., <u>Early Poems</u>, 1900 (entry 2142).

2270/ <u>Spectator</u>, 86 (Feb. 9, 1901), 197-198.
2272 Note on T. H. Warren's "Virgil and Tennyson" in <u>Quarterly</u>
<u>Review</u>, 1901 (entry 2274).

2273 Thistlethwaite, George Parker. "Über die Sprache in Tennysons <u>Idylls of the King</u>, in ihrem Verhältniss zu Malory's
<u>Morte d'Arthur</u> und <u>Mabinogion</u>." <u>Beiblatt zur Anglia</u>, 23
(1901), 473-515.

2274 Warren, Thomas Herbert. "Virgil and Tennyson: A Literary
Parallel." <u>Quarterly Review</u>, 193 (Jan. 1901), 99-129.
Reprinted: <u>Essays of Poets and Poetry Ancient and Modern</u>,
1909 (entry 2545). Noted: <u>Spectator</u> (entry 2270).
A comparison still worth consulting of Virgil and Tennyson.

1902

Books

2275 Collins, John Churton. Introduction. <u>In Memoriam, The</u>
<u>Princess, and Maud</u>, by Alfred, Lord Tennyson. London:
Methuen, 1902.

2276 Elton, Oliver. Tennyson: An Inaugural Lecture. London:
Nutt, 1902.
Reprinted: Modern Studies, 1907 (entry 2451). Less than
sympathetic view of Tennyson.

2277 Illustrated Catalogue of Rare Tennyson Items. London: H.
Sotheran, [1902].

2278 Laughlin, Clara Elizabeth. "The Peace that Came to Tennyson." Stories of Authors' Loves. Philadelphia: Lippincott,
1902. Volume I, pp. 15-34.
Reprinted: Good Words, 1903 (entry 2331).

2279 Lyall, Alfred Comyns. Tennyson. London: Macmillan,
1902. (English Men of Letters)
This biography by a friend of Tennyson is interesting for its
comments on Tennyson's thought.
Reviewed by: Academy (entry 2284); Athenaeum (entry 2287);
H. D. Davray in Mercure de France (entry 2290); Literary World
(London) (entry 2295); F. J. Mather, Jr. in Forum (entry 2333); Nation
(New York) (entry 2298); Public Opinion (entry 2300); Saturday Review
(London) (entry 2301); and Times Literary Supplement (entry 2305).

2280 Payne, William Morton. "In Memoriam." Little Leaders.
Chicago: McClurg, 1902.

2281 Rader, William. The Elegy of Faith: A Study of Tennyson's
In Memoriam. New York: Crowell, 1902.

2282 Shindler, Robert. "Tennyson, Arnold and Clough." On Certain Aspects of Recent English Literature. Leipzig: Teubner,
1902, pp. 17-28. (Neuphilologische Vorträge und Abhandlung,
II)

2283 Van Dyke, Henry. "Alfred Tennyson (1809-1892)." Library
of the World's Best Literature. Ed. C. D. Warner. New
York: Hill, [1902]. Volume XXXVI, pp. 14581-14587.

Periodicals

2284 Academy, 63 (Oct. 18, 1902), 411-412.
Review of A. C. Lyall's Tennyson, 1902 (entry 2279).

2285 Academy, 63 (Dec. 13, 1902), 656.
Discusses In Memoriam.

2286 "An Afternoon with Tennyson." Temple Bar, 126 (Aug. 1902),
216-221.

2287 Athenaeum, Oct. 18, 1902, 513-514.
Review of A. C. Lyall's Tennyson, 1902 (entry 2279).

2288 Chesterton, Gilbert Keith. "The Two Great Victorian Poets:

I. Tennyson." <u>Bookman</u> (New York), 16 (Dec. 1902), 349-351.

2289 Coleman, A.I. de P. "Mr. Lang's Side Glance at Tennyson." <u>Critic</u> (New York), 40 (Feb. 1902), 153.

2290 Davray, Henry D. <u>Mercure de France</u>, 44 (Dec. 1902), 834-835.
Review of A.C. Lyall's <u>Tennyson</u>, 1902 (entry 2279).

2291 Franklin, H.C.T. "Tennyson as a Sea Poet." <u>Temple Bar</u>, 125 (Feb. 1902), 185-191.

2292 Gannett, William Channing. "The Idylls of the King: A Tennyson Study." <u>Poet Lore</u>, 13 (1902), 588-590.

2293 _____. "Tennyson's 'In Memoriam': Suggestions for Study." <u>Poet Lore</u>, 13 (1902), 284-286.

2294 Handly, John Marks. "The Idylls of the Southland." <u>Catholic World</u>, 74 (Feb. 1902), 593-606.

2295 <u>Literary World</u> (London), n.s. 66 (Oct. 24, 1902), 308-309.
Review of A.C. Lyall's <u>Tennyson</u>, 1902 (entry 2279).

2296 McCabe, W. Gordon. "Personal Recollections of Alfred, Lord Tennyson." <u>Century Illustrated Monthly Magazine</u>, 63 (March 1902), 722-737.
Memories of Tennyson's later years.

2297 <u>Nation</u> (New York), 74 (Jan. 16, 1902), 52.
Notes L.S. Livingston's <u>Bibliography</u>, 1901 (entry 2228).

2298 <u>Nation</u> (New York), 75 (Nov. 6, 1902), 366-367.
Review of A.C. Lyall's <u>Tennyson</u>, 1902 (entry 2279).

2299 Potwin, L.S. "The Source of Tennyson's 'The Lady of Shalott.'" <u>Modern Language Notes</u>, 17 (Dec. 1902), 473-477.
Potwin identifies a possible source for part of "The Lady of Shalott."

2300 <u>Public Opinion</u> (New York), 33 (Nov. 6, 1902), 597.
Review of A.C. Lyall's <u>Tennyson</u>, 1902 (entry 2279).

2301 <u>Saturday Review</u> (London), 94 (Oct. 18, 1902), iii-iv.
Review of A.C. Lyall's <u>Tennyson</u>, 1902 (entry 2279).

2302 Schladebach, Kurt. "Tennysons und Wildenbruchs Harolddramen." <u>Studien zur Vergleichenden Litteraturgeschichte</u>, 2 (1902), 215-228.

2303 Seccombe, Thomas. "The Poets Laureate of England." <u>Bookman</u> (New York), 15 (Aug. 1902), 554.

2304 "Tennyson and the Pyrenees." Academy, 63 (Sept. 27, 1902),
      310-311.

2305 Times Literary Supplement, Oct. 10, 1902, p. 297.
      Review of A.C. Lyall's Tennyson, 1902 (entry 2279).

                              1903

Books

2306 Brooke, Stopford Augustus. "Browning and Tennyson." The
      Poetry of Robert Browning. London: Isbister, 1903, pp.
      1-56.
      Brooke's criticism is sensitive and interesting.

2307 Chesterton, Gilbert Keith, and Richard Garnett. Tennyson.
      London: Hodder and Stoughton, 1903. (Bookman Biogra-
      phies)
          The authors of this forty-page book remark: "In Tennyson,
      and in him alone, we find the man who cannot be identified with any
      one of the many tendencies of the age, but has affinities with all."
      The discussion emphasizes Tennyson's poetry's representativeness
      of its era.

2308 Cotterill, H.B. Introduction. The Cup, by Alfred, Lord
      Tennyson. London: Macmillan, 1903.
      Discusses Tennyson's drama.

2309 Gilbert, Levi. "Tennyson and Immortality." Sidelights on
      Immortality. Chicago: Revell, 1903.

2310 Hubbard, Elbert. "Alfred Tennyson." Little Journeys to the
      Homes of English Authors. New York: Putnam, 1903, pp.
      75-100.

2311 McCarthy, Justin Huntly. "Thomas Carlyle--Alfred Tennyson."
      Portraits of the Sixties. New York: Harper, 1903.
          Tennyson on pages 38-44. McCarthy worked for the London
      Morning Star in the 1860s. He remembers Tennyson as the "com-
      manding figure" in any gathering of high society.

2312 Moses, Adolph (Eliezer Asher). Yahvism and Other Discourses
      Louisville: Louisville Section of the Council of Jewish
      Women, 1903, pp. 261-268.

2313 Robertson, John Mackinnon. "De Mortuis: Tennyson."
      Criticism. London: Bonner, 1903. Volume II, pp. 209-
      219.

2314 _____. "Tennyson." Browning and Tennyson as Teachers.
      London: Brown, 1903, pp. 1-83.
      A severe view of Tennyson.

2315 Stevenson, Morley. Spiritual Teaching of the Holy Grail.
      London: Wells, Gardner, and Darton, 1903.

2316 Thomson, J.C. (ed.) Introduction. The Suppressed Poems
      of Alfred, Lord Tennyson, 1830-1862. New York: Harper,
      1903.
         A less than sympathetic view of the poetry. See also: Aca-
      demy (entry 2338); and J.C. Thomson in Harper's Monthly Magazine
      (entry 2339).

2317 Van Dyke, Henry. An Introduction to the Poems of Tennyson.
      Boston: Ginn, 1903.
         An overview of Tennyson's techniques and achievement. Van
      Dyke regards Tennyson as the poet who best expresses the Victorian
      Age's preoccupations.

2318 Ward, Wilfrid. "Tennyson." Problems and Persons. Lon-
      don: Longmans, Green, 1903.
         Of biographical interest.

2319 Watkins, Watkin. The Birds of Tennyson. London: Porter,
      1903. Illustrations by G.E. Lodge.

2320 Weld, Agnes Grace. Glimpses of Tennyson and of Some of
      His Relations and Friends. London: Williams and Norgate,
      1903.
         Weld was the niece of Tennyson's wife. Her firsthand account
      of her relations has some biographical value.

Dissertation

2321 Carlson, Alma S. The Influence of the English Bible on the
      Diction of Alfred Tennyson. Northwestern University, 1903.

Periodicals

2322 Axon, William Edward Armitage. "Tennyson's 'Lover's Tale'--
      Its Original and Analogues." Royal Society of Literature of
      the United Kingdom: Transactions, ser. 2, 24 (1903), 61-79.

2323 Bailey, William Whitman. "Flowers of Tennyson." Education,
      24 (Oct. 1903), 96-101.

2324 "Ballad Poetry." Edinburgh Review, 197 (April 1903), 317.

2325 Coupe, Charles. "Tennysonian Sea-Echoes." American
      Catholic Quarterly Review, 28 (July 1903), 455-463.

2326 Drury, Charles. "Tennyson's 'Lord of Burleigh.'" Notes and
      Queries, 9th ser. 11 (Jan. 3, 1903), 4-5.

2327 Hall, Basil. "Tennyson and Kingsley." Notes and Queries,
      9th ser. 11 (Jan. 17, 1903), 57.

2328 Harrison, Frederic. "Tennyson: A New Estimate." North American Review, 176 (June 1903), 856-867.

2329 Jerram, C.S. "Mr. Churton Collins on Tennyson." Spectator, 90 (March 21, 1903), 453.

2330 Kingsley, Maud Elma. "A Study of 'Idylls of the King.'" Education, 23 (Feb. 1903), 356-370.

2331 Laughlin, Clara Elizabeth. "The Peace that Came to Tennyson." Good Words, 44 (1903), 793-800.
Reprinted from: Stories of Authors' Loves, 1902 (entry 2278).

2332 Literary World (London), n.s. 63 (May 31, 1903), 245.
Discusses In Memoriam.

2333 Mather, F.J., Jr. Forum, 34 (Jan. 1903), 397-398.
Review of A.C. Lyall's Tennyson, 1902 (entry 2279).

2334 Potwin, L.S. "The Prologue to 'In Memoriam,' and Certain Commentaries." Western Reserve University Bulletin, 6 (May 1903), 13-19.

2335 Saturday Review (London), 95 (April 18, 1903), 489-490.
Discusses In Memoriam.

2336 Spectator, 90 (March 14, 1903), 414-415.
Discusses In Memoriam.

2337 "Swinburniana." T.P.'s Weekly, 2 (Dec. 11, 1903), 890.

2338 "Tennyson's Suppressed Poems." Academy, 65 (July 11 and 25, 1903), 45 and 93.

2339 Thomson, J.C. "Tennyson's Suppressed Poems." Harper's Monthly Magazine, 108 (Dec. 1903), 70-74.

2340 Wainwright, John B. "Ben Jonson and Tennyson." Notes and Queries, 9th ser. 12 (Oct. 3, 1903), 277-278.

2341 "With Apologies to Tennyson's 'Sleeping Beauty.'" Punch, 124 (Jan. 14, 1903), 25.
A cartoon.

1904

Books

2342 "Alfred, Lord Tennyson." The Library of Literary Criticism of English and American Authors. Ed. Charles Wells Moulton. Buffalo: Moulton, 1904-1905. Volume VIII, pp. 64-111.

2343 Benson, Arthur Christopher. Alfred Tennyson. New York:
Dutton, 1904. London: Methuen, 1904.
Reviewed by: Academy (entry 2366); Contemporary Review
(entry 2368); and Literary World (London) (entry 2373).

2344 Brotherton, Mary. "Lord Tennyson." Chambers's Cyclopae-
dia of English Literature. Philadelphia: Lippincott, 1904.
Volume III, pp. 540-543.

2345 Burne-Jones, Georgiana. Memorials of Edward Burne-Jones.
2 volumes. New York: Macmillan, 1904.

2346 Chesterton, Gilbert Keith. G. F. Watts. London: Duckworth,
1904.
Tennyson on pages 41 and 73-83.

2347 Conway, Moncure Daniel. Autobiography. Boston: Houghton
Mifflin, 1904. Volume II, pp. 32-38.

2348 Ficker, Georg. Bemerkungen zu Sprache und Wortschatz in
Tennysons "Idylls of the King." Leipzig: Hinrichssche
Buchhandlung, 1904.

2349 Haney, J. L., ed. Early Reviews of English Poets. Philadelphia: Egerton Press, 1904.
Timbuctoo on page 151; Poems, Chiefly Lyrical on pages
152-175; and The Princess on pages 176-186.

2350 Hankin, St. John. "Tennyson." Lost Masterpieces: and
Other Verses. London: Constable, 1904, pp. 16-17.

2351 Hayes, J. W. Tennyson and Scientific Theology. London:
Stock, 1904.
Discusses Tennyson as a philosopher whose thought bears
comparison with that of the best thinkers of his age.

2352 Knight, William. "Tennyson." Retrospects. London: Smith,
Elder, 1904, pp. 46-68.

2353 Kuhns, Oscar. "Browning and Tennyson." Dante and the
English Poets from Chaucer to Tennyson. New York: Holt,
1904, pp. 239-256.

2354 Lilly, William Samuel. "The Mission of Tennyson." Studies
in Religion and Literature. London: Chapman and Hall,
1904, pp. 31-52.
Reprinted from: Fortnightly Review, 1897 (entry 1987).

2355 Lyttleton, Arthur Temple. "Tennyson." Modern Poets of
Faith, Doubt, and Other Essays. London: Murray, 1904,
pp. 1-32.

2356 Meynell, Alice Christiana. Introduction. In Memoriam, by

Alfred, Lord Tennyson. London: Blackie, 1904.
A balanced discussion of the poem.

2357 _____. Introduction. Poems, by Alfred, Lord Tennyson.
London: Blackie, 1904.

2358 Munger, Theodore Thorton. "Interplay of Christianity and
Literature." Essays for the Day. Boston: Houghton Mifflin, 1904, pp. 91-97.

2359 Mustard, Wilfrid Pirt. Classical Echoes in Tennyson. New
York: Macmillan, 1904. (Columbia University Studies in
English, Volume 3)
Mustard cites passages from classical literature, beginning
with the works of Homer, and similar passages from Tennyson.
This book remains a useful reference.
Reviewed by: Athenaeum (entry 2403); and Nation (New York)
(entry 2374).

2360 Negri, Gaetano. "Alfred Tennyson." Ultimi saggi. Milan:
Hoepli, 1904, pp. 243-251.

2361 Pallen, Condé Bénoist. The Meaning of the Idylls of the
King: An Essay in Interpretation. New York: American
Book Co., [1904].
An interesting study that still merits reading.

2362 Stevenson, Morley. Spiritual Teaching of Tennyson's "In
Memoriam": Six Lenten Addresses. London: Gardner,
Darton, 1904.
Stevenson discusses Tennyson as an important thinker on
religion.

2363 Stockwell, Nina. Notes on Tennyson's Passing of Arthur.
London: Simpkin, Marshall, Hamilton, Kent, 1904.
(Normal Tutorial Series)

2364 Ward, Wilfrid. Aubrey de Vere: A Memoir Based on His
Unpublished Diaries and Correspondence. London: 1904.

Dissertation

2365 Wildman, Banks John. A Comparison of Lucretius' "De natura
rerum" and Tennyson's "Lucretius." Chicago, 1904.

Periodicals

2366 Academy, 66 (Feb. 20, 1904), 191.
Review of A.C. Benson's Alfred Tennyson, 1904 (entry 2343).

2367 Collins, John Churton. "Clough and Tennyson." Academy,
66 (Jan. 30, 1904), 133.
See also: W.A. Lewis in Academy (entry 2370).

2368   Contemporary Review, 85 (May 1904), 754-756.
        Review of A.C. Benson's Alfred Tennyson, 1904 (entry 2343).

2369   Dyboski, Roman. "Wortbildung und Wortgebrauch bei Tenny-
        son." Bausteine, 1 (1904), 165-223.

2370   Lewis, W. Aldersey. "Clough and Tennyson." Academy, 66
        (Jan. 16 and Feb. 20, 1904), 82 and 205.
        See also: J.C. Collins in Academy (entry 2367).

2371   Lier, W. "Enoch Arden." Mittelschule und höhere Mädchen-
        schule, 18 (1904), 175-181.

2372   "Literary Sacrilege." Literary World (London), n.s. 69
        (April 22, 1904), 388.

2373   Literary World (London), n.s. 69 (March 11, 1904), 249.
        Review of A.C. Benson's Alfred Tennyson, 1904 (entry 2343).

2374   Nation (New York), 79 (Dec. 29, 1904), 529.
        Review of W.P. Mustard's Classical Echoes, 1904 (entry
2359).

2375   Prideaux, W.F. "FitzGerald's Song in Tennyson's 'Memoir.'"
        Notes and Queries, 10th ser. 2 (Oct. 8, 1904), 285.

2376   _____. "Tennyson's House, Twickenham." Notes and
        Queries, 10th ser. 2 (Oct. 22, 1904), 324.

2377   Rawnsley, Hardwicke Drummond. "Tennyson a South Country
        Man?" Spectator, 92 (April 23, 1904), 639.

2378   Rogers, John. "Tennyson and Leigh Hunt." Academy, 67
        (Sept. 3, 1904), 166-167.

2379   "Tennyson and the Mo 'Allakât." Spectator, 92 (Feb. 13 and
        20, 1904), 256-290.

2380   "Three Poets in One Court Suit." Book-Lover (New York),
        5 (June 1904), 694.

2381   Warren, Thomas Herbert. "Tennyson and Dante." Monthly
        Review, 14 (Jan. 1904), 117-138.
        Reprinted: Essays of Poets and Poetry Ancient and Modern,
1909 (entry 2545). Discusses Tennyson's use of Dante's works.

2382   "Was Purple Tennyson's Favorite Color?" Critic (New York),
        45 (July 1904), 15-16.

2383   Wynn, W.H. "Tennyson's Idylls of the King: An Appre-
        ciation." Lutheran Church Quarterly Review, 34 (Oct.
        1904), 529-555.

1905

Books

2384   Ainger, Alfred. "The Death of Tennyson." Lectures and Essays. London: Macmillan, 1905. Volume II, pp. 114-126.
Reprinted from: Macmillan's Magazine, 1892 (entry 1417).

2385   Boegner, André. La pensée religieuse de Tennyson dans "In Memoriam." Cahors: 1905.
Publication of a dissertation: 1905 (entry 2398).

2386   Brookfield, Charles, and Frances Brookfield. Mrs. Brookfield and Her Circle. 2 volumes. London: Isaac Pitman, 1905.
Of biographical interest.

2387   Dhaleine, L. A Study of Tennyson's Idylls of the King. Bar-le-Duc: Jacquet, 1905.
Publication of a dissertation: 1905 (entry 2399).

2388   Fischer, Thomas A. Tennysonstudien und Anderes: Mit dem Bildnis Tennysons. Leipzig: Wigand, 1905.

2389   Jellinghaus, Paul. Tennysons Drama Harold: Eine Quellenuntersuchung. Borna-Leipzig: Noske, 1905.
Publication of a dissertation: 1905 (entry 2401).

2390   Johnson, Catharine B. William Bodham Donne and His Friends. London: 1905.

2391   Page, H. A. (Alexander Hay Japp). "Alfred Lord Tennyson." Poets and the Poetry of the Nineteenth Century. Ed. Alfred H. Miles. London: Routledge, 1905.

2392   Paterson, Arthur, and Helen Allingham. The Homes of Tennyson: Painted by Helen Allingham, Described by A. Paterson. London: Black, 1905.
Reviewed by: Spectator (entry 2440).

2393   Shorthouse, Joseph Henry. "The 'Morte d'Arthur' and the 'Idylls of the King.'" Literary Remains of J. H. Shorthouse. Ed. Mrs. J. H. Shorthouse. London: Macmillan, 1905. Volume II, pp. 107-122.

2394   Steffen, Paul. Die Alliteration bei Tennyson. Kiel: Fiencke, 1905.
Publication of a dissertation: 1905 (entry 2402).

2395   Stone, John Morris. "A Missing Page from the 'Idylls of the King.'" Studies from Court and Cloister. London: Sands,

1905.
Reprinted from: <u>Dublin Review</u>, 1888 (entry 1242).

2396 Straede, [Karl]. <u>Tennysons "Lucretius": Erklärung des</u>
<u>Gedichtes: Verhältnis zu dem lateinischen Lehrgedicht,</u>
<u>"de rerum natura" des Lucretius.</u> Moldenhauer, 1905.

2397 Thomson, J.C. <u>Bibliography of the Writings of Alfred, Lord</u>
<u>Tennyson.</u> Wimbledon: Thomson, 1905.
Extremely rare. Twenty copies printed. Reprinted: London:
H. Pordes, 1967. See entry 4017 for listing of review.

Dissertations

2398 Boegner, André. <u>La pensée religieuse de Tennyson dans "In</u>
<u>Memoriam."</u> Montauban, [1905?].
Published: 1905 (entry 2385).

2399 Dhaleine, L. <u>A Study on Tennyson's Idylls of the King.</u>
Paris, 1905.
Published: 1905 (entry 2387).

2400 Dyboski, Roman. <u>Tennysons Sprache und Stil.</u> Vienna, 1905.

2401 Jellinghaus, Paul. <u>Tennysons Drama Harold: Eine</u>
<u>Quellenuntersuchung.</u> Münster, 1905.
Published: 1905 (entry 2389).

2402 Steffen, Paul. <u>Die Alliteration bei Tennyson.</u> Kiel, 1905.
Published: 1905 (entry 2394).

Periodicals

2403 <u>Athenaeum</u>, Jan. 28, 1905, p. 110.
Review of W.P. Mustard's <u>Classical Echoes</u>, 1904 (entry
2359).

2404 "The Lincoln Monument to Tennyson." <u>Athenaeum</u>, July 29,
1905), 145.

2405 "The Literature of House-Moving." <u>T.P.'s Weekly</u>, 5 (March
17, 1905), 329.

2406 Magruder, Julia. "Lancelot, Guinevere and Arthur." <u>North</u>
<u>American Review</u>, 180 (March 1905), 375-380.
Replied to by J.E. Robb in <u>North American Review</u> (entry
2407).

2407 Robb, Juliet Everts. "Arthur, Guinevere and Lancelot--An
Open Letter to Miss Julia Magruder." <u>North American Re-</u>
<u>view</u>, 180 (June 1905), 918-926.
A reply to J. Magruder's comments in <u>North American Re-</u>
<u>view</u> (entry 2406).

2408   Salmon, Arthur L. "With Coleridge and Tennyson at Cleve-
       don." Temple Bar, 132 (Aug. 1905), 153-162.
       Reprinted: Eclectic Magazine of Foreign Literature, 145
(Nov. 1905), 512-518.

2409   Sutherland, Allan. "Sunset and Evening Star." Delineator,
       66 (Dec. 1905), 1081-1083.

2410   Times Literary Supplement, Dec. 22, 1905, pp. 453-454.
       Discusses In Memoriam.

                              1906

Books

2411   Benn, Alfred William. The History of English Rationalism
       in the Nineteenth Century. London: Longmans, Green,
       1906. Volume II, pp. 296-300.

2412   Brookfield, Frances Mary. "Alfred Tennyson." The Cam-
       bridge Apostles. New York: Scribner, 1906, pp. 308-330.
       Those unfamiliar with Tennyson's life should use this book
with caution.

2413   Dawson, W.J. Makers of English Poetry. Revised edition.
       New York: Revell, 1906.
       Tennyson on pages 178-274.

2414   Dowden, Edward. "Mr. Tennyson and Mr. Browning." Stud-
       ies in Literature, 1798-1877. London: Kegan Paul, Trench,
       Trübner, 1906, pp. 191-239.
       Reprinted from: Afternoon Lectures on Literature, 1869
(entry 631a). See entry 631A for annotation.

2415   Egan, Maurice Francis. "Imitators of Shakespeare."
       The Ghost in Hamlet. Chicago: McClurg, 1906, pp. 203-
       233.
       Discusses Becket by Tennyson and writings by De Vere.

2416   Ellison, Edith Nicholl. A Child's Recollections of Tennyson.
       New York: Dutton, 1906.
       Reviewed by: Outlook, 1906 (entry 2437).

2417   Gordon, William Clark. The Social Ideals of Alfred Tennyson
       as Related to His Time. Chicago: U. of Chicago P.,
       1906. London: Unwin, 1906.
       Publication of a dissertation: 1906 (entry 2428).
       A sociological study that investigates some of Tennyson's
fundamental views of the roles of people and institutions in society.
Remains informative.
       Reviewed by: Academy (entry 2429); and Spectator (entry
2441).

2418 Griggs, Edward Howard. The Poetry and Philosophy of Tennyson. New York: Huebsch, 1906.
A forty-four-page discussion with a bibliography on pages 40-44.

2419 Harrison, Frederic. "The Burial of Tennyson" and "The Millenary of King Alfred." Memories and Thoughts. New York: Macmillan, 1906, pp. 20-27 and 47-54, respectively. Tennyson also on pp. 31-46.

2420 Hutton, Richard Holt. "Browning and Tennyson," "Newman and Tennyson," and "The Idealism of George Eliot and Mr. Tennyson." Brief Literary Criticisms: Selected from the "Spectator." Ed. Elizabeth M. Roscoe. London: Macmillan, 1906.
"Browning and Tennyson" reprinted from Spectator, 1889 (entry 1268).

2421 Mackie, Alexander. "Tennyson as Botanist, Entomologist, Ornithologist, Geologist." Nature Knowledge in Modern Poetry. London: Longmans, Green, 1906.
Tennyson's use of science for inspiration.

2422 Myall, Laura Hain Friswell. In the Sixties and Seventies. Boston: Turner, 1906.

2423 Rawnsley, Hardwicke Drummond. Homes and Haunts of Famous Authors. London: Darton, 1906.

2424 Rossetti, William Michael. Some Reminiscences. London: Brown, Langham, 1906.
Tennyson in Volume I, pp. 247-259.

2425 Stoker, Bram. Personal Reminiscences of Henry Irving. London: Heinemann, 1906.
Discusses Tennyson and Tennyson's dramatic qualities.

2426 Stuart, Charles. "Alfred Tennyson." The Vision of Christ. Cincinnati: Jennings and Graham, 1906. New York: Eaton and Mains, 1906. Revised edition, pp. 167-232.
(First edition possibly 1896.)

Dissertations

2427 Cross, Ethan. Tennyson's Dramas: A Technical and Critical Study. Chicago, 1906.

2428 Gordon, William Clark. The Social Ideals of Alfred Tennyson as Related to His Time. Chicago, [1906?].
Published: 1906 (entry 2417).

Periodicals

2429 Academy, 71 (Oct. 20, 1906), 391-392.
     Review of W. C. Gordon's The Social Ideals of Alfred Tenny-
son, 1906 (entry 2417).

2430 Butler, Arthur G. "A Walk with Tennyson." Spectator, 97
     (Aug. 25, 1906), 263.
     Reprinted: Eclectic Magazine of Foreign Literature, 147 (Nov.
     1906), 394; and Living Age, 251 (Dec. 1, 1906), 514. A
poem.

2431 Grendon, Felix. "Fitzgerald on Tennyson: or, Tennyson Be-
     fore and After 1842." Sewanee Review, 14 (April 1906),
     161-170.

2432 "In Memoriam after Fifty Years." Edinburgh Review, 203
     (April 1906), 297-318.
     Reprinted: Living Age, 249 (June 9, 1906), 587-602.

2433 Knowles, F. L. "The Idylls of the King." Methodist Review,
     88 (1906), 623-626.

2434 Krahmer, J. "Tennyson als Frauenrechtler." Deutschland
     Monatschrift für die Gesamte Kulter, 4 (Dec. 1906), 359-367.

2435 Living Age, 248 (Feb. 24, 1906), 496-499.
     Discusses In Memoriam.

2436 Mallock, William Hurrell. "Two Poet Laureates on Life."
     National Review, 47 (Aug. 1906), 955-970.
     Reprinted: Living Age, 251 (Oct. 6, 1906), 3-14.

2437 Outlook, 84 (Oct. 20, 1906), 428.
     Review of E. N. Ellison's A Child's Recollections of Tennyson,
     1906 (entry 2416).

2438 Rolfe, William James. "Tennyson's Annotations to 'In Mem-
     oriam.'" Critic (New York), 48 (May 1906), 453-455.

2439 Spectator, 96 (Jan. 6, 1906), 21-22.
     Discusses In Memoriam.

2440 Spectator, 96 (April 28, 1906), 648.
     Review of A. Paterson and H. Allingham's The Homes of Ten-
nyson, 1905 (entry 2392).

2441 Spectator, 97 (Nov. 3, 1906), 686.
     Review of W. C. Gordon's The Social Ideals of Alfred Tenny-
son, 1906 (entry 2417).

2442 Spender, Harold. "Real Tennyson." Living Age, 248 (March
     17, 1906), 696-698.

2443   "Tennyson and Kipling." Bookman (New York), 22 (Feb. 1906), 554-556.

2444   Teza, E. Regia Accademia di scienze, lettere, ed arti in Padova, n. s. 23 (1906), 125-132.

2445   Tyrrell, R. Y. "'In Memoriam' and 'The Door of Humility.'" Academy, 71 (Aug. 18, 1906), 158-159.

2446   Whitewell, C. T. Journal and Transactions of the Leeds Astronomical Society, 1906.
       Mentioned by P. F. Baum in his "Alfred Lord Tennyson" in The Victorian Poets, 1956 (entry 3600), page 46, footnote 3. On Tennyson's astronomy.

1908

Books

2447   Allingham, William. William Allingham: A Diary. Ed. Helen Allingham and D. Radford. London: Macmillan, 1907.
       Allingham and Tennyson were friends. Of biographical interest.

2448   The Choice Collection of the Works of Alfred, Lord Tennyson, Formed by A. E. Jack. New York: Anderson Auction Co., Jan. 28, 1907. 17pp.

2449   Crane, Walter. An Artist's Reminiscences. New York: Macmillan, 1907.
       Tennyson on pages 182-183.

2450   Dyboski, Roman. Tennysons Sprache und Stil. Vienna: Braumüller, 1907. (Wiener Beiträge zur Englischen Philologie, 25)
       Dyboski provides a sound study of Tennyson's style. This book is a standard reference.

2451   Elton, Oliver. "Tennyson: An Inaugural Lecture." Modern Studies. London: Arnold, 1907, pp. 183-207.
       Reprinted from: Tennyson, 1902 (entry 2276).

2452   Genung, John Franklin. The Idylls and the Ages: A Valuation of Tennyson's Idylls of the King, Elucidated in Part by Comparisons between Tennyson and Browning. New York: Crowell, 1907.

2453   Giuliano, A. Essai sur "Locksley Hall" et "Locksley Hall Sixty Years After" d'Alfred Tennyson: Commentaire et Comparaisons. Turin: 1907.
       Giuliano admires Tennyson's skillful use of language and theme.

2454 Gunsaulus, Frank Wakeley. "Alfred Tennyson." The Higher
Ministries of Recent English Poetry. New York: Revell,
[c.1907], pp. 107-177.

2455 Jebb, R.C. "Alfred Lord Tennyson." The English Poets.
Ed. T.H. Ward. New York: Macmillan, 1907. Volume IV,
pp. 755-764.

2456 Jones, Henry. The Immortality of the Soul in the Poems of
Tennyson and Browning. Boston: American Unitarian Association, 1907.
Jones uses the poets to illustrate his contention that religion
and science offer equally valid views of nature.

2457 Maynadier, Howard. "Tennyson." The Arthur of the English
Poets. Boston: Houghton Mifflin, 1907, pp. 410-438.
A better-than-average examination of Tennyson's Arthurian
poetry.

2458 Payne, William Morton. "Alfred Tennyson." The Greater
English Poets of the Nineteenth Century. New York: Holt,
1907, pp. 221-250.

2459 Rances, Maurice. Through English Literature. Paris: Hachette, 1907.

2460 Raybould, W. Notes on Tennyson's "Coming and Passing of
Arthur." London: Simpkin, Marshall, Hamilton, Kent, 1907.
An introductory presentation of the views of critics and notes
on the poetry.

2461 Saintsbury, George. "English and French Poetry." The Later
Nineteenth Century. Edinburgh: Blackwood, 1907, pp. 1-12.

2462 _____. "Tennyson and Browning." A Short History of English Literature. New York: Macmillan, 1907, pp. 727-733.

2463 Smith, Arnold. "Tennyson." The Main Tendencies of Victorian Poetry. London: Simpkin, Marshall, Hamilton, Kent,
1907, pp. 59-104.

2464 Smyser, William Emery. Tennyson. Cincinnati: Eaton and
Mains, 1907.

2465 Tennyson, Hallam, ed. The Works of Alfred, Lord Tennyson.
9 volumes. London and New York: Macmillan, 1907-1908.
This edition and its 1913 single-volume version (entry 2734)
have long been the standard references for scholars studying Tennyson's poetry. See also: Christopher Ricks's edition (entry 4145).
Reviewed by: Academy (entry 2500); E. Faguet in Quarterly
Review (entry 2574); Living Age (entry 2507); Saturday Review (London) (entries 2516 and 2517); and Spectator in 1907 and 1908 (entries
2477, 2518, 2519, and 2520).

Periodicals

2466 Academy, 72 (Jan. 5, 1907), 3.

2467 "Alfred, Lord Tennyson, 1809-1892." Book News Monthly,
      25 (Aug. 1907), 846-854.

2468 Bayne, T. Notes and Queries, 10th ser. 7 (March 9, 1907),
      197.

2469 "Biblical Allusions in Tennyson." Chautauquan, 45 (Feb.
      1907), 375-376.

2470 Doveton, F.B. "Tennyson--or Another." Academy, 73 (July
      20, 1907), 709.
      See also: B.G. Hoare (entry 2475) and E. Talbot (entry
2479).

2471 Fletcher, Robert Huntington. "The Metrical Forms Used by
      Victorian Poets." Journal of English and Germanic Philology,
      7 (1907), 87-91.

2472 Grendon, Felix. "The Influence of Keats Upon the Early Poet-
      ry of Tennyson." Sewanee Review, 15 (July 1907), 285-296.

2473 Hardie, Martin. "The Moxon Tennyson: 1857." Book-Lover's
      Magazine, 7 (1907), 45-51.

2474 Hoare, Barnard George. "Mr. Hardy and Tennyson." Aca-
      demy, 72 (Jan. 19 and 26, 1907), 75 and 100.

2475 _____. "Tennyson or Another." Academy, 73 (Aug. 3,
      1907), 757.
      See also: F.B. Doveton (entry 2470) and E. Talbot (entry
2479).

2476 Paul, Herbert Woodfield. "Is Literature Dying?" Contem-
      porary Review, 91 (April 1907), 472-473.

2477 Spectator, 99 (Dec. 14, 1907), 988-989.
      Review of H. Tennyson, ed., The Works, 1907 (entry 2465).

2478 Spurgeon, Caroline. "Mysticism in English Poetry." Quar-
      terly Review, 207 (Oct. 1907), 453-455.

2479 Talbot, Ethel. "Tennyson, or Another?" Academy, 73 (July
      6, 1907), 654.
      See also: F.B. Doveton (entry 2470) and B.G. Hoare (entry
2475).

2480 "Tennyson's Notes on His Poems." Times Literary Supple-
      ment, Dec. 12, 1907, p. 380.

2481 "Tennyson's Revisions." Academy, 72 (April 20, 1907), 398.

2482 Teza, E. Regia Accademia di Scienze, Lettere, ed Arti in
      Padua, n. s. 24 (1907), 33-49.
      Discusses Tennyson's Oenone.

2483 Thomson, O. R. Howard. "Tennyson's 'The Passing of Ar-
      thur.'" Dial, 43 (Dec. 1, 1907), 367.

2484 Young, A. B. "T. L. Peacock's 'Maid Marian' and Tennyson's
      'Foresters.'" Notes and Queries, 10th ser. 8 (Nov. 2,
      1907), 341-342.

                              1908

Books

2485 Caine, Hall. My Story. London: Heinemann, 1908.

2486 Carr, Joseph William Comyns. Some Eminent Victorians.
      London: Duckworth, 1908.
      Tennyson on pages 112-113 and 193-198.

2487 Gilder, Richard Watson. The Poems of Richard Watson Gil-
      der. Boston: Houghton Mifflin, 1908.
      A poem on pages 206-207. Reprinted from: Critic (New
York), 1892 (entry 1495). See entry 1495 for another reprinting.

2488 Gladstone, William Ewart. Gladstone on Tennyson. [Boston:
      Directors of the Old South Work, 1908.]
      Reprinted in part from: Quarterly Review, 1859 (entry 471).
See entry 471 for other reprintings and for annotation.

2489 Henley, William Ernest. "Tennyson." Views and Reviews:
      Essays in Appreciation. London: Nutt, 1908. Volume I, pp.
      183-188.
      Reprinted: J. D. Jump, ed., Tennyson: The Critical Heritage,
1967 (entry 4013), pp. 444-446.
      Henley compares Tennyson and Keats. He asserts that Ten-
nyson as Poet Laureate is a better poet than Tennyson before the
appointment to the laureateship.

2490 Hinchman, Walter Swain, and Francis B. Gummere. "Alfred
      Tennyson." Lives of Great English Writers from Chaucer to
      Browning. Boston: Houghton Mifflin, 1908, pp. 507-523.

2491 James, Henry. "Tennyson's Drama: Queen Mary and Harold."
      Views and Reviews. Boston: Ball, 1908, pp. 165-204.
      James likes Queen Mary, although the play is fundamentally
undramatic. He dislikes Harold, which he finds unmoving.

2492 McMechan, Archibald McKeller. "Introduction." Select Poems

of Alfred Tennyson. Boston: Heath, 1908.
(Belles-lettres series)

2493 Pearson, Charles William. "Character and Work of Tennyson." Literary and Biographical Essays. Boston: Sherman,
French, 1908, pp. 131-147.

2494 Reade, Willoughby. Notes on the Arthurian Epic and the
Idylls of the King. Alexandria, Virginia: Bell's Potomac
Press, 1908.
A thirty-one-page introduction to the Idylls of the King that
focuses on allegory. Better-than-average commentary.

2495 Schäfer, Bernhard. Englische Gedichte in metrischer Über-
tragung. Lünen a.d. Lippe: 1908.

2496 Shepherd, Henry Elliott. A Commentary upon Tennyson's In
Memoriam. New York: Neale, 1908.

2497 Terry, Ellen. The Story of My Life. London: Hutchinson,
1908.
Mentions Tennyson and the 1881 production of The Cup.

2498 Wise, Thomas J. A Bibliography of the Writings of Alfred,
Lord Tennyson. 2 volumes. London: privately printed by
R. Clay, 1908.
Only one hundred copies were printed.
One should consult J. Carter and G. Pollard's An Enquiry,
1934 (entry 3211) and W. Partington's Thomas J. Wise, 1946 (entry
3373) when using this bibliography. This is still the standard ana-
lytical bibliography, in spite of its flaws and dated information.
Reviewed by: Athenaeum (entry 2556).

Dissertation

2499 Jelinek, Heinrich. Tennysons Lincolnshire Dialektdichtungen.
Vienna, 1908.

Periodicals

2500 Academy, 74 (Feb. 15, 1908), 457-458.
Review of H. Tennyson, ed., The Works, 1907-1908 (entry
2465).

2501 Chevrillon, André. "Note et Souvenirs." Revue de Paris,
June 1, 1908, pp. 591-592.
Discusses Hippolyte Taine's view of Tennyson.

2502 Child, Mary. "The Weird of Sir Launcelot." North American
Review, 188 (Dec. 1908), 903-909.

2503 Contemporary Review, 93 (Feb. 1908), sup. 13-16.
Discusses Tennyson's poetry.

2504 Edgar, Pelham. "English Poetry Since Tennyson." University Magazine, 7 (April 1908), 259-261.

2505 Graham, J.W. "New Facts on Our Survival of Death." Hibbert Journal, 7 (1908), 260-277.

2506 Haultain, Arnold. "From Tennyson to Kipling." Canadian Magazine, 30 (April 1908), 533-536.

2507 Living Age, 256 (Jan. 18, 1908), 180-183.
Review of H. Tennyson, ed., The Works, 1907-1908 (entry 2465).

2508 Lynn, W.T. Notes and Queries, 10th ser. 9 (Jan. 4, 1908), 13.

2509 Mabie, Hamilton Wright. "How to Study Tennyson and Emerson." Ladies' Home Journal, 25 (March 1908), 32.

2510 MacColl, D.S. "Millais's Portrait of Tennyson." Burlington Magazine, 13 (June 1908), 127-128.

2511 McMechan, Archibald McKellar. "Alfred Tennyson, Artist." University Magazine, 7 (Feb. 1908), 53-75.
Reprinted: The Life of a Little College, 1914 (entry 2763).

2512 Murray, J. Malton. "Crossing the Bar." T.P.'s Weekly, 12 (July 3, 1908), 10.

2513 O'Connor, T.P. T.P.'s Weekly, 12 (Dec. 18, 1908), 811.
Mentions Tennyson.

2514 "The Poems of Alfred, Lord Tennyson." Munsey's Magazine, 39 (June 1908), 435-438.

2515 Potts, R.A. "Tennysoniana: Cleopatra." Notes and Queries, 10th ser. 9 (March 7, 1908), 194.
See also: Notes and Queries (entry 2521).

2516 Saturday Review (London), 105 (Jan. 25, 1908), 109-110.
Review of H. Tennyson, ed., The Works, 1907-1908 (entry 2465).

2517 Saturday Review (London), 105 (March 21, 1908), 378.
Review of H. Tennyson, ed., The Works, 1907-1908 (entry 2465).

2518 Spectator, 100 (May 9, 1908), 749-750.
Review of H. Tennyson, ed., The Works, 1907-1908 (entry 2465).

2519 Spectator, 100 (June 27, 1908), 1030-1031.
Review of H. Tennyson, ed., The Works, 1907-1908 (entry 2465).

2520   Spectator, 100 (Sept. 26, 1908), 445-446.
        Review of H. Tennyson, ed., The Works, 1907-1908 (entry
        2465).

2521   "Tennysoniana: Cleopatra." Notes and Queries, 10th ser. 9
        (Feb. 15, 1908), 121-122.
        See also: R. A. Potts (entry 2515). Of bibliographic interest.

2522   Tzeutschler, Artur. "Zu Tennysons 'Locksley Hall': The
        Poem of Amriolkais." Archiv für das Studium der neueren
        Sprachen und Literaturen, 120 (1908), 332-336.

2523   Watson, William. "Orgy on Parnassus: Lines Written in My
        Copy of Tennyson." Fortnightly Review, 89 (April 1, 1908),
        569-570.
        Reprinted: Living Age, 257 (May 2, 1908), 258; Current Lit-
        erature, 44 (June 1908), 678. A poem.

                            1909

Books

2524   Bradley, A. C. "The Long Poem in the Age of Wordsworth."
        Oxford Lectures on Poetry. London: Macmillan, 1909, pp.
        177-208.
        Idylls of the King on pages 192-193.

2525   Chesterton, Gilbert Keith. "Tennyson." Varied Types. New
        York: Dodd, Mead, 1909, pp. 249-257.
        Tennyson also on page 219. Chesterton considers the basic
        aspects of Tennyson's poetry, including its originality, imagery, use
        of science, and depiction of nature. Chesterton admires Tennyson's
        style but not the poet's thinking.

2526   [Churchill, William.] The Marvellous Year. New York:
        Huebsch, 1909.
        Tennyson on pages 65-68.

2527   Fox, Arthur W. Six Studies in Tennyson's "Idylls of the
        King." London: Sunday School Association, 1909.

2528   Gordon, George Angier. Crossing the Bar: A Lyric of Life
        Everlasting. Boston: Pilgrim Press, [c.1909].

2528A   Hayes, J. W. Tennyson and Scientific Theology. London:
        Strock, 1909. Reprinted: Brooklyn: Haskell, 1977.

2529   Kellner, Leon. Die englische Literatur im Zeitalter der Kön-
        igen Viktoria. Leipzig: Tauchnitz, 1909, pp. 259-299.

2530   Ker, William Paton. Tennyson: The Leslie Stephen Lecture
        Delivered in the Senate House, Cambridge, on 11th of Novem-

ber, 1909. Cambridge: Cambridge U. P., 1909.
Reprinted: Collected Essays of W. P. Ker, 1925 (entry 3005).
A short assessment.

2531 Leveloh, Paul. Tennyson und Spenser: Eine Untersuchung
von Spensers Einfluss auf Tennyson mit Berücksichtigung von
Keats. Borna-Leipzig: Noske, 1909.
Publication of a dissertation: 1909 (entry 2550).

2532 Magnus, Laurie. English Literature in the Nineteenth Century.
New York: Putnam, 1909.
Tennyson on pages 224-242 and 280-286.

2533 Mulliner, Beatrice C. Introduction. Tennyson's Shorter
Poems and Lyrics, by Alfred, Lord Tennyson. London: Oxford U. P., 1909.

2534 _____. Introduction. Tennyson's English Idylls and Other
Poems, 1842-1855, by Alfred, Lord Tennyson. London: Oxford U. P., 1909.

2535 O'Hagen, Thomas. "A Study of Tennyson's 'Princess.'"
Essays: Literary, Critical and Historical. Toronto: Briggs,
1909, pp. 9-42.

2536 Peck, Harry Thurston. "The Lyrics of Tennyson." Studies
in Several Literatures. New York: Dodd, Mead, 1909, pp.
67-78.

2537 Rawnsley, Willingham Franklin. Tennyson, 1809-1909: A
Lecture. Ambleside: Middleton, 1909.
Of biographical interest.

2538 Sidgwick, Arthur. Tennyson. London: Sidgwick and Jackson,
1909.
A thirty-four-page discussion.

2539 Slicer, Thomas Roberts. "Tennyson: The Interpreter of Legend and Life." From Poet to Premier. London: Grolier
Society, 1909, pp. 159-191.

2540 Spence, Walter. Idylls of the King: A Spiritual Interpretation.
New York: Cochrane, 1909.

2541 Stork, Charles Wharton. "Heine and Tennyson: An Essay in
Comparative Criticism." Haverford Essays: Studies in Modern Literature. Haverford, Pennsylvania: 1909, pp. 153-182.

2542 Tennyson: A List of Works with References to Periodicals in
the Brooklyn Public Library. New York: Brooklyn Public
Library, 1909.

2543 Thomas, Walter. Littérature Anglaise. Paris: Larousse,
1909.

2544   Warren, Thomas Herbert. The Centenary of Tennyson, 1809-
       1909. Oxford: Clarendon, 1909.
       A short and respectful discussion.

2545   _____. "Virgil and Tennyson: A Literary Parallel,"
       "Tennyson and Dante," and "'In Memoriam' After Fifty
       Years." Essays of Poets and Poetry Ancient and Modern.
       London: Murray, 1909. New York: Dutton, 1909, pp. 172-
       216, 243-269, and 290-325, respectively.
       "Virgil and Tennyson" reprinted from Quarterly Review, 1901
(entry 2274). "Tennyson and Dante" reprinted from Monthly Review,
1904 (entry 2381).
       Not everything Warren states as fact can be relied upon.

2546   Weld, A.G. Tennyson's Religious Life and Teachings. Louis-
       ville: Baptist World Publishing Co., 1909.

2547   Wickham, E.C. The Religious Value of Tennyson's Poetry.
       Lincoln: Lincoln Cathedral, 1909.

2548   Wilkinson, William Cleaver. "Tennyson as Artist in Lyric
       Verse." Some New Literary Valuations. New York: Funk
       and Wagnalls, 1909, pp. 201-250.

Dissertations

2549   Gingerich, Solomon Francis. Wordsworth, Tennyson, and
       Browning: A Study in Human Freedom. Michigan, 1909.
       Published: 1911 (entry 2653).

2550   Leveloh, Paul. Tennyson und Spenser: Eine Untersuchung
       von Spensers Einfluss auf Tennyson mit Berücksichtigung von
       Keats. Marburg, 1909.
       Published: 1909 (entry 2531).

Periodicals

2551   Agresti, A. "Alfred Tennyson." Rassegna Contemporanea, 2
       (Oct. 1909), 77-87.

2552   "Alfred, Lord Tennyson, August 5, 1809-1909." Public Li-
       brary Monthly Bulletin (St. Louis), n.s. 7 (June 1909), 100-
       101.
       Of bibliographical interest.

2553   Allison, William Talbot. "Tennyson's Treatment of the Worth
       of Life." Canadian Magazine, 33 (Aug. 1909), 319-326.

2554   Angeli, D. "Centenario di Alfredo Tennyson." Fanfulla della
       domenica, Aug. 15, 1909.

2555   Arnold, William Harris. "Readings in Tennyson." Nation
       (New York), 88 (May 27, 1909), 534.

2556   Athenaeum, May 8, 1909, 557.
       Review of T.J. Wise's A Bibliography, 1908 (entry 2498).

2557   Barry, William. "Tennyson--a Fragment." Bookman (London), 37 (Oct. 1909), 13-19.

2558   Blake, Warren Barton. "On Tennyson's Centenary." Independent, 67 (Aug. 19, 1909), 398-402.

2559   Boguslawsky, Amalie K. "Tennyson's Women." Book News Monthly, 27 (July 1909), 826-831.

2560   Boynton, Henry Walcott. "Tennyson." Putnam's Magazine, 6 (Aug. 1909), 598-603.

2561   Bremond, Henri. "Le Centenaire de Tennyson." Le Correspondent, 236 (July 15, 1909), 248-269.

2562   Butcher, S.H. "Tennyson." British Academy, 4 (1909), 24-27.

2563   "Le Centenaire de Tennyson." Le Temps, Aug. 11, 1909.

2564   "A Centenary Study of Alfred Tennyson." Academy, 77 (Aug. 7, 1909), 391-392.

2565   Clark, Henry William. "A Reconsideration and Appreciation." Fortnightly Review, 92 (Aug. 1909), 223-238.

2566   Cook, E. Wake. "Appreciations and Depreciations of Tennyson." Academy, 77 (Aug. 28, 1909), 473-474.

2567   Cooper, Alfred B. "Tennyson: The Formative Influences of His First Twenty Years." Bookman (London), 37 (Oct. 1909), 20-28.

2568   Crespi, Angelo. "Alfredo Tennyson." Nuova Antologia di Lettere, Scienze ed Arti, 143 (Oct. 1909), 569-589.

2569   Davray, Henry D. "Tennyson." Mercure de France, 80 (1909), 659-669.

2570   _____. "Tennyson et ses sympathies françaises." Figaro, 1909.

2571   Deatrick, W. Wilburforce. "The Religious Significance of Tennyson's 'In Memoriam.'" Reformed Quarterly Review, 58 (Oct. 1909), 481-498.

2572   Dunne, Marie Aloysia. "The Eschatology of the Poets: A Study in Optimism." American Catholic Quarterly Review, 34 (Oct. 1909), 622-626.

2573 "Echoes of the Tennyson Centenary." Dial, 47 (Sept. 1, 1909), 116.

2574 Faguet, Emile. "The Centenary of Tennyson." Quarterly Review, 210 (April 1909), 305-328.
Discusses, among other items, H. Tennyson, ed., The Works, 1907-1908 (entry 2465) and H. Tennyson's Alfred Lord Tennyson, 1897 (entry 1955).
Faguet asserts that Tennyson's poetry belongs to all humanity and is notable for a pervasive rendering of beauty.

2575 Filon, Augustin. "Le Centenaire de Tennyson à Oxford." Journal des Débats, Sept. 29, 1909, p. 1.
Augustin asserts the importance of Tennyson's poetry.

2576 Grappe, Georges. "Alfred Tennyson." L'Opinion, Aug. 7, 1909.
Tennyson is representative of the spirit of England.

2577 Haney, John Louis. "Tennyson Bibliography." Notes and Queries, 10th ser. 11 (April 24, 1909), 322.

2578 _____. "Tennysoniana." Athenaeum, Aug. 7, 1909, pp. 153-154.

2579 Harrison, Frederic. "Tennyson Centenary." Nineteenth Century and After, 66 (Aug. 1909), 226-233.
Reprinted: Living Age, 262 (Sept. 11, 1909), 643-648.

2580 Hill, N. W. "Tennyson and Terence." Notes and Queries, 10th ser. 12 (Oct. 30, 1909), 346-347.

2581 Hodell, Charles W. "Tennyson, the Thinker." Methodist Review, 91 (July 1909), 539-550.

2582 "Is Tennyson's Influence on the Wane?" Current Literature, 47 (Sept. 1909), 275-278.

2583 James, Charles Canniff. "A Tennyson Pilgrimage, and Tennyson, the Imperialist." Acta Victoriana, Dec. 1909.
Reprinted: 1910 (entry 2623).

2584 Jiriczek, Otto Luitpold. "Tennyson: Eine kritische Würdigung zur hundertsten Wiederkehr seines Geburtstages." Englische Studien, 41 (1909), 28-69.

2585 Jones, Henry. "Tennyson." British Academy, 4 (1909), 131-145.
Reprinted: Hibbert Journal, 8 (Jan. 1910), 264-282; and Essays on Literature and Education, 1924 (entry 2993).
Jones sees a "westering" of Tennyson's reputation but believes that Tennyson's work will outlast its critical reassessment. He believes that Tennyson's poetry has artistic qualities that make it great enough to survive the passions of its age.

2586 Kingsley, Maud Elma. "Examination Questions for Idylls of the King." Education, 30 (Dec. 1909), 245-246.

2587 _____ . "Examination Questions for Tennyson's Princess." Education, 29 (Feb. 1909), 391-393.

2588 Lockwood, Frank C. "Tennyson's Religious Faith." Methodist Review, 91 (Sept. 1909), 783-787.

2589 Lux, James. "Le Centenaire de Tennyson." Revue Bleue, 47 (Aug. 21, 1909), 254-256.

2590 Mercer, Arthur. "'In Memoriam' as a Revelation of the Religious Philosophy of Tennyson." New Church Review, 16 (Oct. 1909), 540-559.

2591 More, Paul Elmer. "Tennyson." Nation (New York), 88 (Jan. 28, 1909), 82-85.

2592 "Our Debt to Tennyson." Spectator, 103 (Aug. 14, 1909), 230-231.

2593 Pancoast, Henry Spackman. "Tennyson and His Time." Book News Monthly, 27 (July 1909), 813-817.

2594 Peck, Harry Thurston. "Human Side of Tennyson." Bookman (New York), 29 (Aug. 1909), 600-609.
Also in: What Is Good English, 1909 (entry 2096).

2595 Pilon, Edmond. "Sites et Personnages." Echo de Paris, Aug. 6, 1909.
Reprinted: 1912 (entry 2686). Tennyson is a careful poet with poetic temperament.

2596 "Poet of Vision." Outlook, 92 (Aug. 7, 1909), 831-833.

2597 Price, Warwick James. "Tennyson's Love Story." Book News Monthly, 27 (July 1909), 823-825.

2598 Rickert, Edith. "Tennyson: A Generation After." Book News Monthly, 27 (July 1909), 819-821.

2599 Ridley, Edwin. "Genius of Tennyson." Westminster Review, 172 (Nov. 1909), 511-514.

2600 Rolfe, William James. "Tennyson's Revisions of His Poems." Nation (New York), 88 (May 6, 1909), 460-461.

2601 Roz, Firmin. "Un poète national de l'Angleterre: Alfred Lord Tennyson." Revue des Deux Mondes, 52 (Aug. 1909), 809-843.
General appreciation of what makes Tennyson a great poet.

2602 Seccombe, Thomas. "A Word about Tennyson." Readers' Review, 2 (Sept. 1909), 125.

2603 "Societies." Athenaeum, Nov. 6, 1909, 561-562.
Discusses the British Academy's activities marking the one-hundredth anniversary of Tennyson's birth.

2604 "Some Nineteenth Century Reviews." Academy, 77 (July 10, 1909), 301.

2605 "Tennyson." Dial, 47 (Aug. 1, 1909), 59-61.

2606 "Tennyson." Times Literary Supplement, Aug. 5, 1909, pp. 281-282.
This article is discussed in "A Great National Poet" in Times Literary Supplement, 1942 (entry 3316).
The article acknowledges Tennyson's poetic greatness and offers a careful assessment of Tennyson's achievements. It contends that the poetry of Poems, 1842, is the most likely of Tennyson's work to stand the test of time.

2607 "Tennyson and the Science of the Nineteenth Century." Popular Science, 75 (Sept. 1909), 306.

2608 "Tennyson and the Tennyson Centenary--a French View." Review of Reviews (New York), 40 (Oct. 1909), 499-500.

2609 "Tennyson Centenary Exhibition." Athenaeum, July 24, 1909, pp. 103-104.

2610 "Tennyson, 1809-1909." Nation (London), 5 (Aug. 7, 1909), 671-672.

2611 "Tennyson, Poe and Shaw." Academy, 76 (Jan. 23, 1909), 703-704.

2612 "Tennyson's 'Amphion.'" Notes and Queries, 9th ser. 3 (June 24, 1909), 484.

2613 Thackeray, Francis St. John. "Darwin and Tennyson." Spectator, 103 (Aug. 7, 1909), 197-198.

2614 Thomas, Ralph. "Tennyson Concordances." Notes and Queries, 10th ser. 11 (April 3, 1909), 261-262.

2615 Tollemache, Lionel Arthur. "Swinburne, the Laureateship, and Tennyson." Guardian, 64 (May 12, 1909), 763.

2616 Tolman, Albert H. "Tennyson and 'The Quarterly Review.'" Dial, 46 (Feb. 16, 1909), 108.

2617 "Two Centenaries." Spectator, 103 (Sept. 18, 1909), 409-410.
Samuel Johnson was born in 1709.

2618 Verrall, A. W. "Aristophanes on Tennyson." New Quarterly, 2 (Jan. 1909), 81-89.

2619 Ward, Wilfrid. "Tennyson's Religious Poetry." Dublin Review, 145 (Oct. 1909), 306-322.
Reprinted: Living Age, 263 (Nov. 27, 1909), 523-533.

2620 Wells, John Edwin. "Variations in the 'Idylls of the King.'"
Nation (New York), 88 (June 3, 1909), 557-558.

1910

Books

2621 Austin, Alfred. "A Vindication of Tennyson." The Bridling of Pegasus: Prose Papers on Poetry. London: Macmillan, 1910, pp. 197-217.
Reprinted from: Macmillan's Magazine, 1881 (entry 978).
Reprinted: Freeport, N. Y.: Books for Libraries, 1967.

2622 Browning, Oscar. Memories of Sixty Years at Eton, Cambridge, and Elsewhere. London: Lane, 1910.
Includes a few memories of Tennyson.

2623 James, Charles Canniff. A Tennyson Pilgrimage, and Tennyson, the Imperialist. Toronto: 1910.
Reprinted from: Acta Victoriana, 1909 (entry 2583).

2624 Kerlin, Robert Thomas. Theocritus in English Literature. Lynchburg, Virginia: Bell, 1910.
Publication of a dissertation: 1910 (entry 2633).

2625 Lauvrière, Emile. Repetition and Parallelism in Tennyson. London: Frowde, 1910.

2626 Le Gallienne, Richard. "Tennyson." Attitudes and Avowals. New York: Lane, [c.1910], pp. 212-226.

2627 Lockyer, Joseph Norman, and Winifred L. Lockyer. Tennyson as a Student and Poet of Nature. London: Macmillan, 1910.
The authors remark that Tennyson is "a poet who, beyond all others who have ever lived, combined the gift of expression with an unceasing interest in the causes of things and in the working out of Nature's laws." J. N. Lockyer was a notable astronomer; he presents considerable evidence supporting Tennyson's scientific sophistication. This book is a standard reference for those interested in Tennyson's use of science and scientific knowledge. Those who regard Tennyson as a poet ignorant of the science of his day are referred to this book, which offers persuasive evidence to the contrary.
Reviewed by: Athenaeum (entry 2635); and Spectator (entry 2670).

2628 Mackail, John William. "Theocritus and Tennyson." Lectures on Greek Poetry. London: Longmans, Green, 1910, pp. 220-226.

2629 More, Paul Elmer. "Tennyson." Shelburne Essays. New York: Putnam, 1910. 7th ser., pp. 64-94.
Reprinted: J. M. Berdan, ed., Modern Essays, 1916 (entry 2813).

2630 Morton, Edward Payson. The Technique of English Non-Dramatic Blank Verse. Chicago: Donnelley, 1910.
Tennyson on pages 124-125. Publication of a dissertation: 1910 (entry 2634).

2631 Saintsbury, George Edward Bateman. "Tennyson and Browning." A History of English Prosody from the Twelfth Century to the Present Day. London: Macmillan, 1910. Volume III, pp. 183-217.
Discusses the style of Tennyson's poetry.

2632 Stedman, Laura, and George M. Gould. Life and Letters of Edmund Clarence Stedman. 2 volumes. New York: Moffat, Yard, 1910.

Dissertations

2633 Kerlin, Robert Thomas. Theocritus in English Literature. Yale, [1910?].
Published: 1910 (entry 2624).

2634 Morton, Edward Payson. The Technique of English Non-Dramatic Blank Verse. Chicago, 1910.
Published: 1910 (entry 2630).

Periodicals

2635 Athenaeum, Dec. 10, 1910, p. 736.
Review of J. N. and W. Lockyer's Tennyson, 1910 (entry 2627).

2636 B., J. F. (J. F. Bense). "Alfred Lord Tennyson." Vragen en Mededeelingen, 1 (May 20, 1910), 226-229.

2637 Chapman, Elizabeth Rachel. "Talks with Tennyson." Putnam's Magazine, 7 (Feb. and March 1910), 546-552 and 746-752.
Describes Chapman's talks with Tennyson about poetry and related topics.

2638 Dawson, Edwin Collas. "Morals of the Round Table: Malory's Morte d'Arthur Compared with the Idylls of the King." Chambers's Journal, 13 (Nov. 1910), 781-784.
Reprinted: Living Age, 267 (Dec. 3, 1910), 606-610.
Dawson perceives the Arthurian story as a consistent presen-

tation of the theme of good men struggling against the world's evils. The basic theme is colored in Malory and Tennyson's works by the eras in which they were written.

2639   Hudson, J. "Tennyson's Birthday." Westminster Review, 174 (Aug. 1910), 210-211.
       A poem.

2640   Meynell, Alice. "Tennyson." Dublin Review, 146 (Jan. 1910), 62-71.

2641   Palmer, J. Foster. "Tennysoniana." Notes and Queries, 11th ser. 2 (Nov. 12, 1910), 394.

2642   Richardson, Charles Francis. "Book of Beginnings." Nation (New York), 91 (Dec. 1, 1910), 520-521.
       Discusses Enoch Arden.

2643   Roz, Firmin. "Une Vie de poète (Alfred Tennyson: A Memoir by His Son)." Bibliothèque Universelle et Revue Suisse, 59 (Nov. 1910), 227-261.
       Discusses H. Tennyson's Alfred Lord Tennyson, 1897 (entry 1955).

2644   Smyser, William Emery. "Romanticism in Tennyson and His Pre-Raphaelite Illustrators." North American Review, 192 (Oct. 1910), 504-515.

2645   "Some Poets of the Victorian Era: V.--Tennyson." Academy, 79 (Aug. 20 and 27, 1910), 173-175 and 198-200.

2646   "Tennyson: 'Oorali.'" Notes and Queries, 11th ser. 2 (Dec. 3, 1910), 453.

2647   "Tennysoniana." Notes and Queries, 11th ser. 2 (Oct. 29, 1910), 341-342.

2648   "Tennyson's 'Margaret.'" Notes and Queries, 11th ser. 2 (July 30, 1910), 94-95.
       See also: entry 2649, below.

2649   "Tennyson's 'Margaret.'" Notes and Queries, 11th ser. 2 (Aug. 13, 1910), 138.
       See also: entry 2648, above.

1911

Books

2650   Ambler, B.G. Alfred, Lord Tennyson: His Homes and Haunts. London: Jack, 1911.
       Reviewed by: Athenaeum (entry 2661).

A Bibliography / 243

2651 Austin, Alfred. The Autobiography of Alfred Austin, Poet
      Laureate, 1835-1910. London: Macmillan, 1911.
      Tennyson in Volume II, pp. 219-231.

2652 di Silvestri-Falconieri, Francesco. Lord Tennyson. Rome:
      Roma Letteraria, 1911.

2653 Gingerich, Solomon Francis. Wordsworth, Tennyson, and
      Browning: A Study in Human Freedom. Ann Arbor: Wahr,
      1911.
      Tennyson on pages 113-175. Publication of a dissertation:
1909 (entry 2549). Emphasizes qualities of spiritual freedom. Reviewed by: Academy (entry 2692).

2654 Lang, Leonora Blanche. The Gateway to Tennyson: Tales
      and Extracts from the Poet's Work. London: Nelson,
      [c.1911].

2655 Mair, G.H. English Literature: Modern. New York: Holt,
      [c.1911]. (Home University Library of Modern Knowledge,
      27)
      Tennyson on pages 194-201.

2656 Price, Walter. Days with the English Poets: Tennyson,
      Browning, Byron. London: Hodder and Stoughton, 1911.

2657 Roz, Firmin. Tennyson. Paris: Bloud, 1911. Boston:
      Ginn, 1911.
      One of the best works in French on Tennyson. Roz analyzes
the qualities that make Tennyson's poetry great.

2658 Tennyson, Hallam, ed. Tennyson and His Friends. London:
      Macmillan, 1911.
      This book is a useful reference containing reminiscences of
Tennyson by many of those who knew him.
      Reviewed by: Academy (entry 2691); P.F. Bicknell in Dial
(entry 2694); Living Age (entry 2701); H.W. Mabie in Literary Di-
gest (entry 2702); C. Metcalfe in Bookman (London) (entry 2703);
Nation (New York) (entry 2704); Spectator (entry 2707); and W.P.
Ward in Dublin Review (entry 2710).

2659 Tipple, Ezra Squier. "Somersby." Some Famous Country
      Parishes. New York: Eaton and Mains, [c.1911], pp. 164-
      199.

Dissertations

2660 Neuner, Karl. Untersuchungen zur Stilistik des Adjektivs in
      Tennysons epischen Dichtungen. Innsbruck, 1911.

Periodicals

2661 Athenaeum, Sept. 9, 1911, p. 295.

Review of B.G. Ambler's <u>Alfred, Lord Tennyson,</u> 1911 (entry 2650).

2662   Brandl, Alois. "Zur Quellenkunde von Tennysons 'Enoch Arden.'" <u>Archiv für das Studium der neueren Sprachen und Literaturen,</u> 126 (1911), 103-108.

2663   "A Crux in Tennyson." <u>Spectator,</u> 107 (Sept. 2 and 9, 1911), 344 and 379-380.
        See also: J.B. Mayor (entry 2667).

2664   Dixon, James Main. "Pragmatism in 'In Memoriam.'" <u>Methodist Review,</u> 93 (1911), 101-111.

2665   Ellacombe, H.N. "Tennyson's 'Flower in the Crannied Wall.'" <u>Notes and Queries,</u> 11th ser. 3 (March 4, 1911), 167.
        See also: <u>Notes and Queries</u> (entry 2674).

2666   Macphail, Alexander. "Lucretius or Scott?" <u>Spectator,</u> 106 (Jan. 28, 1911), 144.
        See also: <u>Spectator</u> (entry 2672).

2667   Mayor, Joseph B. "A Crux in Tennyson." <u>Spectator,</u> 107 (Aug. 26 and Sept. 16, 1911), 310-311 and 414-415.
        See also: <u>Spectator</u> (entry 2663).

2668   Price, Warwick James. "Tennyson's Friendships." <u>Sewanee Review,</u> 19 (April 1911), 228-234.

2669   Quayle, William Alfred. "Tennyson's Men." <u>Methodist Review,</u> 93 (1911), 219-236.

2670   <u>Spectator,</u> 106 (Jan. 21, 1911), 94-95.
        Review of J.N. and W. Lockyer's <u>Tennyson,</u> 1910 (entry 2627).

2671   Stockley, William. "In Memoriam." <u>Queen's Quarterly,</u> 18 (April 1911), 259-272.

2672   "Tennyson and Lucretius or Scott?" <u>Spectator,</u> 106 (Feb. 4, 1911), 180-181.
        See also: A. Macphail (entry 2666).

2673   "The Tennyson Memorial Meetings at Somersby." <u>Spectator,</u> 107 (Aug. 12, 1911), 241-242.

2674   "Tennyson's 'Flower in the Crannied Wall.'" <u>Notes and Queries,</u> 11th ser. 3 (May 6, 1911), 358.
        See also: H.N. Ellacombe (entry 2665).

1912

Books

2675 Choisy, Louis Frédéric. Alfred Tennyson, son spiritualisme, sa personalité morale. Geneva: Kündig, 1912.
Reviewed: Athenaeum (entry 2743). Publication of a dissertation: 1913 (entry 2737).

2676 Collins, John Churton. "Tennyson." The Posthumous Essays of John Churton Collins. Ed. L. C. Collins. London: Dent, 1912, pp. 242-255.
Collins admires Tennyson.

2677 Collins, L. C. Life and Memoirs of John Churton Collins: Written and Compiled by His Son. London: Lane, 1912.

2678 Dixon, William Macneile. "Narrative Poetry in the Nineteenth Century--Tennyson, Morris, Arnold." English Epic and Heroic Poetry. London: Dent, 1912, pp. 302-329.

2679 Douady, Jules. "Enoch Arden." La Mer et les Poètes Anglais. Paris: Hachette, 1912, pp. 262-283.

2680 Fitch, George Hamlin. "Tennyson Leads the Victorian Writers." Modern English Books of Power. New York: Grosset, 1912. San Francisco: Paul Elder, 1912, pp. 96-105.

2681 Gosse, Edmund William. "A First Sight of Tennyson." Portraits and Sketches. London: Heinemann, 1912, pp. 127-134.
Reprinted: Selected Essays, 1928 (entry 3053).

2682 Harrison, Frederic. "Studies in Tennyson." Among My Books. New York: Macmillan, 1912, pp. 284-296.

2683 Lodge, Oliver Joseph. "Attitude of Tennyson Towards Science." Modern Problems. London: Methuen, 1912, pp. 301-307.

2684 MacEwen, V. Knights of the Holy Eucharist. London: Gardner, 1912.
Discusses The Holy Grail's spiritual teachings.

2685 Martin, Werner. Die Quellen zu Tennysons erstem Drama "Queen Mary." Halle: Hohmann, 1912.
Publication of a dissertation: 1912 (entry 2690).

2686 Pilon, E. Sites et Personnages. Paris: Grasset, 1912.
Reprinted from: Echo de Paris, 1909 (entry 2595).

2687 Rawnsley, Willingham Franklin. "Tennyson Centenary." Introduction to the Poets. London: Routledge, 1912, pp. 243-313.

2688 Suddard, S.J. Mary. Essais de littérature anglais. London: Cambridge U.P., 1912.

2689 Watson, Aaron. Tennyson. London: Jack, 1912. (People's Books)
An unoriginal study. Reviewed by: Athenaeum (entry 2693).

Dissertation

2690 Martin, Werner. Die Quellen zu Tennysons erstem Drama Queen Mary. Halle, 1912.
Published: 1912 (entry 2685).

Periodicals

2691 Academy, 82 (Jan. 31, 1912), 37-38.
Review of H. Tennyson, ed., Tennyson and His Friends, 1911 (entry 2658).

2692 Academy, 82 (April 6, 1912), 424.
Review of S. F. Gingerich's Wordsworth, Tennyson, and Browning, 1911 (entry 2653).

2693 Athenaeum, Dec. 7, 1912, p. 688.
Review of A. Watson's Tennyson, 1912 (entry 2689).

2694 Bicknell, P. F. Dial, 52 (March 16, 1912), 221-223.
Review of H. Tennyson, ed., Tennyson and His Friends, 1911 (entry 2658).

2695 Blake, Warren Barton. "Tennyson's 'Poet's Song.'" Spectator, 108 (March 16, 1912), 436.
See also: E. M. Bordes (entry 2696), G. E. Fyson (entry 2699), W. A. Lewis (entry 2700), and J. S. O. Tombs (entry 2708).

2696 Bordes, Elsie M. "Tennyson's 'Poet's Song.'" Spectator, 108 (Feb. 10, 1912), 230.
See also: W. B. Blake (entry 2695), G. E. Fyson (entry 2699), W. A. Lewis (entry 2700), and J. S. O. Tombs (entry 2708).

2697 Carruthers, Adam. "A Tennysonian Interpretation." Canadian Magazine, 39 (Oct. 1912), 526-529.

2698 Clarke, George Herbert. "Browning and Tennyson." Canadian Magazine, 39 (June 1912), 120-132.

2699 Fyson, George E. "Tennyson's 'Poet's Song.'" Spectator, 108 (Feb. 17, 1912), 271.
See also: W. B. Blake (entry 2695), E. M. Bordes (entry 2696), W. A. Lewis (entry 2700), and J. S. O. Tombs (entry 2708).

2700 Lewis, W. Aldresey. "Tennyson's 'Poet's Song.'" Spectator, 108 (March 23, 1912), 475-476.

See also: W.B. Blake (entry 2695), E.M. Bordes (entry 2696), G.E. Fyson (entry 2699), and J.S.O. Tombs (entry 2708).

2701   Living Age, 272 (Jan. 13, 1912), 113-116.
Review of H. Tennyson, ed., Tennyson and His Friends, 1911 (entry 2658).

2702   Mabie, Hamilton Wright. Literary Digest, 44 (March 2, 1912), 431-432.
Review of H. Tennyson, ed., Tennyson and His Friends, 1911 (entry 2658).

2703   Metcalfe, C. Bookman (London), 41 (March 1912), 301.
Review of H. Tennyson, ed., Tennyson and His Friends, 1911 (entry 2658).

2704   Nation (New York), 94 (Feb. 29, 1912), 213.
Review of H. Tennyson, ed., Tennyson and His Friends, 1911 (entry 2658).

2705   "Personal Tennyson." Bookman (New York), 34 (Feb. 1912), 588-590.

2706   "Poet Who Knew and Believed." Outlook, 100 (Feb. 24, 1912), 388-389.

2707   Spectator, 108 (Jan. 6, 1912), 19-20.
Review of H. Tennyson, ed., Tennyson and His Friends, 1911 (entry 2658).

2708   Tombs, J.S.O. "Tennyson's 'Poet's Song.'" Spectator, 108 (Feb. 17, 1912), 271.
See also: W.B. Blake (entry 2695), E.M. Bordes (entry 2696), G.E. Fyson (entry 2699), and W.A. Lewis (entry 2700).

2709   Way, A.S. "Tennyson and Quintus Calaber." Journal of English Studies, 1 (Sept. 1912).

2710   Ward, W.P. Dublin Review, 150 (Jan. 1912), 68-85.
Reprinted: Living Age, 273 (April 27, 1912), 201-211. Review of H. Tennyson, ed., Tennyson and His Friends, 1911 (entry 2658).

1913

Books

2711   Bede, Cuthbert (Edward Bradley). "In Memoriam." A Century of Parody and Imitation. Ed. Walter Jerrold and R.M. Leonard. London: Oxford U.P., 1913, p. 273.

2712   Calverley, Charles Stuart. "Wanderers." A Century of Par-

ody and Imitation. Ed. Walter Jerrold and R.M. Leonard.
London: Oxford U.P., 1913, pp. 296-298.

2713 Carroll, Lewis (Charles Lutwidge Dodgson). "The Three
Voices." A Century of Parody and Imitation. Ed. Walter
Jerrold and R.M. Leonard. London: Oxford U.P., 1913,
pp. 314-321.

2714 Chesterton, Gilbert Keith. "Great Victorian Poets." The
Victorian Age in Literature. New York: Holt, [1913].
Tennyson on pages 160-169 and elsewhere.

2715 Collins, Mortimer. "Hair." A Century of Parody and Imitation. Ed. Walter Jerrold and R.M. Leonard. London:
Oxford U.P., 1913, pp. 287-288.

2716 Cooledge, Charles Edwin. The Sunny Side of Bereavement as
Illustrated in Tennyson's "In Memoriam." Boston: Badger,
[1913].

2717 Dobson, Austin. "Alfred, Lord Tennyson." Collected Poems.
London: Kegan Paul, Trench, Trübner, 1913, p. 319.
Reprinted from: Athenaeum, 1892 (entry 1474). See entry
1474 for other reprinting and for the poem.

2718 Fletcher, Robert Huntington. Tennyson and Browning: A Man-
ual for College Classes and Other Students. Cedar Rapids:
Torch, 1913.

2719 Graves, Alfred Perceval. "Tennyson in Ireland: A Reminiscence." Irish Literary and Musical Studies. London: Mathews, 1913, pp. 1-11.
Reprinted from: Cornhill Magazine, 1897 (entry 1977).

2720 Grünert, Louis. Tennysons Drama Becket: Eine Quellenuntersuchung. Weimar: Wagner, 1913.
Publication of dissertation: 1913 (entry 2738).

2721 Hood, Thomas (the younger). "In Memoriam Technicam." A
Century of Parody and Imitation. Ed. Walter Jerrold and R.
M. Leonard. London: Oxford U.P., 1913, p. 324.

2722 Huckel, Oliver. Through England with Tennyson: A Pilgrimage to Places Associated with the Great Laureate. New York:
Crowell, [1913].

2723 Johnson, Reginald Brimley. Tennyson and His Poetry. London: Harrap, 1913.
How his poetry reveals Tennyson's character.

2724 Lang, Andrew. "Gaily the Troubador." A Century of Parody
and Imitation. Ed. Walter Jerrold and R.M. Leonard.
London: Oxford U.P., 1913, pp. 356-357.

2725 Locker-Lampson, Frederick. "Unfortunate Miss Bailey." A
      Century of Parody and Imitation. Ed. Walter Jerrold and R.
      M. Leonard. London: Oxford U.P., 1913, pp. 268-269.

2726 Murray, Robert Fuller. "The Poet's Hat" and "A Tennysonian
      Fragment." A Century of Parody and Imitation. Ed. Walter
      Jerrold and R.M. Leonard. London: Oxford U.P., 1913, pp.
      382 and 383, respectively.

2727 Plaut, Julius. Das poetische Genus personifizierter Substan-
      tive bei Alfred Lord Tennyson. Heidelberg: Winter, 1913.
      Publication of a dissertation: 1913 (entry 2740).

2728 Rhys, Ernest. Lyric Poetry. London: Dent, 1913, pp. 326-
      333.

2729 Riley, James Whitcomb. "Tennyson: England, Oct. 5, 1892."
      The Complete Works. Ed. Edmund Henry Eitel. Indianapolis:
      Bobbs-Merrill, 1913. Volume IV, p. 229.
      Reprinted from: Critic (New York) (entry 1585). See entry
1585 for poem.

2730 Rossetti, Dante Gabriel. "MacCracken" and "The Brothers."
      A Century of Parody and Imitation. Ed. Walter Jerrold and
      R.M. Leonard. London: Oxford U.P., 1913, pp. 290 and
      290-291, respectively.

2731 Schelling, Felix Emmanuel. "The Victorian Lyrists." The
      English Lyric. Boston: Houghton Mifflin, 1913.
      Tennyson on pages 193-202 and 220-222.

2732 Spurgeon, Caroline. "Philosophical Mystics." Mysticism in
      English Literature. Cambridge: Cambridge U.P., 1913, pp.
      84-88.

2733 Taylor, Tom. "The Laureate's Bust at Trinity." A Century
      of Parody and Imitation. Ed. Walter Jerrold and R.M. Leon-
      ard. London: Oxford U.P., 1913, pp. 266-267.

2734 Tennyson, Hallam, ed. The Works of Tennyson with Notes by
      the Author. London: Macmillan, 1913.
      Single-volume version of The Works, 1907-1908 (entry 2465).
See entry 2465 for annotation.

2735 Warren, T.H. Introduction. The Poems of Alfred Tennyson,
      1830-1870. London: Frowde, 1913.
      Reviewed by: Spectator (entry 2752).

Dissertations

2736 Baumann, Hermann. Über Neubildungen von Wortzusammen-
      setzungen in Tennysons epischen und lyrischen Gedichten.
      Vienna, 1913.

2737 Choisy, Louis-Frédéric. Alfred Tennyson: son spiritualisme sa personalité morale. Geneva, 1913. Published: 1912 (entry 2675).

2738 Grünert, Louis. Tennysons Drama Becket: Eine Quellenuntersuchung. Leipzig, 1913. Published: 1913 (entry 2720).

2739 Pietschmann, Tony. Robin Hood im englischen Drama mit besonderer Berücksichtigung von Tennysons Foresters. Vienna, 1913.

2740 Plaut, Julius. Das poetische Genus personifizierter Substantive bei Alfred Lord Tennyson. Kiel, 1913. Published: 1913 (entry 2727).

2741 Rice, Jessie Folsom. The Influence of Frederick Dennison Maurice on Tennyson. Chicago, [1913?].

Periodicals

2742 Academy, 85 (Dec. 13, 1913), 744. Discusses Tennyson's works.

2743 Athenaeum, March 8, 1913, pp. 283-284. Review of L. F. Choisy's Alfred Tennyson, 1912 (entry 2675).

2744 Baker, H. "Alfred Tennyson: His Misquoted 'Larger Hope' in 'In Memoriam.'" Homilectic Review, 66 (1913), 276-278.

2745 Bannard, T. "Tennyson and Mendelssohn Bartholdy." Monthly Musical Record, 1913, p. 515.

2746 Buckley, Reginald R. "Survivors of Popularity II.--Tennyson." T.P.'s Weekly, 22 (Oct. 24, 1913), 527.

2747 Gibbs, Lincoln R. "Tennyson's Idylls of the King." Methodist Review, 95 (Sept. 1913), 756-763. Poetry and the state.

2748 Lauvrière, Emile. "La Morbidité de Tennyson." Revue Germanique, 9 (1913), 557-565.

2749 Lockhart, A.J. "Arthur Hallam and 'In Memoriam.'" Methodist Review, 95 (1913), 46-65.

2750 Schell, E.A. "Tennyson's 'Ulysses.'" Methodist Review, 95 (March 1913), 192-202. A thorough study.

2751 Span, Reginald B. "Tennyson as a Mystic." Westminster Review, 180 (July 1913), 43-49.

2752 Spectator, 110 (Feb. 22, 1913), 316-317.
      Review of The Poems of Alfred Tennyson, 1913 (entry 2735).

2753 Spectator, 111 (Nov. 8, 1913), 760-761.
      Discusses Tennyson's works.

2754 Stirling, Maria E.A. "Tennyson and Browning: A Defense
      of the Ideal." Canadian Magazine, 40 (Jan. 1913), 294-297.

2755 "Two Lights on Tennyson." Bookman (New York), 36 (Feb.
      1913), 598-600.

1914

Books

2756 Baker, Arthur E. A Concordance to the Poetical and Drama-
      tic Works of Alfred, Lord Tennyson: Including the Poems
      Contained in the "Life of Alfred, Lord Tennyson," and the
      "Suppressed Poems," 1830-1868. London: Kegan Paul,
      Trench, Trübner, 1914. Reprinted: New York: Barnes and
      Noble, 1966.
      Reviewed by: Athenaeum (entry 2773); P.E. More in Nation
      (New York) (entry 2806); T. Walsh in Modern Language Journal,
      1967 (entry 4062); and H.S. Weeks in Library Journal, 1966 (entry
      4007).

2757 Brooks, F.T. Alfred, Lord Tennyson, a Modern Sage. Ma-
      dras: Vyasashrama Book Shop, 1914.

2758 Chubb, Edwin Watts. "Tennyson." Masters of English Liter-
      ature. Chicago: McClurg, 1914, pp. 398-420.

2759 Gladstone, William Ewart. Famous Reviews. Ed. B. John-
      son. London: Pitman, 1914.
      Essay reprinted from: Quarterly Review, 1859 (entry 471).

2760 Hübel, Rudolf. Studien zur Tennysons Becket. Berlin: Tren-
      kel, 1914.
      Publication of a dissertation: 1914 (entry 2770).

2761 Hughes, A.M.D. Biographical sketch. Tennyson: Poems Pub-
      lished in 1842, by Alfred, Lord Tennyson. Oxford: Claren-
      don, 1914.

2762 Hunt, Theodore Whitfield. "Tennyson's 'Idylls of the King.'"
      and "Tennyson's 'In Memoriam.'" English Literary Miscel-
      lany. Oberlin, Ohio: Bibliotheca Sacra Co., 1914, pp. 271-
      318.
      Reprinted from: Bibliotheca Sacra, 1897 (entry 1979) and 1898
      (entry 2058).

2763　McMechan, Archibald McKellar.　"Alfred Tennyson, Artist."
　　　The Life of a Little College and Other Papers.　Boston:
　　　Houghton Mifflin, 1914, pp. 85-120.
　　　Reprinted from: University Magazine, 1908 (entry 2512).

2764　Meyer, Wilhelm.　Tennysons Jugendgedichte in deutscher Über-
　　　setzung.　Münster: 1914.
　　　Publication of a dissertation: 1914 (entry 2771).

2765　Quaritch, Bernard.　Description of an Important Collection of
　　　Holograph Manuscript Poems by Lord Tennyson in the Pos-
　　　session of Bernard Quaritch, and the Holograph Manuscript
　　　of "Sardanapalus" by Lord Byron.　London: 1914.

2766　Snell, Frederick John.　"Alfred Tennyson."　Boys Who Be-
　　　came Famous.　London: Harrap, 1914, pp. 132-142.

2767　Traubel, Horace.　With Walt Whitman in Camden.　3 volumes.
　　　New York: Kennerley, 1914.

2768　Ward, Wilfrid.　"Tennyson at Freshwater."　Men and Matters.
　　　New York: Longmans, Green, 1914, pp. 251-272.
　　　Of biographical interest.

Dissertations

2769　Baunsenwein, Josef.　Die poetischen Bearbeitungen der Balin-
　　　und Balan-sage von Tennyson und Swinburne und ihr Verhält-
　　　nis zu Malory.　Heidelberg, 1914.
　　　This dissertation is listed in R.D. Altick and R. Matthews's
　　　Guide to Doctoral Dissertations in Victorian Literature 1886-1958
　　　(Urbana: U. of Illinois P., 1960) as c. 1914; A. Galimberti lists it
　　　for 1894 in her L'Aedo d'Italia (Palermo: Remo Sandron, 1925).

2770　Hübel, Rudolf.　Studien zur Tennysons Becket.　Giessen, 1914.
　　　Published: 1914 (entry 2760).

2771　Meyer, Wilhelm.　Tennysons Jugendgedichte in deutscher Über-
　　　setzung.　Münster, 1914.
　　　Published: 1914 (entry 2764).

2772　Villard, Léonie.　The Influence of Keats on Tennyson and Ros-
　　　setti.　Paris, 1914.

Periodicals

2773　Athenaeum, Sept. 19, 1914, p. 280.
　　　Review of A.E. Baker's A Concordance, 1914 (entry 2756).

2774　Bensly, Edward.　"'Memmian Naphtha-pits' in Tennyson."
　　　Notes and Queries, 11th ser. 9 (Feb. 14, 1914), 137.
　　　See also: C. Owen (entry 2783) and L.R.M. Strachan (entry
2785).

2775 Crawford, A.W. "Tennyson's 'Maud': A Study of Social Conditions." Canadian Magazine, 43 (May 1914), 29-36.

2776 Dial, 56 (April 1, 1914), 286.

2777 Elton, Oliver. "Poetic Romancers After 1850." British Academy, 6 (1914), 413-431. (Warton Lecture on English Poetry)
Reprinted: A Sheaf of Papers, 1923 (entry 2965).

2778 Lucy, Henry. "Alfred Tennyson: Personal Notes." Nation (New York), 99 (July 16, 1914), 69-71.

2779 McCorkindale, T.B. "Some Elements in the Religious Teaching of Tennyson." Queen's Quarterly, 21 (April 1914), 449-455.

2780 Moeton, P.J. "Tennyson's 'The Palace of Art' en onze tachtiger letterkundige beweging." Bloesem en Wrucht, 3 (1914), 515-538.

2781 Moore, Charles Leonard. "The Asiatic and the Greek Spirit in Literature." Dial, 57 (Sept. 16, 1914), 185-187.

2782 O'Connor, T.P. "Tennyson in Iceland." T.P.'s Weekly, 23 (May 1, 1914), 545-546.

2783 Owen, Cecil. "'Memmian Naphtha-pits' in Tennyson: Medicinal Mummies." Notes and Queries, 11th ser. 10 (Aug. 29, 1914), 176-177.
See also: E. Bensly (entry 2774) and L.R.M. Strachan (entry 2785).

2784 Phelps, William Lyon. "Tennyson's Silence." Modern Language Notes, 29 (April 1914), 126-127.

2785 Strachan, L.R.M. "'Memmian Naphtha-pits' in Tennyson." Notes and Queries, 11th ser. 9 (Jan. 24, 1914), 67.
See also: E. Bensly (entry 2774) and C. Owen (2783).

2786 _____. "'Titmarsh' in an Alleged Poem by Tennyson." Notes and Queries, 9 (June 20, 1914), 487.
See also: Notes and Queries (entry 2789).

2787 Tennyson, Alfred. Bookman (New York), 40 (Nov. 1914), 233.
First publication of a poem by Tennyson. First line: 'O! where is he, the simple fool."

2788 "Tennyson as a Minor Poet." Literary Digest, 48 (March 21, 1914), 619-620.

2789 "'Titmarsh' in an Alleged Poem by Tennyson." Notes and Queries, 11th ser. 10 (July 4, 1914), 16.
See also: L.R.M. Strachan (entry 2786).

1915

Books

2790 Bell, A.F. "Tennyson and Browning." Leaders of English
Literature. London: Bell, 1915, pp. 182-194.

2791 Curzon, George Nathaniel. "Lord Tennyson." Subjects of
the Day. London: Allen and Unwin, [1915], pp. 239-242.

2792 de Sélincourt, Ernest. "English Poetry Since 1815." English
Poets and the National Ideal. London: Oxford U.P., 1915.
Tennyson on pages 99-105.

2793 Frank, Maude Morrison. "Alfred Tennyson." Great Authors
in Their Youth. New York: Holt, 1915, pp. 173-208.

2794 Frodsham, George H. A Bishop's Pleasance. London: Smith,
Elder, 1915.

2795 Gray, W. Forbes. "Alfred, Lord Tennyson." The Poets
Laureate of England. New York: Dutton, 1915, pp. 252-273.

2796 Jennings, James George. "A Note on the Use of Metaphor in
'In Memoriam.'" An Essay on Metaphor in Poetry. London:
Blackie, 1915, pp. 81-94.

2797 Lounsbury, Thomas R. The Life and Times of Tennyson:
1809-1850. New Haven: Yale U.P., 1915. London: Oxford
U.P., 1915.
  Lounsbury died before finishing this book, and it occasionally
appears in need of revision. He defends Tennyson's importance
against what he believed was unfair criticism. This book remains
important, although subsequent scholarship has invalidated some of
Lounsbury's assertions. See E.F. Shannon's Tennyson and the Reviewers, 1952 (entry 3496) for the most important contradiction of
some of Lounsbury's contentions. This book is fundamental to the
study of Tennyson's reputation; its criticism still has value.
  Reviewed by: Athenaeum (entry 2821); Living Age, (entry
2826); B. Mathews in Yale Review (entry 2827); New Republic (entry
2830); C.S. Northup in Dial (entry 2831); and G. Saintsbury in Bookman (London) (entry 2833).

2798 Olivero, Federico. Sulla lirica di Alfred Tennyson. Bari:
Laterza, 1915.

2799 Turnbull, Arthur. Life and Writings of Alfred, Lord Tennyson. New York: Scribner, 1915.

2800 Waugh, Arthur. "The Poetry of Faith and Aspiration." Ret-
icence in Literature and Other Papers. London: Wilson,
[1915], pp. 43-45.

Periodicals

2801　Dupuy, Ernest. "Alfred Tennyson Poète-Lauréat." Revue
　　　Hebdomadaire, 1 (Jan. 1915), 128-144.

2802　Emerson, Oliver Farrar. "Light Upon the Wind." Nation
　　　(New York), 101 (July 1, 1915), 15.
　　　Discusses the word wind in Tennyson's work.

2803　Littell, Philip. "Moral Element in Tennyson's Poetry." New
　　　Republic, 4 (Aug. 21, 1915), 77.

2804　Luce, Morton. "Nature in Tennyson: I. Birds." British Re-
　　　view, 11 (Sept. 1915), 420-432.
　　　Reprinted: Living Age, 287 (Oct. 16, 1915), 156-161.

2805　＿＿＿＿. "Nature in Tennyson: II. Trees." British Re-
　　　view, 12 (Oct. 1915), 102-117.
　　　Reprinted: Living Age, 287 (Dec. 4, 1915), 604-611.

2806　More, Paul Elmer. Nation (New York), 100 (Feb. 25, 1915),
　　　220-221.
　　　Review of A.E. Baker's A Concordance, 1914 (entry 2756).

2807　Owen, Cecil. "Tennyson and Goldsmith: A Parallel." Notes
　　　and Queries, 11th ser. 12 (Aug. 21, 1915), 140.

2808　Willcock, J. "Tennyson and Crabbe." Notes and Queries,
　　　11th ser. 11 (June 12, 1915), 450.

1916

Books

2809　Baker, Arthur Ernest. A Tennyson Dictionary: The Charac-
　　　ters and Place-Names Contained in the Poetical and Dramatic
　　　Works of the Poet, Alphabetically Arranged and Described,
　　　with Synopses of the Poems and Plays. London: Routledge,
　　　1916. Reprinted: New York: Haskell House, 1968.
　　　A handy reference. Reviewed by: Athenaeum (entry 2822);
and P.W. Filby in Library Journal, 1968 (entry 4089).

2810　Grierson, Herbert J.C. "The Tennysons." Cambridge His-
　　　tory of English Literature. Ed. A.W. Ward and A.R. Waller.
　　　Cambridge: Cambridge U.P., 1916. Volume XIII, pp. 25-
　　　53.
　　　A positive assessment of Tennyson.

2811　Hearn, Lafcadio. "Studies in Tennyson (a fragment)." Appre-
　　　ciations of Poetry. Ed. J. Erskine. New York: Dodd,
　　　Mead, 1916, pp. 30-36.
　　　Hearn believes Tennyson's poetry lacks universal appeal.

2812 Mackaye, Percy. "Tennyson." Poems and Plays. New York: Macmillan, 1916. Volume I, pp. 16-20.
A poem.

2813 More, Paul Elmer. "Tennyson." Modern Essays. Ed. J.M. Berdan. New York: Macmillan, 1916, pp. 204-228.
Reprinted from: Shelburne Essays, 1910 (entry 2629).

2814 Quayle, William Alfred. "Tennyson's Men" and "Recovered Yesterdays." Recovered Yesterdays in Literature. New York: Abingdon, 1916, pp. 88-144 and 186-203, respectively.
Classifies the male characters in Tennyson's poetry.

2815 Russell, George. "A Group of Poets." Portraits of the Seventies. New York: Scribner, 1916.
Tennyson on pages 285-286.

2816 Schneider, Fritz. Tennyson und Keats: Eine Untersuchung des Einflusses von Keats auf Tennyson (mit Berücks von Shelley). Weimar: Wagern, 1916.
Publication of a dissertation: 1916 (entry 2820).

2817 [Shorter, Clement.] The Love Story of In Memoriam. Privately printed, 1916.

2818 Thayer, Mary Rebecca. "Alfred Lord Tennyson." The Influence of Horace on the Chief of English Poets of the Nineteenth Century. New Haven: Yale U.P., 1916, pp. 94-101.

2819 Watts-Dunton, Theodore. "Alfred, Lord Tennyson." Old Familiar Faces. London: Jenkins, 1916, pp. 120-176.

Dissertation

2820 Schneider, Fritz. Tennyson und Keats: Eine Untersuchung des Einflusses von Keats auf Tennyson (mit Berücksichtigung von Shelley). Münster, 1916.
Published: 1916 (entry 2816).

Periodicals

2821 Athenaeum, July 1916, pp. 317-318.
Review of T.R. Lounsbury's The Life and Times, 1915 (entry 2797).

2822 Athenaeum, July 1916, p. 318.
Review of A.E. Baker's A Tennyson Dictionary, 1916 (entry 2809).

2823 Blennerhassett, Lady. "Alfred Lord Tennyson." Literarhistor, 1916, pp. 189-236.

2824 Colvin, Sidney. "Box Hill and Its Memories: Keats, Meredith, Tennyson." Scribner's Magazine, 60 (Aug. 1916), 195-
209.

2825 Emerson, Oliver Farrar. "Thackeray and Tennyson." Nation
(New York), 102 (June 1, 1916), 592-593.

2826 Living Age, 291 (Oct. 21, 1916), 187-190.
Review of T.R. Lounsbury's The Life and Times, 1915 (entry
2797).

2827 Matthews, B. Yale Review, 5 (April 1916), 631-633.
Review of T.R. Lounsbury's The Life and Times, 1915 (entry
2797).

2828 Moore, Charles Leonard. "The Passionate Victorians."
Dial, 60 (June 8, 1916), 524.

2829 Moore, John Robert. "Sources of In Memoriam in Tennyson's
Early Poems." Modern Language Notes, 31 (May 1916),
307-309.
Moore notes similarities among three sonnets titled "Love"
in Poems, Chiefly Lyrical (c.1830) and In Memoriam. He asserts
that the sonnets "express the central conception of In Memoriam."

2830 New Republic, 6 (Feb. 19, 1916), 80-81.
Review of T.R. Lounsbury's The Life and Times, 1915 (entry
2797).

2831 Northup, C.S. Dial, 60 (April 27, 1916), 423-424.
Review of T.R. Lounsbury's The Life and Times, 1915 (entry
2797).

2832 Phillips, Charles. "Catholic Note in Tennyson." American
Catholic Quarterly Review, 41 (Oct. 1916), 559-571.

2833 Saintsbury, George. Bookman (London), 50 (Aug. 1916), 130-
133.
Review of T.R. Lounsbury's The Life and Times, 1915 (entry
2797).

1917

Books

2834 Alden, Raymond MacDonald. Alfred Tennyson: How to Know
Him. Indianapolis: Bobbs-Merrill, [c.1917].
Reviewed by: New Republic (entry 2858).

2835 Bradley, Andrew Cecil. The Reaction Against Tennyson.
London: Oxford U.P., 1917. (English Association Pamphlet,
39) 19 p.

Reprinted in: A Miscellany, 1929 (entry 3076); and English Critical Essays, ed. P.M. Jones, 1933 (entry 3195).
A powerful attack on the detractions of Tennyson's achievements. Worth reading to observe a superior critic at work.

2836 Bussmann, Ernst. Tennysons Dialektdichtungen nebst einer Übersicht über den Gebrauch des Dialekts in der englischen Literatur vor Tennyson. Weimar: Wagner, 1917.
Publication of a dissertation: 1917 (entry 2844). Reviewed
by: E. Eckhardt in Englische Studien (entry 2911).

2837 Dhruva, A.B. Kant and Tennyson and Kant and Browning. Bombay: Time, 1917.

2838 Dickinson, Thomas H. The Contemporary Drama of England. Boston: Little, Brown, [c.1917]. London: Murray, 1920. Tennyson on pages 27-29. A negative view of Tennyson's
dramas.

2839 Eagle, Soloman (John Collings Squire). "If Lord Byron Had Written 'The Passing of Arthur.'" Tricks of the Trade. New York: Putnam, 1917, pp. 72-79.

2840 Meynell, Alice. "Some Thoughts of a Reader of Tennyson." Hearts of Controversy. London: Burns and Oates, [1917], pp. 1-22.

2841 Moxon, Thomas Allen. Tennyson's "In Memoriam": Its Message to the Bereaved and Sorrowful. London: Skeffington, 1917. (Books of Consolation)
Sermons.

2842 Robinson, Edna Moore. Tennyson's Use of the Bible. Baltimore: Johns Hopkins, 1917.
Publication of a dissertation: 1917 (entry 2845).
Robinson categorizes the ways Tennyson used the Bible according to six periods in the poet's career. Each period is distinguished by the purposes for which the Bible is used. The organization is clear, although Robinson's reasoning sometimes seems arbitrary. This book is a thorough and useful reference.
Reviewed by: Athenaeum (entry 2847).

2843 Thomas, Edward. "Tennyson." A Literary Pilgrim in England. New York: Dodd, Mead, 1917, pp. 254-262.

Dissertations

2844 Bussmann, Ernst. Tennysons Dialektdichtungen nebst einer Übersicht über den Gebrauch des Dialekts in der englischen Literatur vor Tennyson. Münster, 1917.
Published: 1917 (entry 2836).

2845 Robinson, Edna M. Tennyson's Use of the Bible. Johns Hop-

kins, 1917.
Published: 1917 (entry 2842).   See entry 2842 for annotation.

Periodicals

2846   Ashe, Leslie.   "Tennyson's Rhythms."   Spectator, 119 (Dec.
       15, 1917). 713.

2847   Athenaeum, June 1917, p. 310.
       Review of E.M. Robinson's Tennyson's Use of the Bible,
       1917 (entry 2842).

2848   Bayne, Thomas.   "Tennyson and Grindrod."   Notes and
       Queries, 12th ser. 3 (March 31, 1917), 253.

2849   Bayne, W.   "Tennyson's Rhymes."   Spectator, 119 (Oct. 26,
       1917), 446.
       See also: A.P. Graves (entry 2853), C.R. Haines (entry
       2854), and A.H. Powles (entry 2860).

2850   Birney, L.J.   "What Tennyson Did for the Minister."   Meth-
       odist Review, 99 (Jan. 1917), 22-35.

2851   Bruce, Harold.   "Tennyson and Death."   Sewanee Review, 25
       (Oct. 1917), 443-456.

2852   Carr, Thomas.   "Tennyson Twenty-Five Years After."   Spec-
       tator, 119 (Oct. 13, 1917), 384.
       See also: F.J.C. Hearnshaw (entry 2855).

2853   Graves, Alfred Perceval.   "Tennyson's Rhymes."   Spectator,
       119 (Nov. 3, 1917), 491.
       See also: W. Bayne (entry 2849), C.R. Haines (entry 2854),
       and A.H. Powles (entry 2860).

2854   Haines, C.R.   "Tennyson's Rhymes."   Spectator, 119 (Oct.
       20 and Nov. 24, 1917), 411 and 599.
       See also: W. Bayne (entry 2849), A.P. Graves (entry 2853),
       and A.H. Powles (entry 2860).

2855   Hearnshaw, Fossey John Cobb.   "Tennyson Twenty-Five Years
       After."   Spectator, 119 (Oct. 6 and Nov. 10, 1917), 352-353
       and 522.
       Reprinted: Living Age, 295 (Nov. 24, 1917), 503-506.   See
       also: T. Carr (entry 2852).

2856   Hobson, William A.   "The Religion of Tennyson."   Calcutta
       Review, n.s. 5 (April 1917), 189-199.

2857   Holling, T.E.   "Tennyson's Clerical Characters."   Queen's
       Quarterly, 24 (Jan. 1917), 280-286.

2858   New Republic, 13 (Nov. 3, 1917), 24.
       Review of R.M. Alden's Alfred Tennyson, 1917 (entry 2834).

2859   Palmer, J. Luttrell. "Tennyson's 'Dora.'" Notes and Que-
        ries, 12th ser. 3 (Nov. 1917), 475.

2860   Powles, Allen H. "Tennyson's Rhymes." Spectator, 119 (Oct.
        27, 1917), 446.
        See also: W. Bayne (entry 2849), A.P. Graves (entry 2853),
and C.R. Haines (entry 2860).

2861   "Tennyson's Anachronisms." Spectator, 119 (Oct. 20, 1917),
        411.

2862   "Tennyson's Lost Vogue." Literary Digest, 55 (Nov. 3, 1917),
        29.

2863   Tollemache, Lionel Arthur. "Jowett and Tennyson." Specta-
        tor, 119 (Oct. 20, 1917), 411.

2864   Torretta, L. "Guerra e pace nell'opera di Lord Tennyson."
        Nuova antologia, 1917, pp. 157-164.

1918

Books

2865   Palmer, George Herbert. "Alfred Tennyson." Formative
        Types in English Poetry. Boston: Houghton Mifflin, 1918.
        pp. 223-269.

2866   Vettermann, Ella. Die Balen-dichtungen und ihre Quellen.
        Halle: Niemeyer, 1918. (Zeitschrift für romanische Philolo-
        gie, 60)
        Vettermann finds that Tennyson changed the Balen story into
an entirely new tale only remotely related to the one in Malory's
work.

Periodicals

2867   Dixon, James Main. "Tennyson and Treitschke: A Spiritual
        Forecast." Methodist Review, 101 (July 1918), 524-538.

2868   Mackie, Gascoigne. "Tennyson and Wordsworth." Spectator,
        121 (Nov. 9, 1918), 517.

2869   Phillips, T.M. "Colour in George Meredith and Other Modern
        English Poets." Papers of the Manchester Literary Club, 44
        (1918), 193-195.

2870   _____. "Nature in Modern English Poetry." Manchester
        Quarterly, 37 (Oct. 1918), 268-269.

2871   Sinnett, Alfred Percy. "The Occultism in Tennyson's Poetry."
        Nineteenth Century and After, 83 (March 1918), 582-591.

1919

Books

2872 Browning, Elizabeth Barrett. Alfred Tennyson: Notes and
Comments: With a Defense of the Rhyme System of "The
Dead Pan." London: privately printed by Richard Clay for
T.J. Wise, 1919.
Thirty copies printed. In the first of two letters to R.H.
Horne, Browning compares Tennyson to Keats and Wordsworth.

2873 Cook, Edward. "The Second Thoughts of Poets." Literary
Recreations. London: Macmillan, 1919, pp. 259-270.

2874 Davies, Trevor H. "Tennyson: 'In Memoriam': A Poet's
Plea for Faith." Spiritual Voices in Modern Literature. New
York: Doran, [c.1919], pp. 101-128.

2875 Girardini, Emilio, trans. Poemi drammatici de Alfredo Tennyson. Rome: 1919.
Reviewed by: A. Gabrielli in Nuova Antologia (entry 2886).

2876 Hodgson, Geraldine E. "The Legacy of Tennyson." Criticism
at a Venture. London: Macdonald, [1919], pp. 1-25.

2877 Littell, Philip. "Tennyson." Books and Things. New York:
Harcourt, Brace and Howe, 1919, pp. 167-172.

2878 Nitchie, Elizabeth. Vergil and the English Poets. New York:
Columbia U.P., 1919.
Tennyson on pages 224-233. Publication of a dissertation:
1919 (entry 2885).

2879 Osmond, Percy Herbert. "Tennyson." The Mystical Poets of
the English Church. London: Society for Promoting Christian Knowledge, 1919, pp. 305-310.
Osmond perceives Tennyson's mysticism as lifelong.

2880 Rice, William North. "The Poet of Science." The Poet of
Science and Other Addresses. New York: Abingdon, [c.1919],
pp. 11-45. Discusses Tennyson as "the poet of science."

2881 Roberts, Robert. "The Poet as Seeker--Tennyson." The
Jesus of the Poets and Prophets. London: Student Chris-
tian Movement, 1919, pp. 119-134.
See: That One Face, 1919 (entry 2882, below).

2882 _____. "The Poet as Seeker--Tennyson." That One Face.
New York: Association, 1919, pp. 107-122.
See: The Jesus of the Poets and Prophets, 1919 (entry 2881,
above).

2883 Walker, Hugh, and Mrs. Hugh Walker. "Poetry." Outlines

of Victorian Literature. Cambridge: Cambridge U.P., 1919.
Tennyson on pages 49-58.

Dissertations

2884   Moffatt, J.S. Tennyson, Spenser, and the Renaissance.
North Carolina, 1919.

2885   Nitchie, Elizabeth. Vergil and the English Poets. Columbia,
[1919?].
Published: 1919 (entry 2878).

Periodicals

2886   Gabrielli, Annibale. Nuova Antologia di Lettere, Scienze ed
Arti, 285 (May 1, 1919), 85-91.
Review of Poemi drammatici de Alfredo Tennyson, trans. E.
Girardini, 1919 (entry 2875).

2887   Gosse, Edmund William. "Tennyson's Manuscripts." Times
Literary Supplement, June 12, 1919, p. 325.

2888   Pierpoint, Robert. "Tennyson and Opium." Notes and Queries, 12th ser. 5 (Feb. 1919), 36-37.

2889   von Siebold, Erika. "Tennyson: Synästhen in der englischen
Dichtung der 19. Jahrhunderts." Englischen Studien, 53
(1919-1920), 269-279.

1920

Books

2890   Blore, George Henry. "Alfred Tennyson." Victorian Worthies.
London: Milford, 1920, pp. 150-176.

2891   Browning, Robert. An Opinion of the Writings of Alfred, Lord
Tennyson. London: privately printed by Richard Clay, 1920.
Four letters to Isa Blagden and one to Buxton Forman. The
four letters to Blagden are reprinted in Dearest Isa, ed. E.D. Mc-
Aleer, 1951 (entry 3475). See entry 3475 for annotation.

2892   Bury, J.B. The Idea of Progress: An Inquiry into Its Origin
and Growth. London: 1920.
Mentions Tennyson and "Locksley Hall."

2893   Campbell, James M. "Introduction." The Spiritual Meaning
of "In Memoriam": An Interpretation for the Times, by
James Main Dixon. New York: Abingdon, [c.1920].

2894   Dixon, James Main. The Spiritual Meaning of "In Memoriam":
An Interpretation for the Times. New York: Abingdon,
[c.1920].

2895   Eagle, Solomon (John Collings Squire). "Mr. H.G. Wells and
        Lord Tennyson." Books in General. New York: Knopf,
        1920, pp. 238-243.

2896   Elton, Oliver. "Tennyson." A Survey of English Literature,
        1830-1880. London: Arnold, 1920. Volume I.
        Revised and published in Alfred Tennyson and Matthew Arnold,
        1924 (entry 2990).
            Elton is not overly impressed with Tennyson's poetry, but
        does single out individual works for praise. A systematic evaluation
        of selected poems.

2897   Levey, Sivori. Guinevere and Arthur: Adapted from Tenny-
        son's "Idylls of the King." London: Fountain, [c.1920].
        (Pilgrimage Plays, 4)
        A one-act drama in verse.

2898   _____ . Sir Gareth's Quest: Adapted from Tennyson's
        "Idylls of the King." London: Fountain, [c.1920].
        (Pilgrimage Plays, 3)

2899   Lintner, Robert Casper. "Twilight and Evening Bell." [Coun-
        cil Grove, Kansas: c.1920].

2900   McCabe, Joseph Martin. A Biographical Dictionary of Modern
        Rationalists. London: Watts, 1920.
        Tennyson on pages 787-789.

2901   Pyre, James Francis Augustine. The Formation of Tennyson's
        Style: A Study, Primarily, of the Versification of the Early
        Poems. Madison: U. of Wisconsin P., 1920.
        (University of Wisconsin Studies in Language and Literature,
        12)
            A basic study of the metrics of Tennyson's poetry published
        before 1850. Pyre's commentary is informative.
            Reviewed by: R. Gallienne in New York Times Book Review
        (entry 2937); H. Straus in Nation (New York) (entry 2957); and Times
        Literary Supplement (entry 2942).

2902   Sinnett, Alfred Percy. Tennyson: An Occultist, as His Writ-
        ings Prove. London: Theosophical, 1920.

2903   Smith, Jean Pauline. The Aesthetic Nature of Tennyson. New
        York: White, 1920.

2904   Thorndike, Ashley H. Literature in a Changing Age. New
        York: 1920.
        "Locksley Hall" on page 271.

2905   Van Dyke, Henry. "Introduction." Poems of Tennyson, by
        Alfred, Lord Tennyson. New York: Scribner, 1920, pp.
        xix-cxx.

2906 _____. Studies in Tennyson. New York: Scribner, 1920.

2907 Warren, Kate M. Tennyson. London: National Home-Reading Union, [1920].

2908 Williamson, Claude C.H. "Tennyson and His Ideas." Writers of Three Centuries, 1789-1914. London: Richards, 1920, pp. 170-176.

Dissertation

2909 Hamann, Helmut. Alfred Lord Tennyson und die zeitgenössische Kritik (1830-1860). Jena, 1920.

Periodicals

2910 Bensly, Edward. "Tennyson on Tobacco." Notes and Queries, 12th ser. 6 (Jan. 5, 1920), 280.
See also: J.B. Wainewright (entry 2917).

2911 Eckhardt, E. Englische Studien, 53 (Feb. 1920), 445-447.
Review of E. Bussmann's Tennysons Dialektdichtungen, 1917 (entry 2836).

2912 Gingell, W.H. "Birds in the Highhall-Garden." Notes and Queries, 12th ser. 7 (Sept. 25, 1920), 248.

2913 Omond, T.S. "These Lame Hexameters." Times Literary Supplement, July 29 and Aug. 26, 1920, pp. 488 and 552.
See also: J. Sargeaunt (entry 2914, below).

2914 Sargeaunt, John. "These Lame Hexameters." Times Literary Supplement, July 22 and Aug. 19, 1920, pp. 472 and 536.
See also: T.S. Omond (entry 2913, above).

2915 Sidey, Thomas K. "Some Unnoted Latinisms in Tennyson." Modern Language Notes, 35 (April 1920), 245-246.

2916 Squire, John C. "Tennyson." London Mercury, 2 (Aug. 1920), 443-455.
Reprinted: Essays on Poetry, 1923 (entry 2973).
A thoughtful discussion of Tennyson's relation to the ideas and events of the Victorian Age. Squire perceives Tennyson as struggling with contradictory impulses.

2917 Wainewright, John B. "Tennyson and Tobacco." Notes and Queries, 12th ser. 6 (May 22, 1920), 234.
See also: E. Bensly (entry 2910).

2918 Zuylen van Nijevelt, S. Ivan. "Tennyson's Vertegenwoordiger van het 'Victoria Tijdperk.'" Stemmen des Tijds, Oct. 1920, pp. 350-374.

1921

Books

2919 Broadus, Edmund Kemper. "Alfred Tennyson." The Laureateship. Oxford: Clarendon, 1921, pp. 184-196.

2920 Chesterton, G.K. "Tennyson." The Uses of Diversity. New
York: Dodd, Mead, 1921, pp. 25-33.

2921 Galimberti, Alice. 'I lirici fa Tommaso Moore ad Alfredo
Tennyson: L'Ulysses del Tennyson." Dante nel pensiero
inglese. Florence: LeMonnier, 1921, pp. 212-214.

2922 Holmes, Mabel Dodge. The Poet as Philosopher: A Study of
Three Philosophical Poems: Nosce Teipsum, The Essay on
Man, In Memoriam. Philadelphia: U. of Pennsylvania P.,
1921.
Publication of a dissertation: 1921 (entry 2929). Tennyson
is representative of his time.

2923 Jagger, Hubert. Introduction. Selections from Tennyson.
London: Dent, 1921.

2924 Kellner, Leon. "Alfred (Lord) Tennyson." Die englische Literatur der neuesten Zeit von Dickens bis Shaw. Leipzig:
Tauchnitz, 1921, pp. 150-170.

2925 King, William Henry. "Lord Tennyson." Bookland. London:
Philip, [1921], pp. 216-221.

2926 Lynd, Robert. "Tennyson: A Contemporary Criticism." Art
of Letters. New York: Scribner, 1921, pp. 134-138.

2927 Walker, Hugh. "The New Kings: Tennyson and Browning"
and "Tennyson." The Literature of the Victorian Era. Cambridge: Cambridge U.P., 1921, pp. 287-309 and 374-410,
respectively.

2928 Woodberry, George Edward. "Late Victorian Verse: Browning, Swinburne, Tennyson." Studies of a Littérateur. New
York: Harcourt, Brace, 1921, pp. 37-60.

Dissertations

2929 Holmes, Mabel Dodge. The Poet as Philosopher: A Study of
Three Philosophical Poems: Nosce Teipsum, The Essay on
Man, In Memoriam. Pennsylvania, 1921.
Published: 1921 (entry 2922).

2930 Petermann, Herta. Tennysons kunsttheoretische Urteile.
Würzburg, 1921.

Periodicals

2931 Boas, Frederick Samuel. "'Idylls of the King' in 1921."
      Nineteenth Century and After, 90 (Nov. 1921), 819-830.
      Reprinted: Royal Society of Literature of the United Kingdom:
Transactions, n.s. 2 (1922), 23-42.
      Boas presents an intelligent evaluation of the allegory of Idylls
of the King. He believes the work as a whole represents Tennyson's
world view.

2932 Cornish, Blanche Warre. "Memories of Tennyson." London
      Mercury, 5 (Dec. 1921 and Jan. 1922), 144-155 and 266-275.
      Of biographical interest.

2933 Cross, Tom Peete. "Alfred Tennyson as a Celtist." Modern
      Philology, 18 (Jan. 1921), 485-492.
      Cross asserts that "Tennyson made an honest effort to ground
his Idylls on the most reputable authorities of his day." He maintains that Tennyson tried to keep Idylls of the King consistent with
up-to-date contemporary knowledge of "Celtic antiquities."

2934 Dixon, James Main. "The Rubaiyat and In Memoriam."
      Methodist Review, 104 (May 1921), 353-368.
      A comparison.

2935 Engel, H. "Taines urteil über Tennyson." Zeitscrift für Ver-
      gleichende Litteraturgeschichte, 20 (1921), 8-12.

2936 Leeper, Alex. Notes and Queries, 12th ser. 9 (Sept. 24,
      1921), 248.
      Tennyson's use of the word otherwhere.

2937 Le Gallienne, Richard. New York Times Book Review, Oct.
      9, 1921, p. 9.
      Review of J.F.A. Pyre's The Formation of Tennyson's Style,
1920 (entry 2901).

2938 "Lines by Tennyson." Notes and Queries, 12th ser. 8 (Jan.
      1, 1921), 7.

2939 Pallis, Elisabeth Hude. "Tennysons og Swinburnes Arthurdig-
      te." Edda, 15 (1921), 44-74.

2940 Pinchback, W.H. "Tennyson Queries." Notes and Queries,
      12th ser. 8 (April 23, 1921), 337.

2941 Starnes, De Witt Talmadge. "The Influence of Carlyle upon
      Tennyson." Texas Review, 6 (July 1921), 316-336.

2942 Times Literary Supplement, Nov. 17, 1921, p. 748.
      Review of J.F.A. Pyre's The Formation of Tennyson's Style,
1920 (entry 2901).

2943   Vann, William Harvey. "A Prototype of Tennyson's Arthur."
        Sewanee Review, 29 (Jan. 1921), 98-103.

1922

Books

2944   Beerbohm, Max. Rossetti and His Circle. London: Heine-
        mann, 1922.
        Tennyson on plate 9.

2945   Birrell, Augustine. "Tennyson." Collected Essays and Ad-
        dresses, 1880-1920. New York: Dent, 1922. Volume II,
        pp. 140-143.

2946   Evans, Morris Owen. The Healing of the Nations. Boston:
        Badger, [c.1922].

2947   Inge, William Ralph. The Victorian Age. Cambridge: Cam-
        bridge U.P., 1922. (The Rede Lecture for 1922)

2948   . "The Victorian Age." Outspoken Essays. London:
        Longmans, Green, 1922.
        Tennyson on pages 199-205.

2949   Loudon, K.M. "King Arthur: Malory and Tennyson." Two
        Mystic Poets and Other Essays. Oxford: Blackwell, 1922,
        pp. 31-82.

2950   Ticknor, Caroline. "Two 'Laureates.'" Glimpses of Authors.
        Boston: Houghton Mifflin, 1922, pp. 322-327.

2951   Walker, Janie Roxburgh. "Alfred Tennyson." Stories of the
        Victorian Writers. New York: Macmillan, 1922, pp. 33-42.

Dissertation

2952   Mauss, Aloisia. Stil, Metrik und deren Wechselwirkung in
        Scott, Byron und Tennyson. Innsbruck, 1922.

Periodicals

2953   Arnold, William Harris. "My Tennysons." Scribner's Maga-
        zine, 71 (May 1922), 589-601.
        Reprinted: Ventures in Book Collecting, 1923 (entry 2959).
Of bibliographical interest.

2954   Kern, Alfred Allan. "King Lear and Pelleas and Ettarre."
        Modern Language Notes, 37 (March 1922), 153-157.

2955   Olivero, Federico. "La Leggenda di Ulysse in Tennyson e in
        alcuni poeti irlandesi." Giornale dantesco, 25 (1922), 229-236.
        Reprinted: Studi sur poeti e prosatori inglesi, 1925 (entry 3008).

2956 Ratchford, Fannie E. "The Tennyson Collection in the Wrenn Library." Texas Review, 7 (1922), 95-105.
Of bibliographical interest.

2957 Straus, H. Nation (New York), 114 (Jan. 4, 1922), 23.
Review of J.F.A. Pyre's The Formation of Tennyson's Style, 1920 (entry 2901).

2958 "Tennyson's 'May Queen.'" Notes and Queries, 12th ser. 11 (Sept. 9, 1922), 215.
A parody.

1923

Books

2959 Arnold, William Harris. "My Tennysons." Ventures in Book Collecting. London: Scribner, 1923, pp. 227-258.
Reprinted from: Scribner's Magazine, 1922 (entry 2953).

2960 Beeching, Henry Charles. "In Memoriam," with an Analysis and Notes. London: Methuen, 1923.

2961 Bleibtreu, Karl. "Die Victoria-poesie." Geschichte der eng-lischen Literatur mit Einschluss der amerikanischen. Bern: Bircher, 1923, pp. 226-233.

2962 Cazamian, Madeleine. Le Roman et les Idées en Angleterre: L'Influence de la Science (1860-1890). Strasbourg: Librairie Istra, 1923.
Tennyson on pages 77-78.

2963 Drinkwater, John. Victorian Poetry. London: Hodder and Stoughton, 1923.
Tennyson on pages 54-71 and 140-168. Drinkwater asserts that Tennyson "showed his generation, in a degree unapproached by any other poet who began writing with him, the still fresh and vital possibilities of a great traditional manner."

2964 _____. "Victorian Poets." Outline of Literature. London: George Newnes, 1923, pp. 425-434.
Ranks Tennyson behind Keats as a poet.

2965 Elton, Oliver. "Poetic Romancers After 1850." A Sheaf of Papers. Boston: Small, Maynard, 1923, pp. 45-68.
Reprinted from: British Academy, 1914 (entry 2777).

2966 Fausset, Hugh I'Anson. Tennyson: A Modern Portrait. New York: Appleton, 1923.
This influential biography portrays Tennyson as a man out of touch with reality. Fausset believes that Tennyson's efforts to write about the problems and ideas of the Victorian Age were futile.

Reviewed by: L. Binyon in <u>Bookman</u> (London) (entry 2978);
G.R. Malloch in <u>Algemeen Handelsblad</u> (entry 2980); G. Thomas in
<u>London Quarterly Review</u> (entry 2985); <u>Times Literary Supplement</u>
(entry 2986); and H. Warren in <u>Nineteenth Century and After</u> (entry
2987).

2967 Ferrero, M. <u>Studio su "In Memoriam."</u> Turin: Lattes, 1923.
      6 p.

2968 Hardman, William. <u>A Mid-Victorian Pepys: The Letters and</u>
      <u>Memoirs of Sir William Hardman.</u> Ed. Stewart Marsh Ellis.
      London: Palmer, 1923. New York: Doran, 1923.
      Tennyson on pages 311-312.

2969 Lang, Andrew. "On the Death of Lord Tennyson." <u>The Poeti-</u>
      <u>cal Works.</u> Ed. Mrs. Lang. London: Longmans, Green,
      1923. Volume III, p. 31.

2970 Lowber, J.W. "Tennyson's Science of Religion." <u>World Wide</u>
      <u>Problems or Macrocosmus.</u> Cincinnati: Standard, 1923, pp.
      300-311.

2971 Nicolson, Harold. <u>Tennyson: Aspects of His Life, Character</u>
      <u>and Poetry.</u> London: Constable, 1923. Reprinted: Garden
      City: Anchor Books, Doubleday, 1962.
      Nicolson asserts that "the essential Tennyson is a morbid and
unhappy mystic." His commentary reflects strong reservations about
the merits of Victorian society and hence Tennyson's role as interpreter of society, but his commentary and ideas are sometimes insightful. Perhaps the greatest influence of this book is its presentation of a dual Tennyson: One is a romantic poet whose lyrics have
high literary merit; the other is a moralizing writer whose ideas are
without value. Nicolson has little respect for Tennyson's ability to
think.
      Reviewed by: L. Binyon in <u>Bookman</u> (London) (entry 2978);
G. Thomas in <u>London Quarterly Review</u> (entry 2985); <u>Times Liter-</u>
<u>ary Supplement</u> (entry 2986); and H. Warren in <u>Nineteenth Century</u>
<u>and After</u> (entry 2987).

2972 Sencourt, Robert. "The Mutiny in England--Ruskin and Tenny-
      son." <u>India in English Literature.</u> London: Simpkin, Mar-
      shall, Hamilton, Kent, [c.1923], pp. 441-448.

2973 Squire, J.C. <u>Essays on Poetry.</u> London: Hodder and Stough-
      ton, [1923].
      Tennyson on pages 63-87. Reprinted from: <u>London Mercury</u>
(entry 2916).

2974 Van Dyke, Henry. "Tennyson: In Lucem Transitus, 1892"
      and "In Memoriam." <u>The Poems of Henry Van Dyke.</u> New
      York: Scribner, 1923.
      "Tennyson" reprinted from <u>Critic</u> (New York), 1892 (entry
1637). See entry 1637 for poem.

"In Memoriam"

The record of a faith sublime,
  And hope, through clouds, far-off discerned;
  The incense of a love that burned
Through pain and doubt defying Time:

The story of a soul at strife
  That learned at last to kiss the rod,
  And passed through sorrow up to God,
From living to a higher life:

A light that gleams across the wave
  Of darkness, down the rolling years,
  Piercing the heavy mist of tears--
A rainbow shining o'er a grave.

2975 Williams, Stanley Thomas. Studies in Victorian Literature.
      New York: Dutton, [c.1923].

Dissertation

2976 Dobranz, Gisela. "The Ancient Ballad of Chevy Chase,"
      "The Rime of the Ancient Mariner" (Coleridge), "The Lady
      of Shalott" (Tennyson). Innsbruck, 1923.

Periodicals

2977 Abbott, C. Colleer. "A Short View of the Case Against Ten-
      nyson." Humberside, 1 (Oct. 1923), 5-26.

2978 Binyon, Lawrence. Bookman (London), 64 (April 1923), 23-24.
      Review of H.I'A. Fausset's Tennyson, 1923 (entry 2966) and
H.G. Nicolson's Tennyson, 1923 (entry 2971).

2979 "For and Against Tennyson." Times Literary Supplement,
      April 12, 1923, pp. 237-238.

2980 Malloch, G.R. Algemeen Handelsblad, March 24, 1923.
      Review of H.I'A. Fausset's Tennyson, 1923 (entry 2966).

2981 Morr, Margaret, and Kathryn Skemp. "A Tennyson Festival."
      Popular Educator, 41 (Sept. 1923), 38-42.

2982 Shewan, A. "Repetition in Homer and Tennyson." Classical
      Weekly, 16 (April 2 and 9, 1923), 153-158 and 162-166.

2983 Stenberg, Theodore T. "A Word on the Sources of 'The Charge
      of the Light Brigade.'" Modern Language Notes, 38 (April
      1923), 248-250.

2984 "Tennyson Reinterpreted in Terms of To-Day." Current Opin-
      ion, 75 (Oct. 1923), 421-422.

2985 Thomas, G. London Quarterly Review, 140 (July 1923), 45-
55.
Review of H. I'A. Fausset's Tennyson, 1923 (entry 2966) and
H. G. Nicolson's Tennyson, 1923 (entry 2971).

2986 Times Literary Supplement, March 15, 1923, p. 182.
Notes on H. I'A. Fausset's Tennyson, 1923 (entry 2966) and
H. G. Nicolson's Tennyson, 1923 (entry 2971).

2987 Warren, Thomas Herbert. "The Real Tennyson." Nineteenth
Century and After, 94 (Oct. 1923), 507-519.
Review of H. I'A. Fausset's Tennyson, 1923 (entry 2966) and
H. G. Nicolson's Tennyson, 1923 (entry 2971).

2988 Willcocks, Mary Patricia. "Tennyson." English Review, 36
(Feb. 1923), 171-182.
Reprinted: Between the Old World and the New, 1925 (entry
3011).

1924

Books

2989 Drew, Mary. "Tennyson and Laura Tennant." Acton, Gladstone and Others. London: Nisbet, 1924, pp. 119-130.

2990 Elton, Oliver. Alfred Tennyson and Matthew Arnold. London:
Arnold, 1924.
Tennyson on pages 1-54. Revised version of chapter in A
Survey of English Literature, 1830-1880, 1920 (entry 2896). See
2896 for annotation.

2991 Hixson, Jerome Canady. Tennyson, Romanticist and Romany.
Meadville: the author, 1924.

2992 Hoyt, Arthur S. "Tennyson: The Man and the Poet" and "In
Memoriam: The Way of Faith." The Spiritual Message of
Modern English Poetry. New York: Macmillan, 1924, pp.
67-85 and 89-112, respectively.

2993 Jones, Henry. "Tennyson." Essays on Literature and Education. Ed. H. J. W. Hetherington. London: Hodder and
Stoughton, 1924.
Reprinted from: British Academy, 1909 (entry 2585). See
entry 2585 for another reprinting and for annotation.

2994 Noyes, Alfred. "Tennyson and Some Recent Critics." Some
Aspects of Modern Poetry. New York: Stokes, 1924. Lon-
don: Hodder and Stoughton, 1924, pp. 155-199.
Reprinted separately: 1932 (entry 3176).
Noyes asserts: "The chief indictment that has been brought
against Tennyson will, in fact, be the chief ground upon which he

will be praised by posterity--the fact that he did so completely sum
up and express the great Victorian era in which he lived. " Noyes
provides a first-rate reply to those who denigrate Tennyson's achievements. Important reading for students of Tennyson.

2995 Quinn, John. The Library of John Quinn. New York: Anderson Galleries, 1924.
Tennyson on pages 1009-1111. Of bibliographical interest.

Dissertation

2996 Tropper, Jerica. Der Wortschatz in "The Last Battle" aus
der Arthussage bei Layamon, Huchon, Arthur in Stanzen,
Malory und Tennyson. Innsbruck, 1924.

Periodicals

2997 Ratzka, K. "Tennyson's landbesitz Farringford. " Daheim,
no. 50 (1924).

2998 Sparke, Archibald. "Tennyson's 'The Captain.' " Notes and
Queries, 147 (Sept. 27, 1924), 236.

1925

Books

2999 Arnold, Edwin. "A Day with Lord Tennyson. " Forum Papers. Ed. C.R. Gaston. New York: Duffield, 1925, pp.
192-211.
Reprinted from: Forum, 1891 (entry 1364).

3000 Boas, Guy. Introduction. Tennyson and Browning Contrast-
ed. New York: Nelson, 1925.
Selective edition of poetry.

3001 Cruse, Amy. "The Idylls of the King. " Famous English
Books and Their Stories. New York: Crowell, [1925]. London: Harrap, [1926], pp. 274-284.

3002 Fehr, Bernhard. "Alfred Tennyson. " Die englische Literatur
des 19. und 20. Jahrhunderts. Berlin: Akademische Verlags-
gesellschaft, [1925], pp. 196-205.

3003 Hearn, Lafcadio. "Idylls of the King. " Occidental Gleanings.
New York: Dodd, Mead, 1925. Volume I, pp. 1-23.

3004 Johnson, Reginald Brimley. Story Lives of Nineteenth-Century Authors. London: Gardner, Darton, 1925.

3005 Ker, William Paton. "Tennyson. " Collected Essays of W.P.
Ker. London: Macmillan, 1925. Volume I, pp. 258-276.
Reprinting of: Tennyson, 1909 (entry 2530).

3006 Le Gallienne, Richard. The Romantic '90s. New York: Doubleday, Page, 1925.
Tennyson on pages 52-55 and 115-126.

3007 Northrup, Clark Sutherland. A Register of Bibliographies of the English Language and Literature. New Haven: Yale U. P., 1925.
Tennyson on pages 373-375.

3008 Olivero, Federico. "La leggenda di Ulysse nel Tennyson e in alcuni poeti irlandesi." Studi sur poeti e prosatori inglesi. Turin: Bocca, 1925, pp. 212-232.
Reprinted from: Giornale dantesco, 1922 (entry 2955).

3009 Tuell, Anne Kimball. Mrs. Meynell and Her Literary Generation. New York: Dutton, [c.1925].

3010 Ward, Mrs. E.M. (Henrietta Ward). Memories of Ninety Years. Ed. Isabel G. McAllister. New York: Holt, 1925.
Tennyson on pages 5, 12, 149, and 307. About Tom Taylor, art critic for The Times and collaborator on comedies with Charles Reade, Ward writes: "One day when he and Mrs. Taylor came home the maid informed them that a man of wild appearance insisted upon waiting to see him, and she had put him in the pantry as he did not look reputable enough to be left in the drawing-room. And here they found the great poet Tennyson, eyes twinkling with amusement, quite pleased with his novel reception. Tennyson used to relate the story to his friends gleefully."

3011 Willcocks, Mary Patricia. "Tennyson." Between the Old World and the New. London: Allen and Unwin, [1925].
Reprinted from: English Review, 1923 (entry 2988).

Dissertation

3012 Müller, Erich Guenter. Tennyson: Erlebnis und Dichtung. Marburg, 1925.

Periodicals

3013 Dearmer, Geoffrey. "Tennyson." Literary Digest, 85 (April 4, 1925), 40.
A poem.

3014 Fairchild, Hoxie Neale. "The Classic Poets of English Literature: XII: Alfred Lord Tennyson." Literary Digest International Book Review, 3 (June 1925), 488.

3015 Giordano-Orsini, G.N. "Tennyson e i suoi Critici." La Cultura, 5 (1925-1926), 543-550.

3016 Rawnsley, Willingham Franklin. "Personal Recollections of Tennyson." Nineteenth Century and After, 97 (Jan. and Feb.

1925), 1-9 and 190-196.
Of biographical interest.

3017 Stockley, William Frederick Paul. "'Faith' of 'In Memoriam.'" Catholic World, 120 (March 1925), 801-809.

3018 "Tennyson Songs." Notes and Queries, 149 (Sept. 19, 1925),
213.

3019 Weatherhead, Leslie D. "Tennyson's After-World." London
Quarterly Review, 144 (Oct. 1925), 157-174.

3020 Wilson, Edmund. "Pope and Tennyson." New Republic, 44
(Sept. 16, 1925), 96-97.

1926

Books

3021 Aytoun, William Edmondstoune. "Maud, by Alfred Tennyson."
Notorious Literary Attacks. Ed. G. Mordell. New York:
Boni, 1926, pp. 138-161.
See entry 325.

3022 Benson, Arthur Christopher. "At the Sign of the Hollyhock."
Rambles and Reflections. New York: Putnam, [c.1926], pp.
110-117.

3023 Cameron, Julia Margaret. Victorian Photographs of Famous
Men and Fair Women. London: Hogarth, 1926.
Tennyson on plate 4.

3024 Chubb, Edwin Watts. "Tennyson" and "Emerson on Carlyle
and Tennyson." Stories of Authors, British and American.
New York: Macmillan, 1926, pp. 144-149 and 150-155, respectively.

3025 Japiske, Cornelia G.H. The Dramas of Alfred, Lord Tennyson. London: Macmillan, 1926.
Publication of a dissertation: 1926 (entry 3028).
Japiske admires much of Tennyson's achievement in the dramas, but finds the plays generally less than suited to staging. This
study is unsatisfactory, in spite of a sometimes useful discussion of
the sources for Tennyson's dramas.
Reviewed by: B. Matthews in Outlook (entry 3033).

3026 Mackail, John William. "Tennyson." Studies of English Poets.
London: Longmans, Green, 1926, pp. 227-251.
Ranks Tennyson's poetry high among the best that has been
written.

3027 Postma, J. Tennyson as Seen by His Parodists. New York:

Stechert, 1926. Amsterdam: Paris, 1926. Reprinted: New York: Haskell House, 1966.
Publication of a dissertation: 1926 (entry 3029).
This book is amusing reading, but is not scholarly. It reproduces fifty parodies. Reviewed by: R.B. McKerrow in Review of English Studies (entry 3045).

Dissertations

3028 Japiske, Cornelia Geertrui Hendrika. The Dramas of Alfred Lord Tennyson. Amsterdam, 1926.
Published: 1926 (entry 3025).

3029 Postman, Jelle. Tennyson as Seen by His Parodists. Amsterdam, 1926.
Published: 1926 (entry 3027).

Periodicals

3030 Jiriczek, Otto L. "Die neunte Woge." Beiblatt zur Anglia, 37 (April 1926), 115-121.
Comments on verse 376 of "The Coming of Arthur." See
also: W. Fischer (entry 3043).

3031 Kassel, Charles. "Alfred Tennyson: A Victorian Romance." South Atlantic Quarterly, 25 (April 1926), 139-153.

3032 McKeehan, Irene Pettit. "A Neglected Example of the 'In Memoriam' Stanza." Modern Language Notes, 41 (Dec. 1926), 531-532.

3033 Matthews, B. Outlook, 144 (Dec. 22, 1926), 537-538.
Review of C.G.H. Japiske's The Dramas of Alfred, Lord Tennyson, 1926 (entry 3025).

3034 Pascal, Felicien. "La maison natale d'Alfred Tennyson." Les Annales Polititiques et Littéraires, 87 (Sept. 5, 1926), 255.

1927

Books

3035 Daly, Joseph Francis. The Life of Augustin Daly. New York: Macmillan, 1927.
Discusses Daly's New York and London productions of The Foresters in 1892 and 1893.

3036 Hearn, Lafcadio. "Tennyson and the Great Poetry." A History of English Literature: In a Series of Lectures. Tokyo: Hokuseido, 1927. Volume II, pp. 637-646.

3037 Ruhrmann, Friedrich G. "Tennyson." Studien zur Geschichte
und Charakteristik des Refrains in der englischen Literatur.
Heidelberg: Winter, 1927, pp. 98-109.

3038 Shanks, Edward Buxton. "The Return of Tennyson." Second
Essays on Literature. London: Collins, [c.1927], pp. 163-
176.

Dissertations

3039 Clugston, Phil R. Chapters on Tennyson's Art: With Special
Reference to the Epithet. Wisconsin, 1927.

3040 Kristinus, Heinrich. Die Dramentechnik Tennysons und Shake-
speares Einfluss auf sie. Vienna, 1927.

Periodicals

3041 Armstrong, T. Percy. "Tennyson Portraits by Watts." Notes
and Queries, 153 (Nov. 26, 1927), 394.
See also: L.R.M. Strachan (entry 3047).

3042 Burke, Margaret Mary. "Leadership and Tennyson." Journal
of Applied Sociology, 11 (March 1927), 344-350.

3043 Fischer, W. "Zur 'neunten Woge.'" Beiblatt zur Anglia, 38
(May 1927), 158-159.
See also: O.L. Jiriczek (entry 3030).

3044 Howe, Mark Antony de Wolfe. "The Tennysons at Farringford:
A Victorian Vista: Drawn from the Unpublished Papers of
Mrs. James T. Fields." Cornhill Magazine, n.s. 63 (Oct.
1927), 447-457.
A visit by the American publisher James T. Fields to the
Tennysons.

3045 McK., R.B. (R.B. McKerrow). Review of English Studies,
3 (Oct. 1927), 490.
Review of J. Postma's Tennyson as Seen by His Parodists,
1926 (entry 3027).

3046 Perry, Henry Ten Eyek. "The Tennyson Tragedy." Southwest
Review, 12 (Jan. 1927), 97-112.
Perry believes that Tennyson was unable to harmonize with
his society.

3047 Strachan, L.R.M. "Tennyson Portraits by Watts." Notes
and Queries, 153 (Nov. 12, 1927), 356.
See also: T.P. Armstrong (entry 3041).

3048 "Timbuctoo." Times Literary Supplement, Dec. 1, 1927, p.
916.

1928

In April, the Royal Court Theatre produced Tennyson's play Harold.

Books

3049 Atkins, Gaius Glenn. Reinspecting Victorian Religion. New York: Macmillan, 1928.
The entangled soul in Idylls of the King, and faith and doubt in In Memoriam.

3050 Dobson, Alban. Austin Dobson: Some Notes. London: Oxford U.P. (Humphrey Milford), 1928.

3051 Giordano-Orsini, G.N. La Poesia di Alfred Tennyson: Saggio Critico. Bari: Laterza, 1928. (Biblioteca di Cultura Moderna, 161)
Reviewed by: M. Praz in English Studies (entry 3093).

3052 Gissing, George Robert. Autobiographical and Imaginative Selections. Ed. A.C. Gissing. London: Cape, 1928.

3053 Gosse, Edmund William. "A First Sight of Tennyson." Selected Essays. London: Heinemann, [1928], pp. 111-118.
Reprinted from: Portraits and Sketches, 1912 (entry 2681).

3054 Lee, Ernest Dare. "Tennyson and His Era." The Papers of an Oxford Man. London: Ingpen and Grant, [1928], pp. 161-165.

3055 Loane, George Green. Echoes in Tennyson and Other Essays. London: Stockwell, 1928. 24pp.

3056 McAlpin, Edwin Augustus. "Tennyson and Immortality." Old and New Books as Life Teachers. New York: Doubleday, Doran, 1928, pp. 80-95.

3057 Nisbet, Mrs. Charles Richard. Tennyson and Browning Compared. Charlotte: the author, 1928. 40 pp.

3058 Reid, Forrest. "The Moxon Tennyson." Illustrators of the Sixties. London: Faber and Gwyer, [1928], pp. 36-43.

3059 Whitman, Walt. "A Word About Tennyson." Rivulets of Prose. New York: Greenberg, 1928, pp. 92-98.
Reprinted from: Critic (New York), 1887 (entry 1212). See entry 1212 for other reprintings and for annotation.

Periodicals

3060 "Americana and Tennyson." Times Literary Supplement, May 10, 1928, p. 364.
Of bibliographical interest.

278 / TENNYSON

3061 Birrell, Francis. Nation (London), 43 (April 14, 1928), 45.
Review of the Royal Court Theatre's production of Harold.
Birrell admires the play's verse but faults its tone.

3062 Cressman, Edmund Dresser. "The Classical Poems of Tennyson." Classical Journal, 24 (Nov. 1928), 98-111.

3063 Era, April 11, 1928, p. 6.
Review of the Royal Court Theatre's production of Harold.

3064 "A Glimpse of Tennyson." Notes and Queries, 155 (July 7, 1928), 7.

3065 Jacquart, Rolland R. "One of Those Immortalized by Tennyson." American Hebrew, 121 (May 4, 1928), 965 and 1021.

3066 Jennings, Richard. Spectator, 140 (April 14, 1928), 563-564.
Review of the Royal Court Theatre's production of Harold.
An ambivalent response.

3067 L., S.R. "Revival of Harold." Morning Post (London), April 3, 1928, p. 12.
Review of the Royal Court Theatre's production of Harold.
Finds the play dull.

3068 la Cécilia, Jean. "Tennyson." Notes and Queries, 155 (July 21, 1928), 44.

3069 Macdonell, A.G. London Mercury, 18 (May 1928), 87-88.
Review of the Royal Court Theatre production of Harold.
Likes the play for its characterizations and suitability to the stage.

3070 New Age, April 12, 1928, p. 285.
Review of the Royal Court Theatre's production of Harold.

3071 T. "At the Play." Punch, April 11, 1928, p. 414.
Review of the Royal Court Theatre's production of Harold.
Tepid response to the play.

3072 "Tennyson and William Law." Times Literary Supplement, April 26, 1928, p. 320.

3073 Times (London), April 3, 1928, p. 14.
Review of the Royal Court Theatre's production of Harold.

3074 W., H.M. Daily Telegraph, April 3, 1928, p. 7.
Review of the Royal Court Theatre's production of Harold.

1929

Books

3075   Blunden, Edmund. Nature in English Literature. London:
       Hogarth, 1929, pp. 101-104. (Hogarth Lectures, 9)

3076   Bradley, Andrew Cecil. "The Reaction Against Tennyson."
       A Miscellany. London: Macmillan, 1929, pp. 1-31.
       Reprinted from: The Reaction Against Tennyson, 1917 (entry
2835). See entry 2835 for another reprinting and for annotation.

3077   Granville-Barker, Harley. "Tennyson, Swinburne, Meredith
       and the Theatre." The Eighteen-Seventies: Essays by Fel-
       lows of the Royal Society of Literature. Ed. Harley Gran-
       ville-Barker. Cambridge: Cambridge U.P., 1929, pp. 161-
       191.
       Also published in Fortnightly Review, 1929 (entry 3088).
Likes Queen Mary.

3078   Macnaughton, G.F.A. Tennyson: An Interview. Glasgow:
       Maclehose, 1929.
       Of biographical interest.

3079   Róna, Eva. "The Princess": Tennyson és a nökérdés. Bu-
       dapest: 1929.
       Publication of a dissertation: 1929 (entry 3083).

3080   Tennyson, Alfred, Lord; William Kirby; and Hallam Tennyson.
       Alfred, Lord Tennyson and William Kirby: Unpublished Cor-
       respondence to Which Are Added Some Letters from Hallam,
       Lord Tennyson. Ed. Lorne A. Pierce. Toronto: Macmillan,
       1929.

3081   Weatherhead, Leslie D. "A New Projection of Christian
       Thought Born of the Fear of Death--Tennyson." The After-
       World of the Poets. London: Epworth, [1929], pp. 79-122.
       Tennyson on life after death.

Dissertations

3082   App, August J. "Lancelot in the Poetry of Tennyson." Lan-
       celot in English Literature: His Role and Character. Cath-
       olic University, 1929, pp. 151-175.

3083   Róna, Eva. The Princess: Tennyson és a nökérdés. Buda-
       pest, 1929.
       Published: 1929 (entry 3079).

Periodicals

3084   Daniels, Earl. "The Younger Generation Reads Browning and
       Tennyson." English Journal, 18 (Oct. 1929), 653-661.

3085   Faggi, A. "La Poesia di Tennyson in un libro italiano."
        Marzocco, no. 2 (1929).

3086   Frend, Grace Gilchrist. "Great Victorians: Some Recollec-
        tions of Tennyson, George Eliot and the Rossettis." Book-
        man (London), 77 (Oct. 1929), 9-11.

3087   Granville-Barker, Harley. "Some Victorians Afield: The
        Poet as Dramatist." Theatre Arts Monthly, 13 (May 1929),
        361-372.

3088   _____. "Tennyson, Swinburne, Meredith and the Theatre."
        Fortnightly Review, 131 (May 1929), 655-672.
        Also published in The Eighteen-Seventies, 1929 (entry 3077).

3089   Macy, John. "Tennyson, the Perfect Laureate." Bookman
        (New York), 69 (June 1929), 375-386.

3090   Magnus, Laurie. "Tennyson a Hundred Years After." Corn-
        hill Magazine, n.s. 66 (May 1929), 660-670.
        Commented on in Notes and Queries (entry 3092).

3091   Magnus, Philip M. "Poetry and Society Since Tennyson."
        Edinburgh Review, 249 (April 1929), 301-314.

3092   Notes and Queries, 156 (June 1, 1929), 381.
        Comments on L. Magnus's "Tennyson a Hundred Years After"
        in Cornhill Magazine, 1929 (entry 3090).

3093   Praz, Mario. English Studies, 11 (Aug. 1929), 155.
        Review of G.N. Giordano-Orsini's La Poesia di Alfred Ten-
        nyson, 1928 (entry 3051).

3094   Redgrave, M. "Tennyson in 1929." Cambridge Review, Oct.
        18, 1929, pp. 30-31.

3095   Wright, Herbert G. "Tennyson and Wales." Essays and Stud-
        ies (English Association), 14 (1929), 71-103.
        Wright discusses Tennyson's trips to Wales and compares the
        Mabinogion and Tennyson's "The Marriage of Geraint" and "Geraint
        and Enid."

                            1930

Books

3096   Auslander, Joseph, and Frank Ernest Hill. "Lord Tennyson."
        The Winged Horse. Garden City: Doubleday, Doran, 1930,
        pp. 303-315.

3097   Beck, Georg. Alfred Tennysons ethische Anschauungen. Er-
        langen: Döres, 1930.
        Publication of a dissertation: 1930 (entry 3120).

3098 Benson, Edward Frederic. As We Were: A Victorian Peep-Show. London: Longmans, Green, 1930.

3099 Blos, Ernst. Die politischen Anschauungen Tennysons. Erlangen: Döres, 1930.
Publication of a dissertation: 1930 (entry 3121).

3100 Boss, Eleanor. In Quest of the Grail. London: Marshall, [1930].

3101 Bowden, Margorie Moreland. Tennyson in France. Manchester: Manchester U. P., 1930. (Manchester University Publications in French, no. 5)
Bowden's study is elegantly written and still useful as an introduction to Tennyson's reception in France, although its notation is sloppy. This book would be worth updating and expanding.
Reviewed by: Bookman (London) (entry 3158); A. Brule in Revue Anglo-Américaine (entry 3160); K. R. Gallas in English Studies (entry 3187); and Modern Language Review (entry 3166).

3102 Bryan, J. Ingram. The Philosophy of English Literature. Tokyo: Maruzen, [1930], pp. 218-220.

3103 Carlyle, Thomas. "Tennyson." Representative Essays: English and American. Ed. J. R. Moore. New York: Ginn, 1930, pp. 108-109.

3104 Hacker, John G. Tennyson's Ode to Vergil with Music. Baltimore: privately printed, 1930. 6 p.

3105 Knox, Ronald Arbuthnott. "The Authorship of 'In Memoriam.'" Essays in Satire. New York: Dutton, [c. 1930].

3106 Lucas, Frank Laurence. "Tennyson." Eight Victorian Poets. New York: Macmillan, 1930, pp. 3-19.
Lucas examines the beauties of Tennyson's poetry.

3107 Möllmann, Adelheid. Alfred Tennysons künstlerische Arbeit an seinen Gedichten. Münster: Helios-verlag, 1930.
Publication of a dissertation: 1930 (entry 3123).

3108 Page, Curtis Hidden. "Tennyson: List of References." British Poetry of the Nineteenth Century. New York: Sanborn, 1930, pp. 442-444.

3109 Quiller-Couch, Arthur. "Titania: by Lord T--n." Green Bays: Verses and Parodies. London: Oxford U. P., 1930, pp. 1-2.
A poem.

3110 Scaife, Christopher Henry Oldham. Poetry of Alfred Tennyson: An Essay in Appreciation. London: Cobden-Sanderson, 1930.
Scaife presents a generally negative view of Tennyson's poetry. He believes that most of the poetry is without value.

Reviewed by: E. Lewis in London Mercury (entry 3165);
Times Literary Supplement (entry 3137); and T. E. Welby in Week-
End Review (entry 3141).

3111 Tennyson, Alfred, Lord. Letters to Frederick Tennyson.
Ed. H. J. Schonfield. London: Hogarth, 1930.
Reviewed by: Times Literary Supplement (entry 3138).

3112 Tennyson, Charles (ed.). Introduction. The Devil and the
Lady, by Alfred, Lord Tennyson. London and New York:
Macmillan, 1930.
A play in verse written by Tennyson when he was fifteen
years old. Reviewed by: St. J. Adcock in Bookman (London) (entry
3125).

3113 Weatherhead, Leslie D. "Tennyson." After Death. London:
Epworth, [1930].

3114 Wingfield-Stratford, Esmé Cecil. Those Earnest Victorians.
New York: Morrow, 1930.

3115 _____. The Victorian Tragedy. London: 1930.
Wingfield-Stratford admires Tennyson's "intuition that, though
knowledge might come, wisdom might linger--in other words, that
to improve machines without improving men might lead to progress
in a direction opposite to heavenward."

3116 Wolfe, Humbert. Tennyson. London: Faber and Faber,
1930. (Poets on the Poets, 3)
Wolfe emphasizes Maud in an effort to show that critics who
denigrate Tennyson's poetry are reacting against the Victorian Age
rather than responding to the poems. This short book is one of the
best studies of Maud.
Reviewed by: E. Lewis in London Mercury (entry 3165);
Times Literary Supplement (entry 3137); and T. E. Welby in Week-
End Review (entry 3141).

3117 Woods, George Benjamin. Poetry of the Victorian Period.
New York: Scott, Foresman, [c.1930].
Tennyson bibliography on pages 952-958.

3118 Woods, Margaret L. "Poets of the 'Eighties." The Eighteen-
Eighties: Essays by Fellows of the Royal Society of Literature. Ed. Walter de la Mare. Cambridge: Cambridge U. P.,
1930.
Tennyson on pages 1-2.

Dissertations

3119 Beach, Constance L. The Use of Anglo-Saxon Material by
Scott, Bulwer-Lytton, Kingsley, and Tennyson in the Background of the Anglo-Saxon Revival in England. Chicago, 1930.

3120 Beck, Georg. Alfred Tennysons ethische Anschauungen. Erlangen, 1930.
Published: 1930 (entry 3097).

3121 Blos, Ernst. Die politischen Anschauungen Tennysons. Erlangen, 1930.
Published: 1930 (entry 3099).

3122 King, Lauren Alfred. The Verse Technique of Alfred, Lord
Tennyson. Ohio State, 1930.
Ohio State University Graduate School Abstracts of Doctor's
Dissertations, 3 (1930), 137-146.

3123 Möllmann, Adelheid. Alfred Tennysons künstlerische Arbeit
an seiner Gedichten. Münster, 1930.
Published: 1930 (entry 3107).

3124 Pearce, Helen. The Criticism of Tennyson's Poetry: A Summary with Special Emphasis upon Tennyson's Response to Criticism as a Factor in the Development of his Reputation. California at Berkeley, 1930.
A less than useful study that has been outdated by subsequent
research.

Periodicals

3125 Adcock, St. J. Bookman (London), 77 (March 1930), 336-337.
Review of C. Tennyson, ed., The Devil and the Lady, 1930
(entry 3112).

3126 Bensly, Edward. "Literary Queries: Tennyson." Notes and
Queries, 158 (May 3, 1930), 319.

3127 Bertoni, Giulio. "Ulisse nellas Divina Commedia e nei Poeti
Moderni." Arcadia, 6 (1930).

3128 Brown, Stephen J. "Homeric Simile After Homer." Thought,
4 (March 1930), 597-598.

3129 Burton, Katherine. "Hallam's Review of Tennyson." Modern
Language Notes, 45 (April 1930), 224-225.
Corrects the dating of Hallam's review.

3130 Fausset, Hugh I'Anson. "Alfred Tennyson in Youth." Bookman (London), 79 (Dec. 1930), 168-169.

3131 Hartsock, E. "Poor Tennyson." Personalist, 11 (1930), 28-
31.

3132 Kempling, W. Bailey. "An Apocryphal Tennyson Poem."
Times Literary Supplement, April 3, 1930, p. 298.
See also: A. Rogers (entry 3134) and T. J. Wise (entry 3143).

3133 Notes and Queries, 158 (May 17, 1930), 343.
       Notes A. E. Baker's forthcoming A Concordance to "The Devil
and the Lady," 1931 (entry 3145).

3134 Rogers, Arthur. "An Apocryphal Tennyson Poem." Times
       Literary Supplement, April 3, 1930, p. 298.
       See also: W. B. Kempling (entry 3132) and T. J. Wise (entry
3143).

3135 Sparrow, John. "Tennyson and Thomson's Shorter Poems."
       London Mercury, 21 (March 1930), 428-429.
       Sparrow notes similarities between poems of Tennyson and
Thomson.

3136 "Tennyson Manuscripts." Times Literary Supplement, July 17,
       1930, p. 596.

3137 Times Literary Supplement, Oct. 9, 1930, p. 803.
       Review of H. Wolfe's Tennyson, 1930 (entry 3116) and C. H. O.
Scaife's Poetry of Alfred Tennyson, 1930 (entry 3110).

3138 Times Literary Supplement, Oct. 16, 1930, p. 831.
       Review of Letters to Frederick Tennyson, ed. H. J. Schonfield,
1930 (entry 3111).

3139 "Tours through Literary England: Through the Tennyson Coun-
       try." Saturday Review (London), 150 (Aug. 2, 1930), 139-
       140.

3140 Troxell, Gilbert M. "Tennyson Emergent: Sale of Autograph
       Manuscripts." Saturday Review of Literature (New York), 7
       (Aug. 16, 1930), 60.
       Of bibliographical interest.

3141 Welby, T. E. Week-End Review, Oct. 4, 1930, pp. 457-458.
       Review of H. Wolfe's Tennyson, 1930 (entry 3116) and C. H. O.
Scaife's Poetry of Alfred Tennyson, 1930 (entry 3110).

3142 Wilner, Ortha L. "Tennyson and Lucretius." Classical Jour-
       nal, 1930.

3143 Wise, Thomas James. "An Apocryphal Tennyson Poem."
       Times Literary Supplement, March 27, 1930, p. 274.
       See also: W. B. Kempling (entry 3132) and A. Rogers (entry
3134).

1931

Books

3144 Abercrombie, Lascelles. "Tennyson." Revaluations: Studies
       in Biography. London: Oxford U. P., 1931, pp. 60-76.
       A positive assessment of Tennyson's poetry.

3145 Baker, Arthur Ernest. A Concordance to "The Devil and the
Lady": Being a Supplement to the Concordance to the Works
of the Late Lord Tennyson. London: Golden Vista, 1931.
The standard reference. Reviewed by: H. I'A. Fausset in
Bookman (London) (entry 3186); and Times Literary Supplement (entry
3168). Noted: Notes and Queries, 1930 (entry 3133).

3146 Charteris, Evan. The Life and Letters of Sir Edmund Gosse.
London: Heinemann, 1931.

3147 Chauvet, Paul. "Tennyson." Sept Essais de Littérature anglais. Paris: Figuière, 1931, pp. 151-195.

3148 Crum, Ralph B. "Nature Red in Tooth and Claw: Tennyson's
Problem." Scientific Thought in Poetry. New York: Columbia U. P., 1931, pp. 157-190.
Publication of a dissertation: 1931 (entry 3154). Religion
and science in Tennyson's works.

3149 Halperin, Maurice. "The Last Tournament." Le Roman de
Tristan et Iseult dans la Littérature anglo-américaine au
XIXe et au XXe Siècles. Paris: Jouve, 1931, pp. 31-39.
Publication of a dissertation: 1931 (entry 3155).

3150 Hegner, Anna. Die Evolutionsidee bei Tennyson und Browning.
Wertheim: Bechstein, 1931.
Publication of a dissertation: 1931 (entry 3156).

3151 Hengelhaupt, Margrit. Die Personifikation bei George Meredith. Hannover: Küster, 1931.
Tennyson on pages 3-7. Publication of a dissertation: 1931
(entry 3157).

3152 Lockhart, John Gibson. "Tennyson." Lockhart's Literary
Criticism. Introduction by M. Clive Hildyard. London: Oxford U. P. (Blackwell), 1931, pp. 132-144.

3153 Tennyson, Alfred, Lord. Unpublished Early Poems. Ed.
Charles Tennyson. London: Macmillan, 1931.
Only fifteen hundred copies printed. Reprinted from: Nine-
teenth Century and After, 1931 (entry 3167).
Reviewed by: H. I'A. Fausset in Bookman (London) (entry
3186); R. A. Scott-James in Saturday Review (London) (entry 3194);
Times Literary Supplement (entry 3168); and Week-End Review (entry
3169).

Dissertations

3154 Crum, Ralph B. Scientific Thought in Poetry. Columbia,
1931.
Published: 1931 (entry 3148).

3155 Halperin, Maurice. Le Roman de Tristan et Iseult dans la

Littérature anglo-americiane au XIXe et au XXe Siècles.
Paris, 1931.
Published: 1931 (entry 3149).

3156   Hegner, Anna. Die Evolutionsidee bei Tennyson und Browning.
        Freiburg, 1931.
        Published: 1931 (entry 3150).

3157   Hengelhaupt, Margrit. Die Personification bei George Mere-
        dith. Freiburg, 1931.
        Published: 1931 (entry 3151).

Periodicals

3158   Bookman (London), 80 (April 1931), 31.
        Review of M. M. Bowden's Tennyson in France, 1930 (entry
3101).

3159   Brodribb, C. W. "Tennyson and Froude." Times Literary
        Supplement, Oct. 15 and Dec. 17, 1931, pp. 802 and 1028.
        See also: G. Callender (entry 3161).

3160   Brule, A. Revue Anglo-Américaine, 8 (Feb. 1931), 262-263.
        Review of M. M. Bowden's Tennyson in France, 1930 (entry
3101).

3161   Callender, G. "Tennyson and Froude." Times Literary Sup-
        plement, Oct. 22 and Dec. 31, 1931, pp. 820 and 1053; and
        Jan. 21, 1932, p. 44.
        See also: C. W. Brodribb (entry 3159).

3162   Gillet, Louis. "Pour Tennyson." Nouvelles Littéraires, Oct.
        24, 1931, p. 6.

3163   Hutton, William Holden. "Two Unfamiliar Plays." Church
        Quarterly Review, 111 (Jan. 1931), 314-327.
        Discusses the Royal Court Theatre's 1928 production of Har-
old. He takes the unusual critical point of view that the play had
too little poetry. (The other play is Shakespeare's Timon of Athens.)

3164   Jonson, G. C. Ashton. "Tennyson's 'In Memoriam.'" Poetry
        Review, 22 (May 1931), 181-201.

3165   Lewis, E. London Mercury, 23 (Feb. 1931), 387-388.
        Review of C. H. O. Scaife's Poetry of Alfred Tennyson, 1930
(entry 3110) and H. Wolfe's Tennyson, 1930 (entry 3116).

3166   Modern Language Review, 26 (Jan. 1931), 126.
        Review of M. M. Bowden's Tennyson in France, 1930 (entry
3101).

3167   Tennyson, Charles, ed. "Tennyson's Unpublished Poems."
        Nineteenth Century and After, 109 (March, April, May, and
        June 1931), 367-380, 495-508, 625-636, and 756-764.

Reprinted: Unpublished Early Poems, ed. C. Tennyson, 1931 (entry 3153).

3168 Times Literary Supplement, Dec. 10, 1931, p. 1001.
Review of A.E. Baker's Concordance to "The Devil and the Lady," 1931 (entry 3145) and Unpublished Early Poems, ed. C. Tennyson, 1931 (entry 3153).

3169 Week-End Review, 4 (Dec. 19, 1931), 800-801.
Review of Unpublished Early Poems, ed. C. Tennyson, 1931 (entry 3153).

1932

Books

3170 Auld, William Muir. The Mount of Vision. New York: Macmillan, 1932.
Focusing on "The Ancient Sage," Auld discusses Tennyson's spiritual views.

3171 Bradby, Godfrey Fox. "Tennyson's 'In Memoriam.'" The Brontës and Other Essays. London: Oxford U.P., 1932, pp. 90-112.

3172 Collier, John. "Lord Tennyson." The Great Victorians. Ed. H.J. Massingham and H. Massingham. London: Nicholson and Watson, [1932], pp. 503-516.
Collier emphasizes Tennyson's originality. He indicates how Tennyson portrayed nature and used scientific knowledge.

3173 Füting, Adolf. Tennysons Jugenddrama "The Devil and the Lady." Morburg: Hamel, 1932.
Publication of a dissertation: 1932 (entry 3180).

3174 Gutbier, Elisabeth. Psychologisch-ästhetische Studien zu Tristan-Dichtungen der neueren englischen Literatur. Erlangen: Döres, 1932.
Publication of a dissertation: 1932 (entry 3181).

3175 McFee, Inez Nellie. Story of the Idylls of the King: Tennyson's Idylls of the King in Their Original Form: Also the Stories of These Poems. New York: Stokes, 1932. Illustrated by M.L. Kirk.

3176 Noyes, Alfred. Tennyson. Edinburgh: Blackwood, 1932.
Reprinted from: Some Aspects of Modern Poetry, 1924 (entry 2994). See entry 2994 for annotation

3177 Stevenson, Lionel. "Alfred Tennyson." Darwin Among the Poets. Chicago: U. of Chicago P., 1932, pp. 55-116.
Stevenson traces elements of Darwin's theories of evolution

through Tennyson's work, revealing as he does so much of Tennyson's poetry's debt to science. Tennyson recognized in evolutionary theory the implied hope for progress to a better future and the implied shame of a bestial past. Excellent reading.

3178 Van Doorn, Willem. "Tennyson and the Encroachment of Lyricism." Theory and Practice of English Narrative Verse Since 1833. Amsterdam: De Arbeitersperst, [1932], pp. 163-179.

Dissertations

3179 Donegan, Sylvia Eugenia. The Failure of the Poetical Drama in the Victorian Period: With Special Attention to Browning, Bulwer-Lytton, and Tennyson. Boston U., 1932.

3180 Füting, Adolf. Tennysons Jugenddrama: The Devil and the Lady. Marburg, 1932.
Published: 1932 (entry 3173).

3181 Gutbier, Elisabeth. Psychologisch-ästhetische Studien zu Tristan-Dichtungen der neueren englischen Literatur. Erlangen, 1932.
Published: 1932 (entry 3174).

3182 Morgan, Mary Louis. "Galahad in the Poetry of Tennyson." Galahad in English Literature. Catholic U., 1932, pp. 126-142.

3183 Shipman, Mary Evelyn. The Didactic Element in the Poetry of Tennyson. Boston U., 1932.

Periodicals

3184 Callender, G. "Tennyson and Froude." Times Literary Supplement, Jan. 21, 1932, p. 44.
Last in a series; see entry 3161.

3185 Evans, Benjamin Ifor. "Tennyson and the Origins of the Golden Treasury." Times Literary Supplement, Dec. 8, 1932, p. 941.

3186 Fausset, Hugh I'Anson. Bookman (London), 81 (Jan. 1932), 227.
Review of A.E. Baker's A Concordance to "The Devil and the Lady," 1931 (entry 3145) and Unpublished Early Poems, ed. C. Tennyson, 1931 (entry 3153).

3187 Gallas, K.R. English Studies, 14 (Feb. 1932), 40-41.
Review of M.M. Bowden's Tennyson in France, 1930 (entry 3101).

3188 Osborne, E.A. "Tennyson's 'Holy Grail.'" Times Literary Supplement, Aug. 25, 1932, p. 596.

3189 Peake, Leslie S. "Tennyson and Faith." London Quarterly
Review, 157 (April 9, 1932), 182-189.

3190 _____. "Tennyson and the Search for Immortality: I.
The Pre-Existence of Man." Saturday Review (London), 153
(Feb. 20, 1932), 192.
Discusses the notion that the soul exists prior to its existence
on Earth.

3191 _____. "Tennyson and the Search for Immortality: II.
The Idea of Spiritualism." Saturday Review (London), 153
(Feb. 27, 1932), 216-217.

3192 _____. "Tennyson and the Search for Immortality: III.
Reason and Love." Saturday Review (London), 153 (March
12, 1932), 266.

3193 Rendall, Vernon. "A Tennyson Puzzle?" Saturday Review,
153 (Feb. 13, 1932), 175.
According to Rendall, A.H. Hallam lived on "the long unlove-
ly street" in In Memoriam.

3194 Scott-James, R.A. Saturday Review (London), 153 (Jan. 23,
1932), 102-103.
Review of Unpublished Early Poems, ed. C. Tennyson, 1931
(entry 3153).

1933

Books

3195 Bradley, Andrew Cecil. "The Reaction Against Tennyson."
English Critical Essays. Ed. P.M. Jones. New York: Oxford U.P., 1933. pp. 59-87.
Reprinted from: The Reaction Against Tennyson, 1917 (entry
2835). See entry 2835 for another reprinting and for annotation.

3196 Elton, Oliver. The English Muse: A Sketch. London: 1933.

3197 Evans, B. Ifor. English Poetry in the Later Nineteenth Century. London: Methuen, 1933.
Tennyson's influence.

3198 Fuller, Hester Thackeray. Three Freshwater Friends: Tennyson, Watts, and Mrs. Cameron. Newport, Isle of Wight:
The County Press, 1933.

3199 Gaglio-Morana, V. Alfredo Tennyson: poeta rappresentativo
dell'Inghilterra vittoriana. Palermo: Fratelli Vena, 1933.

3200 Sparrow, John. Introduction. In Memoriam, by Alfred, Lord
Tennyson. London: Nonesuch, 1933.

Sparrow admires the poetry and emotion of In Memoriam, but not its intellectual paucity.

Reviewed by: B. H. Newdigate in London Mercury (entry 3223); and New Statesman and Nation (entry 3224).

3201 Winwar, Frances (Frances Grebanier). Poor Splendid Wings. Boston: Little, Brown, 1933.
Tennyson on pages 121-123.

Periodicals

3202 Bird, W. H. B. "Tennyson in 1833." Times Literary Supplement, Sept. 21, 1933, p. 631.
See also: A. Quiller-Couch (entry 3207).

3203 Howe, Mark Antony de Wolfe. "Victorian Poets: A Side Light." Atlantic Monthly, 152 (Aug. 1933), 226-227.

3204 "In Memoriam: A. H. H." Poetry Review, 24 (1933), 479-481.

3205 Mabbott, Thomas Ollive. "The Correspondence of John Tomlin: Letters from Tennyson and Aubrey De Vere." Notes and Queries, 164 (April 29, 1933), 293-294.

3206 Madan, Geoffrey. "Tennyson and the Letter S." Times Literary Supplement, May 18, 1933, p. 348.

3207 [Quiller-Couch, Arthur.] "Tennyson in 1833." Times Literary Supplement, Sept. 14, 1933, pp. 597-598.
See also: W. H. B. Bird (entry 3202). Reprinted: The Poet as Citizen, 1934 (entry 3213).
Discusses the excellence of In Memoriam.

3208 Richardson, Robert K. "The Idea of Progress in Locksley Hall." Wisconsin Academy of Science, Arts and Letters: Transactions, 28 (1933), 341-361.
Richardson believes that popular acceptance of "Locksley Hall" is representative of popular acceptance of the idea of progress. He contends that "Locksley Hall's" "stanzas, directly, or by easy implication, are the legitimate and authentic product of the entire historical evolution of the factors essential to the idea; embody in a way possible only to verse that emotional element which would appear also a prerequisite of the idea; and suggest, by their presentation of the components of the concept, its adequate definition."

3209 Swift, William H. "Tennyson in the Twentieth Century." Search Quarterly, 3 (April 1933), 341-343.

1934

Books

3210 Bateson, Frederick W. English Poetry and the English Language. London: Oxford U.P. (Clarendon Press), 1934.
Tennyson on pages 101-104 and 124-126.

3211 Carter, John, and Graham Pollard. "Alfred, Lord Tennyson." An Enquiry into the Nature of Certain Nineteenth Century Pamphlets. London: Constable, 1934, pp. 293-343.
Carter and Pollard systematically reveal T.J. Wise's forgeries. This book is essential reading for anyone interested in the bibliographies of nineteenth-century authors.

3212 Cunliffe, John W. "Early Victorian Poets." Leaders of the Victorian Revolution. New York: Appleton-Century, [1934], pp. 130-140.
Cunliffe uses Tennyson's work to illustrate the Victorian society's "smugness."

3213 Quiller-Couch, Arthur. "Tennyson in 1833." The Poet as Citizen, and Other Papers. Cambridge: Cambridge U.P., 1934. New York: Macmillan, 1935, pp. 161-173.
Reprinted from: Times Literary Supplement, 1933 (entry 3207). See entry 3207 for annotation.

3214 Rendall, Vernon. Wild Flowers in Literature. London: Scholartis, 1934.
Tennyson mentioned often.

Dissertation

3215 Scott, Walter B., Jr. Tennyson and His Age, 1850-1875. Princeton, 1934.

Periodicals

3216 Adkins, Nelson F. "Tennyson's 'Charge of the Heavy Brigade': A Bibliographical Note." Notes and Queries, 167 (Sept. 15 and Oct. 13, 1934), 189-190 and 266.

3217 Beaver, Dorothy M. "Mr. Tennyson." Saturday Review of Literature (New York), 11 (Sept. 15, 1934), 108.
Of biographical interest.

3218 Bush, Douglas. "The Personal Note in Tennyson's Classical Poems." University of Toronto Quarterly, 4 (1934), 201-218.

3219 Earls, M. "Wilfrid Ward and Tennyson: Reply." Commonweal, 21 (Nov. 23, 1934), 124.
A reply to M. Sheed (entry 3227).

3220 Howe, Merrill Levi. "Dante Gabriel Rossetti's Comments on Maud." Modern Language Notes, 49 (May 1934), 290-293.
Rossetti felt that Maud lacked vigor and that its social point of view was inappropriate for its characters.

3221 Mansell, Kathryn. "Vitalizing the Idylls of the King." English Journal (High School Edition), 23 (March 1934), 225-227.

3222 Motter, T. H. V. "Arthur Hallam's Centenary: A Bibliographical Note." Yale University Gazette, 8 (1934), 104-109.

3223 Newdigate, B. H. London Mercury, 30 (1934), 648-649.
Review of In Memoriam, introduction by J. Sparrow, 1933 (entry 3200).

3224 New Statesman and Nation, March 10, 1934, p. 364.
Review of In Memoriam, introduction by J. Sparrow, 1933 (entry 3200).

3225 Phelps, William Lyon. "Lancelot and That Forward Hussy Elaine as Seen by 'Godey's.'" Scribner's Magazine, 95 (1934), 434-435.

3226 Pollard, Graham. "Tennyson's 'A Welcome,' 1863." Times Literary Supplement, Feb. 15 and March 15, 1934, pp. 112 and 200.
See also: T. J. Wise (entry 3228). Of bibliographical interest.

3227 Sheed, Masie. "Wilfrid Ward and Tennyson." Commenweal, 21 (Nov. 16, 1934), 87-88.
Replied to by: M. Earls (entry 3219).

3228 Wise, Thomas James. "Tennyson's 'A Welcome,' 1863." Times Literary Supplement, March 8, 1934, p. 168.
See also: G. Pollard (entry 3226).

3229 Zamick, M., ed. "Unpublished Letters of Arthur Henry Hallam from Eton, Now in the John Rylands Library." Bulletin of the John Rylands Library, 18 (1934), 197-248.

1935

Books

3230 Cruse, Amy. The Victorians and Their Reading. Boston: Houghton Mifflin, 1935. London: Allen and Unwin, 1935.
Tennyson and his readers.

3231 Fitzhugh, Harriet Loyd, and Percy R. Fitzhugh. "Alfred Tennyson." Concise Biographical Dictionary. New York: Grosset and Dunlap, [1935], pp. 678-679.

3232 Thompson, James W. "The True History of Tennyson's 'Lord of Burleigh.'" Byways in Bookland. Berkeley: 1935, pp. 121-134.

Dissertations

3233 LeRoy, Gaylord C. The Idea of Progress in Tennyson's Poetry. Harvard, 1935.

3234 Paden, William D. Contributions to the Biography of Tennyson. Yale, 1935.

3235 Poteat, Mary. A Critical Edition of Tennyson's Becket. Duke, 1935.

Periodicals

3236 Brie, Friedrich. "Tennysons Ulysses." Anglia, 59 (1935), 441-447.
Tennyson made the character Ulysses into a Victorian.

3237 Gill, W. W. "Rizpah." Notes and Queries, 169 (Nov. 9, 23, and 30, 1935), 333, 373-374, and 394.
The story of "Rizpah" in other literary works of the nineteenth century.

3238 Phillips, Lawrence. "Successful Prophecies by Men of Letters." Notes and Queries, 169 (Sept. 7, 1935), 175.
Phillips asserts that in "Locksley Hall" Tennyson prophesied "aeroplanes and the League of Nations."

3239 Scott-James, R. A. "Editorial Notes." London Mercury, 31 (1935), 324.
Cambridge's influence on Tennyson.

1936

Books

3240 Beach, Joseph Warren. "Tennyson." The Concept of Nature in Nineteenth-Century English Poetry. New York: Macmillan, 1936.
According to Beach, Tennyson "wished to maintain the distinction between objective and subjective." Tennyson conflicted with nature in his poetry in order to elevate the spiritual world.

3241 Ehrsam, Theodore G.; Robert H. Deily; and Robert M. Smith. "Alfred Lord Tennyson." Bibliographies of Twelve Victorian Authors. New York: Wilson, 1936, pp. 299-362.
This book is an extraordinary achievement in enumerative bibliography. Its chapter on Tennyson has long been the standard bibliographic reference for secondary works related to the poet.

3242   Eliot, T.S. "In Memoriam." Essays Ancient and Modern.
       London: Faber and Faber, 1936. New York: Harcourt,
       Brace, 1936.
           Reprinted: J. Killham, ed., Critical Essays, 1960 (entry
       3697); and J.D. Hunt, ed., Tennyson: In Memoriam, 1970 (entry
       4214); and E.A. Francis, ed., Tennyson, 1980 (entry 4964).
           Eliot asserts: "Tennyson is a great poet, for reasons that
       are perfectly clear. He has three great qualities which are seldom
       found together except in the greatest poets: abundance, variety, and
       complete competence." He also remarks that In Memoriam's "faith
       is a poor thing, but its doubt is a very intense experience." Eliot
       does not admire Tennyson's poetry in general, although he likes In
       Memoriam. This essay is interesting because Eliot wrote it; those
       new to the study of In Memoriam may find it less than helpful.

3243   _____. Introduction. Poems of Tennyson. Nelson Classics
       Series. 1936.
       Not examined.

3244   Roy, P.N. Italian Influence on the Poetry of Tennyson. Be-
       nares: Uttaro, 1936.
       Reviewed by: F. Olivero in English Studies (entry 3262).

3245   Weygandt, Cornelius. The Times of Tennyson: English Vic-
       torian Poetry as It Affected America. New York: Appleton-
       Century, 1936.
           A well written discussion of Tennyson's popularity in America.
       This book is informative and counters some myths about Tennyson's
       reading public.

Dissertation

3246   Hesse, Gerhard. Das politische Element in der Lyrik Swin-
       burnes und Tennysons. Greifswald, 1936.

Periodicals

3247   Carlson, C. Lennart. "A French Review of Tennyson's 1830
       and 1832 Volumes." ELH, 3 (1936), 218-227.

3248   Ehrsam, Theodore George. "Tennyson's Two Sonnets on Po-
       land." Nowy Swiat Niedzielny Dodatek Ilustrowany (New York),
       Jan. 5, 1936, p. 11.

3249   Howell, A.C. "Tennyson's 'Palace of Art'--An Interpretation."
       Studies in Philology, 33 (July 1936), 507-522.
           In an interesting and well argued essay, Howell asserts that
       "The Palace of Art" is autiobiographical, with the "Palace" being
       Cambridge. According to Howell, the poem represents Tennyson's
       disenchantment with Cambridge and its "deadening influence." An
       exacting reader might not be entirely convinced by Howell's arguments,
       but he musters much evidence to support his point of view, and his
       ideas are interesting. This is one of the best essays on Tennyson
       to be published in the 1930s.

3250 Tennyson, Charles. "Tennyson Papers: I. Alfred's Father." Cornhill Magazine, 153 (March 1936), 283-305.
A biographical essay based on the papers of Dr. George Clayton Tennyson, father of Alfred Tennyson.

3251 _____. "Tennyson Papers: II. J. M. Heath's 'Commonplace Book.'" Cornhill Magazine, 153 (April 1936), 426-449.
Some previously unpublished writings of the Tennyson brothers and Hallam are presented.

3252 _____. "Tennyson Papers: III. 'Idylls of the King.'" Cornhill Magazine, 153 (May 1936), 534-557.
Early manuscripts.

3253 _____. "Tennyson Papers: IV. The Making of 'The Princess.'" Cornhill Magazine, 153 (June 1936), 672-680.
Discusses the manuscript of The Princess and what it reveals of Tennyson's methods of composition.

1937

Books

3254 Bush, Douglas. "Tennyson." Mythology and the Romantic Tradition in English Poetry. Cambridge, Mass.: Harvard U. P., 1937, pp. 197-228. (Harvard Studies in English, 18)
Reprinted: New York: Pageant, 1957.
This essay is fundamental to studies of Tennyson's use of classical materials. Bush provides an erudite discussion that covers the backgrounds of the poems and excellent critical evaluations.
Pages 213-216 reprinted: E. A. Francis, ed., Tennyson, 1980 (entry 4964), pp. 163-166.

3255 Cazamian, Madeleine L. Introduction. In Memoriam: Enoch Arden: Le Ruisseau: Ulysse: Les Mangeurs de Lotus, by Alfred, Lord Tennyson. Trans. M. L. Cazamian. Aubier: Editions Montaigne, 1937. (Collections bilingue des classiques étrangers)
Reviewed by: L. Bonnerot in Etudes Anglaises (entry 3269).

3256 Pisanti, G. Ulisse nella poesia di Tennyson e in quella di Pascoli. L. Amendola, 1937.

3257 Routh, H. V. Towards the Twentieth Century. New York: Macmillan, 1937.

Dissertation

3258 Mooney, Emory A., Jr. Tennyson and Modern Science. Cornell, 1937.

Periodicals

3259 Greene, Graham. "Alfred Tennyson Intervenes." Spectator,
      159 (Dec. 10, 1937), 1058.

3260 Grierson, H. J. C. "Croker and Tennyson." Times Literary
      Supplement, April 24, 1937, p. 308.

3261 Millhauser, Milton. "Ringing Grooves." Notes and Queries,
      172 (1937), 45.
      Explicates a phrase from "Locksley Hall."

3262 Olivero, Federico. English Studies, 71 (1937), 415.
      Review of P. N. Roy's Italian Influence on the Poetry of Ten-
      nyson, 1936 (entry 3244).

3263 Potter, George R. "Tennyson and the Biological Theory of
      Mutability in Species." Philological Quarterly, 16 (Oct.
      1937), 321-343.
      Potter examines Tennyson's use of up-to-date scientific knowl-
      edge of nature.

3264 Vissar, G. J. "'The Passing of Arthur' and 'Ymadawiad Ar-
      thur.'" Neophilologus, 23 (1937), 46-52.
      Compares Tennyson's poem with one by T. Gwynn-Jones.

1938

Books

3265 Batho, Edith. "The Victorians and After, 1830-1914."
      Introduction to Literature. Ed. Bonamy Dobrée. London:
      Cresset, 1938.

3266 Hunton, William A. Tennyson and the Victorian Political Mi-
      lieu. New York: Graduate School of New York University,
      1938.
      An eighteen-page summary of a dissertation: 1938 (entry
3267).

Dissertations

3267 Hunton, William A. Tennyson and the Victorian Political Mi-
      lieu. New York, 1938.
      Summary published: 1938 (entry 3266). According to Hunton,
Tennyson was unmoved by lower-class efforts to achieve political lib-
erty. He was a spokesman for England's "dominant class."

3268 Reid, Margaret J. C. The Arthurian Legend. Aberdeen,
      1938.

Periodicals

3268a Boddington, O.-E. "Deux poèmes de Tennyson." Les Langues modernes, Dec. 1938, pp. 549-552.
"Tears, Idle Tears" and "O Swallow, Swallow" translated in
verse.

3269 Bonnerot, L. Etudes Anglaises, 2 (1938), 196-198.
Review of In Memoriam, trans. M. L. Cazamian, 1937 (entry
3255). Likes the book.

3270 Green, Jane. "A Sorrow's Crown of Sorrow." Notes and
Queries, 174 (1938), 436-438.

3271 Starke, F. J. "Tennyson und Virgil: Eine Interpretation von
Tennysons Gedicht 'To Vergil.'" Neuphilologische Monats-
schrift, 9 (1938), 62-73.

3272 Steward, S. M. "Pope and Tennyson: A Possible Parallel."
Notes and Queries, 174 (1938), 133-134.
Steward compares a passage from The Princess with "Ode
on Saint Cecilia's Day."

3273 Strout, Alan Lang. "'Christopher North' on Tennyson."
Review of English Studies, 14 (Oct. 1938), 428-439.
Christopher North (John Wilson) did not understand Tennyson's
poetry (see entry 16).

1939

Books

3274 Groom, Bernard. On the Diction of Tennyson, Browning and
Arnold. London: Oxford U. P. (Clarendon Press), 1939.
(Society for Pure English, 53)
Reprinted: The Diction of Poetry from Spenser to Bridges,
1955 (entry 3578).
Groom examines the peculiarities of Tennyson's style and en-
hances one's appreciation of Tennyson's skill.

3275 Partington, W. Forging Ahead. New York: 1939.
Revised edition: Thomas J. Wise in the Original Cloth, 1946
(entry 3373). Discusses the Wise forgeries.

3276 Young, G. M. The Age of Tennyson. London: Oxford U. P.,
1939. (Warton Lecture on English Poetry)
Reprinted: J. Killham, ed., Critical Essays, 1960 (entry
3697), pp. 25-40. An interesting study.

Dissertation

3277 Bernstein, Ethel. Victorian Morality in the Idylls of the King:
A Study of Tennyson's Use of His Sources. Cornell, 1939.

Periodicals

3278 A. , R. H. , and G. G. L. (George Green Loane?) "Crossing the
Bar." Notes and Queries, 176 (Feb. 4, 1939), 80-81.

3279 C. , T. C. "Tennyson: 'Kapiolani.' " Notes and Queries, 176
(April 8, 1939), 242.

3280 Fucilla, Joseph G. "Bibliographies of Twelve Victorian Authors: A Supplement." Modern Philology, 37 (Aug. 1939),
215-222.
    Tennyson on pages 220-222. Fucilla adds to the listing in
Ehrsam, et al., Bibliographies of Twelve Victorian Authors, 1936
(entry 3241). His listing emphasizes Italian and religious publications.

3281 L. , G. G. (George Green Loane?) "'The Poet': Some Notes on
Tennyson's Early Poem." Notes and Queries, 177 (July 22, 1939),
62-64.

3282 "Lord Tennyson at Aldworth." Poetry Review, 30 (1939),
421-431.

3283 Pitollet, C. "Les Fleurs de Francis Jammes et celles d'Alfred Tennyson." Revue de l'enseignement des langue vivantes,
March 1939, pp. 113-119.

3284 Rose, Felix. "Tennyson and Victor Hugo: Two Poets, Two
Nations, One Epoch." Poetry Review, 30 (1939), 105-117.
See also: F. Rose, 1944 (entry 3359).

3285 Young, George M. "The Age of Tennyson." British Academy,
25 (1939).

1940

Books

3286 Bay, J. Christian. "A Tennyson-Browning Association Copy."
The Fortune of Books. Friends of the Torch, 1940. Chicago: W. M. Hill, 1941, pp. 285-290.

3287 Chew, Samuel C. (ed.) Introduction. Tennyson: Representative Poems. New York: Odyssey, 1941, pp. xi-xlii. (Odyssey Series in Literature)
    Chew tries to show Tennyson's poetic development by discuss-
ing the poet's work chronologically. His criticism is interesting.

3288 de la Mare, Walter. Pleasures and Speculations. London:
Faber and Faber, 1940.

3289 DeVane, William Clyde, and Mabel Phillips DeVane. Introduc-

tion. Selections from Tennyson. New York: Crofts, 1940.
W.C. and M.P. DeVane provide an introduction aimed at college students.

3290 Evans, B. Ifor. A Short History of English Literature. Harmondsworth: 1940.

3291 Johnson, W.S. "Musty, Fusty Christopher." Studies in English in Honor of Raphael Dorman O'Leary and Selden Lincoln Whitcomb. Lawrence: U. of Kansas P., 1940, pp. 40-43.
The background of the word fusty before it appeared in an epigram by Tennyson.

3292 Paden, W.D. "Tennyson and the Reviewers (1829-1835)." Studies in English in Honor of Raphael Dorman O'Leary and Selden Lincoln Whitcomb. Lawrence: U. of Kansas P., 1940, pp. 15-39.
An interesting and only slightly dated essay that takes issue with T.R. Lounsbury's discussion of Tennyson's reception by critics in the early 1830s (The Life and Times of Tennyson, 1915, entry 2797). See also, for further information, E.F. Shannon's Tennyson and His Reviewers, 1952 (entry 3496).

3293 Tabb, John Banister. "Alfred Tennyson," "Tennyson," and "Alfred Tennyson." The Poetry of Father Tabb. Ed. Francis A. Litz. New York: Dodd, Mead, 1940, pp. 350, 452, and 465, respectively.
Three poems, as follows:

Alfred Tennyson

The lordliest at Arthur's Table Round
  No loftier than thou,
The laureate, with England's glory crowned,
  Whom death has knighted now.
Nov. 1892

Tennyson

'Twas fit that with the falling year
  He too should fall;
That he, when Nature heeds, should hear
  The homeward call;
That leaves autumned o'er his bier
  Bespread the pall,
For in their funeral train appear
  The thoughts of all.

Alfred Tennyson

The voice that late with music thrilled
The world, in silence now is stilled.
Or is our loss the larger gain
Of worlds new-wakened to his strain?

Dissertations

3294 Fall, Christine. Frederick Tennyson: A Biographical and Critical Study. Texas, 1940.

3295 Kittelmann, Fritz H. "The Charge of the Light Brigade" von Tennyson. Berlin, 1940.

Periodicals

3296 "Croker on Tennyson." Colophon, n.s. 1, no. 4 (1940), 95-96.
A letter that shows that J.W. Croker wrote the 1833 Quarterly Review article (entry 22) that attacked Tennyson's poetry.

3297 Loane, G. "Illustrations of Tennyson." Notes and Queries, 179 (Oct. 12 and 19, 1940), 258-260 and 274-276.
Tennyson's writings compared with those of other important writers.

3298 Lumiansky, R.M. "Tennyson and Guþrunakviþa." Notes and Queries, 178 (July 13, 1940), 23-24.
Lumiansky suggests a possible source for the line "Home they brought her warrior dead" from The Princess.

3299 McKean, G.R. "Faith in Locksley Hall." Dalhousie Review, 19 (1940), 472-478.

3300 Mooney, E.A., Jr. "Alfred Tennyson's Earliest Shakespeare Parallels." Shakespeare Association Bulletin, 15 (1940), 117-124.

3301 _____. "Tennyson's Earliest Classical Parallels." Classical Journal, 36 (1940), 35-37.
Mooney focuses on The Devil and the Lady.

3302 S., W.W. "The 'Miller's Daughter' with Apologies to Tennyson!" Notes and Queries, 178 (Feb. 3, 1940), 79.
Greek poetry and Tennyson's poem.

1941

Books

3303 Hearn, Lafcadio. Lafcadio Hearn's Lectures on Tennyson.
Ed. Shigetsugu Kishi. Tokyo: Hoduseido, 1941. South Pasadena, California: P.D. and Ione Perkins, 1941.
Kishi was Hearn's "last student in the Imperial University of Tokyo." The book is based on Kishi's notes from lectures given by Hearns.

3304 Marchand, Leslie A. "Tennyson." The Athenaeum: A Mirror

of Victorian Culture. Chapel Hill: U. of North Carolina P.,
1941, pp. 267-282.
Reprinted: New York: Octagon Books, 1971.
This book provides an interesting discussion of the history of
the Athenaeum. His discussion of Tennyson is valuable for its presentation of an important magazine's criticism of Tennyson during
the Victorian era.

Dissertation

3305 Eidson, John O. Tennyson in America: His Reputation and
Influence from 1827-1858. Duke, 1941.
Published: 1943 (entry 3328).

Periodicals

3306 Ratchford, Fannie E. "Idylls of the Hearth: Wise's Forgery
of 'Enoch Arden.'" Southwest Review, 26 (1941), 317-325.

3307 Rutland, William R. "Tennyson and the Theory of Evolution."
Essays and Studies (English Association), 26 (1941).
Evolution and Tennyson's belief in human progress.

1942

Books

3308 Meehan, Francis. Living Upstairs. New York: Dutton, 1942.

3309 Paden, W. D. Tennyson in Egypt: A Study of the Imagery in
His Earlier Work. Lawrence: U. of Kansas P., 1942.
(University of Kansas Humanistic Studies, 27)
Paden examines sources for Tennyson's work and the poet's
development through adolescence. This carefully researched book is
a standard reference for those who study Tennyson. Paden's psychoanalytic interpretations of Tennyson's adolescence are sometimes
heavy-handed. An important and influential study.
Reviewed by: G. Sanders in Modern Language Quarterly (entry
3360); I. Sells in Modern Language Review (entry 3340); and Times
Literary Supplement (entry 3343).

3310 Ratchford, Fannie E. An Exhibition of Manuscripts and Printed Books at the University of Texas, October 1-30, 1942: Alfred, Lord Tennyson, 1809-1892. Austin: U. of Texas P.,
1942.
Of interest to those who wish to work with Tennyson's manuscripts. Reviewed by: Library Quarterly (entry 3354).

Dissertation

3311 Aimée, Sister. The Religious Beliefs of Three Victorian Poets:
Tennyson, Browning, and Arnold, and Their Influence on English Literature. Ottawa, 1942.

Periodicals

3312 Caclamanos, D. "Tennyson's Ideal Man." Times Literary
Supplement, Oct. 17, 1942, pp. 511-513.

3313 Dodds, M. H. "Literary Inaccuracies." Notes and Queries,
183 (Aug. 29, 1942), 144.
Tennyson and Henry Irving disputed over the possible staging
of Becket.

3314 Fausset, Hugh I'Anson. "The Hidden Tennyson." Poetry Review, 33 (1942), 272-275.
Reprinted: Poets and Pundits, 1947 (entry 3387).

3315 "Fifty Years After." Times Literary Supplement, Oct. 10,
1942, p. 499.

3316 "A Great National Poet: England at War: Tennyson's Mystic
Imperialism." Times Literary Supplement, Oct. 10, 1942,
pp. 498 and 501.

3317 Harrison, Thomas P., Jr. "Tennyson's Maud and Shakspere."
Shakespeare Association Bulletin, 17 (1942), 80-85.
Maud and Shakespeare's King Lear, Hamlet, and Romeo and Juliet.

3318 "Memorabilia." Notes and Queries, 183 (Nov. 21, 1942), 301.

3319 Mortimer, Ray. "Books in General." New Statesman and Nation, 24 (Oct. 10 and 17, 1942), 241 and 258.
Discusses Tennyson's poetry.

3320 Motter, T. H. Vail. "Hallam's Suppressed Allusion to Tennyson." PMLA, 57 (1942), 587-589.
On a passage suppressed from A. H. Hallam's Literary Remains (Boston: Ticknor, 1863).

3321 _____. "When Did Tennyson Meet Hallam?" Modern Language Notes, 57 (March 1942), 209-210.
On the basis of sections XXII and XLVI of In Memoriam, Motter deduces that Tennyson and Hallam first met in April 1829.

3322 Nicolson, Harold. "Tennyson: Fifty Years After." Poetry
Review, 33 (Nov. 1942), 333-336.
Nicolson is unenthusiastic about much of Tennyson's poetry,
but urges study of the "pure poetry" that is not didactic.

3323 Quiller-Couch, Arthur. "Tennyson after Fifty Years." Poetry
Review, 33 (1942), 269-271.

3324 Sparke, Archibald. "Literary Inaccuracies." Notes and Queries, 182 (April 25, 1942), 233.

3325 "A Tennyson Emendation." Times Literary Supplement, Oct.
10, 1942, p. 499.

3326 Woods, Margaret L. "My Recollections of Tennyson." Poetry Review, 33 (1942), 276-277.

3327 Yohannan, J. D. "Tennyson and Persian Poetry." Modern Language Notes, 57 (Feb. 1942), 83-92.
See, for reply: W. D. Paden in Modern Language Notes, 1943 (entry 3338). See also: W. D. Paden in Modern Language Notes, 1945 (entry 3371).
Yohannan discusses the influence of Persian poetry on Tennyson's work.

1943

Books

3328 Eidson, John Olin. Tennyson in America: His Reputation and Influence from 1827 to 1858. Athens, Georgia: U. of Georgia P., 1943.
This excellent study is thoroughly researched. Eidson shows that America was initially more receptive to Tennyson's poetry than England, although less happy with the poet's later works. This is the standard study of Tennyson's reputation in nineteenth-century America.
Reviewed by: College English (entry 3332); E. Leisy in Southwest Review (entry 3335); and W. Templeman in Journal of English and Germanic Philology (entry 3342).

3329 Hallam, Arthur Henry. "On Some Characteristics of Modern Poetry and on the Lyrical Poems of Alfred Tennyson." The Writings of Arthur Hallam. Ed. T. H. Vail Motter. New York: Modern Language Association of America, 1943. London: Oxford U. P., 1943.
Reprinted from: Englishman's Magazine, 1831 (entry 9). See entry 9 for other reprintings and for annotation.

Dissertation

3330 Hecht, Maria. Die Wertewelt Tennysons. Vienna, 1943.

Periodicals

3331 Bush, Douglas. "Tennyson's Ulysses and Hamlet." Modern Language Review, 38 (Jan. 1943), 38.
Bush notes the relationship between Hamlet, IV, iv, and a passage in Ulysses.

3332 College English, 5 (1943), 52.
Review of J.O. Eidson's Tennyson in America, 1943 (entry 3328).

3333 D., A. E. "Tennyson on Cleopatra's Needle." Notes and Queries, 184 (Feb. 27, 1943), 136.

3334 Gettmann, Royal A. "Tennyson's Ulysses." Explicator, 1
      (1943), No. 4.

3335 Leisy, E. Southwest Review, 28 (1943), 447-449.
      Review of J.O. Eidson's Tennyson in America, 1943 (entry
3328).

3336 Marie, Rose. "Poetry in the Twilight of the Classics." Col-
      lege English, 5 (1943), 25-30.
      Mentions the influence of the classics on Tennyson.

3337 "Memorabilia." Notes and Queries, 184 (Feb. 27, 1943), 121-
      122.
      The suppressed poems of Tennyson.

3338 Paden, W.D. "Tennyson and Persian Poetry Again." Mod-
      ern Language Notes, 58 (Dec. 1943), 652-656.
      A reply to: J. Yohannan in Modern Language Notes, 1942
(entry 3327). See also: W.D. Paden in Modern Language Notes,
1945 (entry 3371). See, for reply: J. Yohannan (entry 3344). A
criticism of J. Yohannan's "Tennyson and Persian Poetry" (entry
3327).

3339 Price, Fanny. "The Fecundity of Tennyson." Notes and Que-
      ries, 184 (April 24, 1943), 256-257.

3340 Sells, I. Modern Language Review, 38 (1943), 358-359.
      Review of W.D. Paden's Tennyson in Egypt, 1942 (entry 3309).

3341 Shannon, Edgar Finley, Jr. "Tennyson and the Reviewers,
      1830-1842." PMLA, 58 (1943), 181-194.
      See also: J. Green's "Tennyson's Development During the
'Ten Years' Silence' (1832-1842)" in PMLA, 1951 (entry 3484) and
E. F. Shannon's Tennyson and His Reviewers, 1952 (entry 3496).
Chapter II of Tennyson and His Reviewers expands on the themes in
the present article.
      Shannon argues that Tennyson was sensitive to the criticisms
of reviewers and that the poet's revisions of his poetry were influenced by them.

3342 Templeman, William D. Journal of English and Germanic Phi-
      lology, 42 (1943), 607-610.
      Review of J.O. Eidson's Tennyson in America, 1943 (entry
3328).

3343 Times Literary Supplement, Feb. 13, 1943, p. 83.
      Review of W.D. Paden's Tennyson in Egypt, 1942 (entry
3309).

3344 Yohannan, J.D. Modern Language Notes, 58 (Dec. 1943), 656.
      A response to W.D. Paden's criticism (entry 3338) of Yohan-
nan's "Tennyson and Persian Poetry," 1942 (entry 3327).

1944

Books

3345 Auden, W. H. (ed.). Introduction. <u>A Selection from the Po-</u>
<u>ems of Tennyson</u>. New York: Doubleday, 1944.
Auden asserts that Tennyson "had the finest ear, perhaps, of
any English poet; he was also undoubtedly the stupidest; there was
little about melancholia that he didn't know; there was little else that
he did."
Reviewed by: <u>College English</u> (entry 3365); L. Kennedy in
<u>Book Week</u> (entry 3353); F. O. Matthiessen in <u>New York Times Book</u>
<u>Review</u> (entry 3367); G. Mayberry in <u>New Republic</u> (entry 3368); A.
Mizener in <u>Kenyon Review</u> (entry 3369); and R. Mortimer in <u>New</u>
<u>Statesman and Nation</u> (entry 3382).

3346 Ford, George H. <u>Keats and the Victorians: A Study of His</u>
<u>Influence and Rise to Fame, 1821-1895</u>. New Haven: Yale
U. P., 1944.
Ford discusses Keats's influence on Tennyson. A thorough
study.

3347 Grierson, Herbert J. C. <u>Rhetoric and English Composition</u>.
Edinburgh: 1944.
Kipling and Tennyson on pages 62-63.

3348 Grierson, Herbert J. C., and J. C. Smith. <u>A Critical History</u>
<u>of English Poetry</u>. London: Chatto and Windus, 1944. New
York: Oxford U. P., 1946.

Periodicals

3349 Basler, Roy P. "Tennyson the Psychologist." <u>South Atlantic</u>
<u>Quarterly</u>, 43 (April 1944), 143-159.
Reprinted: <u>Sex, Symbolism, and Psychology in Literature</u>,
1948 (entry 3403).
This controversial essay asserts that in <u>Maud</u> Tennyson "pio-
neered the uncharted frontiers of psychological phenomena." Basler
claims much for Tennyson, including insight into psychology that anticipates the works of Freud and Jung.

3350 Brooks, Cleanth. "The Motivation of Tennyson's Weeper."
<u>American Scholar</u>, 1944.
Reprinted: <u>The Well-Wrought Urn</u>, 1947 (entry 3385); and J.
Killham, ed., <u>Critical Essays</u>, 1960 (entry 3697), pp. 177-191. See
<u>The Well-Wrought Urn</u>, 1947 (entry 3384) for annotation. See also:
E. P. Vandiver, Jr., "Tennyson's 'Tears, Idle Tears'" in <u>Explicator</u>,
1963 (entry 3848).

3351 Emery, Clark. "The Background of Tennyson's 'Airy Navies.'"
<u>Isis</u>, 35 (July 1944), 139-147.
Emery discusses a passage from "Locksley Hall" and asserts
that "Tennyson had in mind some kind of aircraft."

3352   Howarth, R.G.   "Tennyson and Ovid."   Notes and Queries,
       186 (Jan. 29, 1944), 69.
       Tennyson misquotes Ovid.

3353   Kennedy, L.   Book Week, Nov. 19, 1944, p. 14.
       Review of: A Selection, ed. W.H. Auden, 1944 (entry 3345).

3354   Library Quarterly, 14 (1944), 92.
       Review of: F.E. Ratchford's An Exhibition of Manuscripts
and Printed Books, 1942 (entry 3310).

3355   M., M.   (M. Munsterberg).   "From Tennyson's Library."
       More Books, 19 (1944), 71-72.
       The Boston Public Library acquired four books once owned
by Tennyson.

3356   M., T.O.   (Thomas Ollive Mabbott?)   "Tennyson and an Auto-
       graph Fiend."   Notes and Queries, 187 (July 1, 1944), 15.

3357   Mabbott, T.O.   "Tennyson's The Poet."   Explicator, 3 (1944),
       Item 9.

3358   Paden, W.D.   "Tennyson's The Poet."   Explicator, 2 (1944),
       Item 56.

3359   Rose, Félix.   "Tennyson et Victor Hugo: deux poètes, deux
       peuples, une époque."   Revue de la pensée français, 3 (1944),
       12-21.
       See also: F. Rose in Poetry Review, 1939 (entry 3284).

3360   Sanders, G.   Modern Language Quarterly, 5 (1944), 379-380.
       Review of W.D. Paden's Tennyson in Egypt, 1942 (entry 3309).

3361   Stevenson, Lionel.   "Tennyson, Browning, and a Romantic Fal-
       lacy."   University of Toronto Quarterly, 13 (Jan. 1944), 175-
       195.
       Stevenson discusses Shelley's influence on Tennyson and how
Tennyson and Browning moved from elitist notions of poetry to concern for common human problems.

1945

Book

3362   Earnest, Ernest.   A Foreword to Literature.   New York:
       1945.
       Tennyson's influence.

Dissertation

3363   Mattes, Eleanor B.   The Religious Influences upon Tennyson's
       In Memoriam.   Yale, 1945.
       Published: 1951 (entry 3481).   See entry 3481 for annotation.

Periodicals

3364 Arms, George. "'Childe Roland' and 'Sir Galahad.'" College English, 6 (1945), 258-262.

3365 College English, 6 (1945), 241.
Review of A Selection, ed. W.H. Auden, 1944 (entry 3345).

3366 Leavis, Frank R. "'Thought' and Emotional Quality: Notes in the Analysis of Poetry." Scrutiny, 1945.
"Break, Break, Break" and "Tears, Idle Tears" criticized.

3367 Matthiessen, F.O. New York Times Book Review, Jan. 28, 1945, p. 4.
Review of A Selection, ed. W.H. Auden, 1944 (entry 3345).

3368 Mayberry, George. New Republic, Jan. 1, 1945, p. 24.
Review of A Selection, ed. W.H. Auden, 1944 (entry 3345).

3369 Mizener, A. Kenyon Review, 7 (1945), 315-318.
Review of A Selection, ed. W.H. Auden, 1944 (entry 3345).

3370 Paden, W.D. "MT. 1352: Jacques de Vitry, the Mensa Philosophica, Hödeken, and Tennyson." Journal of American Folklore, 58 (Jan. 1945), 35-47.
Identifies the source for Tennyson's play The Devil and the Lady.

3371 ———. "Tennyson and Persian Poetry Once More." Modern Language Notes, 60 (April 1945), 284.
See also: J.D. Yohannan in Modern Language Notes, 1942 (entry 3327) and W.D. Paden in Modern Language Notes, 1943 (entry 3338).
More evidence that Tennyson was unfamiliar with Persian poetry when he wrote The Princess.

3372 Templeman, William D. "Leonard Bacon, Nature, and Tennyson." Notes and Queries, Jan. 27, 1945, p. 33.
Suggests an influence by "The Miller's Daughter."

1946

Book

3373 Partington, Wilfred. Thomas J. Wise in the Original Cloth. London: Hale, 1946.
Revised version of Forging Ahead, 1939 (entry 3275).

Dissertation

3374 Donahue, Mary J. Tennyson: Studies in the Ten Years' Si-

lence (1833-1842).   Yale, 1946.
A good study that is worth reading for insight into Tennyson's
creative development.

Periodicals

3375   Basler, Roy P.   "Tennyson's 'Ulysses.'"   Explicator, 4
       (1946), Item 48.
       See also: W. Frost (entry 3378) and C.C. Walcutt (entry
3383).

3376   Carew, Peter.   "One of the 'Six Hundred.'"   Blackwood's
       Edinburgh Magazine, 259 (1946), 40-50.
       Captain Robert Portal's participation in the Crimean War.

3377   d'Agata, Alfio.   "Alcuni punti controversi nell' interpretazione
       dell' 'In Memorima' di A. Tennyson." Anglica, 1 (1946),
       102-107.
       D'Agata discusses Italian mistranslations of In Memoriam.

3378   Frost, William.   "Tennyson's 'Ulysses.'"   Explicator, 4
       (1946), Item 48.
       See also: R.P. Basler (entry 3375) and C.C. Walcutt (entry
3383).

3379   Fuson, Ben W.   "Tennyson's In Memoriam, XI." Explicator,
       4 (1946), Item 34.

3380   Lucas, F.L.   "Croker and Tennyson." Times Literary Sup-
       plement, Nov. 30, 1946, p. 596.

3381   N. , T.W. ; L.R.M. Strachan; and T.A. Notes and Queries,
       190 (April 6 and May 4, 1946), 146 and 196.

3382   Mortimer, Ray.   New Statesman and Nation, 32 (Dec. 28,
       1946), 486-487.
       Review of A Selection, ed. W.H. Auden, 1944 (entry 3345).

3383   Walcutt, Charles C.   "Tennyson's 'Ulysses.'"   Explicator, 4
       (Feb. 1946), Item 28.
       See also: R.P. Basler (entry 3375) and W. Frost (entry 3378).
Discusses the real meaning of the poem.

3384   Waterfield, A.J.   "The Booksale." Notes and Queries, 190
       (Jan. 12, 1946), 14-15.
       A 1929 sale of books from Tennyson's home.

1947

Books

3385   Brooks, Cleanth.   "The Motivation of Tennyson's Weeper."

The Well-Wrought Urn. New York: Harcourt, Brace, 1947.
Reprinted from: American Scholar, 1944 (entry 3350).
This good essay examines the structure of "Tears, Idle
Tears."

3386 Brown, Alan Willard. The Metaphysical Society: Victorian
Minds in Crisis, 1869-1880. New York: Columbia U.P.,
1947.
Tennyson was one of the founders of the Metaphysical Society.
This history of the society is of biographical interest.

3387 Fausset, Hugh I'Anson. "The Hidden Tennyson." Poets and
Pundits: Essays and Addresses. New Haven: Yale U.P.,
1947, pp. 187-191.
Reprinted from Poetry Review, 1942 (entry 3314).

3388 Nicolson, Harold. Tennyson's Two Brothers. Cambridge:
Cambridge U.P., 1947. (The Leslie Stephen Lecture, 1947)
A short discussion. Reviewed by: C.F. Harrold in Modern
Philology (entry 3412).

3389 Squire, John. Introduction. Selected Poems of Tennyson.
New York: Macmillan, 1947.

Dissertations

3390 Carr, Arthur J. The Rhetoric of Tennyson's Values. Illinois,
1947.

3391 Lepke, Arno. Der Todesgedanke und die Unsterblichkeitsidee
in Alfred Tennysons In Memoriam. Marburg, 1947.

Periodicals

3392 Carter, John. "Tennyson's Carmen saeculare." Library, 5th
ser. 2 (Sept.-Dec. 1947), 200-202.

3393 Fairchild, Hoxie N. "Tennyson and Shelley." Times Literary
Supplement, Jan. 11, 1947, p. 23.
Fairchild proposes Shelley's Queen Mab, II., lines 55-66, as
the source for Tennyson's "The Palace of Art."

3394 Haight, Gordon S. "Tennyson's Merlin." Studies in Philology,
44 (July 1947), 549-566.
Haight interprets "Merlin and the Gleam" as an autobiographical poem that expresses some of Tennyson's notions of himself and
others.

3395 Hough, Graham. "The Natural Theology of In Memoriam."
Review of English Studies, 23 (July 1947), 244-256.
Reprinted: J.D. Hunt, ed., Tennyson: In Memoriam, 1970
(entry 4214), pp. 138-154; and Selected Essays, 1978 (entry 4831).
Hough declares: "We find three important elements--the in-
fluence of science, transmitted especially through Lyell's Geology;

the influence of Coleridge, experience at Cambridge; and Tennyson's own religious intuitions, based ultimately on an unanalysable but completely cogent mystical experience." An important study of In Memoriam.

3396 Long, Mason. "The Tennysons and the Brownings." College English, 9 (Dec. 1947), 131-139.
The relationship of the families.

3397 Murray, John. "Croker on Tennyson." Times Literary Supplement, Jan. 18, 1947, p. 37.

3398 Sessions, Ina B. "The Dramatic Monologue." PMLA, 42 (1947), 503-516.

3399 Shannon, Edgar F. "The Proofs of Gareth and Lynette in the Widener Collection." Papers of the Bibliographical Society of America, 41 (Oct. 1947), 321-340.
Shannon shows Tennyson's revisions of the proofs of "Gareth and Lynette" and presents ninety-seven holograph lines from the poem.

3400 Stocking, Fred H. "Tennyson's 'Tears, Idle Tears.'" Explicator, 5, no. 8 (1947), Item 54.

3401 Strout, Alan Lang. "Croker and Tennyson Again." Notes and Queries, 193 (July 26 and Nov. 15, 1947), 317-318 and 498-499.
In the July 26th issue, Strout presents John Wilson Croker's letter in which the critic resigns from the Quarterly Review because of the favorable review (entry 79) of Poems, 1942. In the Nov. 15th issue, Strout presents a letter of January 27, 1833, which accompanied Croker's 1833 (entry 22) attack on Tennyson's Poems, 1833.

3402 T., C.B. "Gabriel Wells." Yale Library Gazette, 21 (1947), 53-54.
Yale acquires part of the manuscript of "Merlin and Vivien."

3403 Wimsatt, W.K., Jr. "The Structure of the 'Conrete Universal' in Literature." PMLA, 57 (March 1947), 278-279.
Includes negative remarks on "Locksley Hall."

1948

Books

3404 Basler, Roy P. "Tennyson's Maud." Sex, Symbolism, and Psychology in Literature. New Brunswick: Rutgers U.P., 1948, pp. 73-93.
Reprinted from: South Atlantic Quarterly, 1944 (entry 3349).
See entry 3349 for annotation.

3405 Baum, Paull F. Tennyson Sixty Years After. Chapel Hill: U. of North Carolina P., 1948.
This book does not rank Tennyson as highly as do other postwar studies. Baum faults Tennyson's lack of intellectualism. In

spite of his low opinion of the poet's ability to think, Baum offers insight into Tennyson's poetry, plays, and stature. This book remains basic reading for Tennysonian scholars.
Reviewed by: N. H. Pearson in Saturday Review of Literature (New York), 1948 (entry 3414).

3406 Chew, Samuel C. "The Nineteenth Century and After (1789-1939)." A Literary History of England. Ed. Albert C. Baugh. New York: Appleton-Century-Crofts, 1948. Reprinted: 1967.

3407 Gernsheim, Helmut. Julia Margaret Cameron. London: Fountain, 1948. Photographs of Tennyson.

Periodicals

3408 Austin, Alfred. "Tennyson's Literary Sensitiveness." National Review, 130 (1948), 56-61.

3409 Bowman, Mary Virginia. "The Hallam-Tennyson Poems (1830)." Studies in Bibliography, 1 (1948-1949), 193-199.

3410 Donahue, Mary Joan. "Tennyson: Two Unpublished Epigrams." Notes and Queries, 193 (Nov. 27, 1948), 521-522.

3411 Friedman, Albert B. "The Tennyson of 1857." More Books, 23 (1948), 15-22.
Friedman discusses the illustrations in the 1857 Moxon edition of Tennyson's Poems (the Pre-Raphaelite edition).

3412 Harrold, C. F. Modern Philology, 46 (1948), 67-68.
Review of H. Nicolson's Tennyson's Two Brothers, 1947 (entry 3388).

3413 Mabbott, T. O. "Tennyson's Merlin." Notes and Queries, 193 (Jan. 10, 1948), 14.

3414 Pearson, N. H. Saturday Review of Literature (New York), 31 (Oct. 30, 1948), 26.
Review of P. F. Baum's Tennyson Sixty Years After, 1948 (entry 3405).

3415 Stevenson, Lionel. "The 'High-Born Maiden' Symbol in Tennyson." PMLA, 63 (March 1948), 234-243.
Reprinted: J. Killham, ed., Critical Essays, 1960 (entry 3697), pp. 126-136.
According to Stevenson: "The symbol conforms with amazing precision to the theory of Jung regarding the archetypal image of the anima, the most frequent unconscious symbol, which Jung regards as representing the unconscious itself." Tennyson derived the "High-Born Maiden" figure from Shelley's Revolt of Islam and Queen Mab and used it in "The Lady of Shalott," "The Palace of Art," "Lady Clara Vere de Vere," "Locksley Hall," The Princess, and Idylls of

the King. As Tennyson matured his powerful literary symbol turned into a "stock-character." Stevenson ties the use of the theme to the circumstances of Tennyson's life.

1949

Books

3416 Nicoll, Allardyce. A History of Late Nineteenth Century Drama: 1850-1900. Cambridge: Cambridge U. P., 1949. Tennyson on pages 258-259.

3417 Tennyson, Charles. Alfred Tennyson. New York: Macmillan, 1949.
This is the standard biography of Tennyson. Charles Tennyson, grandson of Alfred Tennyson, uses private papers, letters, documents, and his own memories (he was born in 1879), to create a full picture of Tennyson. His criticism is also judicious. This book is essential to any Tennysonian library.
Reviewed by: Adelphi (entry 3453); P. F. Baum in South Atlantic Quarterly (entry 3454); E. H. Blakeney in National Review (entry 3419); D. Bush in New Republic (entry 3420); M. St. C. Byrne in English (entry 3456); S. C. Chew in New York Herald Tribune Book Review (entry 3421); College English (entry 3423); A. K. Davis, Jr., in Virginia Quarterly Review (entry 3459); W. C. De Vane in Yale Review (entry 3424); D. Hudson in Spectator (entry 3431); G. Jones in Life and Letters Today (entry 3433); T. H. V. Motter in Modern Language Notes (entry 3467); E. Neff in New York Times Book Review (entry 3436); A. Noyes in Quarterly Review (entry 3437) and Saturday Review of Literature (New York) (entry 3438); J. J. Reilly in Catholic World (entry 3469); W. Robbins in University of Toronto Quarterly (entry 3441); E. F. Shannon, Jr., in Journal of English and Germanic Philology (entry 3472); J. Squire in Illustrated London News (entry 3443); and Times Literary Supplement (entry 3445).
See also: H. Tyler's "I am mad Tom" in Times Literary Supplement (entry 3447).

Dissertation

3418 Bellinger, Rossiter R. Prosodical Studies in Some of Tennyson's Later Poetry. Yale, 1949.

Periodicals

3419 Blakeney, E. H. National Review, 133 (1949), 373-375. Review of C. Tennyson's Alfred Tennyson, 1949 (entry 3417).

3420 Bush, Douglas. New Republic, June 20, 1949, p. 24. Review of C. Tennyson's Alfred Tennyson, 1949 (entry 3417).

3421 Chew, Samuel C. New York Times Herald Tribune Book Review, June 12, 1949, p. 5. Review of C. Tennyson's Alfred Tennyson, 1949 (entry 3417).

3422 Cohen, J. M. "'In Memoriam': A Hundred Years After."
      Cornhill Magazine, 164 (Autumn 1949), 151-164.
      Cohen regards Tennyson's In Memoriam as the poet's most
important achievement. He tends to denigrate Tennyson's poetry in
general.

3423 College English, 11 (1949), 58.
      Review of C. Tennyson's Alfred Tennyson, 1949 (entry 3417).

3424 De Vane, W. C. Yale Review, 39 (1949), 176-178.
      Review of C. Tennyson's Alfred Tennyson, 1949 (entry 3417).

3425 Donahue, Mary Joan. "The Revision of Tennyson's Sir Gala-
      had." Philological Quarterly, 28 (April 1949), 326-329.
      Based on J. M. Heath's Commonplace Book.

3426 _____. "Tennyson's Hail, Briton! and Tithon in the Heath
      Manuscript." PMLA, 64 (June 1949), 385-416.
      See: C. Ricks's "Tennyson's 'Hail, Briton!' and 'Tithon':
Some Corrections" in Review of English Studies, 1964 (entry 3884).
      Donahue discusses an early example of Tennyson's use of the
meter found in In Memoriam and Tennyson's revisions of his poems.

3427 Fairchild, Hoxie N. "'Wild Bells' in Bailey's Festus?" Mod-
      ern Language Notes, 64 (April 1949), 256-258.
      Fairchild compares In Memoriam, section CVI, and the prayer
in Philip James Bailey's Festus.

3428 Hardwick, J. C. "Tennyson's Religion." Modern Churchman,
      39 (Dec. 1949), 317-329.
      Religion in Tennyson's life.

3429 House, Humphrey. Times Literary Supplement, Nov. 4, 1949,
      p. 715.
      House demonstrates that Manley Hopkins wrote one or both of
the Times (London) reviews of Poems, 1842, and The Princess in
1848 (entry 151) and In Memoriam in 1851 (entry 258).

3430 Hudson, Derek. "Tennyson's Aldworth." Spectator, 182 (April
      15, 1949), 507.

3431 _____. Spectator, 183 (Sept. 9, 1949), 330.
      Review of C. Tennyson's Alfred Tennyson, 1949 (entry 3417).

3432 Johnson, E. D. H. "The Lily and the Rose: Symbolic Meaning
      in Tennyson's Maud." PMLA, 64 (Dec. 1949), 1222-1227.
      An interesting essay which suggests that the lily represents
purity and the rose, passion.

3433 Jones, Gwyn. Life and Letters Today, 63 (1949), 166-167.
      Review of C. Tennyson's Alfred Tennyson, 1949 (entry 3417).

3434 Meldrum, Elizabeth. "Tennyson and the Classical Poets."

Contemporary Review, 175 (May 1949), 296-299.
Meldrum discusses possible influences of classical writers on Tennyson, with comments on "Frater Ave atque Vale," "Oenone," and "A Dream of Fair Women."

3435 Mooney, E. A., Jr. "A Note on Astronomy in Tennyson's
       The Princess." Modern Language Notes, 64 (Feb. 1949),
       98-102.
       Discusses "the nebulous star we call the sun" in part IV of
The Princess.

3436 Neff, Emery. New York Times Book Review, July 3, 1949,
       p. 3.
       Review of C. Tennyson's Alfred Tennyson, 1949 (entry 3417).

3437 Noyes, Alfred. "The Real Tennyson." Quarterly Review, 287
       (Oct. 1949), 495-507.
       Review of C. Tennyson's Alfred Tennyson, 1949 (entry 3417).

3438 _____. Saturday Review of Literature, 32 (July 23, 1949),
       19.
       Review of C. Tennyson's Alfred Tennyson, 1949 (entry 3417).

3439 Powys, Atherton. "Alfred, Lord Tennyson." Times Literary
       Supplement, Oct. 7, 1949, p. 649.
       About Tennyson's library at Farringford.

3440 Priestly, F. E. L. "Tennyson's Idylls." University of Toronto
       Quarterly, 19 (Oct. 1949), 35-49.
       Reprinted: J. Killham, ed., Critical Essays, 1960 (entry
3697), pp. 239-255.
       In this excellent study, Priestly asserts: "The Idylls are so
far from being escape that they represent one of Tennyson's most
earnest and important efforts to deal with major problems of his
time." He believes that the Idylls "form a pattern," are allegorical,
and affirm Tennyson's faith in the spiritual and distrust of materialism. He declares: "Tennyson is asserting in the Idylls that Christianity is not so much a set of facts to be argued about as a system
of principles to be lived by; that the proof of these principles is to
be established not by external empirical evidence, but by the power
with which they unify and give stability and meaning to the life of
man and of societies."

3441 Robbins, W. University of Toronto Quarterly, 19 (1949), 109-
       112.
       Review of C. Tennyson's Alfred Tennyson, 1949 (entry 3417).

3442 Shannon, Edgar F., Jr. "The Coachman's Part in the Publi-
       cation of Poems by Two Brothers." Modern Language Notes,
       64 (1949), 107-110.
       Shannon disproves the tradition that his father's coachman
suggested the publication of Poems by Two Brothers by revealing a
letter by Hallam Tennyson that contradicts the story.

3443 Squire, John. Illustrated London News, Sept. 10, 1949, p.
392.
Review of C. Tennyson's Alfred Tennyson, 1949 (entry 3417).

3444 Thaler, Alwin. "Tennyson and Whittier." Philological Quarterly, 28 (1949), 518-519.

3445 Times Literary Supplement, Oct. 14, 1949, p. 664.
Review of C. Tennyson's Alfred Tennyson, 1949 (entry 3417).

3446 Turner, Paul. "The Stupidest English Poet." English Studies,
30 (Feb. 1949), 1-12.
Turner disputes the notion propounded by W. H. Auden (entry
3345), H. Nicolson (entry 2971), and H. I'A. Fausset (entry 2966)
that Tennyson had a poor intellect. He musters much evidence to
support his belief that Tennyson was an advanced thinker.

3447 Tyler, Henry. "I am mad Tom." Times Literary Supplement,
Oct. 21, 1949, p. 681.
Tyler remarks on a passage in C. Tennyson's Alfred Tennyson
(entry 3417).

1950

Books

3448 Bateson, Frederick W. "Romantic Schizophrenia: Tennyson's
'Tears, Idle Tears.'" English Poetry: A Critical Introduction. New York: Longmans, 1950, pp. 223-233.
"Tears, Idle Tears" has public and private levels of expression that are independent of one another.

3449 Bush, Douglas. "Evolution and the Victorian Poets." Science
and English Poetry: A Historical Sketch, 1590-1950. New
York: Oxford U. P., 1950.
Bush asserts: "Although Tennyson was a closer student of
science than other poets, his concern was with man and God rather
than with scientific theories."

3450 Templeman, William Darby. "Tennyson's Locksley Hall and
Thomas Carlyle." Booker Memorial Studies: Eight Essays
on Victorian Literature in Memory of John Manning Booker,
1881-1948. Ed. Hill Shine. Chapel Hill: U. of North Carolina P., 1950, pp. 34-59.
Templeman presents evidence suggesting that "Locksley Hall"
is in large part a "translation" of Book II of Carlyle's Sartor Resartus.

Dissertation

3451 Carrigan, Margaret. Mid-Victorian Criticism as Revealed in
the Criticism of Tennyson, 1850-1870. Cornell, 1950.

3452 Carstensen, Broder. Der junge Tennyson. Kiel, 1950.

Periodicals

3453 Adelphi, 26 (1950), 91-92.
Review of C. Tennyson's Alfred Tennyson, 1949 (entry 3417).

3454 Baum, Paull F. South Atlantic Quarterly, 49 (1950), 96-97.
Review of C. Tennyson's Alfred Tennyson, 1949 (entry 3417).

3455 Bergman, Herbert. "Whitman on His Poetry and Some Poets:
Two Uncollected Interviews." American Notes and Queries,
8 (1950), 163-165.

3456 Byrne, M. St. Clare. English, 8 (1950), 36-37.
Review of C. Tennyson's Alfred Tennyson, 1949 (entry 3417).

3457 Carr, Arthur J. "Tennyson as a Modern Poet." University
of Toronto Quarterly, 19 (1950), 361-382.
Reprinted: J. Killham, ed., Critical Essays, 1960 (entry
3697), pp. 41-64; A. Wright, ed., Victorian Literature, 1961 (entry
3722); and J.D. Hunt, ed., Tennyson: In Memoriam, 1970 (entry
4214), pp. 155-165.
Carr begins by declaring: "The theme of In Memoriam is
loss and the subjective crisis it provokes." He asserts Tennyson's
relevance to modern poetry; in fact, of Tennyson he says, "He is
one of its makers." This challenging, sometimes controversial essay, opens new realms of inquiry into In Memoriam. It anticipates
the critical views of the 1960s.

3458 Cox, Canon Adam. "Tennyson's Elegy." Spectator, 184 (June
16, 1950), 816-817.
In Memoriam one hundred years later.

3459 Davis, Arthur Kyle, Jr. "Mid-Century Tennyson." Virginia
Quarterly Review, 26 (1950), 307-311.
Review of C. Tennyson's Alfred Tennyson, 1949 (entry 3417).

3460 Dunsany, Lord. "The Food of the Imagination." Poetry Review, 41 (1950), 197-198.
Dunsany asserts that "the soil of Earth is the food of the
imagination" and cites "Crossing the Bar" as an example.

3461 Ellmann, Mary Joan. "Tennyson: Revision of In Memoriam,
Section 85." Modern Language Notes, 65 (Jan. 1950), 22-30.
Ellmann "indicates the futility of resting very much of the
history of the composition of In Memoriam on internal evidence" by
comparing manuscript version in J.M. Heath's Commonplace Book
with the published version of In Memoriam, section 85.

3462 _____. "Tennyson: Two Unpublished Letters, 1833-1836."
Modern Language Notes, 65 (1950), 223-228.

3463 Gernsheim, Helmut. Times Literary Supplement, July 21, 1950, p. 460.
A comment on W. D. Paden's "Photographs of Tennyson" in Times Literary Supplement (entry 3468).

3464 James, David G. "Wordsworth and Tennyson." British Academy, 36 (1950), 113-129. (Wharton Lecture on English Poetry)
James compares The Prelude and In Memoriam and declares: "Wordsworth is greater than Tennyson."

3465 Meyerstein, E. H. W., and Charles Tennyson. "A Drayton Echo in Tennyson." Times Literary Supplement, June 2 and 9, 1950, 341 and 357.
See also: E. H. W. Meyerstein, 1951 (entry 3490).

3466 Milmed, Bella Kussy. "In Memoriam a Century Later." Antioch Review, 10 (1950), 471-492.
The modern importance of the poem.

3467 Motter, T. H. V. Modern Language Notes, 65 (1950), 356-357.
Review of C. Tennyson's Alfred Tennyson, 1949 (entry 3417).

3468 Paden, W. D. "Photographs of Tennyson." Times Literary Supplement, June 30, 1950, p. 412.
See also: H. Gernsheim (entry 3463).

3469 Reilly, J. J. Catholic World, 171 (1950), 477-478.
Review of C. Tennyson's Alfred Tennyson, 1949 (entry 3417).

3470 Robertson, David Allan, Jr. "Tennyson and the Mountain-Maid." American Alpine Journal, 7 (1950), 451-454.
Suggests that the maid of "Come Down, O Maid" is the Jungfrau.

3471 Rudman, Harry W. "Tennyson's Crossing the Bar." Explicator, 8 (1950), Item 45.

3472 Shannon, Edgar F., Jr. Journal of English and Germanic Philology, 44 (1950), 263-265.
Review of C. Tennyson's Alfred Tennyson, 1949 (entry 3417).

3473 Ware, Malcome R. "A Note on Tennyson's 'Subtle Beast.'" Notes and Queries, Dec. 23, 1950, p. 564.
Milton echoed in "Guinevere."

3474 White, Frances E. "Unorthodox Tendencies in Tennyson." Review of Religion, 15 (1950), 19-28.

1951

Books

3475 Browning, Robert. Dearest Isa: Robert Browning's Letters
to Isabella Blagden. Ed. Edward C. McAleer. Austin: U.
of Texas P., 1951. Reprinted: Westport: Greenwood, 1970.
    Tennyson is mentioned several times. In a letter dated Jan-
uary 19, 1870, Browning comments on Tennyson's The Holy Grail
and Other Poems: "Well, I go with you a good way in the feeling
about Tennyson's new book: it is all out of my head already. We
look at the object of art in poetry so differently! Here is an Idyll
about a knight being untrue to his friend and yielding to the temptation of that friend's mistress after having engaged to assist him in
his suit. I should judge the conflict in the knight's soul the proper
subject to describe: Tennyson thinks he should describe the castle,
and effect of the moon on its towers, and anything but the soul."

3476 Buckley, Jerome H. "Tennyson--The Two Voices." The Victorian Temper: A Study in Literary Culture. Cambridge,
Mass.: Harvard U. P., 1951. Reprinted: New York: Vin-
tage, 1964, pp. 66-86.
    Buckley mentions Tennyson often throughout this book. He
summarizes what has been written about Tennyson, places the poet
in the literary and intellectual movements of his day, and offers insightful criticism. This excellent book is a standard reference for
students of Victorian literature.

3477 Eidson, John Olin. Charles Stearn Wheeler: Friend of Emerson. Athens, Georgia: U. of Georgia P., 1951.
    The reception of Tennyson's work in America.

3478 Gawsworth, John. Introduction. Poetical Works of Tennyson.
London: Macdonald, 1951.

3479 Irving, Laurence. Henry Irving. London: Faber and Faber,
1951.
    Queen Mary on pages 264-267 and 274-275; Becket on pages
554-562.

3480 Kirkwood, Kenneth Parker. "Maud"--An Essay on Tennyson's
Poem. Ottawa: Le Droit, 1951.
    A multifarious examination of Maud.

3481 Mattes, Eleanor B. "In Memoriam": The Way of a Soul: A
Study of Some Influences That Shaped Tennyson's Poem. New
York: Exposition, 1951.
    Publication of a dissertation: 1945 (entry 3363).
    Mattes attempts to date the composition of passages of In Memo-
riam, and she cites sources for the ideas presented in the poem.
Her datings were useful in 1951, but subsequent research with In
Memoriam's manuscripts have rendered much of her conjecturing
moot. Researchers interested in In Memoriam will find Mattes's

citations of parallels in the poem with works by Wordsworth, Hallam, Isaac Taylor, Carlyle, Lyell, Herschel, and Chambers to be useful, although their status as sources is sometimes unclear.
    Reviewed by: College English (entry 3500); and F.E. White in Review of Religion (entry 3517).

Dissertation

3482 Stange, George R. Tennyson and the Voice of Men: A Study of the Theme of Isolation in His Poetry. Harvard, 1951.

Periodicals

3483 Green, David Bonnell. "Keats and Tennyson." Notes and Queries, 196 (Aug. 18, 1951), 367.

3484 Green, Joyce. "Tennyson's Development During the 'Ten Years' Silence' (1832-1842)." PMLA, 66 (Sept. 1951), 662-697.
    See also: E. F. Shannon's "Tennyson and the Reviewers, 1830-1842" in PMLA, 1943 (entry 3341). Shannon responds to Green in his Tennyson and the Reviewers, 1952 (entry 3496), page 191.
    Green disputes some of Shannon's conclusions in his 1943 article (entry 3341) and analyzes Tennyson's response to his early critics; she provides a careful study of the poet's revisions and their relationship to the comments of critics.

3485 Gwynn, Frederick L. "Tennyson at Leyte Gulf." Pacific Spectator, 5 (1951), 149-160.

3486 Hough, Graham. "Tears, Idle Tears." Hopkins Review, 4 (Spring 1951), 31-36.
    Reprinted: J. Killham, ed., Critical Essays, 1960 (entry 3697), pp. 186-191. Replied to by: L. Spitzer, 1952 (entry 3511).
    The poem "Tears, Idle Tears" presents "a sense of dereliction--arising perhaps from who knows what childish experience."

3487 Jones, Frederick L. "Tennyson's Crossing the Bar." Explicator, 10 (1951), Item 19.
    See also: J. T. Fain, 1952 (entry 3503) and G.G. Langsam, 1952 (entry 3506).
    About "the fusion of separate but associated figures" in the poem.

3488 Jump, J. D. "Shelley and Tennyson." Notes and Queries, 196 (Dec. 8, 1951), 540-541.

3489 McLuhan, H. M. "Tennyson and Picturesque Poetry." Essays in Criticism, 1 (July 1951), 262-282.
    Reprinted: J. Killham, ed., Critical Essays, 1960 (entry 3697), pp. 67-85.
    McLuhan uses A. Hallam's review of Poems, Chiefly Lyrical (entry 9) as background for a consideration of Tennyson's use of landscape in his poetry. An interesting and insightful essay.

320 / TENNYSON

3490   Meyerstein, E.H.W. "A Drayton Echo in Tennyson." Times
       Literary Supplement, March 9, 1951, p. 149.
       See also: E.H.W. Meyerstein, 1950 (entry 3465).

3491   Waterston, Elizabeth Hillman. "Symbolism in Tennyson's Mi-
       nor Poems." University of Toronto Quarterly, 20 (July 1951),
       369-380.
       Reprinted: J. Killham, ed., Critical Essays, 1960 (entry
3697), pp. 113-125.
       Waterston cites many examples of Tennyson's use of symbol-
ism. She indicates that his understanding of symbolism was deep
and extensive.

3492   Werner, Jack. "Arthur Tennyson." Notes and Queries, 196
       (April 14, 1951), 172.

                              1952

Books

3493   Durrell, Lawrence. A Key to Modern British Poetry. Nor-
       man: U. of Oklahoma P., 1952.
       Compares T.S. Eliot's "Gerontion" and Tennyson's "Ulysses."

3494   Estrich, Robert M., and Hans Sperber. "Personal Style and
       Period Style: A Victorian Poet." Three Keys to Language.
       New York: Rinehart, 1952.
       Tennyson's style in "The Revenge." A superior study.

3495   Johnson, E.D.H. "Tennyson." The Alien Vision of Victorian
       Poetry: Sources of the Poetic Imagination in Tennyson, Brown-
       ing, and Arnold. Princeton: Princeton U.P., 1952, pp. 1-
       71. (Princeton Studies in English, 34)
       Johnson discusses Tennyson's "divided will," which creates
conflicts of meaning in Tennyson's poetry. He tries to trace the
poet's attempts to resolve public expectations with private "intuitions."
Interesting.
       Reviewed by: Anglia (entry 3522); J.W. Beach in Modern Lan-
guage Notes (entry 3557); M. Bevington in South Atlantic Quarterly
(entry 3559); A.K. Davis, Jr., in Virginia Quarterly Review (entry
3563); L. Haddakin in Modern Language Review (entry 3565); K. John
in New Statesman and Nation (entry 3525); J.D. Jump in Review of
English Studies (entry 3567); Nation (entry 3508); J.C. Ransom in
Kenyon Review (entry 3538); L. Stevenson in Journal of English and
Germanic Philology (entry 3540); I.J. Suloway in College English
(entry 3514); W.D. Templeman in Personalist (entry 3576); Times
Literary Supplement (entry 3543); P. Turner in English Studies (entry
3619); United States Quarterly Book Review (entry 3516); and J. Wain
in Twentieth Century (entry 3546).

3496   Shannon, Edgar Finley, Jr. Tennyson and the Reviewers: A
       Study of His Literary Reputation and the Influence of the Critics
       upon His Poetry, 1827-1851. Cambridge: Harvard U.P., 1952.

This is a well researched study of the reviews of Tennyson's publications through In Memoriam in 1850, and of the influence of the reviews on Tennyson's poetry. Shannon shows that the reviews were generally more favorable than previously believed. He uses letters and circumstantial evidence to bolster his contention that the criticism markedly influenced Tennyson's writings. This is the standard study of its subject.

Reviewed by: L. Bonnerot in Etudes anglaises (entry 3608), B. A. Booth in Modern Language Notes (entry 3560); R. Halsband in Saturday Review (entry 3524); J. Holloway in Review of English Studies (entry 3566); G. D. McDonald in Library Journal (entry 3536); W. D. Templeman in Journal of English and Germanic Philology (entry 3541); Times Literary Supplement (entry 3544); and United States Quarterly Book Review (entry 3545).

Periodicals

3497 Ball, Donald. "The Characters in Tennyson." Poetry Review, 43 (1952), 87-89.

3498 Blackmur, R. P. "Lord Tennyson's Scissors: 1912-1950." Kenyon Review, 14 (1952), 1-20.
Based on a Tennysonian comment on modern poetry.

3499 Burnam, Tom. "Tennyson's 'Ringing Grooves' and Captain Ahab's Grooved Soul." Modern Language Notes, 67 (1952), 423-424.

3500 College English, 13 (1952), 471.
Review of E. B. Mattes's "In Memoriam," 1951 (entry 3481).

3501 Ed. "Tennyson, or an Imitation." Notes and Queries, 197 (Nov. 8, 1952), 502.
A query about some verses written in the manner of In Memoriam.

3502 Evans, Charles. "Victorian Writers and the Great Exhibition." Notes and Queries, 196 (Feb. 2, 1952), 60.
Tennysonian poem.

3503 Fain, John Tyree. "Tennyson's 'Crossing the Bar.'" Explicator, 10, no. 6 (1952), Item 40.
See also: F. L. Jones, 1951 (entry 3487) and G. G. Langsam (entry 3506).

3504 Gwynn, Frederick L. "Tennyson's 'Tithon,' 'Tears, Idle Tears,' and 'Tithonus.'" PMLA, 67 (1952), 572-575.
Gwynn shows relationships between the versions of "Tithonus" and "Tears, Idle Tears."

3505 Jamieson, Paul F. "Tennyson and His Audience in 1832." Philological Quarterly, 31 (Oct. 1952), 407-413.
Jamieson argues that the Cambridge Apostles provided Tennyson with an importantly encouraging audience.

3506 Langsam, G. Geoffrey. "Tennyson's Crossing the Bar." Explicator, 10 (1952), Item 40.
See also: F. L. Jones, 1951 (entry 3487) and J. T. Fain
(entry 3503).

3507 Moore, John R. "Conan Doyle, Tennyson, and Rasselas."
Nineteenth-Century Fiction, 7 (1952), 221-223.
The influence of Rasselas on Tennyson's The Princess is
discussed.

3508 Nation, Dec. 6, 1952, p. 535.
Review of E. D. H. Johnson's The Alien Vision, 1952 (entry
3495).

3509 Shannon, Edgar F., Jr. "Tennyson's 'Balloon Stanzas.'"
Philological Quarterly, 31 (Oct. 1952), 441-445.
Shannon proposes a balloon ascent at Cambridge, May 19,
1829, involving Richard Monckton Milnes, as the inspiration for the
"balloon stanzas" which originally began "A Dream of Fair Women."

3510 Spector, Robert Donald. "A Dryden Echo in Tennyson."
Notes and Queries, 197 (Nov. 22, 1952), 520.
On "The Lotos-Eaters."

3511 Spitzer, Leo. "Tears, Idle Tears Again." Hopkins Review,
5 (1952), 71-80.
Reprinted: J. Killham, ed., Critical Essays, 1960 (entry
3697), pp. 192-203; and A. Hatcher, ed., Essays, 1962 (entry 3798).
A mild reply to G. Hough's 1951 commentary (entry 3486).
Spitzer provides an erudite discussion of the phrase "some divine
despair."

3512 Stange, G. Robert. "Tennyson's Garden of Art: A Study of
The Hesperides." PMLA, 67 (Sept. 1952), 732-743.
Reprinted: J. Killham, ed., Critical Essays, 1960 (entry
3697), pp. 99-112.
Stange remarks that "The Hesperides" "is a neglected work,
fascinating in itself, which has the additional interest of developing
several motifs and sets of images which are central to much of the
poet's early expression."

3513 Stevenson, Lionel. "The Pertinacious Victorian Poets." University of Toronto Quarterly, 21 (April 1952), 232-245.
Mentions Tennyson.

3514 Suloway, I. J. College English, 14 (1952), 181.
Review of E. D. H. Johnson's The Alien Vision, 1952 (entry
3495).

3515 Tryon, W. S. "Nationalism and International Copyright: Tennyson and Longfellow in America." American Literature, 24
(Nov. 1952), 301-309.
Tryon compares the sales in America of the books of Tennyson and Longfellow.

3516 United States Quarterly Book Review, 8 (1952), 368.
Review of E. D. H. Johnson's The Alien Vision, 1952 (entry
3495).

3517 White, F. E. Review of Religion, 17 (1952), 73-75.
Review of E. B. Mattes's "In Memoriam," 1951 (entry 3481).

1953

Books

3518 Bose, A. Tennyson's "In Memoriam": A Revaluation. Calcutta: General Printers and Publishers, 1953.
Thoughtful and worth consulting.

3519 Chesterton, Gilbert Keith. A Handful of Authors. New York:
Sheed, 1953.
Tennyson on pages 96 and 99, and In Memoriam discussed on
pages 102-106.

3520 Reilly, Mary Paraclita. Aubrey de Vere: Victorian Observer.
Lincoln: U. of Nebraska P., 1953.

Dissertation

3521 Tietze, Frederick I. Tennyson: Science and the Poetic Sensibility. Wisconsin, 1953.
Summary of Doctoral Dissertations, University of Wisconsin,
14 (1954), 452-453.

Periodicals

3522 Anglia, 71 (1953), 360-365.
Review of E. D. H. Johnson's The Alien Vision, 1952 (entry
3495).

3523 Burchell, S. C. "Tennyson's 'Allegory in the Distance.' "
PMLA, 68 (June 1953), 418-424.
Burchell says that the Idylls of the King is "a medley of pure
and symbolic narrative." He asserts that "there is hardly a true
moral allegory in the Idylls."

3524 Halsband, Robert. Saturday Review, March 21, 1953, p. 36.
Review of E. F. Shannon's Tennyson and the Reviewers, 1952
(entry 3496).

3525 John, K. New Statesman and Nation, 45 (March 28, 1953),
374.
Review of E. D. H. Johnson's The Alien Vision, 1952 (entry
3495).

3526-3535 No entries.

3536 McDonald, G. D. Library Journal, Nov. 1, 1953, p. 1896.
    Review of E. F. Shannon's Tennyson and the Reviewers, 1952
(entry 3496).

3537 Paden, W. D. "A Note on the Variants of In Memoriam and
    Lucretius." Library, 5th ser. 8 (1953), 269-273.

3538 Ransom, John Crowe. Kenyon Review, 15 (1953), 335-336.
    Review of E. D. H. Johnson's The Alien Vision, 1952 (entry
3495).

3539 Shannon, Edgar F., Jr. "The Critical Reception of Tenny-
    son's 'Maud.'" PMLA, 68 (June 1953), 397-417.
    This article is more thoroughly researched than most books.
Shannon contends that the reviewers influenced Tennyson's revisions
of Maud and possibly the poet's decision to write Idylls of the King.
His arguments are not entirely convincing but are impressive. Those
who are interested in Tennyson's critical reception in the nineteenth
century should also consult Shannon's Tennyson and the Reviewers,
1952 (entry 3496).

3540 Stevenson, Lionel. Journal of English and Germanic Philology,
    52 (1953), 274-277.
    Review of E. D. H. Johnson's The Alien Vision, 1952 (entry
3495).

3541 Templeman, William D. Journal of English and Germanic Phi-
    lology, 52 (1953), 435-437.
    Review of E. F. Shannon's Tennyson and the Reviewers, 1952
(entry 3496).

3542 Tillotson, Kathleen. "Rugby 1850: Arnold, Clough, Walrond,
    and 'In Memoriam.'" Review of English Studies, n.s. 4
    (April 1953), 122-140.
    Responses to Tennyson's poem.

3543 Times Literary Supplement, Feb. 20, 1953, p. 126.
    Review of E. D. H. Johnson's The Alien Vision, 1952 (entry
3495).

3544 Times Literary Supplement, July 10, 1953, p. 446.
    Review of E. F. Shannon's Tennyson and the Reviewers, 1952
(entry 3496).

3545 United States Quarterly Book Review, 9 (1953), 158-159.
    Review of E. F. Shannon's Tennyson and the Reviewers, 1952
(entry 3496).

3546 Wain, John. "The Strategy of Victorian Poetry." Twentieth
    Century, 153 (1953), 383-390.
    Review of E. D. H. Johnson's The Alien Vision, 1952 (entry
3495).

1954

Books

3547 Evans, B. Ifor. Literature and Science. London: Allen and
Unwin, 1954.
Tennyson on pages 72-78.

3548 Goodman, Paul. "Remarks on 'Morte d'Arthur.'" The Structure of Literature. Chicago: U. of Chicago P., 1954, pp.
216-224.

3549 Hopkins, Kenneth. The Poets Laureate. London: Lane, 1954.

3550 Stanford, William Bedell. The Ulysses Theme: A Study in
the Adaptability of a Traditional Hero. Oxford: Blackwell,
1954.
Tennyson on pages 232-234. Tennyson's poem is placed in
the context of the Ulysses tradition beginning with Homer.

3551 Tennyson, Charles. Six Tennyson Essays. London: Cassell,
1954. Reprinted: Wakefield: S. R. Publishers, 1972.
The contents are: "Tennyson as a Humorist," pp. 1-38;
"Tennyson's Politics," pp. 39-69; "Tennyson's Religion," pp. 70-
124; "Tennyson's Versification," pp. 125-152; "Some Mss. of the
Idylls of the King and a note on Tennyson as a Narrative Poet," pp.
153-187; and "On Reading Tennyson," pp. 188-197.
Charles Tennyson provides six excellent essays on his grandfather. This book is a standard reference on Tennyson.
Reviewed by: L. Bonnerot in Etudes anglaises (entry 3608);
L. Lerner in Encounter (entry 4559); B. Miller in Twentieth Century
(entry 3569); New Statesman and Nation (entry 3571); and Times Literary Supplement (entry 3577).

Dissertations

3552 Green, Joyce M. The Development of the Poetic Imagination
in Tennyson: With Particular Reference to the Juvenilia and
to the Influence of Arthur Hallam. Cambridge, 1954.

3553 Jähne, Anne-Marthe. Tennyson in Deutschland: Die Aufnahme
seiner Werke und die Kritik an seinen Dichtungen und an seiner Persönlichkeit. Marburg, 1954.

3554 Kaufman, Marjorie Ruth. Henry James's Comic Discipline:
The Use of the Comic Structure of His Early Fiction. Minne-
sota, 1954. Dissertation Abstracts, 15 (1955), 2534.
Discusses Tennyson's influence on James.

3555 Langbaum, Robert. The Dramatic Monologue and the Poetry
of Experience: A Study in Dramatic Form. Columbia, 1954.

3556 Wood, Willson E. Alfred Tennyson and His Riddle of the Universe. George Peabody, 1954.

Periodicals

3557   Beach, Joseph Warren.   Modern Language Notes, 69 (1954),
          206-209.
          Review of E. D. H. Johnson's The Alien Vision, 1952 (entry
3495).

3558   Bergman, Herbert.   "Whitman and Tennyson."   Studies in Phi-
          lology, 51 (1954), 492-504.
          The relationship of the two poets.

3559   Bevington, Merle.   South Atlantic Quarterly, 53 (1954), 154-
          155.
          Review of E. D. H. Johnson's The Alien Vision, 1952 (entry
3495).

3560   Booth, Bradford A.   Modern Language Notes, 69 (1954), 203-
          205.
          Review of E. F. Shannon's Tennyson and the Reviewers, 1952
(entry 3496).

3561   Buckler, William E.   "Tennyson's Lucretius Bowdlerized?"
          Review of English Studies, n. s. 5 (July 1954), 269-271.
          Buckler discusses Macmillan's Magazine's omission of lines
188-191 of "Lucretius" when the poem appeared in the May 1868 issue of the magazine.   A letter from David Masson to Alexander Macmillan indicates that the lines were omitted for critical reasons as
well as moral ones.

3562   Chiasson, E. J.   "Tennyson's 'Ulysses'--a Re-interpretation."
          University of Toronto Quarterly, 23 (July 1954), 402-409.
          Reprinted: J. Killham, ed., Critical Essays, 1960 (entry
3697), pp. 164-173.
          Chiasson says "Ulysses" should "be read as the dramatic pre-
sentation of a man who has faith neither in the gods nor consequently
in the necessity of preserving order in his kingdom or in his own
life."

3563   Davis, Arthur Kyle, Jr.   Virginia Quarterly Review, 30 (1954),
          155-160.
          Review of E. D. H. Johnson's The Alien Vision, 1952 (entry
3495).

3564   Eidson, John Olin.   "Charles Stearns Wheeler: Emerson's
          'Good Grecian.'"   New England Quarterly, 27 (1954), 472-
          483.
          Wheeler acted as Tennyson's literary agent in America.

3565   Haddakin, Lilian.   Modern Language Review, 49 (1954), 544-
          545.
          Review of E. D. H. Johnson's The Alien Vision, 1952 (entry
3495).

3566 Holloway, J. Review of English Studies, n.s. 5 (1954), 320-322.
Review of E. F. Shannon's Tennyson and the Reviewers, 1952 (entry 3496).

3567 Jump, J.D. Review of English Studies, n.s. 5 (1954), 98-100.
Review of E. D. H. Johnson's The Alien Vision, 1952 (entry 3495).

3568 Miller, Betty. "Somersby and Background: A Fragment."
Cornhill Magazine, 167 (1954), 361-366.

3569 _____. Twentieth Century, 155 (1954), 473-474.
Review of C. Tennyson's Six Tennyson Essays, 1954 (entry 3551).

3570 Millhauser, Milton. "Tennyson's Princess and Vestiges."
PMLA, 69 (March 1954), 337-343.
Millhauser asserts that Robert Chambers's Vestiges of the Natural History of Creation "was a precipitant but not a determinant of Tennyson's thought." Tennyson assimilated Chambers's "central doctrine" "into the broad, undoctrinal Christianity of his middle and later years."

3571 New Statesman and Nation, 47 (May 22, 1954), 677-678.
Review of C. Tennyson's Six Tennyson Essays, 1954 (entry 3551).

3572 Perrine, Laurence. "Tennyson's In Memoriam." Explicator, 12 (1954), Item 29.

3573 R., V., and J.C. Maxwell. "Virgil and Tennyson." Notes and Queries, n.s. 1 (1954), 449 and 546.
Suggests Virgil as source for "He clasps the crag with crooked hands."

3574 Rudman, Harry W. "Keats and Tennyson on 'Nature, Red in Tooth and Claw." Notes and Queries, n.s. 1 (1954), 293-294.
A comparison.

3575 Stange, G. Robert. "Tennyson's Mythology: A Study of Demeter and Persephone." Journal of English Literary History, 21 (March 1954), 67-80.
Reprinted: J. Killham, ed., Critical Essays, 1960 (entry 3697), pp. 137-150.
Stange declares: "Whatever may be the flaws of Demeter and Persephone, they are not of the sort one finds in minor poetry. The poet may not have entirely succeeded in making his myth bear the modern implication, but of the creative energy and poetic skill he brought to his task there can be no doubt." Stange provides a sophisticated and well written discussion of Tennyson's use and reinterpretation of the classical myth.

3576 Templeman, William D. Personalist, 25 (1954), 201-202.
     Review of E. D. H. Johnson's The Alien Vision, 1952 (entry
3495).

3577 Times Literary Supplement, June 4, 1954, p. 358.
     Review of C. Tennyson's Six Tennyson Essays, 1954 (entry
3551).

1955

Books

3578 Groom, Bernard. The Diction of Poetry from Spenser to
     Bridges. Toronto: U. of Toronto P., 1955.
     See also: B. Groom, On the Diction of Tennyson, Browning,
and Arnold, 1939 (entry 3274).

3579 House, Humphrey. "Tennyson and the Spirit of the Age" and
     "Poetry and Philosophy in In Memoriam." All in Due Time.
     London: Rupert Hart-Davis, 1955, pp. 121-129 and 130-139.
     "Poetry and Philosophy of In Memoriam" reprinted: J. D.
Hunt, ed., Tennyson: In Memoriam, 1970 (entry 4214), pp. 166-
175.

3580 Pearce, Helen. "Homage to Arthur Henry Hallam." The Im-
     age of the Work. Berkeley: U. of California P., 1955, pp.
     113-133.
     About Hallam's essay on poetry and Tennyson's work in the
Englishman's Magazine of Aug. 1831.

Dissertations

3581 Adams, Norman Owens Whitehurst, Jr. Byron and the Early
     Victorians: A Study of His Poetic Influence (1842-1855). Wis-
     consin, 1955. Dissertation Abstracts, 16 (1956), 336-337.
     Tennyson was influenced by Byron, according to Adams.

3582 Daniel, Maggie Browne. A Study of William Dean Howell's Atti-
     tude toward and Criticism of the English and Their Literature.
     Wisconsin, 1955 (?). Summary of Doctoral Dissertations,
     University of Wisconsin, 15 (1955), 603-604.
     Includes Tennyson.

3583 Hübel, Eleanora. König Arthur und seine Tafelrunde bei Al-
     fred Tennyson und E. A. Robinson: ein Vergleich. Vienna,
     1955.

3584 Marshall, George O., Jr. Alfred Tennyson: A Critical Hand-
     book. Texas, 1955.

3585 Semmelmeyer, Ingeborg. Der klassische Hintergrund in Ten-
     nysons Dichtung. Vienna, 1955.

Periodicals

3586 Allott, Miriam. "James Russell Lowell: A Link between Tennyson and Henry James." Review of English Studies, n.s. 6 (1955), 399-401.
Lowell's influence.

3587 _____. "'The Lord of Burleigh' and Henry James's 'A Landscape Painter.'" Notes and Queries, n.s. 2 (1955), 220-221.
Tennyson as source for a story by James.

3588 Burchell, Samuel C. "Tennyson's Dark Night." South Atlantic Quarterly, 54 (Jan. 1955), 75-81.
Burchell discusses the historical significance of In Memoriam.

3589 Crossett, John. "Tennyson and Catullus." Classical Journal, 50 (1955), 313-314.

3590 Dahl, Curtis. "The Victorian Wasteland." College English, 16 (1955), 341-347.
Imagery in Tennyson and others.

3591 Engelberg, Edward. "The Beast Image in Tennyson's Idylls of the King." Journal of English Literary History, 22 (1955), 287-292.
The beast imagery enhances the unity and theme of Idylls of the King.

3592 Healy, Emma Therese. "Virgil and Tennyson." Kentucky Foreign Language Quarterly, 2 (1955), 20-25.

3593 Lerner, Laurence D. "In Memoriam 1955." Essays in Criticism, 5 (1955), 152.
Tennyson's language.

3594 Miller, Betty. "Tennyson and the Sinful Queen." Twentieth Century, 158 (Oct. 1955), 355-363.
Responded to by J. Killham in Notes and Queries, 1958 (entry 3655).
Miller employs psychoanalytic criticism to examine Tennyson's reasons for blaming King Arthur's fall on the sinful queen. This controversial essay seems more provocative than informative.

3595 Munsterberg, Margaret. "Letters from Lady Tennyson." Boston Public Library Quarterly, 7 (1955), 175-191.
The library acquires eighty letters by Emily, Lady Tennyson to Mr. and Mrs. Gatty, 1858-1873.

3596 Pierce, Anne Longfellow. "A Visit to Farringford." Boston University Studies in English, 1 (1955), 96-98.

3597 Sanders, Charles Richard. "Carlyle's Letters." Bulletin of

the John Rylands Library, 38 (1955), 199-224.
Mentions Tennyson.

3598 T., G. "Tennyson and 'The Revenge.'" Notes and Queries,
n.s. 2 (1955), 152.
Suggests a source.

3599 Tennyson, Alfred, Lord. "The Christ of Ammergau." Twentieth Century, 157 (Jan. 1955), 2-3.
Found among the papers of Tennyson's friend James Knowles,
this poem was composed in 1870.

1956

Books

3600 Baum, Paull Franklin. "Alfred Lord Tennyson." The Victor-
ian Poets: A Guide to Research. Ed. Frederic E. Faverty.
Cambridge: Harvard U.P., 1956.
Baum provides a useful but sketchy survey of studies of Ten-
nyson to the early 1950s. Most helpful is its section on criticism,
"Critical Studies," pp. 36-56.

3601 de Selincourt, Aubrey. "Alfred, Lord Tennyson." Six Great
Poets: Chaucer, Pope, Wordsworth, Shelley, Tennyson, the
Brownings. London: Hamilton, 1956.

3602 Nicolson, Harold. The English Sense of Humor, and Other
Essays. London: Constable, 1956. Reprinted: New York:
Funk and Wagnalls, 1968.
Discusses Tennyson's brothers.

3603 Roppen, Georg. "Evolution in the Platonic Tradition." Evolu-
tion and Poetic Belief: A Study in Some Victorian and Modern
Writers. Oslo: Oslo U.P., 1956.
Tennyson and others were more neo-Lamarcian than Darwinian.

3604 Willey, Basil. "Tennyson." More Nineteenth-Century Studies:
A Group of Honest Doubters. London: Chatto and Windus,
1956.
Willey discusses Tennyson's poetry through In Memoriam. He
considers Tennyson to be an honest doubter.

Periodicals

3605 Allott, Kenneth. "An Arnold-Clough Letter: References to
Carlyle and Tennyson." Notes and Queries, n.s. 3 (1956),
267.

3606 Barker, George. "The Face Behind the Poem: An Essay in
Honour of Tennyson." Encounter, 6 (May 1956), 69-72.

3607   Beck, Warren. "Clouds upon Camelot." English Journal, 45
        (1956), 447-454 and 503.
        A survey of the reputation of Idylls of the King with a com-
ment on its unsuitability for schoolroom use.

3608   Bonnerot, L. Etudes anglaises, 9 (1956), 66-68.
        Review of E. F. Shannon's Tennyson and the Reviewers, 1952
(entry 3496) and C. Tennyson's Six Tennyson Essays, 1954 (entry
3551).

3609   Eidson, John Olin. "The Reception of Tennyson's Plays in
        America." Philological Quarterly, 35 (Oct. 1956), 435-443.
        See also: J.O. Eidson, "Tennyson's Minor Plays in America"
in American Notes and Queries, 1965 (entry 3919).
        Eidson surveys American critical response to Tennyson's dra-
mas and regards them as contributing to the decline of the poet's
American reputation.

3610   Esher, Viscount. "Tennyson's Influence on his Times." Es-
        says by Divers Hands: Being the Transactions of the Royal
        Society of Literature, n.s. 28 (1954; published by Oxford U.
        P. in 1956), 35-47.

3611   Gordan, John D. "What's in a Name? Authors and Their
        Pseudonyms." Bulletin of the New York Public Library, 60
        (1956), 107-128.
        Includes the Tennysons.

3612   Greenberg, Robert A. "A Possible Source of Tennyson's
        'Tooth and Claw.'" Modern Language Notes, 71 (1956), 491-
        492.
        Greenberg suggests that Carlyle's Past and Present may have
inspired the image in In Memoriam.

3613   "Harvard Buys Tennyson Manuscripts." Library Journal, 81
        (1956), 888-889.
        The Houghton Library acquires three hundred fifty drafts of
Tennyson's poems.

3614   Hendrick, George. "Enoch Arden in Texas: A Critical Rhap-
        sody." Library Chronicle of University of Texas, 5, no. 4
        (1956), 26-31.
        An 1871 criticism.

3615   Krause, Anna. "Unamuno and Tennyson." Comparative Lit-
        erature, 8 (April 1956), 122-135.
        Krause discusses what the two poets have in common.

3616   Millhauser, Milton. "Tennyson: Artifice and Image." Journal
        of Aesthetics and Art Criticism, 14 (1956), 333-338.
        Tennyson's imagery becomes insincere as he matures.

3617   Shannon, Edgar F., Jr., and W. H. Bond. "Literary Manu-

scripts of Alfred Tennyson in the Harvard College Library."
Harvard Library Bulletin, 10 (Spring 1956), 254-274.
Survey of the collections of Tennysoniana in England and
America.

3618   Sharrock, Roger. "A Reminiscence of In Memoriam in David
       Copperfield." Notes and Queries, n.s. 3 (1956), 502.

3619   Turner, Paul. English Studies, 37 (1956), 32-35.
       Review of E. D. H. Johnson's The Alien Vision, 1952 (entry
3495).

3620   Willard, Charles B. "The Saunders Collection of Whitmania
       in the Brown University Library." Books at Brown, 18, no.
       1 (1956), 14-22.

1957

Books

3621   Fairchild, Hoxie Neale. Religious Trends in English Poetry.
       Volume IV: 1830-1880: Christianity and Romanticism in the
       Victorian Era. New York: Columbia U.P., 1957.
       In her controversial assessment of Tennyson, Fairchild de-
clares that Tennyson "was not a mystic but an emotional pragmatist."

3622   Langbaum, Robert. The Poetry of Experience: The Dramatic
       Monologue in Modern Literary Tradition. London: Chatto and
       Windus, 1957. New York: Random House, 1957.
       Includes interesting comments on Tennyson.

3623   Lewis, Naomi. A Visit to Mrs. Wilcox. London: Cresset,
       1957.

3624   Lucas, F. L. Tennyson. London and New York: Longmans,
       Green, 1957. (Writers and Their Work, 83)
       A forty-page critical biography. Reviewed by: B. Miller in
Twentieth Century (entry 3634); and J. Vallette in Mercure de France
(entry 3640).

3625   Tennyson, Charles. Stars and Markets. London: Chatto and
       Windus, 1957.
       Includes memoirs of Charles Tennyson's grandfather, Alfred.

3626   Wain, John. "A Stranger and Afraid: Notes on Four Victorian
       Poets." Preliminary Essays. London: Macmillan, 1957.
       New York: St. Martin's, 1957 pp. 93-120.

Dissertations

3627   Kissane, James D. The Poetry of Tennyson in Relation to
       Nineteenth-Century Attitudes toward Mythology. Johns Hopkins,
       1957.

3628　Ryals, Clyde de L.　Decadence in British Literature before
the Fin de Siècle.　Pennsylvania, 1957.　Dissertation Abstracts, 17 (1957), 3004.
Chapter 3 discusses Tennyson's poetry through Poems, 1842.
Ryals contends that Tennyson did not understand romantic decadence
even though he was attracted to the poetry of Keats.

3629　Siegenthaler, Walter.　Zum Problem der Anordnung in den
Gedichtsammlungen von Wordsworth und Tennyson.　Bern,
1957.

Periodicals

3629a Fall, Christine.　"An Index of the Letters from Papers of
Frederick Tennyson."　University of Texas Studies in English,
36 (1957), 155-163.

3630　Gordan, John D.　"New in the Berg Collection: 1952-1956."
Bulletin of the New York Public Library, 61 (1957), 303-311
and 353-363.
Includes Tennyson.

3631　Huffman, Clarence.　"The Comrade of my Choice."　Personalist, 38 (1957), 372-375.
Tennyson and Hallam.

3632　Johnson, W. Stacy.　"The Theme of Marriage in Tennyson."
Victorian News Letter, no. 12 (Autumn 1957), 6-8.
According to Johnson: "It is evident that marriage, in Tenny-
son, represents a whole life for man, the basis for a whole society.
True marriage, for him, means a balancing of aggression and pas-
sivity, of physical force and spiritual integrity."

3633　Marshall, George O., Jr.　"Ghost Books."　Notes and Queries,
4 (1957), 154-155.
Corrects a mistaken listing of "Ince" for "Luce" in the CBEL.

3634　Miller, Betty.　Twentieth Century, 161 (1957), 592-594.
Review of F. L. Lucas's Tennyson, 1957 (entry 3624).

3635　Robson, W.W.　"The Dilemma of Tennyson."　Listener, 57
(June 13, 1957), 963-965.
Reprinted: J. Killham, ed., Critical Essays, 1960 (entry
3697), pp. 155-163.
This strongly negative view of Tennyson's poetry includes a
powerful assault on "Locksley Hall Sixty Years After," in particular.

3636　Sanders, Charles Richard.　"Tennyson and the Human Hand."
Victorian News Letter, no. 11 (Spring 1957), 5-14.
An analysis of how Tennyson uses the human hand as a symbol.

3637　Shannon, Edgar F., Jr.　"Alfred Tennyson."　Victorian News
Letter, no. 12 (Autumn 1957), 26-27.
A survey of research materials.

3638 Tennyson, Charles. "The Idylls of the King." Twentieth Century, 161 (March 1957), 277-286.
See also: entry 3639, below. Describes the composition of Idylls of the King.

3639 _____. "Letter from Sir Charles Tennyson." Twentieth Century, 161 (April 1957), 393.
See: entry 3638, above. More on Idylls of the King.

3640 Vallette, Jacques. Mercure de France, 333 (1957), 163.
Review of F. L. Lucas's Tennyson, 1957 (entry 3624).

1958

Books

3641 Buckley, Jerome H. (ed.) "Introduction." Poems of Tennyson. Boston: Houghton Mifflin, 1958. (Riverside Editions)
Buckley remarks about Tennyson: "His poetry deals typically not with the great action seen as an object in itself but with the search through situation and symbol for meaning and the sudden illuminating discovery of purpose. Any reasonably full selection of his verse should indicate his awareness of themes and issues still significant to the modern reader: the moral implications of an amoral science, the need for faith and the necessity of doubt, the isolation of the individual and the extent to which the self must find fulfilment.' This book is excellent for classroom use.

3642 Foakes, Reginald Anthony. "The Rhetoric of Faith." The Romantic Assertion: A Study in the Language of Nineteenth Century Poetry. New Haven: Yale U. P., 1958, pp. 111-138.
An interesting study of imagery that is particularly valuable for its illumination of passages in In Memoriam.

3643 Killham, John. Tennyson and The Princess: Reflections of an Age. London: Athlone (U. of London), 1958.
Killham provides an interesting study of The Princess and those aspects of the Victorian era that the poem responds to. This is a standard reference for the study of The Princess.
Reviewed by: K. Allott in Review of English Studies, (entry 3700); F. Basch in Etudes anglaises, (entry 3703); J. H. Buckley in Journal of English and Germanic Philology (entry 3705); D. Bush in Modern Language Review (entry 3667); B. Miller in Twentieth Century (entry 3678); E. D. Pendry in Studia Neophilologica (entry 3712); and Times Literary Supplement (entry 3661).

3644 Mayhead, Robin. "The Poetry of Tennyson." From Dickens to Hardy. Ed. Boris Ford. Volume VI of Pelican Guide to English Literature. Harmondsworth: Penguin, 1958, pp. 227-244.
A very negative view of the poetry.

3645 Millhauser, Milton. Just Before Darwin. Middletown, Connecticut: Wesleyan U.P., 1958.

Dissertation

3646 McCall, Joseph Darryl, Jr. Factors Affecting the Literary Canon. Florida, 1958. Dissertation Abstracts, 19 (1959), 1744.
  Discussing the career of Tennyson among others, McCall examines how books become classics.

Periodicals

3647 Assad, Thomas J. "Analogy in Tennyson's 'Crossing the Bar.'" Tulane Studies in English, 8 (1958), 153-164.
  A sensible interpretation of value.

3648 B., A.C. "Extant Copies of Tennyson's Timbuctoo." Book Collector, 7 (1958), 296.
  Identifies six extant copies of the pamphlet version.

3649 Barksdale, Richard K. "Arnold and Tennyson on Etna." College Language Association Journal, 2 (1958), 87-103.

3650 Dahl, Curtis. "A Double Frame for Tennyson's Demeter?" Victorian Studies, 1 (June 1958), 356-362.
  Tennyson's "Demeter and Persephone" is "a perhaps unconscious reply to Swinburne's 'Hymn to Proserpine'" as well as a poem intended to teach Christian virtues.

3651 Elliott, Philip L., Jr. "Another Manuscript Version of 'To the Queen.'" Notes and Queries, n.s. 5 (1958), 82-83.

3652 Gibson, Walker. "Behind the Veil: A Distinction Between Poetic and Scientific Language in Tennyson, Lyell, and Darwin." Victorian Studies, 2 (Sept. 1958), 60-68.
  Reprinted: J.D. Hunt, ed., Tennyson: In Memoriam, 1970 (entry 4214), pp. 176-187.
  Gibson remarks: "I submit, then, that Tennyson's 'poetic imagination' can sometimes be examined in terms of his grammar." Tennyson, Lyell, and Darwin were interested in evolution but viewed it in different ways. Tennyson's imagination enabled him to experience the process of evolution.

3653 Gullason, Thomas Arthur. "Tennyson's Influence on Stephen Crane." Notes and Queries, n.s. 5 (1958), 164-165.
  "The Charge of the Light Brigade" and Crane's response.

3654 Johnson, E.D.H. "In Memoriam: The Way of the Poet." Victorian Studies, 2 (Dec. 1958), 139-148.
  Reprinted: J.D. Hunt, ed., Tennyson: In Memoriam, 1970 (entry 4214), pp. 188-199.
  Johnson remarks: "The tendency to regard In Memoriam ex-

clusively as a spiritual autobiography has obscured the importance of
this work as a record of Tennyson's artistic development during the
formative years between 1833 and 1850." He also asserts: "In Memoriam, as a poem of spiritual quest, represents the Way of the
Soul. It is not less surely a poem of aesthetic quest, which sets
forth the Way of the Poet." In Memoriam illustrates the development
of Tennyson's poetic theories.

3655 Killham, John. "Tennyson and the Sinful Queen--A Corrected
      Impression." Notes and Queries, n.s. 5 (1958), 507-511.
      This article replies to B. Miller's "Tennyson and the Sinful
Queen" in Twentieth Century, 1955 (entry 3594).

3656 Korg, Jacob. "The Pattern of Fatality in Tennyson's Poetry."
      Victorian News Letter, no. 14 (Fall 1958), 8-11.
      Korg notes that "Tennyson could not rid himself of the profound conviction that somehow ill would be the final goal of good"
and that Tennyson's poems "fall into a pattern of sudden and disastrous change."

3657 Lewis, Naomi. "Whose Arthur?" New Statesman, 56 (July
      12, 1958), 50-51.
      Comments on Tennyson while reviewing The Once and Future
King by T.H. White.

3658 MacEachen, Dougald B. "Tennyson and the Sonnet." Victorian
      News Letter, no. 14 (Fall 1958), 1-8.
      Tennyson was less than good at writing sonnets.

3659 Miller, Betty. "Camelot at Cambridge." Twentieth Century,
      163 (1958), 133-147.
      Miller presents the notion that the Cambridge Apostles were
a model for the order of the Round Table.

3660 Preyer, Robert. "Tennyson as an Oracular Poet." Modern
      Philology, 55 (May 1958), 239-251.
      Focusing on Tennyson's early poems, Preyer discusses their
"visionary mode."

3661 Times Literary Supplement, Dec. 5, 1958, p. 699.
      Review of J. Killham's Tennyson and The Princess, 1958
(entry 3643).

1959

Books

3662 Madden, William A. "The Burden of the Artist." 1859: Entering an Age of Crisis. Ed. Philip Appleman, William A.
      Madden, and Michael Wolff. Bloomington: Indiana U.P., 1959.
      Includes discussion of the first four Idylls as responses to The
Origin of Species.

3663 Todd, William B. "A Handlist of Thomas J. Wise." Thomas
J. Wise: Centenary Studies. Ed. William B. Todd. Austin:
U. of Texas P., 1959, pp. 80-122.
Todd updates the record of Wise's forgeries.

Dissertations

3664 Brashear, William R. The Concept of the "Living Will" as
an Interpretive Key to Tennyson's Poetry. Princeton, 1959.
Dissertation Abstracts, 20 (1960), 4652.
Brashear illuminates Tennyson's powers of thought by examining the poet from the point of view of nineteenth-century "subjectivism."

3665 Henderson, Stephen Evangelist. A Study of Visualized Detail
in the Poetry of Tennyson, Rossetti and Morris. Wisconsin,
1959. Dissertation Abstracts, 20 (1959), 1015.
Henderson discusses the imagery of the poets and compares
them.

Periodicals

3666 Bevington, Merle M. "Tennyson and Sir James Stephen on
'The Last Great Englishman.'" Notes and Queries, n.s. 6
(1959), 445-446.
The Duke of Wellington similarly described by Tennyson and
Stephen.

3667 Bush, Douglas. Modern Language Review, 54 (1959), 422-423.
Review of J. Killham's Tennyson and The Princess, 1958 (entry 3643).

3668 Duncan, Edgar Hill. "Tennyson: A Modern Appraisal." Tennessee Studies in Literature, 4 (1959), 13-30.
Duncan first surveys critical reactions to Tennyson and then
presents a thoughtful discussion of "Ulysses" as a personal allegory.

3669 Elliott, Philip L., Jr. "Tennyson's 'To Virgil.'" Notes and
Queries, n.s. 6 (1959), 147-148.
The poem in Italy.

3670 Forker, Charles R. "Tennyson's 'Tithonus' and Marston's
Antonio's Revenge." Notes and Queries, n.s. 6 (1959), 445.

3671 Gossman, Ann, and George W. Whiting. "King Arthur's Farewell to Guinevere." Notes and Queries, n.s. 6 (1959), 446-
448.

3672 Hartman, Joan E. "The Manuscripts of Tennyson's 'Gareth
and Lynette.'" Harvard Library Bulletin, 13 (Spring 1959),
239-264.
Hartman provides an informative discussion of the development
of "Gareth and Lynette" in the manuscripts of the poem in the Har-

vard College Library. She provides insight into Tennyson's techniques of composition and style.

3673 Hess, M. Whitcomb. "Tennyson: 1809-1959." Contemporary
      Review, 196 (1959), 183-185.

3674 Jones, Howard Mumford. "The Generation of 1830." Harvard
      Library Bulletin, 13 (1959), 401-414.
      Jones compares Tennyson, Gladstone, Darwin, FitzGerald,
Poe, Holmes, and Lincoln, and he finds in their writings views in
common. Their stylistic similarities illuminate their age as well as
their works.

3675 Lawry, J. S. "Tennyson's 'The Epic': A Gesture of Recovered
      Faith." Modern Language Notes, 74 (1959), 400-403.
      Theme and narrative in "Morte d'Arthur."

3676 Marshall, George O., Jr. "An Incident from Carlyle in Ten-
      nyson's 'Maud.'" Notes and Queries, n. s. 6 (1959), 77-78.

3677 _____. "Textual Changes in a Presentation Copy of Tenny-
      son's Poems (1833)." Library Chronicle of the University of
      Texas, 6, no. 3 (1959), 16-19.

3678 Miller, Betty. Twentieth Century, 165 (1959), 192-193.
      Review of J. Killham's Tennyson and The Princess, 1958 (en-
try 3643).

3679 Millgate, Michael. "Tennyson: Poet and Laureate." Listener,
      57 (1959), 250-251.

3680 Roppen, Georg. "'Ulysses' and Tennyson's Sea Quest."
      English Studies, 40 (April 1959), 77-90.
      According to Roppen, one finds a "synthesis of the Chaotic
feelings of 'The Two Voices,' and integrates the two worlds which
Ulysses explores, that of heroic action and that of spiritual possibility."

3681 Rosenberg, John D. "The Two Kingdoms of In Memoriam."
      Journal of English and Germanic Philology, 58 (April 1959),
      228-240.
      Reprinted: J. D. Hunt, ed., Tennyson: In Memoriam, 1970
(entry 4214), pp. 200-215.
      Rosenberg asserts: "With the 'one far-off event' we confront
Tennyson's final effort at uniting evolutionary science and Christian
faith." Evolutionary science and Christian faith are the "Two Kingdoms."

3682 Ryals, Clyde de L. "The 'Fatal Woman' Symbol in Tennyson."
      PMLA, 74 (1959), 438-443.
      Influenced by Keats, Tennyson uses female figures to repre-
sent his personal conflict between his desire to indulge himself and
his desire to have moral purpose.

3683 _____. "The Nineteenth-Century Cult of Inaction." Tennessee Studies in Literature, 4 (1959), 51-60.
The artistic temperament's withdrawal from a pragmatic society.

3684 _____. "Tennyson's The Lotus-Eaters." Revue des Langues Vivantes, 25 (1959), 474-486.

3685 Shannon, Edgar F., Jr. "Alfred Tennyson's Admission to Cambridge." Times Literary Supplement, March 6, 1959, p. 136.
New information that reveals the date Tennyson entered Cambridge (November 1827) and aspects of his life.

3686 _____. "'Locksley Hall' and Ivanhoe." Notes and Queries, n.s. 6 (1959), 216-217.

3687 Smidt, Kristian. "The Intellectual Quest of the Victorian Poets." English Studies, 40 (1959), 90-102.
Smidt asserts that the Victorian poets' "intellectual dilemma was also an emotional one."

3688 Sonn, Carl Robinson. "Poetic Vision and Religious Certainty in Tennyson's Earlier Poetry." Modern Philology, 57 (1959), 83-93.
The religious and aesthetic impulses are united in Tennyson's poetry.

3689 Stevenson, Lionel. "1859: Year of Fulfillment." The Centennial Review, 3 (1959), 337-356.
Discusses Tennyson and others.

3690 Tener, Robert H. "Bagehot and Tennyson." Times Literary Supplement, Aug. 21, 1959, p. 483.
Shows that Walter Bagehot wrote the review of the Idylls of the King in the National Review, Oct. 1859 (entry 463).

3691 Tennyson, Charles. "Alfred Tennyson and Somersby." Tennyson Chronicle, 10 (Aug. 1959).
Of biographical interest.

3692 _____. "Tennyson's Conversation." Twentieth Century, 165 (1959), 34-44.
Based on family papers.

3693 Wilson, Charles. "Mirror of a Shire: Tennyson's Dialect Poems." Durham University Journal, 52 (1959), 22-28.
Wilson remarks: "Save for Chaucer, no one has portrayed bucolic life with technique so consummate or knowledge so intimate." A well written discussion of the poems and their background.

1960

Books

3694 Altick, Richard D., and William R. Matthews. Guide to Doctoral Dissertations in Victorian Literature 1886-1958. Urbana: U. of Illinois P., 1960.
Contains a useful but unreliable listing of Tennysonian dissertations.

3695 Blunden, Edmund (ed.). Introduction. Selected Poems of Tennyson. New York: Macmillan, 1960. London: Heinemann,
1960.
Reviewed by: L. Bonnerot in Etudes anglaises (entry 3809);
and W. D. Templeman in Personalist (entry 3793).

3696 Buckley, Jerome Hamilton. Tennyson: The Growth of a Poet.
Cambridge, Massachusetts: Harvard U. P., 1960. Boston:
Houghton Mifflin, 1965.
Chapter VI reprinted in part: J. D. Hunt, ed., Tennyson: In
Memoriam, 1970 (entry 4214), pp. 216-223.
This landmark study sets the tone and direction for much of
the Tennysonian scholarship of the 1960s and 1970s. Buckley lays
aside the notion of Tennyson as a divided poet and personality and
focuses on those characteristics that unify his work and life. Although sketchy in places, Buckley's Tennyson presents one of the major arguments for the poet's greatness. When concluding, Buckley
writes: "Laureate for nearly half a century to one of the world's
great ages, Tennyson commanded such public attention as no English
writer before or since has known. Sensitive to the moral and spiritual confusions of his time, familiar with the new sciences, aware
of imminent social change and crisis, he was the voice and sometimes indeed the conscience of Victorian culture; and his work will
endure, even apart from its aesthetic worth, as a mirror of his civilization. Yet the distinction that his critics have repeatedly drawn
between the bard of public sentiments and the earlier poet of private
sensibilities is ultimately untenable. For there was no real break
in Tennyson's career; from the beginning he felt some responsibility
to the society he lived in, and until the end he remained obedient to
the one clear call of his own imagination." This book is a standard
reference.
Reviewed by: P. F. Baum in South Atlantic Quarterly (entry
3728); De L. Ferguson in New York Herald Tribune Book Review
(entry 3732); D. J. Gray in Victorian Studies (entry 3733); G. Hough
in Listener (entry 3735); E. D. H. Johnson in Modern Philology (entry
3736); T. H. Johnson in Saturday Review (entry 3737); J. Killham in
Modern Language Review (entry 3772); R. W. King in Review of English Studies (entry 3773); G. D. Klingopoulos in Spectator (entry 3739);
R. D. McMaster in Dalhousie Review (entry 3741); F. E. L. Priestly
in University of Toronto Quarterly (entry 3780); G. N. Ray in New
York Times Book Review (entry 3746); T. Rogers in English (entry
3786); M. Ross in Queen's Quarterly (entry 3747); D. Smalley in
Journal of English and Germanic Philology (entry 3791); Times Lit-

erary Supplement (entry 3749); J.R. Willingham in Library Journal (entry 3721); and C.R. Woodring in Virginia Quarterly Review (entry 3750).

3697 Killham, John, ed. Critical Essays on the Poetry of Tennyson. London: Routledge and Kegan Paul, 1960. New York: Barnes and Noble, 1960.
Killham gathers previously published essays and provides a useful introduction and an essay of his own. The essays are representative of critical thought of the preceding three decades or so, and the book is a handy reference that is frequently used by both professional scholars and students. This book is a standard reference.
Reviewed by: F.W. Bateson in Spectator (entry 3704); D.J. Gray in Victorian Studies (entry 3733); J. Jones in New Statesman (entry 3708); R.D. McMaster in Dalhousie Review (entry 3741); Times Literary Supplement (entry 3718); and J. Vallette in Mercure de France (entry 3720).

3698 _____. "Tennyson's Maud: The Function of the Imagery." Critical Essays on the Poetry of Tennyson. Ed. John Killham. London: Routledge and Kegan Paul, 1960. New York: Barnes and Noble, 1960, pp. 219-235.
According to Killham, Maud is a composite of images of the human experience.

3699 McLuhan, H.M. "Tennyson and the Romantic Epic." Critical Essays on the Poetry of Tennyson. Ed. John Killham. London: Routledge and Kegan Paul, 1960. New York: Barnes and Noble, 1960, pp. 86-95.
McLuhan tries to show the influence of Theocritus and the Alexandrian poets on Tennyson's poetry.

Periodicals

3700 Allott, Kenneth. Review of English Studies, n.s. 11 (1960), 225-226.
Review of J. Killham's Tennyson and The Princess, 1958 (entry 3643).

3701 Altick, Richard. "Four Victorian Poets and an Exploding Island." Victorian Studies, 3, no. 3 (1960), 249-260.
The reactions of Tennyson, Swinburne, Hopkins, and Bridges to the August 1883 eruption of Krakatoa.

3702 B., C. "Tennyson in Lincolnshire." English, 13 (1960), 22.
The sesquicentennial of Tennyson's birth celebrated.

3703 Basch, F. Etudes anglaises, 8 (1960), 479-480.
Review of J. Killham's Tennyson and The Princess, 1958 (entry 3643).

3704 Bateson, F.W. Spectator, 204 (Jan. 29, 1960), 141.
Review of J. Killham, ed., Critical Essays, 1960 (entry 3697).

3705 Buckley, Jerome H. Journal of English and Germanic Philology, 59 (1960), 164-165.
Review of J. Killham's Tennyson and The Princess, 1958 (entry 3643).

3706 Cameron, Kenneth Walter. "Tennyson to Edward Campbell
Tainsh in 1868." Emerson Society Quarterly, no. 19 (1960),
29-35.

3707 Green, David Bonnell. "Leigh Hunt's Hand in Samuel Carter
Hall's Book of Gems." Keats-Shelley Journal, 8 (1960), 103-
117.
Hunt and Tennyson.

3708 Jones, John. New Statesman, 59 (1960), 196-197.
Review of J. Killham, ed., Critical Essays, 1960 (entry 3697).

3709 Miller, Betty. "Tennyson: The Early Years." Twentieth
Century, 167 (June 1960), 520-529.

3710 Nowell-Smith, Simon. "Tennyson's In Memoriam 1850."
Book Collector, 9 (1960), 76-77.
Nowell-Smith discusses variants in editions.

3711 P., L. "Tennyson's 'The Palace of Art.'" Explicator, 18
(1960), Query 2.

3712 Pendry, E.D. Studia Neophilologica, 21 (1960), 251-255.
Review of J. Killham's Tennyson and The Princess, 1958 (entry 3643).

3713 Richardson, Joanna. "Tennyson in Lincolnshire." Listener,
64 (1960), 796.

3714 Rogers, E.G. "Birdlore in the Poetry of Tennyson." Southern
Folklore Quarterly, 24 (1960), 157-163.

3715 Schweik, Robert C. "The 'Peace or War' Passages in Tennyson's Maud." Notes and Queries, n.s. 7 (1960), 457-458.
The November 1854 issue of Blackwood's Edinburgh Magazine
as a source for the passages.

3716 Shannon, Edgar F., Jr. "The History of a Poem: Tennyson's
Ode on the Death of the Duke of Wellington." Studies in Bibliography, 13 (1960), 149-177.
Shannon presents "an account of the composition, reception,
and revision of the poem and an appendix of variorum readings."

3717 Super, R.H. "Matthew Arnold and Tennyson." Times Literary
Supplement, Oct. 28, 1960, p. 693.
Founded on letters.

3718 Times Literary Supplement, March 11, 1960, p. 162.
Review of J. Killham, ed., Critical Essays, 1960 (entry 3697).

3719 Truss, Tom J., Jr. "Tennysonian Aspects of Maud." University of Mississippi Studies in English, 1 (1960), 105-117.
The aspects of Tennyson's work before Maud that are found in the poem.

3720 Vallette, Jacques. Mercure de France, 339 (1960), 342-344.
Review of J. Killham, ed., Critical Essays, 1960 (entry 3697).

3721 Willingham, J.R. Library Journal, 85 (1960), 4374.
Review of J.H. Buckley's Tennyson, 1960 (entry 3696).

1961

Books

3722 Carr, Arthur J. "Tennyson as a Modern Poet." Victorian Literature: Modern Essays in Criticism. Ed. Austin Wright. New York: Oxford U.P., 1961, pp. 311-333.
Reprinted from: University of Toronto Quarterly, 1950 (entry 3457). See entry 3457 for other reprintings and for annotation.

3723 Marshall, George O., Jr. "Tennyson's 'The Lotos-Eaters': An Essay Toward Appreciation." Creativity and the Arts. Ed. George O. Marshall, Jr. Athens, Georgia: U. of Georgia Center for Continuing Education, 1961, pp. 35-45.
A good, basic introduction to "The Lotos-Eaters."

3724 Wyllie, John Cook, ed. The Tennyson Collection Presented to the University of Virginia in Honor of Edgar Finley Shannon, Jr. Charlottesville: U. of Virginia P., 1961.
A catalogue. Noted by: Papers of the Bibliographical Society of America (entry 3744).

Dissertations

3725 Danzig, Allan Peter. Tennyson: The Endless Quest. Yale, 1961. Dissertation Abstracts, 26 (1965), 3331.
Danzig discusses Tennyson's "dialectic" in terms of the "contrary" and the "harmonization of the the contraries." "Lucretius" and Idylls of the King are prominently discussed.

3726 Smith, Elton Edward. "The Two Voices": A Tennyson Study. Syracuse, 1961. Dissertation Abstracts, 23 (1962), 239.
Published: 1964 (entry 3852).

Periodicals

3727 Barker, George. "The Face behind the Poem." Poetry, 97 (1961), 310-315.
Discusses Tennyson.

3728 Baum, Paull F. South Atlantic Quarterly, 60 (1961), 349.
Review of J.H. Buckley's Tennyson, 1960 (entry 3696).

3729   Britton, John. "Tennyson's 'The Palace of Art,' 1-16." Explicator, 20 (1961), Item 17.

3730   Collins, Rowland L. "Clara Tennyson-D'Eyncourt's Copy of Poems, Chiefly Lyrical: New Facts and New Queries." Notes and Queries, n. s. 8 (1961), 466-468.

3731   Daiches, David. "Imagery and Mood in Tennyson and Whitman." English Studies Today, 11 (1961), 217-232.

3732   Ferguson, De Lancey. New York Herald Tribune Book Review, Jan. 8, 1961, p. 32.
       Review of J. H. Buckley's Tennyson, 1960 (entry 3696).

3733   Gray, Donald J. Victorian Studies, 4 (March 1961), 274-276.
       Discusses recent Tennysoniana, including J. H. Buckley's Tennyson, 1960 (entry 3696) and J. Killham, ed., Critical Essays, 1960 (entry 3697).

3734   Halio, Jay L. "'Prothalamian,' 'Ulysses,' and Intention in Poetry." College English, 22 (1961), 390-394.
       Tennyson's point of view.

3735   Hough, Graham. Listener, June 1, 1961, p. 787.
       Review of J. H. Buckley's Tennyson, 1960 (entry 3696).

3736   Johnson, E. D. H. Modern Philology, 59 (1961), 143-144.
       Review of J. H. Buckley's Tennyson, 1960 (entry 3696).

3737   Johnson, T. H. Saturday Review, 44 (Jan. 28, 1961), 23.
       Review of J. H. Buckley's Tennyson, 1960 (entry 3696).

3738   Kendall, J. L. "A Neglected Theme in Tennyson's In Memoriam." Modern Language Notes, 76 (May 1961), 414-420.
       The theme is failure and defeat.

3739   Klingopoulos, G. D. Spectator, 206 (April 21, 1961), 567-568.
       Review of J. H. Buckley's Tennyson, 1960 (entry 3696).

3740   MacLaren, Malcolm. "Tennyson's Epicurean Lotos-Eaters." Classical Journal, 56 (March 1961), 259-267.
       MacLaren examines the Epicurean aspects of "The Lotos-Eaters." He reveals some of the philosopic substance of the poem.

3741   McMaster, R. D. Dalhousie Review, 40 (1961), 400-402.
       Review of J. H. Buckley's Tennyson, 1960 (entry 3696) and J. Killham, ed., Critical Essays, 1960 (entry 3697).

3742   Marshall, George O., Jr. "Tennyson's 'The Poet': Misseeing Shelley Plain." Philological Quarterly, 40 (Jan. 1961), 156-157.
       Establishes that Shelley's Defense of Poetry was published after "The Poet" was composed.

3743 Paden, W. D. "Twenty New Poems Attributed to Tennyson, Praed, and Landor." Victorian Studies, 4, nos. 3 and 4 (1961), 195-218 and 291-314.
Reprints poems by Tennyson from the Athenaeum, 1828-1829.

3744 Papers of the Bibliographical Society of America, 55 (1961), 409.
Note of J. C. Wyllie, ed., The Tennyson Collection Presented to the University of Virginia, 1961 (entry 3724).

3745 Rand, George I. "Tennyson's Gift to Walt Whitman--A New Letter." Emerson Society Quarterly, no. 24 (1961), 106-109.

3746 Ray, Gordon N. New York Times Book Review, Jan. 1, 1961, p. 5.
Review of J. H. Buckley's Tennyson, 1960 (entry 3696).

3747 Ross, Malcolm. Queen's Quarterly, 68 (1961), 516-517.
Review of J. H. Buckley's Tennyson, 1960 (entry 3696).

3748 Sanders, Charles Richard. "Carlyle and Tennyson." PMLA, 76 (March 1961), 82-97.
A thorough account of the relationship between Carlyle and Tennyson.

3749 Times Literary Supplement, Aug. 11, 1961, p. 535.
Review of J. H. Buckley's Tennyson, 1960 (entry 3696).

3750 Woodring, Carl R. Virginia Quarterly Review, 37 (1961), 157-160.
Review of J. H. Buckley's Tennyson, 1960 (entry 3696).

1962

Books

3751 Benziger, James. "Tennyson." Images of Eternity: Studies in the Poetry of Religious Vision from Wordsworth to T. S. Eliot. Carbondale: U. of Southern Illinois P., 1962, pp. 138-163.
Tennyson's weaknesses and beliefs are examined.

3752 Berry, Francis. "The Voice of Tennyson." Poetry and the Physical Voice. New York: Oxford U. P., 1962.
Berry explores the limitations Tennyson's voice creates for the poetry.

3753 Bose, Amalendu. Chroniclers of Life. Bombay: Longmans, 1962.
Discusses In Memoriam.

3754 DeMott, Benjamin. "The General, the Poet, and the Inquisition." Hells and Benefits: A Report on American Minds, Mat-

ters, and Possibilities. New York: Basic Books, 1962.
Also printed: Kenyon Review, 1962 (entry 3766). See entry
3766 for annotation.

3755 Grigson, Geoffrey. "Alfred Tennyson (1809-92)." Poets in
Their Pride. London: Phoenix House, 1962, pp. 124-135.

3756 Lehmann, John. Ancestors and Friends. London: Eyre and
Spottiswoode, 1962.
Of biographical interest.

3757 Pitt, Valerie. Tennyson Laureate. London: Barrie and
Rockliff, 1962. Toronto: U. of Toronto P., 1963.
Pitt defends Tennyson's greatness. E. D. H. Johnson in his
"Alfred, Lord Tennyson" in The Victorian Poets, 1968 (entry 4068),
complains that this book "is marred by so many factual errors."
Controversial, interesting, and forceful, Pitt's arguments are worth
reading.
Reviewed by: J. E. Baker in Philological Quarterly (entry
3858); L. Bonnerot in Etudes anglaises (entry 3809); A. D. Culler in
Yale Review (entry 3865); R. Fuller in Spectator (entry 3768); J.
Gross in Manchester Guardian Weekly (entry 3771); L. James in Crit-
ical Quarterly (entry 3821); R. Mayne in New Statesman (entry 3777);
A. H. Qureshi in Dalhousie Review (entry 3830); C. Ricks in Listener
(entry 3784); C. de L. Ryals in Victorian Studies (entry 3839); G.
Thomas in English (entry 3846); and Times Literary Supplement (entry 3847).

3758 Richardson, Joanna. The Pre-Eminent Victorian: A Study of
Tennyson. London: Cape, 1962.
A biography that emphasizes Tennyson as Laureate. Well
written.
Reviewed by: L. Bonnerot in Etudes anglaises (entry 3809);
R. Fuller in Spectator (entry 3768); R. Mayne in New Statesman (entry 3777); C. Ricks in Listener (entry 3784); C. de L. Ryals in Victorian Studies (entry 3839); and Times Literary Supplement (entry
3847).

3759 Wilde, Oscar. The Letters of Oscar Wilde. Ed. Rupert Hart-
Davis. London: Hart-Davis, 1962. New York: Harcourt,
Brace and World, 1962.

3760 Young, Andrew. "Tennyson in Lincolnshire." The Poet and
the Landscape. London: Hart-Davis, 1962.
Emphasizes pastoral poetry.

3761 Young, G. M. "The Age of Tennyson." Victorian Essays.
London: Oxford U. P., 1962.

Dissertation

3762 Glasser, Marvin. The Early Poetry of Tennyson and Yeats:
A Comparative Study. New York, 1962. Dissertation Abstracts, 24 (1964), 4174.

Glasser explores how the two poets handled similar problems. A provocative study.

Periodicals

3763 Bishop, Jonathan. "The Unity of In Memoriam." Victorian News Letter, no. 21 (Spring 1962), 9-14.
Reprinted: J. D. Hunt, ed., Tennyson: In Memoriam, 1970 (entry 4214).
Bishop concludes: "It is the reader, then, who achieves the unity of the poem."

3764 Collins, Rowland L. "'Tennyson's Original Issue of Poems, Reviews, etc., 1842-1886': A Compilation by Henry van Dyke." Princeton University Library Chronicle, 24 (1962), 39-50.
The library's holdings of the published works of Tennyson.

3765 Danzig, Allan. "The Contraries: A Central Concept in Tennyson's Poetry." PMLA, 77 (Dec. 1962), 577-585.
Reprinted: S. Kumar, ed., British Victorian Literature, 1969.
The relationships of opposites in Tennyson's work.

3766 DeMott, Benjamin. "The General, the Poet, and the Inquisition." Kenyon Review, 24 (1962), 442-456.
Also printed: Hells and Benefits, 1962 (entry 3753).
Discusses the revolt against Spain's Ferdinand VII in 1830 and Tennyson's involvement. Discusses "The Lotos-Eaters."

3767 Dierckx, J. "King and Archbishop: Henry II and Becket from Tennyson to Fry." Revue des langues vivantes, 27 (1962), 424-435.
Includes a brief and unfavorable mention of Becket.

3768 Fuller, Roy. Spectator, 209 (Nov. 2, 1962), 688.
Review of V. Pitt's Tennyson Laureate, 1962 (entry 3757) and J. Richardson's The Pre-Eminent Victorian, 1962 (entry 3758).

3769 Grant, Stephen Allen. "The Mystical Implications of In Memoriam." Studies in English Literature, 2 (Autumn 1962), 481-495.
Grant discusses Tennyson's mystical experiences and their implications for the interpretation of In Memoriam.

3770 Gridley, Roy. "Confusion of the Seasons in Tennyson's 'The Last Tournament.'" Victorian News Letter, no. 22 (Fall 1962), 14-16.
Irony and symbolism.

3771 Gross, John. Manchester Guardian Weekly, Nov. 1, 1962, p. 11.
Review of V. Pitt's Tennyson Laureate, 1962 (entry 3757).

3772 Killham, John. Modern Language Review, 57 (1962), 144-145.
      Review of J. H. Buckley's Tennyson, 1960 (entry 3696).

3773 King, R.W. Review of English Studies, n.s. 13 (1962), 439.
      Review of J. H. Buckley's Tennyson, 1960 (entry 3696).

3774 Kissane, James. "Victorian Mythology." Victorian Studies,
      6 (Sept. 1962), 5-28.
      Tennyson on pages 25-28.   The poet and the myth of Demeter.

3775 Lewis, Naomi. "Palgrave and his Golden Treasury." Listen-
      er, 67 (1962), 23 and 26.

3776 Marshall, George O., Jr. "Giftbooks, Tennyson, and The
      Tribute (1837)." Georgia Review, 16 (Winter 1962), 459-464.

3777 Mayne, R. New Statesman, 64 (1962), 782.
      Review of V. Pitt's Tennyson Laureate, 1962 (entry 3757) and
J. Richardson's The Pre-Eminent Victorian, 1962 (entry 3758).

3778 Nowell-Smith, Simon. "Tennyson, A.C. and F. Poems by Two
      Brothers, 1827." Book Collector, 11 (1962), 80.
      Note on edition.

3779 Priestly, F.E.L. "Control of Tone in Tennyson's The Prin-
      cess." Langue et Littérature, 6 (1962), 314-315.

3780 _____. "Tennyson." University of Toronto Quarterly, 32
      (Oct. 1962), 102-106.
      Review of J. H. Buckley's Tennyson, 1960 (entry 3696).

3781 Rader, Ralph Wilson. "The Composition of Tennyson's Maud."
      Modern Philology, 59 (May 1962), 265-269.
      Reprinted: Tennyson's Maud, 1963 (entry 3797).
      Rader sheds new light on the way Tennyson composed Maud.

3782 _____. "Tennyson and Rosa Baring." Victorian Studies, 5
      (March 1962), 224-260.
      Reprinted: Tennyson's Maud, 1963 (entry 3797).
      Rader contends that contrary to common opinion, Tennyson's
love for Rosa Baring was serious and had an important effect on
"Locksley Hall," "Locksley Hall Sixty Years After," and other poems.

3783 _____. "Tennyson in the Year of Hallam's Death." PMLA,
      77 (Sept. 1962), 419-424.
      Reprinted: Tennyson's Maud, 1963 (entry 3797).

3784 Ricks, Christopher. Listener, Oct. 25, 1962, p. 678.
      Review of V. Pitt's Tennyson Laureate, 1962 (entry 3757) and
J. Richardson's The Pre-Eminent Victorian, 1962 (entry 3758).

3785 _____. "'Peace and War' and 'Maud.'" Notes and Queries,
      n.s. 9 (1962), 230.

3786 Rogers, Timothy. English, 14 (1962), 26-27.
      Review of J. H. Buckley's Tennyson, 1960 (entry 3696).

3787 Ryals, Clyde de L. "The 'Heavenly Friend': The 'New My-
      thus' of In Memoriam." Personalist, 43 (Summer 1962), 383-
      402.
      Arthur Hallam as Christ figure. Discusses Carlyle's "new
mythus" from Sartor Resartus and Tennyson's conversion of Hallam
into a Christ figure as Tennyson's fulfillment of the "new mythus."

3788 _____. "The Poet as Critic: Appraisals of Tennyson by
      His Contemporaries." Tennessee Studies in Literature, 7
      (1962), 113-125.
      The assessments of Tennyson by his contemporaries are ech-
oed in much of the criticism of the twentieth century.

3789 _____. "Point of View in Tennyson's Ulysses." Archiv
      für das Studium der neueren Sprachen und Literaturen, 199
      (1962), 232-234.
      Ryals does not believe that Ulysses means to begin another
journey: "Ulysses' majestic speech becomes, accordingly, a kind of
dream, a means of escape momentarily from the uncongenial environment of Ithaca."

3790 _____. "The 'Weird Seizures' in The Princess." Texas
      Studies in Literature and Language, 4 (Summer 1962), 268-
      275.
      Tennyson's revisions.

3791 Smalley, Donald. "A New Look at Tennyson--and Especially
      the Idylls." Journal of English and Germanic Philology, 61
      (April 1962), 349-357.
      Review of J. H. Buckley's Tennyson, 1960 (entry 3696). In
this thorough review, Smalley disputes Buckley's positive assessment
of Idylls of the King.

3792 Svaglic, Martin J. "A Framework for Tennyson's In Memo-
      riam." Journal of English and Germanic Philology, 61 (1962),
      810-825.
      A. C. Bradley noted four divisions for In Memoriam; others
noted nine. Svaglic discusses nine divisions, which he finds to be
inherent in the structure of the poem.

3793 Templeman, William D. Personalist, 43 (1962), 132-133.
      Review of Selected Poems, ed. E. Blunden, 1960
      (entry 3695).

3794 Turner, Paul. "Some Ancient Light on Tennyson's Oenone."
      Journal of English and Germanic Philology, 61 (1962), 57-72.
      An erudite investigation of the classical sources for
"Oenone."

350 / TENNYSON

1963

Books

3795 Marshall, George O., Jr. A Tennyson Handbook. New York:
Twayne, 1963.
Designed for college students, this book provides brief back-
grounds for Tennyson's poems and plays.
Reviewed by: C. de L. Ryals in Victorian Poetry, 1964 (en-
try 3888).

3796 Püschel, Brita. Thomas A Becket in der Literatur. Bochum:
Pöppinghaus, 1963. (Beiträge zur Englischen Philologie, 45)

3797 Rader, Ralph Wilson. Tennyson's Maud: The Biographical
Genesis. Berkeley: U. of California P., 1963. London:
Cambridge U. P., 1963. (Perspectives in Criticism, 15)
Rader provides a biographical background that is useful and
important.
Reviewed by: K. Allott in Notes and Queries (entry 3911); G.
Beer in Review of English Studies (entry 3914); J. H. Buckley in Jour-
nal of English and Germanic Philology (entry 3861); R. L. Collins in
Victorian Studies (entry 3864); S. E. Henderson in College English
(entry 3875); J. Killham in Modern Language Review (entry 3877);
C. Ricks in Listener (entry 3881); C. de L. Ryals in Victorian Po-
etry (entry 3887); B. C. Southam in Essays in Criticism (entry 3953);
G. Thomas in English (entry 3895); and Times Literary Supplement
(entry 3896).

3798 Spitzer, Leo. "Tears, Idle Tears Again." Essays on English
and American Literature. Ed. Anna Hatcher. Princeton:
Princeton U. P., 1963.
Reprinted from: Hopkins Review, 1952 (entry 3511). See entry 3511 for another reprinting and for annotation.

3799 Tennyson, Charles. Tennyson Collection, Usher Gallery, Lin-
coln. Lincoln, England: City Libraries, Museum, and Art
Galleries Committee, 1963.
Annotated catalogue of the collection. Reviewed by: T. J.
Brown in Book Collector (entry 3860).

Dissertations

3800 Elliott, Philip Lovin, Jr. A Textual Study of In Memoriam.
Georgia, 1963. Dissertation Abstracts, 24 (1963), 2462.
A study of the variants in the text of In Memoriam in its var-
ious manuscripts and editions.

3801 Kauffman, Corinne Elizabeth. Spenser and Tennyson: A Comparative Study. Texas, 1963. Dissertation Abstracts, 24
(1963), 729.
Kauffman discusses significant similarities between the two
poets and their work.

3802 Lally, Mary Aquin. A Comparative Study of Five Plays on the Becket Story: By Tennyson, Binyon, Eliot, Anouilh, and Fry. Notre Dame, 1963. Dissertation Abstracts, 24 (1963), 2479.
Tennyson's play is representative of nineteenth-century drama.

Periodicals

3803 Ancaster, Lord, and Charles Tennyson. "The Tennyson Society." Times Literary Supplement, June 14, 1963, p. 451.
Publishing plans.

3804 Assad, Thomas J. "Tennyson's 'Break, Break, Break.'" Tulane Studies in English, 12 (1963), 71-80.

3805 _____. "Tennyson's 'Tears, Idle Tears.'" Tulane Studies in English, 13 (1963), 71-83.
Analysis of prosody and structure of the poem.

3806 Ball, Patricia M. "Tennyson and the Romantics." Victorian Poetry, 1 (Jan. 1963), 7-16.
Tennyson shares with the Romantics their "basic fascination with the issue of human identity."

3807 Baum, Paull F. "Crossing the Bar." English Language Notes, 1 (1963), 115-116.

3808 Benton, Richard P. "Tennyson and Lao Tzu." Philosophy East and West, 12 (1963), 233-240.
The translation of Lao Tzu by John Chalmers was a source for Tennyson's "The Ancient Sage."

3809 Bonnerot, Louis. Etudes anglaises, 16 (1963), 291-293.
Review of Selected Poems, ed. E. Blunden, 1960 (entry 3695); V. Pitt's Tennyson Laureate, 1962 (entry 3757); and J. Richardson's The Pre-Eminent Victorian, 1962 (entry 3758).

3810 Brown, T.J. "English Literary Autographs XLV. Lord Tennyson, 1809-1892." Book Collector, 12 (1963), 61.

3811 Burch, Francis F. "Tennyson and Milton: Sources of Reese's 'Tears.'" American Notes and Queries, 1 (1963), 115-117.

3812 Cadbury, William. "The Utility of the Poetic Mask in Tennyson's 'Supposed Confessions.'" Modern Language Quarterly, 24 (1963), 374-385.
Tennyson's use of a persona.

3813 Collins, Rowland L. "The Frederick Tennyson Collection." Publications of the Tennyson Society, a supplement to Victorian Studies, 7 (1963), 57-76.
Catalogue of collection in Lilly Library, Indiana University.

3814 _____. "How Rare Are Montagu Butler's Translations of Tennyson?" Book Collector, 12 (1963), 72-73.

3815 Elliott, Philip L., Jr. "The Charge of the Light Brigade." Notes and Queries, n.s. 10 (1963), 263-264.
See also: C. Ricks (entry 3833).

3816 Fulweiler, Howard. "Mermen and Mermaids: A Note on an 'Alien Vision' in the Poetry of Tennyson, Arnold, and Hopkins." Victorian News Letter, no. 23 (Spring 1963), 16-17.

3817 Goldberg, J. Philip. "Two Tennysonian Allusions to a Poem of Andrew Marvell." Notes and Queries, n.s. 10 (1963), 264-265.
See also: C. Ricks (entry 3833).

3818 Hall, Roland. "Gleanings from Tennyson's Idylls for the O.E.D." Notes and Queries, n.s. 10 (1963), 449.

3819 Hovey, Richard B. "Tennyson's 'Locksley Hall': A Re-Interpretation." Forum (Houston), 4, no. 1 (1963), 24-30.

3820 Huxter, E.W. "Tennyson and Juvenal." Notes and Queries, n.s. 10 (1963), 448-449.

3821 James, Louis. Critical Quarterly, 5 (1963), 277.
Note of V. Pitt's Tennyson Laureate, 1962 (entry 3757).

3822 Litzinger, Boyd. "The Structure of Tennyson's 'The Last Tournament.'" Victorian Poetry, 1 (1963), 53-60.
An interesting analysis.

3823 Marshall, George O., Jr. "Tennyson's 'Oh! That 'twere Possible': A Link between In Memoriam and Maud." PMLA, 78 (June 1963), 225-229.
Marshall analyzes the revising of a passage in Maud and links the theme in the passage to In Memoriam.

3824 _____. "Tennyson's 'Ulysses,' 33-43." Explicator, 21 (Feb. 1963), Item 50.
Marshall takes issue with earlier analyses, particularly of the relationship between Ulysses and his son, Telemachus.

3825 Metzger, Lore. "The Eternal Process: Some Parallels between Goethe's Faust and Tennyson's In Memoriam." Victorian Poetry, 1 (Aug. 1963), 189-196.
A comparison of evolutionary themes.

3826 Miller, J. Hillis. "The Theme of the Disappearance of God in Victorian Poetry." Victorian Studies, 6, no. 3 (1963), 207-227.
Tennyson, Arnold, Browning, and Hopkins respond as Romantics to the absence of God from the world.

3827 Moore, Carlisle. "Faith, Doubt, and Mystical Experience in
In Memoriam." Victorian Studies, 7 (Dec. 1963), 155-169.
Reprinted: J. D. Hunt, ed., Tennyson: In Memoriam, 1970
(entry 4214), pp. 241-258.
Moore provides an overview of the history of critical respons-
es to Tennyson's mysticism in In Memoriam. The trance in the
Somersby garden is fundamental to understanding the mixture of faith
and doubt in the poem.

3828 Pettigrew, John. "Tennyson's 'Ulysses': A Reconciliation of
Opposites." Victorian Poetry, 1 (Jan. 1963), 27-45.
Pettigrew finds unusual complexity in "Ulysses."

3829 Pipes, B. N., Jr. "A Slight Meteorological Disturbance: The
Last Two Stanzas of Tennyson's 'The Poet.'" Victorian Poetry, 1 (1963), 74-76.

3830 Qureshi, A. H. Dalhousie Review, 43 (1963), 409-411.
Review of V. Pitt's Tennyson Laureate, 1962 (entry 3757).

3831 Rader, Ralph Wilson. "Tennyson's 'Strange' Father: The
Comments of a Lincolnshire Neighbour." Notes and Queries,
n. s. 10 (1963), 447-448.

3832 Rehak, Louise Rouse. "On the Use of Martyrs: Tennyson and
Eliot on Thomas Becket." University of Toronto Quarterly,
33 (Oct. 1963), 43-60.

3833 Ricks, Christopher. Notes and Queries, n. s. 10 (1963), 385.
See also: P. L. Elliott, Jr. (entry 3815) and J. P. Goldberg
(entry 3817). A letter.

3834 _____. "Tennyson and Gray." Times Literary Supplement,
June 21, 1963, p. 468.

3835 _____. "The Variants of In Memoriam." Library, 5th ser.
18 (1963), 64.

3836 Ryals, Clyde de L. "The Moral Paradox of the Hero in Idylls
of the King." Journal of English Literary History, 30 (March
1963), 53-69.
King Arthur needs the loyalty of his knights to maintain his
own identity, but he deprives them of their freedom by making them
part of his court. This is an interesting and informative study.

3837 _____. "Percival, Ambrosius, and the Method of Narration
in 'The Holy Grail.'" Neuren Sprachen, 12 (1963), 533-543.
Ryal perceives Ambrosius as a foil to Percival; Ambrosius
reminds the reader that Percival's comments are not to be entirely
trusted.

3838 _____. "Tennyson's Maud." Connotation, 1, no. 1 (1963),
12-32.
Explication.

354 / TENNYSON

3839 _____. Victorian Studies, 7 (1963), 115-117.
Review of V. Pitt's Tennyson Laureate, 1962 (entry 3757) and
J. Richardson's The Pre-Eminent Victorian, 1962 (entry 3758).

3840 St. John-Stevas, Norman. "Bagehot on Tennyson." Times
Literary Supplement, April 26, 1963, p. 314.

3841 Solomon, Stanley J. "Tennyson's Paradoxical King." Victorian Poetry, 1 (Nov. 1963), 258-271.
Solomon calls attention to the paradoxes and ironies in Idylls
of the King, particularly as they relate to King Arthur.

3842 Taafe, James G. "Circle Imagery in Tennyson's In Memoriam." Victorian Poetry, 1 (1963), 123-131.
Dante may have inspired a set of images in In Memoriam.

3843 Templeman, William Darby. "A Consideration of the Fame of
'Locksley Hall.'" Victorian Poetry, 1 (April 1963), 81-103.
This informative article will be of use to anyone interested in
"Locksley Hall." Templeman discusses criticism of the poem from
the time of its publication into the 1960s. Templeman summarizes:
"To conclude, this article gives evidence that 'Locksley Hall' has contributed with great weight, with what may seem surprisingly great
weight, to the establishment and maintenance of Tennyson's hold on
the English-speaking public."

3844 Tennyson, Charles. "The Somersby Tennysons." Publications
of the Tennyson Society, a supplement to Victorian Studies, 7
(1963), 7-55.
For further comment, see also: C. Tennyson's "The Somersby
Tennysons" in Victorian Studies, 1966 (entry 4006).
Tennyson's life is often represented in his poems. During his
youth in Lincolnshire he developed much of his aesthetic--a development shared by his siblings.

3845 Thomas, Gilbert. English, 15 (1963), 155-156.
Review of V. Pitt's Tennyson Laureate, 1962 (entry 3757).

3846 Times Literary Supplement, Feb. 15, 1963, p. 108.
Review of V. Pitt's Tennyson Laureate, 1962 (entry 3757) and
J. Richardson's The Pre-Eminent Victorian, 1962 (entry 3758).

3847 Vandiver, Edward P., Jr. "Tennyson's 'Tears, Idle Tears.'"
Explicator, 21 (1963), Item 53.
Places C. Brooks's observations (entry 3350) in the totality of
The Princess and finds them apt.

1964

Books

3848 Collins, Rowland L. Introduction. The Devil and the Lady,

and Unpublished Early Poems. Ed. Charles Tennyson. Bloomington: Indiana U. P., 1964. (New edition)

3849 Grandsen, K. W. Tennyson: In Memoriam. London: Arnold,
1964. (Studies in English Literature, 22)
Grandsen provides an introduction to In Memoriam. His analysis of the poem and its problems for critics is useful.
Reviewed by: F. Lagarde in Langues modernes (entry 3986).

3850 Inglis-Jones, Elisabeth. The Lord of Burghley. London: Faber, 1964.
A story behind Tennyson's "The Lord of Burleigh."

3851 Ryals, Clyde de L. Theme and Symbol in Tennyson's Poems
to 1850. Philadelphia: U. of Pennsylvania P., 1964. London: Oxford U. P., 1964.
Some of Ryals's readings seem naive, and his organization
seems scattershot, but ultimately his judgments are sound. The dis-
criminating scholar will find much of value in this book.
Reviewed by: J. B. Bennett in Western Humanities Review
(entry 3915); P. Drew in Listener (entry 3867); J. Killham in Modern
Language Review (entry 3929); C. Ricks in Review of English Studies
(entry 3943); L. Stevenson in Victorian Poetry (entry 3889); and Times
Literary Supplement (entry 3897).

3852 Smith, Elton Edward. The Two Voices: A Tennyson Study.
Lincoln: U. of Nebraska P., 1964.
Publication of a dissertation: 1961 (entry 3726).
Smith examines the seeming ambivalence of much of Tennyson's
work by focusing in separate chapters on "Art versus Society," "Sense
versus Soul," "Doubt versus Faith," "Past versus Present," and "Del-
icacy versus Strength." He argues that critics have fragmented Tennyson's work when they should have examined it as a whole.
Reviewed by: J. R. Bennett in Western Humanities Review (entry 3915); P. L. Elliott in South Atlantic Bulletin (entry 4032); R. Gridley in Journal of English and Germanic Philology (entry 3925); G. O.
Marshall, Jr. in Victorian Poetry (entry 3988); M. Millgate in Victorian Studies (entry 3989); J. Newcomer in College English (entry
3991); C. T. Peterson in American Book Collector (entry 3993); R.
Preyer in Modern Philology (entry 3997); D. Smalley in South Atlantic
Quarterly (entry 3951); and H. A. Smith in Modern Language Review
(entry 4004).

3853 Southam, B. C. Introduction. Selected Poems of Lord Tennyson. London: Chatto and Windus, 1964.

3854 Tennyson, Alfred, Lord. The Devil and the Lady, and Unpublished Early Poems. Ed. Charles Tennyson. Bloomington:
Indiana U. P., 1964. (New edition)
Reviewed by: C. Ricks in New York Review of Books (entry
3882); and J. R. Willingham in Library Journal (entry 3900).

3855 Warner, Oliver. English Literature: A Portrait Gallery.

London: Chatto and Windus, 1964.
Includes a sketch of Tennyson.

Dissertations

3856 Engbretson, Nancy Martina. Tennyson's Longer Narrative Po-
ems: The Princess, Maud, and The Idylls of the King. New
York, 1964. Dissertation Abstracts, 28 (1967), 1431A.
Traces the development of Tennyson's art in the longer poems.

3857 Solimine, Joseph, Jr. Tennyson and the Tradition of Burke.
Pennsylvania, 1964. Dissertation Abstracts, 25 (1965), 7249.
Measures Tennyson's political and social ideas against the
tradition of Burke.

Periodicals

3858 Baker, Joseph E. Philological Quarterly, 43 (1964), 573-574.
Review of V. Pitt's Tennyson Laureate, 1962 (entry 3757).

3859 Brashear, William R. "Tennyson's Third Voice: A Note."
Victorian Poetry, 2 (Autumn 1964), 283-286.
Finds a third voice that saves the persona at the end of "The
Two Voices."

3860 Brown, T. J. Book Collector, 13 (1964), 237-242.
Review of C. Tennyson's Tennyson Collection, 1963 (entry
3799).

3861 Buckley, Jerome H. Journal of English and Germanic Philology, 63 (1964), 820-822.
Review of R. W. Rader's Tennyson's Maud, 1963 (entry 3797).

3862 Bufkin, E. C. "Imagery in 'Locksley Hall.'" Victorian Poetry,
2 (Winter 1964), 21-28.
The imagery of time, water, and sky unifies the poem.

3863 Colbeck, Norman. "Variant Bindings on Moxon Authors."
Book Collector, 13 (1964), 356-357.
Includes In Memoriam.

3864 Collins, Rowland L. Victorian Studies, 8 (1964), 85-86.
Review of R. W. Rader's Tennyson's Maud, 1963 (entry 3797).

3865 Culler, A. Dwight. Yale Review, 53 (1964), 440-443.
Review of V. Pitt's Tennyson Laureate, 1962 (entry 3757).

3866 Drew, Philip. "'Aylmer's Field': A Problem for Critics."
Listener, April 2, 1964, pp. 553 and 556-557.
Drew provides an insightful analysis of the narrative of the
poem.

3867 _____. Listener, Oct. 15, 1964, p. 601.
Review of C. de L. Ryals's Theme and Symbol, 1964 (entry 3851).

A Bibliography / 357

3868   Eidson, John Olin. "The First Performance of Tennyson's
       Harold." New England Quarterly, 37 (Sept. 1964), 387-390.
       Harold was performed by the Yale University Dramatic Asso-
ciation on June 19, 1915.

3869   _____. "Tennyson's First Play on the American Stage."
       American Literature, 35 (Jan. 1964), 519-528.
       Eidson discusses the performance of Queen Mary in America
during 1875 through 1878.

3870   _____. "Tennyson's The Foresters on the American Stage."
       Philological Quarterly, 43 (Oct. 1964), 549-557.
       Eidson discusses Augustin Daly's New York production of The
Foresters.

3871   Engbretsen, Nancy M. "The Thematic Evolution of The Idylls
       of the King." Victorian News Letter, no. 26 (Fall 1964), 1-5.
       The Idylls of the King as "social and moral evaluation."

3872   Forsyth, R. A. "The Myth of Nature and the Victorian Com-
       promise of the Imagination." Journal of English Literary His-
       tory, 31 (1964), 213-240.
       Tennyson's poetry is representative of the "compromise."

3873   Fredeman, William E. "Rossetti's Impromtu Portraits of Ten-
       nyson Reading 'Maud.'" Burlington Magazine, 105 (March
       1964), 117-118 and 413.
       Plates 24, 25, 26, page 116, are of Rossetti's drawings of
Tennyson.

3874   Grob, Alan. "Tennyson's The Lotus Eaters: Two Versions
       of Art." Modern Philology, 62 (1964), 118-129.
       Compares the 1832 and 1842 versions of "The Lotos-Eaters."
Interesting.

3875   Henderson, Stephen E. College English, 26 (1964), 64.
       Review of R. W. Rader's Tennyson's Maud, 1963 (entry 3797).

3876   Johnson, Robert O. "Mr. Marquard and Lord Tennyson."
       Research Studies, 32 (1964), 28-38.

3877   Killham, John. Modern Language Review, 59 (1964), 650-651.
       Review of R. W. Rader's Tennyson's Maud, 1963 (entry 3797).

3878   Mitchell, Charles. "The Undying Will of Tennyson's Ulysses."
       Victorian Poetry, 2 (Spring 1964), 87-95.
       In "a soliloquy presented as a dramatic monologue" Ulysses
prepares for death.

3879   Packer, Lona Mosk. "Sun and Shadow: The Nature of Experi-
       ence in Tennyson's 'The Lady of Shalott." Victorian News
       Letter, no. 25 (Spring 1964), 4-8.
       Platonic allegory.

3880 Poston, Lawrence, III. "The Argument of the Geraint-Enid Books in Idylls of the King." Victorian Poetry, 2 (Autumn 1964), 269-275.
Places the Idylls of Geraint and Enid in context.

3881 Ricks, Christopher. Listener, Feb. 27, 1964, pp. 363-364.
Review of R. W. Rader's Tennyson's Maud, 1963 (entry 3797).

3882 _____. New York Review of Books, June 11, 1964, p. 15.
Review of The Devil and the Lady, ed. C. Tennyson, 1964 (entry 3854).

3883 _____. "Tennyson: Three Notes." Modern Philology, 62 (Nov. 1964), 139-141.
Notes: I. "Come Not, When I Am Dead." II. Notes by Palgrave. III. "O Where's He, the Simple Fool."

3884 _____. "Tennyson's 'Hail, Briton!' and 'Tithon': Some Corrections." Review of English Studies, n. s. 15 (Feb. 1964), 53-55.
Ricks discusses the poems as printed in M. J. Donahue's article in PMLA, 1949 (entry 3426).

3885 _____. "Tennyson's Maud." Times Literary Supplement, Dec. 31, 1964, p. 1181.
Ricks discusses R. W. Rader's Tennyson's Maud, 1963 (entry 3797) and supports Rader's ideas concerning the inspiration for the writing of Maud.

3886 _____. "Tennyson's 'Rifle Clubs!!!'" Review of English Studies, n. s. 15 (Nov. 1964), 401-404.
A poem found in Boston College's Baptist Library.

3887 Ryals, Clyde de L. Victorian Poetry, 2 (1964), 133-135.
Review of R. W. Rader's Tennyson's Maud, 1963 (entry 3797).

3888 _____. Victorian Poetry, 2 (1964), 215-217.
Review of G. O. Marshall's A Tennyson Handbook, 1963 (entry 3795).

3889 Stevenson, Lionel. Victorian Poetry, 2 (1964), 287-290.
Review of C. de L. Ryals's Theme and Symbol, 1964 (entry 3851).

3890 Stokes, Edward. "The Metrics of Maud." Victorian Poetry, 2 (Spring 1964), 97-110.
Stokes shows how the metrics in Maud vary according to themes and tone. A thoughtful study.

3891 Talon, Henri A. "Sur un Poème de Tennyson: Essai de critique formelle." Langues modernes, 58 (1964), 32-37.
Talon thoroughly analyzes the language of In Memoriam, section XIII.

3892 Tennyson, Charles. "The Dream in Tennyson's Poetry."
Virginia Quarterly Review, 40 (Spring 1964), 228-248.
Dreams are important to Tennyson's poetry.

3893 _____. "Tennyson and His Times." Lincolnshire Historian,
2, no. 11 (1964).
The poet's allusions to politics.

3894 "Tennysoniana." Times Literary Supplement, July 16, 1964,
p. 640.
Charles Tennyson establishes a Tennyson Research Centre in
the Lincoln City Library.

3895 Thomas, Gilbert. English, 15 (1964), 109-110.
Review of R.W. Rader's Tennyson's Maud, 1963 (entry 3797).

3896 Times Literary Supplement, Feb. 20, 1964, p. 148.
Review of R.W. Rader's Tennyson's Maud, 1963 (entry 3797).

3897 Times Literary Supplement, Aug. 6, 1964, p. 698.
Review of C. de L. Ryals's Theme and Symbol, 1964 (entry
3851).

3898 Todd, William B. "Wise, Wrenn, and Tennyson's Enoch Arden." Book Collector, 13 (1964), 67-68.

3899 Whiting, George Wesley. "The Artist and Tennyson." Rice
University Studies, 50 (1964), 1-84.
Whiting's monograph provides a useful listing of nineteenth-
century English paintings whose subjects are taken from Tennyson's
works.

3900 Willingham, J.R. Library Journal, 89 (1964), 2801.
Review of The Devil and the Lady, ed. C. Tennyson, 1964
(entry 3854).

1965

Books

3901 Bagehot, Walter. The Collected Works of Walter Bagehot.
Ed. Norman St. John-Stevas. Cambridge, Massachusetts:
Harvard U.P., 1965. Volume II, pp. 174-207.
Reprinting of review of Idylls, 1859, from National Review,
1859 (entry 463). See entry 463 for other reprinting and for annota-
tion.

3902 Bakaya, K.N. "Tennyson's Use of the Dramatic Monologue."
Essays Presented to Amy G. Stock. Ed. R.K. Kaul. Jaipur:
Rajasthan, 1965, pp. 95-110.

3903 Grønbech, Vilhelm. Religious Currents in the Nineteenth Cen-

tury.   Trans.   P. M. Mitchell and W. D. Paden.   Lawrence:
U. of Kansas P., 1965.
Discusses Tennyson and others.

3904   Tillotson, Kathleen.   "Tennyson's Serial Poem."   Mid-Victorian
Studies, by Geoffrey Tillotson and Kathleen Tillotson.   London: U. of London (Athlone Press), 1965, pp. 80-109.
Discusses the nineteenth-century critical reception of Idylls
of the King.

Dissertations

3905   Adicks, Richard Rosenbush, Jr.   Structure and Meaning in
Tennyson's Idylls of the King.   Tulane, 1965.   Dissertation
Abstracts, 27 (1966), 764A.
In this interesting dissertation, Adicks discusses the allegorical conflict of Soul and Sense in Idylls of the King.   He finds in the
poetry's humanity, theme of progress, and idealism, ideas that remain meaningful.

3906   Eggenschwiler, David Lee.   Arcadian Myth in the Poetry of
Tennyson and Arnold.   Stanford, 1965.   Dissertation Abstracts,
26 (1966), 6695-6696.
Eggenschwiler perceives Tennyson as a transcendental poet
who uses the Arcadian myths to metaphorically present his intellectual themes.   His comparison of Tennyson and Arnold's approaches
to the Arcadian themes is enlightening.

3907   Hill, James Lewis.   Tennyson and Expressive Art: The Relationship Between Tennyson's Early Poetry and Nineteenth-
Century Esthetic Theory.   Princeton, 1965.   Dissertation Abstracts, 27 (1966), 1786A.
Hill surveys critical responses to Tennyson's work.   He emphasizes Tennyson's originality and downgrades the commonly held
assumptions of Keats and Shelley's influence on the poet's work.   Hill
includes a discussion of how Tennyson's revisions of selected poems
reveal his theory of "expressive art."   An unusually sophisticated
dissertation.

3908   Laurent, Martha Long.   Tennyson and the Poetry of The Germ:
A Study of the Early Pre-Raphaelite Poets' Relation to Tenny-
son.   Georgia, 1965.   Dissertation Abstracts, 26 (1965), 2186.
Laurent examines The Germ, the short-lived publication of the
Pre-Raphaelite Brotherhood of 1850.   She infers direct and indirect
Tennysonian influence on the Pre-Raphaelites.

3909   Moran, William Charles.   Tennyson's Reputation as a Thinker.
Tennessee, 1965.   Dissertation Abstracts, 26 (1966), 4635.
Moran traces the history of opinions of Tennyson's ability to
think.

3910   Wilson, Hugh Hamilton.   The Evolution of Tennyson's Purpose
in the Building of The Idylls of the King.   Wisconsin, 1965.

Dissertation Abstracts, 26 (1965), 3357.
Wilson traces the evolution of Tennyson's thought as revealed
in the development of the Idylls of the King.

Periodicals

3911 Allott, Kenneth. Notes and Queries, n.s. 12 (1965), 73-74.
Review of R.W. Rader's Tennyson's Maud, 1963 (entry 3797).

3912 Assad, Thomas J. "On the Major Poems of Tennyson's 'Enoch
Arden' Volume." Tulane Studies in English, 14 (1965), 29-56.
Assad discusses the poems' unifying themes.

3913 Baldini, Gabriele. "Tennyson conviviale." Rivista di Cultura
Classica e Medievale, 7 (1965), 93-101.

3914 Beer, Gillian. Review of English Studies, n.s. 16 (1965), 442-
443.
Review of R.W. Rader's Tennyson's Maud, 1963 (entry 3797).

3915 Bennett, James B. Western Humanities Review, 19 (1965),
373-375.
Review of C. de L. Ryals's Theme and Symbol, 1964 (entry
3851) and E.E. Smith's The Two Voices, 1964 (entry 3852).

3916 Cadbury, William. "Tennyson's 'The Palace of Art' and the
Rhetoric of Structures." Criticism, 7 (1965), 23-44.
Cadbury asserts that "The Palace of Art" "is about change,
not about art."

3917 Corbes, H. "Alfred Tennyson en Bretagne à la recherche des
légendes arthuriennes." Annales de Bretagne et des Pays de
l'Oest, 72 (1965), 529-536.

3918 Eidson, John O. "Tennyson's Becket on the American Stage."
Emerson Society Quarterly, no. 39 (1965), 15-20.
Irving's tours of Becket in America and the critical reception
of the play.

3919 _____. "Tennyson's Minor Plays in America." American
Notes and Queries, 4 (Oct. 1965), 19-21.
The Cup, The Falcon, and The Promise of May in America.

3920 Elliott, Philip L. "In Memoriam, II and CXXVIII." English
Language Notes, 2 (1965), 275-277.

3921 _____. "In Memoriam, Section XCVI." Victorian Poetry,
3 (1965), 191-192.

3922 Fass, I. Leonard. "Green as a Motif of Alfred Tennyson."
Victorian Poetry, 3 (1965), 139-141.

3923 Fulweiler, Howard W. "Tennyson and the 'Summons from the

Sea.'" Victorian Poetry, 3 (1965), 25-44.
Tennyson's symbolic use of the sea. A thorough study.

3924 Gray, J.M. "'The Lady of Shalott' and Tennyson's Readings
in the Supernatural." Notes and Queries, n.s. 12 (1965),
298-300.

3925 Gridley, Roy. Journal of English and Germanic Philology, 69
(1965), 753-755.
Review of E.E. Smith's The Two Voices, 1964 (entry 3852).

3926 Grosskurth, Phyllis. "Churton Collins: Scourge of the Late
Victorians." University of Toronto Quarterly, 34 (1965), 254-
268.
Grosskurth discusses the career of Collins and his attacks on
Tennyson and others.

3927 Hardie, William. "The Light Brigade." Times Literary Sup-
plement, June 3, 1965, p. 455.
See: C. Tennyson (entry 3955).
Variants in manuscript and published form.

3928 Huebenthal, John. "'Growing Old,' 'Rabbi Ben Ezra,' and
'Tears, Idle Tears.'" Victorian Poetry, 3 (1965), 61-63.

3929 Killham, John. Modern Language Review, 60 (1965), 602-603.
Review of C. de L. Ryals's Theme and Symbol, 1964 (entry
3851).

3930 Kincaid, James R. "Tennyson's 'Crossing the Bar': A Poem
of Frustration." Victorian Poetry, 3 (1965), 57-61.

3931 Kissane, James R. "Tennyson: The Passion of the Past and
the Curse of Time." Journal of English Literary History, 32
(1965), 85-109.
Reprinted: E.A. Francis, ed., Tennyson, 1980 (entry 4964),
pp. 108-132.
Kissane asserts: "Tennyson confessed it, those who knew him
remarked upon it, and commentators have repeatedly emphasized it:
a longing for the 'lost and gone' is the distinctive Tennyson note."
Kissane provides a balanced, forceful, and tough look at the function
of the past in Tennyson's poetry.

3932 Legris, Maurice. "Structure and Allegory in Tennyson's Idylls
of the King." Humanities Association Bulletin, 16, no. 2
(1965), 37-44.
Emphasizes allegory in the narrative.

3933 M., J.C. (J.C. Maxwell). "Tennysonian." Notes and Que-
ries, 12 (1965), 301.
A first use of the word Tennysonian not listed in the Oxford
English Dictionary.

3934 Mattheisen, Paul F. "Gosse's Candid 'Snapshots.'" Victorian

Studies, 8 (1965), 329-354.
Discusses Gosse's views of Tennyson, among others.

3935 Mays, J. C. C. "In Memoriam: An Aspect of Form." University of Toronto Quarterly, 35 (1965), 22-46.
Reprinted: J. D. Hunt, ed., Tennyson: In Memoriam, 1970 (entry 4214), pp. 259-287.
According to Mays, "Tennyson ... gives his poem form by assuming the dramatic role of hero." One of the best essays on In Memoriam.

3936 Melchiori, Giorgio. "Henry James e Tennyson." Arte e Storia, 35 (1965), 339-360.

3937 _____. "Locksley Hall Revisited: Tennyson and Henry James." Review of English Literature, 6, no. 4 (1965), 9-25. Tennyson's influence on Henry James.

3938 Paden, W. D. "Tennyson's The Lover's Tale, R. H. Shepherd and T. J. Wise." Studies in Bibliography, 18 (1965), 111-145.

3939 Perry, John Oliver. "The Relationships of Disparate Voices in Poems." Essays in Criticism, 15 (1965), 49-64.
Discusses "Ulysses."

3940 Ricks, Christopher. "Hallam's 'Youthful Letters' and Tennyson." English Language Notes, 3 (1965), 120-122.

3941 _____. "'Locksley Hall' and the Moâlakât." Notes and Queries, n. s. 12 (1965), 300-301.
The influence of the William Jones translation on Tennyson.

3942 _____. "A Note on Tennyson's Ode on the Death of the Duke of Wellington." Studies in Bibliography, 18 (1965), 282.

3943 _____. Review of English Studies, n. s. 16 (1965), 321-322.
Review of C. de L. Ryals's Theme and Symbol, 1964 (entry 3851).

3944 _____. "Tennyson's Lucretius." Library, 5th ser. 20 (1965), 63-64.
Ricks discusses manuscript and publication of the poem.

3945 _____. "Two Early Poems by Tennyson." Victorian Poetry, 3 (1965), 55-57.

3946 _____. "Two Letters by Browning." Times Literary Supplement, June 3, 1965, p. 464.
Written to Tennyson.

3947 Ryals, Clyde de L. "A Nonexistent Variant in Tennyson's Poems, Chiefly Lyrical, 1830." Book Collector, 14 (1965), 214-215.
Notes an error in T. J. Wise's A Bibliography, 1908 (entry 2498).

3948 Sambrook, A.J. "Cambridge Apostles at a Spanish Tragedy."
English Miscellany, 16 (1965), 183-194.
Discusses Tennyson and the 1830 revolt against Spain's Fer-
dinand VII.

3949 Semmler, Clement. "Brunton Stevens as Literary Critic."
Australian Literary Studies, 2 (1965), 92-102.
Tennyson's influence.

3950 Shaw, W. David, and Carl W. Gartlein. "The Aurora: A
Spiritual Metaphor in Tennyson." Victorian Poetry, 3 (1965),
213-222.
This interesting essay investigates the aurora borealis as an
image in Tennyson's poetry.

3951 Smalley, Donald. South Atlantic Quarterly, 64 (1965), 576.
Review of E.E. Smith's The Two Voices, 1965 (entry 3852).

3952 Smith, R.B. "Sexual Ambivalence in Tennyson." CEA Critic,
27 (1965), 8-9, and 28 (1965), 12.

3953 Southam, B.C. Essays in Criticism, 15 (1965), 130-132.
Review of R.W. Rader's Tennyson's Maud, 1963 (entry 3797).

3954 Tennyson, Charles. "The Tennyson Phonograph Records."
Bulletin of the British Institute of Recorded Sound, no. 3 (Winter 1965), 2-8.
Tennyson made a recording of himself reading his poetry during 1890-1892.

3955 _____. Times Literary Supplement, July 15, 1965, p. 597.
A letter on W. Hardie's "The Light Brigade" (entry 3927).

1966

Books

3956 Buckley, Jerome H. "Tennyson, Lord Alfred (1809-1892)."
Victorian Poets and Prose Writers. New York: Appleton-
Century-Crofts, 1966, pp. 47-51. (Goldentree Bibliographies)
Buckley lists six editions, thirteen biographical sources, and
eighty-nine critical references.

3957 Mendilow, A.A. "Tennyson's Palace of the Sinful Muse."
Studies in English Language and Literature. Ed. Alice Shalvi
and A.A. Mendilow. Jerusalem: Hebrew U., 1966, pp. 155-
189. (Scripta Hierosolymitana, 17)

3958 Steane, J.B. Tennyson. London: Evans, 1966. (Literature
in Perspective)
A basic and learned general discussion of Tennyson's poetry.

Reviewed by: E. Bender in Library Journal (entry 4241); J. L. Bradley in Modern Language Review (entry 4242); Choice (entry 4244); W. Forbes in Aberdeen University Review (entry 4033); F. McCombie in Notes and Queries (entry 4039); and Times Literary Supplement (entry 4006).

3959 Tennyson, Alfred, Lord. Poems, Chiefly Lyrical. Ed. Clyde de L. Ryals. Philadelphia: U. of Pennsylvania P., 1966. (The Matthew Carey Library of English and American Literature, 1)

Dissertations

3960 Burton, Thomas Glen. Tennyson's Use of Biblical Allusions. Vanderbilt, 1966. Dissertation Abstracts, 27 (1966), 742A. Tennyson's allusions to the Bible in such works as In Memoriam, Idylls of the King, Queen Mary, Becket, and Harold.

3961 Cooper, Douglas Wayne. Tennyson's Idylls: A Mythography of the Self. Missouri at Columbia, 1966. Dissertation Abstracts, 27 (1967), 3423A. A Jungian approach to the meaning of the poetry.

3962 Diehl, John Dornfield. The Gospel of Work and Four Victorian Poets. Columbia, 1966. Dissertation Abstracts, 27 (1966), 1028A-1029A. Tennyson's views of the ennobling qualities of work, along with the views of Robert Browning, Clough, and Arnold.

3963 Donohoe, Thomas A. Tennyson After 1859: A Victorian Romantic. Arizona State, 1966. Dissertation Abstracts, 26 (1966), 7295. Donohoe discusses Tennyson as a Romantic poet in the tradition of Wordsworth. Interesting reading.

3964 Gunter, Garland Otho. Archetypal Patterns in the Poetry of Tennyson, 1823-1850. Maryland, 1966. Dissertation Abstracts, 27 (1967), 3010A. This forthrightly Jungian analysis of Tennyson's poetry through In Memoriam investigates the poet's concern with the unconscious mind. Gunter discusses symbolism and the anima.

3965 Hargrave, Harry Allen. The Life and Writings of Arthur Henry Hallam. Vanderbilt, 1966. Dissertation Abstracts, 27 (1966), 1336A-1337A. The focus is on Hallam with special attention paid to his relationship with Tennyson. In Memoriam's biographical significance is also discussed.

3966 Hollis, Valerie Ward. Landscape in the Poetry of Tennyson. Bryn Mawr College, 1966. Dissertation Abstracts, 27 (1967), 3457A-3458A. Hollis uses images of landscape to expose important aspects of Tennyson's thought and development. The poet's use of landscape, she contends, reveals the sensibilities that make Tennyson's style uniquely Tennysonian.

3967 Joseph, Gerhard Joseph. Tennysonian Love: A Strange Diagonal. Minnesota, 1966. Dissertation Abstracts, 27 (1966), 747A. Published: 1968 (entry 4069).
 Tennyson combines Romantic eroticism and Victorian piety in his poetry. He gives his idea of love mythic proportions.

3968 Leach, Chester Raymond, Jr. A Critical Edition of Tennyson's In Memoriam. Michigan, 1966. Dissertation Abstracts, 27 (1967), 2133A.
 Leach emphasizes the unifying aspects of In Memoriam. His introductory discussion divides the poem into four dramatic structures, each defined by a shift in the role of the persona. The text is accompanied by extensive notes.

3969 Otten, Terry Ralph. The Empty Stage: A Comment on the Search for Dramatic Form in the Early Nineteenth Century. Ohio, 1966. Dissertation Abstracts, 27 (1966), 1344A.
 Otten discusses Maud and Becket as examples of Tennyson's handling of dramatic action.

3970 Robb, Kenneth Alan. The Structure of Tennyson's Idylls of the King. Wisconsin, 1966. Dissertation Abstracts, 28 (1967), 640A-641A.
 Unhappy with traditional investigations of the unity of Idylls of the King--investigations that focus on seasonal imagery, animal imagery, or other surface details--Robb seeks to uncover relationships between individual Idylls on the basis of narrative approach and characterization. Often refreshing commentary.

3971 Sears, Richard Duane. The Unity of Tennyson's Idylls of the King. Ohio, 1966. Dissertation Abstracts, 27 (1967), 2545A.
 Sears contends that the poem, regardless of its history of composition, is unified by theme, structure, and ideology.

Periodicals

3972 Adler, Joshua. "The Dilemma in Tennyson's 'The Hesperides.'" Scripta Hierosolymitana (Jerusalem), 17 (1966), 190-208.
 An interesting discussion.

3973 Battaglia, Francis Joseph. "The Use of Contradiction in In Memoriam." English Language Notes, 4 (1966), 41-46.

3974 Cartwright, F. F. "Tennyson's 'Crossing the Bar.'" Country Life, 140 (1966), 1147.
 See: M.G. Jennings (entry 3983)

3975 Corbes, H. "Ernest Renan chez Tennyson." Annales de Bretagne, 73 (1966), 483-486.

3976 Danzig, Allan. "Tennyson's The Princess: A Definition of
Love." Victorian Poetry, 4 (1966), 83-89.
The relationship of man and woman.

3977 Eggers, John Philip. "The Weeding of the Garden: Tennyson's
Geraint Idylls and the Mabinogion." Victorian Poetry, 4
(1966), 45-51.
Tennyson's changes in the story.

3978 Engbretsen, Nancy M. "Tennyson and Modernism." Arts and
Sciences, Winter 1966, pp. 32-36.

3979 Golffing, Francis. "Tennyson's Last Phase: The Poet as
Seer." Southern Review, 2 (1966), 264-285.

3980 Govil, O.P. "An Echo of Tennyson in Browning." Notes and
Queries, 13 (1966), 341.
"Hervé Riel" and "The Lotos-Eaters."

3981 Gray, J.M. "Source and Symbol in 'Geraint and Enid': Tennyson's Doorm and Limours." Victorian Poetry, 4 (1966),
131-132.

3982 _____. "Tennyson and Nennius." Notes and Queries, 13
(1966), 341-342.

3983 Jennings, M.G. Country Life, 140 (1966), 1229.
A letter concerning F.F. Cartwright's "Tennyson's 'Crossing
the Bar'" (entry 3974).

3984 John, Brian. "Tennyson's 'Recollections of the Arabian Nights'
and the Individuation Process." Victorian Poetry, 4 (1966),
275-279.

3985 Kozicki, Henry. "Tennyson's Idylls of the King as Tragic
Drama." Victorian Poetry, 4 (1966), 15-20.
Applies the rituals of Greek tragedy to Idylls of the King. In-
teresting, though a bit dry.

3986 Lagarde, Fernand. Langues modernes, 60 (1966), 210.
Review of K.W. Grandsen's Tennyson, 1964 (entry 3849).

3987 LeMire, Eugene D. "Tennyson's Weeper in Context." University of Windsor Review, 1 (1966), 196-205.
Discusses "Tears, Idle Tears."

3988 Marshall, George O., Jr. Victorian Poetry, 4 (1966), 143-
144.
Review of E.E. Smith's The Two Voices, 1964 (entry 3852).

3989 Millgate, Michael. Victorian Studies, 9 (1966), 211-212.
Review of E.E. Smith's The Two Voices, 1964 (entry 3852).

3990 Millhauser, Milton. "Structure and Symbol in 'Crossing the Bar.'" Victorian Poetry, 4 (1966), 34-39.

3991 Newcomer, James. College English, 27 (1966), 435.
Review of E.E. Smith's The Two Voices, 1964 (entry 3852).

3992 Perrine, Laurence. "When Does Hope Mean Doubt?: The Tone of 'Crossing the Bar.'" Victorian Poetry, 4 (1966), 127-131.

3993 Peterson, Clell T. American Book Collector, 16 (1966), 7.
Review of E.E. Smith's The Two Voices, 1964 (entry 3852).

3994 Pitts, Gordon. "A Reading of Tennyson's 'Ulysses.'" West Virginia University Philological Papers, 15 (1966), 36-42.

3995 Poston, Lawrence, III. "'Peleas and Ettare': Tennyson's 'Troilus.'" Victorian Poetry, 4 (1966), 199-204.

3996 Preyer, Robert. "Alfred Tennyson: The Poetry and Politics of Conservative Vision." Victorian Studies, 9, no. 4 (1966), 325-352.
Tennyson's Christian humanism was not representative of his society.

3997 _____. Modern Philology, 63 (1966), 275-276.
Review of E.E. Smith's The Two Voices, 1964 (entry 3852).

3998 Rackin, Phyllis. "Recent Misreadings of 'Break, Break, Break' and Their Implications for Poetic Theory." Journal of English and Germanic Philology, 65 (1966), 217-228.
Rackin assails reductive criticism, notably that which emphasizes "paradox and striking metaphor" at the expense of other important qualities of a poem. She provides an interesting interpretation of "Break, Break, Break."

3999 Ricks, Christopher. "Tennyson and Persian." English Language Notes, 4 (1966), 46-47.

4000 _____. "Tennyson: 'Armageddon' into 'Timbuctoo.'" Modern Language Review, 61 (1966), 23-24.

4001 _____. "Tennyson's Method of Composition." Proceedings of the British Academy, 52 (1966), 209-230.
See H.H. Lehman's comments on this article in Victorian Studies, 1970 (entry 4260).

4002 Selkirk, J.B. (James Brown). "Exhumations IV: Extracts from J.B. Selkirk's Ethics and Aesthetics of Modern Poetry (1878)." Essays in Criticism, 16 (1966), 73-83.
Reprinted from: entry 879.

4003 Sendry, Joseph. "'The Palace of Art' Revisited." Victorian Poetry, 4 (1966), 149-162.

According to Sendry, "the Soul's progress towards self-awareness becomes a paradigm of universal moral experience."

4004 Smith, H. A. Modern Language Review, 61 (1966), 297-298.
     Review of E. E. Smith's The Two Voices, 1964 (entry 3852).

4005 Solimine, Joseph, Jr. "The Dialectics of Church and State: Tennyson's Historical Plays." Personalist, 47 (1966), 218-233.

4006 Tennyson, Charles. "The Somersby Tennysons: A Postscript." Victorian Studies, 9, no. 3 (1966), 303-305.
     See also: C. Tennyson's "The Somersby Tennysons" in Victorian Studies, 1963 (entry 3844).
     Tennyson presents additional information on the subject. He points out that Tennyson's sister, Cecilia Lushington, had three books published.

4007 Times Literary Supplement, June 9, 1966, p. 516.
     Review of J. B. Steane's Tennyson, 1966 (entry 3958).

4008 Weeks, H. S. Library Journal, 91 (1966), 3692 and 3694.
     Review of 1966 edition of A. E. Baker's A Concordance to the Poetical and Dramatic Works, 1914 (entry 2756).

4009 Weiner, S. Ronald. "The Chord of Self: Tennyson's Maud."
     Literature and Psychology, 16 (1966), 175-183.
     Weiner examines the hero's emotional turmoil.

4010 Wilkenfeld, R. B. "The Shape of Two Voices." Victorian Poetry, 4 (1966), 163-173.
     Tennyson used his "lyrical narrative" to compromise between reality and subjectivity. Interesting.

1967

Books

4011 Anderson, Warren D. "Types of the Classical in Arnold, Tennyson, and Browning." Victorian Essays, a Symposium: Essays on the Occasion of the Centennial of the College of Wooster in Honor of Emeritus Professor Waldo H. Dunn. Ed. Warren D. Anderson and Thomas D. Clareson. Kent, Ohio: Kent State U. P., 1967, pp. 60-70.

4012 Carter, John, and Graham Pollard. The Forgeries of Tennyson's Plays. Oxford: Blackwell, 1967. (Working Paper, 2)
     Contains information not to be found elsewhere. Reviewed by:
     L. S. Thomson in Papers of the Bibliographical Society of America (entry 4059); and Times Literary Supplement (entry 4060).

4013 Jump, John D., ed. Tennyson: The Critical Heritage. London: Routledge and Kegan Paul, 1967. New York: Barnes and Noble, 1967.

Jump presents thirty-five essays, chapters, and extracts from the commentary by Tennyson's contemporaries from 1831 to 1891. This book is surprisingly short of commentary on In Memoriam but is strong on Poems, 1842, and Idylls of the King.

The following entries are reprinted in whole or in part: 8, 9, 16, 22, 36, 64, 66, 69, 79, 89, 90, 159, 222, 322, 403, 415, 463, 471, 534, 537, 643, 875, 1153, 1212, 1252, and 1272.

Reviewed by: I. Armstrong in Victorian Studies (entry 4155); J.L. Bradley in Modern Language Review (entry 4159); J.B. Caird in Library Review (entry 4085); B.J. Inman in Arizona Quarterly (entry 4102); J.C. Maxwell in Notes and Queries (entry 4179); M. Seymour-Smith in Spectator (entry 4050); M. Thorpe in English Studies (entry 4123); and Times Literary Supplement (entry 4125).

See also: I. Armstrong, R.C. Terry, and M. Thorpe in Times Literary Supplement, 1968 (entries 4082, 4122, and 4124).

4014 Robson, W.W. "The Dilemma of Tennyson." Critical Essays. New York: Barnes and Noble, 1967, pp. 191-199.

4015 Ryals, Clyde de L. From the Great Deep: Essays on Idylls of the King. Athens, Ohio: Ohio University Press, 1967.

Ryals remarks of Tennyson: "I make no claim for him as a systematic thinker. I do, however, suggest that Idylls of the King be considered as a philosophical poem." Ryals explores some of the levels of meaning in Idylls of the King in a generally sensible discussion that reveals much of the work's complexity. In spite of his brief disclaimer, Ryals's comments often indicate Tennyson's merits as a thinker.

Reviewed by: J.M. Gray in Tennyson Research Bulletin (entry 4306); E.D.H. Johnson in Victorian Studies (entry 4103). J.D. Jump in English Language Notes (entry 4107). R.O. Preyer in Victorian Poetry (entry 4113); R.W. Rader in Modern Philology (entry 4264); and E.F. Waterman in Library Journal (entry 4063).

4016 Tennyson, Charles, and Christine Fall. Alfred Tennyson: An Annotated Bibliography. Athens, Georgia: U. of Georgia P., 1967.

This bibliography provides a listing of over six hundred editions and secondary works related to Tennyson. It is sloppily, almost casually, put together by both authors and publisher. Along with some good annotations, it provides a significant contribution in a listing of secondary works related to Tennyson's dramas.

Although seemingly intended for students, the book should be used with caution by those who are unfamiliar with Tennyson's canon. Some errors are astonishingly egregious. For example, on pages 67 and 68, Tennyson and Fall list the Westminster Review article on Poems, Chiefly Lyrical twice, as if by two different authors, John Bowring and John Stuart Mill, and as if two different articles. In the Bowring entry is biographical information on the supposed author (attributed to W.J. Fox in entry 8 of the present bibliography); in the Mill entry is a citation plainly from the article cited under Bowring.

This unfortunate sort of lapse is repeated at least once more in the book.

What might have been a handy short bibliography can, unfortunately, only be used effectively by Tennyson specialists and those with a special interest in Tennyson's dramas.

4017   Thomson, J.C.   Bibliography of the Writings of Alfred, Lord Tennyson.   London: H. Pordes, 1967.
Reprinting of rare 1905 edition (entry 2397).   Difficult to use in part because forgeries are listed as genuine.
Reviewed by: Times Literary Supplement (entry 4061).   See also, comments by E.C. Davies in Times Literary Supplement, 1967 (entry 4031).

Dissertations

4018   Al-Khatib, Issam.   The Orientalism of Alfred, Lord Tennyson. Case Western Reserve, 1967.   Dissertation Abstracts, 28 (1968), 4113A-4114A.
Al-Khatib examines Tennyson's use of Eastern myth and the poet's degree of success in reconciling Eastern and Western philosophies.

4019   Goslee, David Frederick.   A More Certain Trumpet: The Effects of Arthur's Ideal upon Individual and Society in Tennyson's Idylls of the King.   Yale, 1967.   Dissertation Abstracts, 28 (1968), 4174A.
Goslee discusses the background of the Idylls of the King and Tennyson's handling of King Arthur and the Arthurian ideal.

4020   Lundquist, James Carl.   The Life Style of Alfred Tennyson. Florida, 1967.   Dissertation Abstracts, 29 (1968), 267A.
Tennyson's manner of living reflected his idealism and melancholia.   The poet's life is examined in five parts: "Alfred Tennyson, Secret Agent," "The Ghost of Arthur Hallam," "Prince Albert's Kiss," "Mr. Tennyson's Abominable Caricature" (about the poet's playwriting), and "Lord Tennyson on the Cross Benches."

4021   Richardson, Robert Edward, Jr.   A Critical Introduction to the Idylls of the King (1859).   Princeton, 1967.   Dissertation Abstracts, 28 (1967), 1825A.
Background, sources, manuscript versions, and early critical reception.   The section on Tennyson's revisions is of particular interest.

4022   Story, Kenneth Ervin.   "Shadow and Substance": The Management of Tone in Tennyson's The Princess.   Tennessee, 1967. Dissertation Abstracts, 28 (1968), 3650A.
A study based on aesthetic rather than social principles.   A long overdue effort to examine The Princess as poetry.

4023   Swingle, Larry James.   Days That Cannot Die: A Romantic Manner of Thought about Time and Human Value.   Wisconsin,

372 / TENNYSON

1967. <u>Dissertation Abstracts</u>, 28 (1967), 646A.
Discusses Tennyson, Keats, and Browning, and <u>In Memoriam</u>.

Periodicals

4024 Adicks, Richard. "The Lily Maid and the Scarlet Sleeve:
      White and Red in Tennyson's <u>Idylls</u>." <u>University Review</u>, 34
      (1967), 65-71.

4025 Agrawala, D. C. "Hopkins on Tennyson." <u>Banasthali Patrika</u>,
      9 (1967), 39-44.

4026 Antippas, Andy P. "Tennyson, Hallam, and <u>The Palace of
      Art</u>." <u>Victorian Poetry</u>, 5 (1967), 294-296.
      The poet's independence of mind.

4027 Assad, Thomas J. "Tennyson's Use of the Tripartite View of
      Man in Three Songs from <u>The Princess</u>." <u>Tulane Studies in
      English</u>, 15 (1967), 31-58.
      Body, mind, and soul.

4028 Ayo, Nicholas. "A Checklist of the Principal Book-Length
      Studies in the Field of English and American Literature De-
      voted to a Single Author's Use of the Bible." <u>Bulletin of Bib-
      liography and Magazine Notes</u>, 25 (1967), 7-8.
      Includes reference to Tennyson.

4029 Buckley, Jerome H. "Tennyson's Irony." <u>Victorian News
      Letter</u>, no. 31 (Spring 1967), 7-10.
      Buckley points out the various forms of irony found in Tenny-
son's work and discusses the poet's use of irony.

4030 Chandler, Alice. "Cousin Clara Vere de Vere." <u>Victorian
      Poetry</u>, 5 (1967), 55-57.
      Chandler discusses the autobiographical aspects of the poem.

4031 Davies, E. C. <u>Times Literary Supplement</u>, Nov. 16, 1967, p.
      1085.
      A letter about the reprinting (entry 4017) of J. C. Thomson's
Bibliography.

4032 Elliott, Phillip L. <u>South Atlantic Bulletin</u>, 32 (Nov. 1967),
      24-25.
      Review of E. E. Smith's <u>The Two Voices</u>, 1964 (entry 3852).

4033 Forbes, William. <u>Aberdeen University Review</u>, 42 (1967), 58-
      60.
      Review of J. B. Steane's <u>Tennyson</u>, 1966 (entry 3958).

4034 Fuson, Ben W. "Tennyson's Chronological Priority over Brown-
      ing in Use of the Dramatic Monologue before 1836."
      <u>Studies</u> (Kobe College, Japan), 13, no. 3 (1967), 1-23.

4035 Gray, J. M. "Tennyson and Geoffrey of Monmouth." Notes
     and Queries, 14 (1967), 52-53.
     A source for Tennyson's work.

4036 Gunter, Richard. "Structure and Style in Poems: A Paradox."
     Style, 1 (1967), 93-106.
     Discusses "The Eagle."

4037 Hamer, Douglas. "Conversation-Notes with Sir Thomas Dyke
     Acland." Notes and Queries, 14 (1967), 65-66.
     Includes notes on Tennyson.

4038 Lees, F. N. "The Dissociation of Sensibility: Arthur Hallam
     and T. S. Eliot." Notes and Queries, 14 (1967), 308-309.
     Mentions the review of Tennyson's poetry by Hallam.

4039 McCombie, F. Notes and Queries, 14 (1967), 399-400.
     Review of J. B. Steane's Tennyson, 1966 (entry 3958).

4040 Millhauser, Milton. "'Magnetic Mockeries': The Background
     of a Phrase." English Language Notes, 5 (1967), 108-113.
     Tennyson's views of electricity and Calvinism.

4041 Noland, Richard W. "Tennyson and Hegel on War." Victorian
     News Letter, no. 31 (Spring 1967), 39-40.

4042 Ostriker, Alicia. "The Three Modes in Tennyson's Prosody."
     PMLA, 82 (1967), 273-284.
     Shifts in the modes in poems written between 1830 and 1842
reflect Tennyson's personal growth.

4043 Palmer, David. "The Laureate in Lyonesse." Listener, 77
     (1967), 815-817.
     The landscape imagery in Idylls of the King.

4044 Pinto, Eva R. "Tennyson's 'Crossing the Bar.'" Country
     Life, 140 (1967), 1024.

4045 Poston, Lawrence, III. "The Two Provinces of Tennyson's
     Idylls." Criticism, 9 (1967), 372-382.
     Unity of didactic and aesthetic themes.

4046 Qureshi, A. H. "The Waste Land Motif in Tennyson." Human-
     ities Association Bulletin, 18, no. 2 (1967), 20-30.

4047 Ricks, Christopher. "An Echo of Tennyson in Browning."
     Notes and Queries, 14 (1967), 374.
     The Princess, VII, lines 136-139 and "Childe Roland to the
Dark Tower Came."

4048 Ryals, Clyde de L. "Idylls of the King: Tennyson's New Re-
     alism." Victorian News Letter, no. 31 (Spring 1967), 5-7.
     Idylls of the King contradicts In Memoriam.

4049 Sendry, Joseph. "In Memoriam and Lycidas." PMLA, 82 (1967), 437-443.
Tennyson's apologies for digressions indicate to Sendry the influence of Milton's poem on that of Tennyson.

4050 Seymour-Smith, Martin. Spectator, Dec. 29, 1967, pp. 817-818.
Review of J. D. Jump, ed., Tennyson, 1967 (entry 4013).

4051 Shaw, W. David. "The Idealist's Dilemma in Idylls of the King." Victorian Poetry, 5 (1967), 41-53.
The work helps its readers to "see, not our past legends, but the total cultural form of our present life as it is involved in the same venture of civilizing nature and investing the wasteland with the flesh and blood of our own redeeming vision."

4052 _____. "The Transcendentalist Problem in Tennyson's Poetry of Debate." Philological Quarterly, 46 (1967), 79-94.
Examines how Tennyson handles problems in "The Two Voices," "The Ancient Sage," and In Memoriam.

4053 Shmiefsky, Marvel. "In Memoriam: Its Seasonal Imagery Reconsidered." Studies in English Literature, 1500-1900, 7 (1967), 721-739.
This interesting essay presents an examination of archetypes in In Memoriam.

4054 Short, Clarice. "Tennyson and 'The Lover's Tale.'" PMLA, 82 (1967), 78-84.
Short presents evidence for dating the composition of sections of the poem and argues for its subjective importance.

4055 Smith, Elton E. "Tennyson Criticism 1923-1966: From Fragmentation to Tension in Polarity." Victorian News Letter, no. 31 (Spring 1967), 1-4.
Discusses important studies of the poet's work.

4056 Smith, M. A. "Autograph Letters." Manchester Review, 11 (1967), 97-120.
Mentions letters by Tennyson in the Manchester Central Library.

4057 Solimine, Joseph. "The Burkean Idea of the State in Tennyson's Poetry: The Vision in Crisis." Huntington Library Quarterly, 30 (1967), 147-165.
In this sophisticated essay, Solimine discusses the influence of Burke's ideas of the state on Tennyson's antipathetic views of the state of the Victorian era.

4058 Sucksmith, H. P. "Tennyson on the Nature of His Own Poetic Genius: Some Recently Discovered Marginalia." Renaissance and Modern Studies, 11 (1967), 84-89.
The poet's comments on a Cornhill Magazine article that discussed Tennyson's indebtedness to earlier great poets.

4059 Thompson, Laurence S. <u>Papers of the Bibliographical Society of America</u>, 61 (1967), 134-135.
Review of J. Carter and G. Pollard's <u>The Forgeries of Tennyson's Plays</u>, 1967 (entry 4012).

4060 <u>Times Literary Supplement</u>, June 1, 1967, p. 496.
Review of J. Carter and G. Pollard's <u>The Forgeries of Tennyson's Plays</u>, 1967 (entry 4012).

4061 <u>Times Literary Supplement</u>, Oct. 26, 1967, p. 1024.
Review of J.C. Thomson's <u>Bibliography</u>, 1967 (c. 1905; entry 4017).

4062 Walsh, Thomas. <u>Modern Language Journal</u>, 51 (1967), 181-182.
Review of A. E. Baker's <u>Concordance to the Poetical and Dramatic Works</u>, 1914, reprinted 1966 (entry 2756).

4063 Waterman, E. F. <u>Library Journal</u>, 92 (1967), 1625.
Review of C. de L. Ryals's <u>From the Great Deep</u>, 1967 (entry 4015).

4064 Wilson, Hugh H. "Tennyson: Unscholarly Arthurian."
<u>Victorian News Letter</u>, no. 32 (Fall 1967), 5-11.
Tennyson drew on secondary sources for some of his knowledge of the Arthurian legends.

1968

Books

4065 Ball, Patricia M. "Inheriting Pegasus: Tennyson, Arnold and Browning." <u>The Central Self: A Study in Romantic and Victorian Imagination</u>. London: Athlone, 1968, pp. 166-200.
Ball examines aspects of Tennyson's imagination and the Romantic qualities of his poetry.

4066 Chapman, Raymond. "Tennyson and Browning." <u>The Victorian Debate: English Literature and Society 1832-1901</u>. London: Weidenfeld and Nicolson, 1968. New York: Basic Books, 1968, pp. 194-206.
Chapman compares Tennyson and Browning and discusses Tennyson's moral themes.

4067 Donoghue, Denis. "From Tennyson to Eliot." <u>The Ordinary Universe: Soundings in Modern Literature</u>. New York: Macmillan, 1968. London: Faber and Faber, 1968, pp. 90-107.
Landscape and Ideas.

4068 Johnson, E. D. H. "Alfred, Lord Tennyson." <u>The Victorian Poets: A Guide to Research</u>. Ed. Frederic E. Faverty.
Cambridge, Massachusetts: Harvard U. P., 1968, pp. 33-80.

Johnson provides an erudite and sensible summary of Tennysonian studies through the mid-1960s.

4069 Joseph, Gerhard. Tennysonian Love: The Strange Diagonal. Minneapolis: U. of Minnesota P., 1968.
Joseph discusses physical and spiritual love in Tennyson's poetry, noting a shift from eroticism to the spiritual that parallels a shift from lyricism to epic legend. Joseph explores the origins of Tennyson's notions of love and the implications of those notions for understanding the poet's character and work.
Reviewed by: Allan Danzig in Victorian Studies (entry 4245); G.O. Marshall, Jr., in Georgia Review (entry 4261); J.R. Reed in Victorian Poetry (entry 4188); C. de L. Ryals in Journal of English and Germanic Philology (entry 4266); and Times Literary Supplement (entry 4272).

Dissertations

4070 Antippas, Andy Peter. The Burden of Poetic Tradition: A Study in the Works of Keats, Tennyson, Arnold, and Morris. Wisconsin, 1968. Dissertation Abstracts, 28 (1968), 4591A-4592A.
Using "The Palace of Art" to exemplify his arguments, Antippas presents Tennyson as a poet who sought to bring poetry back to a realm of shared human experiences.

4071 Boyd, John Douglas. Tennyson's Poetry of Religious Debate: Rhetoric and the Problem of Self. Cornell, 1968. Dissertation Abstracts, 29 (1968), 1531A-1532A.
Boyd examines several of Tennyson's poems as religious debates, contending that critics have misunderstood the poetry. He pays special attention to In Memoriam. His discussion includes a summary of views of Tennyson as a thinker and commentary on the problems Tennyson's religious poetry presents for critics.

4072 Devlin, Francis Patrick. Tennyson's Use of Landscape Imagery. Indiana, 1968. Dissertation Abstracts, 29 (1968), 564A-565A.
A study of the techniques used by Tennyson to evoke landscapes in his poetry and of the uses to which Tennyson puts landscapes.

4073 Eggers, John Philip. The Golden Judgment: A Critical Study of The Idylls of the King in Relation to Its Mythical Background and Victorian Setting. Columbia, 1968. Dissertation Abstracts 29 (1968), 565A-566A.
The meaning and modern relevance of the poetry. See J.P. Eggers's King Arthur's Laureate, 1971 (entry 4276).

4074 Gadziola, David Stanley. The Prophet and the Poet: The Relationship of Thomas Carlyle with Robert Browning, Alfred Tennyson and Arthur Hugh Clough. Maryland, 1968. Dissertation Abstracts International, 30 (1969), 1562A.
Gadziola discusses Carlyle's influence on Tennyson and Carlyle's response to Tennyson's poetry. He maintains that Tennyson came closest of the poets discussed to fulfilling Carlyle's notions of what a poet should do.

4075 McMunn, William Robert. A Critical Edition of the Shorter
Poems of Frederick Tennyson: Edited with a Biographical
Sketch of the Poet. Indiana, 1968. Dissertation Abstracts,
29 (1969), 3104A.
Frederick Tennyson was the brother of Alfred Tennyson. Mc-
Munn provides the shorter poems and commentary. He believes Fred-
erick Tennyson was a good versifier who failed to create his own
poetic style.

4076 Morris, Celia B. The Makaris of Camelot. City University
of New York, 1968. Dissertation Abstracts International, 29
(1968), 1516A-1517A.
Morris compares Tennyson's Idylls of the King, Thomas Malory's Le Morte D'Arthur, and Edwin Arlington Robinson's Merlin and
Lancelot. She finds that ambivalence of allegory and character in
Idylls of the King renders the work into confusion.

4077 Niermeier, Stuart Fraser Cornelius. The Poetic Structure of
In Memoriam. Toronto, 1968. Dissertation Abstracts International, 30 (1970), 4419A-4420A.
Niermeier discusses criticism of In Memoriam and provides an
analysis of the organizing principles of the poem. He perceives in
the poem a blend of poetic forms that he regards as the primary
achievement of Tennyson.

4078 Pappas, John James. Victorian Literature of the Divided Mind:
A Study of the Self in Relation to Nature. Columbia, 1968.
Dissertation Abstracts International, 30 (1969), 693A-694A.
Discusses Tennyson's "The Two Voices" among works by other
writers.

4079 Salome, Rosaline. Tennyson's Idylls: The Relevance of a
Chronology of Composition. Emory, 1968. Dissertation Abstracts, 29 (1969), 2279A-2280A.
The order of the sections of Idylls of the King as commonly
published does not reflect the order of their composition. Salome
examines the poems in the order that they were written in order to
discover continuity of themes and development that might be obscured
by their usual arrangement.

4080 Workman, Charles Thomas. Tennyson's Concept and Use of
the Past. Tulane, 1968. Dissertation Abstracts, 29 (1968),
1883A.
Workman finds that Tennyson uses the idea of the past to provide his best work with philosophical perspective. The past is an important creative element in Tennyson's poetry.

4081 Wymer, Thomas Lee. Romantic to Modern: Tennyson's Aesthetic and Religious Development. Oklahoma, 1968. Dissertation Abstracts, 29 (1968), 242A-243A.
Wymer views Tennyson as representative of the Victorian era.
He tries to create a rational approach to understanding both Tennyson
and his time without interference of prejudices. In Memoriam and
Idylls of the King are examined in particular.

Periodicals

4082 Armstrong, Isobel. Times Literary Supplement, Feb. 1,
1968, p. 117.
See also: R. C. Terry (entry 4122) and M. Thorpe (entry
4124). About J. D. Jump, ed., Tennyson, 1967 (entry 4013).

4083 Assad, Thomas J. "The Touch of Genius in Tennyson's Ear-
liest Lyrics." Tulane Studies in English, 16 (1968), 29-47.
Discusses Tennyson's poetry in Poems by Two Brothers and
Poems, Chiefly Lyrical.

4084 Brashear, William R. "Tennyson's Tragic Vitalism: Idylls
of the King." Victorian Poetry, 6 (1968), 29-49.
Reprinted: The Living Will, 1969 (entry 4132).

4085 Caird, J. B. Library Review, 21 (1968), 269-270.
Review of J. D. Jump, ed., Tennyson, 1967 (entry 4013).

4086 Cameron, A. Barry. "The Extemporaneity of 'Tears, Idle
Tears.'" CEA Critic, 30, no. 8 (1968), 16.

4087 Collins, Winston. "Tennyson and Hopkins." University of
Toronto Quarterly, 38 (1968), 84-95.
A comparison of poems that emphasizes the ideas and qualities
the two poets have in common.

4088 Eidson, John Olin. "Charles Stearns Wheeler, Friend of Emerson." Emerson Society Quarterly, no. 52 (1968), 13-76.
Mentions Tennyson often.

4089 Elliott, Philip L. "Imagery and Unity in the Idylls of the
King." Furman Studies, 15, no. 4 (1968), 22-28.
Seasonal development and unity in Idylls of the King.

4090 Filby, P. W. Library Journal, 93 (1968), 2846.
Review of A. E. Baker's Tennyson Dictionary, 1914, reprinted
1968 (entry 2809).

4091 Fredeman, William E. "'The Sign Betwixt the Meadow and
the Cloud': The Ironic Apotheosis of Tennyson's St. Simeon
Stylites." University of Toronto Quarterly, 38 (1968), 69-83.

4092 Gallagher, Edward J. "A Note on Longfellow and Tennyson."
Notes and Queries, 15 (1968), 415-416.
The image of the "ninth wave" used by both poets.

4093 Goode, John. "Gissing, Morris and English Socialism." Victorian Studies, 12 (1968), 201-226.

4094 Gray, Jon M. "The Creation of Excalibur: An Apparent Incon-
sistency in the Idylls." Victorian Poetry, 6 (1968), 68-69.

4095 _____. "Fact, Form and Fiction in Tennyson's Balin and Balan." Renaissance and Modern Studies, 12 (1968), 90-107.

4096 _____. "Tennyson and Layamon." Notes and Queries, 15 (1968), 176-178.

4097 Hall, P. E. "A Latin Translation of In Memoriam." Book Collector, 17 (1968), 78.
A copy of a translation by O. A. Smith is uncovered.

4098 _____. "Tennyson's Idylls of the King and The Holy Grail." Book Collector, 17 (1968), 218-219.
On the dates of publication. See also: M. Trevanion (entry 4126).

4099 Hill, James L. "Tennyson's 'The Lady of Shalott': The Ambiguity of Commitment." Centennial Review, 12 (1968), 415-429.

4100 Hopkinson, D. M. "Parson Hawker of Morwenstow." History Today, 18 (1968), 38-44.
A friend of Tennyson.

4101 Hornback, Bert G. "Tennyson's 'Break, Break, Break' Again." Victorian News Letter, no. 33 (Spring 1968), 47-48.
Despair, faith, and acceptance in the poem.

4102 Inman, Billie Jo. Arizona Quarterly, 24 (1968), 191-192.
Review of J. D. Jump, ed., Tennyson, 1967 (entry 4013).

4103 Johnson, E. D. H. Victorian Studies, 12 (1968), 113-115.
Review of C. de L. Ryals's From the Great Deep, 1967 (entry 4015).

4104 Jordan, Elaine. "Tennyson's In Memoriam--An Echo of Goethe." Notes and Queries, 15 (1968), 414-415.
Notes an image from Goethe.

4105 Joseph, Gerhard. "The Idea of Mortality in Tennyson's Classical and Arthurian Poems: 'Honor Comes with Mystery.'" Modern Philology, 66 (1968), 136-145.

4106 _____. "Tennyson's Death in Life in Lyric Myth: 'Tears, Idle Tears' and 'Demeter and Persephone.'" Victorian News Letter, no. 34 (Fall 1968), 13-18.

4107 Jump, John D. English Language Notes, 6 (1968), 56-58.
Review of C. de L. Ryals's From the Great Deep, 1967 (entry 4015).

4108 Lagarde, Fernand. "On Tennyson's and Shakespeare's Kates." Caliban, 5, no. 1 (1968), 53-56.

4109   Madden, J.L.   "Peacock, Tennyson and Cleopatra."   Notes
       and Queries, 15 (1968), 416-417.
       About "A Dream of Fair Women."

4110   Moews, Daniel D.   "The 'Prologue' to In Memoriam: A Com-
       mentary on Lines 5, 17, and 32."   Victorian Poetry, 6 (1968),
       185-187.

4111   Monteiro, George.   "Tennyson to Sir Francis Palgrave: A
       Letter."   English Language Notes, 6 (1968), 106-107.
       Presents a letter.

4112   Nowell-Smith, Simon.   "Tennyson's In Memoriam 1850."   Book
       Collector, 17 (1968), 350-351.
       Nowell-Smith disagrees with T.J. Wise's contention that two
first editions were issued.

4113   Preyer, Robert O.   Victorian Poetry, 6 (1968), 209-214.
       Review of C. de L. Ryals's From the Great Deep, 1967 (en-
try 4015).

4114   Reed, John R.   "The Design of Tennyson's 'The Two Voices.'"
       University of Toronto Quarterly, 37 (1968), 186-196.

4115   Scott, P.G.   "Tennyson's Celtic Reading."   Tennyson Research
       Bulletin, 1 (Nov. 1968), paper 2.

4116   Shaw, W. David.   "Gareth's Four Antagonists: A Biblical
       Source."   Victorian News Letter, no. 34 (Fall 1968), 34-35.
       Gareth and the Four Horsemen of the Apocalypse.

4117   _____ .   "The Passion of the Past: Tennyson and Francis
       Grose."   English Language Notes, 5 (1968), 269-277.
       Tennyson presents "an almost Virgilian sense of the pathos
inherent in the simple cycle of human change."

4118   Sifton, Paul G.   "On the European Scene."   Manuscripts, 20
       (Winter 1968), 45-58.
       Mentions manuscripts of Tennyson.

4119   Stange, G. Robert.   "The Victorian City and the Frightened
       Poets."   Victorian Studies, 11 (1968), 627-640.
       Tennyson and others on cities.

4120   Sutherland, Raymond C.   "The 'St. John Sense' Underlying 'The
       Eagle: A Fragment' by Tennyson--'To Whom the Vision
       Came.'"   Studies in the Literary Imagination, 1, no. 1 (1968),
       23-35.
       Themes and relationships.

4121   Tennyson, Charles.   "Tennyson's 'Doubt and Prayer' Sonnet."
       Victorian Poetry, 6 (1968), 1-3.
       Composition of poem.

4122 Terry, R.C. <u>Times Literary Supplement</u>, Feb. 15, 1968, p. 157.
      See also: I. Armstrong (entry 4082) and M. Thorpe (entry 4124). About J.D. Jump, ed., <u>Tennyson</u>, 1967 (entry 4013).

4123 Thorpe, Michael. <u>English Studies</u>, 49 (1968), 362-363.
      Review of J.D. Jump, ed., <u>Tennyson</u>, 1967 (entry 4013).

4124 _____. <u>Times Literary Supplement</u>, March 7, 1968, p. 237.
      See also: I. Armstrong (entry 4082) and R.C. Terry (entry 4122). About J.D. Jump, ed., <u>Tennyson</u>, 1967 (entry 4013).

4125 <u>Times Literary Supplement</u>, Jan. 4, 1968, p. 10.
      Review of J.D. Jump, ed., <u>Tennyson</u>, 1967 (entry 4013).

4126 Trevanion, Michael. "Tennyson's <u>Idylls</u> and <u>The Holy Grail</u>." <u>Book Collector</u>, 17 (1968), 490-491.
      On the dates of publication. See also: P.E. Hall (entry 4098).

4127 Werlich, Egon. "Alfred Lord Tennyson, 'Crossing the Bar': An Essay in the Poem's Meaning and Structural Symbolism." <u>Praxis</u>, 15 (1968), 335-341.

4128 Wiggins, Louise D. "Tennyson's Veiled Statue." <u>English Studies</u>, 49 (1968), 444-445.
      A possible influence of Schiller on an image in <u>In Memoriam</u>.

4129 Wilkenfeld, R.B. "Tennyson's Camelot: The Kingdom of Folly." <u>University of Toronto Quarterly</u>, 37 (1968), 281-294.
      Wilkenfeld discusses the fool as unifying theme in <u>Idylls of the King</u>.

1969

Books

4130 Andrews, Clarence A. "Introduction." <u>Idylls of the King</u>, by Alfred, Lord Tennyson. New York: Airmont, 1969. Toronto: Ryerson, 1969, pp. 3-7.
      Andrews discusses the background of the <u>Idylls of the King</u>.
He remarks: "When Tennyson presented this poem to his Queen, Victoria was ruler over the world's greatest empire, an empire upon which the sun never set. There is implicit in the poem a warning that even the perfect King and the perfect Kingdom cannot survive the loss of faith."

4131 Bergonzi, Bernard. "Feminism and Feminity in <u>The Princess</u>." The Major Victorian Poets: Reconsiderations. Ed. Isobel Armstrong. London: Routledge and Kegan Paul, 1969, pp. 35-50.

Bergonzi remarks: "The Princess is, I suppose, the strangest of Tennyson's well-known poems, and it is also, in a literal sense, one of his most thoughtful: ideas got into the poem more successfully here than elsewhere, and I want to suggest that the eccentricity of its form was dictated by Tennyson's desire to entertain and contemplate ideas, some of them rather disturbing ideas, to which he was not prepared to be formally committed."

4132   Brashear, William R.   The Living Will: A Study of Tennyson
       and Nineteenth-Century Subjectivism.   The Hague: Mouton,
       1969.   (Studies in English Literature, 52)
       "The living will" is victorious in Tennyson's early poetry.
Reviewed by: J. Killham in Yearbook of English Studies (entry 4309);
E. E. Smith in Victorian Poetry (entry 4267); and Times Literary
Supplement (entry 4203).

4133   Burton, Thomas G.   "The Use of Biblical Allusions in Tenny-
       son's Harold."   Essays in Memory of Christine Burleson.   Ed.
       Thomas G. Burton.   Johnson City: East Tennessee State U.,
       1969, pp. 155-163.

4134   Byatt, A.S.   "The Lyric Structure of Tennyson's Maud."   The
       Major Victorian Poets: Reconsiderations.   Ed. Isobel Arm-
       strong.   London: Routledge and Kegan Paul, 1969, pp. 69-92.
       Byatt asserts: "Maud ... is concerned not only with the gen-
eral question 'Were it not better not to be?' but with the practical
question of what it means to have sufficient identity to be capable of
consistent and meaningful action--Hamlet's dramatic problem, and the
dramatic problem of the hero of Maud."   After discussing the lyric
qualities of the poem, Byatt says: "It seems to me that the peculiar
strength of Maud lies in this use of the lyric to combine the particular
and the universal."

4135   Campion, G. Edward.   A Tennyson Dialect Glossary with the
       Dialect Poems.   Lincoln: Lincolnshire Association, 1969.
       Worth consulting for those interested in the Lincolnshire poems.
Includes the seven poems.

4136   Clarke, Austin.   The Celtic Twilight and the Nineties.   Dublin:
       Dolmen, 1969.

4137   Dodsworth, Martin.   "Patterns of Morbidity: Repetition in Ten-
       nyson's Poetry."   The Major Victorian Poets: Reconsiderations
       Ed. Isobel Armstrong.   London: Routledge and Kegan Paul,
       1969, pp. 7-34.
       Dodsworth observes of Tennyson that "no style is easier to
recognize than his, and this is true in spite of the astonishing diversity of forms which he employed."   In this interesting essay, Dodsworth uses Tennyson's repetitiveness to illuminate aspects of the poetry.

4138   Duncan, Edgar H.   "Tennyson's Ulysses and Translations of
       Dante's Inferno: Some Conjectures."   Essays in Memory of

Christine Burleson. Ed. Thomas G. Burton. Johnson City:
East Tennessee State U., 1969, pp. 15-26.

4139 Enzensberger, Christian. Viktorianische Lyrik: Tennyson und
Swinburne in der Geschichte der Entfremdung. Munich: Hau-
ser, 1969. (Literatur als Kunst)
Enzenberger emphasizes the development of Tennyson's poetry.
He presents some interesting ideas about the development of In Memo-
riam.

4140 Gray, J.M. Man and Myth in Victorian England: Tennyson's
The Coming of Arthur. Lincoln, England: Tennyson Society
Research Centre, 1969.
Background and explication. Reviewed by: J. Killham in
Yearbook of English Studies (entry 4309); P. Turner in Notes and
Queries (entry 4274); and Times Literary Supplement (entry 4272).

4141 Killham, John. "Tennyson and FitzGerald." The Victorians.
Ed. Arthur Pollard. London: Cresset, 1969. New York:
Bantam, 1969, pp. 263-291. (The Sphere History of Litera-
ture in the English Language, 6)

4142 Miyoshi, Masao. The Divided Self: A Perspective on the Victorians. New York: New York U. P., 1969.
This book has become a standard reference for students of
Victorian literature. Tennyson is discussed often, with Miyoshi making notably lucid comments on the Idylls of the King.

4143 Reed, John R. Perception and Design in Tennyson's Idylls of
the King. Athens: Ohio U. P., 1969.
Reed begins: "My concept of the moral design in Tennyson's
poetry resembles the pattern of conversion described by Professor
J. H. Buckley in The Victorian Temper.... This moral design is
evident in earlier literature; for example in Saint Augustine's Confessions, if not the parables of Christ.... I am not hereby suggesting
that Tennyson derived his moral views from Augustine, but merely
that the design governing Tennyson's religious imagination was one
of long standing in Christian tradition." Arguing that Tennyson's
point of view in Idylls of the King is clear, and that the poem is not
a muddled allegory, Reed discusses how the work as a whole and in
its parts represents man's effort to fulfill the Christian ideal. This
is an important study of Idylls of the King.
Reviewed by: Choice (entry 4297); C. Fall in Victorian Studies
(entry 4366); J.M. Gray in Tennyson Research Bulletin (entry 4306);
K. McSweeney in Papers on Language and Literature (entry 4562); and
Times Literary Supplement (entry 4322).

4144 Sinfield, Alan. "Matter-moulded Forms of Speech: Tennyson's
Use of Language in In Memoriam." The Major Victorian Po-
ets: Reconsiderations. Ed. Isobel Armstrong. London:
Routledge and Kegan Paul, 1969, pp. 51-67.

4145 Tennyson, Alfred. The Poems of Tennyson. Ed. Christopher
Ricks. London: Longmans, 1969.

This excellent edition includes nearly all of Tennyson's poems, with the exception of a few in manuscripts that were unavailable to Ricks. The annotations are thorough and useful. In general, this edition has supplanted earlier ones and has become the standard reference for scholars. No serious student of Tennyson's poetry should be without a copy. Reviewed by: J. Bayley in Encounter (entry 4439); G. Grigson in Listener (entry 4167); J. Holloway in Spectator (entry 4168); J.D. Jump in Critical Quarterly (entry 4383); J. Killham in Yearbook of English Studies (entry 4309); P. Larkin in New Statesman and Nation (entry 4176); H. L. Lehman in Victorian Studies (entry 4260); J. C. Maxwell in Notes and Queries (entry 4312); J. Pettigrew in Victorian Poetry (entry 4263); and Times Literary Supplement (entry 4202).

4146   Tennyson, Charles. Forward. A Tennyson Dialect Glossary, with the Dialect Poems, by G. Edward Campion. Lincoln: Lincolnshire Association, 1969.

Dissertations

4147   Collins, Winston Lee. The Hero in Tennyson's Longer Poems. Toronto, 1969. Dissertation Abstracts International, 32 (1971), 383A.
      The nature of the hero in Tennyson's poetry, with chapters devoted to The Princess, In Memoriam, Maud, Enoch Arden, and Idylls of the King. Collins finds universality in the moral purpose of Tennyson's heroes.

4148   Kozicki, Henry James. Tennyson's Poetry and the Philosophy of History as Symbolic Form. Wayne State, 1969. Dissertation Abstracts International, 32 (1972), 6394A.
      Kozicki discusses the background for Tennyson's philosophies of history and myth and how they work together in the poetry.

4149   Mitchell, William Richard. Theological Origins of the Christ-Image in Victorian Literature with Special Reference to In Memoriam. Oklahoma, 1969.
      Religious vision, background, and Hallam as image of Christ.

4150   Nodelman, Perry Michael. Art Palace to Evolution: Tennyson's Metaphors of Organization. Yale, 1969. Dissertation Abstracts International, 30 (1969), 1570A-1571A.
      Focusing primarily on Tennyson's In Memoriam and earlier poetry, Nodelman shows how the poet used metaphors to reconcile disperate ideas and aspects of his poetry. A sensible discussion that provides cogent observations on the organization of In Memoriam.

4151   Petrie, Neil H. Psychic Disintegration in the Early Poetry of Tennyson. Kent State, 1969. Dissertation Abstracts International, 30 (1970), 4423A.
      Jungian criticism of archetypes in the early poems. Petrie tries to explain a shift in aesthetics and subject matter in the poetry. The failure of symbol and archetype to reconcile Tennyson's conscious and unconscious selves results in the disintegration of psyche and poetry into incoherence. Interesting.

4152   Simmons, William Kyle. The Passing of Arthur by Alfred,
       Lord Tennyson: An Edition with Variants, Annotated. Ohio,
       1969. Dissertation Abstracts International, 30 (1970), 3958A.
         Good, basic research. Simmons provides some insight into
Tennyson's methods of composition and the progress of the poem
from manuscript to published work.

Periodicals

4153   "Alfred Tennyson flies to the moon--a hitherto unpublished
       poem." Listener, 81 (1969), 33-34.

4154   Antippas, Andy P. "Tennyson's Sinful Soul: Poetic Tradition
       and 'Keats Turned Imbecile.'" Tulane Studies in English, 17
       (1969), 113-134.
       "The Palace of Art" is examined.

4155   Armstrong, Isobel. Victorian Studies, 12 (1969), 482-484.
       Review of J.D. Jump, ed., Tennyson, 1967 (entry 4013).

4156   Assad, Thomas J. "Time and Eternity: Tennyson's 'A Fare-
       well' and 'In the Valley of Cauteretz.'" Tulane Studies in
       English, 17 (1969), 93-111.

4157   August, Eugene R. "Tennyson and Teilhard: The Faith of
       In Memoriam." PMLA, 84 (1969), 217-226.
         August sees In Memoriam as anticipating Pierre Teilhard de
Chardin's efforts to reconcile religion and science. He finds the
faith of the poem to be strong in its sense of progress.

4158   Bishop, Morchard. Times Literary Supplement, Aug. 28, 1969,
       p. 954.
         A letter on C. Ricks's "The Tennyson Manuscripts" (entry
4190).

4159   Bradley, J.L. Modern Language Review, 64 (1969), 656-657.
       Review of J.D. Jump, ed., Tennyson, 1967 (entry 4013).

4160   Chandler, Alice. "Tennyson's Maud and the Song of Songs."
       Victorian Poetry, 7 (1969), 91-104.
       The Bible and allegory in Maud.

4161   Closs, A. Times Literary Supplement, Aug. 28, 1969, p. 954.
         A letter on C. Ricks's "The Tennyson Manuscripts" (entry
4190).

4162   Crawford, John W. "A Unifying Element in Tennyson's Maud."
       Victorian Poetry, 7 (1969), 64-66.
         The change in colors of the rose is a "nationalistic, propagan-
distic device."

4163   D'Avanzo, Mario L. "Lyric 95 of In Memoriam: Poetry and
       Vision." Research Studies, 37 (1969), 149-154.
       Music as metaphor.

4164   Ferguson, John. "Catullus and Tennyson." English Studies
       in Africa, 12 (1969), 41-58.
       The classics and Tennyson.

4165   Gaskell, Philip. Times Literary Supplement, Sept. 18, 1969,
       p. 1026.
       A letter on C. Ricks's "The Tennyson Manuscripts" (entry
4190).

4166   Gray, J. M. "Knightly Combats in Malory's Tale of Sir Gar-
       eth and Tennyson's 'Gareth and Lynette.'" Notes and Queries,
       16 (1969), 207-208.

4167   Grigson, Geoffrey. Listener, 81 (1969), 385-386.
       Review of The Poems of Tennyson, ed. C. Ricks, 1969 (entry
4145).

4168   Holloway, John. Spectator, 222 (1969), 338-339.
       Review of The Poems of Tennyson, ed. C. Ricks, 1969 (entry
4145).

4169   Hume, Robert D., and Toby A. Olshin. "Ambrosius in 'The
       Holy Grail': Source and Function." Notes and Queries, 16
       (1969), 208-209.
       Links Ambrosius to King Arthur.

4170   Humphreys, A. R. "Oration on Sir Charles Tennyson." Tenny-
       son Research Bulletin, 1, no. 3 (Nov. 1969), 55-56.

4171   Kaplan, Fred. "Woven Paces and Waving Hands: Tennyson's
       Merlin as Fallen Artist." Victorian Poetry, 7 (1969), 285-298.
       "Merlin and Vivien" presents Tennyson's concerns about the
limitations of imagination and creativity. The poet perceives imagination as capable of destroying itself by creating its own nemesis.

4172   Kay, Donald. "'The Holy Grail' and Tennyson's Quest for Po-
       etic Identity." Arlington Quarterly, 2, no. 1 (1969), 58-70.
       Allegorical interpretation.

4173   Kincaid, James R. "Tennyson's Mariners and Spenser's De-
       spair: The Argument of 'The Lotus-Eaters.'" Papers on
       Language and Literature, 5 (1969), 273-281.
       Ambiguity in the poem.

4174   Kramer, Dale. "Metaphor and Meaning in 'Crossing the Bar.'"
       Ball State University Forum, 10, no. 3 (1969), 44-47.

4175   Landesberg, Frances H. "Huge Men on Huge Horses: Heroes
       in Obscurity." Tennyson Research Bulletin, 1, no. 3 (Nov.
       1969), 57-60.
       Background for the poem.

4176 Larkin, P. New Statesman and Nation, 77 (1969), 363-364.
      Review of The Poems of Tennyson, ed. C. Ricks, 1969 (entry
4145).

4177 Lewin, Lois S. "The Blameless King? The Conceptual Flaw
      in Tennyson's Arthur." Ball State University Forum, 10, no.
      3 (1969), 32-41.

4178 Marshall, George O., Jr. "Tennyson's 'The Sisters' and
      'Porphyria's Lover.'" Browning Newsletter, 3 (1969), 9-11.

4179 Maxwell, J.C. Notes and Queries, 16 (1969), 232-233.
      Review of J.D. Jump, ed., Tennyson, 1967 (entry 4013).

4180 Meinhold, George D. "The Idylls of the King and the Mabino-
      gion." Tennyson Research Bulletin, 1, no. 3 (Nov. 1969),
      61-63.

4181 Merriman, James D. "The Poet as Heroic Thief: Tennyson's
      'The Hesperides' Re-examined." Victorian Newsletter, no.
      35 (Spring 1969), 1-5.
      The poet and the sisters in opposition.

4182 Millhauser, Milton. "A Plurality of After-Worlds: Isaac Tay-
      lor and Alfred Tennyson." Hartford Studies in Literature, 1,
      no. 1 (1969), 37-49.
      Taylor's influence on poems by Tennyson.

4183 _____. "Tennyson, Vestiges and the Dark Side of Science."
      Victorian Newsletter, no. 35 (Spring 1969), 22-25.
      An influence on Tennyson.

4184 Miyoshi, Masao. "Narrative Sequence and the Moral System:
      Three Tristram Poems." Victorian Newsletter, no. 35 (1969),
      5-10.
      A "technique of obfuscation" in a poem by Tennyson.

4185 Nishimae, Yoshimi. "The Tennyson Manuscripts at Trinity
      College, Cambridge." Hiroshima Studies in English Language
      and Literature, 16, nos. 1 and 2 (1969), 48-54.

4186 Nowell-Smith, Simon. "Tennyson's Tiresias, 1885." Library,
      5th ser. 24 (1969), 55-56.
      Variant versions.

4187 Perrine, Laurence. "Tennyson and Robinson: Legalistic Mor-
      alism vs. Situation Ethics." Colby Library Quarterly, 8
      (1969), 416-433.
      The Arthurian poems of Edward Arlington Robinson and Ten-
nyson's Idylls of the King.

4188 Reed, John R. Victorian Poetry, 7 (1969), 171-174.
      Review of G. Joseph's Tennysonian Love, 1968 (entry 4069).

4189 Ricks, Christopher. "Tennyson as a Love-Poet." Malahat
      Review, 12 (1969), 73-88.

4190 _____. "The Tennyson Manuscripts." Times Literary Sup-
      plement, Aug. 21, 1969, pp. 918-922.
      See also: M. Bishop (entry 4158), A. Closs (entry 4161), P.
Gaskell (entry 4165), and C. Ricks (entry 4191). Also discussed by
H.H. Lehman in Victorian Studies, 1970 (entry 4260).
      Ricks presents previously unpublished poetry and copies of
texts corrected by Tennyson.

4191 _____. Times Literary Supplement, Sept. 11, 1969, p.
      1002.
      A letter on C. Ricks's "The Tennyson Manuscripts" (entry
4190).

4192 Russo, Antonino. "Fedeltà storica, struttura, ispirazione
      epico storica e poesia nei drammi storici di Alfred Tennyson."
      Annali del Liceo Classico Garibaldi di Palermo, 5-6 (1968-
      1969), 374-410.

4193 Ryals, Clyde de L. "Browning's Fifine at the Fair: Some
      Further Sources and Influences." English Language Notes,
      7 (1969), 46-51.

4194 Scott, P.G. "Tennyson and Clough." Tennyson Research Bul-
      letin, 1, no. 3 (Nov. 1969), 64-70.
      The relationship of the poets. Of biographical interest.

4195 "Shalott and Other Ladies." Times Literary Supplement, April
      3, 1969, pp. 367-368.

4196 Shaw, W. David. "Idylls of the King: A Dialectical Reading."
      Victorian Poetry, 7 (1969), 175-190.

4197 Smith, James L. "William McGonagall and the Poet Laureate."
      Studies in Scottish Literature, 7 (1969), 21-34.
      Discusses the funeral of Tennyson.

4198 Sochatoff, A. Fred. "Four Variations on the Becket Theme in
      Modern Drama." Modern Drama, 12 (1969), 83-91.
      Mention's Tennyson's play.

4199 Solimine, Joseph, Jr. "The Idylls of the King: The Rise,
      Decline, and Fall of the State." Personalist, 50 (1969), 105-
      116.
      Allegory of the Christian state.

4200 "The Sources of 'Enoch Arden' and 'Aylmer's Field.'" Notes
      and Queries, 16 (1969), 84.
      Notes an error in The Poems of Tennyson, ed. C. Ricks,
1969 (entry 4145).

4201   Tennyson, Charles. "Sir Charles Tennyson Remembers His
       Grandfather." Listener, 82 (1969), 548-550.

4202   Times Literary Supplement, April 3, 1969, pp. 367-368.
       Review of The Poems of Tennyson, ed. C. Ricks, 1969 (entry
4145).

4203   Times Literary Supplement, Nov. 13, 1969, p. 1298.
       Review of W. B. Brashear's The Living Will, 1969 (entry
4132).

4204   Todd, William B. "Some Wiseian Advertisements." Book
       Collector, 18 (1969), 219-220.
       Lists Tennysonian works while discussing Wise's advertise-
ments.

4205   Walton, James. "Tennyson's Patrimony: From 'The Outcast'
       to 'Maud.'" Texas Studies in Literature and Language, 11
       (1969), 733-759.
       Internal conflict in Tennyson.

4206   Wheeler, Edd. "Tennyson's In Memoriam as a Gauge of Vic-
       torian Aesthetics." Studies in Humanities, 1 (Winter 1969-
       1970), 31-36.

4207   Wilkinson, L. P. "Virgil, Dryden, and Tennyson." Times
       Literary Supplement, Oct. 9, 1969, p. 1159.
       "Morte d'Arthur."

                              1970

Books

4208   Bloom, Harold. "Tennyson, Hallam, and Romantic Tradition."
       The Ringers in the Tower: Studies in Romantic Tradition.
       Chicago: U. of Chicago P., 1970, pp. 145-154.

4209   Burnshaw, Stanley. The Seamless Web. New York: Braziller,
       1970.

4210   Colville, Derek. "Tennyson." Victorian Poetry and the Ro-
       mantic Religion. Albany: State U. of New York P., 1970,
       pp. 167-238.
       Colville asserts: "The Romantic influence which Tennyson
showed directly and crudely in his earliest work is just as omnipres-
ent in his full development, but there he controls and moulds it to
the point of original creation...." An insightful discussion.

4211   Cooper, Robert M. Lost on Both Sides: Dante Gabriel Ros-
       setti: Critic and Poet. Athens, Ohio: Ohio U. P., 1970.
       Rossetti's views on Tennyson mentioned often.

4212   Goldfarb, Russell M.   "Alfred Tennyson's 'Lancelot and Elaine'
       and 'Pelleas and Ettare.'"   Sexual Repression and Victorian
       Literature.   Lewisburg, Pennsylvania: Bucknell U.P., 1970.
       Psychoanalytical.

4213   Groom, Bernard.   On the Diction of Tennyson, Browning, and
       Arnold.   Hamden, Connecticut: Archon, 1970.
       Reviewed by: D. Roll-Hansen in English Studies (entry 4479).

4214   Hunt, John Dixon, ed.   Tennyson: In Memoriam: A Case-
       book.   London: Macmillan, 1970.   (Macmillan Casebook Se-
       ries)
       A good introductory collection of writings about In Memoriam,
       emphasizing studies from the 1940s, 1950s, and 1960s, although rep-
       resentative   reviews from the 1850s are included.
       Reviewed by: Times Literary Supplement (entry 4324).

4215   Kissane, James D.   Alfred Tennyson.   New York: Twayne,
       1970.   (Twayne English Authors Series, 110)
       This is a basic introduction to Tennyson's achievements, or-
       ganized by genres: lyric, narrative, and dramatic poetry.

4216   Langbaum, Robert.   "The Dynamic Unity of In Memoriam."
       The Modern Spirit: Essays on the Continuity of Nineteenth
       and Twentieth Century Literature.   New York: Oxford U.P.,
       1970, pp. 51-75.
       A careful assessment.

4217   MacBeth, George.   Introduction.   Alfred Lord Tennyson: The
       Falling Splendour, by Alfred, Lord Tennyson.   London: Mac-
       millan, 1970.
       Selected poetry.   Reviewed by: Times Literary Supplement
(entry 4323).

4218   Peckham, Morse.   "Escape from Charisma."   Victorian Rev-
       olutionaries: Speculations on Some Heroes of a Cultural Cri-
       sis.   New York: Braziller, 1970, pp. 8-43.
       A psychoanalytical interpretation of Tennyson's King Arthur.

4219   Scott, P.G.   Tennyson's Enoch Arden: A Victorian Best-
       Seller.   Lincoln, England: Tennyson Research Centre, 1970.
       Scott discusses the background of the composition of Enoch
Arden and its reception.   A useful study.
       Reviewed by: C. Fall in Victorian Studies (entry 4366); Times
Literary Supplement (entry 4273); and M.C. Wiebe in Queen's Quar-
terly (entry 4405).

4220   Victoria, Queen, and Alfred Tennyson, et al.   Dear and Hon-
       oured Lady: The Correspondence Between Queen Victoria and
       Alfred Tennyson.   Ed. Hope Dyson and Charles Tennyson.
       London: Macmillan, 1970.   Rutherford, New Jersey: Fair-
       leigh Dickinson U.P., 1971.
       Dyson and Tennyson provide thorough notes and commentary
for the correspondence between the Queen and the Laureate.

Reviewed by: C.C. Barfoot in English Studies (entry 4240);
K. Cushman in Library Journal (entry 4299); and Times Literary
Supplement (entry 4272).

4221 Warren, Thomas H. "Tennyson and Dante." Essays of Poets
and Poetry, Ancient and Modern. Port Washington, New
York: Kennikat, 1970, pp. 241-269.

4222 Wheeler, Edd. "Tennyson's In Memoriam as a Gauge of Victorian Aesthetics." Studies in the Humanities. Ed. William
F. Grayburn. Indiana: Indiana U. of Pennsylvania, 1970,
pp. 31-36.

Dissertations

4223 Busskohl, James Lester. Studies in Tennyson's Prosody.
Southern Illinois, 1970. Dissertation Abstracts International,
31 (1971), 3497A.
Tennyson's verse is considered within the English tradition of
prosody.

4224 Clark, Barbara Anne Roberts. Critical Annotations for Tennyson's Maud. Georgia, 1970. Dissertation Abstracts International, 31 (1971), 4113A.
The annotations present the opinions of various critics.

4225 Coffin, Lawrence Irving. Empiricism and Mysticism in Tennyson's Poetry. S.U. of New York at Albany, 1970. Dissertation Abstracts International, 31 (1970), 2870A-2871A.
The ironic combination of the mystical and empirical in some
of Tennyson's poems.

4226 Collins, Joseph Johnson, Jr. The Tennysonian Hero: Stages
on Life's Way. Florida State, 1970. Dissertation Abstracts
International, 31 (1971), 4759A.
Collins uses Kierkegaardian philosophy to illuminate Tennyson's
heroes and ethos in Maud and earlier poems.

4227 Francis, Elizabeth Ahlgren. Narrative Strains in Tennyson's
Poetry: History, Apocalypse, and Romance. Yale, 1970.
Dissertation Abstracts International, 31 (1970), 2874A.
Francis examines admirable qualities of Tennyson's early po-
ems and discusses how history and romance illuminate important as-
pects of his characters in The Princess and Idylls of the King.

4228 Grattan, Robert Merle. The Marriage of Geraint and Geraint
and Enid by Alfred, Lord Tennyson: An Edition with Variants,
Annotated. Ohio, 1970. Dissertation Abstracts International,
31 (1971), 4160A.

4229 Haas, Kenneth William, Jr. Gareth and Lynette by Alfred,
Lord Tennyson: An Edition with Variants, Annotated. Ohio,
1970. Dissertation Abstracts International, 31 (1971), 4119A.
Reveals new information on Tennyson's methods of composition.

4230 Hoge, James Otey. The Letters of Emily Lady Tennyson. Virginia, 1970. Dissertation Abstracts International, 31 (1971), 4718A. Published: 1974 (entry 4518). See entry 4518 for annotation.

4231 Lovenheim, Barbara Irene. The Apocalyptic Vision in Victorian Literature. Rochester, 1970. Dissertation Abstracts International, 31 (1971), 4127A.
The belief that English civilization was on the verge of collapse in Thomas Carlyle, Charles Dickens, Matthew Arnold, and Alfred, Lord Tennyson. Interesting discussion.

4232 Miller, Elliot Stuart. The Victorian Domestic Realists. Ohio State, 1970. Dissertation Abstracts International, 31 (1971), 3557A.
The home as sanctuary from and barrier to the evils of the wider world in the works of several Victorian writers. Miller's examination of the development of domestic realism is enlightening.

4233 Pfordresher, John Charles. A Complete Variorum Edition of Alfred, Lord Tennyson's Idylls of the King. Minnesota, 1970. Dissertation Abstracts International, 32 (1971), 449A. Published: 1973 (entry 4419). See entry 4419 for annotation.

4234 Thompson, John Allen. From the Hesperides to Camelot: The Aesthetic Conflict of Alfred Lord Tennyson Reflected in the Themes, Symbols, and Personae of His Poetry. Tulane, 1970. Dissertation Abstracts International, 31 (1970), 2891A-2892A.
Thompson provides an intelligent discussion of Tennyson's efforts to reconcile a private aesthetic vision with the seeming realities of Victorian society. He contends that Tennyson begins and ends with a private vision after traversing aesthetic responses to the world.

4235 Wilxman, Louise. A Critical Study of Tennyson's In Memoriam. Ohio State, 1970. Dissertation Abstracts International, 31 (1971), 3569A.
Wilxman discusses Tennyson's grief, evolution, and imagery in the poem, and its expression of the poet's experiences.

Periodicals

4236 Adey, Lionel. "Tennyson's Sorrow and Her Lying Lip." Victorian Poetry, 8 (1970), 261-263.
A lyric from In Memoriam, section III.

4237 Adler, Thomas P. "The Uses of Knowledge in Tennyson's Merlin and Vivien." Texas Studies in Literature and Language, 11 (1970), 1397-1403.
Adler discusses the similarities between Book IX of Milton's Paradise Lost and "Merlin and Vivien." Merlin is tempted by Vivien the way Eve is tempted by Satan, and in yielding to temptation, he brings sin to Camelot.

4238   Alaya, Flavia. "Tennyson's 'The Lady of Shalott': The Tri-
       umph of Art." Victorian Poetry, 8 (1970), 273-289.
       The Lady and the spirit of the artist.

4239 Assad, Thomas J. "Tennyson's 'Courage, Poor Heart of Stone.'"
       Tulane Studies in English, 18 (1970), 73-80.
       Assad analyzes a lyric from Maud and shows how it enhances
the themes of the poem.

4240 Barfoot, C.C. English Studies, 51 (1970), 490.
       Review of Dear and Honoured Lady, ed. H. Dyson and C. Ten-
nyson, 1970 (entry 4220).

4241 Bender, Elaine. Library Journal, 95 (1970), 159.
       Review of J. B. Steane's Tennyson, 1966 (entry 3958).

4242 Bradley, J.L. Modern Language Review, 65 (1970), 156.
       Review of J. B. Steane's Tennyson, 1966 (entry 3958).

4243 Cannon, Garland. "'The Lady of Shallott' and The Arabian
       Nights' Tales." Victorian Poetry, 8 (Winter 1970), 344-346.
       Sources for Tennyson's poem.

4244 Choice, 7 (1970), 387.
       Review of J. B. Steane's Tennyson, 1966 (entry 3958).

4245 Danzig, Allan. Victorian Studies, 13 (1970), 372.
       Review of G. Joseph's Tennysonian Love, 1968 (entry 4069).

4246 Elliott, Philip L. "Tennyson's In Memoriam, XLI, 9-12." Ex-
       plicator, 28 (1970), Item 66.

4247 Ewart, Gavin. "2001--The Tennyson/Hardy Poem." Listener,
       83 (1970), 480.
       A poetic parody.

4248 Fredeman, William E. "The Bibliographical Significance of a
       Publisher's Archive: The Macmillan Papers." Studies in Bib-
       liography, 23 (1970), 183-190.
       Discusses Alexander Macmillan's letters to Tennyson, in the
British Museum.

4249 Fricke, Donna G. "Tennyson's The Hesperides: East of Eden
       and Variations on the Theme." Tennyson Research Bulletin,
       1, no. 4 (Nov. 1970), 99-103.
       Creation and myth in the poem.

4250 Gray, J.M. "A Feature Characterizing Lancelot in Tennyson's
       'Lancelot and Elaine.'" Notes and Queries, 17 (1970), 15.

4251 _____. "The Purpose of an Epic List in 'The Coming of
       Arthur.'" Victorian Poetry, 8 (1970), 339-341.

4252 _____. "A Study in Idyl: Tennyson's The Coming of Arthur." Renaissance and Modern Studies, 14 (1970), 111-150.
A close study of the poetry's sources and meanings.

4253 _____. "Two Transcendental Ladies of Tennyson's Idylls:
The Lady of the Lake and Vivien." Tennyson Research Bulletin, 1, no. 4 (Nov. 1970), 104-105.

4254 Hirsch, Gordon D. "Tennyson's Commedia." Victorian Poetry, 8 (1970), 93-106.
Dantesque elements in In Memoriam.

4255 Hunt, John D. "The Symbolist Vision of In Memoriam." Victorian Poetry, 8 (1970), 187-198.
Hunt suggests that in In Memoriam Tennyson anticipates the
symbolist poets, notably Yeats.

4256 Langford, Thomas A. "The 'Phases of Passion' in Tennyson's
Maud." South Central Bulletin, 30 (1970), 204-208.
Symbolism and the "phases of passion" in Maud.

4257 Lavabre, Simone. "Une lecture de Maud." Caliban, 7 (1970),
25-34.

4258 Lee, B.S. "Two Arthurian Tales: What Tennyson Did to Malory." University of Cape Town Studies in English, 1 (1970),
1-18.

4259 Leggett, B.J. "Dante, Byron, and Tennyson's Ulysses." Tennessee Studies in Literature, 15 (1970), 143-159.
Leggett asserts that Byron influenced Tennyson's writing of
"Ulysses" as much as Dante. He points in particular to Childe Harold's Pilgrimage, Canto III, for parallels between Byron's work and
that of Tennyson.

4260 Lehman, Herbert H. Victorian Studies, 13 (1970), 425-427.
Review of The Poems of Tennyson, ed. C. Ricks, 1969 (entry
4145). Discusses also, C. Ricks's "The Tennyson Manuscripts" in
Times Literary Supplement, 1969 (entry 4190), and "Tennyson's Method of Composition" in British Academy, 1966 (entry 4001).

4261 Marshall, George O., Jr. Georgia Review, 24 (1970), 261-262.
Review of G. Joseph's Tennysonian Love, 1968 (entry 4069).

4262 Motter, T.H. Vail. "Tennyson's Lines to Adelaide Kemble."
Times Literary Supplement, July 16, 1970, p. 780.

4263 Pettigrew, John. Victorian Poetry, 8 (1970), 161-168.
Review of The Poems of Tennyson, ed. C. Ricks, 1969 (entry
4145).

4264 Rader, Ralph W. Modern Philology, 67 (1970), 386-388.
Review of C. de L. Ryals's From the Great Deep, 1967 (entry
4015).

4265 Ricks, Christopher. "Tennyson's 'To E. FitzGerald.'" Library, 5th ser. 25 (1970), 156.
On FitzGerald's age.

4266 Ryals, Clyde de L. Journal of English and Germanic Philology, 59 (1970), 540-543.
Review of G. Joseph's Tennysonian Love, 1968 (entry 4069).

4267 Smith, Elton E. Victorian Poetry, 8 (1970), 65-67.
Review of W. B. Brashear's The Living Will, 1969 (entry 4132).

4268 Smith, James L. "William McGonagall and the Poet Laureate." Studies in Scottish Literature, 7 (1970), 21-28.

4269 Sonstroem, David. "'Crossing the Bar' as Last Word." Victorian Poetry, 8 (1970), 55-60.
The poem sums up Tennyson's point of view.

4270 Stock, A. G. "Tennyson and the Imprisoned Lady." Banasthali Patrika, 14 (1970), 1-12.

4271 Tennyson, Charles. "A Poet's Child: The Early Days of Lionel Tennyson." Tennyson Research Bulletin, 1, no. 4 (Nov. 1970), 91-98.

4272 Times Literary Supplement, Jan. 8, 1970, p. 28.
Review of G. Joseph's Tennysonian Love, 1968 (entry 4069), J. M. Gray's Man and Myth, 1969 (entry 4140), and Dear and Honoured Lady, ed. H. Dyson and C. Tennyson, 1970 (entry 4220).

4273 Times Literary Supplement, Nov. 20, 1970, p. 1346.
Review of P. G. Scott's Tennyson's Enoch Arden, 1970 (entry 4219).

4274 Turner, Paul. Notes and Queries, 17 (1970), 274.
Review of J. M. Gray's Man and Myth, 1969 (entry 4140).

4275 Weinstock, Donald J. "Tennysonian Echoes in 'The Love Song of J. Alfred Prufrock.'" English Language Notes, 7 (1970), 213-214.

1971

Books

4276 Eggers, J. Philip. King Arthur's Laureate: A Study of Tennyson's Idylls of the King. New York: New York U. P., 1971.
Eggers declares: "This study is an attempt to capture the social meaning of the poem from various perspectives--its place in literary tradition, its effect upon readers of Tennyson's day, its relation to Arthurian sources, its competition with rival Arthurian poems,

its growth as a series of installments, and its structure as a completed work of art." Eggers's writing is clear and stylistically admirable. He provides a sensible summary of Victorian responses to Idylls of the King and of other Victorian versions of the Arthurian legends, and he presents cogent criticism of his own. This book is a fundamental reference for those interested in Idylls of the King.
  Reviewed by: J.M. Gray in Tennyson Research Bulletin (entry 4306); and E.E. Smith in Clio (entry 4492). See also: K. McSweeney in Papers on Language and Literature, 1974 (entry 4562).

4277 Gray, J.M. Tennyson's Doppelgänger: Balin and Balan. Lincoln, England: Tennyson Society, 1971. (Tennyson Society Monographs, 3)
  The brothers represent different aspects of the self. Reviewed by: D.R. Davis in Essays in Criticism (entry 4448); C. Fall in Victorian Studies (entry 4366); Times Literary Supplement (entry 4326); and M.G. Wiebe in Queen's Quarterly (entry 4405).

4278 Hunt, John D. "Tennyson, 1809-1892." English Poetry: Select Bibliographical Guides. Ed. A.E. Dyson. London: Oxford U.P., 1971, pp. 265-283.

4279 Knight, G. Wilson. "Poetry and the Arts: Tennyson, Browning, O'Shaughnessy, Yeats" and "Excalibur: An Essay on Tennyson." Neglected Powers: Essays on Nineteenth and Twentieth Century Literature. New York: Barnes and Noble, 1971. London: Routledge and Kegan Paul, 1971, pp. 243-259 and 419-429, respectively.

4280 Lucas, John. "Politics and the Poet's Role." Literature and Politics in the Nineteenth Century. London: Methuen, 1971, pp. 7-43.
  Shelley's influence on Tennyson.

4281 Millhauser, Milton. Fire and Ice: The Influence of Science on Tennyson's Poetry. Lincoln, England: Tennyson Society, 1971.
  Scientific imagery is important to Tennyson's poetry.

4282 Norst, Marlene J. "Enoch Arden in the German Alps: A Comparative Study of Tennyson's Enoch Arden and Duboc's Walpra." Affinities: Essays in German and English Literature. Ed. R.W. Last. London: Wolff, 1971, pp. 52-67.
  The influence of Tennyson on Duboc.

4283 Sinfield, Alan. The Language of Tennyson's In Memoriam. New York: Barnes and Noble, 1971. Oxford: Blackwell, 1971. (Language and Style Series, 9)
  Sinfield provides an illuminating linguistic analysis of In Memoriam. He investigates the complexities beneath the surface of the poem.
  Reviewed by: Choice (entry 4298); C. Fall in Victorian Studies (entry 4366); K. McSweeney in Papers on Language and Literature

(entry 4562); P.G. Scott in Tennyson Research Bulletin (entry 4317); and Times Literary Supplement (entry 4326).

4284 Southam, Brian C. Tennyson. Harlow, Essex: Longmans, 1971. (Writers and Their Work, 218)
      Reviewed by: Times Literary Supplement (entry 4325).

Dissertations

4285 Crawford, James Slater, IV. Alfred, Lord Tennyson: The Mythopoeic Resolution of Ambivalence in His Poetry. Columbia, 1971. Dissertation Abstracts International, 34 (1974), 7743A-7744A.
      A psychoanalytical study that investigates evidence in the poetry of Tennyson's identification with women, latent homosexuality, and search for sexual identity.

4286 Fischer, Arthur H. Tennyson as Playwright: A Study of His Dramatic Career. Denver, 1971. Dissertation Abstracts International, 32 (1971), 1681A.
      A general study of the history of Tennyson's interest in writing dramas and of the merits of the plays. Fischer finds much worthwhile poetry and insight in some of the poet's dramatic writings, and he analyzes how they often fail.

4287 Hagen, June Steffensen. Facsimile Edition of Tennyson's 1842 Poems, with Critical Variorum and Introduction (In Two Volumes). New York, 1971. Dissertation Abstracts International, 32 (1972), 3951A-3952A.
      Tennyson's work has characteristics of modern poetry.

4288 Loeppert, Theodore Walters. The Felt Perception of Order: Musicality in the Works of Carlyle, Tennyson, and Walter Pater. Northwestern, 1971. Dissertation Abstracts International, 32 (1972), 4618A.
      Music as metaphor and Romanticism in Tennyson.

4289 Pratt, Linda Ray. "The Neutral Territory Between Two Worlds": A Comparative Study of Alfred Tennyson and T.S. Eliot. Emory, 1971. Dissertation Abstracts International, 32 (1972), 4017A.
      Pratt notes significant similarities between Tennyson and Eliot, although she finds that the effect of poetic tradition on each varies.

4290 Prince, Jeffrey Robert. Havens of Intensity: Aestheticism in the Poetry of Keats, Tennyson and Yeats. Virginia, 1971. Dissertation Abstracts International, 32 (1972), 4629A-4630A.
      Tennyson's role in nineteenth-century Aestheticism.

4291 Vent, Maryanne Ciardullo. Tennyson's Idylls of the King and the Victorian Periodical Press. Fordham, 1971. Dissertation Abstracts International, 32 (1971), 2071A.
      The critical response to the poetry.

4292 Ziemann, Gwendolyn Timmons. Fate, Chance, and Free Will in Nineteenth Century Tristram and Iseult Legends. Arizona State, 1971. Dissertation Abstracts International, 32 (1971), 2659A.
A comparison of how Tennyson, Arnold, Hardy, Swinburne, and Symons handle the Tristram and Iseult legends.

Periodicals

4293 Adicks, Richard. "'The Garden Trees': A Collaboration Between Tennyson and Hallam." Tennyson Research Bulletin, 1, no. 5 (1971), 147.
A collaborative sonnet.

4294 Bertram, James. "Tennyson's 'In Memoriam': A Verse Tribute by Tom Arnold." Notes and Queries, 18 (1971), 99-100.

4295 Campbell, Nancy. "Another Letter to Queen Victoria." Tennyson Research Bulletin, 1, no. 5 (1971), 150.
Variants for August 1883 letter by Tennyson.

4296 Chakraborty, S.C. "Bird and Animal Imagery in Tennyson." Panjab University Research Bulletin (Arts), 2, no. 2 (1971), 27-37.

4297 Choice, 8 (1971), 228.
Review of J.R. Reed's Perception and Design, 1969 (entry 4143).

4298 Choice, 8 (1971), 1021.
Review of A. Sinfield's The Language, 1971 (entry 4283).

4299 Cushman, K. Library Journal, 96 (1971), 4089.
Review of Dear and Honoured Lady, ed. H. Dyson and C. Tennyson, 1970 (entry 4220).

4300 Duncan-Jones, Katherine. "A Note on Tennyson's 'Claribel.'" Victorian Poetry, 9 (1971), 348-350.
"Claribel" is "a Romantic evocation of emotion through natural objects."

4301 Elliott, Philip L. "Tennyson's 'Sir Galahad.'" Victorian Poetry, 9 (1971), 445-452.
Analyzes the poem's merits.

4302 Findlay, Leonard M. "Swinburne and Tennyson." Victorian Poetry, 9 (1971), 217-236.
A comparative study of the poets' relationship.

4303 Fleissner, Robert F. "Tennyson's Hesperidean Xanadu: The Anagogical Thread." Research Studies, 39 (1971), 40-46.

4304 Gray, J.M. "An Allusion to Paradise Regained in Merlin and Vivien." Tennyson Research Bulletin, 1, no. 5 (1971), 150.

4305 _____ . "An Origin for Tennyson's Characterization of Percivale in The Holy Grail." Notes and Queries, 18 (1971),
416-417.
Malory and Tennyson.

4306 _____ . Tennyson Research Bulletin, 1, no. 5 (1971), 142-
145.
Review of C. de L. Ryals's From the Great Deep, 1967 (entry 4015); J. R. Reed's Perception and Design, 1969 (entry 4143); and
J. P. Eggers's King Arthur's Laureate, 1971 (entry 4276).

4307 Gunter, G. O. "Life and Death Symbols in Tennyson's 'Mariana.'" South Atlantic Bulletin, 36, no. 3 (1971), 64-67.

4308 Harrison, James. "Tennyson and Evolution." Durham University Journal, 33 (1971), 26-31.

4309 Killham, John. Yearbook of English Studies, 1 (1971), 302-
304.
Review of W. R. Brashear's The Living Will, 1969 (entry
4132); J. M. Gray's Man and Myth, 1969 (entry 4140); and The Poems
of Tennyson, ed. C. Ricks, 1969 (entry 4145).

4310 Lewis, Saunders. "Morte d'Arthur a'r Passing of Arthur."
Y Traethedydd, 126 (1971), 3-11.
T. Gwynn Jones influenced by Tennyson.

4311 McCullough, Joseph B., and Claude C. Brew. "A Study of the
Publication of Tennyson's Idylls of the King." Papers of the
Bibliographical Society of America, 65 (1971), 156-169.
The authors cover editions of Idylls of the King published dur-
ing the poet's lifetime and provide notes reflecting recent scholarship.

4312 Maxwell, J. C. Notes and Queries, 18 (1971), 274-275.
Review of The Poems of Tennyson, ed. C. Ricks, 1969 (entry
4145).

4313 Niermeier, Stuart F. C. "The Problem of the In Memoriam
Manuscripts." Harvard Library Bulletin, 19 (1971), 149-159.

4314 Ross, Malcolm. "Time, the Timeless, and the Timely: Notes
on a Victorian Poem." Proceedings and Transactions of the
Royal Society of Canada, 9 (1971), 219-234.
The uses of time in In Memoriam.

4315 Scott, P. G. "Tennyson and The Hymn-books Again." Tennyson Research Bulletin, 1, no. 5 (1971), 151.

4316 _____ . "Tennyson and the Macmillan Papers." Tennyson
Research Bulletin, 1, no. 5 (1971), 146-147.
The correspondence of Hallam Tennyson with Macmillan is in
the British Museum.

4317 _____ . Tennyson Research Bulletin, 1, no. 5 (1971), 142.
Review of A. Sinfield's The Language, 1971 (entry 4283).

4318 Shaw, W. David. "In Memoriam and the Rhetoric of Confes-
sion." Journal of English Literary History, 38 (1971), 80-
103.

4319 Storch, R. F. "The Fugitive from the Ancestral Hearth: Tennyson's 'Ulysses.'" Texas Studies in Literature and Language,
13 (1971), 281-297.
"Ulysses" reflects an important aspect of Western civilization:
the conflict between the drive for personal fulfillment and social duty.
Victorian readers would not have detected the irony perceived by recent critics, according to Storch, because the poem spoke directly to
their society.

4320 Sundaram, P. S. "Tennyson's 'Ulysses.'" Rajasthan University Studies in English, 5 (1971), 11-16.

4321 Tennyson, Charles. "Tennyson: Mind and Method." Tennyson
Research Bulletin, 1, no. 5 (1971), 127-136.

4322 Times Literary Supplement, March 19, 1971, p. 236.
Review of J. R. Reed's Perception and Design, 1969 (entry
4143).

4323 Times Literary Supplement, April 2, 1971, p. 382.
Review of G. MacBeth's The Falling Splendour, 1970 (entry
4217).

4324 Times Literary Supplement, April 30, 1971, p. 500.
Review of J. D. Hunt, ed., Tennyson: In Memoriam, 1970
(entry 4214).

4325 Times Literary Supplement, June 11, 1971, p. 682.
Review of B. C. Southam's Tennyson, 1971 (entry 4284).

4326 Times Literary Supplement, June 25, 1971, p. 727.
Review of J. M. Gray's Tennyson's Doppelgänger, 1971 (entry
4277) and A. Sinfield's The Language, 1971 (entry 4283).

4327 Tobias, Richard C. "Tennyson's Painted Shell." Victorian
Newsletter, no. 39 (Spring 1971), 7-10.

4328 University of Rochester Library Bulletin, 26 (1971), 170.
The library receives three letters by Tennyson and materials
related to his funeral.

4329 Vyas, H. K. "Lifting the Veil." Banasthali Patrika, 16 (1971),
37-41.
Tennyson's "The Lady of Shalott" and T. S. Eliot's "Marina."

4330 Wajid, R. A. "Tennyson's 'Tears, Idle Tears.'" Rajasthan
University Studies in English, 5 (1971), 31-35.

4331 Yamada, Taiji. "Tennyson's 'Lucretius': An Interpretation."
Hitotsubashi Journal of Arts and Sciences (Tokyo), 12, no. 1
(1971), 20-25.

4332 Zuckermann, Joanne P. "Tennyson's In Memoriam as Love
Poetry." Dalhousie Review, 51 (1971), 202-217.

1972

Books

4333 Armstrong, Isobel. Victorian Scrutinies: Reviews of Poetry
1830-1870. London: Athlone, 1972.
Reprints reviews on Tennyson (entries 8, 9, 16, 79, 173, and
227), Arnold, Browning, and Clough. Supplies bibliographies of further reviews. Introduction includes "Issues Raised by Tennyson's
Early Poetry," pages 14-31.

4334 Campbell, Nancie. Tennyson in Lincoln: A Catalogue of the
Collections in the Research Centre. 2 volumes. Lincoln:
Tennyson Society, 1972-1973.
Reviewed by: F. Hill in Tennyson Research Bulletin (entry
4551); K. McSweeney in Modern Language Review (entry 4724); E. F.
Shannon, Jr., in Victorian Studies (entry 4487); and Times Literary
Supplement, 1972 and 1974 (entries 4402 and 4594). See also: B. S.
C. Harding in Times Literary Supplement, 1972 (entry 4375).

4335 Edgar, Irving. "The Psychological Sources of Poetic Creative
Expression and Tennyson's 'In Memoriam.'" Essays in English Literature and History. New York: Philosophical Library, 1972, pp. 1-14.

4336 Gent, Margaret. "'To Flinch from Modern Varnish': The
Appeal of the Past to the Victorian Imagination." Victorian
Poetry. Ed. Malcolm Bradbury and David Palmer. London:
E. Arnold, 1972, pp. 11-35.

4337 Hellstrom, Ward. On the Poems of Tennyson. Gainesville:
U. of Florida P., 1972.
Hellstrom discusses Tennyson's poetry's Christian implications
for Victorian readers. Although his topic is not original, Hellstrom's
discussion of the whole of Tennyson's poetic achievement makes this
book more balanced and informative than most.
Reviewed by: L. G. Bailey in Victorian Studies (entry 4697);
C. C. Barfoot in English Studies (entry 4439); R. P. Draper in Aber-
deen University Review (entry 4541); G. Joseph in Georgia Review
(entry 4462); H. Kozicki in Criticism (entry 4465); J. C. Maxwell in
Notes and Queries (entry 4661); Prairie Schooner (entry 4568); H.
Sergeant in English (entry 4486); and P. Turner in Review of English
Studies (entry 4597).

4338 Hunt, John Dixon. "The Poetry of Distance: Tennyson's Idylls

of the King." Victorian Poetry. Ed. Malcolm Bradbury and
David Palmer. London: E. Arnold, 1972. New York:
Crane, Russak, 1972, pp. 89-121. (Stratford-Upon-Avon
Studies, 15)
The "possibilities of distance in landscapes, pictures, and
the past."

4339 Lang, Cecil Y. Introduction. Tennyson in Lincoln: A Catalogue of the Collections in the Research Centre, by Nancie
Campbell. Lincoln, England: Tennyson Society, 1972. Volume I.

4340 Otten, Terry. "Tennyson's Maud and Becket." The Deserted
Stage: The Search for Dramatic Form in Nineteenth-Century
England. Athens, Ohio: Ohio U. P., 1972, pp. 76-107.

4341 Ray, Gordon N. "Tennyson Reads Maud." Romantic and Vic-
torian: Studies in Memory of William H. Marshall. Ed. W.
Paul Elledge and Richard L. Hoffman. Rutherford, N. J.:
Fairleigh Dickinson U. P., 1972, pp. 290-317.
Ray presents and discusses notes taken by James Knowles of
a reading of Maud given by Tennyson.

4342 Revell, Peter, and Sian Allsobrook. A Catalogue of the Tennyson Collection in the Library of University College, Cardiff.
Cardiff: University College, 1972.
Reviewed by: L. Madden in Tennyson Research Bulletin (entry
4469).

4343 Ricks, Christopher B. Tennyson. New York: Macmillan,
1972. (Masters of World Literature Series)
This book is a good introduction to the life and work of Ten-
nyson. Ricks's insights into the poetry are valuable.
Reviewed by: J. Bayley in Encounter (entry 4440); Choice (en-
try 4361); Economist (entry 4365); N. Lewis in New Statesman and
Nation (entry 4387); K. McSweeney in Papers on Language and Lit-
erature (entry 4562); J. C. Maxwell in Notes and Queries (entry 4661);
J. D. Rosenberg in New York Times Book Review (entry 4480); H.
Sergeant in Britannica Book of the Year (entry 4485); W. D. Shaw in
Victorian Studies (entry 4489); B. C. Southam in Review of English
Studies (entry 4493); G. Thomas in English (entry 4497); Times Lit-
erary Supplement (entry 4403); and C. Wilmer in Spectator (entry
4407). See also: W. H. Auden in Listener, 1972 (entry 4356) and
T. R. Schuck in Notes and Queries, 1976 (entry 4733).

4344 Rutland, William R. "The Theory of Evolution in English Poetry." The Becoming of God: An Outline of Man's Conception
of Cosmic Process. Oxford: Blackwell, 1972, pp. 27-54.

4345 Sulloway, Alison G. Gerard Manley Hopkins and the Victorian
Temper. New York: Columbia U. P., 1972.

4346 Tennyson, Alfred, Lord. A Collection of Poems by Alfred Ten-

nyson. Ed. Christopher Ricks. Garden City, N.Y.: International Collectors Library, 1972.
Illustrated by Barnett I. Plotkin.

4347 _____ . Tennyson's Poetry. Ed. Robert W. Hill. New York: Norton, 1972. (Norton Critical Edition)

4348 Tilling, Philip M. "Local Dialect and the Poet: A Comparison of the Findings in the Survey of English Dialects with Dialect in Tennyson's Lincolnshire Poems." Patterns in the Folk Speech of the British Isles. Ed. Martyn F. Wakelin. London: Athlone (U. of London), 1972, pp. 88-108.
A linguistic study that offers insight into Tennyson's purposes in the dialect poems.

Dissertations

4349 Barnett, Gail Zech. The Endless Journey: An Ontogenetic Study of Three Poets. Maryland, 1972. Dissertation Abstracts International, 33 (1972), 2314A.
The discovery of self in the poetry of Tennyson, Coleridge, and T.S. Eliot.

4350 Briney, John O. Alfred Tennyson's The Lover's Tale: An Interpretation. Michigan State, 1972. Dissertation Abstracts International, 33 (1973), 5113A.

4351 Kolb, Gwin Jackson, II. Letters of Arthur Henry Hallam to the Tennyson Family. Virginia, 1972. Dissertation Abstracts International, 36 (1975), 2198A.
Of biographical interest.

4352 Morris, Christopher D. World into Word: Tennyson, Ruskin, Hopkins, and the Nineteenth-Century Loss of Certainty. S.U. of New York at Buffalo, 1972. Dissertation Abstracts International, 33 (1973), 4427A.
The "de-centering" philosophy of Jacques Derrida applied to the works of Tennyson and others.

4353 Reese, Theodore Irving, III. The Character and Role of Guenevere in the Nineteenth Century. Brandeis, 1972. Dissertation Abstracts International, 33 (1973), 5138A-5139A.
Reese discusses the works of many authors but devotes a chapter to Idylls of the King. He examines Tennyson's use of Guinevere for moral and other themes.

4354 Schwalbaum, Joan. The Balance of Contradiction in Marvell and Tennyson. Columbia, 1972. Dissertation Abstracts International, 33 (1972), 2904A.
Compares and contrasts themes and points of view of the poets.

4355 Whall, Raymond Anthony, Jr. Escapes from Time in the Poetry of Alfred Lord Tennyson. Colorado, 1972. Dissertation Abstracts International, 33 (1973), 4371A-4372A.

"Transcendence of Process," "Historical Transcendence," and "Mystical Transcendence" are terms given by Whall to Tennyson's efforts to reconcile faith and doubt by transcending temporal limitations in his poetry. Interesting.

Periodicals

4356   Auden, W. H.   "The Poet of No More--W. H. Auden Offers Some Personal Reflections on Tennyson." Listener, 88 (1972), 181.
Auden also discusses C. Ricks's Tennyson, 1972 (entry 4343).

4357   Boyd, John D.   "In Memoriam and the 'Logic of Feeling.'" Victorian Poetry, 10 (1972), 95-110.
The logic and psychology of In Memoriam and the engagement of readers in the philosophic crisis of the poem.

4358   Bruns, Gerald L.   "'The Irony of Nature': Tennyson's Idylls and the Problem of Culture." Majallat Majma^{C}al-Lughah al-^{C}Arabíyah (Cairo), 2 (1972), 38-45.

4359   Cancel, Rafael A.   "Two Studies on Theatre." Revista de Letras, 4 (1972), 257-279.
Becket and Le malentendu.

4360   Chakraborty, S. C.   "Character-Imagery in Tennyson." Panjab University Research Bulletin (Arts), 3, no. 1 (1972), 45-58.

4361   Choice, 9 (1972), 817.
Review of C. Ricks's Tennyson, 1972 (entry 4343).

4362   Devlin, Francis P.   "Dramatic Irony in the Early Sections of Tennyson's In Memoriam." Papers on Language and Literature, 8 (1972), 172-183.
Dramatic irony created by symbols.

4363   Ditsky, John M.   "Whitman-Tennyson Correspondence: A Summary and Commentary." Walt Whitman Review, 18 (1972), 75-82.

4364   Drake, Constance.   "A Topical Dating for 'Locksley Hall Sixty Years After.'" Victorian Poetry, 10 (1972), 307-320.
On the basis of internal evidence, Drake suggests that "Locksley Hall Sixty Years After" was composed between 1882 and 1884, not in 1886 as commonly believed.

4365   Economist, 244 (1972), 49.
Review of C. Ricks's Tennyson, 1972 (entry 4343).

4366   Fall, Christine.   Victorian Studies, 16 (1972), 110-111.
Review of J. R. Reed's Perception and Design, 1969 (entry 4143); P. G. Scott's Tennyson's Enoch Arden, 1970 (entry 4219), J. M. Gray's Tennyson's Doppelgänger, 1971 (entry 4277), and A. Sinfield's The Language, 1971 (entry 4283).

4367   Ford, Ford Madox. "Poeta Nascitur." Poetry, 121 (1972),
        41-45.
        Reminiscences in 1927 of Tennyson, Browning, and Patmore.

4368   Fredeman, William E. "'The Sphere of Common Duties': The
        Domestic Solution in Tennyson's Poetry." Bulletin of the John
        Rylands Library, 54 (1972), 357-383.

4369   Gransden, K. W. "The Figure of Lazarus in Tennyson and
        Browning." Ariel (Calgary), 3, no. 1 (1972), 93-98.

4370   Grattan, Robert M. "'Men from Beasts': A View on Conver-
        sion in Tennyson's Idylls of the King." West Virginia Univer-
        sity Philological Papers, 19 (1972), 29-40.
        The failure of conversion and its significance in Idylls of the
King.

4371   Gray, J. M. "Arthurian Invention in Merlin and Vivien." Ten-
        nyson Research Bulletin, 2, no. 1 (1972), 36.

4372   _____. "The Iconography of Pellam's Castle in Balin and
        Balan." Tennyson Research Bulletin, 2, no. 1 (1972), 29-30.

4373   Griffiths, David N. "Tennyson and Gladstone." Tennyson Re-
        search Bulletin, 2, no. 1 (1972), 1-5.

4374   Hall, P. E. "The Bereaved Bride." Tennyson Research Bul-
        letin, 2, no. 1 (1972), 35.
        About In Memoriam.

4375   Harding, Bruce S. C. Times Literary Supplement, June 16,
        1972, p. 689.
        A letter regarding N. Campbell's Tennyson in Lincoln, volume
I, 1972 (entry 4334).

4376   Hargrave, Harry A. "Kind Hearts and Coronets." Victorian
        Institute Journal, 1 (1972), 31-38.
        The relationship of Tennyson and Charles Dickens.

4377   Harrison, James. "Tennyson and Embryology." Humanities
        Research Bulletin, 23, no. 2 (1972), 28-32.

4378   Hoge, James O. "Emily Tennyson's Narrative for Her Sons."
        Texas Studies in Literature and Language, 14 (1972), 93-106.
        The three versions of Emily Tennyson's account of her court-
ship and early years of marriage with Alfred Tennyson.

4379   Hussain, Syed Muzaffer. "Traces of Sufism in Tennyson's
        Poetry." Tennyson Research Bulletin, 2, no. 1 (1972), 6-14.

4380   Jerman, Bernard. "The Death of Tennyson." Acta Neophilo-
        logica, 5 (1972), 31-44.
        The death and funeral as representative of Victorian views of
death.

4381 Jones, Horace P. "Southern Parodies on Tennyson's 'Charge
      of the Light Brigade.'" Louisiana Studies, 11 (1972), 315-320.

4382 Joseph, Gerhard. "Tennyson's Concepts of Knowledge, Wis-
      dom, and Pallas Athene." Modern Philology, 69 (1972), 314-
      322.
      How the poet handles the concepts in his poetry.

4383 Jump, John D. Critical Quarterly, 14 (1972), 285-286.
      Review of The Poems of Tennyson, ed. C. Ricks, 1969 (entry
4145).

4384 Kincaid, James R. "Tennyson's 'Gareth and Lynette.'" Texas
      Studies in Literature and Language, 13 (1972), 663-671.
      The comic ending of "Gareth and Lynette" sets up a contrast
for the following tales of Idylls of the King.

4385 Landow, George P. "Hartley Coleridge's Two Sonnets to Al-
      fred Tennyson." Tennyson Research Bulletin, 2 (1972), 37-38.

4386 _____. "The Page Proofs of ll. 1-132 of the 1842 Version
      of 'The Miller's Daughter.'" Tennyson Research Bulletin, 2,
      no. 1 (1972), 31-34.

4387 Lewis, N. New Statesman and Nation, 84 (1972), 475-476.
      Review of C. Ricks's Tennyson, 1972 (entry 4343).

4388 "Lionel Tennyson: A Letter from F.T. Palgrave to Lord Ten-
      nyson." Tennyson Research Bulletin, 2, no. 1 (1972), 15-24.

4389 Martin, David M. "The Triumph of the Grail: Capitulation of
      Self in Tennyson's Poetic Career." Research Studies, 40
      (1972), 135-139.

4390 Mason, Michael Y. "In Memoriam: The Dramatization of Sor-
      row." Victorian Poetry, 10 (1972), 161-177.
      Dissociation, the "pathetic fallacy," and dealing with grief.

4391 Metcalfe, Priscilla. Times Literary Supplement, June 23,
      1972, p. 719.
      Letter about James Knowles and Tennyson.

4392 Milne, Fred L. "Yeats's 'The Cap and the Bells': A Probable
      Indebtedness to Tennyson's Maud." Ariel (Calgary), 3, no. 3
      (1972), 69-79.
      A Tennysonian influence on a poem by Yeats.

4393 Niermeier, Stuart F.C. "In Memoriam and The Excursion: A
      Matter of Comparison." Victorian Newsletter, no. 41 (Spring
      1972), 20-22.
      Wordsworth's influence on Tennyson.

4394 Paulin, T. "Tennyson in Hardy's 'A Sign Seeker.'" Notes and
      Queries, 19 (1972), 265.

4395 Rutenberg, Daniel. "Crisscrossing the Bar: Tennyson and Lionel Johnson on Death." Victorian Poetry, 10 (1972), 179-180.
"Crossing the Bar" and "In Falmouth Harbor" compared.

4396 Scott, P. G. "The Proof of Tennyson's Achilles Over the Trench." Tennyson Research Bulletin, 2, no. 1 (1972), 38-39.
Scott notes corrections of the proof of the poem for Nineteenth Century.

4397 _____. "Tennyson's Celtic Reading." Tennyson Research Bulletin, 2 (1972), 4-8.
The sources for Tennyson's knowledge of the Arthurian legends.

4398 Shaw, W. David. "Imagination and Intellect in Tennyson's 'Lucretius.'" Modern Language Quarterly, 33 (1972), 130-139.
In this careful study, Shaw shows how "Lucretius" focuses on the conflict between intellect and imagination.

4399 Simpson, Arthur L., Jr. "Aurora as Artist: A Reinterpretation of Tennyson's Tithonus." Philological Quarterly, 51 (1972), 905-921.
"Tithonus" presents a "rejection of the life of the 'pure' artist."

4400 Stevens, L. Robert. "Tennyson's Aesthetic Logic." Southern Humanities Review, 6 (1972), 328-332.
Nihilism in Tennyson's poetry and its implications for Tennyson's aesthetics.

4401 Tennyson, Charles. "Tennyson and Browning." Browning Society Notes, 3, no. 2 (Dec. 1972), 10-22.

4402 Times Literary Supplement, May 26, 1972, p. 606.
Review of N. Campbell's Tennyson in Lincoln, Volume I, 1972 (entry 4334). See also: B. S. C. Harding (entry 4375).

4403 Times Literary Supplement, Aug. 25, 1972, p. 988.
Review of C. Ricks's Tennyson, 1972 (entry 4343).

4404 Verschoor, E. N. E. "'Much Abides': Alfred Lord Tennyson (1809-1892)." Fort Hare Papers, 5 (1972), 286-301.

4405 Wiebe, M. G. Queen's Quarterly, 79 (1972), 118-119.
Review of P. G. Scott's Tennyson's Enoch Arden, 1970 (entry 4219) and J. M. Gray's Tennyson's Doppelgänger, 1971 (entry 4277).

4406 Williams, Melvin G. "In Memoriam: A Broad Church Poem." Costerus, 4 (1972), 223-233.

4407 Wilmer, Clive. Spectator, 229 (1972), 364-365.
Review of C. Ricks's Tennyson, 1972 (entry 4343).

1973

Books

4408 Bergonzi, Bernard. "Feminism and Femininity in 'The Princess.'" The Turn of a Century: Essays on Victorian and
Modern English Literature. London: Macmillan, 1973. New
York: Barnes and Noble/Harper, 1973, pp. 1-16.

4409 Buckler, William E., ed. The Major Victorian Poets: Tennyson, Browning, Arnold. Boston: Houghton Mifflin, 1973.
(Riverside Edition)

4410 Conrad, Peter. The Victorian Treasure-House. London: Collins, 1973.
Tennyson on pages 206-209. Tennyson compared to Arnold.

4411 Drew, Philip. "Tennyson and the Dramatic Monologue: A
Study of 'Maud.'" Tennyson. Ed. D.J. Palmer. Athens,
Ohio: Ohio U.P., 1973. London: Bell, 1973, pp. 115-146.
(Writers and Their Background)

4412 Hunt, John D. "'Story Painters and Picture Writers': Tennyson's Idylls and Victorian Painting." Tennyson. Ed. D.J.
Palmer. Athens, Ohio: Ohio U.P., 1973. London: Bell,
1973, pp. 180-202. (Writers and Their Background)
Images and arrangements Tennyson's work shares with paintings.

4413 Jump, John D. "Tennyson's Religious Faith and Doubt." Tennyson. Ed. D.J. Palmer. Athens, Ohio: Ohio U.P., 1973.
London: Bell, 1973, pp. 89-114. (Writers and Their Background)
According to Jump: "The interesting question about Tennyson's
religious faith and doubt is not what reasons he gives for his doubt
and for his faith but how he communicates these states of mind in his
poetry."

4414 Killham, John. "Tennyson and Victorian Social Values." Tennyson. Ed. D.J. Palmer. Athens, Ohio: Ohio U.P., 1973.
London: Bell, 1973, pp. 147-179. (Writers and Their Background)
Tennyson's poetry in the context of Victorian conflicts between
practices and ideals.

4415 Madden, Lionel. Sir Charles Tennyson: An Annotated Bibliography of His Published Writings. Lincoln, England: Tennyson Society, 1973.

4416 _____. "Tennyson: A Reader's Guide." Tennyson. Ed.
D.J. Palmer. Athens, Ohio: Ohio U.P., 1973. London:
Bell, 1973, pp. 1-22. (Writers and Their Background)

A Bibliography / 409

4417   Palmer, D.J., ed. Tennyson. Athens, Ohio: Ohio U.P.,
       1973. London: Bell, 1973. (Writers and Their Background)
       A gathering of essays. See entries 4411, 4412, 4413, 4414,
4416, 4418, 4422, 4426, and 4427.
       Reviewed by: L.G. Bailey in Victorian Studies (entry 4696);
D. Kwinn in Library Journal (entry 4467); L. Lerner in Encounter
(entry 4559); K. McSweeney in Papers on Language and Literature
(entry 4562); H. Sergeant in English (entry 4486); Times Literary
Supplement (entry 4499); R. Trickett in Review of English Studies
(entry 4596); P. Turner in Notes and Queries (entry 4675); and G.M.
White in American Book Collector (entry 4678).

4418   _____. "Tennyson's Romantic Heritage." Tennyson. Ed.
       D.J. Palmer. Athens, Ohio: Ohio U.P., 1973. London:
       Bell, 1973, pp. 23-51. (Writers and Their Work)
       According to Palmer: "Beginning in the aftermath of the Ro-
mantic movement, Tennyson's development, as it is reflected in the
volumes of 1830, 1832 and 1842, is a Romantic progression from in-
troverted and inert states of mind towards emancipated consciousness."

4419   Pfordresher, John (ed.). "Introduction." A Variorum Edition
       of Tennyson's Idylls of the King, by Alfred, Lord Tennyson.
       New York: Columbia U.P., 1973. Publication of a disserta-
       tion: 1970 (entry 4233).
       This is a thorough edition that includes Tennyson's prose drafts
of the poems as well as variants from the different poems. This
book is valuable for its information on Tennyson's manuscripts and
Pfordresher's insight into Tennyson's methods of composition.
       Reviewed by: U.C. Knoepflmacher in Victorian Studies (entry
4555); K. McSweeney in Papers on Language and Literature (entry
4562); J.R. Reed in Modern Philology (entry 4669); and P.G. Scott
in Tennyson Research Bulletin (entry 4482).

4420   Priestly, Francis E.L. Language and Structure in Tennyson's
       Poetry. London: Deutsch, 1973. (The Language Library)
       Priestly traces Tennyson's poetic development through the in-
creasingly sophisticated use of language.
       Reviewed by: L.G. Bailey in Victorian Studies (entry 4696);
K. McSweeney in Papers on Language and Literature (entry 4562); L.
Madden in Tennyson Research Bulletin (entry 4469); C. Moore in
Queen's Quarterly (entry 4563); Times Literary Supplement (entry
4593); and P. Turner in Review of English Studies (entry 4597).

4421   Rosenberg, John D. The Fall of Camelot: A Study of Tenny-
       son's "Idylls of the King." Cambridge, Massachusetts: Har-
       vard U.P. (Belknap), 1973.
       Rosenberg presents an interesting, provocative, and original
study of Idylls of the King. He presents his ideas in prose worthy
of its subject. His discussion indicates new ways for understanding
Tennyson's great work. Rosenberg asserts: "At the heart of Arthur's
story is the dual cycle of his coming and promised return. The
Idylls, incorporating this cycle into its structure, is itself a kind of

literary second coming of Arthur, a resurrection in Victorian England
of the long sequence of Arthuriads extending back before Malory and
forward through Spenser, Dryden, Scott, and Tennyson. The poem
takes on the quality of a self-fulfilling prophecy and validates itself,
like Scripture, by foretelling in one passage what is fulfilled in the
next."
        Reviewed by: C.C. Barfoot in English Studies (entry 4623);
Choice (entry 4535); J.M. Gray in Tennyson Research Bulletin (entry
4545) and Victorian Studies (entry 4641); G. Joseph in Virginia Quarterly Review (entry 4553); D. Kwinn in Library Journal (entry 4557);
K. McSweeney in Queen's Quarterly (entry 4561); J. Pfordresher in
Criticism (entry 4668); M. Ross in Dalhousie Review (entry 4573); C.
de L. Ryals in South Atlantic Quarterly (entry 4670); R. Sale in Hudson Philology (entry 4815); and P. Turner in Notes and Queries (entry
4744). See also: J.M. Gray in Tennyson Research Bulletin, 1975
(entry 4640).

4422   Shaw, M. "Tennyson and His Public 1827-1859." Tennyson.
        Ed. D.J. Palmer. Athens, Ohio: Ohio U.P., 1973. London:
        Bell, 1973, pp. 52-88. (Writers and Their Background)
        Shaw notes: "Tennyson was compelled to consider the question
of popularity more seriously than any previous poet."

4423   Stevens, L. Robert. "The Logic of Tennyson's Aestheticism."
        Studies in Relevance: Romantic and Victorian Writers in 1972.
        Ed. Thomas M. Harwell. Salzburg: Dr. James Hogg, Insti-
        tute für Englische Sprache und Literatur, University of Salz-
        burg, 1973, pp. 114-122.

4424   Tennyson, Alfred. Selected Poems. Ed. Michael Millgate.
        New York: Oxford U.P., 1973. (New Oxford English Series)

4425   _____. Tennyson. Ed. Kingsley Amis. Baltimore: Pen-
        guin, 1973. (Poet to Poet)
        A selective edition.

4426   Tennyson, Charles. "Tennyson as Poet Laureate." Tennyson.
        Ed. D.J. Palmer. Athens, Ohio: Ohio U.P., 1973. London:
        Bell, 1973, pp. 203-225.
        "Tennyson was without doubt the most successful of all our Po-
ets Laureate, even if we include Spenser and Ben Jonson in the list,
as, strictly speaking, we should not," remarks Charles Tennyson.
His essay discusses the poet's contributions to the Laureateship.

4427   Thomson, Peter. "Tennyson's Plays and Their Production."
        Tennyson. Ed. D.J. Palmer. Athens, Ohio: Ohio U.P.,
        1973. London: Bell, 1973, pp. 226-254. (Writers and Their
        Background)

Dissertations

4428   Belden, Daniel Morgan, Jr. The Hero as Failure in an Age of
        Hero Worship: Five Victorian Writers. Michigan, 1973. Dis-

sertation Abstracts International, 35 (1974), 393A-394A.
Tennyson's views of heroes and the ambiguity of the heroes in his poetry. Also discusses Thackeray, Dickens, Arnold, and Conrad.

4429　Franklin, Stephen Lyle. The Dilemma of Time: Time as a Shaping Force in the Writings of Carlyle, Arnold, Browning, Dickens, and Tennyson. Illinois at Urbana-Champaign, 1973. Dissertation Abstracts International, 34 (1974), 5966A.
Franklin investigates how Tennyson and other writers come to terms with modern conceptions of time. He finds Tennyson to be the most modern of the writers in his understanding of time.

4430　Gliserman, Susan M. Literature as Historical Document: Tennyson and the Nineteenth-Century Science Writers, 1830-1854. Indiana, 1973. Dissertation Abstracts International, 34 (1974), 4201A.

4431　Mounger, Samuel Gwin. Will Within Will: Religious Thought in the Poetry of Tennyson. Virginia, 1973. Dissertation Abstracts International, 34 (1974), 5113A-5114A.
Tennyson's work within the Christian tradition. Of particular interest are the comments on free will in the poetry.

4432　Petch, Simon Stonehouse. Tennyson: The Passion of the Past. Princeton, 1973. Dissertation Abstracts International, 34 (1973), 1929A.
Tennyson's views of the past and their relation to the principal themes of the poetry.

4433　Powers, Samuel Bernard. The Development of Tennyson's English Idyls. Pennsylvania, 1973. Dissertation Abstracts International, 34 (1974), 5199A-5200A.
A critical examination of Tennyson's English idylls and their significance for Tennyson's work as a whole. Powers contradicts the old notion of "two Tennysons," one private and the other public.

4434　Schlager, Herbert C. The Marriage Theme in the Poetry and Plays of Alfred Tennyson. New York, 1973. Dissertation Abstracts International, 34 (1974), 5122A.
Marriage as a central concept in Tennyson's work.

4435　Shea, Michael Timothy. I. The "Uncreating Word": The Poetical Identities of William Cowper. II. Milton: The "Sociable Angle" of Paradise Lost. III. Browning and Tennyson and the Uses of the Past. Rutgers and S.U. of New Jersey, 1973. Dissertation Abstracts International, 34 (1973), 2578A-2579A.
Contrasts the views of Browning and Tennyson on England's cultural tradition.

4436　Stevenson, Catherine Barnes. Narrative Form and Point of View in The Princess, Maud, and Idylls of the King. New York, 1973. Dissertation Abstracts International, 34 (1973), 1255A-1256A.

Stevenson tries to reveal the genuine complexity of Tennyson's thought and narratives.

Periodicals

4437 Adlard, John. "Hopkins and Tennyson: An Echo." Notes and Queries, 20 (1973), 252.

4438 Allentuck, Marcia. "New Light on Rossetti and the Moxon Tennyson." Apollo, 97 (1973), 176.

4439 Barfoot, C.C. English Studies, 54 (1973), 363.
Review of W. Hellstrom's On the Poems of Tennyson, 1972 (entry 4337).

4440 Bayley, John. "The Touch of a Vanished Hand." Encounter, 41 (July 1973), 51-55.
Review of The Poems of Tennyson, ed. C. Ricks, 1969 (entry 4145) and C. Ricks's Tennyson, 1972 (entry 4343).

4441 Brantlinger, Patrick. "A Reading of Morris' The Defense of Guenevere and Other Poems." Victorian Newsletter, no. 44 (1973), 18-24.

4442 Cameron, Kenneth W., ed. "Victorian Notebook: Literary Clippings from Nineteenth-Century American Newspapers Concerning Tennyson, Scott, Shelley, Browning, Kingsley and Others." American Transcendental Quarterly, no. 19 (1973), supplement 1-54.

4443 Campbell, Patrick. "Four Unpublished Pieces from the Trinity Manuscript of Poems by Two Brothers." Notes and Queries, 20 (1973), 87-90.
Four poems by Charles Tennyson.

4444 Collins, Joseph J. "Tennyson and Kierkegaard." Victorian Poetry, 11 (1973), 345-350.

4445 _____. "Tennyson and the Spasmodics." Victorian Newsletter, no. 43 (Spring 1973), 24-28.
Denies the influence of the Spasmodics on Tennyson.

4446 Collins, Winston. "The Princess: The Education of the Prince." Victorian Poetry, 11 (1973), 285-294.
The growth of the Prince's character unifies the poem. Presents a positive view of the poem as a whole.

4447 "A Colloquium on Tennyson." Listener, 89 (1973), 302-305.

4448 Davis, Derek R. Essays in Criticism, 23 (1973), 95-101.
Review of J.M. Gray's Tennyson's Doppelgänger, 1971 (entry 4277).

4449 Eaton, Richard Bozman. "Chart of Tennyson's Descendants." Victorian Poetry, 11 (1973), 38.

4450 Elvin, Laurence. "Farringford." Tennyson Research Bulletin, 2 (1973), 82-83.

4451 Fichter, Andrew. "Ode and Elegy: Idea and Form in Tennyson's Early Poetry." Journal of English Literary History, 40 (1973), 398-427.
Conflict between form and content, logic and Romanticism.
This controversial essay retains its interest.

4452 Fleissner, Robert F. "The 'Cross-' of 'Crossing the Bar.'" Research Studies, 41 (1973), 139-140.

4453 Freeman, James A. "Tennyson, 'Lucretius' and the 'Breasts of Helen.'" Victorian Poetry, 11 (1973), 69-75.
An interpretation of Lucretius' third dream.

4454 Gillen, Francis. "Tennyson and the Human Norm: A Study of Hubris and Human Commitment in Three Poems by Tennyson." Costerus, 8 (1973), 57-64.

4455 Goslee, David F. "Spatial and Temporal Vision in Early Tennyson." Victorian Poetry, 11 (1973), 323-329.

4456 Gray, J.M. "Horse Sense in Tennyson's 'Walking to the Mail.'" Tennyson Research Bulletin, 2 (1973), 73-74.

4457 Grosskurth, Phyllis. "Tennyson, Froude, and Queen Mary." Tennyson Research Bulletin, 2 (1973), 44-54.

4458 Hagen, June Steffensen. "The 'Crescent Promise' of 'Locksley Hall': A Crisis in Poetic Creativity." Victorian Poetry, 11 (1973), 169-171.

4459 _____. "Tennyson Praises the Spasmodics: A Second Conversation with the Scottish Mr. Mitchell." Tennyson Research Bulletin, 2 (1973), 74-75.

4460 Hoge, James O. "Tennyson and Emily Sellwood: Two Unpublished Letter Fragments." Tennyson Research Bulletin, 2 (1973), 55-57.

4461 Jahn, E.M. "Drawings of Farringford." Tennyson Research Bulletin, 2 (1973), 82.

4462 Joseph, Gerhard. Georgia Review, 27 (1973), 607-610.
Review of W. Hellstrom's On the Poems of Tennyson, 1972 (entry 4337).

4463 _____. "Poe and Tennyson." PMLA, 88 (1973), 418-428.
An illuminating comparative essay that reveals similar responses to Romanticism in the two poets.

4464 Kalita, Dwight. "Life as Spirit: A Phenomenology of Mystic Poetry." Christianity and Literature, 23, no. 1 (1973), 7-24.

4465 Kozicki, Henry. Criticism, 15 (1973), 374-377.
Review of W. Hellstrom's On the Poems of Tennyson, 1972 (entry 4337).

4466 _____. "Wave and Fire Imagery in Tennyson's Idylls." Victorian Newsletter, no. 43 (Spring 1973), 21-23.

4467 Kwinn, D. Library Journal, 98 (1973), 2862.
Review of D.J. Palmer, ed., Tennyson, 1973 (entry 4417).

4468 McSweeney, Kerry. "The Pattern of Natural Consolation in In Memoriam." Victorian Poetry, 11 (1973), 87-99.
Nature consoles and reconciles.

4469 Madden, Lionel. Tennyson Research Bulletin, 2 (1973), 66-67.
Review of P. Revell and S. Allsobrook's A Catalogue, 1972 (entry 4342) and F.E.L. Priestly's Language and Structure, 1973 (entry 4420).

4470 Martin, David M. "Romantic Perspectivism in Tennyson's 'The Lady of Shalott.'" Victorian Poetry, 11 (1973), 255-256.

4471 Mermin, Dorothy M. "Tennyson's Maud: A Thematic Analysis." Texas Studies in Literature and Language, 15 (1973), 267-277.
According to Mermin, Maud is a full expression of a major theme of Tennyson's poetry: love of the past.

4472 Millard, Charles W. "Julia Margaret Cameron and Tennyson's Idylls of the King." Harvard Library Bulletin, 21 (1973), 187-201.
Millard discusses Cameron's photographs that illustrate Tennyson's poems.

4473 Pfordresher, John. "A Bibliographic History of Alfred Tennyson's Idylls of the King." Studies in Bibliography, 26 (1973), 193-218.
Pfordresher lists the manuscripts and proofs for Idylls of the King, and he discusses the composition of the poem. This is an important bibliographic article.

4474 Pittman, Philip McM. "Tennyson in Xanadu." Victorians Institute Journal, 2 (1973), 45-60.

4475 Pratt, Linda R. "The Holy Grail: Subversion and Revival of a Tradition in Tennyson and T.S. Eliot." Victorian Poetry, 11 (1973), 307-321.
Pratt conveys the idea that Tennyson was more thematically innovative than Eliot in his handling of the Grail legends. She perceives Eliot as expressing a desire for religious salvation and Tenny-

son as expressing a belief that man must seek secular solutions to his problems. Interesting.

4476 Richardson, Joanna. "The Most English of Englishmen: An Impression of Tennyson." History Today, 23 (1973), 776-784.

4477 Ricks, Christopher. "Query on Poem from Trinity Notebook." Notes and Queries, 20 (1973), 221.
About "That old Teuton."

4478 Robbins, Tony. "Tennyson's 'Ulysses': The Significance of the Homeric and Dantesque Backgrounds." Victorian Poetry, 11 (1973), 177-193.
Tennyson's themes of heroism and action were inspired by Homer and Dante.

4479 Roll-Hansen, Diderik. English Studies, 54 (1973), 404.
Review of B. Groom's On the Diction of Tennyson, Browning, and Arnold, 1970 (entry 4213).

4480 Rosenberg, John D. New York Times Book Review, March 18, 1973, pp. 7-8.
Review of C. Ricks's Tennyson, 1972 (entry 4343).

4481 Ross, Alastair. "Tennyson's Syntax." Listener, 89 (1973), 377.

4482 Scott, P.G. Tennyson Research Bulletin, 2 (1973), 65-66.
Review of A Variorum Edition, ed. J. Pfordresher, 1973 (entry 4419).

4483 Sendry, Joseph. "The In Memoriam Manuscripts: Some Solutions to the Problem." Harvard Library Bulletin, 21 (1973), 202-220.
See also: J. Sendry's "The In Memoriam Manuscripts" in Harvard Library Bulletin, 1974 (entry 4580). Sendry strives to identify the manuscripts.

4484 _____. "Tennyson's 'Butcher's Books' as Aids to Composition." Victorian Poetry, 11 (1973), 55-59.

4485 Sergeant, Howard. Britannica Book of the Year, 1973, p. 430.
Review of C. Ricks's Tennyson, 1972 (entry 4343).

4486 _____. English, 22 (1973), 78-80.
Review of W. Hellstrom's On the Poems of Tennyson, 1972 (entry 4337) and D.J. Palmer, ed., Tennyson, 1973 (entry 4417).

4487 Shannon, Edgar F., Jr. Victorian Studies, 16 (1973), 363-364.
Review of N. Campbell's Tennyson in Lincoln, volume I, 1972 (entry 4334).

4488 Shaw, W. David. "Tennyson's 'Tithonus' and the Problem of

Mortality." Philological Quarterly, 52 (1973), 274-285.
Shaw finds elements of classical and Romantic tradition in "Tithonus." He believes the poem reconciles ideas present in "Ulysses" and In Memoriam.

4489 _____. Victorian Studies, 16 (1973), 467-468.
Review of C. Ricks's Tennyson, 1972 (entry 4343).

4490 Sinclair, David. "The First Pirated Edition of Tennyson's Poems." Book Collector, 22 (1973), 177-188.
James Campbell and Poems.

4491 Slinn, E. Warwick. "Deception and Artifice in Idylls of the King." Victorian Poetry, 11 (1973), 1-14.
Warwick investigates the theme of deception in Idylls of the King and shows the fundamental role it plays in the poem.

4492 Smith, Elton E. Clio, 2 (1973), 198-200.
Review of J. P. Eggers's King Arthur's Luareate, 1971 (entry 4276).

4493 Southam, B. C. Review of English Studies, 24 (1973), 505-508.
Review of C. Ricks's Tennyson, 1972 (entry 4343).

4494 Stevens, R. L. "The Exorcism of England's Gothic Demon." Midwest Quarterly, 14 (1973), 151-164.

4495 Tarr, Roger L., and D. R. M. Wilkinson. "Carlyle, Tennyson, and 'Sincere' Literary Justice." PMLA, 88 (1973), 136-138.

4496 "Tennyson's 'Masters.'" Tennyson Research Bulletin, 2 (1973), 81.

4497 Thomas, Gilbert. English, 22 (1973), 32-33.
Review of C. Ricks's Tennyson, 1972 (entry 4343).

4498 Tierney, Frank M. "The Causes of the Revival of the Rondeau in Nineteenth Century England." Revue de l'Université d'Ottawa, 43 (1973), 96-113.

4499 Times Literary Supplement, July 20, 1973, p. 831.
Review of D. J. Palmer, ed., Tennyson, 1973 (entry 4417).

4500 Tyree, Donald W. "A Bibliographical Item on 'The Charge of the Light Brigade.'" Tennyson Research Bulletin, 2 (1973), 75.

4501 Yamada, Taiji. "Art and Artifice in 'The Palace of Art.'" Hitotsubashi Journal of Arts and Sciences (Tokyo), 14, no. 1 (1973), 45-52.

1974

Books

4502 Culler, A. Dwight. "Tennyson, we cannot live in art."
Nineteenth-Century Literary Perspectives: Essays in Honor
of Lionel Stevenson. Ed. Clyde de L. Ryals. Durham, North
Carolina: Duke U. P., 1974, pp. 77-92.

4503 Faas, Egbert. Poésie al Psychogramm: Die dramatisch-
monologische Verdichtung im viktorianischen Zeitalter. Munich: Fink, 1974.

4504 Figueroa, John J. "Poetry and the Teaching of Poetry." Literary Studies: Essays in the Memory of Francis A. Drumm.
Worcester, Massachusetts: College of the Holy Cross, 1974,
pp. 207-227.

4505 Fleissner, Robert F. "Like 'Pythagoras' Comparison of the
Universe with Number': A Frost-Tennyson Correlation."
Frost: Centennial Essays. Ed. J. L. Tharpe and Peggy W.
Prenshaw. Jackson, Mississippi: U. P. of Mississippi, 1974,
pp. 207-220.

4506 Gray, J. M. Serialism in the Idylls: Lists. Nottingham: the
author, 1974. 18 pp.

4507 _____. Serialism in the Idylls: Songs. Nottingham: the
author, 1974. 23 pp.

4508 _____. Tennyson's Idylls: Cyclic Imagery and Syntax.
Nottingham: the author, 1974. 19 pp.

4509 Jenkins, Elizabeth. Tennyson and Dr. Gully. Lincoln, England: Tennyson Society, 1974. 19 pp.

4510 Jump, John D. (ed.) Introduction. In Memoriam, Maud, and
Other Poems, by Alfred, Lord Tennyson. London: Dent,
1974. (Everyman's Library) Totowa, New Jersey: Rowman
and Littlefield, 1975.
Reviewed by: C. C. Barfoot in English Studies (entry 4698);
J. C. Maxwell in Notes and Queries (entry 4725); and I. Ousby in
Durham University Journal (entry 4666).

4511 Marshall, George O., Jr. Tennyson in Parody and Jest: An
Essay and a Selection. Lincoln, England: Tennyson Society,
1974. 31 pp.

4512 Moorman, Mary. Poets and Historians: A Family Inheritance.
Lincoln, England: Tennyson Society, 1974. 16 pp.

4513 Stange, G. Robert. "The 'Voyages' of Tennyson and Baudelaire." Nineteenth-Century Literary Perspectives: Essays in

Honor of Lionel Stevenson. Ed. Clyde de L. Ryals. Durham, North Carolina: Duke U. P., 1974, pp. 93-103.

4514 Tennyson, Alfred, Lord. In Memoriam. Ed. Robert H. Ross. New York: Norton, 1974. (Norton Critical Edition)

4515 Tennyson, Charles. Alfred Tennyson and Somersby. Lincoln, England: Tennyson Society, 1974. Revised edition. 15 pp.

4516 _____. Tennyson and His Times. Lincoln, England: Tennyson Society, 1974. 16 pp.

4517 _____, and Hope Dyson. Tennyson, Lincolnshire and Australia: A Contribution to the Lincolnshire Celebrations of the Bicentenary of Matthew Flinders, March 16th-May 31st 1974. Lincoln, England: Lincolnshire Society and Tennyson Society, 1974. 18 pp.
Reviewed by: P. Collins in Times Literary Supplement (entry 4538).

4518 Tennyson, Emily, Lady. The Letters of Emily Lady Tennyson. Ed. James O. Hoge. University Park: Pennsylvania State U. P., 1974.
Publication of a dissertation: 1970 (entry 4230). Hoge presents a gathering of three hundred ninety-two of Emily, Lady Tennyson's letters and provides informative notes.
Reviewed by: A. Bell in Times Literary Supplement (entry 4624); N. H. Campbell in Tennyson Research Bulletin (entry 4533); Choice (entry 4628); J. S. Hagen in Arnoldian (entry 4863); J. Kolb in South Atlantic Bulletin (entry 4718); J. Marcus in Victorian Studies (entry 4658); and R. B. Martin in Review of English Studies (entry 4804).

Dissertations

4519 Aaron, Jonathan. The Idea of the Novelistic Form: A Study of Four Victorian "Verse-Novels" by Clough, Tennyson, and Browning. Yale, 1974. Dissertation Abstracts International, 35 (1974), 2928A.
Aaron discusses nineteenth- and twentieth-century critical notions of the "verse novel" and in chapter IV relates them to Maud.

4520 Beusse, Jeffrey Henry. "The New Strong Wine of Love": Tennyson's Attitudes Toward Love and Marriage. Washington, 1974. Dissertation Abstracts International, 35 (1975), 4416A.
Beusse emphasizes Tennyson's ambivalent feelings about marriage.

4521 Ferrell, Mary Key Wynne. Tennyson's "Ulysses": An Analysis According to Coleridge's Critical Principles. Georgia, 1974. Dissertation Abstracts International, 35 (1975), 6664A.
The symbolic import of "Ulysses" is analyzed on the basis of Coleridge's ideas of unity achieved by reconciling opposites.

4522   Gillett, Peter Joseph. Poetic Processes of the Early Tenny-
       son. Wisconsin-Madison, 1974. Dissertation Abstracts Inter-
       national, 35 (1975), 7904A.
       Tennyson's unconscious mind and its role in the poet's crea-
tive development.

4523   Hinton, Ernestine Gibson. Technique in Tennyson's Maud.
       Georgia, 1974. Dissertation Abstracts International, 35
       (1975), 5348A.
       Devices, language, themes, and imagery.

4524   Miller, John Arthur. Tennyson's Paired Poems. McMaster,
       1974. Dissertation Abstracts International, 35 (1975), 5417A-
       5418A.
       The paired poems of Tennyson, such as "The Merman" and
"The Mermaid" and "Locksley Hall" and "Locksley Hall Sixty Years
After," and their significance for understanding the whole of Tenny-
son's work.

4525   Organ, Dennis Michael. Tennyson's Dramas: A Critical Study.
       Texas Tech, 1974. Dissertation Abstracts International, 35
       (1975), 6675A-6676A.
       Published: 1979 (entry 4905). See entry 4905 for annotation.

4526   Sawyer, Paul Lincoln. The Old Wound of the World: The
       Eden Myth in Tennyson and Ruskin. Columbia, 1974. Disser-
       tation Abstracts International, 35 (1975), 6109A-6110A.
       The Victorian theme of the loss of childhood in the writings of
Tennyson and Ruskin. Special note taken of "Oenone," "Hesperides,"
"The Lotos-Eaters," "The Palace of Art," In Memoriam, and Idylls
of the King. Sawyer presents some interesting ideas.

4527   Taylor, Edward Allan. Tennyson and the Elusive Gleam: The
       Problem of Transcendence from "The Mystic" to "The Ancient
       Sage." Illinois at Urbana-Champaign, 1974. Dissertation Ab-
       stracts International, 35 (1974), 481A-482A.
       Tennyson's search for spiritual truth. Illuminating commen-
tary, particularly on Idylls of the King.

Periodicals

4528   Adler, Joshua. "Tennyson's 'Mother of Sorrows': 'Rizpah.'"
       Victorian Poetry, 12 (1974), 363-369.
       Irony and meaning in Tennyson's poem.

4529   Adler, T. P. "An Echo of Daniel in Tennyson's 'Ulysses.'"
       Tennyson Research Bulletin, 2 (1974), 128-130.

4530   Appleman, Philip. "The Dread Factor: Eliot, Tennyson, and
       the Shaping of Science." Columbia Forum, n.s. 3 (Fall 1974),
       32-38.

4531   Bovey, John. "The Lady of Shalott." Cornhill Magazine, 180
       (1974), 240-254.

4532   Breen, Jennifer. "Wilfred Owen: 'Greater Love' and Late
        Romanticism." English Literature in Transition (1880-1920),
        17 (1974), 173-183.
            Cites "Cramped in that Funnelled Hole" (1917) as a parody of
Tennyson's "The Charge of the Light Brigade."

4533   Campbell, N. H. Tennyson Research Bulletin, 2 (1974), 118-
        119.
            Review of E. Tennyson's Letters, ed. J. O. Hoge, 1974 (entry
4518).

4534   Chepiga, Michael J. "'The Wholesome Madness of an Hour':
        An Examination of the Ironic Implications of Tennyson's Idylls
        of the King." Victorians Institute Journal, 3 (1974), 61-72.

4535   Choice, 11 (1974), 440.
            Review of J. D. Rosenberg's The Fall of Camelot, 1973 (entry
4421).

4536   Christopher, J. R. "The Death of Robin Hood." Eildon Tree,
        1, no. 1 (1974), 16-18.
            Discusses The Foresters.

4537   Collins, Philip. "Tennyson and Australia: A New Letter."
        Tennyson Research Bulletin, 2 (1974), 131-134.

4538   _____. Times Literary Supplement, Oct. 25, 1974, p.
        1184.
            Review of C. Tennyson and Hope Dyson's Tennyson, Lincoln-
shire and Australia (entry 4517).

4539   Collins, Winston. "'Maud': Tennyson's Point of War." Ten-
        nyson Research Bulletin, 2 (1974), 126-128.

4540   Cox, James T. "A New Date for Wiseian Forgery: Tennyson's
        'Trial' Issue of Becket (1879)." Papers of the Bibliographical
        Society of America, 68 (1974), 335-336.

4541   Draper, Ronald P. Aberdeen University Review, 45 (1974),
        419-421.
            Review of W. Hellstrom's On the Poems of Tennyson, 1972
(entry 4337).

4542   Faverty, Frederic E. "The Brownings and Their Contemporar-
        ies." Browning Institute Studies, 2 (1974), 61-80.

4543   Fricke, D. C. "A Study of Myth and Archetype in 'Enoch Ar-
        den.'" Tennyson Research Bulletin, 2 (1974), 106-115.

4544   Goslee, David F. "Character and Structure in Tennyson's
        The Princess." Studies in English Literature, 1500-1900, 14
        (1974), 563-573.
            Ida's visions bring her into conflict with her world and the
structure of the poem.

4545 Gray, J. M. Tennyson Research Bulletin, 2 (1974), 119-120.
      Review of J. D. Rosenberg's The Fall of Camelot, 1973 (entry
4421). See also: J. M. Gray in Tennyson Research Bulletin, 1975
(entry 4640) and in Victorian Studies, 1975 (entry 4641).

4546 Gunter, Garland O. "Archetypal Patterns in 'The Lady of
      Shalott.'" Victorians Institute Journal, 3 (1974), 85-93.

4547 Hargrave, Harry A. "Arthur Hallam's 'Theodicaea': An Influ-
      ence on In Memoriam." Victorians Institute Journal, 3
      (1974), 103-109.

4548 Hargrove, Nancy D. "Landscape as Symbol in Tennyson and
      T. S. Eliot." Victorians Institute Journal, 3 (1974), 73-83.

4549 Harrs, R. "Floral Motifs in Idylls of the King." Tennyson
      Research Bulletin, 2 (1974), 124-126.

4550 Helterman, Jeffrey. "Narrative Modes and the Dynamics of
      Passion in The Idylls of the King." Victorians Institute Jour-
      nal, 3 (1974), 45-59.

4551 Hill, F. Tennyson Research Bulletin, 2 (1974), 117-118.
      Review of N. Campbell's Tennyson in Lincoln, 1972 (entry
4334).

4552 Hunter, W. "Tennyson as a Smoker." Tennyson Research
      Bulletin, 2 (1974), 134-135.

4553 Joseph, Gerhard. "Tennyson's 'Idylls': Attack and Defense."
      Virginia Quarterly Review, 50 (1974), 152-156.
      Review of J. D. Rosenberg's The Fall of Camelot, 1973 (entry
4421).

4554 Kincaid, James R. "Rhetorical Irony, the Dramatic Monologue,
      and Tennyson's Poems (1842)." Philological Quarterly, 53
      (1974), 220-236.

4555 Knoepflmacher, U. C. Victorian Studies, 17 (1974), 344-347.
      Review of A Variorum Edition, ed. J. Pfordresher, 1973 (en-
try 4419).

4556 Kolb, Jack. "The Hero and His Worshippers: The History of
      Arthur Henry Hallam's Letters." Bulletin of the John Rylands
      Library, 56 (1974), 150-173.

4557 Kwinn, D. Library Journal, 99 (1974), 760.
      Review of J. D. Rosenberg's The Fall of Camelot, 1973 (entry
4421).

4558 Landow, George P. "Closing the Frame: Having Faith and
      Keeping Faith in Tennyson's 'The Passing of Arthur.'" Bulle-
      tin of the John Rylands Library, 56 (1974), 423-442.

Arthur is tested three times in "The Passing of Arthur" and he passes each time. Landow presents a positive view of the Idylls of the King.

4559 Lerner, Laurence. "Victorian Masters: Treatments of Browning and Tennyson." Encounter, 43 (July 1974), 60-64.
Review of D. J. Palmer's Tennyson, 1973 (entry 4417) and C. Tennyson's Six Tennyson Essays, 1954 (entry 3551).

4560 Libera, Sharon Mayer. "John Tyndall and Tennyson's 'Lucretius.'" Victorian Newsletter, no. 45 (Spring 1974), 19-22.

4561 McSweeney, Kerry. Queen's Quarterly, 81 (1974), 473-474.
Review of J. D. Rosenberg's The Fall of Camelot, 1973 (entry 4421).

4562 _____. "The State of Tennyson Criticism." Papers on Language and Literature, 10 (1974), 433-446.
Review of J. R. Reed's Perception and Design, 1969 (entry 4143), J. P. Eggers's King Arthur's Laureate, 1971 (entry 4276), A. Sinfield's The Language, 1971 (entry 4283), C. B. Ricks's Tennyson, 1972 (entry 4343), D. J. Palmer, ed., Tennyson, 1973 (entry 4417), J. Pfordresher's A Variorum Edition, 1973 (entry 4419), and F. E. L. Priestly's Language and Structure, 1973 (entry 4420).
McSweeney focuses on the negative, moralizing aspects of criticism of Tennyson's works and uses seven books to illustrate his point of view.

4563 Moore, C. Queen's Quarterly, 81 (1974), 649-650.
Review of F. E. L. Priestly's Language and Structure, 1973 (entry 4420).

4564 Morris, Celia. "From Malory to Tennyson: Spiritual Triumph to Spiritual Defeat." Mosaic, 7, no. 3 (1974), 87-98.
In Malory's work the characters believe in their duties; in Tennyson's poem, the characters represent nineteenth-century evasion of Christian faith.

4565 Pfeiffer, Karl L. "Interpretation and Marxismus: Überlegungen zur marxistischen Methode aus Anlass von Christian Enzensbergers Viktorianische Lyrik." Anglia, 92 (1974), 349-379.

4566 Pollard, Arthur. "Tennyson and the Roman Poets." Tennyson Research Bulletin, 2 (1974), 58-62.

4567 Portnoy, William E. "Wilde's Debt to Tennyson in Dorian Gray." English Literature in Transition (1880-1920), 17 (1974), 259-261.
Wilde borrowed extensively from Tennyson, as shown in the parallels between Tennyson's "The Lady of Shalott" and part of Dorian Gray.

4568 Prairie Schooner, 48 (1974), 89.

Review of W. Hellstrom's On the Poems of Tennyson, 1972 (entry 4337).

4569 Priestly, F. E. L. "Locksley Hall Revisited." Queen's Quarterly, 81 (1974), 512-532.
Priestly compares the Locksley Hall poems to illustrate their complexity and value.

4570 Puckett, Harry. "Subjunctive Imagination in In Memoriam." Victorian Poetry, 12 (1974), 97-124.
Responded to by A. Sinfield, "That Which Is" in Victorian Poetry, 1976 (entry 4739).
The subjunctive is used in In Memoriam to show growth in imagination.

4571 Ricks, Christopher. "The Lincoln Ms. from 'The Coming of Arthur.'" Tennyson Research Bulletin, 2 (1974), 68-72.

4572 Rosenberg, John D. "Tennyson and the Landscape of Consciousness." Victorian Poetry, 12 (1974), 303-310.
Rosenberg analyzes Tennyson's mythical landscapes, with attention to In Memoriam.

4573 Ross, Malcolm. Dalhousie Review, 54 (1974), 572-574.
Review of J. D. Rosenberg's The Fall of Camelot, 1973 (entry 4421).

4574 Sait, James E. "Edward Tennyson: Two Letters and a Poem." Tennyson Research Bulletin, 2 (1974), 137-138.

4575 _____. "Tennyson, Mesmerism, and the Prince's 'Weird Seizures.'" Yearbook of English Studies, 4 (1974), 203-211.

4576 Sale, Roger. "Tennyson as Great Poet." Hudson Review, 27 (1974), 443-450.
Review of J. D. Rosenberg's The Fall of Camelot, 1973 (entry 4421).

4577 Scott, P. G. "John Addington Symonds and the Reaction Against Tennyson." Tennyson Research Bulletin, 2 (1974), 85-95.

4578 _____. "Tennyson and Charles Kingsley." Tennyson Research Bulletin, 2 (1974), 135-136.

4579 Scrivner, Buford, Jr. "Question and Answer: The Philosophic Progression of In Memoriam." Cithara, 14, no. 1 (1974), 43-59.

4580 Sendry, Joseph. "The In Memoriam Manuscripts: Additional Evidence." Harvard Library Bulletin, 22 (1974), 47-48.
See also: J. Sendry's "The In Memoriam Manuscripts" in Harvard Library Bulletin, 1973 (entry 4483).

4581   Shaw, W. David. "Tennyson's Late Elegies." Victorian Po-
       etry, 12 (1974), 1-12.
       Shaw discusses Tennyson's austere style in such poems as
"In the Garden at Swainston," "To the Marquis of Dufferin and Ava,"
and "Crossing the Bar."

4582   Smith, Harold J. "The Mirror of Art: Mallarmé's 'Heriodi-
       ade' and Tennyson's 'The Lady of Shalott.'" Romance Notes,
       16 (1974), 91-94.

4583   Spatz, Jonas. "Love and Death in Tennyson's Maud." Texas
       Studies in Literature and Language, 16 (1974), 503-510.
       Maud is Tennyson's statement on the relationship between love
and aggression.

4584   Staines, David. "The Prose Drafts of Tennyson's Idylls of the
       King." Harvard Library Bulletin, 22 (1974), 280-308.
       Staines presents material from Tennyson's prose drafts.

4585   _____. "Tennyson's 'The Holy Grail': The Tragedy of Per-
       civale." Modern Language Review, 69 (1974), 745-756.
       According to Staines, the quest for the Holy Grail is Perci-
vale's personal tragedy. This article presents much valuable information on the sources for the Grail story and on Tennyson's render-
ings of the source material.

4586   Stevenson, Catherine B. "The Aesthetic Function of the 'Weird
       Seizures' in The Princess." Victorian Newsletter, no. 45
       (Spring 1974), 22-25.

4587   _____. "An Early Version of 'Sweet and Low.'" Tennyson
       Research Bulletin, 2 (1974), 130-131.

4588   Tannacito, Dan J. "Tennyson." Victorian Poetry, 12 (1974),
       279-284.
       Survey of works on Tennyson.

4589   Tennyson, Charles. "James Spedding and Alfred Tennyson."
       Tennyson Research Bulletin, 2 (1974), 96-105.

4590   _____. "Tennyson and Twickenham." Tennyson Research
       Bulletin, 2 (1974), 78-81.

4591   _____. "Tennyson in North Wales in 1870?" Tennyson Re-
       search Bulletin, 2 (1974), 139-141.

4592   _____, and C. Ricks. "Tennyson's 'Marblethorpe.'" Ten-
       nyson Research Bulletin, 2 (1974), 121-123.

4593   Times Literary Supplement, March 15, 1974, p. 267.
       Review of F. E. L. Priestly's Language and Structure, 1973
(entry 4420).

4594   Times Literary Supplement, Nov. 8, 1974, p. 1246.
        Review of N. Campbell's Tennyson in Lincoln, volume II,
1973 (entry 4334).

4595   Timko, Michael. "Arnold, Tennyson, and the English Idyl:
        Ancient Criticism and Modern Poetry." Texas Studies in Lit-
        erature and Language, 16 (1974), 135-146.
        Arnold's disparagement of Tennyson's work was a subjective
reaction based in large part on Arnold's misunderstanding of Tennyson's poetry.

4596   Trickett, Rachel. Review of English Studies, 25 (1974), 349-
        351.
        Review of D. J. Palmer, ed. , Tennyson, 1973 (entry 4417).

4597   Turner, Paul. Review of English Studies, 25 (1974), 357-359.
        Review of W. Hellstrom's On the Poems of Tennyson, 1972
(entry 4337) and F. E. L. Priestly's Language and Structure, 1973 (entry 4420).

4598   Ward, Arthur D. "'Ulysses' and 'Tithonus': Tunnel-Vision
        and Idle Tears." Victorian Poetry, 12 (1974), 311-319.
        Contrasts the characters of Ulysses and Tithonus to illustrate
the nature of each.

4599   Ware, Thomas C. "The Impact of Tennyson on the King Cop-
        hetua Legend." Victorians Institute Journal, 3 (1974), 95-102.

4600   Wiebe, M. G. "The Maid of Astolat: A Trial Printing of Ten-
        nyson's 'Elaine' and 'Guinevere' Idylls." Book Collector, 23
        (1974), 355-360.
        Revisions of the poems.

4601   Wilkenfeld, Roger B. "'Columbus' and 'Ulysses': Notes on
        the Development of a Tennysonian Theme." Victorian Poetry,
        12 (1974), 170-174.
        Columbus is a more mature and insightful character than
Ulysses.

4602   Wilkins, Mary C. "Some Birmingham Comments on the Genius
        of Tennyson." Tennyson Research Bulletin, 2 (1974), 76-78.

4603   Wilson, James D. "Tennyson's Emendations to Wordsworth's
        'Tintern Abbey.'" Wordsworth Circle, 5 (1974), 7-8.
        Tennyson's emendations of 'Tintern Abbey' in the poet's copy
of Wordsworth's Poetical Works show Tennyson to be insensitive as
a critic to elements in Wordsworth's work that are also prominent in
Tennyson's poetry.

4604   Wordsworth, Jonathan. "'What Is It, that Has Been Done?':
        The Central Problem of Maud." Essays in Criticism, 24
        (1974), 356-362.

1975

Books

4605 Christ, Carol T. The Finer Optic: The Aesthetic of Partic-
      ularity in Victorian Poetry. New Haven: Yale, 1975.
      Tennyson discussed often throughout, most notably on pages
17-29. Christ notes of Tennyson, along with other cogent observations: "The descriptions in his poems are characterized by a remarkable visual precision."

4606 Johnson, Wendell Stacy. "Marriage and Divorce in Tennyson."
      Sex and Marriage in Victorian Poetry. Ithaca: Cornell U. P.,
      1975, pp. 110-184.
      Johnson remarks of Tennyson: "The frustrated and failed
marriages in his poetry suggest that he finds in life not union but a
divorce, a conflict, of contrasting, complementary, and partial
values--values, not people."

4607 Kincaid, James R. Tennyson's Major Poems: The Comic and
      Ironic Patterns. New Haven: Yale U. P., 1975.
      Kincaid divides Tennyson's poems by comedy--"mythic
pattern"--and irony--"mythos of winter." With good sense and insight, Kincaid provides a revealing and provocative study of the major poems. His interpretations are controversial because of the
seeming arbitrariness of his applications of the terms comedy and
irony, but their originality is refreshing and interesting.
      Reviewed by: J. H. Buckley in Journal of English and German-
ic Philology (entry 4774); D. A. Dillon in Library Journal (entry
4631); G. Joseph in English Language Notes (entry 4716); J. Jump in
Critical Quarterly (entry 4717); J. Korg in Victorian Poetry (entry
4719); H. Kozicki in Victorian Studies (entry 4720); K. McSweeney in
Modern Language Notes (entry 4801); R. G. Martin in Tennyson Research Bulletin (entry 4660); K. L. Pfeiffer in Anglia (entry 5093); L.
Poston in Ohio Review (entry 4808); C. de L. Ryals in Clio (entry
4732); and W. D. Shaw in Modern Language Quarterly (entry 4737).

4608 Tennyson, Charles, and Hope Dyson. The Tennysons: Back-
      ground to Genius. London: Macmillan, 1975.
      Tennyson and Dyson present a history of the Tennyson family
from the eighteenth century through the nineteenth. Biographers will
find much useful information in this book; Tennyson specialists will
find particularly interesting the appendix, "Tennyson's Conversation,"
based on notes taken by Hallam Tennyson when he was a schoolboy of
conversations with his father.
      Reviewed by: A. Bell in Times Literary Supplement (entry
4624); G. Grigson in Country Life (entry 4642); F. Hill in Tennyson
Research Bulletin (entry 4647); A. N. Jeffers in Sewanee Review (entry 4789); and A. R. Lee in Studies (entry 4800).

Dissertations

4609 Bailey, Leslie George. The Statelier Eden: Tennyson in the

1850's. Indiana, 1975. <u>Dissertation Abstracts International</u>, <u>36</u> (1976), 7429A-7430A.
Tennyson's belief in an immutable and transcendent law and how it colors his thought and poetry.

4610 Berlin, James Arthur. <u>The Ideal Poet: The Aesthetic Thought of Tennyson, Browning, and Arnold and Its Relation to German Idealism.</u> Michigan, 1975. <u>Dissertation Abstracts International,</u> 36 (1975), 1486A.
German idealism's role in the ethos of the poets.

4611 Coyle, Kathleen Mildred. <u>"Madhouse Cells": The Love Poem Sequences of Clough, Tennyson, Arnold, Meredith and Rossetti.</u> Washington U., 1975. <u>Dissertation Abstracts International,</u> 36 (1976), 8071A-8072A.
Coyle discusses <u>Amours de Voyage, Maud, Switzerland, Modern Love,</u> and <u>The House of Life</u> as autobiographical searches for spiritual order.

4612 Crabbe, Katharyn Frances Wood. <u>The Framework and the Chord: Ethical Themes in Tennyson's Idylls of the King.</u> Oregon, 1975. <u>Dissertation Abstracts International,</u> 36 (1976), 6111A-6112A.
<u>Activism</u> as manifested by <u>life, use,</u> and <u>fame</u> in <u>Idylls of the King</u> and other poems.

4613 Dillard, Philip Edward. <u>The Influence of Thomas Carlyle upon the Poetry of Alfred Tennyson.</u> Georgia, 1975. <u>Dissertation Abstracts International,</u> 36 (1976), 8044A.
Carlylean themes in Tennyson's work.

4614 Johnston, Priscilla Winthrop. <u>Keats and Tennyson: Two Modes in Nineteenth-Century Classical Myth.</u> Brown, 1975. <u>Dissertation Abstracts International,</u> 37 (1976), 332A.
Similarities and contrasts in the poets' uses of classical mythology.

4615 Moritz, Albert Frank. <u>Tennyson and the Defense of Romantic Faith.</u> Marquette, 1975. <u>Dissertation Abstracts International,</u> 36 (1976), 6709A.
Tennyson extends and further develops the Romanticism of his predecessors.

4616 O'Neill, James Norman. <u>Tennyson's Maud: A Reexamination of Its Biographical Genesis and Aesthetic Merits.</u> Bowling Green State, 1975. <u>Dissertation Abstracts International,</u> 36 (1976), 5324A.
O'Neill argues for Tennyson's control over the emotional content of <u>Maud.</u>

4617 Parker, Cheryl Leigh. <u>The Ever-Poising Wave: The Articulation of Change in Tennyson's Poems.</u> California at San Diego, 1975. <u>Dissertation Abstracts International,</u> 36 (1975), 1532A-1533A.

The psychological and aesthetic unifying factors of Tennyson's poetry.

4618   Rosenbaum, Jean Louise Watson. Tennyson's Idylls of the
       King: A Critical Analysis. Ohio, 1975. Dissertation Ab-
       stracts International, 36 (1976), 6714A.
       The structure, themes, and characters of Idylls of the King
present a complex philosophical point of view.

4619   Rosenblum, Dolores Mary. The Forms of Space in Tennyson's
       Poetry. Cornell, 1975. Dissertation Abstracts International,
       36 (1975), 909A-910A.
       Tennyson presents his ideas in terms of space and time.

4620   Ward, Arthur Douglas. Death and Eroticism in the Poetry of
       Keats and Tennyson. California at Berkeley, 1975. Disser-
       tation Abstracts International, 37 (1976), 344A-345A.
       A comparison of how Keats and Tennyson unite death and sex-
uality in their poetry.

Periodicals

4621   Adler, Joshua. "A Further Note on Tennyson's 'Subtle Beast.'"
       Notes and Queries, 22 (1975), 437-439.

4622   Allen, S.C. "Tennyson, Sappho and 'The Lady of Shalott.'"
       Tennyson Research Bulletin, 2 (1975), 171-172.

4623   Barfoot, C.C. English Studies, 56 (1975), 438.
       Review of J.D. Rosenberg's The Fall of Camelot, 1973 (entry
4421).

4624   Bell, A. Times Literary Supplement, March 14, 1975, p. 274.
       Review of E. Tennyson's Letters, ed. J.O. Hoge, 1974 (entry
4518) and C. Tennyson and H. Dyson's The Tennysons, 1975 (entry
4608).

4625   Brown, Lloyd W. "Jones (Baraka) and His Literary Heritage
       in The System of Dante's Hell." Obsidian, 1, no. 1 (1975),
       5-17.

4626   Burton, Thomas G. "Speaking Out in Idylls of the King."
       Tennessee Philological Bulletin, 12, no. 1 (1975), 5-11.

4627   Carlson, Patricia Ann. "'The Play's the Thing'?: The Dra-
       matic Impulse in Victorian Theatre and the Plays of Alfred,
       Lord Tennyson." Victorians Institute Journal, 4 (1975), 1-12.

4628   Choice, 11 (1975), 1311.
       Review of E. Tennyson's Letters, ed. J.O. Hoge, 1974 (entry
4518).

4629   Culler, A. Dwight. "Monodrama and the Dramatic Monologue."
       PMLA, 90 (May 1975), 366-385.

A Bibliography / 429

Culler examines the development of monodrama and the dramatic monologue and places such poems as "Locksley Hall" and "Ulysses" in the subgenre of monodramas. He disputes the interpretations of the poems as ironic monologues. An enlightening and informative essay.

4630 Devlin, Francis P. "A 'Cinematic' Approach to Tennyson's Descriptive Art." Literature/Film Quarterly, 3 (1975), 132-144.

4631 Dillon, D. A. Library Journal, 100 (1975), 1926.
Review of J. R. Kincaid's Tennyson's Major Poems, 1975 (entry 4607).

4632 Fielding, K. J. "Tennyson for Rector: A Note." Tennyson Research Bulletin, 2 (1975), 168-171.

4633 Fleissner, Robert F. "Frost and Tennyson: Factual as Well as 'Archetypal.'" American Notes and Queries, 14 (1975), 53-55.

4634 Fontana, Ernest. "Tennyson's In Memoriam, XCV, 64." Explicator, 33 (1975), Item 51.
The "boundless day" of lines 53-64 is the summer solstice and represents eternal life.

4635 _____. "Virginal Hysteria in Tennyson's The Hesperides." Concerning Poetry, 8, no. 2 (1975), 17-20.
Fontana suggests that The Hesperides is about masculine sexuality rather than creativity.

4636 Fowler, H. Ramsey. "Tennyson's 'Demeter and Persephone': New Poem, New Myth." Intepretations, 7 (1975), 22-29.

4637 Friedman, Norman. "Hallam on Tennyson: An Early Aesthetic Doctrine and Modernism." Studies in the Literary Imagination, 8, no. 2 (1975), 37-62.
Friedman discusses Hallam's essay "On Some of the Characteristics of Modern Poetry" (entry 9) and its section on Tennyson's Poems, Chiefly Lyrical.

4638 Gliserman, Susan. "Early Victorian Science Writers and Tennyson's In Memoriam: A Study in Cultural Exchange." Victorian Studies, 18, nos. 3 and 4 (1975), 277-308 and 437-459.
Tennyson used scientific writings as rhetorical models for In Memoriam, and the poem helped Victorians to emotionally understand new scientific advances.

4639 Goslee, David F. "The Stages in Tennyson's Composition of 'Balin and Balan.'" Huntington Library Quarterly, 38 (1975), 247-268.
A close examination of Tennyson's development of "Balin and Balan" from Malory's ethos to his own, over a period of fifteen years.

4640 Gray, J. M. Tennyson Research Bulletin, 2 (1975), 164.
      Comments on J. D. Rosenberg's The Fall of Camelot, 1973
(entry 4421). See also: J. M. Gray, Tennyson Research Bulletin,
1974 (entry 4545), and Victorian Studies, 1975 (entry 4641), below.

4641 _____. Victorian Studies, 19 (1975), 122-123.
      Review of J. D. Rosenberg's The Fall of Camelot, 1973 (entry
4421). See also: J. M. Gray, Tennyson Research Bulletin, 1974 and
1975 (entries 4545 and 4640, above).

4642 Grigson, Geoffrey. Country Life, 157 (1975), 112-113.
      Review of C. Tennyson and H. Dyson's The Tennysons, 1975
(entry 4608).

4643 Hagen, June Steffensen. "Reality and Reflection in 'The Lady
      of Shalott.'" American Notes and Queries, 14 (1975), 7-8.

4644 _____. "Tennyson Answers Coleridge's Complaint." Amer-
      ican Notes and Queries, 13 (1975), 86-87.

4645 _____. "Tennyson's Revisions of the Last Stanza of 'Audley
      Court.'" Costerus, 4 (1975), 39-49.
      A discussion of how the page proofs of the 1842 "Audley Court"
illustrate the control Tennyson exercised over his work.

4646 Harrison, James. "The Role of Anachronism in The Princess."
      English Studies in Canada, 1 (1975), 304-316.

4647 Hill, F. Tennyson Research Bulletin, 2 (1975), 162.
      Review of C. Tennyson and H. Dyson's The Tennysons, 1975
(entry 4608).

4648 Hixson, J. C. "Cauteretz Revisited." Tennyson Research Bul-
      letin, 2 (1975), 145-149.

4649 Hoge, James O. "Keatsian Love-making in Tennyson's 'Tithon-
      us.'" Victorians Institute Journal, 4 (1975), 13-16.

4650 Hollander, John. "Tennyson's Melody." Georgia Review, 29
      (1975), 676-703.
      The relationship between the music of Tennyson's poetry and
sense, theme, image, and reader. A sophisticated analysis of the
musical qualities of the poetry.

4651 Hunter, W. "Punch on Tennyson's Becket." Tennyson Re-
      search Bulletin, 2 (1975), 174-175.

4652 Kolb, Jack. "When Did Tennyson Meet Rose Baring?" Victori-
      an Newsletter, 48 (Fall 1975), 26-28.

4653 Kozicki, Henry. "Philosophy of History in Tennyson's Poetry
      to the 1842 Poems." Journal of English Literary History, 42
      (1975), 88-106.

Background for history in Tennyson's poetry and interpretation of the poet's use of history.

4654 _____. "The 'Medieval Ideal' in Tennyson's The Princess."
Criticism, 17 (1975), 121-130.
A study of the mixture of past and present in Tennyson's poem.

4655 Leach, T. "The Tennysons and the Massingberds." Tennyson Research Bulletin, 2 (1975), 155-159.

4656 Librach, Ronald S. "Myth and Romance in Idylls of the King."
Dalhousie Review, 55 (1975), 511-525.
King Arthur as expression of ideals and the unity of humanity and nature.

4657 McGhee, Richard D. "In Memoriam: The Ways of an Artist."
Studia Neophilologica, 47 (1975), 333-352.

4658 Marcus, J. Victorian Studies, 19 (1975), 270-272.
Review of E. Tennyson's Letters, ed. J. O. Hoge, 1974 (entry 4518).

4659 Martin, R. B. Times Literary Supplement, June 6, 1975, p. 626.
A letter declaring Martin's intention to write a biography of Tennyson (entry 4970).

4660 Martin, R. G. Tennyson Research Bulletin, 2 (1975), 162-163.
Review of J. R. Kincaid's Tennyson's Major Poems, 1975 (entry 4607).

4661 Maxwell, J. C. Notes and Queries, 22 (1975), 463-464.
Review of W. Hellstrom's On the Poems of Tennyson, 1972 (entry 4337) and C. Ricks's Tennyson, 1972 (entry 4343).

4662 Meyers, T. L. "An Interview with Tennyson on Poe." Tennyson Research Bulletin, 2 (1975), 167-168.

4663 Miller, J. C. "Tennyson and the Chancellor's Medal, 1828."
Tennyson Research Bulletin, 2 (1975), 165-166.

4664 Nash, Walter. "Horace and In Memoriam." Neophilologus, 59 (1975), 466-475.

4665 _____. "Tennyson: 'The Epic' and 'The Old "Morte."'"
Cambridge Quarterly, 6 (1975), 326-349.

4666 Ousby, Ian. Durham University Journal, 68 (1975), 109-110.
Review of In Memoriam, ed. J. D. Jump, 1974 (entry 4510).

4667 Pachori, Satya S. "Tennyson's Early Poems and Their Hindu Imagery." Literature East and West, 19 (1975), 132-138.

4668 Pfordresher, J. Criticism, 17 (1975), 100-102.
Review of J. D. Rosenberg's The Fall of Camelot, 1973 (entry 4421).

4669 Reed, J. R. Modern Philology, 72 (1975), 437-439.
Review of A Variorum Edition, ed. J. Pfordresher, 1973 (entry 4419).

4670 Ryals, Clyde de L. South Atlantic Quarterly, 74 (1975), 277-278.
Review of J. D. Rosenberg's The Fall of Camelot, 1973 (entry 4421).

4671 Sait, James E. "Tennyson's The Princess and Queen Mary: Two Examinations of Sex and Politics." Durham University Journal, 37 (1975), 70-78.

4672 Stevenson, Catherine Barnes. "Tennyson's 'Mutability Canto': Time, Memory, and Art in The Princess." Victorian Poetry, 13 (1975), 21-33.
The Princess shows that Art alone can defy Time.

4673 Story, Kenneth E. "Theme and Image in The Princess." Tennessee Studies in Literature, 20 (1975), 50-59.
The Princess shows that growth in personality is gained only through relationships with others.

4674 Tennyson, Charles. "Tennyson's Philosophy." Tennyson Research Bulletin, 2 (1975), 150-154.

4675 Turner, Paul. Notes and Queries, 22 (1975), 461-463.
Review of D. J. Palmer's Tennyson, 1975 (entry 4417).

4676 Weissman, Judith. "Tess of the D'Urbervilles: A Demystification of the Eternal Triangle of Tennyson's Idylls of the King." Colby Library Quarterly, 11 (1975), 189-197.
Weissman discusses an allusion to the relationship among Guinevere, Arthur, and Lancelot in Tennyson's poem, and how that relationship informs the one among Tess, Alec, and Angel in Hardy's novel. She asserts that Hardy attacks Tennyson's view of sex.

4677 Whitbread, L. G. "Tennyson's 'In the Garden at Swainston.'" Victorian Poetry, 13 (1975), 61-69.

4678 White, G. M. American Book Collector, 25 (1975), 10-11.
Review of D. J. Palmer's Tennyson, 1973 (entry 4417).

1976

Books

4679 Altholz, Joseph L., ed. The Mind and Art of Victorian Eng-

land. Minneapolis: U. of Minnesota P., 1976.
Tennyson mentioned often, notably by Robert Langbaum, pages 20-27, and David J. DeLaura, pages 40-46.

4680 Ball, Patricia Mary. The Heart's Events: The Victorian Poetry of Relationships. London: Athlone, 1976. Atlantic Highlands, New Jersey: Humanities, 1976.

4681 Bloom, Harold. "Tennyson: In the Shadow of Keats." Poetry and Repression. New Haven: Yale U. P., 1976, pp. 143-174. Reprinted: E. A. Francis, ed., Tennyson, 1980 (entry 4964), pages 28-52.
Bloom declares: "My concern will be with Tennyson's revisionist genius for internalizing Keats, a process we might have thought impossible but for Tennyson's incredible rhetorical skill."

4682 Cluysenaar, Anne. Aspects of Literary Stylistics: A Discussion of Dominant Structures in Verse and Prose. London: Batsford, 1976. New York: St. Martin's, 1976.

4683 Eichler, Rolf. "Alfred Tennyson: Becket." Das englische Drama im 18. und 19. Jahrhundert: Interpretationen. Ed. Heinz Kosok. Berlin: Schmidt, 1976, pp. 254-266.

4684 Going, William T. "The Tennysons and the Rossettis: Sonneteering Families." Scanty Plot of Ground: Studies in the Victorian Sonnet. The Hague: Mouton, 1976, pp. 40-60. (Studies in English Literature, 106)

4685 Gunter, Garland O. "Symbols of Individuation in Tennyson's The Princess." A Festschrift for Professor Marguerite Roberts, on the Occasion of Her Retirement from Westhampton College, University of Richmond, Virginia. Ed. Frieda Elaine Penninger. Richmond: U. of Richmond, 1976, pp. 74-86.

4686 Hunt, John Dixon, and David Palmer. "Tennyson." English Poetry. Ed. Alan Sinfield. London: Sussex, 1976, pp. 130-147.

4687 Kabiljo-Šutić, Simha. "Tenison i njegov sonet 'Crna Gora.'" Uporedna istraživanja. Ed. Nikša Stipčević. Belgrade: Inst. za književnost i umetnost, 1979. Volume I, pages 501-545.

4688 Preyer, Robert O. "The Burden of Culture and the Dialectic of Literature." Evolution of Consciousness: Studies in Polarity: Essays in Honor of Owen Barfield. Ed. Shirley Sugerman. Middletown: Wesleyan U. P., 1976, pp. 98-105.

4689 Shaw, William David. Tennyson's Style. Ithaca: Cornell U. P., 1976.
In this thorough study, Shaw counters the comments of those who disparage Tennyson's style and provides an erudite elucidation of its character and complexity. This book would be a good place to begin

reading for anyone interested in Tennyson's stylistics and their background.

Reviewed by: F. Austin in English Studies (entry 4980); J. Bayley in Times Literary Supplement (entry 4844); Choice (entry 4776); B. M. Goff in Southern Humanities Review (entry 4860); G. Joseph in Victorian Studies (entry 4791); F. Kaplan in English Language Notes (entry 4872); J. R. Kincaid in Journal of English and Germanic Philology (entry 4875); C. J. Meyers in Dalhousie Review (entry 4806); J. R. Reed in Criticism (entry 4809); S. R. Rounds in Library Journal (entry 4731); C. de L. Ryals in South Atlantic Quarterly (entry 4883); A. Sinfield in Victorian Poetry (entry 4816); and P. Turner in Review of English Studies (entry 4896).

4690 Tennyson, Alfred. Poems. London: Scolar, 1976.
Reprints Moxon edition of 1857. Reviewed by: V. Neuburg in Times Literary Supplement (entry 4727).

4691 Turner, Paul. Tennyson. London: Routledge and Kegan Paul, 1976.
An introduction to Tennyson, his poetry, and its background. Informative.
Reviewed by: C. C. Barfoot in English Studies (entry 4771); D. A. Dillon in Library Journal (entry 4778); G. Grigson Country Life (entry 4712); C. J. Horne in Journal of the Australasian Universities Language and Literature Association (entry 4876); K. McSweeney in Modern Language Review (entry 4947); R. B. Martin in Review of English Studies (entry 4805); and S. Shatto in Notes and Queries (entry 4886).

Dissertations

4692 Cowan, James Alton. The Tristan Legend: A Barometer of Love and Art in the Victorian Period. Louisiana State U. and Agricultural and Mechanical College, 1976. Dissertation Abstracts International, 37 (1977), 7138A-7139A.

4693 Esch, Robert Morley. Creature of Glorious Promise: A Study of the Intellectual Milieu of Arthur Hallam, W. E. Gladstone, Alfred Tennyson, and Their Circle 1826-1833. Wisconsin-Madison, 1976. Dissertation Abstracts International, 37 (1977), 6494A.
Focuses on Hallam and his relationships.

4694 Fuller, Gerry William. The Aesthetic Significance of Tennyson's Revisions for the 1842 Poems. Catholic U. of America, 1976. Dissertation Abstracts International, 37 (1976), 1562A-1563A.
Fuller finds Tennyson's revisions to be part of the poet's aesthetic development.

4695 Hughes, Linda Kay. Tennyson's Dramatic Monologues: The Wisdom of Experience. Missouri-Columbia, 1976. Dissertation Abstracts International, 37 (1977), 5851A.

Examines the themes and other significant qualities of Tenny-son's dramatic monologues.

Periodicals

4696 Bailey, L.G. Victorian Studies, 19 (1976), 427-430.
Review of D.J. Palmer, ed., Tennyson, 1973 (entry 4417)
and F.E.L. Priestly's Language and Structure, 1973 (entry 4420).

4697 _____. Victorian Studies, 19 (1976), 549.
Review of W. Hellstrom's On the Poems of Tennyson, 1972
(entry 4337).

4698 Barfoot, C.C. English Studies, 57 (1976), 436.
Review of In Memoriam, ed. J.D. Jump, 1974 (entry 4510).

4699 Bischoff, Brigitte. "Tennyson, Mrs. Gaskell, and the Weaver
Poet." Victorian Poetry, 14 (1976), 356-358.

4700 Boyd, John D. "In Memoriam, Section CXXI." Victorian Poetry, 14 (1976), 161-164.

4701 _____. "The Principle of Analogy and the Immortality Question in Tennyson's In Memoriam." University of Toronto
Quarterly, 45 (1976), 123-138.
Boyd investigates the uses of analogy in In Memoriam, the
unifying aspects of analogy, and its consequences for the poem.

4702 Collins, Winston. "Enoch Arden, Tennyson's Heroic Fisher-
man." Victorian Poetry, 14 (1976), 47-53.

4703 Dietrich, Manfred. "Unity and Symbolic Structure in Tennyson's The Princess." English Studies in Canada, 2 (1976),
182-202.

4704 Durham, Margery Stricker. "Tennyson's Wellington Ode and
the Cosmology of Love." Victorian Poetry, 14 (1976), 277-
292.

4705 England, Eugene. "Tuckerman's Sonnet I: 10: The First
Post-Symbolist Poem." Southern Review, 12 (1976), 323-347.

4706 Fabreguet, Philippe. "Un Exemple d'Information Littéraire:
L'Image de Tennyson dans la Revue des Deux-Mondes dans la
Première Moitié du XIXe siècle." Confluents, 2, no. 1 (1976),
33-52.

4707 Fass, Barbara. "Christina Rossetti and St. Agnes' Eve."
Victorian Poetry, 14 (1976), 33-46.

4708 Francis, Elizabeth A. "Tennyson's Political Poetry, 1852-
1855." Victorian Poetry, 14 (1976), 113-123.
Francis provides an informative background for Tennyson's
early political views.

4709   Gallant, Christine. "Tennyson's Use of the Nature Goddess in 'The Hesperides,' 'Tithonus,' and 'Demeter and Persephone.'" Victorian Poetry, 14 (1976), 155-160.

4710   Goslee, David F. "Three Stages of Tennyson's 'Tiresias.'" Journal of English and Germanic Philology, 75 (1976), 154-167.
      Goslee discusses the two 1833 versions of "Tiresias" and the 1883 one. Each version, according to Goslee, represents a shift in Tennyson's psychological concerns. The first version was written before Hallam's death and represents a loss of innocence; the second was written after Hallam's death and represents Tennyson's alienation from the world; and the third, alienation with hope for redemption.

4711   Gray, J.M. "Tennyson's Guinevere and Francis Grose." Tennyson Research Bulletin, 2 (1976), 172.

4712   Grigson, Geoffrey. Country Life, 160 (1976), 923-924.
      Review of P. Turner's Tennyson, 1976 (entry 4691).

4713   Helsinger, Elizabeth K. "Ruskin and the Poets: Alterations in Autobiography." Modern Philology, 74 (1976), 142-170.
      Discusses Tennyson, Arnold, and Browning.

4714   Hoge, James O., Jr. "Tennyson in East Anglia: September 1876." Notes and Queries, 23 (1976), 399-401.

4715   _____. "Tennyson on Shakespeare: His Talk about the Plays." Texas Studies in Literature and Language, 18 (1976), 147-170.

4716   Joseph, Gerhard. English Language Notes, 13 (1976), 307-310.
      Review of J.R. Kincaid's Tennyson's Major Poems, 1975 (entry 4607).

4717   Jump, John D. "Comedy, Irony, and the Criticism of Tennyson." Critical Quarterly, 18, no. 2 (1976), 67-73.
      Discusses J.R. Kincaid's Tennyson's Major Poems, 1975 (entry 4607).

4718   Kolb, Jack. South Atlantic Bulletin, 41, no. 2 (1976), 150-153.
      Review of E. Tennyson's Letters, ed. J.O. Hoge, 1974 (entry 4518).

4719   Korg, Jacob. Victorian Poetry, 14 (1976), 172-174.
      Review of J.R. Kincaid's Tennyson's Major Poems, 1975 (entry 4607).

4720   Kozicki, Henry. Victorian Studies, 19 (1976), 547-550.
      Review of J.R. Kincaid's Tennyson's Major Poems, 1975 (entry 4607).

4721 Laird, Robert G. "Tennyson and 'The Bar of Michael Angelo':
      A Possible Source for In Memoriam LXXXVII. 40." Victorian
      Poetry, 14 (1976), 253-255.

4722 _____. "Tennyson and the 'Most Burlesque Barbarous Ex-
      periment.'" English Studies in Canada, 2 (1976), 439-451.

4723 Leonard, David Charles. "Chambers' 'Mental Constitution of
      Animals' from Vestiges of the Natural History of Creation and
      Tennyson's 'Poems 54-56' from In Memoriam." Unisa English
      Studies, 14, no. 1 (1976), 34-37.

4724 McSweeney, Kerry. Modern Language Review, 71 (1976), 145-
      146.
         Review of N. Campbell's Tennyson in Lincoln, volumes I and
      II, 1972 (entry 4334).

4725 Maxwell, J.C. Notes and Queries, 23 (1976), 98.
         Review of In Memoriam, ed. J.D. Jump, 1974 (entry 4510).

4726 Montabrut, Maurice. "Tennyson, le dit et le non-dit dans
      Enoch Arden (1864) ou le sens d'une nostalgie." Caliban, 13
      (1976), 69-79.

4727 Neuburg, V. Times Literary Supplement, Oct. 22, 1976, p.
      1337.
         Review of Poems, 1976 (entry 4690).

4728 N., J.M. (J.M. Newton). "Alive or Dead?" Cambridge
      Quarterly, 7 (1976), 81-82.

4729 Puckett, Harry. Victorian Poetry, 14 (1976), 340.
         A response to A. Sinfield's "That Which Is" in Victorian Poet-
      ry, 1976 (entry 4739).

4730 Radford, Colin, and Sally Minogue. "The Complexity of Crit-
      icism: Its Logic and Rhetoric." Journal of Aesthetics and
      Art Criticism, 34 (1976), 411-429.

4731 Rounds, S.R. Library Journal, 101 (1976), 2178.
         Review of W.D. Shaw's Tennyson's Style, 1976 (entry 4689).

4732 Ryals, Clyde de L. Clio, 6 (1976), 114-115.
         Review of J.R. Kincaid's Tennyson's Major Poems, 1975 (en-
      try 4607).

4733 Schuck, Thomas R. "Christopher Ricks's Tennyson and the
      Laureate's Publication History." Notes and Queries, 23 (1976),
      63.
         See: C. Ricks's Tennyson, 1972 (entry 4343).

4734 Sendry, Joseph. "Tennyson." Victorian Poetry, 14 (1976),
      237-245.
         Review of Tennysonian studies.

4735 Shatto, Susan. "Byron, Dickens, Tennyson, and the Monstrous Efts." Yearbook of English Studies, 6 (1976), 144-155. About the megalosaur.

4736 Shaw, W. David. "Consolation and Catharsis in In Memoriam." Modern Language Quarterly, 37 (1976), 47-67.

4737 _____. Modern Language Quarterly, 37 (1976), 202-205. Review of J.R. Kincaid's Tennyson's Major Poems, 1975 (entry 4607).

4738 Sinfield, Alan. "Tennyson's Imagery." Neophilologus, 60 (1976), 466-479.
Sinfield perceives similarities between Tennyson's imagery and that of the Symbolists. He investigates aspects of Tennyson's imagery that seem to be neither metaphor nor simile but are, instead, "fantasy" and "displacement." He illustrates his ideas with Maud, "Lucretius," and "The Last Tournament."

4739 _____. "'That Which Is': The Platonic Indicative in In Memoriam XCV." Victorian Poetry, 14 (1976), 247-252.
A response to H. Puckett's "Subjunctive Imagination in In Memoriam" in Victorian Poetry, 1974 (entry 4570). Responded to H. Puckett in Victorian Poetry, 1976 (entry 4729).
Sinfield believes that the phrase "that which is" (In Memoriam, XCV, line 39) refers to the Platonic concept of "Absolute Reality" and that from section XCV on the indicative dominates the subjunctive in In Memoriam; affirmation supplants doubt.

4740 Soule, George H., Jr. "Walt Whitman's 'Pictures': An Alternative to Tennyson's 'Palace of Art.'" Emerson Society Quarterly, 22 (1976), 39-47.

4741 Stratford, Jenny. "Tennyson's 'The Victim' and Charlotte Yonge's A Book of Golden Deeds of All Times and All Lands, 1864." Library, 31 (1976), 140-142.

4742 Sypher, F.J. "Politics in the Poetry of Tennyson." Victorian Poetry, 14 (1976), 101-112.
Places the political verse of Tennyson in the whole of his canon.

4743 Tobin, J.J.M. "'Ulysses': A Possible Source in Horace." Notes and Queries, 23 (1976), 395.

4744 Turner, P. Notes and Queries, 23 (1976), 426. Review of J.D. Rosenberg's The Fall of Camelot, 1973 (entry 4421).

4745 Welch, James Donald. "Tennyson's Landscapes of Time and a Reading of 'The Kraken.'" Victorian Poetry, 14 (1976), 197-204.
Landscape as imagery for two kinds of time, one active and the other quiescent.

4746 Wilson, Stephen Clifford. "Swinburne, Tennyson and The Sisters." Notes and Queries, 23 (1976), 406-408.

1977

Books

4747 Brantlinger, Patrick. "The Ambiguities of Progress." The Spirit of Reform: British Literature and Politics, 1832-1867. Cambridge, Massachusetts: Harvard U.P., 1977, pp. 181-203.
Tennyson, among many others.

4748 Brashear, William R. "The Boundless Deep: Tennyson." The Gorgon's Head: A Study in Tragedy and Despair. Athens, Georgia: U. of Georgia P., 1977, pp. 27-48.
About "Tennyson's vision of infinity."

4749 Carlyle, Thomas, and Jane Welsh Carlyle. The Collected Letters of Thomas and Jane Welsh Carlyle. Ed. Charles Richard Sanders and Kenneth J. Fielding. Durham, North Carolina: Duke U.P., 1977.

4750 Christ, Carol. "Victorian Masculinity and the Angel in the House." A Widening Sphere: Changing Roles of Victorian Women. Ed. Martha Vicinus. Bloomington: Indiana U.P., 1977, pp. 146-162.

4751 Culler, Arthur Dwight. The Poetry of Tennyson. New Haven: Yale U.P., 1977.
Emphasizing Tennyson's early poetry, Culler provides insightful and original readings of individual poems while tracing important themes through the poet's works. One of the best modern studies of Tennyson's poetry.
Reviewed by: F. Austin in English Studies (entry 4981); J. Bayley in Times Literary Supplement (entry 4844); J.D. Boyd in Victorian Poetry (entry 4849); D.R. Faulkner in Yale Review (entry 4858); D. Grumbach in New York Times Book Review (entry 4784); W. Hellstrom in South Atlantic Quarterly (entry 4864); E. Jordan in Essays in Criticism (entry 4939); G. Joseph in Review (entry 4940); J. Kissane in Victorian Studies (entry 4876); J. Kolb in Modern Philology (entry 5008); K. McSweeney in Yearbook of English Studies (entry 5013); C.J. Meyers in Dalhousie Review (entry 4880); P.G. Scott in Tennyson Research Bulletin (entry 4811); W.D. Shaw in Modern Language Quarterly (entry 4890); D.O. Tomlinson in Arnoldian (entry 4895); and W. Waring in Library Journal (entry 4823).

4752 Eichler, Rolf. Die Entdeckung des Dialog bei Byron, Shelley, Swinburne und Tennyson. Heidelberg: Winter, 1977.

4753 Holloway, John. The Proud Knowledge: Poetry, Insight and the Self, 1620-1920. London: Routledge and Kegan Paul, 1977.

The Holy Grail on pages 150-157; Maud on pages 195-207; and Tennyson also on pages 211-212 and 219.

4754 Landow, George P. "Moses Striking the Rock: Typological Symbolism in Victorian Poetry." Literary Uses of Typology: From the Late Middle Ages to the Present. Ed. Earl Miner. Princeton: Princeton U.P., 1977, pp. 315-344. Redemption in In Memoriam, section CXXXI.

4755 Lozynsky, Artem, and John R. Reed. Introduction. A Whitman Disciple Visits Tennyson: An Interview Describing Dr. Richard Maurice Bucke's Visit of 9 August 1891 at Aldworth, by Horace Logo Traubel. Lincoln: Tennyson Society, 1977. (Tennyson Society Monographs, 8)

4756 Meisel, Martin. "'Half Sick of Shadows': The Aesthetic Dialogue in Pre-Raphaelite Painting." Nature and the Victorian Imagination. Ed. U.C. Knoepflmacher and G.B. Tennyson. Berkeley: U. of California P., 1977, pp. 309-340.

4757 Sanders, Charles R. "Tennyson and the Human Hand." Carlyle's Friendships and Other Studies. Durham, North Carolina: Duke U.P., 1977.

4758 Smith, Eric. "Tennyson--In Memoriam." By Mourning Tongues: Studies in English Elegy. Ipswich: Boydell, 1977. Totowa, New Jersey: Rowman and Littlefield, 1977, pp. 100-134.

4759 Traubel, Horace Logo. A Whitman Disciple Visits Tennyson: An Interview Describing Dr. Richard Maurice Bucke's Visit of 9 August 1891 at Aldworth. Ed. Artem Lozynsky and John R. Reed. Lincoln, England: Tennyson Society, 1977. (Tennyson Society Monographs, 8)

Dissertations

4760 Boardman, Steven. Private Vision vs. Social Responsibility: A Study of the Poetic Imagination of Tennyson, Browning, and Arnold. Temple, 1977. Dissertation Abstracts International, 38 (1977), 2135A.
The independence of poetic imagination of the three poets.

4761 Bonner, Arnold Frank. Tennyson's Narrative Treatment of Married Love. North Carolina at Chapel Hill, 1977. Dissertation Abstracts International, 38 (1977), 3510A.
Narrative technique and Tennyson's views on married love.

4762 Fortune, Ronald John. Dialectical Characterization in Victorian Literature. Purdue, 1977. Dissertation Abstracts International, 39 (1978), 895A-896A.
Discusses Tennyson's In Memoriam and works by other writers.

4763 Franzese, Anthony Joseph. The Faithful Mind: Studies in Lit-

erary Structures. Oregon, 1977. Dissertation Abstracts International, 38 (1977), 3514A.
The plot and structural meaning of In Memoriam and other works.

4764 Kennedy, Ian Hodge Caldwell. Five Essays on Tennyson's Poetry. Virginia, 1977. Dissertation Abstracts International, 39 (1978), 898A-899A.
"Alfred Tennyson's Bildungsgang: Notes on His Early Reading," "In Memoriam and the Tradition of Pastoral Elegy," "'God's Just Wrath': Doubts and Fears in Tennyson's Maud," "The Crisis of Language in Tennyson's Maud," and "'Broken by the Worm': Love and Death in Tennyson's Poetry." For further annotations, see entries 4792, 4793, and 4874.

4765 Nord, Martha Humphreys Andrews. A People's Voice: The Rhetorical Art of Tennyson's Public Poetry. Vanderbilt, 1977. Dissertation Abstracts International, 38 (1977), 1414A-1415A.
Tennyson as idealizing and inspiring poet.

4766 Simpson, David Lon. Four Philosophical Poems: Ideas of Order in Donne, Pope, Tennyson, and Eliot. Columbia, 1977. Dissertation Abstracts International, 38 (1977), 2781A.
Discusses In Memoriam as well as Donne's Anniversaries, Pope's Essay on Man, and Eliot's Four Quartets. In Memoriam asserts a spiritual order in response to the discoveries of naturalistic science.

4767 Taylor, Beverly White. Wandering Fires: Studies in Medieval and Nineteenth-Century Arthurian Literary Tradition. Duke, 1977. Dissertation Abstracts International, 38 (1977), 4853A-4854A.
Tennyson, Arnold, Morris, Swinburne, and others were interested in maintaining medieval Arthurian tradition even while interpreting it. Tennyson is more faithful than the other poets to Malory and the medieval Arthurian tradition.

4768 Tobin, David Ned. The Presence of the Past: T.S. Eliot's Victorian Inheritance. Princeton, 1977. Dissertation Abstracts International, 38 (1977), 5469A.
Includes discussion of Eliot's response to the works of Tennyson. Presents some interesting ideas, particularly on In Memoriam and Four Quartets.

4769 Yearwood, John Charles, Jr. A Catalogue of the Tennyson Manuscripts at Trinity College, Cambridge. Texas at Austin, 1977. Dissertation Abstracts International, 41 (1980), 1621A.
A detailed description of the Tennyson manuscripts donated by Hallam Tennyson to Trinity College in 1924. The collection includes approximately one third of extant Tennyson manuscripts.

4770 Young, Robert Stephen. Tennyson and Swinburne and the Metaphor of Love: The Quest for Spiritual Values in Nineteenth

Century England. Arizona, 1977. <u>Dissertation Abstracts International</u>, 38 (1977), 2820A.

As a response to materialism, love is used by Tennyson and Swinburne to develop concepts of spiritual meaning and social unity.

Periodicals

4771 Barfoot, C. C. <u>English Studies</u>, 58 (1977), 535.
Review of P. Turner's <u>Tennyson</u>, 1976 (entry 4691).

4772 "Best Regards." <u>Listener</u>, 98 (1977), 173.
Anecdotes about Tennyson and Alfred Austin.

4773 Boyd, Zelda, and Julian Boyd. "To Lose the Name of Action: The Semantics of Action and Motion in Tennyson's Poetry." <u>PTL</u>, 2 (1977), 21-32.
The authors declare: "This paper has two purposes: to introduce a theoretical framework, and to say something about Tennyson's poetry. The theoretical apparatus we use is 'linguistic' insofar as it deals with certain semantic features of English verbs."

4774 Buckley, Jerome H. <u>Journal of English and Germanic Philology</u>, 75 (1977), 450-453.
Review of J. R. Kincaid's <u>Tennyson's Major Poems</u>, 1975 (entry 4607).

4775 Cervo, Nathan A. "The 'Aesthetic' Poetry of Keats and Tennyson." <u>Northern New England Review</u>, 2, no. 2 (1977), 46-56.

4776 <u>Choice</u>, 14 (1977), 378.
Review of W. D. Shaw's <u>Tennyson's Style</u>, 1976 (entry 4689).

4777 Davies, James A. "Dylan Thomas's 'One Warm Saturday' and Tennyson's <u>Maud</u>." <u>Studies in Short Fiction</u>, 14 (1977), 284-286.
Davies uses <u>Maud</u> to illuminate the meaning of Thomas's story.

4778 Dillon, D. A. <u>Library Journal</u>, 102 (1977), 388.
Review of P. Turner's <u>Tennyson</u>, 1976 (entry 4691).

4779 Edwards, P. D. "Tennyson and the Young Person." <u>Victorian Poetry</u>, 15 (1977), 78-82.

4780 Ewbank, David R. "Kidding the Victorian Poets: A Collection of Parodies." <u>Victorian Poetry</u>, 15 (1977), 66-74.
Includes a poem attributed to Tennyson.

4781 Gillett, Peter J. "Tennyson's Mind at the Work of Creation." <u>Victorian Poetry</u>, 15 (1977), 321-333.
An interesting discussion of the manner in which Tennyson put words together. Gillett argues that Tennyson was more interested in the sequences of words than in their sounds.

4782 Giordano, Frank R., Jr. "The 'Red-Ribbed Hollow,' Suicide, and Part III in Maud." Notes and Queries, 24 (1977), 402-404.

4783 Gray, J.M. "The Red Knight in Tennyson's 'The Last Tournament' and Malory." Notes and Queries, 24 (1977), 405-407.

4784 Grumbach, D. New York Times Book Review, Sept. 11, 1977, p. 20.
Review of A.D. Culler's The Poetry of Tennyson, 1977 (entry 4751).

4785 Hill, F. "The Cracroft Diary." Tennyson Research Bulletin, 3 (1977), 26-29.

4786 Hoge, James O., Jr. "Jowett on Tennyson's Maud: A New Letter." Notes and Queries, 24 (1977), 16-18.

4787 Hughes, Linda K. "Tennyson's 'Columbus': 'Sense at War with Soul' Again." Victorian Poetry, 15 (1977), 171-176.
Tennyson's response to Victorian materialism.

4788 _____. "Tennyson's Demeter: The Compassionate Poet." Publications of the Missouri Philological Association, 2 (1977), 33-38.

4789 Jeffares, A.N. Sewanee Review, 85 (1977), 301-317.
Review of C. Tennyson and H. Dyson's The Tennysons, 1975 (entry 4608).

4790 Joseph, Gerhard. "Tennyson's Optics: The Eagle's Gaze." PMLA, 92 (1977), 420-428.
A beautiful essay on the conflicting attractions and distressing qualities of near and far perspectives for Tennyson.

4791 _____. Victorian Studies, 21 (1977), 109-111.
Review of W.D. Shaw's Tennyson's Style, 1976 (entry 4689).

4792 Kennedy, Ian H.C. "The Crisis of Language in Tennyson's Maud." Texas Studies in Literature and Language, 19 (1977), 161-178.
The "fears about the nature and value of language" in In Memoriam "well up again and find in Maud their fullest and most moving expression." See Kennedy's dissertation: entry 4764.

4793 _____. "In Memoriam and the Tradition of Pastoral Elegy." Victorian Poetry, 15 (1977), 351-366.
Kennedy examines Tennyson's handling of the conventions of the pastoral elegy in In Memoriam and draws some interesting conclusions about Tennyson's manipulation of the conventions and the implications of that manipulation for the poem's meaning. See Kennedy's dissertation: entry 4764.

4794 Kilroy, James. "The Chiastic Structure of In Memoriam, A. H.H." Philological Quarterly, 56 (1977), 358-373.

Kilroy proposes the rhetorical structure of the chiasmus as a way of relating the sections of In Memoriam to one another.

4795   Kincaid, James R. "Tennyson's Ironic Camelot: Arthur Breathes His Last." Philological Quarterly, 56 (1977), 241-245.
Tennyson exalts Arthur to heighten the contrast between the character and the failed Arthurian civilization.

4796   Kolb, Jack. "Arthur Hallam and Emily Tennyson." Review of English Studies, 28 (1977), 32-48.

4797   Kotzin, Michael C. "Tennyson and Pre-Raphaelitism: Symbolism and Point of View in 'Mariana' and 'The Awakening Conscience.'" Pre-Raphaelite Review, 1 (1977), 91-101.
Kotzin finds similarities in point of view between such paintings as Holman Hunt's The Awakening Conscience and such Tennysonian poems as "Mariana."

4798   Kozicki, Henry. "A Dialectic of History in Tennyson's Idylls." Victorian Studies, 20 (1977), 141-157.
The Idylls of the King illustrates the rise and decline of civilization through archetypal historical processes. The forces that destroy Camelot then create its dialectical opposite.

4799   _____. "'Meaning' in Tennyson's In Memoriam." Studies in English Literature, 1500-1900, 17 (1977), 673-694.
According to Kozicki, the persona of In Memoriam moves toward happiness "not through perceptions of design or supernaturalism, but through his developing consciousness, his willed construction of 'meaning' in the disastrous past, and his faith in a God."

4800   Lee, A. R. Studies, 65 (1977), 86-89.
Review of C. Tennyson and H. Dyson's The Tennysons, 1975 (entry 4608).

4801   McSweeney, Kerry. Modern Language Review, 72 (1977), 926-928.
Review of J. R. Kincaid's Tennyson's Major Poems, 1975 (entry 4607).

4802   _____. "Tennyson's Quarrel with Himself: The Tristram Group of Idylls." Victorian Poetry, 15 (1977), 49-59.
McSweeney links the Tristram poems--"Balin and Balan," "Pelleas and Ettarre," and "The Last Tournament"--with psychological and sexual themes. His close reading of "The Last Tournament" provides an interesting view of Tristram.

4803   Malbone, Raymond G. "In Memoriam XV." Explicator, 35, no. 3 (1977), 6-8.

4804   Martin, R. B. Review of English Studies, 28 (1977), 362-363.
Review of E. Tennyson's Letters, ed. J. O. Hoge, 1974 (entry 4518).

4805 _____ . Review of English Studies, 28 (1977), 490-492.
Review of P. Turner's Tennyson, 1976 (entry 4691).

4806 Meyers, C.J. Dalhousie Review, 57 (1977), 375-376.
Review of W. D. Shaw's Tennyson's Style, 1976 (entry 4689).

4807 Nishimae, Yoshimi. "Tennyson and Australia: The Poet Laureate from an Australian Standpoint." Hiroshima Studies in
English Language and Literature, 22, nos. 2 and 3 (1977),
66-83.
Japanese, with abstract in English on pages 84-85.

4808 Poston, Lawrence. Ohio Review, 18 (Spring/Summer 1977),
103-105.
Review of J. R. Kincaid's Tennyson's Major Poems, 1975 (entry 4607).

4809 Reed, John R. Criticism, 19 (1977), 282.
Review of W. D. Shaw's Tennyson's Style, 1976 (entry 4689).

4810 Scott, P. "The Cloughs Visit the Tennysons, 1861." Tennyson Research Bulletin, 3 (1977), 10-13.

4811 Scott, P.G. Tennyson Research Bulletin, 3 (1977), 31-32.
Review of A. D. Culler's The Poetry of Tennyson, 1977 (entry
4751).

4812 Sendry, Joseph. "Tennyson." Victorian Poetry, 15 (1977),
279-288.
A survey of recent studies of Tennyson.

4813 Shannon, Edgar F., Jr. "Alfred Tennyson as a Poet for Our
Time." Virginia Quarterly Review, 53 (1977), 692-707.
Tennyson's poetry is accessible to and has meaning for the
modern general reader.

4814 Shaw, Marion. "In Memoriam and Popular Religious Poetry."
Victorian Poetry, 15 (1977), 1-8.
Shaw points out similarities between hymns of the eighteenth
and nineteenth centuries and In Memoriam.

4815 Sinfield, Alan. Modern Philology, 74 (1977), 431-433.
Review of J. D. Rosenberg's The Fall of Camelot, 1973 (entry
4421).

4816 _____ . Victorian Poetry, 15 (1977), 289.
Review of W. D. Shaw's Tennyson's Style, 1976 (entry 4689).

4817 Staines, David. "Tennyson's Mysticism: A Personal Testimo-
ny." Notes and Queries, 24 (1977), 404-405.
Staines presents a draft of a letter by Tennyson to Benjamin
Paul Blood in which Tennyson discusses his own mysticism.

4818 Stevenson, Catherine Barnes. "Tennyson on Women's Rights." Tennyson Research Bulletin, 3 (1977), 23-25.

4819 Thesing, W.B. "Tennyson and the City: Historical Tremours and Hysterical Tremblings." Tennyson Research Bulletin, 3 (1977), 14-22.

4820 Vogel, C.S. "Heart of Stone: An Emblem for Conversion." Victorian Newsletter, no. 51 (Spring 1977), 21-25.

4821 Waller, John O. "Francis Turner Palgrave's Criticisms of Tennyson's In Memoriam." Victorian Newsletter, no. 52 (Fall 1977), 13-17.

4822 Ward, Hayden. "Tennyson's Light Brigade and Kipling's." Kipling Journal, 44 (March 1977), 15-17.
Compares Kipling's "The Last of the Light Brigade" with Tennyson's "The Charge of the Light Brigade."

4823 Waring, Walter. Library Journal, 102 (1977), 2262.
Review of A.D. Culler's The Poetry of Tennyson, 1977 (entry 4751).

4824 Waterston, Elizabeth. "Tennyson and the Church Bells." Dalhousie Review, 57 (1977), 18-27.
Waterston discusses the sounds of bells in Tennyson's poetry. She perceives "a chain of change in Tennyson's life and thought and in his times" in the "sequence of references" to bells. An interesting study.

1978

Books

4825 Allen, Peter. The Cambridge Apostles: The Early Years. Cambridge: Cambridge U.P., 1978.
Discusses Tennyson at Cambridge.

4826 Eagleton, Terry. "Tennyson: Politics and Sexuality in The Princess and In Memoriam." 1848: The Sociology of Literature. Ed. Francis Barker, John Coombes, Peter Hulme, Colin Mercer, and David Musselwhite. Colchester, England: University of Essex, 1978, pp. 97-106.

4827 Elliott, Philip L. The Making of the Memoir. Greenville, South Carolina: Furman University, 1978.
Short discussion of Hallam Tennyson's Alfred Lord Tennyson.

4828 Gaskell, Philip. From Writer to Reader: Studies in Editorial Method. London: Oxford U.P., 1978.
Discusses "Oenone" on pages 118-141.

4829   Goldfarb, Clara R., and Russell M. Goldfarb. Spiritualism
       and Nineteenth-Century Letters. Cranbury, New Jersey:
       Fairleigh Dickinson U.P., 1978.

4830   Henderson, Philip. Tennyson: Poet and Prophet. London:
       Routledge and Kegan Paul, 1978.
       An introduction to the life and works of Tennyson. Reviewed
by: J. Bayley in Times Literary Supplement (entry 4844); Blackwood's (entry 4846); Booklist (entry 4847); Choice (entry 4918); Economist (entry 4921); G. Grigson in Country Life (entry 4862); J.S.
Hagen in Victorian Studies (entry 5005); P. Honan in Notes and Queries (entry 4933); J. Irons in Studies (entry 4938); R. Jackson in
Encounter (entry 4868); E. Jordan in Essays in Criticism (entry
4939); S. Shatto in Modern Language Review (entry 5028); P. Turner
in British Book News (entry 4896); and K. Wilson in Arnoldian (entry
4898).

4831   Hough, Graham. "The Natural Theology of In Memoriam."
       Selected Essays. London: Cambridge U.P., 1978, pp. 110-
       125.
       Reprinted from Review of English Studies, 1947 (entry 3395).

4832   Lerner, Laurence. "An Essay on The Princess." The Vic-
       torians. Ed. Laurence Lerner. New York: Holmes and
       Meier, 1978, pp. 209-222.

4833   Tillotson, Geoffrey A. A View of Victorian Literature. Lon-
       don: Oxford U.P. (Clarendon), 1978.
       Tennyson on pages 286-327. A general assessment of the po-
etry.

4834   Trevelyan, Raleigh. A Pre-Raphaelite Circle. London: Chat-
       to and Windus, 1978. Totowa, New Jersey: Rowman and Lit-
       tlefield, 1978.
       About Pauline Trevelyan.

Dissertations

4835   Caughran, Barbara Ferguson. Christian Allegory in Tennyson's
       "Idylls of the King." Alabama, 1978. Dissertation Abstracts
       International, 39 (1978), 5521A.
       Christian allegory and the structure of Idylls of the King.
King Arthur as Christ and other characters as Christian symbols.

4836   Jablow, Betsy Lynn. Illustrated Texts from Dickens to James.
       Stanford, 1978. Dissertation Abstracts International, 38 (1978),
       7345A.
       Tennyson's poems illustrated by Pre-Raphaelites.

4837   Mazzeno, Laurence W., III. The Influence of Thomas Car-
       lyle's Writings on Alfred Tennyson's Concept of the Hero in
       Idylls of the King. Tulane, 1978. Dissertation Abstracts In-
       ternational, 39 (1978), 1595A.
       King Arthur as Carlylean hero.

4838 Oates, David Dean. The Shape of Hope in Victorian Fiction.
      Emory, 1978. Dissertation Abstracts International, 39 (1978),
      4281A-4282A.
      Includes loss and hope in the 1859 Idylls of the King.

4839 Osborne, Richard L. Personative and Mythopoeic Dimensions
      in Tennyson's Poetry. New York, 1978. Dissertation Ab-
      stracts International, 39 (1978), 3602A.
      Mythopoesis and personae in Tennyson's poems.

4840 Peltason, Timothy Walter Hopkins. The Emergence of the Self
      in Tennyson's Poetry: 1830-1850. Yale, 1978. Dissertation
      Abstracts International, 40 (1979), 874A.
      Peltason discusses poems that present an emerging poet or an
enclosed one, with notable attention to "The Kraken," "Mariana,"
"The Lady of Shalott," and "Recollections of the Arabian Nights."
He also discusses such works as In Memoriam as accounts of the
self.

4841 Storey, Michael Louis. The Tennysonian Monologue: A Study
      in Classification. Catholic U. of America, 1978. Disserta-
      tion Abstracts International, 39 (1978), 1603A.
      Storey tries to establish a clear structural definition for what
constitutes a Tennysonian dramatic monologue. A challenging and
interesting study.

4842 Tarhuni, Tohami T. The Imro-Elkhaisianism of Tennyson's
      Locksley Hall. Northern Colorado, 1978. Dissertation Ab-
      stracts International, 39 (1979), 6784A.
      The influence of Imro-Elkhais' Moallaka on "Locksley Hall."

Periodicals

4843 Altieri, Charles. "Arnold and Tennyson: The Plight of Vic-
      torian Lyricism as Context of Modernism." Criticism, 20
      (1978), 281-306.
      Altieri examines a conflict between self-expression and objec-
tivity in Victorian lyricism that Tennyson and Arnold partly solve in
a Modern way.

4844 Bayley, John. "The Dynamics of the Static." Times Literary
      Supplement, March 3, 1978, p. 246.
      Review of W. D. Shaw's Tennyson's Style, 1976 (entry 4689);
A. D. Culler's The Poetry of Tennyson, 1977 (entry 4751); and P.
Henderson's Tennyson, 1978 (entry 4830).

4845 Belcher, Margaret E. "'Sane But Shattered': The Ending of
      Tennyson's Maud." AUMLA (Journal of the Australasian Uni-
      versity Language and Literature Association), no. 50 (1978),
      224-234.

4846 Blackwood's, 323 (1978), 552.
      Review of P. Henderson's Tennyson, 1978 (entry 4830).

4847   Booklist, 75 (1978), 19.
       Review of P. Henderson's Tennyson, 1978 (entry 4830).

4848   Boos, Florence S. "Medievalism in Alfred Tennyson and Wil-
       liam Morris." Victorians Institute Journal, 7 (1978), 19-24.

4849   Boyd, John D. Victorian Poetry, 16 (1978), 285-289.
       Review of A. D. Culler's The Poetry of Tennyson, 1977 (entry
4751).

4850   Bruns, Gerald L. "'The Lesser Faith': Hope and Reversal
       in Tennyson's In Memoriam." Journal of English and German-
       ic Philology, 77 (1978), 247-264.
       How the concepts of modern thinkers, notably Merleau-Ponty,
can illuminate difficult passages of In Memoriam.

4851   Cervo, Nathan. "Tennyson, Hallam, Mill and Arnold: Some
       Nineteenth-Century Background to the Pre-Raphaelite Ques-
       tion." Victorians Institute Journal, 7 (1978), 57-67.

4852   Colley, Ann C. "Alfred Tennyson's 'Four Crises': Another
       View of the Water Cure." Tennyson Research Bulletin, 3
       (1978), 64-68.

4853   _____. "The Conflict between Tradition and Modern Values
       in Tennyson's The Princess." Bucknell Review, 24, no. 1
       (1978), 37-48.

4854   Comley, Nancy R. "Marvell, Tennyson, and 'The Islet': An
       Inversion of Pastoral." Victorian Poetry, 16 (1978), 270-274.
       "The Islet," according to Comley, is a parody of Marvell's
"A Dialogue Between Thysis and Dorinda."

4855   Crabbe, Katharyn. "The Function of Fantasy in Tennyson's
       The Holy Grail." Cithara, 17, no. 2 (1978), 52-62.

4856   _____. "Tennyson, Faith, and the Fantastic." Tennyson
       Research Bulletin, 3 (1978), 55-63.

4857   Crawford, John W. "A Unifying Element in Tennyson's Maud."
       Costerus, 14 (1978), 89-92.

4858   Faulkner, D. R. Yale Review, 67 (1978), 440-447.
       Review of A. D. Culler's The Poetry of Tennyson (entry 4751).

4859   Fleissner, Robert F. "Frost and Tennyson: New Points."
       American Notes and Queries, 16 (1978), 72-73.

4860   Goff, B. M. Southern Humanities Review, 12 (1978), 378-379.
       Review of W. D. Shaw's Tennyson's Style, 1976 (entry 4689).

4861   Gray, J. M. "Tennyson's Idylls of the King." Explicator, 36,
       no. 1 (1978), 43-44.

4862   Grigson, Geoffrey. Country Life, 163 (1978), 1107.
       Review of P. Henderson's Tennyson, 1978 (entry 4830).

4863   Hagen, J.S. Arnoldian, 6, no. 1 (1978), 21-23.
       Review of E. L. Tennyson's The Letters of Emily Lady Ten-
nyson, ed. J.O. Hoge, 1974 (entry 4518).

4864   Hellstrom, W. South Atlantic Quarterly, 77 (1978), 531-532.
       Review of A. D. Culler's The Poetry of Tennyson, 1977 (entry
4751).

4865   Hill, F. "The Disinheritance Tradition Reconsidered." Ten-
       nyson Research Bulletin, 3 (1978), 41-54.

4866   Hoge, James O., Jr. "Talks and Walks: Tennyson's Remarks
       and Observations, 1870-92." Journal of English and Germanic
       Philology, 77 (1978), 53-71.
       Presents Audrey Boyle Tennyson's records of Tennyson's re-
marks and observations.

4867   Horne, Colin J. AUMLA (Journal of the Australasian Univer-
       sity Language and Literature Association), no. 49 (1978), 103-
       104.
       Review of P. Turner's Tennyson, 1976 (entry 4691).

4868   Jackson, R. Encounter, 51, no. 1 (1978), 73.
       Review of P. Henderson's Tennyson, 1978 (entry 4830).

4869   Johnston, Priscilla. "Tennyson's Demeter and Persephone
       Theme: Memory and the 'Good Solid' Past." Texas Studies
       in Literature and Language, 20 (1978), 68-92.
       Johnston uncovers important themes in Tennyson's poetry by
examining the poet's use of the Demeter and Persephone myth.

4870   Jones, John Bush. "Tennyson, Forster, and the Punch Con-
       nection." Victorian Periodicals Newsletter, 11 (Dec. 1978),
       118-120.
       See also: J. A. Davies in Victorian Periodicals Review, 1980
(entries 4992 and 4993); and J. B. Jones (entry 5006).

4871   Joseph, Gerhard. "Victorian Frames: The Windows and Mir-
       rors of Browning, Arnold, and Tennyson." Victorian Poetry,
       16 (1978), 70-87.
       Window as view of the world; mirror as introspection.

4872   Kaplan, Fred. English Language Notes, 15 (1978), 313-316.
       Review of W. D. Shaw's Tennyson's Style, 1976 (entry 4689).

4873   Kashiwagi, Hideo. "Natsume Soseki's Launcelot and Guinevere:
       A Comparative Study of 'Kairoko.'" Essays in Foreign Lan-
       guages and Literature, 24 (1978), 33-81 (back section; in Jap-
       anese). Summary, pages 386-388 (front section; in English).

4874   Kennedy, Ian H.C.   "Alfred Tennyson's Bildungsgang: Notes
       on His Early Reading."   Philological Quarterly, 57 (1978),
       82-103.
       The influence of Goethe and Bulwer-Lytton on Tennyson's
poetry.   See Kennedy's dissertation: entry 4764.

4875   Kincaid, James R.   Journal of English and Germanic Philology,
       77 (1978), 456-458.
       Review of W.D. Shaw's Tennyson's Style, 1976 (entry 4869).

4876   Kissane, James.   Victorian Studies, 22 (1978), 96-98.
       Review of A.D. Culler's The Poetry of Tennyson, 1977 (entry
4751).

4877   McSweeney, Kerry.   "Swinburne's Tennyson."   Victorian Stud-
       ies, 22 (1978), 5-28.
       McSweeney perceives the heart of the conflict between Swin-
burne's sensibilities and those of Tennyson in Tennyson's belief in
immortality and Swinburne's lack of such belief.   Interesting account
of the poets' relationship.

4878   Mantell, Deborah Byrd.   "The Princess: Tennyson's Eminent-
       ly Shakespearian Poem."   Texas Studies in Literature and
       Language, 20 (1978), 48-67.
       Mantell discusses how Victorian ideas about Shakespeare could
have influenced Tennyson.

4879   Mason, H.A.   "The First Setting of Tennyson's 'Morte
       D'Arthur.'"   Essays and Studies, 31 (1978), 98-114.
       Mason finds the poem to be concerned with Tennyson's unhap-
piness over Arthur Hallam's death and that many of the poem's trap-
pings are superficial.

4880   Meyers, C.J.   Dalhousie Review, 58 (1978), 584-587.
       Review of A.D. Culler's The Poetry of Tennyson, 1977 (entry
4751).

4881   Petch, Simon S.   "Tennyson: Mood and Myth."   Sydney Stud-
       ies in English, 4 (1978-1979), 18-30.

4882   Redfern, Roger A.   "Walking in Tennyson's Shadow: Along
       the Bluestone Heath, Lincolnshire."   Country Life, 163 (1978),
       1634-1636.

4883   Ryals, Clyde de L.   South Atlantic Quarterly, 77 (1978), 130-
       131.
       Review of W.D. Shaw's Tennyson's Style, 1976 (entry 4689).

4884   Savory, J.J.   "Tennyson's In Memoriam and The Book of Job."
       Notes and Queries, 25 (1978), 237-238.

4885   Sendry, Joseph.   "Tennyson."   Victorian Poetry, 16 (1978),
       261-269.
       A survey of the previous year's published work on Tennyson.

4886   Shatto, Susan. Notes and Queries, 25 (1978), 263-264.
        Review of P. Turner's Tennyson, 1976 (entry 4691).

4887   _____. "'The First Written Sections of In Memoriam.'"
        Notes and Queries, 25 (1978), 233-237.

4888   _____. "Tennyson's Library." Book Collector, 27 (1978),
        494-513.
        An interesting summary of the books Tennyson owned and of
his reading habits. The standard short introduction to a complicated
subject.

4889   _____. "Tennyson's Revisions of In Memoriam." Victorian
        Poetry, 16 (1978), 341-356.
        Shatto presents a sophisticated study of Tennyson's artful re-
visions of In Memoriam.

4890   Shaw, W. David. Modern Language Quarterly, 39 (1978), 82-
        85.
        Review of A. D. Culler's The Poetry of Tennyson, 1977 (entry
4751).

4891   Siemens, Lloyd. "A Full Look at the Worst: Hardy and the
        Poetry of Optimism." Wascana Review, 13, no. 1 (1978),
        3-17.
        Hardy's poetry compared to that of Tennyson and Browning.

4892   Sloan, Gary. "Yeats, Tennyson, and 'Innisfree.'" Victorian
        Newsletter, no. 54 (Fall 1978), 29-31.

4893   Starzyk, Lawrence J. "The Will to Die: Tennyson's Poetics
        of Self-Transformation." Humanities Association Review/La
        Revue de l'Association des Humanités, 29 (1978), 21-36.

4894   Timko, Michael. "'The Central Wish': Human Passion and
        Comic Love in Tennyson's Idyls." Victorian Poetry, 16 (1978),
        1-15.
        A study of Tennyson's domestic idyls.

4895   Tomlinson, D. O. Arnoldian, 6, no. 1 (1978), 15-17.
        Review of A. D. Culler's The Poetry of Tennyson, 1977 (entry
4751).

4896   Turner, Paul. British Book News, May 1978, pp. 411-412.
        Review of P. Henderson's Tennyson, 1978 (entry 4830).

4897   _____. Review of English Studies, 29 (1978), 503-504.
        Review of W. D. Shaw's Tennyson's Style, 1976 (entry 4689).

4898   Wilson, K. Arnoldian, 6, no. 1 (1978), 17-20.
        Review of P. Henderson's Tennyson, 1978 (entry 4830).

4899   Wiseman, Christopher. "'Tithonus' and Tennyson's Elegaic
        Vision." English Studies in Canada, 4 (1978), 212-223.

1979

Books

4900 Dawson, Carl. "In Memoriam: The Uses of Dante and Words-
      worth." Victorian Noon: English Literature in 1850. Balti-
      more: Johns Hopkins U. P., 1979, pp. 36-51.
      Discusses In Memoriam in relation to its era of publication.

4901 Hagen, June Steffensen. Tennyson and His Publishers. Lon-
      don: Macmillan, 1979. University Park: Pennsylvania State
      U. P., 1979.
      An account of Tennyson's business life and the role it played
in his art.
      Reviewed by: P. Collins in Times Literary Supplement (entry
4990); G. Grigson in Country Life (entry 5003); G. Joseph in Victorian Studies (entry 5081); B. Maidment in Tennyson Research Bulletin
(entry 4948); A. Pollard in British Book News (entry 5021); P. G.
Scott in Library (entry 5100); and D. Tomlinson in Arnoldian (entry
5112).

4902 [No entry]

4903 Kozicki, Henry. Tennyson and Clio: History in the Major
      Poems. Baltimore: Johns Hopkins U. P., 1979.
      Kozicki presents a challenging, complex, and controversial
study of the development of Tennyson's philosophy of history.
      Reviewed by: P. Brantlinger in Criticism (entry 4985); G. L.
Bruns in English Language Notes (entry 5060); A. D. Culler in Arnoldian (entry 5062); M. L. Greenberg in Journal of English and Germanic Philology (entry 5125); G. Joseph in Victorian Studies (entry
5081); and E. D. Mackerness in Notes and Queries (entry 5128).

4904 Nishimae, Yoshimi. Tennyson kenkyu: Sono shoki shishu no
      sekai. Tokyo: Chukyo, 1979.
      Discusses the early poetry.

4905 Organ, Dennis M. Tennyson's Dramas: A Critical Study.
      Lubbock: Texas Tech U. P., 1979.
      Publication of a dissertation: 1974 (entry 4525). A careful
and lucid evaluation of the plays. Reviewed by: T. Otten in Victorian Studies (entry 5020).

4906 Pattison, Robert. Tennyson and Tradition. Cambridge, Mas-
      sachusetts: Harvard U. P., 1979.
      Reviewed by: P. Brantlinger in Criticism (entry 4985); A. D.
Culler in Arnoldian (entry 5062); W. Hellstrom in Journal of English
and Germanic Philology (entry 5074); G. Joseph in Victorian Studies
(entry 5081); H. Kozicki in Modern Philology (entry 5085); L. Lerner
in Encounter (entry 5087); J. M. Gray in Tennyson Research Bulletin
(entry 5072); B. Pavlock in Victorian Poetry (entry 5021a); and J. R.
Reed in Clio (entry 5095).

4907 Sharma, Virendra. Studies in Victorian Verse Drama: An
Appraisal of the Poetic Plays of Browning, Tennyson and Oth-
er Victorians. Salzburg: Institut für Englische Sprache und
Literatur, 1979.
Reviewed by: T. Otten in Victorian Studies (entry 5020).

4908 Waterston, Elizabeth. "Crawford, Tennyson and the Domestic
Idyll." The Crawford Symposium. Ed. Frank M. Tierney.
Ottawa: U. of Ottawa P., 1979, pp. 61-77.

Dissertations

4909 Churchill, Robert Joseph. Mysticism and Religious Experience
in Carlyle, Tennyson, and Browning. Nebraska-Lincoln,
1979. Dissertation Abstracts International, 40 (1980), 4604A.
Discusses Tennyson's mystical visions and their role in the
poetry. Special attention paid to mysticism in In Memoriam.

4910 Friesen, Edward Henry. Tennyson's Use of the Arthurian
Myth: A Study of the Characters in Tennyson's Idylls of the
King. Indiana U. of Pennsylvania, 1979. Dissertation Ab-
stracts International, 40 (1980), 4052A.
Idylls of the King as portrait of sense in conflict with soul.
Includes evaluation of characterizations and of the work as part of
the Arthurian tradition.

4911 Jacobs, Joanne Ciske. The Tristram Myth in Arnold, Tennyson and Swinburne: Sources and Moral Vision. Notre Dame,
1979. Dissertation Abstracts International, 40 (1980), 4013A.
Contrasts Tennyson's rendering of the story with Malory's as
well as Arnold's and Swinburne's. Finds lust at the heart of the relationship between Tristram and Isolt in Tennyson's version.

4912 Kenig, Lea. Tennyson's Maud: The Betrayal of Reason. Columbia, 1979. Dissertation Abstracts International, 40 (1979),
271A.
In this original and sometimes surprising study, Kenig portrays
Maud as a cynical work in which optimism is negated by insanity and
incoherent form.

4913 Poland, Peter Davies. "The Christ That Is to Be": A Study
of Tennyson's Religious Thought. State U. of New York at
Stony Brook, 1979. Dissertation Abstracts International, 40
(1979), 2078A.
Tennyson and the Broad Church movement.

Periodicals

4914 Adams, Michael C.C. "Tennyson's Crimean War Poetry: A
Cross-Cultural Approach." Journal of the History of Ideas,
40 (1979), 405-422.

4915 Aspinwall, Bernard. "Alfred, Lord Tennyson's 'Old College

Friend.'" <u>Notes and Queries</u>, 26 (1979), 298-299.
About Tennyson's friend Robert Monteith.

4916 Baker, F. T. "Sir Francis Hill, C. B. E., Litt. D., F. S. A.,
D. L." <u>Tennyson Research Bulletin</u>, 3, no. 3 (Nov. 1979),
135-136.

4917 Baker, William. "Tiresias and Other Poems: Watts Dunton's
Marked Copy of <u>Tiresias</u> and His Review of It." <u>Tennyson
Research Bulletin</u>, 3, no. 3 (Nov. 1979), 122-125.

4918 <u>Choice</u>, 15 (1979), 1517.
Review of P. Henderson's <u>Tennyson</u>, 1978 (entry 4830).

4919 Dahl, Curtis. "'To Fight Aloud' and 'The Charge of the Light
Brigade': Dickinson on Tennyson." <u>New England Quarterly</u>,
52 (1979), 94-99.

4920 Draper, Anita B. "The Artistic Contribution of the 'Weird
Seizures' to <u>The Princess</u>." <u>Victorian Poetry</u>, 17 (1979),
180-191.

4921 <u>Economist</u>, 266 (1979), 106.
Review of P. Henderson's <u>Tennyson</u>, 1978 (entry 4830).

4922 Ehrenpreis, Anne Henry. "Edward Lear Sings Tennyson's
Songs." <u>Harvard Library Bulletin</u>, 27 (1979), 65-85.

4923 Elliott, Philip. "Tennyson and Spiritualism." <u>Tennyson Research Bulletin</u>, 3, no. 3 (Nov. 1979), 89-100.
Elliott discusses the spiritualist movement in Tennyson's life
and work. He concludes that although spiritualism very much interested Tennyson, it did not play a notable role in the poetry.

4924 Findlay, Leonard. "Tennyson, Landor and Ulysses." <u>Victorian
Studies Association of Western Canada Newsletter</u>, 5, no. 1
(1979), 11-16.

4925 Fletcher, Pauline. "Romantic and Anti-Romantic Gardens in
Tennyson and Swinburne." <u>Studies in Romanticism</u>, 18 (1979),
81-97.
Traces the garden as symbol in Tennyson's poetry.

4926 Flynn, Philip. "Hallam and Tennyson: The 'Theodicaea Novissima' and In Memoriam." <u>Studies in English Literature,
1500-1900</u>, 19 (1979), 705-720.
Hallam and Tennyson's thoughts about evil.

4927 Gates, Barbara. "Victorian Attitudes Toward Suicide and Mr.
Tennyson's 'Despair.'" <u>Tennyson Research Bulletin</u>, 3, no. 3
(Nov. 1979), 101-110.
Gates discusses the cultural milieu for the discussion of sui-
cide in "Despair."

4928 Gilmour, Robin. "Dickens, Tennyson, and the Past." Dicken-
sian, 75 (1979), 131-142.

4929 Gray, J.M. "Further Milton Echoes in Idylls of the King."
Tennyson Research Bulletin, 3, no. 3 (Nov. 1979), 134-135.

4930 Hagen, June Steffensen. "Tennyson's Troubled Years with
Moxon & Co.: A Publishing Relationship." Browning Institute
Studies in Victorian Literary and Cultural History, 7 (1979),
21-30.

4931 _____. "Tennyson's Use of the Impersonative Mode in a
Minor Art Cluster." Susquehanna University Studies, 11
(1979), 15-23.

4932 Homans, Margaret. "Tennyson and the Spaces of Life." ELH,
46 (1979), 693-709.
The struggle for self-identity in Idylls of the King.

4933 Honan, P. Notes and Queries, 26 (1979), 266-267.
Review of P. Henderson's Tennyson, 1978 (entry 4830).

4934 Hughes, Linda K. "Dramatis and Private Personae: 'Ulysses'
Revisited." Victorian Poetry, 17 (1979), 192-203.

4935 _____. "From 'Tithon' to 'Tithonus': Tennyson as Mourner
and Monologist." Philological Quarterly, 58 (1979), 82-89.

4936 _____. "The Reader as Mariner: Tennyson's 'Lotos-
Eaters.'" English Language Notes, 16 (1979), 300-308.

4937 _____. "Tennyson's 'Mermaid' Poems: An Additional
Source." Tennyson Research Bulletin, 3, no. 3 (Nov. 1979),
127-133.
Hughes suggests that Walter Scott's The Pirate is a source
for "The Mermaid" and "The Merman."

4938 Irons, J. Studies: An Irish Quarterly Review, 68 (1979), 135-
137.
Review of P. Henderson's Tennyson, 1978 (entry 4830).

4939 Jordan, E. Essays in Criticism, 29 (1979), 175-191.
Review of A.D. Culler's The Poetry of Tennyson, 1977 (entry
4751) and P. Henderson's Tennyson, 1978 (entry 4830).

4940 Joseph, Gerhard. "Imperial Criticism." Review, 1 (1979),
75-80.
Review of A.D. Culler's The Poetry of Tennyson, 1977 (entry
4751).

4941 Kearny, Anthony. "A Borrowing from In Memoriam in David
Copperfield." Notes and Queries, 26 (1979), 306-307.

4942 Kendall, J. L. "Gem Imagery in Tennyson's Maud." Victorian Poetry, 17 (1979), 389-394.

4943 Leonard, David Charles. "Tennyson, Chambers, and Recapitulation." Victorian Newsletter, no. 56 (Fall 1979), 7-10.

4944 Lourie, Margaret A. "Below the Thunders of the Upper Deep: Tennyson as Romantic Revisionist." Studies in Romanticism, 18 (1979), 3-27.
Tennyson's similarities to and differences from his Romantic predecessors and successors.

4945 McCarron, William E. "Tennyson, Donne, and All the King's Men." American Notes and Queries, 17 (1979), 140-141.

4946 McLaine, Allan H. "Some Echoes of Burns in Tennyson." Studies in Scottish Literature, 14 (1979), 249-252.

4947 McSweeney, K. Modern Language Review, 74 (1979), 673-674. Review of P. Turner's Tennyson, 1976 (entry 4691).

4948 Maidment, B. E. Tennyson Research Bulletin, 3, no. 3 (Nov. 1979), 119.
Review of J. S. Hagen's Tennyson and His Publishers, 1979 (entry 4901).

4949 Marks, Patricia. "Henry Hallam in Fraser's." Tennyson Research Bulletin, 3, no. 3 (Nov. 1979), 125-126.

4950 Mazzeno, Laurence W. "Tennyson and Henry James." Tennyson Research Bulletin, 3, no. 3 (Nov. 1979), 111-116.
Argues that James viewed Tennyson's work somewhat more favorably than scholars have heretofore indicated.

4951 Nishimae, Yoshimi. "A Study of Tennyson's Maud's Imagery: With Special Reference to Images of Animals, Jewels, Stones, and Flowers." Hiroshima Studies in English Language and Literature, 24 (1979), 17-28 (in Japanese) and 29-30 (abstract in English).

4952 Pavlock, Barbara R. "'Frater Ave atque Vale': Tennyson and Catullus." Victorian Poetry, 17 (1979), 365-376.

4953 Richardson, Joanna. "Emily, Lady Tennyson." History Today, 29 (1979), 188-193.

4954 Sendry, Joseph. "In Memoriam: The Minor Manuscripts." Harvard Library Bulletin, 27 (1979), 36-64.
Discusses twenty-three fragments and their places in the history of the composition of In Memoriam.

4955 _____. "Tennyson." Victorian Poetry, 17 (1979), 251-257. Survey of publications on Tennyson in 1978.

4956 Shannon, Edgar F., Jr., and Christopher Ricks. "A Further
History of Tennyson's Ode on the Death of the Duke of Wellington: The Manuscript at Trinity College and the Galley
Proof at Lincoln." Studies in Bibliography, 32 (1979), 125-
157.
The development of the poem traced through manuscripts and
revised proofs.
See also: A. Day and P.G. Scott in Studies in Bibliography,
1982 (entry 5124).

4957 Sherry, James J. "Tennyson: The Paradox of the Sign."
Victorian Poetry, 17 (1979), 204-216.
Tennyson's language and style.

4958 Stevenson, Catherine Barnes. "Emily Tennyson in Her Own
Right: The Unpublished Manuscripts." Victorians Institute
Journal, 8 (1979), 31-44.

4959 Talbot, Norman. "Best of Three Falls: James Thomson
(B.V.) v. Alfred, Lord Tennyson." Southern Review (Adelaide,
Australia), 12 (1979), 227-245.

4960 "Tennyson in Young England." Tennyson Research Bulletin,
3, no. 3 (Nov. 1979), 136.

4961 Tobin, J.J.M. "'Ulysses' and Troilus and Cressida." Tennyson Research Bulletin, 3, no. 3 (Nov. 1979), 120-121.

4962 Waller, John O. "Tennyson and Philip James Bailey's Festus."
Bulletin of Research in the Humanities, 82 (1979), 105-123.
Discusses Tennyson's annotations of the work.

1980

Books

4963 Buckler, William E. "The Tennysonian Imagination," "Tennysonian Madness: Mighty Collisions in the Imagination," "En-
larging the 'miniature epic': The Panic Subtext in Tennyson's
Oenone," "Tennyson's The Lotos-Eaters: Emblem of a New
Poetry," "In Defense of Locksley Hall," "Tennyson's Function
of Poetry at the Present Time: A Parabolic Reading of The
Princess," "In Memoriam in Aesthetic Context," and "Tennyson's Maud: New Critical Perspectives." The Victorian Imagination: Essays in Aesthetic Exploration. New York: New
York U.P., 1980, pp. 36-63, 64-91, 92-100, 101-118, 119-131,
132-163, 164-207, and 208-226, respectively.
Buckler presents a series of insightful essays that will inform
college students and enlighten scholars. He perceives in Tennyson's
poetry models for Victorian literary aesthetics and for the creative
imagination. For instance, in "The Tennysonian Imagination," he
asserts that after penetrating "to itness--having put 'keen Discovery'

to its ultimate creative uses as 'Discovery' of nature, man, and
ourselves--then we may occasionally, in our most favored moments,
make the imaginative leap into the consciousness of a reality that
absorbs into itself all of the individual tactilities to which we have
brought the authority of the bodily eye and which gives them full place
as sensuous symbolic gateways to a reality different in kind from
themselves, making even Time and Space mere modes of consciousness. That, both as concept and as process, is the essence of the
Tennysonian, and of the Victorian, imagination." The essays stimu-
late interest and ideas.
    Reviewed by: E. F. Shannon, Jr., in Tennyson Research Bul-
letin (entry 5137).

4964 Francis, Elizabeth A. "Introduction" and "Late Poems." Ten-
     nyson: A Collection of Critical Essays. Ed. Elizabeth A.
     Francis. Englewood Cliffs, New Jersey: Prentice-Hall, 1980,
     pp. 1-17 and 189-214, respectively. (A Spectrum Book)
    This book is a gathering of previously published essays and
is a helpful introduction to Tennyson's work. In her introduction,
Francis declares: "Throughout his career Tennyson sought power.
Despite the complexity of some of his works, he also sought simplicity and the ability to live in a constantly moving and tangible present
undeterred by regret for the past or longing for future joy." Francis's comments are informative and gracefully expressed.
    Reviewed by: P. Collins in Tennyson Research Bulletin (en-
try 5117).

4965 Gray, James Martin. Thro' the Vision of the Night: A Study
     of Source, Evolution and Structure in Tennyson's "Idylls of the
     King." Edinburgh: Edinburgh U. P., 1980. Montreal: McGill-
     Queens U. P., 1980.
    Gray investigates Tennyson's indebtedness to and rendering of
poetic tradition.
    Reviewed by: F. Kermode in London Review of Books (entry
5007); J. Lucas in Times Higher Education Supplement (entry 5012);
W. Nash in Tennyson Research Bulletin (entry 5019); S. Shatto in
Notes and Queries (entry 5139); and W. D. Shaw in University of Toronto Quarterly (entry 5105).

4966 Hargrave, Harry A. "Tennyson's 'Little Hamlet': Shake-
     spearean Parallels in Maud." A Fair Day in the Affections:
     Literary Essays in Honor of Robert B. White, Jr. Ed. Jack
     M. Durant and M. Thomas Hester. Raleigh: Winston, 1980,
     pp. 151-158.

4967 Hobson, Anthony Robert. The Art and Life of J.W. Waterhouse,
     RA, 1847-1917. London: Cassell, 1980. New York: Rizzoli,
     1980.

4968 Landow, George P. Victorian Types, Victorian Shadows: Bib-
     lical Typology in Victorian Literature, Art, and Thought. Bos-
     ton: Routledge and Kegan Paul, 1980.
    Landow discusses In Memoriam among many diverse works by
diverse authors.

4969   Macey, Samuel L.   Clocks and the Cosmos: Time in Western
       Life and Thought.   Hamden, Connecticut: Archon Books,
       1980.
       Tennyson's Devil and the Lady on page 209.

4970   Martin, Robert Bernard.   Tennyson: The Unquiet Heart.   Lon-
       don: Faber, 1980.   New York: Oxford U. P., 1980.
       Martin's biography of Tennyson features thorough and up-to-
date research that uses the literary scholarship of the last thirty
years to reveal the personality of the complex poet.   Written in a
fine style, the book is a good, readable study of Tennyson's life and
career that emphasizes the private character of the poet over analysis
of his works.   Martin's judgments are sound, and his book probably
should supplant that of Charles Tennyson (entry 3417) as the standard
biography.
       Reviewed by: J. Atlas in New York Times Book Review (en-
try 4978); J. Bayley in New York Review of Books (entry 4983); J.
H. Buckley in Victorian Studies (entry 5061); A. D. Culler in Journal
of English and Germanic Philology (entry 5119); A. Day in Tennyson
Research Bulletin (entry 4996); Economist (entry 4999); R. Engen in
Antiquarian Bookman Monthly Review (entry 5067); G. Grigson in Country Life (entry 5004); R. Howard in Yale Review (entry 5076); J. Hunter in Hudson Review (entry 5077); G. Joseph in Victorian Poetry
(entry 5080); J. Kelly in British Book News (entry 5082); F. Kermode
in London Review of Books (entry 5007); H. Kozicki in Western Humanities Review (entry 5086); P. Larkin in Times Literary Supplement (entry 5010); L. Lerner in Encounter (entry 5087); J. Lucas in
Times Higher Education Supplement (entry 5012); A. Motion in New
Scholar (entry 5018); S. Pickering in Sewanee Review (entry 5131);
S. Shatto in Notes and Queries (entry 5138); H. Tennyson in Listener
(entry 5036); and A. Wilson in Spectator (entry 5040).

4971   Metcalf, Priscilla.   James Knowles, Victorian Editor and Ar-
       chitect.   London: Oxford U. P. (Clarendon), 1980.
       Knowles was an important friend of Tennyson.

4972   Wheatcroft, Andrew.   The Tennyson Album: A Biography in
       Original Photographs.   London: Routledge and Kegan Paul,
       1980.
       Reviewed by: J. Atlas in New York Times Book Review (en-
try 4978); J. Bayley in New York Review of Books (entry 4983); J.
H. Buckley in Victorian Studies (entry 5061); R. Engen in Antiquarian
Bookman Monthly Review (entry 5067); S. Monod in Literary Review
(Edinburgh) (entry 5017); H. Tennyson in Listener (entry 5036); and
A. Wilson in Spectator (entry 5040).

Dissertations

4973   Ahern, Carolyn Clark.   Wordsworth, Tennyson, and the Uses
       of Disorder: A Study of The Prelude and In Memoriam.   Cor-
       nell, 1980.   Dissertation Abstracts International, 41 (1980),
       1061 A.
       Ahern believes that the work of Wordsworth was a source of

inspiration for Tennyson. She compares The Prelude and In Memoriam.

4974 Lee, William Lamborn. Interpreting Insane Characters in King Lear, The Duchess of Malfi, Rasselas, Maud, and As I Lay Dying: Toward a Theory. (Volume I and II.) Dissertation Abstracts International, 41 (1980), 2094A.
Lee contends that critics in general have misunderstood the essential problem of madness in Maud: readers cannot be sure where madness begins and ends in the poem's hero, society, and structure. Interesting commentary.

4975 Yarbrough, Bonnie Thames. Tennyson's Historical Trilogy: A Study of the Dramatic Hero. Pennsylvania State, 1980. Dissertation Abstracts International, 41 (1981), 4407A.
Yarbrough presents an analysis of the title characters of Queen Mary, Harold, and Becket. Central to the characters, she contends, is their struggle for a sense of self.

Periodicals

4976 Abbott, H. Porter. "Letters to the Self: The Cloistered Writer in Nonretrospective Fiction." PMLA, 95 (1980), 23-41.
Abbott asserts: "If among whole literary works cast as diaries there is any single paradigmatic example in which the form is endorsed as an agent both for the soul's self-expression and for the soul's discovery of truth, it is not a novel but Tennyson's long elegy, In Memoriam." Abbott discusses In Memoriam as a kind of diary.

4977 Aspinwall, Barnard. "Did Tennyson Consider Joining the Catholic Church in 1849?" Notes and Queries, 27 (1980), 208-209.

4978 Atlas, J. New York Times Book Review, Dec. 14, 1980, pp. 1 and 26-27.
Review of R.B. Martin's Tennyson, 1980 (entry 4970) and A. Wheatcroft's The Tennyson Album, 1980 (entry 4972).

4979 Auerbach, Nina. "The Rise of the Fallen Woman." Nineteenth-Century Fiction, 35 (June 1980), 29-52.
Tennyson and Idylls of the King discussed primarily on pages 30-31. Auerbach observes: "For Browning and Tennyson, then, the fallen woman becomes the abased figurehead of a fallen culture; her imaginative resonance justifies the punishment to which she is subjected."

4980 Austin, F. English Studies, 61 (1980), 376-379.
Review of W.D. Shaw's Tennyson's Style, 1976 (entry 4689).

4981 _____. English Studies, 61 (1980), 472-475.
Review of A.D. Culler's The Poetry of Tennyson, 1977 (entry 4751).

4982 Baker, Christopher P. "Milton's Nativity Ode and In Memoriam CVI." Victorian Poetry, 18 (1980), 202-203.

4983 Bayley, John. "The All-Star Victorian." New York Review
of Books, Dec. 18, 1980, pp. 42 and 44-49.
Review of R.B. Martin's Tennyson, 1980 (entry 4970) and A.
Wheatcroft's The Tennyson Album, 1980 (entry 4972).

4984 Bennett, James R. "Maud, Part III: Maud's Battle-Song."
Victorian Poetry, 18 (1980), 35-49.

4985 Brantlinger, Patrick. Criticism, 22 (1980), 378-379.
Review of H. Kozicki's Tennyson and Clio, 1979 (entry 4903)
and R. Pattison's Tennyson and Tradition, 1979 (entry 4906).

4986 Buckler, William E. "A Precarious Turning: Tennyson's Redemption of Literature and Life from Medievalism." Browning Institute Studies, 8 (1980), 85-102.

4987 Buckley, William K. "Alfred Tennyson's Early Poetry (1830-
1850): A Semantic Field That Exhibits the Search for the
Self." Interpretations, 12 (1980), 53-69.

4988 Burnet, Archie. "Tennyson's 'Mariana': Two Parallels."
Notes and Queries, 27 (1980), 207-208.

4989 Carroll, R.A. "The Tennyson Sales." Tennyson Research
Bulletin, 3, no. 4 (Nov. 1980), 141-146.

4990 Collins, P. Times Literary Supplement, Feb. 29, 1980, p.
242.
Review of J.S. Hagen's Tennyson and His Publishers, 1979
(entry 4901).

4991 Dale, Peter Allan. "'Gracious Lies': The Meaning of Metaphor in In Memoriam." Victorian Poetry, 18 (1980), 147-167.
Dale explores the notion that Tennyson used language and metaphor to express spiritual truth. He focuses on the words breath
and spirit in metaphors that express the presence of God and the spirit of Hallam in In Memoriam. An interesting study.

4992 Davies, James A. "Tennyson, Forster, and the Punch Connection: A Reply." Victorian Periodicals Review, 13 (1980), 64-
65.
See also: J.B. Jones in Victorian Periodicals Newsletter,
1978 (entry 4870), and in Victorian Periodicals Review, 1980 (entry
5006); and J.A. Davies in Victorian Periodicals Review (entry 4993),
below.

4993 _____. "'Tennyson, Forster, and the Punch Connection':
Again." Victorian Periodicals Review, 13 (1980), 103-105.
See also: J.B. Jones in Victorian Periodicals Newsletter,
1978 (entry 4870), and in Victorian Periodicals Review, 1980 (entry
5006); and J.A. Davies in Victorian Periodicals Review (entry 4992),
above.

4994 Day, Aidan. "G. S. Faber and Tennyson: A Note on the Question of Influence." Notes and Queries, 27 (1980), 520-522.

4995 ———. "Two Unrecorded Stages in the Revision of Tennyson's 'Oenone' for Poems, 1842." Library, 6th ser., 2 (1980), 315-325.

4996 ———. Tennyson Research Bulletin, 3, no. 4 (Nov. 1980), 165-166.
Review of R. B. Martin's Tennyson, 1980 (entry 4970).

4997 Dilligan, Robert. "Computers and Style: The Prosody of In Memoriam." Victorian Poetry, 18 (1980), 179-196.
With the help of computer analysis, Dilligan examines the relationship between syntax and meter in In Memoriam.

4998 Dunn, Richard J. "Vision and Revision: In Memoriam XCV." Victorian Poetry, 18 (1980), 135-146.
According to Dunn, In Memoriam, XCV, moves from the limitations of memories to the expansive possibilities, and that the section itself is an example of imaginative growth.

4999 Economist, Nov. 29, 1980, pp. 82-83.
Review of R. B. Martin's Tennyson, 1980 (entry 4970).

5000 Fleissner, Robert F. "A Possible Source for 'Forgive O Lord.'" Notes on Contemporary Literature, 10, no. 4 (1980), 9-10.

5001 Greene, Michael E. "Tennyson's 'Disastrous Day': Time in Section 72 of In Memoriam." Literatur in Wissenschaft und Unterricht, 13 (1980), 29-33.

5002 ———. "Tennyson's 'Gray shadow, once a man': Erotic Imagery and Dramatic Structure in 'Tithonus.'" Victorian Poetry, 18 (1980), 293-300.
Greene declares: "Although 'Tithonus' is one of the more erotic poems of the nineteenth century, its sexual element is so integrally a vehicle for its statement that the reader tends to concentrate on the larger implications of the narrative. Critics may refer in passing to the eroticism of the poem, but little close attention has been given to it. The sexuality of the poem is nevertheless a critical part of its pattern and is pervasive, even though understated."

5003 Grigson, G. Country Life, 167 (1980), 699-700.
Review of J. S. Hagen's Tennyson and His Publishers, 1979 (entry 4901).

5004 ———. Country Life, 168 (1980), 1837-1838.
Review of R. B. Martin's Tennyson, 1980 (entry 4970).

5005 Hagen, June Steffensen. Victorian Studies, 23 (1980), 271-273.
Review of P. Henderson's Tennyson, 1978 (entry 4830).

5006 Jones, John Bush. "The Punch Connection II: or, et tu, Tennyson?" Victorian Periodicals Review, 13 (1980), 66-69.
See also: J.A. Davies in Victorian Periodicals Review, 1980
(entries 4992 and 4993), and J.B. Jones in Victorian Periodicals
Newsletter, 1978 (entry 4870).

5007 Kermode, F. London Review of Books, Nov. 6, 1980, pp.
4-6.
Review of J.M. Gray's Thro' the Vision of the Night, 1980
(entry 4965) and R.B. Martin's Tennyson, 1980 (entry 4970).

5008 Kolb, Jack. Modern Philology, 77 (1980), 349-352.
Review of A.D. Culler's The Poetry of Tennyson, 1977 (entry
4751).

5009 Kramer, Lawrence. "The 'Intimations' Ode and Victorian Romanticism." Victorian Poetry, 18 (1980), 315-335.
The possible influence of Wordsworth's poem on In Memoriam.

5010 Larkin, P. Times Literary Supplement, Nov. 7, 1980, p.
1247.
Review of R.B. Martin's Tennyson, 1980 (entry 4970).

5011 Lohrli, Anne. "The Chancellor's Verse-Medal." Victorian
Poetry, 18 (1980), 81-84.

5012 Lucas, John. Times Higher Education Supplement, Nov. 21,
1980, p. 14.
Review of J.M. Gray's Thro' the Vision of the Night, 1980
(entry 4965) and R.B. Martin's Tennyson, 1980 (entry 4970).

5013 McSweeney, Kerry. Yearbook of English Studies, 10 (1980),
315-316.
Review of A.D. Culler's The Poetry of Tennyson, 1977 (entry
4751).

5014 Martin, R.B. "An Unpublished Early Poem by Alfred Tennyson." Tennyson Research Bulletin, 3, no. 4 (Nov. 1980),
147-149.
Presentation and discussion of "To Georgina 1834."

5015 Maxwell, Bennett. "The Steytler Recordings of Alfred, Lord
Tennyson: A History." Tennyson Research Bulletin, 3, no.
4 (Nov. 1980), 150-157.
An account of how Charles R.C. Steytler recorded Tennyson
reading poetry on May 15, 1890 by using wax cylinders and an Edison
recording machine.

5016 Metcalf, Priscilla. "Letter to the Editor on Aldworth." Tennyson Research Bulletin, 3, no. 4 (Nov. 1980), 161.
On what Aldworth would have looked like in Tennyson's time.

5017 Monod, S. Literary Review (Edinburgh), Nov. 14, 1980, pp.
32-33.

Review of A. Wheatcroft's The Tennyson Album, 1980 (entry 4972).

5018 Motion, A. New Scholar, Dec. 12, 1980, p. 16.
Review of R. B. Martin's Tennyson, 1980 (entry 4970).

5019 Nash, Walter. Tennyson Research Bulletin, 3, no. 4 (Nov. 1980), 168-169.
Review of J. M. Gray's Thro' the Vision of the Night, 1980 (entry 4965).

5020 Otten, Terry. Victorian Studies, 24 (1980), 136-138.
Review of D. M. Organ's Tennyson's Drama, 1979 (entry 4905) and V. Sharma's Studies in Victorian Verse Drama, 1979 (entry 4907).

5021 Pollard, A. British Book News, June 1980, p. 370.
Review of J. S. Hagen's Tennyson and His Publishers, 1979 (entry 4901).

5021a Pavlock, Barbara. Victorian Poetry, 18 (Winter 1980), 415-418.
Review of R. Pattison's Tennyson and Tradition, 1979 (entry 4906).

5022 Poston, Lawrence. "'Satan' Montgomery and In Memoriam." Tennyson Research Bulletin, 3, no. 4 (Nov. 1980), 162-163.

5023 Rosenblum, Dolores Ryback. "The Act of Writing In Memoriam." Victorian Poetry, 18 (1980), 119-134.
Rosenblum examines those sections of the poem that discuss the act of writing In Memoriam. Rosenblum writes: "Despite the emergence of a line of development, the poem proceeds by many returns and retractions, particularly in those sections which consider the relation between language and the inexpressible. This essay attempts to trace that tentative line which Tennyson wrests, with difficulty, out of an obsessive circularity. This is not to say, however, that the final arrangement of the poem represents the biographical process by which Tennyson came to terms with his grief. Ultimately, In Memoriam records no process beyond that of its own unfolding."

5024 Scott, Patrick. "Three Literary Sources for Clough's 'Farewell, My Highland Lassie.'" English Language Notes, 17 (1980), 192-195.

5025 Scott, Patrick Greig. "'Flowering in a Lonely Word': Tennyson and the Victorian Study of Language." Victorian Poetry, 18 (1980), 371-381.

5026 Sendry, Joseph. "In Memoriam: Twentieth-Century Criticism." Victorian Poetry, 18 (1980), 105-118.
Sendry presents a useful introduction to the major critical views of In Memoriam, with an emphasis on the criticism of the 1960s and 1970s.

5027 _____. "Tennyson." Victorian Poetry, 18 (1980), 282-292.
A survey of 1979 publications on Tennyson.

5028 Shatto, Susan. Modern Language Review, 75 (1980), 371-373.
Review of P. Henderson's Tennyson, 1978 (entry 4830).

5029 _____. "The Sotheby's Sale of Tennyson Papers." Victorian Papers, 18 (1980), 309-312.

5030 _____. "Tennyson's In Memoriam: Section 123 in the Manuscripts." Library, 6th ser., 2 (1980), 304-314.

5031 Shaw, Marion. "The Opening Section of In Memoriam: First
and Second Thoughts." Notes and Queries, 27 (1980), 522-
525.

5032 _____. "Palgrave's In Memoriam." Victorian Poetry, 18
(1980), 199-201.

5033 Shaw, W. David. "The Agnostic Tradition in Victorian Poetry." Criticism, 22 (1980), 116-139.
Includes Tennyson among others.

5034 Stevenson, Catherine Barnes. "Druids, Bards, and Tennyson's
Merlin." Victorian Newsletter, no. 57 (Spring 1980), 14-23.

5035 _____. "Tennyson's Dying Swans: Mythology and the Definition of the Poet's Role." Studies in English Literature,
1500-1900, 20 (1980), 621-635.

5036 Tennyson, H. Listener, 104 (1980), 549-551.
Review of R.B. Martin's Tennyson, 1980 (entry 4970) and A.
Wheatcroft's The Tennyson Album, 1980 (entry 4972).

5037 Welch, Dennis M. "Distance and Progress in In Memoriam."
Victorian Poetry, 18 (1980), 169-177.
According to Welch: "In Memoriam deals with the 'Way' of
the soul and of the human race. Tennyson points out the way by
changing the concern in the poem from grief over the past to hope
in the future."

5038 Wickens, G. Glen. "The Two Sides of Early Victorian Science
and the Unity of 'The Princess.'" Victorian Studies, 23 (1980),
369-388.
Wickens asserts: "The attitude towards evolution worked out
in The Princess is deeply rooted in Tennyson's complex response to
the two sides of pre-Darwinian science."

5039 Wilkins, Mary. "Tennyson's Water Cures." Tennyson Research Bulletin, 3, no. 4 (Nov. 1980), 158-159.

5040 Wilson, A. Spectator, Nov. 8, 1980, pp. 19-20.
Review of R.B. Martin's Tennyson, 1980 (entry 4970) and A.
Wheatcroft's The Tennyson Album, 1980 (entry 4972).

1981

Books

5041   Bayley, John. "Tennyson and the Idea of Decadence." Studies
       in Tennyson. Ed. Hallam Tennyson. Totowa, New Jersey:
       Barnes and Noble, 1981, pp. 186-205.

5042   Collins, Philip. "Tennyson In and Out of Time." Studies in
       Tennyson. Ed. Hallam Tennyson. Totowa, New Jersey:
       Barnes and Noble, 1981, pp. 131-154.
       History and myth in Tennyson's work.

5043   Fredeman, William E. "One Word More: On Tennyson's
       Dramatic Monologues." Studies in Tennyson. Ed. Hallam
       Tennyson. Totowa, New Jersey: Barnes and Noble, 1981, pp.
       169-185.

5044   Hair, Donald S. Domestic and Heroic in Tennyson's Poetry.
       Toronto: U. of Toronto P., 1981.
       Hair argues that Tennyson adapted the pastoral tradition of
poetry to the purpose of exhalting the ideal of the family.
       Reviewed by: R. Pattison in Victorian Studies (entry 5130).

5044a Hallam, Arthur Henry. The Letters of Arthur Henry Hallam.
       Ed. Jack Kolb. Columbus, Ohio: Ohio State U.P., 1981.
       Reviewed by: P.L. Elliott in Victorian Studies (entry 5142);
and D.G. Riede in Victorian Poetry (entry 5134).

5045   Korg, Jacob. "Astronomical Imagery in Victorian Poetry."
       Victorian Science and Victorian Values: Literary Perspectives.
       Ed. James Paradis and Thomas Postlewait. New York: New
       York Academy of Sciences, 1981, pp. 137-158.

5046   McSweeney, Kerry. Tennyson and Swinburne as Romantic Nat-
       uralists. Toronto: U. of Toronto P., 1981.
       Reviewed by: D.G. Riede in Journal of English and Germanic
Philology (entry 5133).

5047   Mason, Michael. "The Timing of In Memoriam." Studies in
       Tennyson. Ed. Hallam Tennyson. Totowa, New Jersey:
       Barnes and Noble, 1981, pp. 151-168.

5048   Radford, Colin, and Sally Minoque. "The Logical Richness of
       Criticism: An Analysis of Ricks on Tennyson." The Nature
       of Criticism. Brighton: Harvester, 1981. New Jersey: Hu-
       manities, 1981, pp. 84-114.

5049   Redpath, Theodore. "Tennyson and the Literature of Greece
       and Rome." Studies in Tennyson. Ed. Hallam Tennyson.
       Totowa, New Jersey: Barnes and Noble, 1981, pp. 105-130.
       Classical influences on Tennyson.

5050   Ricks, Christopher. "Tennyson Inheriting the Earth." <u>Studies</u>
       <u>in Tennyson</u>. Ed. Hallam Tennyson. Totowa, New Jersey:
       Barnes and Noble, 1981, pp. 66-104.

5051   Robson, W. W. "The Present Value of Tennyson." <u>Studies in</u>
       <u>Tennyson</u>. Ed. Hallam Tennyson. Totowa, New Jersey:
       Barnes and Noble, 1981, pp. 45-65.

5052   Tennyson, Alfred, Lord. <u>The Letters of Alfred Lord Tenny-</u>
       <u>son, Volume I: 1821-1850.</u> Ed. Cecil Y. Lang and Edgar F.
       Shannon, Jr. Cambridge: Harvard U. P. (Belknap), 1981.
       This important contribution to Tennysonian studies includes an
excellent introduction to the letters and their bibliography and to Alfred and Emily Tennyson.
       Reviewed by: P. L. Elliott in <u>Victorian Studies</u> (entry 5142);
and L. K. Hughes in <u>Victorian Poetry</u> (entry 5127).

5053   Tennyson, Emily. <u>Lady Tennyson's Journal</u>. Ed. James O.
       Hoge. Charlottesville: U. P. of Virginia, 1981.
       Reviewed by: P. L. Elliott in <u>Victorian Studies</u> (entry 5142);
and H. Tennyson in <u>Tennyson Research Bulletin</u> (entry 5111).

5054   Tennyson, Hallam, ed. <u>Studies in Tennyson</u>. Totowa, New
       Jersey: Barnes and Noble, 1981.
       A gathering of essays. See entries 5041, 5042, 5043, 5047,
5049, 5050, and 5051.
       Reviewed by: P. L. Elliott in <u>Victorian Studies</u> (entry 5142);
and D. Palmer in <u>Tennyson Research Bulletin</u> (entry 5091).

5055   Wordsworth, Ann. "An Art That Will Not Abandon the Self to
       Language: Bloom, Tennyson and the Blind World of the Wish."
       <u>Untying the Text: A Post-Structuralist Reader</u>. Ed. Robert
       Young. Boston: Routledge, 1981, pp. 207-222.

Dissertation

5056   Sparer, Jonathon Douglas. <u>Gareth's Function in Tennyson's</u>
       <u>"Idylls of the King" and "Arthur's Vast Design."</u> Toledo,
       1981. <u>Dissertation Abstracts International</u>, 42 (1981), 2690A-
       2691A.
       Sparer discusses Gareth as the moral character against which
the others in <u>Idylls of the King</u> are measured. He perceives in "Arthur's Vast Design" the king's effort to promote moral evolution.

Periodicals

5057   Bennett, James R. "The Historical Abuse of Literature: Ten-
       nyson's Maud: A Monodrama and the Crimean War." <u>English</u>
       <u>Studies</u>, 62 (Jan. 1981), 34-45.

5058   Bonney, William W. "The Grounds of Vision in Tennyson's
       'The Holy Grail.'" <u>Victorians Institute Journal</u>, 10 (1981),
       89-110.

5059   Bryant, Hallman B.   "The African Genesis of Tennyson's 'Timbuctoo.'"   Tennyson Research Bulletin, 3, no. 5 (Nov. 1981),
196-202.

5060   Bruns, G. L.   English Language Notes, 18 (1981), 150-151.
Review of H. Kozicki's Tennyson and Clio, 1979 (entry 4903).

5061   Buckley, J. H.   Victorian Studies, 24 (1981), 511-513.
Review of R. B. Martin's Tennyson, 1980 (entry 4970) and A.
Wheatcroft's The Tennyson Album, 1980 (entry 4972).

5062   Culler, A. D.   Arnoldian, 8, no. 2 (1981), 69-74.
Review of H. Kozicki's Tennyson and Clio, 1979 (entry 4903)
and R. Pattison's Tennyson and Tradition, 1979 (entry 4906).

5063   Day, Aidan.   "The Lincoln Manuscript Fragment of Tennyson's
'The Passing of Arthur.'"   Library, 3 (1981), 343-346.

5064   _____.   "Notable Acquisitions by the Tennyson Research
Centre: Tennyson's Annotated Copy of William Trollope's
Pentalogia Graeca and an Unlisted MS Poem."   Tennyson Re-
search Bulletin, 3, no. 5 (Nov. 1981), 203-208.

5065   _____.   "A Tennyson Discovery."   Times Literary Supplement, Dec. 11, 1981, p. 1449.
A recently discovered poem "'Yours & caetera' O how cold!"

5066   Elliott, Philip L.   "Materials for a Life of A. T."   Notes and
Queries, 28 (Oct. 1981), 415-418.

5067   Engen, R.   Antiquarian Bookman Monthly Review, 8 (1981),
228-231.
Review of R. B. Martin's Tennyson, 1980 (entry 4970) and A.
Wheatcroft's The Tennyson Album, 1980 (entry 4972).

5068   Fertel, Randy J.   "Antipastoral and the Attack on Naturalism
in Tennyson's Idylls of the King."   Victorian Poetry, 19 (Winter 1981), 337-350.
According to Fertel, "the Idylls attack philosophical naturalism" and that "In his attack, Tennyson adopts an antipastoral strategy: the subtle subversion of pastoral conventions to illuminate pastoral's false idealism, hollow sentimentality, and vicious passivity."

5069   Findlay, L. M.   "Sensation and Memory in Tennyson's 'Ulysses.'"   Victorian Poetry, 19 (Summer 1981), 139-149.
Findlay observes: "Sensory references and figurative language
collaborate effectively to give this poem immediacy and unity and to
encourage our participation in Ulysses' mental life; but our memories
are not identical with his.   The allusive fabric of the poem controls
its larger meanings--one might say its ethical import--in an aptly
unobtrusive way that curbs the claims of Ulysses."

5070   Gibson, Mary Ellis.   "Approaches to Character in Browning

and Tennyson: Two Examples of Metrical Style." Language
and Style, 14 (Winter 1981), 34-51.

5071 Glowka, Arthur Wayne. "Tennyson's Tailoring of Source in
the Geraint Idylls." Victorian Poetry, 19 (Autumn 1981),
302-307.
Clothing symbolism in Tennyson's Geraint poems.

5072 Gray, J. M. Tennyson Research Bulletin, 3, no. 5 (Nov. 1981),
215-216.
Review of R. Pattison's Tennyson and Tradition, 1979 (entry
4906).

5073 Harrison, Antony H. "Irony in Tennyson's 'Little Hamlet.'"
Journal of General Education, 32 (Winter 1981), 271-286.

5074 Hellstrom, W. Journal of English and Germanic Philology,
80 (1981), 147-149.
Review of R. Pattison's Tennyson and Tradition, 1979 (entry
4906).

5075 Hoeveler, Diane Long. "Manly-Women and Womanly-Men:
Tennyson's Androgynous Ideal." Michigan Occasional Papers
in Women's Studies, 19 (1981), 1-19.

5076 Howard, R. Yale Review, 70 (1981), 616-621.
Review of R. B. Martin's Tennyson, 1980 (entry 4970).

5077 Hunter, J. Hudson Review, 34 (1981), 138-140.
Review of R. B. Martin's Tennyson, 1980 (entry 4970).

5078 Johnston, Eileen T. "Hallam's Review of Tennyson: Its Con-
texts and Significance." Texas Studies in Literature and Language, 23 (Spring 1981), 1-26.

5079 Joseph, Gerhard. "Tennyson's Three Women: The Thought
within the Image." Victorian Poetry, 19 (Spring 1981), 1-18.
A study of "the three queens of the Idylls of the King who appear at Arthur's coronation and escort him at his death to Avilion."

5080 _____. Victorian Poetry, 19 (1981), 196-199.
Review of R. B. Martin's Tennyson, 1980 (entry 4970).

5081 _____. Victorian Studies, 24 (1981), 235-237.
Review of J. S. Hagen's Tennyson and His Publishers, 1979
(entry 4901); H. Kozicki's Tennyson and Clio, 1979 (entry 4903); and
R. Pattison's Tennyson and Tradition, 1979 (entry 4906).

5082 Kelly, J. British Book News, Jan. 1981, p. 51.
Review of R. B. Martin's Tennyson, 1980 (entry 4970).

5083 Knies, Earl A. "The Diary of James Henry Mangles." Tennyson Research Bulletin, 3, no. 5 (Nov. 1981), 185-191.

5084 Kostamlatský, Samuel. "Analysis of the Rhythm Effects in Alfred Tennyson's Poem 'Crossing the Bar.'" Brno Studies in English, 14 (1981), 133-137.

5085 Kozicki, Henry. Modern Philology, 79 (1981), 210-213. Review of R. Pattison's Tennyson and Tradition, 1979 (entry 4906).

5086 _____. Western Humanities Review, 35 (1981), 273-276. Review of R.B. Martin's Tennyson, 1980 (entry 4970).

5087 Lerner, Laurence. Encounter, June 1981, pp. 72-76. Review of R.B. Martin's Tennyson, 1980 (entry 4970), and R. Pattison's Tennyson and Tradition, 1979 (entry 4906).

5088 Maidment, Brian. Tennyson Research Bulletin, 3, no. 5 (Nov. 1981), 210-211. Discusses E.F. Shannon's article on "Lucretius" (entry 5103).

5089 Mattheisen, Paul F. "Tennyson and Carlyle: A Source for 'The Eagle.'" Victorian Newsletter, no. 60 (Fall 1981), 1-3.

5090 Paden, W.D. "Tennyson's The New Timon, R.H. Shepherd and Henry Buxton Forman." Studies in Bibliography, 34 (1981), 262-266.

5091 Palmer, David. Tennyson Research Bulletin, 3, no. 5 (Nov. 1981), 213-215. Review of H. Tennyson, ed., Studies in Tennyson, 1981 (entry 5054).

5092 Peters, Robert L. "John Addington Symonds: Three Letters to the Tennysons." Tennyson Research Bulletin, 3, no. 5 (Nov. 1981), 192-195.

5093 Pfeiffer, K.L. Anglia, 99 (1981), 522-525. Review of J.R. Kincaid's Tennyson's Major Poems, 1975 (entry 4607).

5094 Pollard, Arthur. "In Memoriam as a Personal Poem." Tennyson Research Bulletin, 3, no. 5 (Nov. 1981), 175-184.

5095 Reed, John R. Clio (Fort Wayne), 11 (Fall 1981), 97-101. Review of R. Pattison's Tennyson and Tradition, 1979 (entry 4906).

5096 _____. "Tennyson, Browning, and the Victorian Idyll." Studies in Browning and His Circle, 9, no. 1 (Spring 1981), 27-31.

5097 Rogers, William N., II. "Tennyson's Poetry of Social Converses: 'To Ulysses.'" Victorian Poetry, 19 (Winter 1981), 351-366.

Rogers discusses the poem and the poet's relationship with William Gifford Palgrave.

5098 Rosenbaum, Jean Watson. "Apples and Milkmaids: The Vision-ary Experience in Tennyson's The Holy Grail." Studia Mys-tica, 4 (Summer 1981), 11-35.

5099 Saunders, Mary. "Tennyson's 'Ulysses' as Rhetorical Mono-logue." Victorian Newsletter, no. 60 (Fall 1981), 20-24.

5100 Scott, Patrick Greig. Library, 3 (1981), 167-171.
Review of J.S. Hagen's Tennyson and His Publishers, 1979 (entry 4901).

5101 Sendry, Joseph. "Tennyson." Victorian Poetry, 19 (Autumn 1981), 288-298.
A survey of 1980 publications on Tennyson.

5102 Shannon, Edgar F., Jr. "Poetry as Vision: Sight and Insight in 'The Lady of Shalott.'" Victorian Poetry, 19 (Autumn 1981), 207-223.
According to Shannon, the poem "explores parabolically the quality of poetry derived from two opposing postulates and advocates expression rather than imitation as the essential impetus for art."

5103 _____. "The Publication of Tennyson's 'Lucretius.'" Stud-ies in Bibliography, 34 (1981), 146-186.
Discussed by B. Maidment, entry 5088.

5104 Shaw, W. David. "Projection and Empathy in Victorian Poet-ry." Victorian Poetry, 19 (Winter 1981), 315-336.
This essay focuses on the poetic theories of Arthur Henry Hallam and W.J. Fox. Shaw discusses the influence of their theories on Tennyson.

5105 _____. University of Toronto Quarterly, 50, no. 4 (1981), 125-126.
Review of J.M. Gray's Thro' the Vision of the Night, 1980 (entry 4965).

5106 Sopher, H. "The 'Puzzling Plainness' of 'Break, Break, Break': Its Deep and Surface Structure." Victorian Poetry, 19 (Spring 1981), 87-93.
Linguistic analysis.

5107 Stein, Richard L. "The Pre-Raphaelite Tennyson." Victorian Studies, 24 (Spring 1981), 279-301.
Stein discusses the 1857 illustrated edition of Tennyson's po-ems. The essay includes illustrations by Daniel Maclise, Dante Ga-briel Rossetti, William Holman Hunt, and John Everett Millais. Stein contends that the illustrations' unconventionality makes them funda-mentally Tennysonian. He declares: "The emotional depth of the Pre-Raphaelite illustrations was a way of keeping faith with the spirit

of the poetry; for all their divergence from literal accuracy, it was
a sign of aesthetic allegiance."

5108 Stevenson, Catherine Barnes. "How It Struck a Contemporary:
Tennyson's 'Lancelot and Elaine' and Pre-Raphaelite Art."
Victorian Newsletter, no. 60 (Fall 1981), 8-14.

5109 _____. "Swinburne and Tennyson's Tristram." Victorian
Poetry, 19 (Summer 1981), 185-189.
Stevenson argues that "The Last Tournament" is a response
to Swinburne, and that "Tristram is a fleshly poet whose attitudes
and poetic imagery resemble Swinburne's." She concludes: "But
before Swinburne could issue his version of the Tristram legend,
Tennyson created a Tristram who reveals the dangers of Swinburnean
art and whose aesthetic and moral aberrations are punished by a
swift, violent death. Perhaps, through Tristram's poetically just
death Tennyson rid himself of a feared poetic rival."

5110 [No entry.]

5111 Tennyson, Hallam. Tennyson Research Bulletin, 3, no. 5
(Nov. 1981), 211-213.
Review of Emily, Lady Tennyson's Lady Tennyson's Journal,
ed. J. O. Hoge, 1981 (entry 5053).

5112 Tomlinson, D. Arnoldian, 8, no. 2 (1981), 75-76.
Review of J. S. Hagen's Tennyson and His Publishers, 1979
(entry 4901).

5113 Trapp, J. B. "Mantua's Tennyson Manuscript." Times Literary Supplement, Sept. 18, 1981, p. 1081.
Discusses an Italian manuscript of "To Virgil."

1982

A partial listing.

Books

5113a Tennyson, Alfred, Lord. Tennyson: In Memoriam. Ed. Susan Shatto and Marion Shaw. Oxford: Clarendon, 1982.

Periodicals

5114 Bornstein, George. "Last Romantic or Last Victorian: Yeats,
Tennyson, and Browning." Yeats Annual, 1 (1982), 114-132.
Bornstein asserts: "The early Tennyson strove for a poetry
of exquisite sensation deeply derived from romantic examples; after
the 'decade of silence,' however, his verse began to incorporate the
very 'reflection' which Hallam had praised him for refining away."
Bornstein examines Tennyson and Browning as prototypes for Yeats.

5115 Canham, Stephen. "Robert B. Martin, Tennyson: The Unquiet Heart." Biography, 5, no. 1 (Winter 1982), 74-87.
An interview of R.B. Martin.

5116 Collins, Philip. "Sir Charles Tennyson: Further Reminiscences of his Grandfather." Tennyson Research Bulletin, 4,
no. 1 (Nov. 1982), 8-15.

5117 _____. Tennyson Research Bulletin, 4, no. 1 (Nov. 1982),
35-37.
Review of E.A. Francis, ed., Tennyson, 1980 (entry 4964).

5118 Collins, Thomas J. "Three Additional Letters from Browning
to the Tennysons." Tennyson Research Bulletin, 4, no. 1
(Nov. 1982), 25-27.
Prints two letters to Hallam Tennyson, dated Dec. 1st and
15th, 1883, and one letter to Alfred, Lord Tennyson, dated April
27, 1886.

5119 Culler, A. Dwight. Journal of English and Germanic Philology,
81 (Jan. 1982), 133-135.
Review of R.B. Martin's Tennyson, 1980 (entry 4970).

5120 Culver, Marcia C. "The Death and Birth of an Epic: Tennyson's 'Morte d'Arthur.'" Victorian Poetry, 20 (Spring 1982),
51-61.
Culver asserts about "Morte d'Arthur": "Begun in despair and
grief amidst the wreckage of the Arthurian dream which was to have
been 'the chief work of his manhood,' the poem ended in hope and a
new beginning."

5121 Day, Aidan. "Edward FitzGerald to the Tennysons: Three
Letters." Notes and Queries, 29 (Aug. 1982), 303-307.

5122 [_____.] "Letters from Emily Tennyson Jesse to Ellen Hallam and an 1865 Tennyson Presentation Copy Acquired by the
Tennyson Research Centre." Tennyson Research Bulletin, 4,
no. 1 (Nov. 1982), 29-31.

5123 _____. "Voices in a Dream: The Language of Skepticism
in Tennyson's 'The Hesperides.'" Victorian Newsletter, no.
62 (Fall 1982), 13-21.
Day believes that "while Romantic metaphorical and symbolic
modes characteristically emphasize a vision of continuity and unity,
in Tennyson's subversive use of myth in 'The Hesperides,' his examination of a sense of discontinuity, we see him using the language of
Romanticism against itself."

5124 Day, Aidan, and P.G. Scott. "Tennyson's Ode on the Death
of the Duke of Wellington: Addenda to Shannon and Ricks."
Studies in Bibliography, 35 (1982), 318-324.
See also: E.F. Shannon, Jr., and C. Ricks in Studies in
Bibliography, 1979 (entry 4956).

5125 Greenberg, Mark L. Journal of English and Germanic Philology, 81 (Jan. 1982), 135-139.
      Review of H. Kozicki's Tennyson and Clio, 1979 (entry 4903).

5126 Harland, Catherine R. "The Modernity of Tennyson's Tristram." Studies in English Literature 1500-1900, 22 (Autumn 1982), 647-657.
      Harland asserts: "What is fundamentally important about Tristram is not the particular set of ideas with which Tennyson associates him, but the fact that he is torn between ideas and is partially incapacitated by this psychomachia."

5127 Hughes, Linda K. Victorian Poetry, 20 (Summer 1982), 199-204.
      Review of The Letters of Alfred Lord Tennyson, Volume I, ed. C. Y. Lang and E. F. Shannon, Jr., 1981 (entry 5052).

5128 Mackerness, E. D. Notes and Queries, 29 (Oct. 1982), 458-460.
      Review of H. Kozicki's Tennyson and Clio, 1980 (entry 4903).

5129 Menand, Louis. "The Victorian Historical Sense and Modernism." Victorian Newsletter, no. 61 (Spring 1982), 5-8.
      Menand asserts that after Hallam's death "Tennyson had found his true poetic mode, and almost overnight he had changed from an accomplished and minor disciple of Keats into the major poetic voice of his time. The mode was the elegy...."

5130 Pattison, Robert. Victorian Studies, 25 (Summer 1982), 510-511.
      Review of D. S. Hair's Domestic and Heroic in Tennyson's Poetry, 1981 (entry 5044).

5131 Pickering, Sam. Sewanee Review, 90, no. 4 (Oct.-Dec. 1982), xciv-c.
      Review of R. B. Martin's Tennyson: The Unquiet Heart, 1980 (entry 4970).

5132 Pollard, Arthur. "Three Horace Translations by Tennyson." Tennyson Research Bulletin, 4, no. 1 (Nov. 1982), 16-24.

5133 Riede, David G. Journal of English and Germanic Philology, 81 (Oct. 1982), 587-588.
      Review of K. McSweeney's Tennyson and Swinburne as Romantic Naturalists, 1981 (entry 5046).

5134 _____ . Victorian Poetry, 20 (Summer 1982), 205-208.
      Review of A. H. Hallam's The Letters of Arthur Henry Hallam, ed. J. Kolb, 1979 (entry 5044a).

5135 Rosenberg, John D. "The Mistaken Point of In Memoriam, Section LXXII." Tennyson Research Bulletin, 4, no. 1 (Nov. 1982), 3-7.

Suggests a correction of an error in punctuation in Section LXXII of the authoritative editions of In Memoriam.

5136 Sendry, Joseph. "Tennyson." Victorian Poetry, 20 (Summer 1982), 182-191.
A survey of Tennysonian publications in 1981.

5137 Shannon, Edgar F., Jr. Tennyson Research Bulletin, 4, no. 1 (Nov. 1982), 34-35.
Review of W. E. Buckler's The Victorian Imagination, 1980 (entry 4963).

5138 Shatto, Susan. Notes and Queries, 29 (June 1982), 247-249.
Review of R. B. Martin's Tennyson, 1980 (entry 4970).

5139 _____ . Notes and Queries, 29 (June 1982), 247-249.
Review of J. M. Gray's Thro' the Vision of the Night, 1980 (entry 4965).

5140 Tucker, Herbert F., Jr. "Tennyson's Narrative of Desire: The Lover's Tale." Victorian Newsletter, no. 62 (Fall 1982), 21-30.
Tucker suggests of "The Lover's Tale" that "Tennyson kept returning to this poem as he did because it took up thematically-- and with an analytic rigor we usually hesitate to attribute to him-- imaginative problems of emotional relationship that lay at the heart of virtually all his subsequent work...."

5141 Warren, Roger. "'Now folds the lily all her sweetness up': Tennyson and Edward Fairfax." Tennyson Research Bulletin, 4, no. 1 (Nov. 1982), 28.

1983

A partial listing.

Periodicals

5142 Elliott, Philip L. Victorian Studies, 26 (Winter 1983), 248-250.
Review of The Letters of Alfred Lord Tennyson, Volume I, ed. C. Y. Lang and E. F. Shannon, Jr., 1981 (entry 5052); A. H. Hallam's The Letters of Arthur Henry Hallam, ed. J. Kolb, 1979 (entry 5044a); E. Tennyson's Lady Tennyson's Journals, ed. J. O. Hoge, 1981 (entry 5053); and H. Tennyson, ed., Studies in Tennyson, 1981 (entry 5054).

5143 Gilbert, Elliot L. "The Female King: Tennyson's Arthurian Apocalypse." PMLA, 98 (Oct. 1983).
Gilbert argues that "the restrained, almost maidenly Victorian monarch," Tennyson's King Arthur, was the inevitable characterization for the Victorian era. He shows how Arthur and Idylls of the King reflect the major political and social events of nineteenth-century

England and how Tennyson incorporated current issues, including the "Women Question" and the Victorian sense of historical belatedness as major themes in the poem. Gilbert concludes: "From his long, dark Arthurian speculation, Tennyson seems to be saying, the century can only move inexorably forward through fin-de-siècle hedonism into the fragmentation and alienation of a modernist waste land." This is an impressively researched and provocative essay.

5144 Harris, Jack. "The Pre-Raphaelites and the Moxon Tennyson." Journal of Pre-Raphaelite Studies, 3 (May 1983), 26-37.
    Includes illustrations by John Everett Millais, William Holman Hunt, and Dante Gabriel Rossetti. Harris provides an account of the history of the publication of the 1857 edition of Tennyson's poetry. Interesting.

5145 Sparer, J. Douglas. "Arthur's Vast Design." Victorian Poetry, 21 (Summer 1983), 119-131.
    According to Sparer, Tennyson uses Camelot as representation of Arthur's plan to make the knights of Camelot into better men. Sparer declares "that Camelot indeed possessed a functional objective reality for its knights. The formative influence of its gate, gardens, hall, windows, and four great zones all attest to the substance of the city. An actual Camelot was always a necessity for Arthur to achieve his vast design." This is a well argued essay.

5146 Tucker, Herbert F., Jr. "Strange Comfort: A Reading of Tennyson's Unpublished Juvenalia." Victorian Poetry, 21 (Spring 1983), 1-25.
    Tucker begins: "Although Tennyson's earliest surviving poems ostensibly concern heaven, hell, the devil, and the battle of good with evil, in fact they are remarkably amoral performances, explosions of a precocious verbal gift that may be most precocious in its cool exploration of the sources of its peculiar power."

5147 _____. "Tennyson and the Measure of Doom." PMLA, 98 (Jan. 1983), 8-20.
    Tucker examines Tennyson's work as poetry concerned with ends, with inevitable fatality. He finds that Tennyson used poetic rhythm, the "measure," to convey an understanding of human doom. According to Tucker, Tennyson "intended his rhythms to imitate the pulse of inevitability that he felt within the core of human experience and that he intuited beyond its further reaches and to express the deep if somewhat narrow range of moods that arise in acknowledging, and submitting to, the inevitable."

Author-Editor Index

(By entry number)

Entry numbers for book-length studies, including dissertations, are underlined.

A., R.H. 3278
A., T. 3381
Aaron, Jonathan 4519
Abbott, C. Colleer 2977
Abbott, H. Porter 4976
Abercrombie, Lascelles 3144
Ackermann, R. 2161, 2162, 2163
Adam, Graeme Mercer 1897
Adams, Annie see Fields, Annie
Adams, Francis 1811, 2087
Adams, H. 786
Adams, Michael C.C. 4914
Adams, Norman Owens Whitehurst,
  Jr. 3581
Adcock, St. J. 3125
Adey, Lionel 4236
Adicks, Richard Rosenbush, Jr.
  3905, 4024, 4293
Adkins, Nelson F. 3216
Adler, John 4437
Adler, Joshua 3972, 4528, 4621
Adler, Thomas P. 4237, 4529
Agrawala, D.C. 4025
Agresti, A. 2551
Ahern, Carolyn Clark 4973
Aimée, Sister 3311
Ainger, Alfred 1252, 1417, 2384
Alaya, Flavia 4238
Albee, John 1960
Alden, Raymond MacDonald 2834
Aldrich, Thomas Bailey 1299, 1418
Alford, Henry 649
Alger, George W. 1913
Alger, W.R. 417
Al-Khatib, Issam 4018
Allen, G.C. 2137
Allen, Grant 1425
Allen, Katherine 2103
Allen, Peter 4825
Allen, S.C. 4622
Allentuck, Marcia 4438
Allingham, Helen (painter) 2392,
  2447

Allingham, William 2447
Allison, William Talbot 2553
Allott, Kenneth 3605, 3700, 3911
Allott, Miriam 3586, 3587
Allsobrook, Sian 4342
Althaus, Friedrich 1881
Altholz, Joseph L. 4679
Altick, Richard D. 3694, 3701
Altieri, Charles 4843
Ambler, B.G. 2650
Amis, Kingsley 4425
Ancaster, Lord 3803
Anderson, Warren D. 4011
Andrews, Clarence A. 4130
Andrews, Samuel 1065
Angeli, D. 2554
Antippas, Andy Peter 4026, 4070,
  4154
App, August J. 3082
Appleman, Philip 3662, 4530
Archer, William 1013, 1145
Argyll, Duke of 1695
Arms, George 3364
Armstrong, Isobel 4082, 4131, 4134,
  4137, 4144, 4155, 4333
Armstrong, Richard A. 2026
Armstrong, T. Percy 3041
Arnold, Edwin 1364, 1426, 2999
Arnold, William Harris 2555, 2953,
  2959
Aronstein, Philipp 2104, 2165
Ashe, Leslie 2846
Asher, David 563, 1071
Asher, Eliezer see Moses, Adolph
Aspinwall, Bernard 4915, 4977
Assad, Thomas J. 3647, 3804, 3805,
  3912, 4027, 4083, 4156, 4239
Atkins, Gaius Glenn 3049
Atlas, J. 4978
Auden, W.H. (Wystan Hugh Auden)
  3345, 4356
Auerbach, Nina 4979
August, Eugene R. 4157
Auld, William Muir 3170

Auslander, Joseph 3096
Austin, Alfred (pseud. Lamia) 634, 643, 978, 1248, 1259, 1260, 1429, 1430, 2621, 3408
Austin, F. 4980, 4981
Axon, William Edward Armitage 880, 913, 1365, 2042, 2322
Axson, Stockton 1798
Ayo, Nicholas 4028
Aytoun, William Edmondstoune 85, 86, 99, 325, 419, 644, 1288, 1289, 1293, 3021
Azarias, Brother see Mullany, Patrick Francis

B. 326
B., A.C. 3648
B., C. 3702
Bacon, George B. 500
Bacon, Thomas R. 1181, 1182
Bagehot, Walter 463, 537, 904, 3901
Bailey, Albert Edward 1939
Bailey, Leslie George 4609, 4696, 4697
Bailey, William Whitman 2323
Bakaya, K.N. 3902
Baker, Arthur Ernest 2756, 2809, 3145
Baker, Christopher P. 4982
Baker, F.T. 4916
Baker, H. 2744
Baker, Joseph E. 3858
Baker, Myron Eugene 2041
Baker, William 4917
Baldini, Gabriele 3913
Ball, Donald 3497
Ball, Patricia M. 3806, 4065, 4680
Bannard, T. 2745
Barera, Eugenio 1898
Baret, Adrien 1146, 1697(?)
Barfoot, C.C. 4240, 4439, 4623, 4698, 4771
Barker, Francis 4826
Barker, George 3606, 3727
Barksdale, Richard K. 3649
Barnes, S.D. 2169
Barnett, Gail Zech 4349
Barot, Odysse 774
Barrett, Elizabeth see Browning, Elizabeth Barrett
Barry, E. Milner 743
Barry, William 2557
Barthélemy, A. 2043
Basch, F. 3703
Baskerville, W.M. 1963
Basler, Roy P. 3349, 3375, 3404

Bates, Charlotte Riske 1115
Bateson, Frederick W. 3210, 3448, 3704
Batho, Edith 3265
Battaglia, Francis Joseph 3973
Baugh, Albert C. 3406
Baum, Paull Franklin 3405, 3454, 3600, 3728, 3807
Baumann, Hermann 2736
Bausenwein, Joseph 2769
Baxter, Wynne E. 538
Bay, J. Christian 3286
Bayley, John 4440, 4844, 4983, 5041
Bayne, Peter 441, 459, 881, 882, 883, 884, 885, 886, 887, 888, 889, 890, 891, 905, 1814
Bayne, Thomas 1261, 1366, 1431, 2106, 2468, 2848
Bayne, W. 2849
Beach, Constance L. 3119
Beach, Joseph Warren 3240, 3557
Beale, Dorothea 1432
Beatty, Arthur 1815
Beaver, Dorothy M. 3217
Beck, Georg 3097, 3120
Beck, Warren 3607
Bede, Cuthbert pseud. for Bradley, Edward (see)
Beeching, Henry Charles 1183, 2960
Beer, Gillian 3914
Beerbohm, Max 2944
Beers, Henry Augustin 1147, 2027, 2215
Belcher, Margaret E. 4845
Belden, Daniel Morgan, Jr. 4428
Beljame, Al 2216
Bell, A. 4624
Bell, A.F. 2790
Bell, Robert 4, 13
Bellezza, Paolo 1799, 1816, 1860
Bellinger, Rossiter R. 3418
Belrose, Louis, Jr. 1171
Bender, Elaine 4214
Benn, Alfred William 2411
Bennett, James B. 3915
Bennett, James R. 4984, 5057
Bennett, William Cox 321, 1172, 1184
Bense, J.F. 2636
Bensly, Edward 2774, 2910, 3126
Benson, Arthur Christopher 2343, 3022
Benson, Edward Frederic 3098
Benton, Richard P. 3808
Benziger, James 3751
Berdan, J.M. 2813

Bergman, Herbert 3455, 3558
Bergonzi, Bernard 4131, 4408
Berlin, James Arthur 4610
Bernstein, Ethel 3277
Berry, Francis 3752
Bertoni, Giulio 3127
Bertram, James 4294
Beusse, Jeffrey Henry 4520
Bevington, Merle M. 3559, 3666
Bicknell, P.F. 2694
Binyon, Lawrence 2978
Bird, W.H.B. 3203
Birney, L.J. 2850
Birrell, Augustine 2945
Birrell, Francis 3061
Bischoff, Brigitte 4699
Bishop, Jonathan 3763
Bishop, Morchard 4158
Bixby, James T. 1301
Black, William George 1074
Blackburne 467
Blackmur, R.P. 3498
Blair, D. 593, 653, 702
Blake, Warren Barton 2558, 2695
Blakeney, E.H. 1434, 1435, 1661, 3419
Blanloeil, A. 1038
Bleibtreu, Karl 1436, 2961
Blémont, Emile 703
Blennerhassett, C. de L. 2107, 2823
Block, Louis James 1882, 1915
Bloom, Harold 4208, 4681
Blore, George Henry 2890
Blos, Ernst 3099, 3121
Blunden, Edmund 3075, 3695
Boardman, Steven 4760
Boas, Frederick Samuel 2931
Boas, Guy 3000
Boase, Frederic 2217
Boddington, O.-E. 3268a
Boedeker, Augusta 2044
Boegner, André 2385, 2398
Boguslawsky, Amalie K. 2559
Bolton, Sarah (Knowles) 1290
Bond, W.H. 3617
Bonner, Arnold Frank 4761
Bonnerot, Louis 3269, 3608, 3809
Bonney, William W. 5058
Boodle, R.W. 980, 1229
Boos, Florence S. 4848
Booth, Bradford A. 3560
Bordes, Elsie M. 2696
Bornstein, George 5114
Boss, Eleanor 3100
Boswell, R. Bruce 1438
Boucher, L. 824
Bouchier, Jonathan 594, 606, 704, 892, 893, 1155, 1230, 1231,

2045, 2172
Bouchor, Maurice 1700
Bourdillon, Francis William 1439, 1662
Bovey, John 4531
Bowden, Marjorie Moreland (Sansom) 3101
Bowen, Robert Adger 1968
Bowker, R.R. 1232
Bowman, Mary Virginia 3409
Boyd, John Douglas 4071, 4357, 4700, 4701, 4849
Boyd, Julian 4773
Boyd, Zelda 4773
Boynton, Henry Walcot 2560
Brachvogel, Udo 1916
Bradbury, Godfrey Fox 3171
Bradbury, Malcolm 4336, 4338
Bradley, Andrew Cecil 2218, 2524, 2835, 3076, 3195
Bradley, E.T. 1440
Bradley, Edward 573, 700, 701, 914, 1073, 1228, 2711
Bradley, J.L. 4159, 4242
Brandl, Alois 1441, 2662
Brantlinger, Patrick 4441, 4747, 4985
Brashear, William R. 3664, 3859, 4084, 4132, 4748
Breachan 514
Breen, Jennifer 4532
Bremond, Henri 2561
Brew, Claude C. 4311
Brewer, E. Cobham 894, 895, 915, 916
Bricard, Georges 2046
Brie, Friedrich 3236
Brightwell, D. Barron 630, 645, 917
Brimley, George 322, 450
Briney, John O. 4350
Brinton, D.G. 444
Bristed, Charles Astor 100, 134
Britton, John 3729
Broadus, Edmund Kemper 2919
Brodribb, C.W. 3159
Brody, George M. 739, 784
Brooke, Stopford Augustus 1442, 1800, 2306
Brookfield, Charles 2386
Brookfield, Frances Mary 2386, 2412
Brookfield, Mrs. W.H. 1819
Brooks, Cleanth 3350, 3385
Brooks, Elbridge Streeter 1663, 2138
Brooks, F.T. 2757
Brotherton, Mary 2344
Brown, Alan Willard 3386
Brown, Anna Robertson 1443

Brown, Calvin S. 1940, 1969
Brown, James Bucham 879, 900, 4002
Brown, John 252
Brown, Lloyd W. 4625
Brown, Stephen J. 3128
Brown, T.J. 3810, 3860
Browne, Irving 1444
Browne, W.H. 706, 744, 790
Browning, Elizabeth Barrett 90, 1861, 1941, 2088, 2872
Browning, Oscar 2622
Browning, Robert 2088, 2891, 3475
Browning, Robert B. 2088
Browning, Orestes A. 192
Bruce, Harold 2851
Brule, A. 3160
Bruns, Gerald L. 4358, 4850, 5060
Bryan, J. Ingram 3102
Bryant, Hallman B. 5059
Bryden, Robert 2089
Buchan, T. Winter 1262
Buchanan, Robert Williams 707, 735, 1173, 1445
Buckler, William E. 3561, 4409, 4963, 4986
Buckley, Jerome H. 3476, 3641, 3696, 3705, 3861, 3956, 4029, 4774, 5061
Buckley, Reginald R. 2746
Buckley, W.E. 953, 954, 955, 1041, 1303, 1367
Buckley, William K. 4987
Bucknill, John Charles 327
Bufkin, Ernest C. 3862
Bullen, A.H. 791
Bulwer-Lytton, Edward 21, 114
Burch, Francis F. 3811
Burchell, Samuel C. 3523, 3588
Burke, Margaret Mary 3042
Burnam, Tom 3499
Burne-Jones, Georgiana 2345
Burnet, Archie 4988
Burnshaw, Stanley 4209
Burroughs, John 1701
Burton, Katherine 3129
Burton, Richard 1702
Burton, Thomas Glen 3960, 4133, 4138, 4626
Bury, J.B. 2892
Bush, Douglas 3218, 3254, 3331, 3420, 3449, 3667
Busskohl, James Lester 4223
Bussmann, Ernst 2836, 2844
Butcher, S.H. 2562
Butler, Arthur G. 2430

Butler, Fanny Kemble 92
Butler, H. Montagu 1394
Byatt, A.S. 4134
Byrne, M. St. Clare 3456

C., C.C. 453
C., T.C. 3279
Caclamanos, D. 3312
Cadbury, William 3812, 3916
Caine, Hall 1117, 2485
Caird, J.B. 4085
Callender, G. 3161, 3184
Calverley, Charles Stuart 736, 2712
Camerini, E. 654, 780
Cameron, A. Barry 4086
Cameron, H.H. Hay 1664
Cameron, Julia Margaret 781, 1664, 1665, 3023
Cameron, Kenneth Walter 3706, 4442
Cameron, P. 1917
Campbell, James M. 2893
Campbell, N.H. 4533
Campbell, Nancie 4334, 4339
Campbell, Nancy 4295
Campbell, Patrick 4443
Campion, G. Edward 4135, 4146
Cancel, Rafael A. 4359
Canebrake, Thomas 1185
Canham, Stephen 5115
Cannon, Garland 4243
Canton, William 1666, 1970, 2173
Capen, S.H.R. 2238
Carew, Peter 3376
Carlson, Alma S. 2321
Carlson, C. Lennart 3247
Carlson, Patricia Ann 4627
Carlyle, Jane Welsh 4749
Carlyle, Thomas 1118, 3103, 4749
Carpenter, William Boyd 1667, 2219
Carr, Arthur J. 3390, 3457, 3722
Carr, Joseph William Comyns 2486
Carr, Thomas 2852
Carrigan, Margaret 3451
Carroll, Lewis (pseud. for Charles Lutwidge Dodgson) 523, 2239, 2713
Carroll, R.A. 4989
Carruthers, Adam 2697
Carstensen, Broder 3452
Carter, John 3211, 3392, 4012
Cartwright, F.F. 3974
Cary, Elisabeth Luther 2028
Case, William Arthur 50
Caswell, C.J. 1304, 1368, 1369

Cattle, Frederic 1263
Caughran, Barbara Ferguson 4835
Cazamian, Madeleine L. 2962, 3255
Cervo, Nathan A. 4775, 4851
Challsteth, A. 574
Chakraborty, S. C. 4296, 4360
Chamberlain, N. H. 1020
Chandler, Alice 4030, 4160
Chapman, Edward Mortimer 2220
Chapman, Elizabeth Rachel 1148, 1214, 2637
Chapman, Raymond 4066
Charteris, Evan 3146
Chasles, Philarète 42
Chauvet, Paul 3147
Cheetham, Samuel 607
Cheney, John Vance 1305, 1395
Chepiga, Michael J. 4534
Cherbuliez, Victor see Valbert, G.
Chesson, Nora Hopper 2139
Chesterton, Gilbert Keith 2174, 2175, 2288, 2307, 2346, 2525, 2714, 2920, 3519
Chestnutt, J. 1447
Chevrillon, André 2501
Chew, Samuel Claggett 3287, 3406, 3421
Chiasson, E. J. 3562
Chignell, T. W. 969
Child, Mary 2502
Chimenti, Francesco 1942
Chivers, Thomas Holley 197
Choisy, Louis Frédéric 2675, 2737
Chorley, Henry Fothergill 52, 198, 199
Chretien, Charles Peter 173
Christ, Carol T. 4605, 4750
Christopher, J. R. 4536
Chubb, Edwin Watts 2758, 3024
Church, Alfred John 1353
Churchill, Robert Joseph 4909
Churchill, William 2526
Clark, Barbara Anne Roberts 4224
Clark, Henry William 2565
Clark, John Scott 2140
Clark, Thomas Arkle 2221
Clark, William 1971
Clarke, Austin 4136
Clarke, George Herbert 2698
Clarke, Helen A. 1704
Clarke, Henry V. 1449
Clarke, Hyde 825
Clarke, James Freeman 38
Clarke, Marcus 826
Clements, H. H. 117
Clifford, John R. S. 827, 851

Closs, A. 4161
Clough, Arthur Hugh 631
Clugston, Phil R. 3039
Cluysenaar, Anne 4682
Cobbe, Frances Power 1450
Cochrane, Robert 1215
Coffin, Lawrence Irving 4225
Cohen, J. M. 3422
Colbeck, Norman 3863
Cole, Samuel Valentine 1076, 1451
Coleman, A. I. de P. 2289
Coleridge, Henry N. 35
Coleridge, Sara 138
Coleridge, Samuel Taylor 35
Colley, Ann C. 4852, 4853
Collier, John 3172
Collier, William Francis 2141
Collins, John Churton 919, 956, 983, 1354, 2142, 2176, 2275, 2367, 2676
Collins, Joseph Johnson, Jr. 4226, 4444, 4445
Collins, L. C. 2677
Collins, Mortimer 2715
Collins, Philip 4537, 4538, 4990, 5042, 5116, 5117
Collins, Rowland L. 3730, 3764, 3813, 3814, 3848, 3864
Collins, Thomas J. 5118
Collins, Wilkie 336(?), 337(?)
Collins, Winston Lee 4087, 4147, 4446, 4539, 4702
Colville, Derek 4210
Colvin, Sidney 710, 984, 2824
Comley, Nancy R. 4854
Compton-Rickett, Arthur 2029
Conrad, Peter 4410
Conway, Moncure Daniel 1014, 1452, 2347
Cook, Albert S. 1370, 1371
Cook, E. Wake 2566
Cook, Edward 2873
Cooke, George Willis 1149
Cooke, John Esten 194
Cooledge, Charles Edwin 1291, 2716
Coombes, John 4826
Cooper, Alfred B. 2567
Cooper, Douglas Wayne 3961
Cooper, Robert M. 4211
Corbes, H. 3917, 3975
Cornish, Blanche (Ritchie) Warre 2932
Corson, Mrs. C. R. 530
Cotterill, H. B. 2308
Coupe, Charles 2325
Courthope, William John 745, 795, 2222

Cowan, James Alton 4692
Cox, Canon Adam 3458
Cox, James T. 4540
Coyle, Kathleen Mildred 4611
Crabbe, Katharyn Frances Wood 4612, 4855, 4856
Craggs, John 852
Cranch, Christopher Pearse 782
Crane, Walter 2449
Crawford, A.W. 2775
Crawford, James Slater, IV 4285
Crawford, John W. 4162, 4857
Crespi, Angelo 2568
Cressman, Edmund Dresser 3062
Croker, John Wilson 22
Cross, Ethan Allen 2427
Cross, Tom Peete 2933
Crossett, John 3589
Crum, Ralph B. 3148, 3154
Cruse, Amy 3001, 3230
Culler, Arthur Dwight 3865, 4502 4629, 4751, 5062, 5119
Culver, Marcia C. 5120
Cunliffe, John W. 3212
Cunningham, Allan 23
Currier, Mary M. 2240
Curtis, George William 341, 424(?), 541
Curzon, George Nathaniel 2791
Cushman, Keith 4299
Cusins, W.G. 906
Cuthbertson, Evan J. 2030

D., A.E. 3333
Dabbs, George 1973
d'Agata, Alfio 3377
Dahl, Curtis 3590, 3650, 4919
Daiches, David 3731
D'Albeville, J.W. 1461
Dale, Peter Allan 4991
Dallas, Eneas Sweetland 342
Daly, Joseph Francis 3035
Daniel, Maggie Browne 3582
Daniels, Earl 3084
D'Annunzio, G. 1462
Danzig, Allan Peter 3725, 3765, 3976, 4245
Darmesteter, Mary James 1463
D'Avanzo, Mario L. 4163
Davidson, H.A. 2223
Davidson, Thomas 1249
Davies, E.C. 4031
Davies, James 746
Davies, James A. 4777, 4992, 4993
Davies, Joseph J. 1372, 1826
Davies, Samuel D. 1710
Davies, Trevor H. 2874

Davies, W.W. 1464
Davis, Arthur Kyle, Jr. 3459, 3563
Davis, Derek R. 4448
Davray, Henry D. 2177, 2290, 2569, 2570
Dawson, Carl 4900
Dawson, Edwin Collas 2638
Dawson, George 1216
Dawson, Samuel Edward 1015
Dawson, William James 1292, 2090, 2413
Day, Aidan 4994, 4995, 4996, 5063, 5064, 5065, 5121, 5122, 5123, 5124
Dearmer, Geoffrey 3013
Deatrick, W. Wilburforce 2571
De Blowitz 1466
Dees, R.R. 747
Deily, Robert H. 3241
Déjob, Ch. 2178
de Laprade, Victor 646
de la Mare, Walter 3118, 3288
DeMott, Benjamin 3754, 3766
de P., F. 1467
de Selincourt, Aubrey 3601
de Sélincourt, Ernest 2792
Dessommes, Georges 2241
DeVane, Mabel Phillips 3289
DeVane, William Clyde 3289, 3424
de Vere, Aubrey 174, 1468, 1469, 1470, 1711
Devey, Joseph 737
Devlin, Francis Patrick 4072, 4362, 4630
De Witt, A. 1712
de Wyzewa, Téodor 1471, 1899
Dhaleine, L. 2387, 2399
d'Haussey, Baron 24
Dhruva, A.B. 2837
Dickinson, Thomas H. 2838
Dicksee, Herbert 1296
Didier, Eugene L. 1042, 2242
Diehl, John Dornfield 3962
Dierckx, J. 3767
Dieter, Ferdinand 1473
Dietrich, Manfred 4703
Dillard, Philip Edward 4613
Dilligan, Robert 4997
Dillon, D.A. 4631, 4778
di Silvestri-Falconieri, Francesco 2652
Ditsky, John M. 4363
Dixon, Hepworth 343, 542
Dixon, James Main 2664, 2867, 2894, 2934
Dixon, William Macneile 1801, 1900, 2678

Dobranz, Gisela 2976
Dobrée, Bonamy 3265
Dobson, Alban 3050
Dobson, Austin 712, 1474, 2717
Dodds, M. H. 3313
Dodgson, Charles Lutwidge see
    Carroll, Lewis
Dodsworth, Martin 4137
Döllen, Dr. 344
Donahue, Mary Joan 3374, 3410,
    3425, 3426
Donegan, Sylvia Eugenie 3179
Donoghue, Denis 4067
Donohoe, Thomas A. 3963
Doran, John 467
Dorchester, Daniel, Jr. 1883
Doré, Gustave 586, 587, 588, 589,
    603
Dorsey, Anna Vernon 1233
Douady, Jules 2679
Doveton, F. B. 2470
Dowden, Edward 608, 631a, 875,
    1189, 1225, 1475, 1901, 2414
Drake, Constance 4364
Draper, Anita B. 4920
Draper, Ronald P. 4541
Draycott, Charles 2111
Drew, Mary (Gladstone) 2989
Drew, Philip 3866, 3867, 4411
Drinkwater, John 2963, 2964
Dronsart, M. 1919, 1975
Drury, Charles 2326
Duboc, C. E. see Waldmueller, R.
Duclaux, Mary see Darmesteter,
    Mary James
Dudley, Arthur 425
Duncan, Edgar Hill 3668, 4138
Duncan-Jones, Katherine 4300
Dunn, Richard J. 4998
Dunne, Marie Aloysia 2572
Dunsany, Lord 3460
Dupuy, Ernest 2801
Durant, Jack M. 4966
Durham, Margery Stricker 4704
Durrell, Lawrence 3493
Dutoit, M. 2179
Duyckinck, Evert A. 44, 55
Dwight, John Sullivan 41, 140
Dyboski, Roman 2369, 2400, 2450
Dyneley, Mortimer 1159
Dyson, A. E. 4278
Dyson, Hope 4220, 4608

Eagle, Solomon pseud. for Squire,
    John Collings (see)
Eagleton, Terry 4826
Earle, John Charles 853

Earls, M. 3219
Earnest, Ernest 3362
Eaton, Richard Bozman 4449
Eckhardt, E. 2911
Edgar, Irving 4335
Edgar, Pelham 2504
Edwards, P. D. 4779
Egan, Maurice Francis 1122,
    1480, 2415
Eggenschwiler, David Lee 3906
Eggers, John Philip 3977, 4073,
    4276
Ehrenpreis, Anne Henry 4922
Ehrsam, Theodore George 3241,
    3248
Eichler, Rolf 4683, 4752
Eidson, John Olin 3305, 3328,
    3477, 3564, 3609, 3868, 3869,
    3870, 3918, 3919, 4088
Eitel, Edmund Henry 2729
Elgee, Jane Francesca see Wilde,
    Jane Francesca Elgee
Eliot, George (pseud. for Mary
    Ann Evans) 355
Eliot, T. S. (Thomas Stearns
    Eliot) 3242, 3243
Ellacombe, H. N. 2665
Elledge, W. Paul 4341
Elliot, Arthur 1884
Elliott, J. J. 1715
Elliott, Philip Lovin, Jr. 3651,
    3669, 3800, 3815, 3920, 3921,
    4032, 4089, 4246, 4301, 4827,
    4923, 5066, 5142
Ellis, A. S. 2048
Ellis, Stewart Marsh 2968
Ellison, Edith Nicholl 2416
Ellmann, Mary Joan 3461, 3462
Elsdale, Henry 845, 876
Elton, Oliver 2276, 2451, 2777,
    2896, 2965, 2990, 3196
Elvin, Laurence 4450
Emerson, G. R. 575
Emerson, Oliver Farrar 2802,
    2825
Emerson, Ralph Waldo 87
Emery, Clark 3351
Engbretson, Nancy Martina 3856,
    3871, 3978
Engel, H. 2935
Engelberg, Edward 3591
Engen, R. 5067
England, Eugene 4705
Enzensberger, Christian 4139
Eric, George 1178
Erskine, John 2811
Esch, Robert Morley 4693
Escott, Thomas Hay Sweet, 1160,
    2049

Esher, Viscount 3610
Estrich, Robert M. 3494
Etienne, Louis 296, 503
Evans, Benjamin Ifor 3185, 3197,
  3290, 3547
Evans, Charles 3502
Evans, Howard 1082
Evans, Mary Ann see Eliot,
  George
Evans, Morris Owen 2946
Everett, Charles Carroll 504, 1717,
  2224
Ewart, Gavin 4247
Ewbank, David R. 4780
Ewer, Ferdinand C. 357
Ewing, Thomas J. 1309

F. 298
Faas, Egbert 4503
Fabreguet, Philippe 4706
Faggi, A. 3085
Faguet, Emile 2574
Fain, John Tyree 3503
Fairchild, Hoxie Neale 3014, 3393,
  3427, 3621
Fall, Christine 3294, 3629a, 4016,
  4366
Fambri, Paulo 1023
Farrar, Frederick William 1482,
  1944
Fass, Barbara 4707
Fass, I. Leonard 3922
Faulkner, D. R. 4858
Fausset, Hugh I'Anson 2966, 3130,
  3186, 3314, 3387
Faverty, Frederic E. 4542
Fehr, Bernhard 3002
Felton, Cornelius C. 61
Fenn, Alice Maude 1024
Ferguson, De Lancey 3732
Ferguson, John 4164
Ferrell, Mary Key Wynne 4521
Ferrero, M. 2967
Fertel, Randy J. 5068
Fichter, Andrew 4451
Ficker, Georg 2348
Fielding, Kenneth J. 4632, 4749
Fields, Annie (Adams) 1718,
  1827, 1902
Figueroa, John J. 4504
Filby, P.W. 4090
Filon, Augustin 1123, 1483, 1885,
  2575
Finch, F. M. 175
Findlay, Leonard M. 4302, 4924,
  5069
Finlayson, Thomas Campbell 1668

Fischer, Arthur H. 4286
Fischer, Heinrich 314
Fischer, Thomas A. 2091, 2388
Fischer, W. 3043
Fisher, Charles 2050, 2180
Fisher, George P. 256
Fitch, George Hamlin 2680
Fitzhopkins 610
Fitzhugh, Harriet Lloyd 3231
Fitzhugh, Percy R. 3231
Fleissner, Robert F. 4303, 4452,
  4505, 4633, 4859, 5000
Fletcher, Pauline 4925
Fletcher, Robert Huntington 2471,
  2718
Flynn, Philip 4926
Foakes, Reginald Anthony 3642
Fontana, Ernest 4634, 4635
Foote, G.W. 970
Forbes, William 4033
Ford, Boris 3644
Ford, C. Lawrence 2051, 2052,
  2112
Ford, Ford Madox 4367
Ford, George H. 3346
Forgues, E.D. 125, 495
Forker, Charles R. 3670
Forman, Harry Buxton 658, 685,
  1862
Formentin, C. H. 1485
Formont, M. 1110
Forshaw, Charles F. 1486
Forster, John 25, 62, 145, 208,
  360
Forster, Joseph 2031
Forsyth, R. A. 3872
Fortune, Ronald John 4762
Fowler, H. Ramsey 4636
Fowler, William J. 1487
Fox, Arthur W. 2527
Fox, William Johnson 8, 26, 98,
  361
Francis, Beata 1669
Francis, Elizabeth Ahlgren 4227,
  4708, 4964
Frank, Maude Morrison 2793
Franklin, H.C.T. 2291
Franklin, Stephen Lyle 4429
Franzese, Anthony Joseph 4763
Fredeman, William E. 3873, 4091,
  4248, 4368, 5043
Freedland, H.W. 442
Freeman, James A. 4453
Frend, Grace Gilchrist 3086
Fricke, Douglas C. 4543
Fricke, Donna G. 4249
Friedman, Albert B. 3411
Friedman, Norman 4637
Friesen, Edward Henry 4910

Friswell, James Hain 647, 687
Friswell, Laura Hain see
  Myall, Laura Hain Friswell
Frodsham, George H. 2794
Frost, William 3378
Fruit, John Phelps 1310
Fuchs, R. 1234
Fucilla, Joseph G. 3280
Fulford, William 428
Fuller, Gerry William 4694
Fuller, Hester Thackeray 3198
Fuller, Margaret 45, 63
Fuller, Roy 3768
Fullerton, John 659
Fulweiler, Howard W. 3816, 3923
Furnivall, Frederick James 714,
  748
Fuson, Ben W. 3379, 4034
Füting, Adolf 3173, 3180
Fyson, George E. 2699

G., C.A.L. 749
Gabrielli, Annibale 2886
Gadziola, David Stanley 4074
Gage, Minot G. 1264
Gaglio-Morana, V. 3199
Galimberti, Alice 2921
Gallagher, Edward J. 4092
Gallant, Christine 4709
Gallas, K.R. 3187
Galton, Arthur 1111
Gannett, William Channing 2292,
  2293
Gannon, Nicholas J. 293
Garden, Francis 64
Gardiner, Robert F. 1190
Garnett, Richard 1490, 2307
Garrod, Herbert B. 1265
Gartlein, Carl W. 3950
Gaskell, Philip 4165, 4828
Gates, Barbara 4927
Gates, Lewis Edwards 1491, 2143,
  2181
Gatty, Alfred 496, 715, 750, 854,
  907, 957, 1025, 1191, 1373, 1492
Gatty, Margaret 429, 595
Gaultier, Bon pseud. for Aytoun,
  William Edmondstoune, and Mar-
  tin, Theodore (see)
Gawsworth, John 3478
Gent, Margaret 4336
Genung, John Franklin 1066, 2452
Gerhart, Robert Leighton 958
Gernsheim, Helmut 3407, 3463
Gettmann, Royal A. 3334
Gibbs, Lincoln R. 2747
Gibson, Mary Ellis 5070

Gibson, Walker 3652
Gilbert, Elliot L. 5143
Gilbert, Levi 2309
Gilbert, William S. 1067
Gilchrist, Herbert Harlakenden
  1174
Gilder, Richard Watson 1495, 2487
Gilfillan, George 103, 126, 181,
  443
Gill, W.K. 2182
Gill, W.W. 3237
Gillen, Francis 4454
Gillet, Louis 3162
Gillett, Peter Joseph 4522, 4781
Gilmour, Robin 4928
Gingell, W.H. 2912
Gingerich, Solomon Francis 2549,
  2653
Giordano, Frank R., Jr. 4782
Giordano-Orsini, G.N. 3015, 3051
Girardini, Emilio 2875
Gissing, A.C. 3052
Gissing, George Robert 3052
Giuliano, A. 2453
Gladstone, William Ewert 363(?),
  471, 908, 1175, 1192, 1311,
  2488, 2759
Glasser, Marvin 3762
Gliserman, Susan M. 4430, 4638
Glowka, Arthur Wayne 5071
Godwin, Edward William 1863
Goff, B.M. 4860
Going, William T. 4684
Goldberg, J. Philip 3817
Goldfarb, Clara R. 4829
Goldfarb, Russell M. 4212, 4829
Golffing, Francis 3979
Gomont, Henri Augustin 560, 564
Goode, John 4093
Goodman, Paul 3548
Gordan, John D. 3611, 3630
Gordon, George Angier 2528
Gordon, William Clark 2417, 2428
Goslee, David Frederick 4019,
  4455, 4544, 4639, 4710
Gosse, Edmund William 922, 1266,
  1497, 1670, 1976, 2053, 2681,
  2887, 3053
Gossman, Ann 3671
Gostwick, Joseph 783
Gould, George M. 2632
Govil, O.P. 3980
Gower, Ronald Sutherland 1039
Graham, J.E. 2054
Graham, J.W. 2505
Graham, Peter Anderson 1355,
  1374
Grandsen, K.W. 3849, 4369
Grant, Charles 570

Grant, Stephen Allen 3769
Granville-Barker, Harley 3077, 3087, 3088
Grappe, Georges 2576
Grattan, Robert Merle 4228, 4370
Graves, Alfred Perceval 1977, 2719, 2853
Gray, Donald J. 3733
Gray, J. M. 3924, 3981, 3982, 4035, 4097, 4098, 4140, 4166, 4250, 4251, 4252, 4253, 4277, 4304, 4305, 4306, 4371, 4372, 4456, 4506, 4507, 4508, 4545, 4640, 4641, 4711, 4783, 4861, 4929, 5072
Gray, James Martin 4965
Gray, Jon M. 4094, 4095, 4096
Gray, W. Forbes 2795
Grebanier, Frances see Winwar, Frances
Green, David Bonnell 3483, 3707
Green, Jane 3270
Green, Joyce M. 3484, 3552
Green, S. G. 1161, 1489(?)
Greenberg, Mark L. 5125
Greenberg, Robert A. 3612
Greene, Graham 3259
Greene, Michael E. 5001, 5002
Gregory, D. S. 2113
Grendon, Felix 2431, 2472
Greswell, William 1396
Gridley, Roy 3770, 3925
Grierson, Herbert John Clifford 2810, 3260, 3347, 3348
Griffiths, David N. 4373
Griggs, Edward Howard 2418
Grigson, Geoffrey 3755, 4167, 4642, 4712, 4862, 5003, 5004
Grindon, Leopold Hartley 1217
Griswold, Hattie Tyng 1176, 1498, 2032
Griswold, Rufus W. 65
Grob, Alan 3874
Groom, Bernard 3274, 3578, 4213
Grønbech, Vilhelm 3903
Gross, John 3771
Grosskurth, Phyllis 3926, 4457
Groth, Ernst 1375
Grove, George 576, 577
Grumbach, D. 4784
Grünert, Louis 2720, 2738
Gullason, Thomas Arthur 3653
Gummere, Francis B. 2490
Gunsaulus, Frank Wakeley 2454
Gunter, Garland Otho 3964, 4307, 4546, 4685
Gunter, Richard 4036
Gurteen, Stephen Humphreys Villiers 1864

Gutbier, Elisabeth 3174, 3181
Gwynn, Frederick L. 3485, 3504
Gwynn, Stephen Lucius 1828, 1978, 2092

H. 454
H., J. 367
Haas, Kenneth William, Jr. 4229
Hacker, John G. 3104
Haddakin, Lilian 3565
Haddow, R. 1829
Hadley, James 176, 738
Hagen, J. O. 829
Hagen, June Steffensen 4287, 4458, 4459, 4643, 4644, 4645, 4863, 4901, 4930, 4931, 5005
Haight, Elizabeth Hazelton 2183
Haight, Gordon S. 3394
Haines, C. R. 2854
Hair, Donald S. 5044
Hale, Edward Everett 368
Hale, Edward Everett, Jr. 1722
Hales, John W. 1500, 1671
Halio, Jay L. 3734
Hall, Basil 2327
Hall, P. E. 4374
Hall, Roland 3818
Hallam, Arthur Henry 9, 1672, 1865, 3329, 5044a
Halperin, Maurice 3149, 3155
Halsband, Robert 3524
Halsey, F. W. 1501
Halsey, John J. 1723
Hamann, Albert 1162, 1172
Hamann, Helmut 2909
Hamer, Douglas 4037
Hamerton, Philip Gilbert 524
Hamilton, Walter 877, 1068
Handly, John Marks 2294
Haney, John Louis 2349, 2577, 2578
Hankin, St. John 2350
Hardie, Martin 2473
Hardie, William 3927
Hardin, M. C. 1920
Harding, Bruce S. C. 4375
Hardman, William 2968
Hardwick, J. C. 3428
Hare, Julius C. 129
Harford-Battersby, D. 2184
Hargrave, Harry Allen 3965, 4376, 4547, 4966
Hargrove, Nancy D. 4548
Harland, Catherine R. 5126
Harris, Jack 5144
Harrison, Antony H. 5073
Harrison, Frederic 1724, 2144, 2328, 2419, 2579, 2682

Harrison, James 4308, 4377, 4646
Harrison, Thomas P., Jr. 3317
Harrold, C.F. 3412
Harrs, R. 4549
Hart, John S. 214
Hart-Davis, Rupert 3759
Hartman, Joan E. 3673
Hartsock, E. 3131
Harwell, Thomas M. 4423
Hasell, Elizabeth J. 472, 544,
  799, 1124
Hatcher, Anna 3798
Hatton, Joseph 1294, 1725
Haultain, Arnold 2506
Havens, Charles E. 369
Haweis, Hugh Reginald 688, 1295
Hawkins, Frederick 1125
Hayes, J.W. 2351, 2528a
Hayne, William H. 1502
Hayward, Abraham 689, 948
Healy, Emma Therese 3592
Healy, John 896
Hearn, Lafcadio 2811, 3003, 3036,
  3303
Hearnshaw, Fossey John Cobb 2855
Hecht, Maria 3330
Hegner, Anna 3150, 3156
Hellstrom, Ward 4337, 4864, 5074
Helsinger, Elizabeth K. 4713
Helterman, Jeffrey 4550
Henderson, Philip 4830
Henderson, Stephen Evangelist 3665,
  3875
Hendrick, George 3614
Hendrickson, L. 526
Hengelhaupt, Margrit 3151, 3157
Henley, William Ernest 2489
Henry, H.T. 2055
Heraud, Edith 878
Herford, Oliver 2145
Heron, Robert Matthew 1083
Hess, M. Whitcomb 3673
Hesse, Gerhard 3246
Hester, M. Thomas 4966
Hervey, T.K. 279
Hetherington, H.J.W. 2993
Heywood, J.C. 846
Higgs, William 1314
Hill, F. 4551, 4647, 4785, 4865
Hill, Frank Ernest 3096
Hill, James Lewis 3907, 4099
Hill, N.W. 2580
Hill, Robert W. 4347
Hillis, Newell Dwight 2093
Hilton, Arthur Clement 751
Himes, John A. 752
Hinchman, Walter Swain 2490
Hinckley, Henry B. 2056

Hinton, Ernestine Gibson 4523
Hirsch, Gordon D. 4254
Hirst, Henry B. 149
Hixson, J.C. 4648
Hixson, Jerome Canady 2991
Hoare, Barnard George 2474, 2475
Hobson, Anthony Robert 4967
Hobson, William A. 2856
Hodell, Charles W. 2114, 2581
Hodgkins, Louise Manning 1866
Hodgson, Geraldine E. 2876
Hodgson, S.H. 971
Hoeveler, Diane Long 5075
Hoffman, Richard L. 4341
Hogben, John 1084
Hoge, James Otey, Jr. 4230,
  4378, 4460, 4518, 4649, 4714,
  4715, 4786, 4866
Hollander, John 4650
Holling, T.E. 2857
Hollis, Valerie Ward 3966
Holloway, John 3566, 4168, 4753
Hollowell, J. Hirst 1026
Holmes, Mabel Dodge 2922, 2929
Homans, Margaret 4932
Honan, Park 4933
Hood, Thomas (the younger) 2721
Hooper, Joseph 1045
Hope, Henry Gerald 2057
Hopkins, Kenneth 3549
Hopkins, Manley 151, 258, 275(?)
Hopkinson, D.M. 4100
Hornback, Bert G. 4101
Horne, Colin J. 4867
Horne, Richard Henry 90
Horton, Robert Forman 2146
Hoskyns-Abrahall, J. 1085, 1193
Hough, Graham 3395, 3486, 3735,
  4831
House, Humphrey 3429, 3579
Hovey, Richard B. 3819
Howard, R. 5076
Howarth, R.G. 3352
Howe, Mark Antony de Wolfe 3044,
  3203
Howe, Merrill Levi 3220
Howell, A.C. 3249
Howells, William Dean 662, 716,
  800, 856, 924, 1867
Howitt, William 123, 152
Hoyt, Arthur S. 1726, 2992
Hubbard, Elbert 2310
Hübel, Eleanora 3583
Hübel, Rudolf 2760, 2770
Huckel, Oliver 2722
Hudson, Derek 3430, 3431
Hudson, J. 2639
Huebenthal, John 3928

Huffman, Clarence 3631
Hughes, A. M. D. 2761
Hughes, Linda Kay 4695, 4787, 4788, 4934, 4935, 4936, 4937, 5127
Hulme, Peter 4826
Hume, Robert D. 4169
Humphreys, A. R. 4170
Hunt, John Dixon 4214, 4255, 4278, 4338, 4412, 4686
Hunt, Leigh 10, 66, 218
Hunt, Theodore Whitfield 1979, 2058, 2762
Hunter, J. 5077
Hunter, W. 4552, 4651
Hunter, William A. 3266, 3267
Hussain, Syed Muzaffer 4379
Hutchinson, J. 753
Hutton, Laurence 1267
Hutton, Richard Holt 717, 820, 847, 1163, 1268, 1802, 1921(?), 2420
Hutton, William Holden 3163
Huxley, Thomas Henry 1504
Huxter, E. W. 3820

Inge, William Ralph 2947, 2948
Ingleby, C. Mansfield 280
Inglis-Jones, Elisabeth 3850
Ingram, John K. 590
Inman, Billie Jo 4102
Innes, Arthur Donald 1673
Irons, J. 4938
Irving, Laurence 3479
Irving, Walter pseud. for Brody, George M. (see)

J. 377
Jablow, Betsy Lynn 4836
Jack, Albert E. 2059, 2115, 2244, 2448
Jackson, R. 4868
Jacobs, Joanne Ciske 4911
Jacobs, Joseph 1397, 1507, 1868
Jacottet, Henri 1236
Jacquart, Rolland R. 3065
Jagger, Hubert 2923
Jahn, E. M. 4461
Jähne, Anne-Marthe 3553
James, A. 1194
James, Charles Canniff 2583, 2623
James, David G. 3464
James, Henry 802, 2491
James, Louis 3821
Jamieson, Paul F. 3505
Japiske, Cornelia Geertrui Hendrika 3025, 3028

Japp, Alexander Hay see Page, H. A.
Jarratt, F. 2116
Jebb, R. C. 611, 803(?), 831(?), 2455
Jeffares, A. N. 4789
Jelinek, Heinrich 2499
Jellinghaus, Paul 2389, 2401
Jenkins, Elizabeth 4509
Jenkinson, Arthur 1398
Jennings, Henry James 1069, 1886
Jennings, James George 2796
Jennings, M. G. 3983
Jennings, Richard 3066
Jerdan, William 14, 68, 153, 221
Jerman, Bernard 4380
Jerome, Jerome Klapka 1218
Jerram, C. S. 2329
Jerrold, Walter 1981, 2711, 2712, 2713, 2715, 2721, 2724, 2725, 2726, 2730, 2733
Jessup, A. 2245
Jiriczek, Otto Luitpold 2584, 3030
John, Brian 3984
John, K. 3525
Johnson, B. 2759
Johnson, Catherine B. 2390
Johnson, Edward Dudley Hume 3432, 3495, 3654, 3736, 4068, 4103
Johnson, L. 1508
Johnson, Reginald Brimley 2723, 3004
Johnson, Robert O. 3876
Johnson, Rossiter 1509
Johnson, T. H. 3737
Johnson, Wendell Stacy 3291, 3632, 4606
Johnston, Eileen T. 5078
Johnston, Priscilla Winthrop 4614, 4869
Jones, D. M. 1510
Jones, Frederick L. 3487
Jones, Gwyn 3433
Jones, Henry 2456, 2585, 2993
Jones, Howard Mumford 3674
Jones, Horace P. 4381
Jones, John 3708
Jones, John Bush 4870, 5006
Jones, P. M. 3195
Jones, Richard D. 1356, 1869, 1878
Jonson, G. C. Ashton 3164
Jordan, Elaine 4104, 4939
Joseph, Gerhard Joseph 3967, 4069, 4105, 4106, 4382, 4462, 4463, 4553, 4716, 4790, 4791, 4871, 4940, 5079, 5080, 5081

Jump, John D. 3488, 3567, 4013, 4107, 4383, 4413, 4510, 4717
Jusserand, Jules Jean 1870

Kabiljo-Sutić, Simha 4687
Kalisch, Carl 1674, 1693
Kalita, Dwight 4464
Kaplan, Fred 4171, 4872
Karkaria, R. P. 2246
Kashiwagi, Hideo 4873
Kassel, Charles 3031
Kauffman, Corinne Elizabeth 3801
Kaufman, Marjorie Ruth 3554
Kaul, R. K. 3902
Kay, Donald 4172
Kearny, Anthony 4941
Keeling, A. E. 1511
Kellner, Leon 2060, 2529, 2924
Kellogg, D. B. 1727
Kellogg, D. O. 1952
Kelly, J. 5082
Kemble, Fanny see Butler, Fanny Kemble
Kemble, John 663(?)
Kempling, W. Bailey 3132
Kendall, J. L. 3738, 4942
Kenig, Lea 4912
Kennedy, Ian Hodge Caldwell 4764, 4792, 4793, 4874
Kennedy, L. 3353
Kennedy, William Sloane 2061
Kenyon, Frederic G. 1941
Kenyon, James Banjamin 2062, 2225
Ker, William Paton 2530, 3005
Kerlin, Robert Thomas 2624, 2633
Kermode, F. 5007
Kern, Alfred Allan 2954
Kernahan, Coulson 2226
Killham, John 3643, 3655, 3697, 3698, 3772, 3877, 3929, 4141, 4309, 4414
Kilroy, James 4794
Kincaid, James R. 3930, 4173, 4384, 4554, 4607, 4795, 4875
King, Lauren Alfred 3122
King, R. W. 3773
King, William Henry 2925
Kingsley, Charles 222, 379, 460, 461, 1219
Kingsley, Maud Elma 2330, 2586, 2587
Kirby, William 3080
Kirk, M. L. 3175
Kirkwood, Kenneth Parker 3480
Kishi, Shigetsugu 3303
Kissane, James D. 3627, 3774, 3931, 4215, 4876

Kittelmann, Fritz H. 3295
Kitton, F. G. 1887
Klingopoulos, G. D. 3739
Knies, Earl A. 5083
Knight, G. Wilson 4279
Knight, Joseph 718
Knight, William 1903, 1982, 2352
Knoepflmacher, Ulrich Camillus 4555, 4756
Knowles, F. L. 2433
Knowles, James T. 664, 755, 1512, 1728, 1729
Knowles, Sarah see Bolton, Sarah
Knox, Ronald Arbuthnott 3105
Koeppel, Emil 1983, 2094, 2185
Kolb, Gwin Jackson, II 4351
Kolb, Jack 4556, 4652, 4718, 4796, 5008, 5044a
König, Robert 1513, 1830
Korg, Jacob 3656, 4719, 5045
Kostamlatský, Samuel 5084
Kotzin, Michael C. 4797
Kozicki, Henry James 3985, 4148, 4465, 4466, 4653, 4654, 4720, 4798, 4799, 4903, 5085, 5086
Krahmer, J. 2434
Kramer, Dale 4174
Kramer, Lawrence 5009
Kristinus, Heinrich 3040
Kuhns, Oscar 2353
Kwinn, D. 4467, 4557
Kynaston, Herbert 1730

L., S. R. 3067
la Cécilia, Jean 3068
Lagarde, Fernand 3986, 4108
Laird, Robert G. 4721, 4722
Lally, Mary Aquin 3802
Lambert, Agnes 1731
Lamia see Austin, Alfred
Lamont, Alexander 1269
Lancaster, H. H. 545
Landesberg, Frances H. 4175
Landow, George P. 4385, 4386, 4558, 4968
Lang, Andrew 804, 1984, 2227, 2247, 2724, 2969
Lang, Cecil Y. 4339, 5052
Lang, Leonora Blanche 2654, 2969
Langbaum, Robert 3555, 3622, 4216
Langford, Thomas A. 4256
Langsam, G. Geoffrey 3506
Larkin, P. 4176, 5010
Last, R. W. 4282
Lathrop, G. P. 990, 1086, 1087, 1733
Laughlin, Clara Elizabeth 2278, 2331

Laurent, Martha Long 3908
Lauvrière, Emile 2625, 2748
Lavabre, Simone 4257
Lawrenny, H. 666
Lawry, J.S. 3675
Layard, George Somes 1803
Lea, Henry Charles 94
Leach, Chester Raymond, Jr. 3968
Leach, T. 4655
Leary, T.H.L. 720
Leavis, Frank R. 3366
Lee, A.R. 4800
Lee, B.S. 4258
Lee, Ernest Dare 3054
Lee, George 2186
Lee, John 2064
Lee, W. 474
Lee, William Lamborn 4974
Leeper, Alex 2936
Lees, F.N. 4038
Lees, Frederic 2187
Le Gallienne, Richard 1522, 1523,
    1734, 1871, 2626, 2937, 3006
Leggett, B.J. 4259
Legris, Maurice 3932
Lehman, Herbert H. 4260
Lehmann, John 3756
Leisy, E. 3335
LeMire, Eugene D. 3987
Leonard, David Charles 4723, 4943
Leonard, R.M. 2711, 2712, 2713,
    2715, 2721, 2724, 2725, 2726,
    2730, 2733
Lepke, Arno 3391
LeRoy, Gaylord C. 3233
Lerner, Laurence D. 3593, 4559,
    4832, 5087
Lester, George 1270, 1318, 1357,
    1985, 1986
Leveloh, Paul 2531, 2550
Levey, Sivori 2897, 2898
Lewes, George Henry 225, 337(?)
Lewin, Lois S. 4177
Lewis, E. 3165
Lewis, Naomi 3623, 3657, 3775,
    4387
Lewis, Saunders 4310
Lewis, W. Aldersey 2370, 2700
Libera, Sharon Mayer 4560
Librach, Ronald S. 4656
Lier, W. 2371
Lillie, Lucy C. 1524
Lilly, William Samuel 1987, 2354
Lindsay, James 1904
Lintner, Robert Casper 2899
Littell, Philip 2803, 2877
Little, Charles J. 1238
Littledale, Harold 1675
Litz, Francis A. 3293

Litzinger, Boyd 3822
Livingston, Luther Samuel 2122,
    2228
Loane, George Green 3055, 3278,
    3281, 3297
Locker-Lampson, Frederick 2725
Lockhart, A.J. 2749
Lockhart, John Gibson 3152
Lockwood, Frank C. 2588
Lockyer, Joseph Norman 2627
Lockyer, Winifred L. 2627
Lodge, Oliver Joseph 2683
Loeppert, Theodore Walters 4288
Lohrli, Anne 5011
Loliée, Frédéric 1532
Long, Mason 3396
Longfellow, Henry Wadsworth 859
Looten, C. 1738, 2147
Lord, John 1897
Loudon, K.M. 2949
Lounsbury, Thomas Raynesford
    456, 1271, 2797
Lourie, Margaret A. 4944
Lovenheim, Barbara Irene 4231
Lowber, J.W. 2970
Lowell, James Russell 155, 549
Lozynsky, Artem 4755, 4759
Lucas, Frank Laurence 3106,
    3380, 3624
Lucas, John 4280, 5012
Luce, Morton 1676, 1872, 2069,
    2229, 2804, 2805
Lucy, Henry 2778
Ludlow, J.M. 476, 550, 579
Lumiansky, R.M. 3298
Lundquist, James Carl 4020
Lushington, Franklin 227
Lux, James 2589
Lyall, Alfred Comyns 1992, 2279
Lyall, William 897
Lynd, Robert 2926
Lynn, W.T. 2508
Lyon, William Henry 1399
Lyttleton, Arthur Temple 2355

M., J.L. 506
M., T.W. 3381
Mabbott, Thomas Ollive 3205,
    3356(?), 3357, 3413
Mabie, Hamilton Wright 1239,
    1544, 1545, 1993, 1994, 2509,
    2702
McAleer, Edward C. 3475
McAllister, Isabel G. 3010
McAlpin, Edwin Augustus 3056
MacArthur, James 1558
Macaulay, G.C. 1400, 1677, 1678
MacBeth, George 4217

McCabe, Joseph Martin 2900
McCabe, W. Gordon 2296
McCall, Joseph Darryl, Jr. 3646
MacCallum, Mungo William 1804
McCarron, William E. 4945
McCarthy, Justin Huntly 1559, 2311
MacColl, D.S. 2510
McCombie, F. 4039
McCorkindale, T.B. 2779
McCrie, George 785
McCullough, Joseph B. 4311
McDonald, G.D. 3536
MacDonell, A.G. 3069
McDonnell, A.C. 1945
MacEachen, Dougald B. 3658
MacEwen, V. 2684
Macey, Samuel L. 4969
McFee, Inez Nellie (Canfield) 3175
McGhee, Richard D. 4657
McGiffert, Margaret C. 1995
McGill, Anna Blanche 2197
Mackail, John William 1095, 2628, 3026
Mackay, Charles 807
Mackay, Eric pseud. for Eric, George (see)
Mackaye, Percy 2812
McKean, G.R. 3299
McKeehan, Irene Pettit 3032
McKeller, W.H. 2070
Mackerness, E.D. 5128
McKerrow, R.B. 3045
Mackie, Alexander 2421
Mackie, Gascoigne 2868
McLaine, Allan H. 4946
MacLaren, Malcolm 3740
McLuhan, H.M. 3489, 3699
McMaster, R.D. 3741
McMechan, Archibald McKellar 2492, 2511, 2763
Macmillan, Alexander 477
McMunn, William Robert 4075
Macnaughton, G.F.A. 3078
McNicoll, Thomas 513
Macphail, Alexander 2666
Macphail, W.M. 1401
Macquoid, Thomas R. 1560
McSweeney, Kerry 4468, 4561, 4562, 4724, 4801, 4802, 4877, 4947, 5013, 5046
Macy, John 3089
Madan, Geoffrey 3206
Madden, J.L. 4109
Madden, Lionel 4415, 4416, 4469
Madden, William A. 3662
Maddyn, D. Owen 478
Magnus, Laurie 2532, 3090
Magnus, Philip M. 3091

Magruder, Julia 2406
Maidment, Brian E. 4948, 5088
Mair, G.H. 2655
Malan, Edward 1047, 1131
Malbone, Raymond G. 4803
Malcolm, E.H. 833
Mallarmé, Stéphane 1546, 1946
Malloch, G.R. 2980
Mallock, William Hurrell 993, 1070, 2436
Mann, Robert James 415
Mansell, Kathryn 3221
Mantell, Deborah Byrd 4878
Manuel, J. 834
Marble, Annie Russell 2255, 2256
Marchand, Leslie A. 3304
Marcus, J. 4658
Margulies, David 2102
Marie, Rose 3336
Marks, Patricia 4949
Marshall, Ed 1326
Marshall, George O., Jr. 3584, 3633, 3676, 3677, 3723, 3742, 3776, 3795, 3823, 3824, 3988, 4178, 4261, 4511
Marshall, James see Mather, Marshall
Marston, John Westland 159, 229
Martin, David M. 4389, 4470
Martin, Edwin 1741
Martin, Robert Bernard 4659, 4660, 4804, 4805, 4970, 5014
Martin, Theodore 99, 644, 1288, 1289, 1293, 1548
Martin, Werner 2685, 2690
Mason, C. 1378
Mason, H.A. 4879
Mason, Michael Y. 4390, 5047
Massey, Gerald 262, 263, 388, 389
Massingham, Harold John 3172
Massingham, Hugh 3172
Masson, D. 1679
Masson, Gustave 479
Masterman, Charles Frederick Gurney 2148
Mather, F.J., Jr. 2333
Mather, Marshall (pseud. for James Marshall) 1402
Mathews, C.E. 1040
Mattes, Eleanor B. 3363, 3481
Mattheisen, Paul F. 3934, 5089
Matthews, B. 2827, 3033
Matthews, J. 1549
Matthews, William R. 3694
Matthiessen, F.O. 3367
Matthison, Arthur 696
Mauss, Aloisia 2952
Maxwell, Bennett 5015

Maxwell, J.C. 3573, 3933, 4179, 4312, 4661, 4725
Mayberry, George 3368
Mayhead, Robin 3644
Mayhew, A.L. 1048
Maynadier, Howard 2457
Mayne, R. 3777
Mayor, J.E.B. 230
Mayor, Joseph B. 1150, 2667
Mays, J.C.C. 3935
Mazzeno, Laurence W., III 4837, 4950
Meakin, Budgett 2123
Meehan, Francis 3308
Meinhold, George D. 4180
Meisel, Martin 4756
Meissner, L. 516
Melchiori, Giorgio 3936, 3937
Meldrum, Elizabeth 3434
Menand, Louis 5129
Mendilow, A.A. 3957
Mercer, Arthur 2590
Mercer, Colin 4826
Merivale, Charles 2033
Merivale, Judith Anne 2033
Mermin, Dorothy M. 4471
Merriman, James D. 4181
Metcalfe, C. 2703
Metcalfe, Priscilla 4391, 4971, 5016
Metzger, Lore 3825
Meyer, Wilhelm 2764, 2771
Meyers, C.J. 4806, 4880
Meyers, Terry L. 4662
Meyerstein, E.H.W. 3465, 3490
Meynell, Alice Christiana Thompson 2356, 2357, 2640, 2840
Mill, John Stuart 36
Millar, J.H. 1996
Millard, Charles W. 4472
Miller, Bessie Porter 1220
Miller, Betty 3568, 3569, 3594, 3634, 3659, 3678, 3709
Miller, Elliott Stuart 4232
Miller, Hugh 390(?)
Miller, J.C. 4663
Miller, J. Hillis 3826
Miller, Joaquin 1550
Miller, John Arthur 4524
Millgate, Michael 3679, 3989, 4424
Millhauser, Milton 3261, 3570, 3616, 3645, 3990, 4040, 4182, 4183, 4281
Milmed, Bella Kussy 3466
Milne, Fred L. 4392
Milnes, Richard Monckton 69
Milsand, Joseph 264, 509, 1680
Mims, Edwin 2258
Minckwitz, M.J. 2259
Minogue, Sally 4730, 5048

Mitchell, Charles 3878
Mitchell, P.M. 3903
Mitchell, William Richard 4149
Miyoshi, Masao 4142, 4184
Mizener, A. 3369
Moeton, P.J. 2780
Moews, Daniel D. 4110
Moffatt, J.S. 2884
Moggridge, M.W. 898
Moir, David M. 276
Möllmann, Adelheid 3107, 3123
Monod, S. 5017
Montabrut, Maurice 4726
Montégut, Emile 480, 580, 1250
Monteiro, George 4111
Monti, G. 1681
Mooney, Emory A., Jr. 3258, 3300, 3301, 3435
Moore, C. 4563
Moore, Carlisle 3827
Moore, Charles Leonard 2781, 2828
Moore, John Murray 1997, 2071, 2124, 2230
Moore, John Robert 2829, 3103, 3507
Moorman, Mary 4512
Moran, William Charles 3909
Mordell, G. 3021
More, Paul Elmer 2591, 2629, 2806, 2813
Morgan, Mary Louis 3182
Morin, E. 434
Moritz, Albert Frank 4615
Morr, Margaret 2981
Morris, Celia B. 4076, 4564
Morris, Christopher D. 4352
Morris, Lewis 1552
Morshead, E.D.A. 1092, 1093, 1094
Mortimer, Ray 3319, 3382
Morton, Edward Payson 2630, 2634
Moseley, W.M. 1998
Moses, Adolph 2312
Motion, A. 5018
Motter, T.H. Vail 3222, 3320, 3321, 3329, 3467, 4262
Moulton, Louise Chandler 1553, 1554
Mounger, Samuel Gwin 4431
Mount, C.B. 1379, 1555
Moxon, Thomas Allen 2841
Mozley, Anne 481
Mozley, J.R. 669
Mudge, J. 2125
Mühlefeld, Karl 2231
Mullany, Patrick Francis 1403
Müller, Erich Guenter 3012
Mulliner, Beatrice C. 2533, 2534
Munger, Theodore Thorton 2358

Munsterberg, Margaret 3355, 3595
Murray, J. Malton 2512
Murray, John 3397
Murray, Robert Fuller 2726
Musselwhite, David 4826
Mustard, Wilfrid Pirt 2072, 2073
  2095, 2126, 2198, 2359
Myall, Laura Hain Friswell 2422
Myers, E. 1050
Myers, Frederick William Henry
  1272, 1556, 1682, 1744

Napier, George G. 1404
Napier, Macvey 40(?)
Nash, Walter 4664, 4665, 5019
Neff, Emery 3436
Negri, Gaetano 1683, 2074, 2360
Nencioni, Enrico 998, 1029, 1051,
  1052, 1564, 1947
Neuberg, V. 4727
Neuner, Karl 2660
Newcomer, James 3991
Newdigate, B. H. 3223
Newton, J. M. 4728
Nichol, John 483
Nicoll, Allardyce 3416
Nicoll, Willaim Robertson 972,
  1861, 1862, 1865
Nicolson, Harold George 2971,
  3322, 3388, 3602
Niermeier, Stuart Fraser Cornelius
  4077, 4313, 4393
Niessl von Mayendorf, Erwin 1879
Nisbet, Mrs. Charles Richard 3057
Nishimae, Yoshimi 4185, 4807,
  4904, 4951
Nitchie, Elizabeth 2878, 2885
Nodelman, Perry Michael 4150
Noel, Roden Berkeley Wriothesley
  1132, 1151, 1565, 1566
Noland, Richard W. 4041
Nord, Martha Humphreys Andrews
  4765
Norst, Marlene J. 4282
North, Christopher (pseud. for John
  Wilson) 15, 16, 416
North, Ernest Dressel 1567
Northrup, Clark Sutherland 2831,
  3007
Nowell-Smith, Simon 3710, 3778,
  4112, 4186
Noyes, Alfred 2994, 3176, 3437,
  3438
Nutt, Alfred 1221

Oakley, J. H. I. 724
Oates, David Dean 4838

Oates, John 1805
O'Brien, D. 2127
O'Connor, T. P. 2513, 2782
O'Connor, V. C. Scott 2000
O'Connor, W. A. 1251
O'Hagen, Thomas 2149, 2535
Oliphant, Margaret O. W. 676,
  725, 1200, 1332, 1405, 1569
Olivero, Federico 2798, 2955,
  3008, 3262
Olshin, Toby A. 4169
Omond, T. S. 2913
O'Neill, James Norman 4616
Organ, Dennis Michael 4525, 4905
Ortensi, Ulisse 2201
Osborne, E. A. 3188
Osborne, Richard L. 4839
Osmond, Percy Herbert 2879
Ostriker, Alicia 4042
Otten, Terry Ralph 3969, 4340,
  5020
Ousby, Ian 4666
Owen, Cecil 2783, 2807

P., C. H. 571
P., H. W. 265
P., L. 3711
Pachori, Satya S. 4667
Packer, Lona Mosk 3879
Paden, William D. 3234, 3292,
  3309, 3338, 3358, 3370, 3371,
  3468, 3537, 3743, 3903, 3938,
  5090
Page, Curtis Hidden 3108
Page, H. A. (pseud. for Alexander
  Hay Japp) 561, 2391
Paget, R. H. 2262
Paget, Walter 1296
Pain, Barry 1406
Painter, F. V. N. 1750
Palgrave, Francis Turner 484,
  1570, 1948
Pallen, Condé Bénoist 1133, 2361
Pallis, Elisabeth Hude 2939
Palmer, David 4043, 4336, 4338,
  4411, 4412, 4413, 4414, 4416,
  4417, 4418, 4422, 4426, 4427,
  4686, 5091
Palmer, George Herbert 2865
Palmer, J. Foster 2641
Palmer, J. Luttrell 2859
Pancoast, Henry Spackman 2593
Pappas, John James 4078
Paradis, James 5045
Parker, Cheryl Leigh 4617
Parkin, George R. 2001
Parnell, John 1684

Parsons, Eugene 1273, 1332, 1380, 1407, 1572, 1838, 1929, 1930, 1931, 2076, 2150
Partington, Wilfred George 3275, 3373
Pascal, Felicien 3034
Paterson, Arthur 2392
Patmore, Coventry 161, 234, 235, 394, 485, 486
Pattison, Robert 4906, 5130
Paul, Herbert Woodfield 1573, 1752, 2232, 2476
Paulin, T. 4394
Pavlock, Barbara R. 4952, 5021a
Payne, Frederic Taylor 909
Payne, William Morton 1201, 1334, 1574, 1575, 2280, 2458
Peacock, Edward 963
Peacock, Florence 1576
Peake, Leslie Sillman 3189, 3190, 3191, 3192
Pearce, Helen 3124, 3580
Pearce, Maresco 531
Pearson, Charles William 2493
Pearson, N. H. 3414
Peck, Harry Thurston 2096, 2536, 2594
Peckman, Morse 4218
Peltason, Timothy Walter Hopkins 4840
Pendry, E. D. 3712
Penninger, Frieda Elaine 4685
Perrine, Laurence 3572, 3992, 4187
Perriwig, John 28
Perry, Henry Ten Eyek 3046
Perry, John Oliver 3939
Petch, Simon Stonehouse 4432, 4881
Petermann, Herta 2930
Peters, Robert L. 5092
Peterson, Clell T. 3993
Petrie, Neil H. 4145
Pettigrew, John 3828, 4263
Pfeiffer, Karl L. 4565, 5093
Pfordresher, John Charles 4233, 4419, 4473, 4668
Phelps, William Lyon 2784, 3225
Phillips, Charles 2832
Phillips, Lawrence 3238
Phillips, T. M. 2869, 2870
Phillips, W. 931
Pickering, Sam 5131
Picton, J. A. 761, 776, 812, 1031
Pierce, Anne Longfellow 3596
Pierce, Lorne A. 3080
Pierpoint, Robert 2888
Pietschmann, Tony 2739
Pilon, Edmond 2595, 2686

Pinchback, W. H. 2940
Pinto, Eva R. 4044
Pipes, B. N., Jr. 3829
Pisanti, G. 3256
Pitollet, C. 3283
Pitt, Valerie 3757
Pittman, Philip McM. 4474
Pitts, Gordon 3994
Placci, C. 1000
Platner, John Winthrop 2263
Plaut, Julius 2727, 2740
Poe, Edgar Allan 43, 74, 88, 96, 106, 107, 108, 109, 177, 178, 237
Poland, Peter Davies 4913
Pollard, Arthur 4141, 4566, 5021, 5094, 5132
Pollard, Graham 3211, 3226, 4012
Pollock, Walter Herries 1891
Porter, C. 1336
Portnoy, William E. 4567
Postlewait, Thomas 5045
Postma, J. 3027, 3029
Poston, Lawrence, III 3880, 3995, 4045, 4808, 5022
Poteat, Mary 3235
Potter, George Reuben 3263
Potts, R. A. 2515
Potwin, L. S. 2299, 2334
Powell, Thomas 172
Powers, Samuel Bernard 4433
Powles, Allen H. 2860
Powys, Atherton 3439
Pratt, Linda Ray 4289, 4475
Praz, Mario 3093
Prenshaw, Peggy W. 4505
Preyer, Robert O. 3660, 3996, 3997, 4113, 4688
Price, Fanny 3339
Price, Thomas R. 1579
Price, Walter 2656
Price, Warwick James 2597, 2668
Prideaux, William Francis 1580, 2375, 2376
Priestly, Francis E. L. 3440, 3779, 3780, 4420, 4569
Prince, Jeffrey Robert 4290
Priolo, Paolo 527
Prothero, Rowland 1166
Puckett, Harry 4570, 4729
Purton, H. B. 777
Püschel, Brita 3796
Pyre, James Francis Augustine 1958, 2901

Quaritch, Bernard 2765
Quayle, William Alfred 1949, 2669, 2814

Quesnel, Léo 762, 899
Quiller-Couch, Arthur 1755, 3109,
    3207, 3213, 3323
Quinn, John 2995
Qureshi, A. H. 3830, 4046

R., V. 3573
Rackin, Phyllis 3998
Rader, Ralph Wilson 3781, 3782,
    3783, 3797, 3831, 4264
Rader, William 2281
Radford, Colin 4730, 5048
Radford, D. 2447
Radford, G. H. 1806
Ragey, Le Père 2097
Raleigh, Walter S. 815
Ramage, C. T. 763, 764
Rances, Maurice 2459
Rand, George I. 3745
Rand, Theodore H. 1381
Ransom, John Crowe 3538
Ratchford, Fannie E. 2956, 3306,
    3310
Ratzka, K. 2997
Rawnsley, Hardwicke Drummond
    765, 816, 1274, 1685, 1932,
    2151, 2377, 2423
Rawnsley, Willingham Franklin
    1582, 1583, 2537, 2687, 3016
Ray, Gordon N. 3746, 4341
Ray, Luzerne 111
Raybould, W. 2460
Read, William A. 2128
Reade, Willoughby 2494
Reardon, Timothy Henry 1053, 1950
Redfern, Roger A. 4882
Redgrave, M. 3094
Redpath, Theodore 5049
Reed, Henry 497
Reed, John R. 4114, 4143, 4188,
    4669, 4755, 4759, 4809, 5095,
    5096
Rees, R. Wilkins 2202
Reese, Theodore Irving, III 4353
Reeve, Henry 1337
Rehak, Louise Rouse 3832
Reid, Forrest 3058
Reid, Margaret J. C. 3268
Reid, Thomas Wemyss 1297
Reilly, J. J. 3469
Reilly, Mary Paraclita 3520
Renaud, Armand 532, 582
Rendall, Vernon 3193, 3214
Revell, Peter 4342
Reynolds, Helen M. 1756
Reynolds, Llywarch 964
Rhys, John 1358
Rice, Jessie Folsom 2741

Rice, William North 2880
Richards, William C. 76
Richardson, Charles Francis 2642
Richardson, D. L. 277
Richardson, Joanna 3713, 3758,
    4476, 4953
Richardson, Robert Edward, Jr.
    4021
Richardson, Robert K. 3208
Rickert, Edith 2598
Ricks, Christopher 3784, 3785,
    3833, 3834, 3835, 3881, 3882,
    3883, 3884, 3885, 3886, 3940,
    3941, 3942, 3943, 3944, 3945,
    3946, 3999, 4000, 4001, 4047,
    4145, 4189, 4190, 4191, 4265,
    4343, 4346, 4477, 4571, 4592,
    4956, 5050
Rideing, William H. 2002
Ridley, Edwin 2599
Riede, David George 5133, 5134
Riley, James Whitcomb 1585, 2729
Ritchie, Anne Isabella Thackeray
    1054, 1408, 1686
Robb, Juliet Everts 2407
Robb, Kenneth Alan 3970
Robbins, Tony 4478
Robbins, W. 3441
Roberts, Robert 1586, 2881, 2882
Robertson, David Allen, Jr. 3470
Robertson, Frederick William 278,
    451, 525
Robertson, John Mackinnon 1252,
    2313, 2314
Robinson, A. Mary F. 934
Robinson, Edna Moore 2842, 2845
Robson, W. W. 3635, 4014, 5051
Rodriguez, Francesco 1338, 1359
Rogers, Arthur 3134
Rogers, E. G. 3714
Rogers, John 2378
Rogers, Timothy 3786
Rogers, William N., II 5097
Rolfe, William James 1096, 1134,
    1152, 1202, 1203, 1587, 1892,
    2003, 2034, 2035, 2264, 2265,
    2438, 2600
Roll-Hansen, Diderik 4479
Rôna, Eva 3079, 3083
Roppen, Georg 3603, 3680
Roscoe, Elizabeth M. 2420
Roscoe, William Caldwell 399, 498
Rose, Felix 3284, 3359
Rosenbaum, Jean Louise Watson
    4618, 5098
Rosenberg, John D. 3681, 4421,
    4480, 4572, 5135
Rosenblum, Dolores Mary 4619
Rosenblum, Dolores Ryback 5023

Ross, Alastair 4481
Ross, Malcolm 3747, 4314, 4573
Ross, Robert H. 4514
Rossetti, Dante Gabriel 2730
Rossetti, William Michael 2424
Rounds, S. R. 4731
Routh, H. V. 3257
Rowe, F. J. 1409
Roy, P. N. 3244
Royce, Josiah 1204, 2036
Roz, Firmin 2601, 2643, 2657
Rudman, Harry W. 3471, 3574
Ruhrmann, Friedrich G. 3037
Rupprecht, Johann Georg 1687, 1694
Russell, George William Erskine 2815
Russell, John 936
Russo, Antonio 4192
Rutenberg, Daniel 4395
Rutland, William R. 3307, 4344
Ryals, Clyde de L. 3628, 3682, 3683, 3684, 3787, 3788, 3789, 3790, 3836, 3837, 3838, 3839, 3851, 3887, 3888, 3947, 3959, 4015, 4048, 4193, 4266, 4502, 4513, 4670, 4732, 4883

S., J. 268
S., J. O. 435
S., W. W. 3302
Saint-Cère, Jacques 1588
Saintsbury, George Edward Bateman 965, 1873, 1906, 2461, 2462, 2631, 2833
Sait, James E. 4574, 4575, 4671
Sale, Roger 4576
Salmon, Arthur L. 2408
Salome, Rosaline 4079
Salt, Henry Stephens 1097, 1222, 1339, 1688
Sambrook, A. J. 3948
Sanders, Charles Richard 3597, 3636, 3748, 4749, 4757
Sanders, G. 3360
Sandys, J. Edwin 766
Sangster, Margaret E. 1590
Sargeaunt, John 2914
Sarrazin, Gabriel 1240, 1253, 1276
Saunders, Mary 5099
Savage, W. H. 1843
Savory, J. J. 4884
Sawyer, Paul Lincoln 4526
Scaife, Christopher Henry Oldham 3110
Schäfer, Bernhard 2495
Scharf, Lewis 973, 975

Schell, E. A. 2750
Schelling, Felix Emmanuel 2731
Scherer, Edmond 678, 1017, 1254
Schladebach, Kurt 2302
Schlager, Herbert C. 4434
Schmerler, Heinrich Emil 1255
Schmidt, Rudolf 692
Schneider, Fritz 2816, 2820
Schonfield, H. J. 3111
Schooling, J. Holt 1844
Schrumpf, G. A. 640
Schuck, Thomas R. 4733
Schuman, A. T. 1893
Schwalbaum, Joan 4354
Schweik, Robert C. 3715
Scott, J. Loughran 2233
Scott, Patrick 4810, 5024
Scott, Patrick Greig 4115, 4194, 4219, 4315, 4316, 4317, 4396, 4397, 4482, 4577, 4578, 4811, 5025, 5100, 5124
Scott, Robert 583(?)
Scott, Walter B., Jr. 3215
Scott-James, R. A. 3194, 3239
Scrivner, Buford, Jr. 4579
Scudder, Vida Dutton 2098
Seaman, Owen 1907
Sears, Richard Duane 3971
Seccombe, Thomas 2303, 2602
Selkirk, J. B. pseud. for Brown, James Bucham (see)
Sells, I. 3340
Semmelmeyer, Ingeborg 3585
Semmler, Clement 3949
Sencourt, Robert 2972
Sendry, Joseph 4003, 4049, 4483, 4484, 4580, 4734, 4812, 4885, 4954, 4955, 5026, 5027, 5101, 5136
Sergeant, Howard 4485, 4486
Sessions, Ina B. 3398
Seymour-Smith, Martin 4050
Shairp, John Campbell 1360
Shakespeare, Charles 1032
Shalvi, Alice 3957
Shanks, Edward Buxton 3038
Shannon, Edgar Finley, Jr. 3341, 3399, 3442, 3472, 3496, 3509, 3539, 3617, 3637, 3685, 3686, 3716, 4487, 4813, 4956, 5052, 5102, 5103, 5137
Sharma, Virendra 4907
Sharp, Amy 1361
Sharp, Elizabeth A. 2099
Sharp, Robert Farquharson 2152
Sharrock, Roger 3618
Shatto, Susan 4735, 4886, 4887, 4888, 4889, 5028, 5029, 5030, 5113a, 5138, 5139

Shaw, Marion 4422, 4814, 5031, 5032, 5113a
Shaw, W. David 3950, 4051, 4052, 4116, 4117, 4196, 4318, 4398, 4488, 4489, 4581, 4689, 4736, 4737, 4890, 5033, 5104, 5105
Shaw, William J. 1223
Shaylor, Joseph 2234
Shea, Michael Timothy 4435
Sheed, Maisie (Ward) 3227
Shepard, William pseud. for Walsh, William Shepard (see)
Shepherd, Henry Elliott 1340, 1383, 1760, 2496
Shepherd, Richard Herne 572, 648, 910, 1100, 1205, 1908
Sherry, James J. 4957
Shewan, A. 2982
Shields, Charles W. 2079
Shindler, Robert 2282
Shipman, Mary Evelyn 3183
Shmiefsky, Marvel 4053
Shoemaker, W. L. 938, 1055
Shorey, Paul 1761
Short, Clarice 4054
Short, Jeremy 401
Shorter, Clement King 1224, 1951, 2817
Shorthouse, Joseph Henry 2393
Sidey, Thomas K. 2915
Sidgwick, Arthur 2538
Siegenthaler, Walter 3629
Siemens, Lloyd 4891
Sifton, Paul G. 4118
Simcox, George Augustus 729, 1595
Simmons, William Kyle 4152
Simms, William Gilmore 243
Simpson, Arthur L., Jr. 4399
Simpson, David Lon 4766
Simpson, Richard 693
Simpson, William 518
Sinclair, David 4490
Sinclair, W. 2006
Sinfield, Alan 4144, 4283, 4686, 4738, 4739, 4815, 4816
Singer, S. W. 244
Sinnett, Alfred Percy 2871, 2902
Skeat, Walter William 584, 769, 939
Skemp, Kathryn 2981
Slater, John Herbert 1807
Slicer, Thomas Roberts 2539
Slinn, E. Warwick 4491
Sloan, Gary 4892
Smalley, Donald 3791, 3951
Smalley, George W. 1874
Smedley, Menella B. 619
Smidt, Kristian 3687

Smith, Albert 269
Smith, Arnold 2463
Smith, Byron Caldwell 1952
Smith, C. C. 245, 490
Smith, Charles Alphonso 2007
Smith, Elton Edward 3726, 3852, 4055, 4267, 4492
Smith, Eric 4758
Smith, George 620
Smith, George Barnett 1003
Smith, Goldwin 403
Smith, H. A. 4004
Smith, Harold J. 4582
Smith, James Cruickshank 3348
Smith, James L. 4197, 4268
Smith, Jean Pauline 2903
Smith, Jephson Huband 740
Smith, M. A. 4056
Smith, R. B. 3952
Smith, Robert M. 3241
Smith, William Henry 179
Smyser, William Emery 2464, 2644
Sneath, Elias Hershey 2153
Snell, Frederick John 2766
Snow, Jane Elliott 2235
Sochatoff, A. Fred 4198
Solimine, Joseph, Jr. 3857, 4005, 4057, 4199
Solomon, Stanley J. 3841
Sonn, Carl Robinson 3688
Sonstroem, David 4269
Sopher, H. 5106
Soule, George H., Jr. 4740
Southam, Brian C. 3853, 3953, 4284, 4493
Span, Reginald B. 2751
Sparer, Jonathan Douglas 5056, 5145
Sparke, Archibald 2998, 3324
Sparrow, John 3135, 3200
Sparvel-Bayly, J. A. 940
Spatz, Jonas 4583
Spector, Robert Donald 3510
Spedding, James 89, 911
Spence, R. M. 864, 2080, 2130
Spence, Walter 2540
Spender, Harold 2009, 2442
Sperber, Hans 3494
Spitzer, Leo 3511, 3798
Spurgeon, Caroline Frances Eleanor 2478, 2732
Squire, John Collings 2839, 2895, 2916, 2973, 3389, 3443
Staines, David 4584, 4585, 4817
Stanford, William Bedell 3550
Stange, George Robert 3482, 3512, 3575, 4119, 4513
Stanley, Hiram M. 1767, 1768, 1953
Starke, F. J. 3271

Starnes, De Witt Talmadge 2941
Starzyk, Lawrence J. 4893
Statham, H. H. 865
Stead, William Taylor 1599, 1769
Steane, J. B. 3958
Stedman, Edmund Clarence 694,
  778, 1410, 1909, 2632
Stedman, Laura 2632
Steffen, Paul 2394, 2402
Steigler, G. 1600
Stein, Richard L. 5107
Stenberg, Theodore T. 2983
Stephen, Leslie 2037
Stephens, F. G. 566
Stephenson, Nathaniel Wright 1386
Sterling, John 79, 129
Sterne, Ernest Staveley 1411
Stevens, L. Robert 4400, 4423
Stevens, R. L. 4494
Stevenson, Catherine Barnes 4436,
  4586, 4587, 4672, 4818, 4958,
  5034, 5035, 5108, 5109
Stevenson, Lionel 3177, 3361, 3415,
  3513, 3540, 3689, 3889
Stevenson, Morley 2315, 2362
Steward, S. M. 3272
Stewart, George 1601, 1690
Stipčević, Nikša 4687
Stirling, James Hutchinson 492, 604
Stirling, Maria E. A. 2754
Stitt, E. F. R. 1602
St. John-Stevas, Norman 3840,
  3901
Stock, A. G. 4270
Stocking, Fred H. 3400
Stockley, William Frederick Paul
  2671, 3017
Stockwell, Nina 2363
Stoddard, Richard Henry 436, 731,
  1006, 1139, 1603
Stoddart, A. M. 2209
Stoker, Bram 2425
Stokes, Edward 3890
Stone, John Morris 1242, 2395
Stone, Samuel John 842
Storch, R. F. 4319
Storey, Michael Louis 4841
Stork, Charles Wharton 2541
Story, Kenneth Ervin 4022, 4673
Strachan, L. R. M. 2785, 2786,
  3047, 3381
Strachey, Edward 1770
Straede, Karl 2396
Stratford, Jenny 4741
Straus, H. 2957
Strong, Augustus Hopkins 1954
Strout, Alan Lang 3273, 3401
Stuart, Charles 2426
Sucksmith, Harvey Peter 4058

Suddard, S. J. Mary 2688
Sugerman, Shirley 4688
Sulloway, Alison G. 4345
Suloway, I. J. 3514
Sundaram, P. S. 4320
Super, R. H. 3717
Sutherland, Allan 2409
Sutherland, Raymond C. 4120
Sutton, Henry 167
Svaglic, Martin J. 3792
Swanwick, Anna 1412
Sweeney, Helen M. 1894
Swift, William H. 3209
Swinburne, Algernon Charles 697,
  1007, 1008, 1153, 1243, 1772,
  1808
Swingle, Larry James 4023
Symonds, John Addington 866, 1773
Sypher, Francis Jacques 4742

T. 287
T. 3071
T., C. B. 3402
T., G. 3598
Taafe, James G. 3842
Tabb, John Banister 1387, 1604,
  3293
Taine, Hippolyte Adolphe 519,
  520, 521, 534
Tainsh, Edward Campbell 605,
  1774
Talbot, Ethel 2479
Talbot, Norman 4959
Talfourd, Thomas Noon 128
Talon, Henri A. 3891
Tannacito, Dan J. 4588
Tarbox, Increase N. 248
Tarhuni, Tohami T. 4842
Tarr, Roger L. 4495
Taylor, Achilles 1413
Taylor, Bayard 499, 822, 867,
  949
Taylor, Beverly White 4767
Taylor, Edward Allan 4527
Taylor, Henry 1225
Taylor, John 585
Taylor, Tom 2733
Taylor, W. V. 1850
Teeling, Bartle 1851
Temple, Joseph 2081
Templeman, William Darby 3342,
  3372, 3450, 3541, 3576, 3793,
  3843
Tener, Robert H. 3690
Tennyson, Alfred 586, 587, 588,
  589, 603, 641, 781, 1400, 1409,
  1606, 1664, 1667, 1668, 1965,
  2034, 2035, 2099, 2142, 2150,

2216, 2233, 2275, 2283, 2308, 2316, 2356, 2357, 2465 (standard edition), 2533, 2534, 2734, 2735, 2761, 2787, 2875, 2905, 2923, 3000, 3080, 3111, 3112, 3153, 3167, 3175, 3200, 3235, 3243, 3255, 3287, 3345, 3389, 3478, 3599, 3641, 3695, 3743, 3848, 3853, 3854, 3959, 3968, 4130, 4135, 4145, 4152, 4217, 4220, 4228, 4229, 4233, 4287, 4346, 4347, 4409, 4419, 4424, 4425, 4510, 4511, 4514, 4690, 5052, 5065, 5113a

Tennyson, Charles 3112, 3153, 3167, 3250, 3251, 3252, 3253, 3417, 3465, 3551, 3625, 3638, 3639, 3691, 3692, 3799, 3803, 3844, 3848, 3854, 3892, 3893, 3954, 3955, 4006, 4016, 4121, 4146, 4201, 4220, 4271, 4321, 4401, 4426, 4515, 4516, 4517, 4589, 4590, 4591, 4592, 4608, 4674

Tennyson, Emily 4230, 4518, 5053

Tennyson, G. B. 4756

Tennyson, Hallam (the elder) 1875, 1955, 2465, 2658, 2734, 3080

Tennyson, Hallam (the younger) 5036, 5041, 5042, 5043, 5047, 5049, 5050, 5051, 5054, 5111

Terry, Ellen 2497

Terry, F. C. Birbeck 1629

Terry, R. C. 4122

Teza, E. 2444, 2482

Thackeray, Francis St. John 1853, 2613

Thaler, Alwin 3444

Tharpe, J. L. 4505

Thayer, Mary Rebecca 2818

Thayer, Stephen Henry 1630

Thayer, W. R. 1343

Thesing, W. B. 4819

Theuriet, André 1631

Thistlethwaite, George Parker 1910, 1912, 2273

Thomas, E. M. 1207

Thomas, Edward 2843

Thomas, G. 2985

Thomas, Gilbert 3845, 3895, 4497

Thomas, Ralph 2614

Thomas, Walter 2543

Thomas, William 733

Thompson, Alexander Hamilton 2236

Thompson, Francis 2015, 2016, 2017

Thompson, James W. 3232

Thompson, John Allen 4234

Thompson, John R. 271, 308(?), 409(?), 439(?)

Thompson, Laurence S. 4059

Thomson, Joseph Charles 2316, 2339, 2397, 4017

Thomson, O. R. Howard 2483

Thomson, Peter 4427

Thorndike, Ashley H. 2904

Thorpe, Michael 4123, 4124

Thurston, Charles T. 33

Ticknor, Caroline 2950

Tierney, Frank M. 4498, 4908

Tietze, Frederick I. 3521

Tilling, Philip M. 4348

Tillotson, Geoffrey 3904, 4833

Tillotson, Kathleen 3542, 3904

Timko, Michael 4595, 4894

Tipple, Ezra Squier 2659

Tobias, Richard C. 4327

Tobin, J. J. M. 4743, 4768, 4961

Todd, William B. 3663, 3898, 4204

Todhunter, John 1633

Tollemache, Lionel Arthur 779, 2615, 2863

Tolman, Albert H. 2616

Tombs, J. S. O. 2708

Tomlinson, D. O. 4895, 5112

Torretta, L. 2864

Toynbee, Paget 1247

Traill, Henry Duff 1634, 1854, 2018, 2154

Trapp, J. B. 5113

Traubel, Horace Logo 2767, 4755, 4759

Trench, Richard Chenevix 591

Trent, William Peterfield 2083, 2100, 2212

Trevanion, Michael 4126

Trevelyan, Raleigh 4834

Trevvett, Florence 2155

Trickett, Rachel 4596

Tropper, Jerica 2996

Troxell, Gilbert M. 3140

Truman, Joseph 2019

Truss, Tom J., Jr. 3719

Tryon, W. S. 3515

Tucker, Herbert F., Jr. 5140, 5146, 5147

Tuckerman, Henry Theodore 112, 115

Tuell, Anne Kimball 3009

Turnball, Arthur 2799

Turner, Paul 3446, 3619, 3794, 4274, 4597, 4675, 4691, 4744, 4896, 4897

Tyler, Henry 3447

Tyree, Donald W. 4500

Tyrrell, R. Y. 2445

Tzeutschler, Artur 2522

Unwin, S. Philip 1779
Urban, Sylvanus 1344, 1636

Valbert, G. 2020
Valdes, Edgar 2021
Vallette, Jacques 3640, 3720
Vandiver, Edward P., Jr. 3847
van Doorn, Willem 3178
Van Dyke, Henry J., Jr. 1064,
    1209, 1256, 1282, 1283, 1345,
    1390, 1637, 1638, 1780, 1956,
    2022, 2156, 2283, 2317, 2905,
    2906, 2974
Vann, William Harvey 2943
Venables, Edmund 1639
Vent, Maryanne Ciardullo 4291
Vermorel, A. 557
Verrall, A.W. 2618
Verschoor, E.N.E. 4404
Vettermann, Ella 2866
Victor, O.J. 458
Victoria, Queen 4220
Villard, Léonie 2772
Vince, C.A. 2084
Vissar, G.J. 3264
Vogel, C.S. 4820
von Siebold, Erika 2889
Vyas, H.K. 4329

W. 272, 412
W., C.B. 273
W., H.M. 3074
W., W. 318
Wace, Walter E. 974
Wain, John 3546, 3626
Wainewright, John B. 2340, 2917
Wajid, R.A. 4330
Wakelin, Martyn F. 4348
Walcutt, Charles C. 3383
Waldau, Otto 1640
Waldmueller, R. (pseud. for C.E.
    Duboc) 627, 628
Walford, E. 1641
Walford, L.B. 1642, 1782
Walker, Hugh 1876, 1957, 2883,
    2927
Walker, Mrs. Hugh 2883
Walker, Janie Roxburgh . 2951
Walker, Thomas 1019
Walkley, A.B. 1643, 1781
Wallace, Percy M. 1414
Waller, A.R. 2810
Waller, John O. 4821, 4962
Wallis, Alfred 1108

Walsh, Henry C. 1257
Walsh, Thomas 4062
Walsh, Walter 1783
Walsh, William Shepard 1018,
    1113
Walter, John 494
Walters, John Cuming 1298, 1346,
    1347, 1691, 1856, 1896
Walton, James 4205
Ward, A.W. 2810
Ward, Arthur Douglas 4598, 4620
Ward, Hayden 4822
Ward, Mrs. E.M. (Henrietta
    Ward) 3010
Ward, Julius H. 872, 946
Ward, Louisa Edith 2157
Ward, Maisie see Sheed, Maisie
Ward, Mary Augusta 1141
Ward, Richard 2157
Ward, W.P. 2710
Ward, Wilfrid 1937, 2023, 2318,
    2364, 2619, 2768
Ward, William Godman 2038
Ware, Malcolme R. 3473
Ware, Thomas C. 4599
Warfield, Ethelbert D. 1644
Waring, Walter 4823
Warner, Oliver 3855
Warren, J. Leicester 569
Warren, Kate M. 2907
Warren, Roger 5141
Warren, Thomas Herbert 1391,
    1645, 2274, 2381, 2544, 2545,
    2735, 2987, 4221
Waterfield, A.J. 3384
Waterman, E.F. 4063
Waterston, Elizabeth 4824, 4908
Waterston, Elizabeth Hillman 3491
Watkins, Watkin 2319
Watson, Aaron 2689
Watson, William 1348, 1646, 1647,
    1648, 2101, 2523
Watts, Henry Edward 535
Watts, Theodore see Watts-Dunton,
    Theodore
Watts-Dunton, Theodore 1142,
    1210, 1284(?), 1285, 1392, 1393,
    1649, 1650, 1651, 1652, 1653,
    1785, 1786, 1787, 2819
Waugh, Arthur 1415, 1654, 1788,
    1789, 1790, 1857, 1858, 2213,
    2214, 2800
Way, A.S. 2709
Weatherhead, Leslie D. 3019,
    3081, 3113
Webb, W. Trego 1791, 1938
Wedgwood, Julia 1792
Wedmore, Frederick 1011, 1036,
    1793

Weeks, H. S. 4008
Weigand, W. 1286
Weiner, S. Ronald 4009
Weinstock, Donald J. 4275
Weiss, August 1655
Weiss, J. 873
Weissman, Judith 4676
Welby, Thomas Earle 3141
Welch, Dennis M. 5037
Welch, James Donald 4745
Weld, Agnes Grace 1794, 2024,
  2320, 2546
Wells, John Edwin 2620
Werlich, Egon 4127
Werner, Jack 3492
Westercamp, F. W. 2136
Weygandt, Cornelius 3245
Whall, Raymond Anthony, Jr. 4355
Wheatcroft, Andrew 4972
Wheeler, Edd 4206, 4222
Whipple, Edwin P. 113, 130
Whitbread, L. G. 4677
White, Frances E. 3474, 3517
White, G. M. 4678
White, James W. 1349
White, Walter 2039
Whitewell, C. T. 2446
Whiting, George Wesley 3671,
  3899
Whitman, Walt 413, 1212, 1226,
  1227, 2040, 3059
Whymper, A. 2085
Wickens, G. Glen 5038
Wickham, E. C. 2547
Wiebe, M. G. 4405, 4600
Wiggins, Louise D. 4128
Wilcock, A. B. 1350
Wilde, Jane Francesca Elgee 1362
Wilde, Oscar 3759
Wilde, Lady T. H. S. see Wilde,
  Jane Francesca Elgee
Wildman, Banks John 2365
Wilkenfeld, Roger B. 4010, 4129,
  4601
Wilkins, Mary C. 4602, 5039
Wilkinson, D. R. M. 4495
Wilkinson, L. P. 4207
Wilkinson, William Cleaver 2548
Willard, Charles B. 3620
Willcock, J. 2808
Willcocks, Mary Patricia 2988, 3011
Willey, Basil 3604
Williams, J. E. Hodder 2175
Williams, Melvin G. 4406
Williams, Sparks Henderson 734
Williams, Stanley Thomas 2975
Williamson, Claude C. H. 2908
Willingham, J. R. 3721, 3900
Wilmer, Clive 4407

Wilner, Ortha L. 3142
Wilson, A. 5040
Wilson, Charles 3693
Wilson, Edmund 3020
Wilson, Epiphanius 1657
Wilson, Henry Schütz 1809
Wilson, Hugh Hamilton 3910, 4064
Wilson, James D. 4603
Wilson, John see North, Chris-
  topher
Wilson, K. 4898
Wilson, Stephen Clifford 4746
Wilson, William 1037
Wilxman, Louise 4235
Wimsatt, W. K., Jr. 3403
Wingfield-Stratford, Esmé Cecil
  3114, 3115
Winn, Edith Lynwood 1363
Winter, William 1416, 1692
Winterwood, Geoffrey 1658
Winwar, Frances (pseud. for
  Frances Vinciguerra Grebanier)
  3201
Wise, Thomas James 1859, 1861,
  1862, 1865, 2025, 2498, 3143,
  3228
Wiseman, Christopher 4899
Wolfe, Humbert 3116
Wolff, Michael 3662
Wood, Willson E. 3556
Woodberry, George Edward 1144,
  1170, 1213, 1351, 2928
Woodring, Carl R. 3750
Woods, George Benjamin 3117
Woods, M. A. 1796
Woods, Margaret L. 3118, 3326
Wordsworth, Ann 5055
Wordsworth, Jonathan 4604
Workard, Job J. B. 559
Workman, Charles Thomas 4080
Wright, Austin 3722
Wright, Herbert Gladstone 3095
Wright, W. H. K. 1012
Wülker, Richard Paul 1877, 1880,
  1911
Wüllenweber, Walther 1258, 1287
Wyllie, John Cook 3724
Wymer, Thomas Lee 4081
Wynn, W. H. 2383

Y. 414
Yamada, Taiji 4331, 4501
Yarbrough, Bonnie Thames 4975
Yardley, E. 1659
Yates, Amos pseud. for Macmil-
  lan, Alexander (see)
Yates, Edmund Hodgson 848

Yearwood, John Charles, Jr.   4769
Yohannan, J. D.   3327, 3344
Young, A. B.   2484
Young, Andrew   3760
Young, George M.   3276, 3285, 3761
Young, Robert Stephen   4770, 5055

Zamick, M.   3229
Ziemann, Gwendolyn Timmons 4292
Zimmern, Helen   1797
Zocco, Irene   2158
Zuckermann, Joanne P.   4332
Zuylen van Nijevelt, S. Ivan   2918

Subject Index

(By entry number)

Entry numbers for book-length studies, including dissertations, are underlined. Readers interested in aspects of Tennyson's character or career might find the sections beginning "Tennyson as ... " and "Tennyson's ... " to be helpful. Also, broad studies are mentioned under "Tennyson's ... ," such as "Tennyson's work in general."

Acland, Thomas Dyke 4037
Addison, Joseph 2172
Africa 5059
Age of Tennyson (1897) (by H. Walker) 1957, 1965, 1989, 2078
agnosticism 5033
Aldworth 1425, 1887, 3282, 3430, 5016
Alfred, King 2419
Alfred, Lord Tennyson (1911) (by B.G. Ambler) 2650, 2661
Alfred Lord Tennyson (1892) (by A. Waugh) 1415, 1458, 1523, 1592, 1713, 1735, 1765, 1922, 1934
Alfred, Lord Tennyson, ed. G. MacBeth (1970) 4217, 4323
Alfred Lord Tennyson: A Memoir (1897) (by H. Tennyson, the elder) 1955, 1959, 1962, 1964, 1966, 1967, 1970, 1972-1975, 1978, 1981, 1984, 1988, 1990-1994, 1996, 1999, 2004, 2005, 2008, 2016, 2020, 2022, 2047, 2054, 2067, 2070, 2075, 2104, 2107, 2110, 2161, 2177, 2574, 2643, 4827
Alfred, Lord Tennyson and His Friends (1893) (by J.M. Cameron) 1665, 1747, 1759
Alfred Tennyson (1917) (by R.M. Alden) 2834, 2858
Alfred Tennyson (1904) (by A.C. Benson) 2343, 2366, 2368, 2373
Alfred Tennyson (1912) (by L.F. Choisy) 2675, 2737, 2743
Alfred Tennyson (1900) (by R.F. Horton) 2146, 2205, 2209, 2248
Alfred Tennyson (1901) (A. Lang) 2227, 2237, 2251, 2261, 2268
Alfred Tennyson (1949) (by C. Tennyson) 3417, 3419, 3420, 3421, 3423, 3424, 3431, 3433, 3436-3438, 3441, 3443, 3445, 3447, 3453, 3454, 3456, 3459, 3467, 3469, 3472
The Alien Vision of Victorian Poetry (1952) (by E.D.H. Johnson) 3495, 3508, 3514, 3516, 3522, 3525, 3538, 3540, 3543, 3546, 3557, 3559, 3563, 3565, 3567, 3576, 3619
All the King's Men (by R.P. Warren) 4945
allegory 1783
Allingham, William 2447
Ambrosius 3837, 4169
America 318, 1544, 3060, 3245, 3305, 3328, 3477, 3515, 3609, 3918, 3919
American Whig Review 106
"Anacreontics" 6
"The Ancient Sage" 2106, 2112, 2116, 2130, 3170, 4052
Anglo-Saxon 3119
animals 1376, 4951
Antonio's Revenge (by J. Marston) 3670
Arcadian myth 3906
architecture in Tennyson's work 1427
Aristophanes 2618
"Armageddon" 4000
Arnold, Matthew 1801, 1876, 2282, 2678, 2990, 3274, 3311, 3495, 3542, 3578, 3605, 3649, 3717, 3826, 3906, 3962, 4011, 4065, 4070, 4213, 4231, 4292, 4333, 4409, 4410, 4428, 4429, 4595, 4610, 4611, 4713, 4760, 4843, 4851, 4871, 4911
art in Tennyson's work 1427

Arthur, King 718, 748, 755, 1258, 1287, 1346, 1806, 1886, 2406, 2407, 2457, 2943, 2949, 3583, 3594, 3655, 3671, 3836, 3840, 4019, 4169, 4177, 4218, 4558, 4656, 4795, 4835, 4837, 5056, 5143, 5145
Arthurian literature 607, 1258, 1287, 1300, 1358, 1804, 1864, 1877, 1880, 2457, 2494, 2996, 3268, 3364, 3917, 4767, 4910
astronomy 2446, 5045
Athenaeum 3304, 3743
"Audley Court" 4645
aurora borealis in Tennyson's poetry 3950
Austin, Alfred 2651, 4772
Australia 4537, 4807
The Awakening Conscience (painting by W. H. Hunt) 4797
"Aylmer's Field" 582, 651, 963, 968, 1367, 1379, 1555, 3866, 4200

Bacon, Francis 1243
Bacon, Leonard 3372
Bagehot, Walter 3690, 3840
Bailey, Philip James 3427, 4962
"Balin and Balan" 2769, 2866, 4095, 4277, 4372, 4639, 4802; sources 2866
Ballads and Other Poems (1880) reviews 959, 965-967, 979, 981, 984, 985, 988-990, 993, 998, 1000, 1002, 1003, 1009, 1012
Baring, Rosa 3782, 4652
Baudelaire, Charles 4513
Becket: reviews 1081, 1095, 1098, 1102, 1103, 1105, 1106, 1114, 1117, 1119, 1121, 1122, 1124, 1125, 1127, 1130, 1139, 1141, 1143, 1144, 1165; reviews of performances 1696, 1698, 1699, 1708, 1709, 1714, 1716, 1721, 1725, 1743, 1751, 1778, 1782, 1793; in general 1689, 1700, 1731, 1863, 2415, 2760, 2770, 3313, 3767, 3802, 3969, 4198, 4340, 4359, 4651, 4683; characterizations 4975; critical edition 3235; forgeries 4540; the king in 1130; about performances 3479, 3918; sources 2720, 2738
Becket, as Arranged for the Stage by Henry Irving 1781
Becket, Thomas 1731, 3767, 3796, 3802, 3832, 4975

bells (as image and sound) 4824
Bible 775, 1282, 1357, 1910, 1912, 1985, 2321, 2469, 2842, 2845, 3960, 4028, 4116, 4133, 4160, 4884, 4968
bibliography of Tennyson 304, 569, 572, 702, 910, 1034, 1422, 1567, 1660, 1719, 1753, 1807, 1844, 1900, 1908, 1943, 2013, 2025, 2034, 2102, 2115, 2122, 2140, 2142, 2149, 2159, 2164, 2228, 2265, 2277, 2397, 2448, 2498, 2515, 2521, 2542, 2552, 2577, 2578, 2953, 2956, 2959, 2995, 3007, 3060, 3108, 3117, 3129, 3132, 3134, 3140, 3143, 3211, 3216, 3222, 3226, 3241, 3280, 3304, 3305, 3328, 3409, 3429, 3633, 3637, 3694, 3724, 3764, 3799, 3810, 3946, 3956, 4012, 4016, 4017, 4028, 4112, 4248, 4278, 4311, 4334, 4339, 4341, 4416, 4473, 4490, 4500, 4734, 4812, 4885, 4955, 5026, 5027, 5101, 5136
The Bibliography of Tennyson (1896) (by R. H. Shepherd) 1908, 1925
Bibliography of the First Editions in Book Form of the Works of Alfred, Lord Tennyson (1901) (by L. S. Livingston) 2228, 2297
Bibliography of the Writings of Alfred, Lord Tennyson (1905; rpt. 1967) (by J. C. Thomson) 2397, 4017, 4031, 4061
A Bibliography of the Writings of Alfred, Lord Tennyson (1908) (by T. J. Wise) 2498, 2556; errors in 3947
biography of Tennyson 434, 740, 972, 974, 1018, 1034, 1039, 1054, 1069, 1118, 1176, 1225, 1264, 1266, 1270, 1275, 1279, 1297, 1304, 1325, 1327, 1355, 1362, 1374, 1398, 1407, 1408, 1415, 1430, 1478, 1524, 1566, 1586, 1587, 1599, 1626, 1639, 1653, 1664, 1665, 1686, 1691, 1728, 1729, 1773, 1785, 1794, 1799, 1816, 1819, 1851, 1861, 1875, 1881, 1887, 1896, 1902, 1918, 1919, 1937, 1941, 1944, 1955, 1976, 1977, 1982, 2000, 2012, 2015, 2030, 2032-2034, 2037, 2039, 2050, 2059, 2076, 2089, 2091, 2094, 2097, 2141, 2146, 2147, 2151, 2157, 2174, 2175, 2179, 2217, 2221, 2233, 2234, 2239, 2278, 2279, 2296,

2307, 2311, 2318, 2320, 2331,
2343, 2346, 2386, 2388, 2412,
2416, 2424, 2425, 2447, 2449,
2464, 2485, 2486, 2490, 2497,
2537, 2567, 2622, 2632, 2637,
2651, 2657, 2658, 2681, 2719,
2757, 2761, 2766, 2768, 2784,
2793, 2795, 2797, 2799, 2900,
2907, 2932, 2944, 2951, 2966,
2968, 2971, 2992, 3004, 3010,
3012, 3016, 3023, 3031, 3041,
3047, 3053, 3078, 3086, 3095,
3098, 3130, 3144, 3198, 3215,
3217, 3231, 3234, 3250, 3326,
3374, 3386, 3396, 3407, 3417,
3452, 3463, 3468, 3475, 3624,
3625, 3685, 3691, 3692, 3709,
3727, 3748, 3756, 3758, 3782,
3783, 3844, 3855, 3933, 3954,
3965, 4006, 4020, 4058, 4201,
4343, 4351, 4367, 4378, 4459,
4476, 4518, 4590, 4591, 4659,
4662, 4691, 4693, 4715, 4755,
4759, 4810, 4830, 4865, 4866,
4901, 4930, 4970, 4972, 4977,
5015, 5044a, 5052, 5053, 5115,
5116, 5118, 5121
birds 2021, 2132, 2182, 2184,
2200, 2319, 2421, 2801, 2912,
3714, 4296
Blackwood's Edinburgh Magazine
3715
Blagden, Isabella 3457
Book of Gems 3707
A Book of Golden Deeds (by C.
Yonge) 4741
Boston College 3886
"Break, Break, Break" 3366,
3804, 4101, 5106; misreadings of
3998; linguistic analysis of 5106
Bridges, Robert 3701
Bright, John 2081, 2084
British Academy 2603
Brittany 3917
Brookfield, Mrs. W.H. 2386
Brown University 3620
Browning, Elizabeth Barrett 503,
1681, 1941, 2088, 3396, 3601
Browning, Robert 537, 567, 631a,
632, 875, 904, 1268, 1310, 1408,
1489, 1602, 1717, 1798, 1801,
1876, 2041, 2088, 2156, 2220,
2224, 2306, 2314, 2353, 2414,
2420, 2452, 2456, 2462, 2549,
2631, 2653, 2656, 2698, 2718,
2754, 2790, 2837, 2927, 2928,
3000, 3057, 3084, 3150, 3156,
3179, 3274, 3286, 3311, 3361,
3396, 3475, 3495, 3578, 3601,

3826, 3962, 3980, 4011, 4023,
4034, 4047, 4065, 4066, 4074,
4178, 4193, 4213, 4279, 4333,
4367, 4369, 4401, 4409, 4429,
4435, 4519, 4542, 4559, 4610,
4713, 4760, 4871, 4891, 4907,
4909, 5070, 5096, 5114, 5118
Bucke, Richard Maurice 4755,
4759
Bulwer-Lytton, Edward 116, 118,
119, 120, 122, 3119, 3179,
4874
Burke, Edmund 3857, 4057
Burne-Jones, Edward 2345
Burns, Robert 4946
busts of Tennyson 449, 2733
Butler, Montagu 3814
Byron, George Gordon, Lord 24,
689, 948, 1054, 1408, 2222,
2656, 2765, 2839, 2952, 3581,
4259, 4735, 4752

The Cabinet Edition (1874) 789
Caine, Hall 2485
Calaber, Quintus 2709
Calvinism 4040
Cambridge 1639, 2412, 3239, 3395
Cambridge Apostles 2412, 3505,
3659, 3685, 4825
Camelot 5145
Cameron, Julia Margaret 3198,
3407, 4472
Campbell, James 4490
"The Cap and the Bells" (by W.B.
Yeats) 4392
"The Captain" 2998
Carlyle, Jane Welsh 4749
Carlyle, Thomas 561, 905, 1366,
2311, 2941, 3024, 3450, 3597,
3605, 3612, 3676, 3748, 4074,
4231, 4288, 4429, 4495, 4613,
4749, 4837, 4909, 5089
cartoons 1075
A Catalogue of the Tennyson Col-
lection in the Library of Univer-
sity College, Cardiff (1972) (by
P. Revell and S. Allsobrook)
4342, 4469
Catullus, Gaius Valerius 2072,
3589, 4952
Celt 2933
"The Charge of the Heavy Brigade"
3216
"The Charge of the Light Brigade":
in general 351, 353, 357, 408,
724, 3295, 3376, 3815, 3833,
4381, 4822; bibliography 4500;
influence of 3653, 4822, 4919;

meter 721; parodied 4532;
sources 2983; variants 3927,
3955
Chaucer, Geoffrey 1220, 1821,
3601
"Childe Roland to the Dark Tower
Came" (by R. Browning) 4047
A Child's Recollections of Tennyson
(1906) (by E. N. Ellison) 2416,
2437
Christ 1084, 2881, 2882
"The Christ of Ammergau" 3599
Christian Examiner 58
Christmas 1318, 1986, 2114, 2264
cities 4119, 4819
"Claribel" 4300
Classical Echoes in Tennyson (1904)
(by W. P. Mustard) 2359, 2374,
2403
Cleopatra 2515, 2521, 4109
"Cleopatra's Needle" 3333
Clough, Arthur Hugh 631, 2282,
2367, 2370, 3542, 3605, 3962,
4074, 4194, 4333, 4519, 4611,
4810, 5024
"Cockney School" of poetry 22
Coleridge, Hartley 4385
Coleridge, Samuel Taylor 2408,
2976, 3395, 4349, 4521, 4644
Collins, John Churton 1438, 1580,
2329, 2676, 2677, 3926
color 2869, 3922, 4024
Columbus 4601
"Columbus" 1178, 1179, 4601,
4787
"Columbus at Seville" (by J. Ellis)
1178, 1179
"Come Down, O Maid" 3470
"Come Not, When I Am Dead" 3883
"The Coming of Arthur": in general
1409, 2460, 4140, 4251, 4252;
critics on 2460; manuscript
4571; sources for 1258, 1287;
verse 376 of 3030, 3043
A Commentary on Tennyson's In
Memoriam (1901) (by A. C. Bradley) 2218, 2254, 2267
A Concordance to "The Devil and
the Lady" (1931) (by A. E. Baker)
3133, 3145, 3168, 3186
A Concordance to the Poetical and
Dramatic Works of Alfred, Lord
Tennyson (1914) (by A. E. Baker)
2756, 2773, 2806, 4007, 4062
concordances to works of Tennyson
630, 645, 2756, 3145; about concordances 2614
"Confessions of a Sensitive Mind"
913

Congreve, William 686
Conrad, Joseph 4428
Conway, Moncure Daniel 2347
Cophetua, King 4599
copyrights 3515
Cornwall 2049
Cowper, William 1359, 4435
Crabbe, George 2056, 2808
Crane, Stephen 3653
Crimean War 3376, 4914, 5057
Critical Essays on the Poetry of
Tennyson (1960) (ed. J. Killham)
3697, 3704, 3708, 3718, 3720,
3733, 3741
critics on Tennyson 16, 41, 89,
106, 134, 176, 210, 248, 277,
282, 286, 290, 364, 565, 978,
1055, 1276, 1395, 1407, 1467,
1477, 1572, 1761, 2140, 2245-
2247, 2262, 2329, 2501, 2604,
2608, 2621, 2909, 2926, 2935,
2994, 3015, 3024, 3101, 3124,
3129, 3176, 3247, 3273, 3292,
3304, 3341, 3429, 3451, 3484,
3496, 3539, 3553, 3580, 3582,
3600, 3607, 3609, 3614, 3668,
3690, 3788, 3827, 3841, 3843,
3904, 3926, 4013, 4025, 4038,
4055, 4068, 4214, 4219, 4224,
4276, 4291, 4333, 4442, 4562,
4588, 4595, 4602, 4651, 4706,
4730, 4734, 4812, 4821, 4885,
4917, 4950, 4955, 5026, 5048,
5078, 5101, 5136
Croker, John Wilson 18, 20, 31,
3260, 3296, 3380, 3397, 3401
Cromwell, Oliver 892, 901, 931, 940
"Crossing the Bar" 1730, 1791,
1971, 2202, 2213, 2512, 2528,
3278, 3460, 3471, 3487, 3503,
3506, 3647, 3807, 3930, 3974,
3983, 3990, 3992, 4044, 4127,
4174, 4269, 4395, 4452, 5084
Cunningham, Allan 29
The Cup: reviews see The Cup and
The Falcon; reviews of performances 977, 986, 987, 992, 994,
995, 996, 999, 1004, 1005, 1010,
1011; in general 2308; about performances 2497, 3919
The Cup and The Falcon: reviews
1072, 1077, 1087, 1092, 1101,
1109

Daly, Augustin 3035
Dante Alighieri 776, 1853, 2353,
2381, 2545, 3127, 3842, 4138,
4221, 4254, 4259, 4478, 4900

"Daphne" 1382
Darwin, Charles 1243, 1808, 2613, 3177, 3645, 3652, 3674
David Copperfield (by C. Dickens) 3618, 4941
"The Day Dream" 1129
Dear and Honoured Lady, ed. H. Dyson and C. Tennyson (1970) 4220, 4240, 4272, 4299
death 2851, 3391, 4395, 4620
The Death of Oenone: reviews 1455, 1479, 1494, 1506, 1508, 1528, 1531, 1563, 1571, 1575, 1578, 1593, 1649, 1652, 1703; in general 1733
"Death of the Old Year" 701
decadence 5041
The Defense of Guenevere (by W. Morris) 4441
Defense of Poetry (by P.B. Shelley) 3742
Demeter 4788
Demeter 1259, 1265, 1277, 1278, 1284, 1307, 1308, 1317, 1319, 1324, 1332, 1334, 1336, 1343, 1351, 1703
"Demeter and Persephone" 3575, 3650, 3774, 4106, 4636, 4709, 4869
De Musset, Alfred 735, 884, 1008, 1153, 2083, 2100
"De Profundis" 1016
"De rerum natura" 2365, 2396
"Despair": in general 970, 1014, 1026, 1032, 1802, 4927; background for 4927; parodied 1007; religion in 1019
de Vere, Aubrey 1122, 2364, 3205, 3520
The Devil and the Lady: review 3125; in general 3112, 3173, 3180, 3848, 4969; classicism 3301; concordance 3145; sources 3370
The Devil and the Lady, ed. C. Tennyson (1930) 3112, 3125; 1964 edition 3854, 3882, 3900
de Vitry, Jacques 3370
"A Dialogue Between Thysis and Dorinda" (by A. Marvell) 4854
Dickens, Charles 2175, 4231, 4376, 4428, 4429, 4735, 4928, 4941
Dickinson, Emily 4919
dictionaries to Tennyson's works 2809
La Divina Commedia (by Dante) 3127, 4138
divorce 4606

Dobson, Austin 3050
Domestic and Heroic in Tennyson's Poetry (1981) (by D.S. Hair) 5044, 5130
Donne, John 4766, 4945
Donne, William Bodham 2390
doom in Tennyson's poetry 5147
"Dora" 713, 2859
Doré, Gustave 623
Dorian Gray (by O. Wilde) 4567
"Doubt and Prayer" 4121
Doyle, Arthur Conan 3507
The Dramas of Alfred, Lord Tennyson (1962) (by C.G.H. Japiske) 3025, 3028, 3033
dramatic monologue 3398
Drayton, Michael 3465, 3490
"A Dream of Fair Women" 883, 953, 1363, 1476, 1629, 3434, 3509, 4109
dreams in Tennyson's poetry 3892
Dryden, John 3510, 4207
Duke of Wellington see Ode on the Death of the Duke of Wellington
duty 1602
"The Dying Swan" 5035

"The Eagle" 3573, 4036, 4120, 5089
Early Editions (1894) (J.H. Slater) 1807, 1859
The Early Poems of Alfred Lord Tennyson, ed. J.C. Collins 2142, 2168, 2170, 2176, 2189, 2191, 2204, 2206, 2208, 2244, 2269
Eden 4526
editions 641, 1257, 1400, 1409, 1414, 1606, 1677, 1678, 1956, 2034, 2035, 2099, 2150, 2216, 2233, 2275, 2308, 2316, 2356, 2357, 2465, 2654, 2734, 2735, 2761, 2787, 2905, 2923, 3000, 3080, 3111, 3153, 3167, 3205, 3235, 3243, 3251, 3268, 3287, 3289, 3389, 3462, 3478, 3641, 3695, 3848, 3853, 3854, 3959, 4111, 4130, 4135, 4145, 4152, 4153, 4217, 4220, 4228, 4229, 4233, 4295, 4346, 4347, 4409, 4419, 4424, 4425, 4510, 4511, 4514, 4690, 4817, 5052, 5065, 5113a
Elaine 3225
"Elaine" see "Lancelot and Elaine"
"Eleanor" 17
Eliot, George 2420, 3086

Eliot, T.S.   3493, 3832, 4038,
  4289, 4329, 4349, 4475, 4548,
  4766, 4768
Elizabeth I   834
Ellis, Joseph   1178, 1179
embryology   4377
Emerson, Ralph Waldo   2509,
  3024, 3477, 3564, 4088
England   2038, 2722
"English Idyls"   2099
"Enid"   493; illustrated   603
Enoch Arden   4702
Enoch Arden: reviews   536, 539-
  545, 547-549, 551-558, 566, 583,
  651; in general   537, 538, 562,
  580, 582, 692, 825, 828, 833,
  904, 1162, 1216, 1250, 1377,
  1940, 2155, 2178, 2216, 2257,
  2371, 2642, 2662, 2679, 3614,
  3898, 3912, 4200, 4219, 4282,
  4543, 4702, 4726; background
  4219; bigamy in   538, 542, 559;
  dramatized   696; forged   3306;
  immorality of   542; parodied
  571; reception   4219; sources for
  2238, 2662
"The Epic"   3675, 4665
eroticism   4620
Essay on Man (by A. Pope)   2922,
  2929
Essays on Lord Tennyson's Idylls
  of the King (1893) (by H. Littledale)   1675, 1706, 1736, 1746,
  1757, 1763, 1788
Etna   3649
evolution   1787, 3150, 3156, 3177,
  3263, 3307, 3449, 3603, 3652,
  3681, 4308, 4344, 5038
Examiner (London)   154
The Excursion (by W. Wordsworth)
  4393
An Exhibition of Manuscripts (1942)
  (by F.E. Ratchford)   3310, 3354
Eyre Defence Fund   579

Fabbri, Cora   1681
Faber, G.S.   4994
The Faerie Queen (by E. Spenser)
  2061
Fairfax, Edward   5141
faith in Tennyson's work   1667,
  1876, 2026, 2169, 2355, 2800,
  3189, 4846
The Falcon: reviews see The Cup
  and The Falcon; reviews of performances   921, 927, 928, 929,
  933, 945, 950; about performances   3919

The Fall of Camelot (1973) (by J.
  D. Rosenberg)   4421, 4535,
  4545, 4553, 4557, 4561, 4573,
  4576, 4623, 4640, 4641, 4668,
  4670, 4744, 4815
the fallen woman   4979
"A Farewell"   439, 4156
"Farewell, My Highland Lassie"
  (by A. Clough)   5024
Farragut, Admiral David Glasgow
  1509
Farringford   1425, 2997, 3044,
  3439, 3596, 4450, 4461
"Fatima"   373
Faust (by W. von Goethe)   3825
feminism   168, 307
Festus (by P.J. Bailey)   3427,
  4962
Fields, James T.   3044
Fields, Mrs. James T.   3044
Fifine at the Fair (by R. Browning)
  4193
FitzGerald, Edward   2375, 2431,
  3674, 4141, 4265, 5121
Flinders, Matthew   4517
Florence   312
"Flower in the Crannied Wall"
  2665, 2674
flowers   1855, 2323, 3283, 4951
The Foresters, Robin Hood and
  Maid Marian: reviews   1428,
  1433, 1437, 1460, 1464, 1496,
  1503, 1505, 1526, 1529, 1547,
  1561, 1574, 1591, 1623, 1646,
  1703; reviews of performances
  1424, 1453, 1459, 1540, 1543;
  in general   1392, 1559, 1624,
  1625, 1643, 2484; Maid Marian
  1624, 1625, 1643; parodied
  1484; about performances   1416,
  1720, 3035, 3870; Robin Hood
  2739, 4536
forgeries   1108, 3211, 3275, 3306,
  3373, 3663, 4012, 4540
The Forgeries of Tennyson's Plays
  (1967) (by J. Carter and G. Pollard)   4012, 4059, 4060
Forman, Henry Buxton   5090
The Formation of Tennyson's Style
  (1920) (by J.F.A. Pyre)   2901,
  2937, 2942, 2957
Forster, John   4870, 4992, 4993,
  5006
Fox, William Johnson   5104
"A Fragment"   6
France   1546, 1946, 2570, 2608,
  3101
Fraser's Magazine   4949
"Frater Ave atque Vale"   3434, 4952

freedom 2153, 2549, 2653
French poetry 2461
Freshwater 2000, 2768, 3198
Freud, Sigmund 3349, 3404
From the Great Deep (1967) (by
    C. de L. Ryals) 4015, 4063,
    4103, 4107, 4113, 4264, 4306
Frost, Robert 4505, 4633, 4859
Froude, James 1471, 3159, 3161,
    3184, 4457
fusty in Tennyson's work 3291

Galahad 3182
"The Garden Trees" 4293
gardens 4925
Gareth 4116, 5056
Gareth and Lynette reviews 699,
    710, 714, 718, 719, 722, 725,
    727, 729, 730, 732, 744, 749,
    756, 767, 773; in general 743, 747,
    766, 894, 1678, 2898, 4166,
    4384; edition 4229; manuscripts
    3672; revisions of 3399
Gaskell, Elizabeth 4699
Gatty, Mr. and Mrs. 3595
The Gem: A Literary Annual 6
gems 4942, 4951
Geoffrey of Monmouth 4035
"Geraint and Enid" 1400, 3095,
    3880, 3977, 5071
The Germ 3908
Germany 3553, 4610
"Gerontion" (by T. S. Eliot) 3493
Gilchrist, Anne 1174
Gissing, George Robert 3052, 4093
Gladstone, William Ewart 1194,
    1254, 1683, 2074, 3674, 4373,
    4693
Gladstone on the New "Locksley Hall"
    (by W. E. Gladstone) 1175, 1188
God 2153, 3826
Goethe, Johann Wolfgang von 1025,
    3825, 4104, 4874
The Golden Treasury 3185, 3775
Goldsmith, Oliver 2807
Gosse, Edmund 3146, 3934
Gothicism 4494
Gray, Thomas 826, 3834
The Greater Victorian Poets (1895)
    (by H. Walker) 1876, 1888, 1914
green 3922
Grose, Francis 4711
Guinevere 2406, 2407, 3594, 3655,
    3671, 4353, 4711
"Guinevere" 1917, 2897, 3473, 4600;
    illustrated 587
Gully, Dr. 4509
Guþrunakviþa 3298

"Hail, Briton" 3426, 3884
Hall, Samuel Carter 3707
Hallam, Arthur Henry (see also:
    In Memoriam) 252, 907, 1047,
    1131, 1312, 1326, 1672, 1865,
    3129, 3193, 3222, 3229, 3251,
    3320, 3321, 3409, 3489, 3552,
    3580, 3631, 3783, 3787, 3940,
    3965, 4026, 4038, 4149, 4208,
    4293, 4351, 4547, 4556, 4637,
    4693, 4796, 4851, 4879, 4926,
    4949, 5044a, 5078, 5104
Hallam, Ellen 5122
Hamlet (by W. Shakespeare) 3317,
    3331
A Handbook to the Works of Alfred,
    Lord Tennyson (1872) (by M.
    Luce) 1872, 1923, 1924, 1928,
    1933
Hardman, William 2968
Hardy, Thomas 2474, 4292, 4394,
    4676, 4891
Harold 4975
Harold: reviews 823, 840, 850,
    855-858, 860-863, 866, 872-874,
    3061, 3063, 3066, 3067, 3069,
    3070, 3071, 3073, 3074; in gen-
    eral 865, 2302, 2389, 2401,
    2491; Bible in 4133; characteri-
    zations 4975; Harold 4975; about
    performances 3163, 3868
Harrison, Frederick 2245, 2262
Harvard University 3613, 3617,
    3672
Havelock, Henry 2057
Hearn, Lafcadio 3303
Heath, J. M. 3251
Hegel, Georg 4041
Heine, Heinrich 735, 2541
Heinrich, Max 2257
Henry II 3767
Herbert, George 235
"Heriodiade" (by S. Mallarmé)
    4582
"Hervé Riel" (by R. Browning)
    3980
"The Hesperides" 3512, 3972,
    4181, 4249, 4303, 4635, 4709,
    5123
Hiawatha (by H. W. Longfellow) 352
Hill, Francis 4916
Hindu imagery 4667
Holmes, Oliver Wendell (the elder)
    1894, 3674
Holy Grail 1221, 3100, 4475
The Holy Grail: reviews 633, 635,
    636, 649, 655, 656, 658, 662,
    663, 666, 667, 669, 670, 671,
    672, 673, 675, 676, 677, 682,

684; in general 664, 759, 1082, 1221, 1677, 2315, 3188, 4098, 4126, 4169, 4172, 4585, 4753, 4855, 5058; allegory 4172; characters 3837; narration 3837; Percivale 4305, 4585; sources 4305, 4585; spiritual teachings 2684; visionary experience in 5098

Homer 435, 2183, 2198, 2982, 3128, 4478

The Homes and Haunts of Alfred, Lord Tennyson (1892) (by G.G. Napier) 1404, 1584

The Homes of Tennyson (1905) (by A. Paterson and H. Allingham) 2392, 2440

Hopkins, Gerard Manley 3701, 3826, 4087, 4345, 4352, 4437

Horace 2073, 2082, 2818, 4664, 4743, 5132

Howells, William Dean 3582

Hugo, Victor 512, 2178, 3284, 3359

humor in Tennyson 1854

Hunt, Leigh 2378, 3707

Hunt, William Holman 4797

Hutton, Richard Holt 748

"Hymn to Proserpine" (by A.C. Swinburne) 3650

Iceland 2782

Idylls of the King, 1859: reviews 463-470, 472-475, 479-483, 485-491, 494, 500-502, 504, 509, 3901; in general 471, 476, 510, 653, 4838; illustrated 527, 588; language 479; and Malory's Le Morte d'Arthur 607; morality 476

Idylls of the King, entire: in general 770, 845, 876, 916, 980, 1052, 1216, 1221, 1229, 1242, 1250, 1257, 1386, 1401, 1675, 1680, 1829, 1890, 2044, 2058, 2093, 2223, 2292, 2330, 2361, 2383, 2387, 2395, 2399, 2433, 2452, 2494, 2524, 2527, 2540, 2586, 2620, 2762, 2931, 3001, 3003, 3175, 3221, 3440, 3523, 3594, 3639, 3655, 3671, 3690, 3791, 3836, 3841, 3856, 3871, 3961, 3970, 4015, 4019, 4021, 4024, 4045, 4048, 4051, 4073, 4084, 4094, 4130, 4143, 4187, 4196, 4276, 4338, 4353, 4358, 4370, 4419, 4421, 4491, 4506, 4507, 4508, 4534, 4549, 4550, 4564, 4618, 4626,

4656, 4798, 4861, 4932, 4965, 5143; allegory 750, 876, 1133, 1177, 2494, 2931, 3440, 3523, 3905, 3932, 4199, 4835; antipastoralism 5068; background 1675, 1804, 1864, 1869, 1878, 2494, 3659, 4019, 4073, 4130, 4276; bibliography 4473; Camelot in 5145; characterizations 3970, 4253, 4910, 4979, 5056, 5079, 5143; composition of 3638, 4079, 4473; critical reception 3904, 4276, 4291; development 980, 1862, 1869, 1878, 2069, 3871, 3910, 4965; diction 887; dramatized 2897, 2898; early editions 4311; entangled soul 3049; ethical themes 4612; fool in 4129; Greek tragedy and 3985; hero in 4837; illustrated 781, 3175, 4472; imagery 3591, 4043, 4089, 4412, 4466, 5145; influence of 4676; influences on 4837, 4929; and In Memoriam 4048; introductions 1675, 2494, 4021; language 1910, 1912, 2273, 2348, 3818; Mabinogion 2273, 4180; manuscripts 3252, 3551, 4473; morality 3277; Le Morte d'Arthur (by T. Malory) 2273, 2273, 2638, 4076, 4166, 4564; narrative of 3523, 3551, 3932, 3970, 4436, 4550; and The Origin of Species 3662; philosophy 4618, 5068; poetry and the state 2747; proofs of 4473; prose drafts of 4584; religion in 3440, 4835; reputation 3607, 3904; revisions 1862, 1869, 1878; and Robert Browning 2452; social themes 5143; sources 3277, 4965; structure 876, 3905, 3932, 4835, 4965; Tennyson's thought in 3910, 5143; three queens of 5079; Tristram group 4802; unity of 3971, 4089, 4129; variorum edition 4233, 4419; and Victorian paintings 4412; For further information, see separate listings for individual tales.

Illustrations of Tennyson (by J.C. Collins) 1354, 1385, 1522

Illustrations to Vivien (by G. Doré) 592

imagination 4171

imperialism 2135, 2583, 2623, 3316

Imro-Elkhais 4842

"In Falmouth Harbor" (by L. Johnson) 4395

Inferno (by Dante) 4138
influences on Tennyson 441, 459,
910, 919, 1054, 1258, 1287,
1298, 1354, 1408, 1740, 1876,
2038, 2061, 2128, 2183, 2321,
2381, 2415, 2469, 2472, 2531,
2550, 2567, 2741, 2772, 2816,
2818, 2820, 2941, 3040, 3119,
3177, 3239, 3244, 3327, 3336,
3338, 3344, 3361, 3363, 3371,
3395, 3434, 3473, 3481, 3496,
3507, 3510, 3552, 3570, 3573,
3581, 3598, 3676, 3715, 3842,
3960, 4018, 4035, 4049, 4057,
4058, 4074, 4133, 4182, 4183,
4259, 4280, 4281, 4304, 4305,
4445, 4478, 4529, 4547, 4599,
4610, 4613, 4638, 4681, 4837,
4874, 4900, 4937, 4946, 4965,
4966, 5009, 5027, 5049, 5089,
5104, 5109
In Memoriam: reviews 182, 185-
194, 196, 200-203, 206, 208-217,
219-221, 225-229, 231-236, 238,
239, 241-243, 245-250, 253,
256, 258, 261, 268, 270, 272,
274, 275, 282, 286, 290, 298,
305, 310, 326, 3223, 3224; in
general 222, 265, 278, 417,
428, 429, 442, 497, 525, 657,
741, 827, 854, 864, 882, 888,
907, 955, 1031, 1051, 1066,
1083, 1148, 1291, 1330, 1356,
1373, 1383, 1388, 1397, 1668,
1704, 1749, 1760, 1796, 1815,
1892, 1929, 1949, 1956, 1979,
1980, 2098, 2113, 2149, 2218,
2250, 2275, 2280, 2281, 2285,
2293, 2332, 2334, 2335, 2336,
2356, 2410, 2432, 2435, 2439,
2445, 2496, 2545, 2664, 2671,
2716, 2762, 2960, 2967, 3105,
3164, 3171, 3200, 3202, 3204,
3207, 3213, 3242, 3422, 3457,
3458, 3464, 3466, 3501, 3518,
3519, 3542, 3572, 3579, 3588,
3642, 3654, 3722, 3753, 3763,
3825, 3849, 3935, 3973, 4023,
4052, 4206, 4222, 4235, 4255,
4318, 4335, 4357, 4374, 4390,
4406, 4468, 4579, 4657, 4664,
4723, 4736, 4758, 4762, 4763,
4766, 4799, 4814, 4826, 4850,
4884, 4887, 4900, 4973, 4976,
5022, 5023, 5031, 5032, 5037,
5047, 5094, 5113a; about editions
of 4112; act of writing 5023;
analogy 4701; and Arthur Henry
Hallam 252, 471, 2749, 3193,

3965, 4991; Arthur Hallam as
Christ figure 3787, 4149; as a
personal poem 5094; as diary
4976; as love poetry 4332; and
Bible 775, 4968; and The Book of
Job 4884; casebook 4214; compan-
ions to 1214, 1704; composition of
3363, 3481, 4887, 4954; critical
edition 3968, 4514; critics of 4821,
5026; death 3391; development of
1205; doubt 3049, 3827; dramatic
irony in 4362; evolution 3681,
3825; failure and defeat 3738; faith
273, 2281, 2874, 2992, 3017,
3049, 3681, 3827, 4157; form
3935; God in 4991; and Idylls of
the King 4048; imagery 3612,
3842, 4053; immortality 3391,
4701; index to 523; influence of
3618, 4941; influences on 3363,
3395, 3481, 3842, 4049, 4104,
4128, 4254, 4393, 4547, 4638, 4831,
4973, 5009; in Latin 4097; introductions to 1249; Italian mis-
translations of 3377; language
3593, 3891, 4144, 4283, 4318,
4570; love story 2817, 4332;
manuscripts 4313, 4483, 4580,
4954, 5030; and Maud 3823;
meaning 4799; message of 2841;
metaphor in 2796, 4991; meter
704, 712, 733, 757, 2003, 2007;
misquotations 2744; moral
thought 264, 1356, 4926; mysticism 3769, 3827, 4909; nature
4468; on evil 4926; parodied
2711, 2721; pastoral elegy 4793;
philosophy 522, 2922, 2929,
3579, 4357, 4579, 5037; pragmatism 2664; the Prologue 4110;
prosody of In Memoriam, analyzed
by computer 4997; punctuation
error in section LXXII 5135;
readers 3763; religion in 885,
982, 2385, 2398, 2571, 2590,
2841, 3363, 3395, 3481, 4149,
4157, 4831; revisions 3461,
4889; and The Rubáiyát of Omar
Khayyám 2934; science 4157,
4723; section II 3920; section III
4236; section XI 3379; section
XIII 3891; section XV 4803; section XXII 3321; section XLI 4246;
section XLVI 3321; section LIV
2051, 2080; section LXXII 5001,
5135; section LXXXV 3461; section LXXXVII 4721; section XCV
4634, 4729, 4739, 4998; section
XCVI 3921; section CVI 3427,

4982; section CXXI 4700; section CXXIII 5030; section CXXVIII 3920; section CXXXI 4754; sorrow 4390; sources 2829, 2933, 3612; spiritual themes 1249, 1403, 2362, 2893, 2894, 4157; stanza 531, 3032; structure 260, 827, 1066, 2114, 2218, 2264, 3792, 3968, 4077, 4150, 4763, 4794; subjunctive in 4570, 4729, 4739; Tennyson's annotations to 2438; the three Christmases in 2114, 2264; time in 4314; twentieth-century criticism of 5026; unity of 4216; variant binding 3863; variants 3537, 3710, 3800, 3835; and Wordsworth's The Prelude 4973

"In Memoriam": The Way of the Soul (1951) (by E. B. Mattes) 3481, 3500, 3517
In Memoriam, etc., trans. M. L. Cazamian (1937) 3255, 3269
In Memoriam, Maud, and Other Poems, ed. J. D. Jump (1974) 4510, 4666, 4698, 4725
In Tennyson Land (by J. C. Walters) 1298, 1302, 1316, 1321, 1322, 1329, 1331, 1341
"In the Garden at Swainston" 4677
"In the Valley of Cauteretz" 4156
Ireland 1977, 2719, 2955, 3008
irony in Tennyson's work 4029
Irving, Henry 1885, 2425, 3313, 3479
Irving, Washington 917
"Isabel" 455
Isle of Wight 2002
"The Islet" 4854
the isolation theme in Tennyson's poetry 3482
Italian Influence on the Poetry of Tennyson (1936) (by P. N. Roy) 3244, 3262
Italy 3244
Ivanhoe (by W. Scott) 3686

Jack, A. E. 2448
James, Henry 3554, 3586-3587, 3936, 4950
Jammes, Francis 3283
Jesse, Emily Tennyson 5122
Johnson, Lionel 4395
Johnson, Samuel 2617
Jones, Thomas Gwynn 3264, 4310
Jonson, Ben 87, 2340
Jowett, Benjamin 2863, 4786
Jung, Carl Gustav 3349, 3404

Juvenal 3820

"Kairoko" (by N. Soseki) 4873
Kane, Dr. Elisha 2079
Kant, Immanuel 2837
"Kapiolani" 3279
Keats, John: in general 463, 2128, 2531, 2550, 2824, 2872, 2964, 3483, 3574, 4023, 4070, 4290, 4614, 4620, 4775; influence on Tennyson 2472, 2772, 2816, 2820, 3346, 3682, 3907, 4649, 4681
The Keepsake 37
Kemble, Adelaide 4262
A Key to Tennyson's "In Memoriam" (by A. Gatty) 907, 1027
Kierkegaard, Sören 4444
King Arthur's Laureate (1971) (by J. P. Eggers) 4276, 4306, 4492, 4562
King Lear (by W. Shakespeare) 2954, 3317, 4974
Kingsley, Charles 2327, 3119, 4578
Kipling, Rudyard 2443, 2506, 3347, 4822
Kirby, William 3080
Knights of the Round Table 932
Knowles, James 3599, 4391, 4971
Krakatoa 3701

"Lady Clara Vere de Vere": parodied 1907
"Lady Clare" 1091
"The Lady of Shalott": in general 167, 991, 1443, 2976, 3924, 4099, 4195, 4238, 4329, 4470, 4531, 4546, 4582, 4622, 4643, 5102; allegory 167, 3879; sources 2299, 4243
Lady of the Lake 4253
Lady Tennyson's Journal (1981) (ed. J. O. Hoge) 5053, 5111, 5142
Lamartine, Alphonse 1681
Lamb, Charles 1431, 1659
Lancelot 2406, 2407, 2502, 3082, 3225, 4250
Lancelot (by E. A. Robinson) 4076
"Lancelot and Elaine" 506, 594, 595, 598, 915, 1180, 1710, 4212, 4250, 4600, 5108; illustrated 586
Landor, Walter Savage 3743, 4924
landscape 4548
"A Landscape Painter" (by H. James) 3587

Lang, Andrew 2289
language, Victorian study of 5025
Language and Structure in Tenny-
son's Poetry (1973) (by F. E. L.
Priestly) 4420, 4469, 4562,
4563, 4593, 4597, 4696
The Language of Tennyson's In
Memoriam (1971) (by A. Sinfield)
4283, 4298, 4317, 4326, 4366,
4562
Lao Tzu 3808
"The Last of the Light Brigade"
(by R. Kipling) 4822
"The Last Tournament" 690, 691,
706, 708, 711, 716, 720, 728,
3149, 3155, 3174, 3181, 3770,
3822, 4184, 4292, 4783, 4802,
4911, 5109, 5126
Latin 2829
Law, William 3072
Layamon 2996
Lazarus 4369
Lear, Edward 4922
Leaves of Grass (by W. Whitman)
413
Leben und Werke Alfred Lord Ten-
nysons (1899) (by T. A. Fischer)
2091, 2110, 2119, 2162
Lessons from My Masters (by Peter
Bayne) 942, 962
The Letters of Alfred Lord Tennyson, Volume I: 1821-1850 (1981)
(ed. C. Y. Lang and E. F. Shannon, Jr.) 5052, 5127, 5142
The Letters of Arthur Henry Hallam
(1981) (ed. J. Kolb) 5044a,
5134, 5142
The Letters of Emily Lady Tenny-
son (1974) (ed. J. O. Hoge) 4518,
4533, 4624, 4628, 4658, 4718,
4804, 4863
Letters to Frederick Tennyson (by
Alfred, Lord Tennyson), ed. H. J.
Schonfield (1930) 311, 3138
Leyte Gulf 3485
The Library Edition (1872) 705
life after death 1349, 1732, 1998,
2153, 2309, 2464, 2505, 2528,
3019, 3056, 3081, 3113, 3391
The Life and Times of Tennyson:
1809-1850 (1915) (by T. R. Lounsbury) 2797, 2821, 2826, 2827,
2830, 2831, 2833
"Lilian" 1237
Lincoln, Abraham 3674
Lincolnshire 765, 1298, 1347,
1353, 1372, 2063, 2499, 3702,
3713, 3760, 3831, 4135, 4882
Lincolnshire dialect 2499, 4135

The Living Will (1969) (by W. R.
Brashear) 4132, 4203, 4267,
4309
Lockhart, John 1057, 1058
"Locksley Hall": in general 62,
70, 79, 80, 81, 88, 180, 222,
230, 257, 264, 453, 774, 806,
807, 812, 925, 939, 964, 1187,
1492, 1940, 2102, 2453, 2522,
2892, 2904, 3403, 3686, 3819,
3937, 4458; "airy navies" (from
line 124) 3351; as prophecy
1190, 3238; background 3782;
faith in 3299; idea of progress
3208; imagery 3862; influence of
222; influences on 4842; language
2453; liberalism 1159; line 182
of 3261, 3499; and "Locksley
Hall Sixty Years After" 1163,
1172, 1192, 1197, 1202, 1271,
1771, 1802, 1809, 1940, 2036,
2453, 4569; and Moâlakât 3941,
4842; moral thought 264; optimism of 1192; parodied 99,
269, 736; about parodies of 700;
philosophy of 1185, 2036; reputation 3843; sources 3450
Locksley Hall Sixty Years After:
reviews 1167, 1168, 1181-1183,
1186, 1188, 1191, 1195, 1199,
1200-1201, 1204, 1208, 1210-1211,
1213, 1940; in general 1175,
1198, 2453, 3635; background
3782; dating of composition
4364; language 2453; and "Locksley Hall" 1163, 1172, 1184,
1192, 1197, 1202, 1271, 1771,
1802, 1809, 1940, 2036, 2453,
4569; pessimism of 1192, 2036;
philosophy of 2036; replies to
1223
Longfellow, Henry Wadsworth 43,
108, 352, 622, 1294, 1359,
1916, 3515, 4092
"The Lord of Burleigh" 2326, 3232,
3587, 3850
Lord Tennyson (1884) (by H. J.
Jennings) 1069, 1094, 1099
"The Lotos-Eaters" 431, 888,
914, 3510, 3684, 3723, 3740,
3755, 3766, 3874, 3980, 4173,
4936
love 1602, 4770
"Love" 2829
love in Tennyson's work 3967,
4069, 4520
"The Lover's Tale" 648, 2322,
3938, 4054
The Lover's Tale: reviews 912,

918, 920, 922-924, 930, 935,
937, 941, 944, 947; in general
4350, 5140
"The Love Song of J. Alfred Prufrock" (by T.S. Eliot) 4275
Lowell, James Russell 3586
Lucretius 2103, 2365, 2396, 3142
"Lucretius": in general 611, 612,
614-616, 626, 2365, 2396,
3537, 3561, 3944, 4331, 4398,
4453, 4560; line 61 of 4453;
and Lucretius 2103, 2666,
2672; publication of 5088, 5103
Lycidas (by J. Milton) 4049
Lyell, Charles 515, 3395, 3652
Lyrical Poems, ed. F.T. Palgrave
(1885) 1120, 1128, 1136

mabinogion 2273, 3095, 3977,
4180
McGonagall, William 4197, 4268
Maclise, Daniel 507
Macmillan, Alexander 4248, 4316
Maid Marian 1624, 1625, 1643
Maid Marian (by T.L. Peacock)
2484
Mallarmé, Stéphane 1485, 4582
Malory, Thomas 2769, 2866,
2949, 2996, 4166, 4258, 4564,
4783
Man and Myth in Victorian England
(1969) (by J.M. Gray) 4140,
4272, 4274, 4309
Mangles, James Henry 5083
manuscripts of Tennyson 2765,
2887, 3136, 3140, 3252, 3253,
3310, 3399, 3402, 3613, 3617,
3630, 3651, 3672, 3800, 3927,
3944, 4056, 4118, 4158, 4161,
4165, 4185, 4190, 4191, 4260,
4313, 4328, 4334, 4443, 4473,
4483, 4571, 4580, 4769, 4954,
4956, 5030, 5063, 5064, 5124
Manzoni, Alessandro 1860
"Marblethorpe" 4592
"Margaret" 2648, 2649
"Mariana" 960, 4307, 4797, 4988
"Marina" (by T.S. Eliot) 4329
marriage 889, 3632, 4434, 4520,
4606, 4761
"The Marriage of Geraint" 1400,
3095
Marston, John 3670
Martin, Robert Bernard 5115
Marvell, Andrew 3817, 3833, 4354,
4854
Mary, Queen 4457, 4975
Materials for a Life of A.T. (1895)

(by H. Tennyson, the elder)
1875, 1919, 5066
Maud: reviews 324, 325, 327,
329-338, 341-343, 345-350, 354-
356, 358-360, 362-366, 368,
370, 372, 374-380, 382, 383,
385, 386, 388, 392-398, 400,
401, 404-407, 409-413, 421,
422, 424, 425, 430, 433, 437,
458; in general 320, 367, 390,
391, 414, 415, 419, 423, 428,
444, 456, 477, 526, 532, 1029,
1110, 1598, 2102, 2275, 3021,
3116, 3317, 3480, 3719, 3785,
3797, 3838, 3856, 3885, 3969,
4009, 4205, 4224, 4239, 4256,
4257, 4340, 4411, 4471, 4519,
4523, 4583, 4604, 4616, 4753,
4777, 4786, 4792, 4875, 4912;
allegory 4160; as autobiography
4611; background 3719, 3797,
4616; Bible 4160; commerce in
387, 403; composition 3782; and
Crimean War 5057; critical reception of 3539; development
1100, 4616; ending of 4845; gems
in 4942, 4951; hero of 4009;
and Hiawatha (by H.W. Longfellow) 352; imagery of 3698,
4942, 4951; influence of 4392;
influences on 3676, 4966; and
In Memoriam 3823; insanity in
4974; irony in 5073; language
4792; and Leaves of Grass (by W.
Whitman) 413; love and aggression in 4583; lyric 4134; metrics 3890; narrative 4436; Part
III 4782, 4984; and the past
4471; psychology in 3349, 3404;
replies to 321; revisions of
890; D.G. Rossetti on 3220,
3873; and Shakespeare 4966;
sources 3715; structure 4134;
symbolism in 3432, 4256; Tennyson reading 3873, 4341; unity
of 4857; versification 426
Maurice, Frederick Dennison 2741
"The May Queen" 93, 97, 2958
the meaning of life 1744
medieval themes in Tennyson's
work 849, 4848, 4986
medievalism 4986
megalosaur 4735
"Memmian Naphtha-pits" 2774,
2783, 2785
memorial to Tennyson 1827, 1839
Memories of the Tennysons (1900)
(by H.D. Rawnsley) 2151, 2160,
2194, 2196, 2260, 2264

Mendelssohn, Felix 2745
Meredith, George 2824, 2869, 3077, 3088, 3151, 3157, 4611
Merivale, Charles 2033
Merlin 3413, 4171, 5034
Merlin (by E. A. Robinson) 4076
"Merlin and the Gleam" 3394
"Merlin and Vivien": in general 4171, 4237, 4304, 4371; illustrated 589; manuscripts 3402
"The Mermaid" 4937
"The Merman" 4937
mesmerism 4575
The Metaphysical Society 3386
Meynell, Alice 3009
Mill, John Stuart 2144, 4851
Millais, John Everett 2510
"The Miller's Daughter" 1267, 1438, 3302, 3372, 4386
Milnes, Richard Monckton 1297
Milton, John 117, 1064, 1083, 3473, 3811, 4049, 4237, 4435, 4929, 4982
The Mind of Tennyson (1900) (by E. H. Sneath) 2153, 2193
"Miranda" (by W. Shakespeare) 1710
Moâlakât 2379, 3941, 4842
Moby Dick (by H. Melville) 3499
Modernism 3978
Monteith, Robert 4915
monument to Tennyson 2079, 2404
Moore, Thomas 34, 2921
Morning Post (Boston) 73
Morris, William 849, 1471, 2678, 3665, 4070, 4093, 4441, 4848
"Morte d'Arthur" 79, 96, 895, 3548, 3675, 4207, 4879, 5120; parodied 86, 1289
Le Morte d'Arthur (by T. Malory) 607, 2273, 2638, 4076, 4166
Moxon and Co. 4930
the Moxon Poems see Poems, illustrated, 1857
music 4288
Musset, Alfred De see De Musset, Alfred
"My Early Love" 102, 104
mysticism 4909

narrative form in Tennyson's work 4436
narrative poetry 2678
nature goddess 4709
nature in Tennyson's work 1269, 1355, 1376, 1687, 1694, 1786, 1855, 1876, 1997, 2021, 2132, 2138, 2143, 2182, 2184, 2200, 2319, 2323, 2421, 2627, 2804,

2805, 2870, 3075, 3172, 3240, 3263, 3574, 3714, 3872, 4296
Nennius 3982
Newman, John Henry 1921, 2420
New Single-Volume Edition (1884) 1126
The New Timon: A Poetical Romance (by E. Bulwer-Lytton) 116, 118, 119, 120, 122
"The New Timon and the Poets" 5090
Nichol, John 1903
"No More" 6
North, Christopher (pseud. for John Wilson) 3273
"The Northern Farmer, New Style" 674, 683, 880, 1372
"The Northern Farmer, Old Style" 550, 563, 683, 880, 1372
Notes and Marginalia (by J. H. Smith) 742

occultism in Tennyson's work 2871, 2902
"Ode on Saint Cecilia's Day" (by A. Pope) 3272
Ode on the Death of the Duke of Wellington: reviews 279, 285, 288, 291, 292, 294, 302, 303, 309; in general 746, 763, 764, 772, 3666, 3942, 4704, 4956, 5124; composition of 3716, 4956, 5124; manuscripts 4956, 5124
"Oenone": in general 888, 2482, 3434, 4828; classical sources 3794; revisions of 4995
On the Diction of Tennyson, Browning, and Arnold (1970) (by B. Groom) 4213, 4479
"On the Morning of Christ's Nativity" (by J. Milton) 4982
On the Poems of Tennyson (1972) (by W. Hellstrom) 4337, 4439, 4462, 4465, 4486, 4541, 4568, 4597, 4661, 4697
The Once and Future King (1958) (by T. H. White) 3657
"One Warm Saturday" (by D. Thomas) 4777
opium and Tennyson 454, 2888
"Oriana" 295
The Origin of Species (by C. Darwin) 3662
O'Shaughnessy, Arthur William Edgar 4279
"O Swallow, Swallow" translated 3268a
otherwhere in Tennyson's work 2936

Our Living Poets (by H. B. Forman)
745
"The Outcast" 4205
Ovid 3352
"O where is he, the simple fool"
2787, 3883
"The Owl" 16

paintings of Tennyson's works
3899
"The Palace of Art": in general
606, 883, 954, 1251, 2780, 3711,
3729, 3916, 4003, 4026, 4070,
4154, 4501, 4740; autobiographical 3249; sources 3393
Palgrave, Francis T. 3775,
3883, 4111, 4388, 4821, 5032
Palgrave, William Gifford 5097
Paradise Lost (by J. Milton)
4237, 4435
Paradise Regained (by J. Milton)
4304
Parkes, Henry 1538
parodies 85, 86, 99, 571, 644,
768, 1007, 1067, 1068, 1288,
1289, 1293, 1406, 1484, 1907,
2711, 2712, 2713, 2715, 2721,
2724, 2725, 2726, 2730, 2733,
2958, 3027, 3029, 3109, 4247,
4381, 4532, 4780
Pascoli, Giovanni 3256
"The Passing of Arthur": in general 1409, 2064, 2363, 2460,
2483, 2839, 3264, 4152, 4310,
4558; critics on 2460; editions
4152; manuscripts 5063
Past and Present (by T. Carlyle)
3612
pastoral poetry 5044
Pater, Walter 4288
Patmore, Coventry 4367
Les Pauvres Gens (by V. Hugo)
2178
peace in the works of Tennyson
2864
Peacock, Thomas Love 2484, 4109
"Pelleas and Ettarre" 2954, 3995,
4212, 4802
Pentalogia Graeca (by W. Trollope)
5064
Perception and Design in Tennyson's
Idylls of the King (1969) (by J. R.
Reed) 4143, 4297, 4306, 4322,
4366, 4562
Percival 3837, 4305, 4585
Persian language 3999
Persian poetry 3327, 3338, 3344,
3371

The Pirate (by W. Scott) 4937
plagiarism 1042, 1045, 1046,
1178, 2242, 2253
Poe, Edgar Allan 1509, 1916,
2611, 3674, 4463, 4662; influenced by Tennyson 301
Poemi drammatici de Alfredo Tennyson (1919) (by E. Girardini)
2875, 2886
Poems, 1833: reviews 12-14, 17,
18, 20-22, 25-27, 30, 32, 36,
39, 41; in general 3247; revisions 3677
Poems, 1842: reviews 46-54, 56-
62, 64-80, 82-84, 89, 92, 94,
101, 107, 111, 151, 156, 161, 173,
174, 179, 180, 256, 305, 693,
911, 1056; in general 369, 952,
1001, 1337, 2357, 2606, 4287,
4554; editions 2761, 4490; revisions 4694; variorum edition
4287
Poems, illustrated, 1857: reviews
446, 448, 452, 4727; in general
1803, 2473, 2644, 3058, 3411,
4438, 4836, 5107; edition 4690;
history of publication of 5144
poems about Tennyson 1260, 1285,
1299, 1418, 1426, 1429, 1432,
1439, 1445, 1451, 1468-1470,
1474, 1495, 1498, 1502, 1504,
1512, 1548, 1552-1554, 1556,
1565, 1569, 1570, 1582, 1583,
1585, 1595, 1604, 1633, 1637,
1645, 1647, 1648, 1650, 1657,
1684, 1685, 1702, 1772, 1893,
1968, 2019, 2101, 2350, 2430,
2487, 2523, 2639, 2717, 2729,
2812, 2969, 2974, 3013, 3293,
4294, 4385
Poems before Congress (by E. B.
Browning) 503
Poems by Two Brothers: reviews
1, 2; in general 1715, 1748,
1758, 1777, 3442, 3778, 4083,
4443
Poems, Chiefly Lyrical: reviews
4, 5, 7-11, 15-17, 26, 36, 38,
39, 41, 1672, 2349, 3329; editions 3959; variants 3947
The Poems of Alfred Tennyson,
1830-1870, ed. T. H. Warren
(1913) 2735, 2752
The Poems of Tennyson, ed. C.
Ricks (1969) 4145, 4167, 4168,
4176, 4200, 4202, 4260, 4263,
4309, 4312, 4383, 4439
poems to Tennyson 859, 938, 1115,
1171, 1247, 1248, 1274, 1387, 1391

La Poesia di Alfred Tennyson (1928)
(by G. N. Giordano-Orsini) 3051,
3093
"The Poet" 3281, 3357, 3358,
3742, 3829
the poet laureateship (see also:
Tennyson as poet laureate) 184,
197-199, 218, 223, 224, 240,
1306, 1342, 1519-1521, 1579,
1581, 1600, 1656, 1891, 2303,
2615, 2919
poetic theory 3998
Poetry of Alfred Tennyson (1930)
(by C. H. O. Scaife) 3110, 3137,
3141, 3165
The Poetry of Tennyson (1977) (by
A. D. Culler) 4751, 4784,
4811, 4823, 4844, 4849, 4858,
4864, 4876, 4880, 4890, 4895,
4939, 4940, 4981, 5008, 5013
The Poetry of Tennyson (1899) (by
H. Van Dyke) 1256, 1315, 1320,
1323, 1328, 1348, 1735
Poland 3248
Pope, Alexander 2922, 2929, 3020,
3272, 3601, 4766
"Porphyria's Lover" (by R. Brown-
ing) 4178
Portugal 484
Praed, Winthrop Mackworth 3743
The Pre-Eminent Victorian (1962)
(J. Richardson) 3758, 3768,
3777, 3784, 3809, 3839, 3847
The Prelude (by W. Wordsworth)
3464, 4973
Pre-Raphaelite art 5108
Pre-Raphaelite painting 4756
Pre-Raphaelite Poems see Poems,
illustrated, 1857
Pre-Raphaelites 4834, 5144
Pre-Raphaelitism 4797, 4851
A Primer of Tennyson (1896) (by
W. M. Dixon) 1900, 1926, 1927
The Princess: reviews 131-133,
135-166, 168-171, 173-176, 179,
299, 738, 2349; in general 169,
222, 263, 518, 576, 782, 997,
1015, 1044, 1104, 1112, 1414,
1939, 2099, 2249, 2259, 2275,
2535, 2587, 3079, 3083, 3272,
3643, 3779, 3847, 3856, 4022,
4027, 4646, 4654, 4672, 4673,
4685, 4826, 4832, 4853; bibliography 2159; composition 3253;
evolution and 5038; feminism
4131, 4408; femininity 4131,
4408; Ida 4544; illustrations for
507; influences on 3507, 3570;
love 3976; manuscripts 3253;

narrative 4436; parodied in music 1067; part IV of 3435; the
Prince 4446; relationship of
man and woman 3976; science
and 5038; section VII, lines
136-139 4047; sex and politics
4671; Shakespeare and 4878;
sources 3298; structure 4544,
4703; symbolism 4703; "Tears,
Idle Tears" see separate entry;
tone 3779, 4022; unity 4703;
"weird seizures" 3790, 4575,
4586, 4920; women's rights 307,
1015
progress 2892, 3208, 3233, 3307,
4747
The Promise of May: reviews of
performances 1021, 1022, 1028,
1030, 1033, 1035, 1036; about
performances 3919; production
1145
proofs of Tennyson's works 3399,
4386, 4396, 4473, 4956
psychology in Tennyson's work
3349
Punch 4651, 4870, 4992, 4993, 5006
purple 2382
Pyrenees 1085, 1193, 2304

Quaritch, Bernard 2765
Quarterly Review 18, 20, 31, 81,
477, 2616
Queen Mab (by P. B. Shelley) 3393
Queen Mary: reviews 786-790,
792-805, 808-811, 813, 814, 817-
821, 824, 829, 831, 844; in general 784, 834, 865, 1023, 2491,
3077, 3088; about performances
830, 832, 835, 836, 837, 838,
839, 841, 3479, 3869; characterizations 4975; sex and politics
4671; sources 2685, 2690
Quinn, John 2995

Rasselas (by S. Johnson) 3507, 4974
rationalism 2411, 2900
the Reaction against Tennyson 4577
"Recollections of the Arabian Nights"
3984
recordings of Tennyson reading
3954, 5015
Records of Tennyson, Ruskin,
Browning (1892) (by A. Ritchie)
1408, 1457, 1472, 1530, 1562,
1594, 1596
red 4024
religion 2456

religion in Tennyson's poetry (see
    also: Tennyson's religion) 511, 785,
    878, 896, 1413, 1448, 1482, 1510,
    1644, 1667, 1717, 1750, 1792,
    1876, 1920, 1998, 2006, 2097,
    2148, 2219, 2224, 2315, 2358,
    2362, 2385, 2398, 2426, 2456,
    2469, 2540, 2546, 2547, 2571,
    2590, 2619, 2779, 2832, 2842,
    2845, 2850, 2881, 2882, 2970,
    3049, 3148, 3154, 3189, 3190,
    3191, 3192, 3363, 3440, 3474,
    3481, 3681, 3688, 3751, 4071,
    4149, 4337, 4413, 4431, 4909
The Remains in Verse and Prose
    of Arthur Henry Hallam 252
the Renaissance 2884
Renan, Ernest 1399, 3975
"The Revenge" 3494, 3598
Revue des Deux-Mondes 4706
Ricks, Christopher 5048
"Rifle Clubs!!!" 3886
The Rime of the Ancient Mariner
    (by S. T. Coleridge) 2976
"Ring Out, Wild Bells" 210
"Rizpah" 1461, 3237, 4528
Robin Hood 2739, 4536
Robinson, Edward Arlington 4187
the Romantics 3806
Romeo and Juliet (by W. Shake-
    speare) 3317
rondeau 4498
Rossetti, Christina 4707
Rossetti, Dante Gabriel 2772,
    2944, 3086, 3220, 3665, 3873,
    4211, 4438, 4611
Rossetti, William Michael 2424
the Rossettis 4684
The Rubáiyát of Omar Khayyâm
    2934
Ruskin, John 435, 561, 905, 1408,
    2144, 2972, 4352, 4526, 4713

"Saint Agnes" 37
"Saint Simeon Stylites" 888, 4091
Saint Thomas of Canterbury (by A.
    de Vere) 1122
Sappho 4622
"Sardanapalus" (by Lord Byron) 2765
Sartor Resartus (by T. Carlyle)
    3450, 3787
satires 632, 1243, 1808, 3105
Schiller, Friedrich 1681, 4128
science 1701, 2180, 2456, 2607,
    3258, 4530, 5038
Scott, Walter 903, 1155, 1230,
    2666, 2672, 2952, 3119
the sea 3923

"Sea Dreams" 582
Selected Poems of Tennyson, ed.
    E. Blunden (1960) 3695, 3793,
    3809
A Selection from the Poems of
    Tennyson, ed. W. H. Auden
    (1944) 3345, 3353, 3365, 3367,
    3368, 3369, 3382
Sellwood, Emily 4460
sexual ambivalence in Tennyson's
    work 3952
Shakespeare, William 211, 1096,
    1216, 1220, 1243, 1548, 1710,
    1779, 1910, 1912, 2175, 2415,
    3040, 3163, 3300, 3317, 4108,
    4715, 4878, 4966
Shaw, George Bernard 2611
Shelley, Percy Bysshe 251, 463,
    791, 843, 1083, 2816, 2820,
    3361, 3393, 3488, 3601, 3742,
    3907, 4280, 4752
Shepherd, Ettrick 936
Shepherd, Richard Herne 3938,
    5090
Shorthouse, Joseph Henry 2393
Sidney, Philip 909
"A Sign Seeker" (by T. Hardy)
    4394
"Sir Galahad" 4301
"The Sisters" 4178, 4746; drama-
    tized 33, 1218
Six Tennyson Essays (1954) (by C.
    Tennyson) 3551, 3569, 3571,
    3577, 3608, 4559
Skepticism 1930
"The Sleeping Beauty" 957, 2341
Smedley, Edward 40
Smith, Alexander 300, 402
Smith, Byron Caldwell 1952
Smith, O. A. 4097
The Social Ideals of Alfred Tenny-
    son as Related to His Time
    (1906) (by W. C. Gordon) 2417,
    2428, 2429, 2441
Somersby 2659, 2673, 3568, 3691,
    3844, 4006, 4515
sorrow in Tennyson 760, 1681
Soseki, Natsume 4873
Sotheby's sale of Tennyson papers
    5029
the soul before birth 3190
Spain 3755, 3766, 3948
the Spasmodics 4445, 4459
Spedding, James 4589
Spenser, Edmund 211, 2061, 2531,
    2550, 2884, 3801, 4173
Spenser, W. R. 585
spiritualism 1235, 3191, 4829,
    4923

"St. Agnes' Eve" 1370
"Stanzas" 40
Stedman, Edmund Clarence 2632
Stephen, James 3666
Stevens, Brunton 3949
Steytler, Charles R.C. 5015
Strauss, Richard 2257
Studies in Tennyson (1981) (ed. H.
  Tennyson, the younger) 5054,
  5091, 5142
Studies in Victorian Verse Drama
  (1979) (by V. Sharma) 4907,
  5020
A Study ... of ... the Princess (by
  S.E. Dawson) 1015, 1043,
  1050, 1088
A Study of the Works of Tennyson
  (by E.C. Tainsh) 608, 613,
  618, 621, 1707, 1774, 1789,
  1795
Subjectivism 4132
Sufism 4379
supernatural 971
"Supposed Confessions of a Second-
  rate Sensitive Mind" 3812
The Suppressed Poems of Alfred,
  Lord Tennyson, 1830-1862, ed.
  J.C. Thomson (1903) 2316,
  2338, 2339
Surrey 1024
"Sweet and Low" 308, 4587
Swinburne, Algernon Charles 978,
  1344, 2337, 2615, 2621, 2769,
  2928, 2939, 3077, 3088, 3246,
  3650, 3701, 4139, 4292, 4302,
  4746, 4752, 4770, 4877, 4911,
  4925, 5046, 5109
Symonds, John Addington 4577,
  5092
Symons, Arthur 4292

Taine, Hippolyte Adolphe 884,
  2501, 2935
Tainsh, Edward Campbell 3706
The Tale of Balen (by A.C. Swin-
  burne) 2769
Tales from Tennyson (1900) (by G.C.
  Allen) 2137, 2192
Taylor, Henry 1225
Taylor, Isaac 4182
Taylor, Jeremy 438
The Teaching of Tennyson (1894)
  (J. Oates) 1805, 1889, 2117
"Tears, Idle Tears" 577, 3350,
  3366, 3385, 3400, 3448, 3486,
  3504, 3511, 3798, 3805, 3847,
  3928, 3987, 4086, 4106, 4330;
  translated 3268a

Teilhard, Pierre 4157
Tennant, Laura 2989
Tennyson, Audrey Boyle 4866
Tennyson, Charles (Tennyson's
  brother) 591, 3388, 3602,
  4443
Tennyson, Charles (the younger)
  4170, 4201, 4415, 5116
Tennyson, Edward 4574
Tennyson, Emily, Lady 1932,
  3595, 4230, 4518, 4378, 4518,
  4796, 4953, 4958, 5053
Tennyson, George Clayton (father
  of Alfred Tennyson) 3250
Tennyson, Frederick 3111, 3294,
  3388, 3602, 3629a, 3813, 4075
Tennyson, Hallam (the elder) 3080,
  3442, 4316, 5118
Tennyson, Lionel 4271, 4388
Tennyson (1894) (by S.A. Brooke)
  1800, 1810, 1814, 1817, 1818,
  1824, 1833, 1835, 1842, 1846,
  1848, 1884
Tennyson (1960) (by J.H. Buckley)
  3696, 3721, 3728, 3732, 3733,
  3735-3737, 3739, 3741, 3746,
  3747, 3749, 3750, 3772, 3773,
  3780, 3786, 3791
Tennyson (1898) (by E.L. Cary)
  2028, 2065, 2109
Tennyson (1898) (by E.J. Cuthbertson) 2030, 2066
Tennyson (1923) (by H.I'A. Fausset)
  2966, 2978, 2980, 2985-2987
Tennyson (1980) (ed. E.A. Francis)
  4964, 5117
Tennyson (1899) (by S. Gwynn)
  2092, 2105, 2108, 2118, 2120,
  2127, 2129
Tennyson (1978) (by P. Henderson)
  4830, 4844, 4846, 4847, 4862,
  4868, 4896, 4898, 4918, 4921,
  4933, 4938-4939, 5005, 5028
Tennyson (1899) (by E. Koeppel)
  2094, 2163
Tennyson (1957) (by F.L. Lucas)
  3624, 3634, 3640
Tennyson (1902) (by A.C. Lyall)
  2279, 2284, 2287, 2290, 2295,
  2298, 2300, 2301, 2305, 2333
Tennyson (1980) (by R.B. Martin)
  4970, 4978, 4983, 4996, 4999,
  5004, 5007, 5010, 5012, 5018,
  5036, 5040, 5061, 5067, 5076,
  5077, 5080, 5082, 5086, 5087,
  5115, 5119, 5131, 5138
Tennyson (1923) (by H. Nicolson)
  2971, 2978, 2985, 2986, 2987
Tennyson (1973) (ed. D.J. Palmer)

4417, 4467, 4486, 4499, 4559, 4562, 4596, 4675, 4678, 4696
Tennyson (1972) (by C. Ricks) 4343, 4356, 4361, 4365, 4387, 4403, 4407, 4440, 4480, 4485, 4489, 4493, 4497, 4562, 4661, 4733
Tennyson (1971) (by B.C. Southam) 4284, 4325
Tennyson (1966) (by J.B. Steane) 3958, 4006, 4033, 4039, 4241, 4242, 4244
Tennyson (1976) (by P. Turner) 4691, 4712, 4771, 4778, 4805, 4867, 4886, 4947
Tennyson (1891) (by J.C. Walters) 1691, 1822, 1834, 1857
Tennyson (1912) (by A. Watson) 2689, 2693
Tennyson (1930) (by H. Wolfe) 3116, 3137, 3141, 3165
Tennyson: In Memoriam (1964) (by K.W. Grandsen) 3849, 3986
Tennyson: In Memoriam (1970) (ed. J.D. Hunt) 4214, 4324
Tennyson: The Critical Heritage (1967) (ed. J.D. Jump) 4013, 4050, 4082, 4085, 4102, 4122-4125, 4155, 4159, 4179
The Tennyson Album (1980) (by A. Wheatcroft) 4972, 4978, 4983, 5017, 5036, 5040, 5061, 5067
Tennyson and Clio (1979) (by H. Kozicki) 4903, 4985, 5060, 5062, 5081, 5125, 5128
Tennyson and His Friends (1911) (by H. Tennyson) 2658, 2691, 2694, 2701-2704, 2707, 2710
Tennyson and His Pre-Raphaelite Illustrators (1894) (by G.S. Layard) 1803, 1825, 1832, 1836, 1841, 1849
Tennyson and His Publishers (1979) (by J.S. Hagen) 4901, 4948, 4990, 5003, 5021, 5081, 5100, 5112
Tennyson and "In Memoriam" (1892) (by J. Jacobs) 1397, 1705, 1737, 1745, 1766
Tennyson and Swinburne as Romantic Naturalists (1981) (by K. McSweeney) 5046, 5133
Tennyson and The Princess (1958) (by J. Killham) 3643, 3661, 3667, 3678, 3700, 3703, 3705, 3712
Tennyson and the Reviewers (1952) (by E.F. Shannon, Jr.) 3496, 3524, 3536, 3541, 3544, 3545, 3560, 3566, 3608
Tennyson and Tradition (1979) (by

R. Pattison) 4906, 4985, 5012a, 5062, 5072, 5074, 5081, 5085, 5087, 5095
Tennyson as: a botanist 753, 1217, 1245, 1855, 2421; critic 4603; an entomologist 2421; feminist 2434; a geologist 2421; a humorist 1854, 3551; a love poet 4189; a minor poet 2788; a modern poet 3457; a national poet 2071, 2576, 2601, 3316; an occultist 2902; an ornithologist 2421, 3714; poet for modern age 4813; a poet for women 1532, 1631; poet laureate 184, 197-199, 218, 223, 224, 240, 427, 2801, 2919, 2950, 3089, 3549, 3679, 3758, 4426; poet of humanity 2124; a poet of the past 110, 313, 3931, 4080, 4336, 4432, 4435, 4471, 4653, 4903, 4906, 4928, 5042; a prophet 73, 124, 289, 1272, 1682, 2029, 2596, 3238, 3351, 3660, 3979; representative of his age 534, 1070, 1301, 1339, 1412, 1688, 1792, 1800, 1897, 1913, 1957, 2143, 2181, 2307, 2317, 2417, 2593, 2680, 2916, 2922, 2929, 2973, 2994, 3046, 3054, 3176, 3199, 3212, 3215, 3276, 3285, 3579, 3643, 3761, 3996, 4081, 4516; a smoker 4552; a social poet 91, 98; a spiritualist 1235; a teacher 69, 142, 561, 1434, 1475, 1482, 1510, 1644, 1661, 1691, 1756, 1805, 2031, 2125, 2148, 2314, 2315, 2362, 2546, 2779, 3183
Tennyson as a Religious Teacher (1900) (by C.F.G. Masterman) 2148, 2190, 2195, 2207
Tennyson as Seen by His Parodists (1926) (J. Postma) 3027, 3045
Tennyson Centenary Exhibition 2609
The Tennyson Collection (1961) (ed. J.C. Wyllie) 3724, 3744
Tennyson Collection, Usher Gallery, Lincoln (1963) (by C. Tennyson) 3799, 3860
Tennyson-D'Eyncourt, Clara 3730
A Tennyson Dictionary (1916) (by A.E. Baker) 2809, 2822, 4089
A Tennyson Handbook (1963) (by G. O. Marshall, Jr.) 3795, 3888
Tennysonian (as a word) 3933
Tennysoniana (by R.H. Shepherd) 910, 1048

Tennysonian Love (1968) (by G. Joseph) 3967, 4069, 4188, 4245, 4261, 4266, 4272
Tennyson in America (1943) (by J.O. Eidson) 3328, 3332, 3335, 3342
Tennyson in Egypt (1942) (by W.D. Paden) 3309, 3340, 3343, 3360
Tennyson in France (1930) (by M.M. Bowder) 3101, 3158, 3160, 3166, 3187
Tennyson in Lincoln (1972-1973) (by N. Campbell) 4334, 4375, 4402, 4487, 4551, 4594, 4724
Tennyson Laureate (1962) (by V. Pitt) 3757, 3768, 3771, 3777, 3784, 3809, 3821, 3830, 3839, 3846, 3847, 3858, 3865
Tennyson, Lincolnshire and Australia (1974) (by C. Tennyson and H. Dyson) 4517, 4538
Tennyson Research Centre 3894, 4334
Tennyson, Ruskin, Mill (1900) (by F. Harrison) 2144, 2166, 2121, 2171, 2188, 2199, 2203, 2212
Tennyson Sixty Years After (1948) (by P.F. Baum) 3405, 3414
The Tennysons (1975) (by C. Tennyson and H. Dyson) 4608, 4624, 4642, 4647, 4789, 4800
Tennyson's: aesthetics 2903, 3688, 3907, 4081, 4234, 4290, 4400, 4423, 4617, 4694, 4775; afterworld 3019; alliteration 2394, 2402; annotations 2438, 2480, 4962; apocalyptic vision 4231; archaic words 7, 1969, 1995, 2861; Arthurian poetry 607, 638, 697, 717, 2457, 2939, 3583, 3657, 4064, 4258, 4795, 4910, mortality in 4105, parodied 768, sources for 4397, 4767; artistry 26, 62, 152, 737, 1273, 1430, 1545, 1742, 1800, 2041, 2511, 2763, 3039, 3107, 3123, 4630, 4781; astronomy 2446, 3435, 5045; audience 521, 886, 1271, 1466, 1670, 1727, 2746, 2811, 3230, 3245, 3305, 3328, 3477, 3505, 3515, 3542, 4319, 4422, 4638; baronetcy 568; birthday 3702; blank verse 1150, 1958, 2630, 2634; career 1034, 1501, 1517, 3646, 4286, 4389, 4900; Celtic reading 4115; character 496, 1430, 1651, 2041, 2050, 2096, 2493, 2594, 2675, 2737, 3553, 3913; characteriza-

tions 1132, 1151, 2857, 3312, 3497, 3837, 4108, 4147, 4226, 4305, 4360, 4428, 4446, 4910, 4975, 4979, 5070, 5075, 5079, 5143; classical poetry 1752, 2232, 2359, 3062, 3218, 3575, 5132, mortality in 4105; classicism 1752, 2183, 2232, 2359, 2396, 2781, 2818, 3062, 3142, 3254, 3301, 3302, 3336, 3434, 3550, 3575, 3585, 3627, 3699, 3794, 3906, 3985, 4011, 4478, 4488, 4566, 4572, 4614, 4743, 5049, 5132; clerical characters 2857; death 1394, 1411, 1417-1423, 1426, 1429, 1432, 1436, 1439, 1445, 1447, 1450-1452, 1465, 1468-1470, 1473, 1474, 1480, 1490, 1493, 1495, 1497-1499, 1502, 1507, 1512-1516, 1534-1537, 1548, 1550, 1552-1554, 1556, 1557, 1565, 1569, 1570, 1573, 1579, 1582, 1585, 1590, 1595, 1601, 1604, 1607-1609, 1630, 1632, 1636-1638, 1640, 1645, 1647, 1648, 1650, 1651, 1655, 1657, 1658, 1684, 1685, 1772, 1862, 1905, 2101, 2313, 2384, 2487, 2717, 2729, 2969, 2974, 3293, 4380; development 3552, 3654, 3696, 4420, 4433, 4522, 4694; dialect poems 3693, 4135, 4146, 4348; dialogue 4752; diction 440, 887, 2321, 3274, 3578, 4213; dramas in general 1013, 1255, 1692, 1876, 1879, 1885, 1911, 1915, 2011, 2136, 2427, 2838, 3025, 3028, 3040, 3077, 3087, 3088, 3179, 3416, 3609, 3919, 4005, 4012, 4286, 4427, 4525, 4627, 4905, 4907, 4975; dramatic poetry 1255, 2875, 3555, 3622, 3902, 4034, 4192, 4503, 4554, 4629, 4695, 4841, 5043; early poetry (see also: Tennyson's poetry in general) 572, 573, 581, 593, 602, 1040, 1079, 1080, 1239, 1246, 1350, 1876, 2037, 2142, 2168, 2170, 2176, 2189, 2191, 2204, 2206, 2208, 2244, 2269, 2173, 2472, 2534, 2793, 2797, 2829, 2901, 3153, 3167, 3309, 3452, 3552, 3604, 3628, 3660, 3688, 3709, 3762, 3848, 3851, 3907, 3945, 3964, 4083, 4132, 4150, 4151, 4333, 4455, 4522, 4653, 4667, 4706, 4840, 4904, 4987, 5146, translated 2764, 2771;

elegiac vision 4899; elegies 5129; English idyls 4433, 4595, 4894, 4908, 5096; environment 2038, 2722, 3139; epic poetry 2660, 2736; epigrams 3410; epithets 3039; eroticism 5002; ethical views 3097; family 1441, 1576, 1622, 1851, 2048, 2151, 2198, 2320, 2810, 3044, 3250, 3251, 3388, 3396, 3602, 3831, 3844, 4006, 4075, 4271, 4351, 4449, 4608, 4684, 4810; fancy 8, 12, 72; friendships 1741, 2000, 2028, 2320, 2658, 2668, 3198, 4100, 4693; funeral 1440, 1445, 1456, 1488, 1504, 1518, 1541, 1542, 1560, 1583, 1633, 1695, 2419, 4197, 4328, 4380; glibness 8; handwriting 1844; homes 596, 661, 848, 1298, 1404, 1425, 1589, 1936, 2028, 2310, 2376, 2392, 2423, 2650, 2997, 3034, 3139, 5016; idea of progress 3233; idealism 2420; imagery 25, 80, 142, 1948, 2382, 3309, 3590, 3616, 3665, 3698, 3731, 3862, 3950, 4296, 4360, 4630, 4667, 4738, 4757, 4824, 4871, 4925, 5002, 5045, 5145; imagination 9, 23, 25, 1430, 1723, 3460, 3552, 4054, 4760, 4781, 4963; imperialism 3316; influence 853, 1544, 2582, 2876, 3197, 3362, 3372, 3457, 3554, 3587, 3610, 3653, 3899, 3908, 3937, 3949, 3980, 4047, 4193, 4275, 4310, 4392, 4567, 4676, 4768, 4941, 5024, religious 3311, spiritual 1280; intellect 36, 232, 3446, 3909; inventiveness 7, 1723; landscape 1948, 3489, 3966, 4043, 4067, 4072, 4572; language 23, 41, 69, 132, 173, 258, 479, 485, 815, 1340, 1380, 1960, 2128, 2369, 2400, 2450, 2499, 2660, 2736, 2802, 2836, 2844, 2915, 3347, 3390, 3593, 3652, 4135, 4283, 4348, 4420, 4481, 4931, 4937; late elegies 4581; later poetry 3418, 4964; leadership 3042; library 3355, 3384, 3439, 4888; lyrics 2536, 2548, 2728, 2731, 2736, 2798, 2921, 3178, 3246, 4083, 4565, 4843; metaphors 4150, 4288; method of composition 4001, 4321, 4484, 4781; metrics 758, 1150, 1938, 2471, 2495, 2952, 3890, 5070; mission 1987,

2354; moral themes 1240, 1253, 1483, 2803, 3097, 3120, 3390, 4066; morbidity 2748; mysticism 879, 2258, 2478, 2732, 2751, 2879, 3316, 3769, 4002, 4464, 4817, 4909; mythical landscapes 4572; narrative poetry 2678, 3551, 3856, 4761; nature poetry 1687, 1694; nihilism 4400; optimism 1272, 1682, 2572; Orientalism 4018; originality 8, 29, 74, 151, 678, 1723, 3172, 3907; paired poems 4524; parodies 4511, 4780, 4854; passion 2014; pastoral poetry 3760; peerage 1049, 1059, 1062, 1071, 1097; pension of 1845 114; perspectives 4790; pessimism 2036; philosophy 522, 1060, 1097, 1185, 1222, 1272, 1349, 1434, 1682, 1691, 1856, 2036, 2153, 2351, 2418, 2732, 2922, 2929, 3102, 3740, 4018, 4080, 4148, 4674, 4903; physical voice 3752; poetry illustrated 1296, 1669; poetry in general: (most of the following entries are cited elsewhere in this Index; each is notable for its broad view of Tennyson's poetry) 18, 20, 24, 28, 29, 31, 36, 45, 55, 63, 87, 88, 90, 91, 97, 103, 110, 112, 115, 117, 121, 123, 125, 126, 174, 179, 181, 195, 222, 262, 264, 276, 278, 296, 297, 314, 322, 323, 344, 369, 389, 399, 418, 428, 432, 434, 436, 441, 443, 450, 451, 457, 459-461, 471, 480, 492, 495, 496, 498, 503, 508, 513, 520, 534, 535, 546, 560, 564, 570, 574, 590, 597, 599, 604, 605, 627-629, 634, 643, 646, 647, 654, 659, 678, 685, 697, 703, 707, 737, 739, 740, 762, 778, 780, 783, 842, 846, 867, 886, 897, 900, 905, 908, 909, 949, 1008, 1038, 1054, 1063, 1090, 1129, 1132, 1151, 1212, 1219, 1226, 1227, 1233, 1236, 1240, 1251-1253, 1256, 1296, 1360, 1361, 1407, 1408, 1410, 1463, 1466, 1483, 1546, 1558, 1603, 1666, 1669, 1670, 1680, 1726, 1754, 1800, 1801, 1942, 1945, 1946, 2017, 2026, 2035, 2038, 2040, 2090, 2150, 2167, 2229, 2231, 2236, 2240, 2241, 2288, 2316, 2317, 2338, 2339, 2391, 2413,

2418, 2454, 2455, 2458, 2461,
2463, 2488, 2492, 2503, 2514,
2525, 2533, 2534, 2574, 2575,
2585, 2595, 2601, 2606, 2627,
2631, 2637, 2645, 2656, 2657,
2676, 2686, 2687, 2714, 2723,
2727, 2735, 2740, 2759, 2765,
2777, 2788, 2792, 2795, 2811,
2815, 2865, 2872, 2873, 2883,
2889, 2896, 2905, 2923, 2928,
2961, 2963-2965, 2990, 2992,
2993, 3000, 3012, 3014, 3026,
3036, 3051, 3057, 3059, 3103,
3106, 3107, 3110, 3116, 3118,
3123, 3144, 3183, 3196-3197, 3210,
3242-3243, 3255, 3287, 3289,
3319, 3322, 3323, 3337, 3345,
3348, 3361, 3389, 3398, 3455,
3457, 3475, 3478, 3482, 3495,
3502, 3513, 3601, 3606, 3626,
3627, 3629, 3635, 3641, 3644,
3656, 3664, 3683, 3687, 3695,
3697, 3743, 3765, 3853, 3872,
3912, 3957, 3958, 4030, 4042,
4070, 4071, 4117, 4137, 4139,
4148, 4175, 4205, 4217, 4223,
4225, 4227, 4234, 4279, 4285,
4289, 4337, 4346, 4347, 4349,
4354, 4355, 4368, 4379, 4431,
4432, 4454, 4504, 4510, 4512,
4524, 4527, 4605, 4607, 4617,
4619, 4620, 4680, 4686, 4751,
4764, 4765, 4773, 4833, 4839,
4869, 4891, 4893, 4894, 4903,
4914, 4923, 4963, 5044, 5129,
5147; poetry of the 1850's
4609, 4708; poetry's musicality
38, 52, 1483, 1611, 1612, 4650;
point of view 3734; political
views 156, 478, 1627, 1876,
3099, 3121, 3246, 3266, 3267,
3551, 3857, 3893, 4708, 4742;
popularity 2746, 2811, 3245,
4422; portraits of men 2669,
2814, 5075; portraits of women
41, 132, 420, 1220, 1931, 2235,
2559, 3415, 3682, 5075, 5079;
prosody 3418, 4042, 4223; pseu-
donyms 3611; publishers 1610,
1734, 2187, 2214, 4901, 4930;
rank among poets 23, 39, 45,
53, 64, 72, 90, 95, 96, 100,
107, 117, 124, 173, 179, 225,
235, 237, 445, 1064, 1471,
1722, 1768, 1953, 2835, 2964,
3026, 3195, 3242, 3464; relation
to modern life 2143, 2181, 2984,
3084, 3094, 3209, 3258, 3457,
3466, 3498, 3722, 4813, 5051;

religious beliefs (see also: separate entry, religion in Tennyson's poetry) 200, 233, 289,
298, 625, 752, 1349, 1448,
1628, 1667, 1691, 1717, 1769,
1784, 1792, 1838, 1843, 1876,
1929, 1954, 2023, 2148, 2153,
2169, 2186, 2351, 2362, 2528a,
2546, 2588, 2590, 2675, 2737,
2779, 2856, 2970, 3148, 3154,
3170, 3311, 3395, 3428, 3551,
3570, 3604, 3621, 3681, 3688,
3903, 4081, 4149, 4413, 4877,
4909, 4913, 4977; reputation 90,
1345, 2077, 2797, 2835, 3076,
3195, 3245, 3305, 3328, 3496,
3553, 3909; revisions 52, 56,
68, 89, 92, 1381, 1862, 2481,
2600, 3341, 3399, 3461, 3484,
3496, 3539, 3677, 3716, 3823,
3874, 4645, 4694, 4889, 4995;
rhymes 2849, 2853, 2854, 2860;
rhythms 2846, 5084, 5147; romanticism 42, 151, 1491, 2215,
2644, 2991, 3806, 3826, 3963,
3967, 4023, 4065, 4208, 4210,
4288, 4418, 4451, 4463, 4470,
4488, 4615, 4944, 5046, 5114,
5123; science 771, 1701, 1787,
2180, 2279, 2351, 2421, 2446,
2528a, 2607, 2627, 2683, 2880,
2962, 2970, 3148, 3150, 3154,
3156, 3172, 3177, 3258, 3263,
3307, 3349, 3351, 3435, 3449,
3521, 3547, 3570, 3603, 3652,
3681, 4040, 4183, 4281, 4308,
4344, 4430, 4638, 5038, 5045;
sea poetry 2291, 2325, 3923;
skill; 52, 60, 151, 159, 678,
737, 1564, 2008, 3274, 3578;
social commentary 162, 1627,
2417, 2428; social philosophy
779, 1876, 2417, 2428, 2434;
social themes 1240, 1253, 1876,
2417, 2428, 5143; social views
3857, 3962, 4414, 4520, 4770,
4787; songs 1882, 3018, 4922;
set to music 906; sonnets 271,
591, 1606, 2829, 3248, 3658,
4293, 4684, 4687; sources 1258,
1354, 2238, 2299, 2322, 2662,
2685, 2690, 2720, 3025, 4035,
4064, 4116, 4243, 4397, 4937,
4965, 4973, 5089; spiritual views
4527; style 488, 2400, 2450,
2660, 2901, 2952, 2963, 3274,
3494, 3578, 3966, 4137, 4682,
4689, 4957; supernaturalism
3924; symbolism 3491, 3636,

3851, 3923, 4824, 4925, 5071;
talent 519; theories 2930, 3654;
thought 9, 46, 113, 264, 631a,
1215, 1339, 1442, 1463, 1680,
1688, 2144, 2153, 2210, 2279,
2351, 2362, 2414, 2581, 2637,
2908, 3115, 3345, 3446, 3570,
3664, 3687, 3909, 3910, 4015,
4026, 4057, 4231, 4382, 4436,
4610, 4926; translations of Horace 5132; unpublished juvenalia
5146; use of architecture 681;
versification 910, 2901, 3122,
3551; view of Shakespeare
4715; vision of infinity 4748;
weltanschauung 2165, 2436,
2931, 3330; work in general:
(most of the following entries
are cited elsewhere in this Index;
each is notable for its broad view
of Tennyson's work) 847, 877,
934, 946, 958, 969, 972, 973,
974-976, 1006, 1053, 1065, 1070,
1111, 1113, 1123, 1146, 1147,
1149, 1152, 1173, 1215, 1224,
1238, 1273, 1290, 1292, 1295,
1305, 1338, 1352, 1359, 1362,
1390, 1396, 1398, 1402, 1405,
1415, 1444, 1449, 1480, 1493,
1511, 1533, 1564, 1588, 1597,
1607, 1634, 1663, 1671, 1673,
1674, 1676, 1679, 1690, 1691,
1693, 1697, 1718, 1738, 1739,
1769, 1775, 1797, 1798, 1799,
1811, 1816, 1820, 1830, 1850,
1866, 1867, 1868, 1870, 1872,
1873, 1874, 1876, 1883, 1898,
1899, 1900, 1904, 1906, 1909,
1947, 1950, 1951, 1952, 1963,
1983, 2001, 2024, 2027, 2028,
2043, 2046, 2055, 2060, 2062,
2068, 2077, 2087, 2091, 2092,
2137, 2139, 2144, 2147, 2152,
2154, 2164, 2201, 2225, 2226,
2227, 2230, 2276, 2282, 2283,
2328, 2342, 2344, 2352, 2360,
2388, 2442, 2451, 2459, 2462,
2464, 2465, 2467, 2476, 2477,
2489, 2493, 2500, 2507, 2509,
2516, 2517, 2518, 2519, 2520,
2526, 2529, 2530, 2532, 2538,
2539, 2543, 2544, 2551, 2554,
2555, 2558, 2560, 2561, 2562,
2563, 2564, 2565, 2566, 2568,
2569, 2574, 2576, 2579, 2583,
2584, 2585, 2589, 2591, 2597,
2598, 2599, 2602, 2605, 2608,
2610, 2623, 2625, 2626, 2629,
2636, 2640, 2654, 2655, 2676,

2680, 2682, 2688, 2689, 2718,
2742, 2753, 2757, 2758, 2790,
2791, 2797, 2799, 2810, 2813,
2819, 2823, 2824, 2840, 2843,
2852, 2855, 2864, 2877, 2890,
2891, 2906, 2907, 2918, 2920,
2924, 2925, 2927, 2945, 2947,
2948, 2963, 2966, 2971, 2975,
2977, 2979, 2982, 2984, 2988,
2993, 2994, 3002, 3005, 3006,
3011, 3024, 3037, 3038, 3055,
3065, 3067, 3090, 3092, 3094,
3096, 3115, 3147, 3152, 3162,
3172, 3176, 3214, 3215, 3265,
3288, 3290, 3297, 3303, 3314,
3315, 3387, 3405, 3406, 3417,
3476, 3519, 3551, 3556, 3584,
3624, 3673, 3674, 3689, 3696,
3725, 3726, 3757, 3795, 3852,
3922, 4066, 4142, 4215, 4232,
4284, 4343, 4352, 4369, 4404,
4417, 4429, 4434, 4502, 4679,
4688, 4691, 4722, 4830, 4856,
4881, 4906, 4963, 4964, 4970,
5042, 5050, 5054, 5055
Tennyson's Doppelgänger (1971) (by
J. M. Gray) 4277, 4326, 4366,
4405, 4448
Tennyson's Drama (1979) (by D. M.
Organ) 4905, 5020
Tennyson's Enoch Arden (1970) (by
P. G. Scott) 4219, 4273, 4366,
4405
Tennyson's Idylls of the King and
Arthurian Story from the XVIth
Century (1894) (by M. W. Mac-
Callum) 1804, 1823, 1828, 1831,
1835, 1837, 1845, 1847, 1858,
1884
Tennyson's In Memoriam (1884) (by
J. F. Genung) 1066, 1078, 1086,
1088, 1093
Tennyson's Life and Poetry (1892)
(by E. Parsons) 1407, 1454
Tennyson's Major Poems (1975) (by
J. R. Kincaid) 4607, 4631, 4660,
4716, 4717, 4719, 4720, 4732,
4737, 4774, 4801, 4808, 5093
Tennyson's Maud (1963) (by R. W.
Rader) 3797, 3861, 3864, 3875,
3877, 3881, 3885, 3887, 3895,
3896, 3911, 3914, 3953
The Tennyson Society 3803
Tennyson's Songs Set to Music by
Various Composers (ed. W. G.
Cusins) 943, 961
Tennyson's Style (1976) (by W. D.
Shaw) 4689, 4731, 4776, 4791,
4806, 4809, 4816, 4844, 4860,
4872, 4875, 4883, 4896, 4980

Tennyson's Two Brothers (1947)
  (by H. Nicolson) 3388, 3412
Tennyson's Use of the Bible (1917)
  (E. M. Robinson) 2842, 2845
Terence 2580
Terry, Ellen 2497
Tess of the D'Urbervilles (by T.
  Hardy) 4676
texts of Tennyson's works 702,
  871
Thackeray, William Makepeace
  2825, 4428
"That old Teuton" 4477
Theme and Symbol in Tennyson's
  Poems to 1850 (1964) (by C. de
  L. Ryals) 3851, 3867, 3889,
  3897, 3915, 3929, 3943
Theocritus 694, 1411, 1909, 2624,
  2633, 2628, 3699
"Theodicaea Novissima" (by A.
  Hallam) 4547, 4926
Thomas, Dylan 4777
Thomson, James 3135, 4959
Three Aspects of the Late Alfred
  Lord Tennyson (1901) (by J. M.
  Moore) 2230, 2252
Thro' the Vision of the Night
  (1980) (by J. M. Gray) 4965,
  5007, 5012, 5019, 5105, 5139
Timbuctoo 3, 516, 2123, 2349,
  3048, 3648, 4000, 5059
time 4429, 4745
Timon of Athens (by W. Shake-
  speare) 3163
"Tintern Abbey" (by W. Words-
  worth) 4603
Tiresias: reviews 1117, 1135,
  1138, 1140, 1142, 1154, 1156-
  1158, 1160, 1161, 1166, 1169,
  1170; in general 4710; critics
  of 4917; variants 4186, 4710
"Tithon" 3426, 3504, 3884, 4935
Tithonus 4598
"Tithonus" 3504, 3670, 4399,
  4488, 4598, 4649, 4709, 4899,
  4935, 5002
"Titmarsh" 2786, 2789
tobacco 1486, 2910, 2917
"To E. FitzGerald" 4265
"To Georgina 1834" 5014
Tomlin, John 3205
"To-morrow" 1262
"To the Queen" 852, 3651
"To Ulysses" 5097
"To Virgil" 3104, 3271, 3669;
  manuscripts 5113
translations 1389, 2042, 2134,
  2764, 2771, 3255, 3268, 3377,
  3814

trees 1244, 1855, 2805
Trevelyan, Pauline 4834
The Tribute 40, 3776
Trinity College 4185
Tristan (Tristram) 4802, 5109, 5126
Tristan (Tristram) and Iseult (Isol-
  de) 3149, 3155, 3174, 3181,
  3292, 4692, 4911
Trollope, William 5064
Twickenham 2376, 4590
"The Two Voices" 66, 151, 530,
  891, 2713, 3680, 3859, 4010,
  4052, 4078, 4114
The Two Voices (1964) (by E. E.
  Smith) 3852, 3915, 3925, 3951,
  3988, 3989, 3991, 3993, 3997,
  4004, 4032
Tyndall, John 4560

Ulysses 2955, 3008, 3127, 3236,
  3256, 3550, 4598, 4601, 4924
"Ulysses": in general 95, 888,
  2750, 2921, 2955, 3008, 3236,
  3331, 3334, 3375, 3378, 3383,
  3493, 3562, 3680, 3734, 3789,
  3824, 3828, 3878, 3939, 3994,
  4138, 4259, 4319, 4320, 4478,
  4521, 4529, 4601, 4924, 4934,
  4961, 5069; allegory 3668; audience of 4319; background 1371,
  3550, 4598; memory in 5069;
  sources for 4743
Unamuno y Jugo, Miguel de 3615
Under the Microscope (by A. C.
  Swinburne) 717
University of Rochester 4328
University of Texas 3310
University of Virginia 3724
Unpublished Early Poetry, ed. C.
  Tennyson (1931) 3153, 3168,
  3169, 3186, 3194

Valete (1893) (by H. D. Rawnsley)
  1685, 1764
value of life 2553
A Variorum Edition of Tennyson's
  Idylls of the King, ed. J. Pfor-
  dresher (1973) 4419, 4482,
  4555, 4562, 4669
"Vastness" 1137
Vestiges of the Natural History of
  Creation (by R. Chambers)
  3570, 4183, 4723
"The Victim" 619, 4741
Victoria, Queen 4220, 4295
The Victorian Imagination (1980) (by
  W. E. Buckler) 4963, 5137

Victorian Poets (1891) (by A.
  Sharp) 1361, 1384
Virgil 816, 919, 1354, 1468,
  2095, 2126, 2133, 2270, 2274,
  2545, 2878, 2885, 3271, 3573,
  3592, 4207
La Vita e le opere di Alfredo Ten-
  nyson (1894) (by P. Bellezza)
  1799, 1812, 1813
Vivien 4253
"Vivien" see "Merlin and Vivien"
Voices of the Night (by Longfellow)
  43
Vox Clamantis (by E. Mackay)
  1178, 1179
"The Voyage" 4513
"The Voyage of Maeldune" 1309

Wales 3095
"Walking to the Mail" 4456
war in Tennyson's work 2864,
  4041
Ward, Louisa Edith 2157
Ward, Wilfred 3219, 3227
waste land motif in Tennyson's
  work 4046
Waterhouse, J.W. 4967
Watts, G.F. 2346, 3198
Watts-Dunton, Theodore 4917
"weird seizures" (in The Princess)
  3790, 4575, 4586, 4920
"A Welcome to Alexandra" 3226,
  3228
Wells, H.G. 2895
Wheeler, Charles Stearn 3477,
  3564, 4088
Whipple, Edwin P. 106
white 4024
White, T.H. 3657
White, Walter 2039

Whitman, Walt 413, 1701, 2767,
  3455, 3558, 3620, 3731, 3745,
  4363, 4740
Whittier, John Greenleaf 1487,
  3444
Wilde, Oscar 3759, 4567
"Will" 871
Wilson, John 3273
wind in Tennyson's work 2802
The Window 652, 679, 688
Wise, Thomas James 3211, 3275,
  3306, 3373, 3663, 3898, 3938,
  4204, 4540
women's rights 307, 2434, 4818
Wordsworth, William 318, 463,
  537, 567, 752, 904, 1017, 2010,
  2156, 2524, 2549, 2653, 2868,
  2872, 3464, 3601, 3629, 3963,
  4393, 4603, 4900, 4973, 5009
Wordsworth, Tennyson, and Browning (1911) (by S.F. Gingerich)
  2653, 2692
work 3962
The Works of Alfred, Lord Tennyson, ed. H. Tennyson, the elder (1907-1908) 2465, 2477,
  2500, 2507, 2516, 2517, 2518,
  2519, 2520, 2574
Wycherley, William 686

Yale University 3868
Yeats, William Butler 3762, 4279,
  4290, 4392, 4892, 5114
"Ymadawiad Arthur" (by T. Gwynn-
  Jones) 3264
Yonge, Charlotte 4741
young people 4779
"'Yours & caetera' O how cold!"
  5065